CAREER

OPPORTUNITIES

in

AGRICULTURE, FOOD, AND NATURAL RESOURCES

SUSAN ECHAORE-MCDAVID AND RICHARD A. MCDAVID

Ferguson's

An Infobase Learning Company

To
Santiago D. Echaore, Sr., and Frances D. Echaore,
who tilled the land
first in the Philippines
and then in the United States

Career Opportunities in Agriculture, Food, and Natural Resources

Copyright © 2011 by Susan Echaore-McDavid and Richard A. McDavid

Ferguson's
An Infobase Learning Company
132 West 31st Street
New York NY 10001

Library of Congress Cataloging-in-Publication Data
Echaore-McDavid, Susan.
   Career opportunities in agriculture, food, and natural resources / Susan Echaore-McDavid and Richard A. McDavid.
      p. cm.
   Includes bibliographical references and index.
   ISBN-13: 978-0-8160-7456-3 (hardcover : alk. paper)
   1. Agriculture—Vocational guidance—Juvenile literature. I. McDavid, Richard A. II. Title.
   S494.5.A4E24 2010
   630.203—dc22   2009051103

Ferguson's books are available at special discounts when purchased in bulk quantities for businesses, associations, institutions, or sales promotions. Please call our Special Sales Department in New York at (212) 967-8800 or (800) 322-8755.

You can find Ferguson's on the World Wide Web at http://www.infobasepublishing.com

Text design by Kerry Casey
Composition by Hermitage Publishing Services
Cover printed by Sheridan Books, Ann Arbor, Mich.
Book printed and bound by Sheridan Books, Ann Arbor, Mich.
Date printed: October 2010
Printed in the United States of America

10 9 8 7 6 5 4 3 2 1

This book is printed on acid-free paper.

CONTENTS

INTRODUCTION

We are all likely to see or use something every day that relates to agriculture, whether we are at home, in school, at a shopping mall, in a hospital, or walking or driving down the street. We may live in a rural area, a large city, or a suburb. Look around us. Wherever we are, whatever we do, agriculture affects our lives. Without agriculture, we would not have foods to eat, clothes to wear, buildings to live in, books to read, paper to write on, pets to keep as companions, nor flowers to decorate the inside and outside of our homes.

Most of us think of agriculture as farming. When we shop for our food, we are aware that it is grown on farms. However, unless we patronize farmers' markets, most of us rarely encounter real farmers and many of us do not give much thought to where our food originates. We buy our food at well-stocked supermarkets and take it home without as much as an inkling as to how it came to be stocked on the stores' shelves.

In actuality, agriculture is much more than the production, marketing, and distribution of food. People involved in the agriculture industry also work to produce raw materials for clothing, shelter, energy, and medicine, as well as to provide opportunities for recreation. Farms and ranches are only two types of places where agricultural production occurs. Dairies, fish hatcheries, nurseries, greenhouse facilities, forests, and rangelands are also places where plants and animals are raised for food and other agricultural products.

Moreover, there are more people employed in the agriculture industry than farmers, ranchers, and farm and ranch hands, although these familiar individuals do represent the majority of agricultural workers. In fact, millions of people pursue opportunities in a wide range of fields in agriculture, including food production, fishing and fisheries, forestry, horticultural services, business, scientific research, education, veterinary medicine, food science, the environment, pet services, and tourism, among others. Agricultural employment can be found in both rural and urban settings, and include occupations to pursue in both indoor and outdoor environments. This book, *Career Opportunities in Agriculture, Food, and Natural Resources*, explores 99 of these diverse occupations.

A Brief History of Agriculture

Agriculture is commonly thought to be the foundation of all civilizations. Developing agriculture was the major step that people took to make the transition from living the nomadic life of hunters and gatherers to living a settled life.

In favorable locations of the world, people noticed that some of the food they ate could be grown deliberately by planting seeds and monitoring their growth until fruits, grains, and other foods were ready for harvest. They also learned to domesticate animals for food purposes by restricting their ability to wander. As they became more adept at managing crops and animals, people became more reliant on these newfound agricultural techniques and less dependent on hunting wild game or gathering wild vegetation. Because fewer individuals could cultivate enough food to feed many people, they began to establish permanent settlements in which to live all year. In these villages, more members of tribes or communities could begin to pursue other occupations. They could be soldiers, craftspersons, scribes, tradespeople, or builders, and pursue many other occupations on a full-time basis. Over centuries, agriculture enabled humans to develop cities and nations.

Agriculture developed in areas where such conditions as favorable climate, adequate supplies of water, and the lay of the land were conducive to the long-term cultivation of crops and the husbandry of domestic animals. Many historians believe that agriculture first originated approximately 10,000 years ago in the Middle East in a historic region that James H. Breasted, an American historian, named the Fertile Crescent, because it was shaped like the quarter-moon. It stretched from the eastern shore of the Mediterranean Sea to the Persian Gulf. Both the Tigris River and the Euphrates River flowed through the region, and the Nile River fed into the western part of it. (Today, this area consists of parts of the modern countries of Egypt, Israel, the West Bank, Gaza Strip, Jordan, Lebanon, Syria, Turkey, Iran, Iraq, and Kuwait.) Agriculture spread to other parts of the world from the Fertile Crescent. Some historians believe that agriculture also arose independently during other historical eras in various places around the globe, including South Asia, Papua, and the Americas.

The complete history of agriculture would fill many volumes. In summary, the development of agriculture progressed slowly through the centuries. Each nation contributed innovations and technologies that improved agricultural output, altered social structures, and introduced new foods. The most rapid innovations in agriculture occurred within the last century. Many of those changes took place in the United States and are the result of efforts made through both government involvement and the entrepreneurial spirit.

Agriculture is a dynamic industry and continues to change in our present day. New knowledge from a wide range of scientific, engineering, and technological disciplines will contribute to more exciting innovations and opportunities in the years to come.

Agricultural Jobs and Careers

Career Opportunities in Agriculture, Food, and Natural Resources describes a wide range of possible careers including agricultural producers, business specialists, scientists, technicians, managers, educators, communicators, tradespeople, and service professionals, among others. This book describes 99 occupations that are available in the following agricultural and agricultural-related fields.

Farming

Farmers and farm laborers are among the most familiar people who work in agriculture. They produce all types of crops and livestock for commercial purposes. They work on small and large crop farms, fruit and nut orchards, cattle ranches, dairy farms, chicken farms, plant nurseries, flower farms, tree farms, and many other agricultural operations in rural, suburban, and urban settings.

The first two sections of this book are dedicated to the men and women who are responsible for providing us with food, as well as the raw materials for clothing, buildings, fuel, medicines, and other products. The first section profiles some of the different types of farmers, while the second section covers staff members whose responsibilities range from performing physical labor to supervising and managing entire work crews.

Aquaculture and Commercial Fishing

When we buy fish and shellfish in groceries, at restaurants, or other locations, we often do not appreciate the hard, risky work that some workers perform to bring these foods to the marketplace. Some of the seafood we eat may have been caught in its natural habitats in open seas, lakes, and rivers. They may have been born wild or bred in hatcheries and then released. Other fish and shellfish may have been born and raised in controlled environments along seacoasts or at inland locations.

In section three of this book you will learn about commercial fishers and aquaculturists who catch or raise large quantities of fish for sale in all kinds of markets. You will also learn about scientists and other experts who are involved in the study, management, and administration of fisheries and hatcheries to ensure that there is a sufficient and safe food supply.

Forest Production and Management

For many people, there are few things as pleasurable as visiting or living in forest areas. These ecosystems are teeming with all kinds of animal and plant life, although their most visible attribute is their trees. Forests cleanse our environment and provide natural resources in abundance. Whether forests are located in remote wildernesses or closer to population centers, a variety of experts work to maintain their health and vitality.

Section four of *Career Opportunities in Agriculture, Food, and Natural Resources,* describes some of the men and women who work "behind the scenes" to study and maintain both private and public forests. These professionals, technicians, and managers work to protect and conserve forests so that future generations may enjoy forests and use the resources they provide.

Agriscience

Scientists and engineers play a valuable role in agriculture, food processing, and the management and conservation of natural resources. They conduct research:

- to gain further knowledge in their areas of expertise
- to solve specific problems in a wide range of areas, including crop production, animal husbandry, aquaculture, farm management, horticulture, food safety, food manufacturing, public health, forestry conservation, the environment, and so on
- to invent new machinery, processes, systems, and other technologies that are useful and affordable to agricultural producers, food processing companies, and others
- to create and manufacture quality commercial products

In this section you will discover how many scientists and engineers work to help agriculture advance in new directions. They may work in academic, private, or government settings.

Agricultural Services

To establish and maintain successful enterprises, agricultural producers and other agricultural-related entrepreneurs must be adept at running their daily operations. They must plan their work activities, meet their business goals, buy supplies, maintain equipment, pay bills and taxes, sell their products, maintain records, follow regulations, and so on.

Many business owners seek help from experts in areas about which they are unfamiliar or when they do not have the time or staff to handle the tasks.

In this section, you will read about some occupations that are involved in providing various technical and business services to agricultural producers and other businesses. You will also learn about government officials who make sure that agricultural enterprises comply with appropriate laws and regulations.

Agribusiness

Agriculture is an economic endeavor as much as it is about producing food and other products. In fact, it is a major segment of the U.S. economy as a whole. In order for this economic sector to thrive and continue producing, many types of business professionals contribute their knowledge and skills to help agricultural enterprises of all kinds flourish and succeed.

This section of the book describes some business experts who help agricultural producers make wise business decisions. For example, a business specialist might assist farmers with finding buyers for their goods, obtaining financial loans, assessing property value, or purchasing appropriate supplies or equipment. Agribusiness experts work in both the private and public sectors.

Food and Beverage Industries

Many of the foods we buy in grocery stores are ready to eat or drink, such as cheeses, baked goods, and juices. Many other foods, such as meat and pasta noodles, are cut, cleaned, or otherwise prepared for us to make into meals. Some foods, such as frozen and canned foods, are already made and require only that we cook or reheat them. All these convenient foods are processed, packaged, and distributed by small and large food and beverage companies.

Food and beverage companies continually develop new products to satisfy the needs of their customers, whether they are consumers, grocery stores, or restaurants or other foodservice establishments. Food and beverage firms employ scientists, technologists, technicians, engineers, chefs, and others to create and manufacture safe, nutritious, and cost-effective food products. In this section you will learn about some of these professions.

Floral, Gardening, and Landscaping Services

The ornamental horticultural industry, another segment of agriculture, offers a variety of career options. It includes such businesses as floral shops, nurseries, and landscaping services. Workers in this industry help individuals, businesses, government agencies, and other establishments use flowers and ornamental plants to enhance their living and working spaces. For example, many of our public places are characterized by lawns, flower gardens, and trees that are arranged in a pleasing fashion.

In this section you will learn about professionals who design beautiful flower arrangements or exterior landscapes. You will learn about careers of the experts who plan, install, and maintain lush public and private landscaped grounds.

Pet and Animal Services

Do you own a pet? Did you know that the pet industry is also agricultural? In fact, it is a rapidly growing agricultural industry.

Every year, millions of people in the United States purchase billions of dollars in products and services for their dogs, cats, horses, fishes, and other pets. They buy food, medicine, and pet supplies, as well as hire various services to help them groom, exercise, and care for their pets. Pet owners also seek help from animal experts to train their pets or to modify undesirable behavior exhibited by their pets.

In this section of *Career Opportunities in Agriculture, Food, and Natural Resources* you will learn about the various career options that are available in the pet industry, including business entrepreneurs, animal trainers, and animal caretakers. This section also profiles the men and women in government who enforce animal laws, regulations, and codes to make sure that pets and other animals are treated humanely.

Veterinary Medicine

Veterinarians and their support staffs provide essential health care to all types of animals, from livestock to pets to wildlife to exotic animals kept in zoos. They diagnose and treat animal patients, perform surgeries, and advise owners about how to care for their animals. Some veterinarians become experts in a particular medical discipline such as veterinary cardiology, pathology, toxicology, or dermatology.

Veterinarians, as well as veterinary para-professionals, are also involved in research and development in public, private, and government laboratories. In addition, they play a valuable role in protecting the public health. For example, they participate in investigating disease outbreaks, monitoring the importation and exportation of animals, and evaluating the safety of newly developed medications. In this section, you will learn more about the work that veterinarians and veterinary technicians do in different work settings.

Natural Resources Management and Conservation

Air, water, soil, minerals, and wildlife are a few examples of natural resources that are found on Earth. They are all essential to the survival and well-being of human beings. Many are renewable, while others cease to exist once depleted or destroyed. The United States and all the other countries in the world enact laws and regulations to protect and conserve the natural resources and the ecosystems in which they exist.

Many professionals, technicians, and others are involved with the study, management, and conservation of natural resources on both public and private lands. They may be engaged in conducting scientific research; creating conservation policies and plans; enforcing environmental laws and regulations; helping landowners, communities, and governments conserve and manage fragile ecosystems; or caring for injured, sick, or displaced wildlife. In this section of *Career Opportunities in Agriculture, Food, and Natural Resources* you will learn about some of these career options.

Travel, Tourism, and Recreation

Many people like to travel to the countryside or the great outdoors to enjoy the scenery as well as to experience new adventures. The opportunities for day and overnight trips are plentiful in the United States and throughout the world. People visit parks to hike, swim, boat, fish, camp, and take part in many other fun outdoor activities. Many also talk with park rangers to learn about the wildlife, plants, topography, history, and other aspects of the parks they visit.

In many rural communities, agritourism and ecotourism entrepreneurs offer visitors the chance to experience the local culture and natural resources through tours, activities, products, and hospitality services. Agritourism and ecotourism are two growing segments of the tourism industry. Both types of tourism contribute to the economic well-being of local communities as well as raise awareness about agriculture and the environment.

In this section of the book you will learn about some of the entrepreneurs, guides, and nature experts who are involved in helping travelers have great adventures on their trips.

Education and Communications

The last section of *Career Opportunities in Agriculture, Food, and Natural Resources* covers occupations in the agricultural education and agricultural communication fields.

This book will profile agricultural educators who teach in traditional and nonformal educational settings. Some educators work in middle schools and high schools where they are part of vocational agriculture programs. Other educators work as part-time or full-time instructors and professors at colleges and universities. Some agricultural educators work within the Cooperative Extension System where they develop and implement nonformal educational programs in the areas of agriculture, natural resources, 4-H youth development, family and consumer sciences, and community and economic development.

Agricultural businesses, food companies, government agencies, schools, nonprofit organizations, and many other organizations rely on specialists to document and distribute essential information to the public and, in particular, to their current and prospective customers. These men and women create various types of informational materials, which may be published in print, in digital media, on the Internet, or in other forms of media. In this section you will learn about journalists, public relations specialists, and other experts who engage in agricultural communications.

Job Outlook

Two industries—the food manufacturing industry and the agriculture, forestry, and fishing industry—employ a large population of workers in the United States. In 2006, the latter industry employed about 2 million people, including self-employed workers, while the former employed about 1.5 million, according to the U.S. Bureau of Labor Statistics (BLS). Job opportunities in both industries are found throughout the United States.

During the 2008–18 period, the BLS reports that job growth in the food manufacturing industry is expected to be minimal. Employment in the agriculture, forestry, and fishing industry is predicted to show little or no change in job growth during this period. Despite the lack of job growth in both industries, opportunities will continue to be available for qualified workers.

Many other job opportunities are available in other fields besides agricultural production and food manufacturing. These include such fields as research, business services, veterinary medicine, landscaping services, education, and natural resources management. Job growth varies among the different fields and occupations. For example, the BLS reported that employment of these occupations, which are covered in this book, should increase by the following rates during 2008–18:

- agricultural engineers, 12 percent
- animal scientists, 13 percent
- animal trainers, 20 percent
- environmental science and protection technicians, 29 percent
- firefighters, 19 percent
- food technologists and scientists, 16 percent
- foresters, 12 percent
- grounds maintenance workers, 18 percent
- landscape architects, 20 percent
- nonfarm animal caretakers, 21 percent
- soil and plant scientists, 15 percent
- veterinarians, 33 percent
- veterinary technicians and technologists, 36 percent
- wildlife biologists, 13 percent

In addition to job growth, employers in all industries will need to replace workers who advance to higher positions, transfer to other jobs or career fields, retire, or leave the workforce for various reasons.

Keep in mind that the number of job opportunities typically reflects the state of the economy. During economic downturns, employers in both the public and private sectors usually hire fewer new employees and may lay off staff.

Start Exploring Your Options

Career Opportunities in Agriculture, Food, and Natural Resources provides you with basic information for 99 professions. When you come across occupations that sound intriguing, take the time to learn more about them. The references mentioned throughout the book and in the appendixes can help you further research careers that interest you. In addition, here are a few other things you might do to explore a profession or field in more depth:

- read books about the profession or field
- read professional and trade magazines, journals, newspapers, and other print and online periodicals
- visit Web sites of professional societies, unions, trade associations, businesses, and other organizations related to your desired occupation
- talk with people who work in those occupations that interest you
- contact businesses and other organizations to ask to visit work settings
- browse through career resources that are available at libraries and career centers
- obtain part-time, seasonal, volunteer, or internship positions in the areas that interest you

As you explore various occupations, you will discover the kind of careers you might like, as well as those you would not like at all. You will also be gaining valuable knowledge and experience. Furthermore, you will be building a network of contacts that may be able to help with your next steps—obtaining further education, training, and jobs.

A Special Note to High School Students

Now is the time to start preparing for your future career, whether it is in agriculture, food science, natural resources management, or another field. You will need a well-rounded background to enter the workforce after high school graduation or to continue your education at a vocational school, trade school, college, or university.

Regardless of the occupation you are considering—farmer, technician, administrative worker, professional, manager, entrepreneur, or other—you will need a strong foundation in English, mathematics, science, and social studies. Having strong writing, public-speaking, computing, critical-thinking, and problem-solving skills is also essential to performing well in your future jobs.

Let your high school counselor and teachers know about your interest in pursuing a career in agriculture or other fields. They can help you choose appropriate classes, as well as advise you on the various career options that are available. They can also help you learn about educational programs and schools that can provide you with the proper training and education to enter different fields.

You can also start exploring different apprenticeship programs, vocational schools, trade schools, colleges, or universities on your own. Check out pamphlets, catalogs, and other written materials on different programs and schools. You should be able to find such materials at your career guidance center, school library, or public library. In addition, you can learn about different postsecondary schools on the World Wide Web.

This Book Is Yours

Career Opportunities in Agriculture, Food, and Natural Resources was written with you, the reader, in mind. Use it to help you search for the career of your dreams. Remember, only you can make your career goals and dreams come true. Believe in yourself. You can do it. We, the authors, know you can. Good luck!

—Susan Echaore-McDavid
and Richard A. McDavid

ACKNOWLEDGMENTS

Our appreciation for the Internet grows with each book that we write. We sincerely give thanks to the many owners of Web sites that we visited to learn about the 99 occupations in *Career Opportunities in Agriculture, Food, and Natural Resources*. This includes the Web sites and blogs created by professionals, colleges, businesses, nonprofit organizations, government agencies, and others. Without individuals and organizations willing to share information about occupations and careers on the Internet, completing this book would have been an even more difficult job.

We also could not have written this book without the help of the many experts in their various fields. We especially want to thank the following individuals and groups for taking the time out of their busy schedules to answer our questions:

Judith Barth, Ph.D., Assistant Director, Operations, Colorado State University Extension, Fort Collins, Colorado

Tara Lea Brown, Pacific Northwest Aerial Applicators Alliance

Michael Cheng, CHE, Director/Associate Professor, Culinology and Hospitality Management, Southwest Minnesota State University, Marshall, Minnesota

Kenneth W. Degg, Director of Education and Safety, National Agricultural Aviation Association

Scott Deitrick, American Vineyard Foundation

Don Dressler, Consultant, Irvine, California

Mary C. Fabrizio, Associate Professor of Marine Science, Department of Fisheries Science, Virginia Institute of Marine Science, Gloucester Point, Virginia

Jim Ferris, Silviculturist, Michigan Department of Natural Resources

Terry Gage, California Agricultural Aircraft Association

Daniel Kluepfel, USDA-ARS Research Leader, Crops Pathology and Genetics Research Unit, Department of Plant Pathology, University of California, Davis

Andrew Loftus, Loftus Consulting, Annapolis, Maryland

Chris Longly, Deputy Executive Director, National Auctioneers Association

Wayne Nishijima, Associate Dean and Associate Director for Cooperative Extension, College of Tropical Agriculture and Human Resources, University of Hawaii at Manoa

Cecelia A. Stortzum, Branch Chief, Outreach and Recruitment, USDA Agricultural Research Service, Administrative and Financial Management Office of Outreach, Diversity and Equal Opportunity, Beltsville, Maryland

Lisa Townson, Extension Specialist, Program Development and Evaluation, University of New Hampshire Cooperative Extension, Durham, New Hampshire

Mary Weber, Employment Officer, USDA, REE, AFM, Beltsville, Maryland

James A. Wolpert, Viticulture Extension Specialist, Department of Viticulture and Enology, University of California, Davis

Furthermore, we would like to express our appreciation to our editors, James Chambers, Matt Anderson, and Sarah Dalton, for their patience with us, and most of all, for their confidence in us. Thank you!

HOW TO USE THIS BOOK

Career Opportunities in Agriculture, Food, and Natural Resources provides basic information about 99 occupations that are available in various fields, including farming, aquaculture, forestry, natural resources management, business, food processing, pet services, tourism, education, and communication, among others.

This book will describe what the 99 occupations are like and what the requirements are for entering each profession. You will also get a general idea of the salaries, job markets, and advancement prospects available for the different occupations.

Sources of Information

The information presented in *Career Opportunities in Agriculture, Food, and Natural Resources* comes from a variety of sources. Books and periodicals related to the different occupations were read by the authors, along with research reports, pamphlets, and other materials created by professionals, professional associations, federal agencies, businesses, and other organizations. Job descriptions, work guidelines, and other work-related materials for the different occupations were also studied by the authors. In addition, transportation experts, professional and trade associations, and others were consulted.

The World Wide Web was also an essential source for information. The authors visited a wide range of Web sites to learn about each of the occupations that are described in this book. These Web sites included those belonging to government agencies, trade associations, professional societies, private companies, academic departments, nonprofit organizations, and more.

How This Book Is Organized

Career Opportunities in Agriculture, Food, and Natural Resources is designed to be easy to use and read. Altogether there are 99 job profiles in 14 sections. A section may have as few as three profiles or as many as 11 profiles, and the profiles are usually two or three pages long. All profiles follow the same format so that you may read the profiles or sections in whatever order you prefer.

The Job Profiles

Each of the 99 profiles starts with the *Career Profile*—a summary of the job's major duties, salary, job outlook, and opportunities for promotion. A profile also sums up general requirements and special skills needed for the job, as well as personality traits that successful professionals may share. The *Career Ladder* section is a visual presentation of a typical career path.

The rest of each occupational profile is divided into the following parts:

- *Position Description* describes what an occupation is and its major responsibilities and duties.
- *Salaries* presents a general range of the wages that professionals may earn.
- *Employment Prospects* provides a general survey of the job market for an occupation.

- *Advancement Prospects* discusses some options that individuals may pursue to advance in their careers.
- *Education and Training* describes the educational qualifications for entering a profession.
- *Special Requirements* covers licenses, certificates, or registrations that professionals, tradespeople, and others may be required to possess. This section also mentions any other special qualifications individuals must fulfill to become employed.
- *Experience, Skills, and Personality Traits* generally describes the job requirements needed for entry-level positions. It also talks about some basic employability skills that employers expect job candidates to have. In addition, this part describes some personality traits that successful professionals have in common.
- *Unions and Associations* provides the names of some professional associations and labor unions that professionals are eligible to join.
- *Tips for Entry* offers general advice for gaining work experience, improving employability, and finding jobs. In many profiles, it also gives suggestions for finding more information on the World Wide Web.

Additional Resources

At the end of the book are five appendixes that provide additional resources for the occupations described in *Career Opportunities in Agriculture, Food, and Natural Resources*. Appendix I provides Internet resources for you to learn about educational programs for some of the professions described in this book. Appendix II presents contact information for professional unions and associations that are mentioned in this book.

Appendix III provides a list of Web sites for federal agencies that are concerned with agriculture, food, the environment, natural resources management, and other related fields. Appendix IV gives a listing of resources on the World Wide Web, which can help you learn more about the various occupations in this book.

In addition, *Career Opportunities in Agriculture, Food, and Natural Resources* provides a glossary that defines some of the terms used in this book. This book also has a bibliography. It lists the titles of periodicals, books, and other resources to help you learn more about the professions that interest you.

The World Wide Web

Throughout *Career Opportunities in Agriculture, Food, and Natural Resources*, Web site addresses for online resources are provided so that you can learn more on your own. All the Web sites were accessible as this book was being written. Since its publication, Web site owners may have changed Web site addresses, removed the Web pages to which you have been referred, or shut down their Web sites completely. Should you come across a URL that does not function, you may still be able to find the Web site by entering its title or the name of the organization or individual into a search engine.

FARMING

FARMER

Duties: Oversee commercial agricultural operations; perform farming, marketing, management, and administrative duties as required

Alternate Title(s): Agriculturist, Grower, Rancher, Orchardist; Chicken Farmer, Mushroom Farmer, Cattle Rancher, or other title that reflects a type of farmer

Salary Range: $20,000 to $97,000

Employment Prospects: Fair

Advancement Prospects: Poor

Prerequisites:

    Education or Training—On-the-job training; formal education in agriculture encouraged

    Experience—Several years of farming experience

    Special Skills and Personality Traits—Leadership, management, planning, organizational, problem-solving, interpersonal, communication, conflict-resolution, computer, writing, business, finance, and marketing skills; self-motivated, patient, friendly, resourceful, resilient, determined, and decisive personality traits

    Special Requirements—Possess appropriate government licenses, permits, and certificates

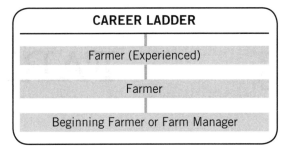

CAREER LADDER

Farmer (Experienced)

Farmer

Beginning Farmer or Farm Manager

Position Description

Farmers play a valuable and essential role to all people around the world. These men and women supply much of the fruits, vegetables, grains, eggs, milk, meats, poultry, and fish that we consume. Farmers also produce raw materials that we use to make our clothing, furniture, buildings, fuel, pharmaceuticals, and other products. They cultivate trees, ornamental plants, and turfgrass that we buy to landscape our homes, buildings, schools, shopping centers, parks, highways, and other places. In addition, Farmers breed and raise animals for food, recreation, and other purposes.

Farmers are their own bosses. They produce crops and livestock for commercial purposes. They might own or lease their land. In the United States, the majority of farm operations are owned by families. Some of these farms have been in operation for several generations. Family farms range in size from a few acres to large-scale operations that consist of several thousand acres. Nonfamily farms are defined as those owned by corporations or farmers' cooperatives; they are overseen by hired managers.

Farmers are usually known by the type of products they raise. They choose crops and livestock according to their interests and consumer demands. Farmers also consider such factors as competition, region, climate, and the availability and condition of natural resources.

Crop farmers cultivate row crops on arable lands for food, livestock feed, fiber, or fuel. They might grow one or more types of grains, vegetables, fruits, herbs, or fiber plants. Vineyard growers raise grapevines, while orchardists produce fruit or nut trees such as cherry, peach, orange, olive, walnut, and macadamia trees.

Ranchers dedicate themselves to tending one or more types of livestock on open land and in pens or corrals. Many ranchers raise cattle, hogs, emus, or other livestock to sell to other ranchers or to meat processors. Some ranchers nurture animals, such as horses or bulls, for breeding purposes. Dairy farmers rear cows, goats, or other animals to produce milk. These farmers may process the milk at their farms or transport it to dairy processing facilities. Poultry farmers tend chickens, ducks, or other fowl for eggs or meat. Fish farmers raise trout, salmon, or other fish or shellfish in ponds to sell for food, fish bait, and pets.

Horticultural growers are involved in the production of ornamental plants such as flowers, shrubbery, and turfgrass. These farmers also produce flower, fruit, and vegetable starter plants for consumers. Tree farmers tend acres of pine or other hardwoods to harvest for lumber, fiber, Christmas trees, and other products.

Farming is a complex occupation in which growers make various technical, management, and administrative decisions every day. Farmers are knowledgeable about agricultural practices, agricultural science, biological sciences, and business administration. They also understand farm management, nutrition, genetics, water quality, erosion control, pest control, farm equipment and machinery, marketing, finance, labor, and food processing. Farmers follow farming methods that meet their business goals, as well as their personal interests and philosophies. For example, Farmers who practice organic farming grow crops without any manufactured chemicals such as synthetic pesticides and fertilizers.

Marketing crops is a major aspect of farming. Farmers sell their products to local, national, and international markets in various ways. Many of them sell some or all of their harvested crops to food processors, food distributors, grocery stores, produce markets, and restaurants. Some Farmers enter into agreements with companies to raise crops solely for them.

Some Farmers are members of farmers' cooperatives through which they market their products. These cooperatives are businesses that the members own jointly to share marketing and other resources. Some Farmers sell their products directly to the public at farmers' markets or at their own farms.

Farmers also use other venues to sell their goods. For example, some Farmers sell finished products (such as jams, soaps, or flower wreaths) made from their harvested crops. Other examples are Farmers who set up agritourism operations to offer customers activities at their farms, such as corn mazes, farm tours, petting zoos, or picking their own fruits and vegetables.

Farming is a risky business. Many uncontrollable factors affect Farmers' profits every year. For example, extreme temperatures, droughts, or heavy rains can destroy crops; or the market demand for crops may be lower than Farmers had expected. Government aid is often made available to Farmers when they experience extreme loss to their crops and livestock due to a natural or man-made disaster.

Farmers perform daily and seasonal routines, which rarely vary from year to year. They execute many duties that are particular to the type of farm they operate. Dairy, poultry, livestock, and fish Farmers feed and care for animals and maintain the barns, coops, pens, ponds, and other structures where the animals live. Many of these Farmers also manage the breeding of animals. Crop Farmers, orchardists, vineyard growers, and horticultural growers perform a wide range of tasks concerned with tilling, planting, cultivating, and harvesting. These Farmers also deal with pest control and the fertilization of plants.

All Farmers perform many similar farming and business tasks. For example, they:

- plan what crops and livestock they will raise
- schedule weekly, monthly, and yearly work activities
- purchase necessary supplies and equipment
- direct and coordinate their daily activities and those of their employees
- formulate operational procedures, standards, and policies
- plan and administer budgets
- pay bills, insurance payments, government fees, taxes, and salaries
- keep licenses and permits up-to-date
- comply with local, state, and federal laws and regulations regarding agriculture, food safety, the environment, business operations, land use, and labor
- meet with agents of companies that are interested in purchasing their products
- operate and maintain farm machinery and systems

Most Farmers hire one or more employees, including family members, to assist them with their farming and business responsibilities. Their employees might work full time, part time, or on a seasonal basis. During busy times, such as crop harvesting, many Farmers hire additional temporary workers. Some farmers do their own selection and hiring of temporary workers, while others use the services of private labor contractors.

To improve the success of their operations, Farmers keep up with agricultural developments, new technologies, commodity futures, government programs, and other areas. Many Farmers take advantage of educational programs and technical advice offered by Cooperative Extension Service offices, farm bureaus, and other farm organizations.

Farming is a tough job in which men and women work outdoors in all kinds of weather. They are exposed to chemicals, dust, machinery, sun, and other conditions that put them at risk for illness, injuries, and death. Hence, Farmers are continually alert and follow various safety precautions, such as wearing safety equipment when applying pesticides.

Farmers often work long hours every day to complete their many tasks. Because of the financial insecurity of farming, some Farmers work full time or part time to supplement their income.

Salaries

Annual farm income for Farmers varies each year. According to the May 2008 Occupational Employment Statistics survey by the U.S. Bureau of Labor Statistics

(BLS), the estimated annual wage for most Farmers ranged from $19,920 to $96,630.

Employment Prospects

In 2007, according to the U.S. Department of Agriculture (USDA), approximately 2.1 million farms were in operation, of which the majority were family-run farms. The USDA defines a farm as any establishment that sells at least $1,000 worth of agricultural products during a year. In the United States, the trend has been toward larger farms, which may be operated by families or non-family organizations.

According to the BLS, approximately 1 million Farmers were self-employed in the United States in 2008. It further states that during the 2008 to 2018 period, the employment of Farmers should decrease by 8 percent. However, opportunities are available for individuals who are willing to invest their money, patience, and hard work in establishing successful farms. Some agricultural experts report that almost 50 percent of today's Farmers will be reaching retirement age in the coming decade.

Advancement Prospects

Farmers advance according to their own ambitions and interests. They gauge their progress by achieving their business goals and objectives. For example, some Farmers buy more land to expand their operations. Most, if not all, Farmers measure their success by being able to make a comfortable living from their profits.

Education and Training

No formal training is required for individuals to become Farmers. Many experts in the field encourage individuals to pursue higher education to handle the complex farming, business, and marketing problems and issues that modern Farmers face. Many Farmers have earned college degrees in agronomy, botany, environmental studies, food science, and other disciplines in the agricultural or biological sciences.

Farmers learn their skills on the job. They also complete courses, workshops, and other educational programs offered through colleges, the Cooperative Extension Service offices, farm bureaus, farmers' cooperatives, and other organizations. Farmers also gain valuable knowledge by networking with colleagues, attending trade shows, and reading relevant books, trade journals, and other materials.

Special Requirements

Farmers must obtain the proper local and state licenses and permits to operate their businesses. For specific information, contact your local government office that oversees business licensing.

Farmers must also acquire proper permits to perform specific activities such as pesticide application. In addition, Farmers may be required to be registered or certified with the proper government agency to sell certain products, such as organic vegetables. Furthermore, Farmers must pass regular government inspections of their products and facilities.

Experience, Special Skills, and Personality Traits

Individuals generally need several years of working on farms to obtain sufficient technical and management experience to become self-employed Farmers.

Farmers must have excellent leadership, management, planning, organizational, and problem-solving skills. They also need effective interpersonal, communication, and conflict-resolution skills, as they must be able to get along with many people from diverse backgrounds. In addition, Farmers need strong computer, writing, business, finance, and marketing skills. Being self-motivated, patient, friendly, resourceful, resilient, determined, and decisive are some personality traits that successful Farmers share.

Unions and Associations

Many Farmers join local, state, or national professional associations and other farming organizations that serve their particular farming interests. For example, many Farmers become members of their local or state farm bureau to take advantage of networking opportunities, training programs, and other services and resources.

Tips for Entry

1. Are you a high school student? Enroll in a few agriculture classes if your school offers them. This may help you determine if a farming career might interest you.
2. You may need to move to another county or state in order to buy or lease land to start the type of farming that interests you.
3. Check with your local or state farm bureau for information about organizations that help new Farmers establish their businesses.
4. Learn more about agriculture and farming. You might start by visiting the Web sites of these organizations: the U.S. Department of Agriculture (www.usda.gov); the American Farm Bureau (www.fb.org); and the Farmland Information Center (www.farmlandinfo.org). For more links, see Appendix IV.

ORGANIC FARMER

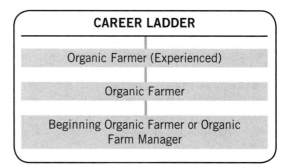

Position Description

Organic Farmers are known for using sustainable methods to produce commercial crops and livestock for food, fiber, and other purposes. These farmers range from market gardeners to small family farmers to large-scale corporate growers. They grow a wide range of common and specialty products, including grains, vegetables, fruits, nuts, herbs, mushrooms, honey, meat, poultry, eggs, flowers, and ornamental plants. Organic farming is labor intensive; thus, many Organic Farmers run small operations. It is also common for Organic Farmers to raise a few kinds of crops and livestock on their farms. For example, an Organic Farmer might grow tomatoes, walnuts, and herbs, along with raising chickens and turkeys.

Organic Farmers promote biodiversity and rely on the natural behavior and adaptation of animals, plants, and soils to their environments. These farmers produce crops and livestock according to their interests, market demands, potential profits, the local climate and weather, soil conditions, and other considerations.

Unlike conventional farmers, organic producers do not use synthetic chemicals to help them raise farm products. For example, organic livestock are not injected with antibiotics when animals are ill, nor are they given growth hormones. Another example is the practice of natural pest management to handle weeds, insects, rodents, deer, and other pests. Organic Farmers believe that sudden and massive outbreaks of pests are usually short-lived, as they are soon cut back by natural predators, parasites, and disease agents. Farmers might aid the natural process by using such mechanical controls as row covers and traps.

The fundamental basis of organic farming is building up healthy soils that in turn produce healthy plants that are more likely to be resistant to disease and insect pests. Organic Farmers nourish the living matter in soils by utilizing such methods as crop rotation, planting cover crops, and applying compost and manure to the land. They also use other nonsynthetic forms of fertilizers such as seed meal as well as add natural forms of vitamins and minerals to soil.

In the United States, Organic Farmers must adhere to strict regulations and standards established by the U.S. Department of Agriculture (USDA) regarding the production, processing, and labeling of organic products. For example, the USDA stipulates that only organic or untreated seeds must be used and livestock must have access to pastures and rangelands. In addition, these farmers must keep accurate records of their production processes, including how their crops or livestock were raised, where they were tended, what products were applied to them, and where the food products were stored.

Organic Farmers market their products locally, regionally, nationwide, and globally. Some farmers sell their products through Organic Farmers' cooperatives or collectives. Others arrange with food buyers, food distributors, and grocery stores (including food cooperatives, natural food stores, and major supermarkets) to buy their products.

Many Organic Farmers sell some or all of their products directly to the public in various ways. They set up booths at farmers' markets. They maintain stands on or near their farms as well as take orders from customers by phone or by e-mail. Some farmers participate in community-supported agriculture programs in which customers can purchase a basket of a farmer's weekly harvest. Customers usually pay a fixed price in advance for a few weeks or the whole season. The food is either delivered to the customers or they pick it up at the farm or another designated location.

Some Organic Farmers also make jams, dried fruit, jerky, soaps, or other finished products to sell to customers. Still others create farm tours, mazes, pick-your-own vegetable patches, and other entertaining activities for customers to experience for a fee.

Organic Farmers perform physically hard tasks every day. They feed and care for animals. They prepare the land for planting crops. They irrigate fields and cultivate plants throughout the season. They harvest crops and butcher livestock. Dairy farmers milk their animals. All farmers clean and maintain barns, storage rooms, coops, and other farm structures. They also operate and maintain farm equipment, machinery, and systems. Furthermore, Organic Farmers troubleshoot problems as they occur.

Many farmers hire family members and nonfamily to assist them on a permanent or temporary basis. Farmers direct and supervise the work activities of their employees. They also provide employees with technical and safety training as needed.

Along with performing their farm duties, farmers are responsible for completing various administrative tasks. For example, they devise work plans and schedules; plan and administer budgets; purchase supplies and equipment; pay bills, taxes, and salaries; and keep records. Organic Farmers also set aside time to develop marketing strategies as well as stay up-to-date with commodity futures and developments in organic agriculture.

Organic Farmers work long hours throughout the year, particularly during harvesting season and other busy times. Some farmers continue to work full time or part time in other occupations to supplement their farming incomes.

Salaries

Annual farm income for Organic Farmers varies each year. Their annual net profit is determined after subtracting the total operating expenses from gross annual sales. It is common for small business owners to be unprofitable during their first years in operation.

According to the May 2008 Occupational Employment Statistics survey by the U.S. Bureau of Labor Statistics (BLS), the estimated annual wage for most farmers ranged from $19,920 to $96,630.

Employment Prospects

Organic farming is practiced in all 50 states. The USDA Economic Research Service reports that organic farming is one of the fastest-growing segments of U.S. agriculture. In 1994, according to the Organic Farming Research Foundation Web site, there were between 2,500 and 3,000 Organic Farmers in the United States. In 2007, approximately 13,000 farmers were certified as organic producers in the country. In general, experts in the field express confidence that the organic industry will continue to grow in the United States as well as worldwide.

The BLS reports that nearly 1 million farmers were self-employed in the United States in 2008. It further states that during the 2008 to 2018 period, employment of farmers should decrease by 8 percent. However, opportunities are available for individuals who are willing to invest their money, patience, and hard work in establishing successful farms. Some agricultural experts report that almost 50 percent of today's farmers will be reaching retirement age in the coming decade.

Although opportunities for Organic Farmers are favorable, their success depends on their ambition, competition, the demand for their products, and other factors.

Advancement Prospects

As entrepreneurs, Organic Farmers determine their own terms of advancement. Many measure their success by earning higher incomes, by expanding their businesses, and through job satisfaction.

Education and Training

No formal training is required for individuals to become Organic Farmers. Many farmers, however, have earned college degrees in agronomy, animal science, botany, environmental studies, food science, and other disciplines in the agricultural or biological sciences.

Experts in the field encourage individuals to pursue higher education to handle the complex farming, business, and marketing problems and issues that modern farmers face.

Organic Farmers learn their skills on the job. They also gain valuable knowledge by networking with colleagues, attending trade shows, and reading relevant books, trade journals, USDA pamphlets, and other materials. Additionally, farmers enroll in relevant agriculture and business workshops and courses offered through colleges, Cooperative Extension Service offices, farm bureaus, Organic Farmers' cooperatives, and organizations that support organic farming education and research.

Special Requirements

Farmers must obtain the proper local and state licenses and permits to operate their businesses. Requirements for businesses vary among states. For specific information, contact your local government office that oversees business licensing.

To market organic farm products, farmers must have their operations certified by the USDA through a state, private, or nonprofit organization accredited by the USDA. Organic farmers may be exempt from certification if they sell less than $5,000 in organic farm products.

Once their operations are certified, farmers can attach the "USDA Certified Organic" seal to their products, packaging, and marketing materials. To maintain their certification, farmers must submit annual plans for production systems, maintain accurate records, and undergo regular inspections of their operations. For more information about USDA certification, visit the USDA National Organic Program Web site at www. ams.usda.gov/nop.

Experience, Special Skills, and Personality Traits

Individuals generally need several years of work experience on farms to obtain sufficient technical and management experience to become self-employed farmers. To be Organic Farmers, individuals must have a strong understanding of how ecological systems work as well as of the principles and methodologies of organic agriculture.

To maintain profitable businesses, Organic Farmers must have excellent business and marketing skills. They also need effective leadership, planning, organizational, problem-solving, and self-management skills. Having strong computer, writing, and record-keeping skills is also important. Successful Organic Farmers share several personality traits including being caring, patient, observant, innovative, flexible, persistent, and self-motivated.

Unions and Associations

Organic Farmers can join associations at the local, state, national, and international levels to take advantage of networking opportunities, training programs, educational resources, and other services and resources. Various organizations serve the general interests of farmers, such as local and state farm bureaus. Other organizations serve particular concerns of Organic Farmers. For example, the Organic Trade Association is a national organization to which many Organic Farmers belong. For contact information, see Appendix II.

Tips for Entry

1. Learn as much as you can about organic farming before getting into it. For example, talk with several Organic Farmers to learn about their farms and how and why they chose to practice organic farming. Be sure you understand what is and is not involved in this sustainable practice.

2. If you have a conventional farm, be prepared to take several years to convert it into an organic operation that meets USDA standards and regulations.

3. Use the Internet to learn more about organic agriculture. You might start by visiting the Organic Trade Association Web site (www.ota. com); the Organic Farming Research Foundation Web site (ofrf.org); and HowtogoOrganic.com. For more links, see Appendix IV.

CROP FARMER

Duties: Oversee commercial crop farming operations; perform farming, marketing, management, and administrative duties as required

Alternate Title(s): Cotton Farmer, Vegetable Farmer, other title that reflects the type of crops being grown

Salary Range: $20,000 to $97,000

Employment Prospects: Fair

Advancement Prospects: Poor

Prerequisites:

    Education or Training—On-the-job training; formal education in agriculture encouraged

    Experience—Several years of farming experience

    Special Skills and Personality Traits—Communication, writing, computer, business, finance, marketing, interpersonal, self-management, planning,

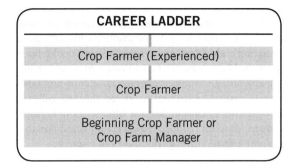

organizational, problem-solving, and conflict-resolution skills; determined, decisive, self-motivated, patient, resilient, and resourceful personality traits

    Special Requirements—Possess appropriate government licenses, permits, and certificates

Position Description

Crop Farmers are skilled experts at raising all kinds of crops for food, animal feed, fiber, fuel, and aesthetics, or to be made into a variety of manufactured products such as paper, medicines, clothing, building materials, furniture, or tools. These farmers grow grains, vegetables, herbs, mushrooms, fruits, nuts, flowers, ornamental plants, trees, turfgrass, cotton, tobacco, and various other types of crops. They may produce one or more types of crops in fields, orchards, nurseries, and greenhouses. Some farmers use conventional methods to produce their crops, while others follow sustainable agricultural practices.

Crop Farmers sell their products to local, national, and international markets. Many farmers market their harvested crops directly to food processors, food distributors, grocery stores, produce markets, and restaurants. Some farmers enter into agreements with companies to raise crops solely for them. Locally, Crop Farmers may sell their products directly to the public at farmers' markets or at their own farms.

Crop Farmers own or lease their land for farming. As self-employed practitioners and business owners, Crop Farmers are responsible for the success of their operations. Each day, these growers make various technical, managerial, and business decisions. They apply science and business principles and techniques to perform their tasks. Agronomy, soil science, weed science,

plant pathology, pest management, marketing, sales, financial management, and labor management are some of the disciplines about which they are knowledgeable.

Crop Farmers live and work in every state of the United States. They grow crops that are suitable for their geographic location, type of soil, terrain, and climate. Farmers also take into consideration the availability of water. Apple crops, for example, are grown in the cool, moist, temperate climates of Washington or Wisconsin, while mango crops are cultivated in the subtropical climate of Hawaii, and olive crops are raised in semiarid areas of California. Rice farmers find favorable conditions in Louisiana and California in locations where water is abundant and the climate is warm for much of the year. Crop Farmers in the Midwest find the plains areas to be best for growing wheat, corn, soybeans, and other grains.

Some farmers raise specialty crops, which are crops that have not been commercially grown in their area before. They may be common crops, such as lettuce, berries, or ornamental plants, or they may be exotic crops such as Asian vegetables, herbs, or mushrooms. These farmers may grow specialty crops to sell to niche food markets or to industries that use such plants to produce new medicines or make finished products that have the qualities that these plants provide. Some Crop Farmers produce new plant species by adapting them to their local conditions through selective breeding. Other

Crop Farmers grow new types of crops that are developed by biotechnological techniques. These genetically modified crops are designed to resist disease or pests, and have other desired characteristics such as specific flavors.

Although Crop Farmers manage different types of crops that are suitable for their particular region, they follow the same basic steps to produce their crops. Crop Farmers:

- study their soil, local climate conditions, and market demands to determine which crops to plant
- prepare their soil for planting
- manage pests and plant diseases
- tend their crops by managing weeds and providing sufficient water
- harvest their crops at the proper time and store them until they are ready to use
- sell their harvested crops

To one extent or another, Crop Farmers use machines to manage their crop production. For example, Crop Farmers who grow row crops of such vegetables as broccoli, peppers, lettuce, or cabbage may use tractors to plow their land, but they manage weeds, install irrigation systems, and pick the ripe harvest by using hand tools. Their land for each crop generally consists of a few acres. On the other hand, Crop Farmers who grow grains such as wheat, barley, or rye need vast expanses of land, on which they plow, plant, and harvest their crops through mechanical means by using large machines to dig the soil, distribute seeds, and collect the harvest. Crop Farmers who manage orchards either use mechanical means—tree shaker machines—or pick fruit by hand to complete their harvest. These Crop Farmers prune their trees by hand.

Technology also plays an important role in the life of Crop Farmers. These farmers may use global positioning systems and geographic information systems technologies to measure their harvest and optimize the efficient use of their lands. Increasingly, Crop Farmers also use computers to keep track of planting schedules, sales records, machine maintenance records, and inventory records.

Many Crop Farmers hire one or more employees, including family members, to assist with the day-to-day operations of their farms. During busy times, such as the harvesting of crops, farmers may hire as many as hundreds of temporary farm laborers to perform routine tasks. Farmers employ these temporary workers directly or use the services of private labor contractors.

Throughout their careers, Crop Farmers continue to learn about different methods of managing crops and land. For example, more of these producers seek ways to minimize the erosion of soil and the leeching of harmful chemicals into the water supply by using fewer synthetic fertilizers and insecticides, and by using sustainable and organic farming techniques. They spread mulch around plants, rotate their crops, utilize insect and plant species to draw harmful pests and diseases away from their crops, and use chemical-free fertilizers and compost to enrich their soil and provide nutrients to their crops. In addition, they use different methods of tilling to help revitalize soil that has been depleted from overuse.

All farming is intense and demanding work, and crop farming is no exception. Crop Farmers exert themselves physically. They work outdoors in all weather conditions. They also work indoors to manage their finances, repair equipment, arrange for the sale of their harvests, and maintain records of their farm activities. They may be exposed to dangerous chemicals. These experts also risk injury when using heavy equipment or lifting heavy objects. Hence, Farmers are continually alert and follow various safety precautions, such as wearing safety equipment when applying pesticides.

Crop Farmers work all year and put in long hours each week. During growing seasons, they work from sunup to sundown every day.

Salaries

Annual farm income for Crop Farmers varies each year, depending on such factors as the size of their farm, how much crops they produce and sell, and the market value for their crops. Their annual net profit is determined after subtracting the total operating expenses from gross annual sales.

The U.S. Bureau of Labor Statistics reports in its May 2008 Occupational Employment Statistics survey that the estimated annual wage for most farmers ranged from $19,920 to $96,630.

Employment Prospects

According to some agricultural experts, many farmers will be reaching retirement age in the coming decade. Therefore, opportunities will be available for individuals to become Crop Farmers, as long as they are willing to invest money and hard work to establish their farms. The state of the economy and the demand for the types of crops that farmers grow also influence how successful farmers are each year. As in some other enterprises, it is common for farmers to be unprofitable during the first few years in business.

In 2007, the U.S. Department of Agriculture reported that there were about 2.1 million farms in the United States, which includes all types of crop and livestock operations. In the United States, the trend has been toward larger farms. Most farms are family-owned.

Because of the financial insecurity of farming, some Crop Farmers work full-time, part-time, or seasonal jobs to supplement their income. Some Crop Farmers continue working in their occupations in education, business, technology, engineering, and other fields.

Advancement Prospects

Crop Farmers gauge their success by being able to make a comfortable living from the profits earned by their operations. They also measure their progress by achieving their business goals and objectives. For example, a Crop Farmer might successfully enter new markets for their products or purchase more land for farming.

Education and Training

There are no educational standards for individuals to become Crop Farmers. However, many experts in the field encourage individuals to pursue higher education to handle the complex farming, business, and marketing problems and issues that modern farmers face. Many Crop Farmers have earned college degrees in agronomy or another related field in agricultural or biological sciences.

Crop Farmers learn their skills on the job while working as farm laborers, supervisors, and managers. Many have also learned about crop production, farm management, marketing, and business practices by completing agricultural courses in high school or college. In addition, many Crop Farmers have taken advantage of informal educational programs that are provided by local Cooperative Extension Service offices, farmers' cooperatives, and trade associations.

Special Requirements

Crop Farmers must obtain the proper local and state licenses and permits to operate their businesses. Requirements for businesses vary among states. For specific information, contact your local government office that oversees business licensing.

They also must acquire proper permits to perform specific activities such as pesticide application. To sell organic products, Crop Farmers are required to be registered or certified with the appropriate govern-ment agency. Furthermore, these farmers must pass regular government inspections of their products and facilities.

Experience, Special Skills, and Personality Traits

Individuals need several years of experience working on farms to obtain sufficient technical and manage-ment knowledge and skills to become Crop Farmers. Some farmers had worked their way up from being farmhands to managers before establishing their own farms.

Crop Farmers need strong communication, writing, computer, business, finance, and marketing skills to maintain successful businesses. In addition, they should have excellent interpersonal, self-management, plan-ning, organizational, problem-solving, and conflict-resolution skills. Successful Crop Farmers share such personality traits as being determined, decisive, self-motivated, patient, resilient, and resourceful.

Unions and Associations

Many Crop Farmers belong to local, state, or national professional and trade associations and other organiza-tions that serve their particular farming interests. By joining such organizations, farmers have the opportu-nity to network with peers, as well as take advantage of training programs, technical or business advice, and other professional services and resources.

Crop Farmers may also be members of farmers' cooperatives through which they market their prod-ucts. Cooperatives are business organizations that the members own jointly to share various resources.

Tips for Entry

1. Participate in 4-H and FFA while you are still in school to learn fundamental agricultural skills.
2. Learn how to do basic maintenance and minor repair work on farm equipment and machinery.
3. To encourage individuals interested in becom-ing farmers, many agricultural programs, such as Cooperative Extension Service, offer resources for finding farmlands for sale or lease, bank loans, and starting small businesses and farms.
4. Use the Internet to learn more about crop pro-duction. You might start by visiting the U.S. Department of Agriculture Web site at www.usda.gov. For more links, see Appendix IV.

HORTICULTURAL GROWER

Position Description

Horticulture is a branch of agriculture that pertains to the science and practice of cultivating edible and ornamental plants. Vegetables, fruits, flowers, foliage, vines, trees, groundcover, and turfgrass are all examples of horticultural crops sold by commercial farms, nurseries, and greenhouse companies. The agricultural producers who engage in raising these specialties are known as Horticultural Growers. They sell the plant starts and plugs, bedding plants, potted plants, vines, bushes, trees, and other products that customers grow in their own gardens and farms and use for the interior or exterior landscaping of their homes, office buildings, malls, parks, school campuses, roadsides, and so forth. Some Horticultural Growers raise and harvest full-grown crops, such as flowers, to sell to retail businesses, plant distributors, or the public.

Like all agricultural producers, Horticultural Growers make various technical, management, and administrative decisions every day to ensure their operations run efficiently and safely. They apply the knowledge and skills of many areas to their work, including horticultural science, biology, horticultural crop production and processing, human resources, business, administration, finance, marketing, and sales.

These agricultural producers grow their plants in fields as well as in pots and other containers. Many of them also cultivate plants in controlled environments inside greenhouses, which are made of glass or plastic. Some plants are started from seed, which are sown into ground or in containers. Other plants are propagated from existing ones. Growers use various propagation methods to take leaves, stems, roots, or other parts of plants and start them in containers or in the ground.

Horticultural Growers choose plants to grow according to the demands of their markets. Many Horticultural Growers raise a variety of plants and species at their operations. Some growers concentrate on producing one or more varieties of certain plants, such as turfgrass, orchids, or conifers for Christmas trees. Others choose to produce crops, such as drought-resistant plants, native plants, or organic plants, that are aimed at specific markets. Some growers specialize by practicing certain farming methods. For example, growers might follow such sustainable practices as organic farming, permaculture, or the use of integrated pest management.

Whether they have small or large operations, Horticultural Growers hire one or more employees, including family members, on a part-time or full-time basis to help them complete their various production, business, and marketing duties. They may also employ additional agricultural laborers to work during the growing or harvest season. Some growers do their own selection and hiring of temporary workers, while others use the services of private labor contractors.

Horticultural Growers perform many duties to ensure that their operations run smoothly. They determine which and how many plants to grow by taking into consideration such factors as environmental conditions, the growing seasons of plants, and the needs of their customers. They plan weekly, monthly, and annual work schedules for themselves and their employees. They select and purchase materials and supplies, such as seeds, fertilizers, and herbicides. They also make sure that tools, equipment, and structures are maintained and repaired, if needed. Some growers prepare fields for planting, sowing, or propagating plants, while other growers supervise and direct their employees in these activities.

Horticultural Growers monitor the growth of their plants and troubleshoot problems, such as plant diseases, pest infestations, and weed growth. These growers also exercise quality control to ensure their products meet their customers' satisfaction. For example, they might remove substandard products from batches of plants that are to be shipped to customers. Some growers are involved in the development of new varieties of species that may enhance their appeal to customers; for example, a grower might be interested in producing plants that require less watering.

In addition, Horticultural Growers manage a wide range of tasks to manage their businesses. For example, they:

- develop and implement marketing plans
- formulate standard operational procedures and work standard policies
- plan and administer budgets
- maintain accurate business records, such as inventory logs and sales invoices
- pay bills, insurance payments, license fees, taxes, and salaries
- keep licenses and permits up to date
- comply with local, state, and federal laws and regulations regarding agriculture, food safety, the environment, business operations, land use, labor, and employment
- meet with agents of companies that are interested in purchasing their products
- promote their business by joining and networking with farmers' cooperatives, trade associations, local chambers of commerce, and other organizations
- stay abreast with horticultural developments, technologies, and market trends and prices

Producing horticultural crops is a physically demanding and intense job. Horticultural Growers must work outdoors in all kinds of weather. While working in greenhouses, they deal with very hot temperatures. They are exposed to chemicals, dust, machinery, sunlight, and other conditions that put them at risk for illnesses or injuries. Because farming is a risky business, their work can often be stressful as they deal with such issues as crop failures, employee problems, bad weather, and poor sales.

To build a successful business, Horticultural Growers work long hours, for six or seven days a week.

Salaries

Annual farm income for Horticultural Growers varies each year. Their annual net profit is determined after subtracting the total operating expenses from gross annual sales. It is common for small business owners to be unprofitable during their first years in operation. Some growers hold other jobs to supplement their income.

According to the May 2008 Occupational Employment Statistics survey by the U.S. Bureau of Labor Statistics, the estimated annual wage for most farmers ranged from $19,920 to $96,630.

Employment Prospects

Horticultural Growers set up farms, nurseries, and greenhouse companies throughout the United States. They establish wholesale or retail operations. They may sell to local, regional, national, or international markets.

Opportunities are available for individuals who are willing to invest their money, patience, and hard work into establishing successful agricultural operations. The success of horticultural operations depends on various factors, including the growers' ambition, business and marketing skills, competition, demand for products, and the state of the economy.

Some experts in the field report that prospects for Horticultural Growers, in general, should be favorable because customers continually buy ornamental plants for landscaping homes, businesses, and public areas. However, during economic downturns, consumers make fewer purchases.

Advancement Prospects

Horticultural Growers advance according to their own ambitions and interests. Like many entrepreneurs, they gauge their progress by achieving their business goals and objectives. Most, if not all, agricultural producers measure their success by being able to make a comfortable living from the profits of their operations.

Education and Training

Individuals do not need any formal training to become Horticultural Growers. They learn their skills on the job. They also complete formal and information courses in agriculture, horticulture, and business offered through colleges, Cooperative Extension Service offices, farm bureaus, farmers' cooperatives, and other organizations. In addition, they gain valuable knowledge by networking with colleagues and through self-study.

Some experts in the field encourage individuals to pursue higher education to handle the complex farming, business, and marketing problems and issues that modern farmers face.

Special Requirements

Horticultural Growers must obtain the proper local and state licenses and permits to operate their businesses. Requirements for businesses vary among states. For specific information, contact your local government office that oversees business licensing.

They also must acquire proper permits to perform specific activities such as pesticide application. In addition, these growers may be required to be registered or certified with the proper government agency to sell certain products, such as organic vegetables. Furthermore, Horticultural Growers must pass regular government inspections of their products and facilities.

Experience, Special Skills, and Personality Traits

Individuals should have several years of experience working in the horticultural industry, particularly in the type of operations that they wish to establish. Some Horticultural Growers worked their way up from being farmhands to managers before establishing their own farms, nurseries, or greenhouse companies.

To do well, Horticultural Growers need strong business, finance, and marketing skills. In addition, they must have excellent leadership, management, planning, organizational, and problem-solving skills. Having effective interpersonal, communication, and conflict-resolution skills is also essential, as they must be able to get along with many people from diverse backgrounds. Being self-motivated, determined, persistent, creative, flexible, and decisive are some personality traits that successful Horticultural Growers have in common.

Unions and Associations

Horticultural Growers can join trade associations, professional societies, farmers' cooperatives, and other agricultural organizations that serve their particular interests. By joining such organizations, they can take advantage of continuing education, current research studies, networking opportunities, and other services and resources. For example, some growers belong to farmers' cooperatives through which they market their products. These cooperatives are business organizations that the members own jointly to share various resources.

Tips for Entry

1. While in school, get a part-time or summer job with a nursery, seed company, gardening service, landscaping firm, or similar type of business to gain experience working with horticultural crops.

2. Experts suggest that prospective growers choose horticultural crops that satisfy the needs of their intended customers rather than themselves.

3. Take advantage of resources that are available from the U.S. Small Business Administration. This federal agency provides information and training programs to assist individuals with establishing and maintaining their small businesses.

4. Will you be seeking a bank loan to start your business? Be sure you have carefully prepared business and marketing plans to present to the loan officer. You might ask someone, such as a business or agricultural expert, to review your plans for thoroughness and detail, as well as for logic and comprehension.

5. Use the Internet to learn more about the production of horticultural crops. To get a list of relevant Web sites, enter any of these keywords into a search engine: *nursery production, greenhouse growers,* or *horticultural crop production.* For some links, see Appendix IV.

LIVESTOCK RANCHER

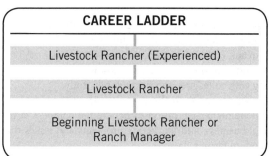

Duties: Oversee commercial livestock operations; perform farming, marketing, management, and administrative duties as required

Alternate Title(s): Cattle Rancher, Dairy Farmer, Horse Rancher, or other title that reflects a type of livestock producer

Salary Range: $20,000 to $97,000

Employment Prospects: Fair

Advancement Prospects: Poor

Prerequisites:

   Education or Training—On-the-job training; formal education in agriculture encouraged

   Experience—Several years of ranching experience

   Special Skills and Personality Traits—Business, marketing, negotiation, organizational, decision-making, critical-thinking, leadership, interpersonal, and communications skills; self-motivated, detail-oriented, patient, determined, persistent, flexible, and confident personality traits

   Special Requirements—Possess appropriate government licenses, permits, and certificates

Position Description

Livestock is the word used to collectively describe domestic farm animals, particularly cows, sheep, goats, pigs, and horses. Some wild or semidomesticated animals (such as elk and llamas) and large birds (such as emus and ostriches) are also considered livestock when they are managed in controlled conditions. Most livestock is raised on farm properties, more commonly known as ranches. The men and women who own or lease ranch operations are called Livestock Ranchers.

Livestock Ranchers raise their animals for commercial purposes. Many ranchers market livestock for their meat or milk. Some ranchers sell animal by-products, such as wool, leather, or fat to various markets, which use the by-products to make fiber, pharmaceuticals, livestock feed, soap, and other finished products. Some ranchers breed animals to sell to other ranchers, who grow them as livestock or use them as working stock. Some livestock producers raise animals to show at fairs and other exhibitions, where they may be auctioned. Other ranchers rear livestock, such as horses, for sports or recreational riding.

Most Livestock Ranchers produce one type of animal, such as sheep or cows. They usually hold job titles that reflect the type of livestock they tend, such as cattle rancher, dairy farmer, or horse rancher. Some Livestock Ranchers engage in raising animals for specialty markets. Increasingly, the demand for certain game meats such as venison, elk, ostrich, buffalo, and rabbit provides enterprising ranchers who live in favorable locations the opportunity to supply such meats to restaurants, food stores, and food processing companies. Other Livestock Ranchers raise llamas or alpacas for their wool as an alternative to sheep's wool.

In recent years, more Livestock Ranchers have begun to use the organic method of raising livestock. Organic ranchers feed their herds or flocks only pesticide-free food that was grown in soils supplemented solely with nonchemical fertilizers. In the United States, these organic ranchers adhere to standards established by the U.S. Department of Agriculture (USDA). For example, organic ranchers must not use antibiotics or hormones on their livestock; they must only give their livestock totally organic feed; and they must breed their herds with only organically-raised animals that meet the desired characteristics and quality.

Livestock ranches usually consist of several acres of land on which animals can graze. Some Livestock Ranchers set aside land to grow crops, such as hay, oats, and rye, to feed their herds or flocks. Ranchers also provide barns or sheds to shelter their animals from inclement weather, cold temperatures, and the night. Although some livestock animals spend their days in pens or corrals, many ranchers allow their animals to feed in open-range environments. Livestock Ranchers erect fences over long distances to keep their herds or flocks within the boundaries of their ranch property. Fences also help keep natural predators, such as coyotes or wolves, from attacking the livestock. While roaming large pastures, livestock animals help prevent wildfires in remote locations and control ground cover and weeds by keeping overgrowth in check.

In addition to caring for and keeping track of their herds or flocks, Livestock Ranchers need to be experts at running a business. To keep their operations profitable, Livestock Managers manage a budget and keep abreast of land values and market prices for their livestock. Livestock Ranchers also must be familiar with operating and maintaining farm equipment, have a working understanding of veterinary science and animal nutrition, and be knowledgeable about basic crop management.

Livestock Ranchers perform a wide range of tasks, both directly with their animals and around their ranch properties. Some of their duties include:

- deciding where to graze their animals
- selecting which animals to use for breeding purposes
- providing sufficient water and supplemental foods to their animals
- setting out salt licks or blocks, which provide animals with such necessary minerals as sodium, calcium, and iron
- monitoring their animals closely for signs of illness or injury
- assisting animals with the birthing of their young
- milking animals such as goats or cows
- butchering and processing meat for sale
- tagging animals with ear tags or ear notches for identification purposes
- selling animals and their by-products such as milk, wool, manure, bones, or horns
- plowing land, planting seeds, and cultivating, irrigating, and harvesting crops
- cleaning farm equipment, corrals, and barn facilities
- maintaining ranch buildings and equipment
- building and repairing fences
- keeping records of accounts and ranch activities

Livestock Ranchers are responsible for their own business success. They continually learn new ranching, husbandry, management, and marketing methods, as well as keep up with commodity futures, agricultural trends, new technologies, proposed legislations and government programs, and other areas.

Like all agricultural producers, Livestock Ranchers establish marketing plans for their operations. They sell their products to local, national, and international markets in various ways. Some ranchers sell their livestock or by-products directly to food processors, food distributors, meat markets, and restaurants, while others make contractual arrangements with companies to sell their products specifically to those businesses. Some Livestock Ranchers market their products directly to the public by selling their products at their ranches or at farmers' markets.

Many Livestock Ranchers seek other ways to bring in additional income. For example, ranchers might sell their animals' manure to gardeners, other farmers, horticulturists, or commercial fertilizer suppliers. Goat or sheep ranchers may offer grazing services to property owners who wish to control the spread of undergrowth, wild grasses, weeds, or shrubbery on their lands. Some cattle and horse ranchers have started agritourism operations in which they offer activities to attract tourists, such as cattle drives, horseback rides, and hunting trips. Ranchers may also provide tourists with an opportunity to stay overnight for several days or weeks at their ranches.

Ranching is sometimes isolating work, as ranches are generally located some distance away from population centers. Livestock Ranchers spend much of their time alone or with a few ranch employees while working outdoors with their animals or performing other tasks. Ranchers attend to their business tasks indoors in offices.

Ranch work is physically strenuous. Livestock Ranchers handle live animals that are large, heavy, and strong, and may risk injury. They work in all kinds of weather conditions. Ranchers often drive trucks or other vehicles around their ranch properties but also do much of their range work on horseback.

Livestock Ranchers work long hours every day of the week. Their workweeks may be as long as 60 hours or more. Some ranchers also work at other jobs to supplement their income.

Salaries

Annual farm income for Livestock Ranchers varies each year. Their annual net profit is determined after subtracting the total operating expenses from gross annual sales. It is common for small business owners to be unprofitable during their first years in operation.

According to the May 2008 Occupational Employment Statistics survey by the U.S. Bureau of Labor Statistics (BLS), the estimated annual wage for most farmers, including Livestock Ranchers, ranged between $19,920 and $96,630.

Employment Prospects

The number of farms, including livestock operations, has been declining over the last several decades in the United States. According to some agricultural experts, there has been a trend toward larger farms. The USDA reports that in 2007 there were about 2 million farms in operation. The majority of them were family-run operations.

Opportunities to start livestock ranches are available to individuals who are willing to invest their money, patience, and hard work into establishing successful operations. The BLS reports that nearly 1 million farmers, including Livestock Ranchers, were self-employed in the United States. It further states that during the 2008 to 2018 period, the employment of farmers should decrease by 8 percent. Some agricultural experts report that almost 50 percent of today's farmers will be reaching retirement age in the coming decade.

Advancement Prospects

Livestock Ranchers define their own measure of success according to their own ambitions and interests. Like many entrepreneurs, they determine their progress by achieving specific business goals and objectives, such as earning certain annual incomes and expanding their operations. Most, if not all, Livestock Ranchers pursue advancement through job satisfaction and the ability to make a comfortable living from the profits of their operations.

Education and Training

There are no standard educational requirements for individuals to become Livestock Ranchers. However, many experts in the field encourage individuals to obtain formal training in raising livestock. Many ranchers have completed high school or college courses in animal science, farm management, business, and marketing. Some Livestock Ranchers have earned college degrees in agriculture, animal science, zoology, biological science, or other disciplines.

Livestock Ranchers learn their skills on the job while they work as ranch hands and managers. They also complete informal courses in agriculture and business offered through colleges, Cooperative Extension Service offices, farm bureaus, farmers' cooperatives, and other organizations. These ranchers also gain valuable knowledge through self-study and by networking with colleagues.

Special Requirements

Livestock Ranchers must obtain the proper local and state licenses and permits to operate their businesses. Requirements for businesses vary among states. For specific information, contact your local government office that oversees business licensing.

In addition, Farmers may be required to be registered or certified with the proper government agency to sell organic products.

Experience, Special Skills, and Personality Traits

To be successful Livestock Ranchers, individuals usually need several years of experience working on ranches to obtain sufficient technical and management experience.

Livestock Ranchers need strong business, marketing, negotiation, organizational, decision-making, and critical-thinking skills. They also must have excellent leadership, interpersonal, and communications skills to work well with employees, fellow ranchers, bankers, suppliers, and many others from diverse backgrounds. Being self-motivated, detail-oriented, patient, determined, persistent, flexible, and confident are some personality traits that successful Livestock Ranchers have in common.

Unions and Associations

Livestock Ranchers can join local, state, or national professional associations and other farming organizations that serve their particular farming interests. As members of such groups, these ranchers can take advantage of networking opportunities, training programs, and other professional services and resources.

Ranchers may also be members of farmers' cooperatives through which they market their products. These cooperatives are business organizations that the members own jointly to share various resources.

Tips for Entry

1. Enroll in animal husbandry classes at your high school or community college, if they are available. Obtain a part-time job or volunteer at a livestock ranch to gain experience.
2. Take advantage of educational programs offered by your local Cooperative Extension Service office that can help you learn more about livestock production and marketing.
3. Be willing to relocate to find jobs as a ranch hand or ranch manager.
4. Use the Internet to learn more about livestock and livestock ranching. You might start by visiting these Web sites: Virtual Livestock Library at Oklahoma State University (www.139.78.104.1/library); and Ohioline-Farm: Livestock (ohioline.osu.edu/lines/stock.html). For more links, see Appendix IV.

DAIRY FARMER

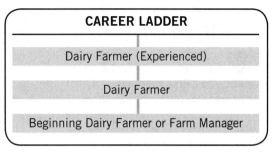

Position Description

Milk is one of our most nutritious foods. It is packed with protein, vitamins, and minerals that build and sustain healthy muscles and bones, as well as stave off diseases that result from vitamin deficiencies. Throughout history, people have drunk milk that came from many animals, including goats, sheep, horses, donkeys, buffaloes, camels, and reindeer. Cows, however, are the most common animals used for the purpose of providing milk for humans because they produce milk in sufficient quantities to be distributed widely. Cows can supply milk for as many as 320 days; individually each cow can produce an average of six gallons of milk a day. They begin producing milk when they have given birth to calves. They continue to furnish milk even after their calves have been weaned.

Agricultural producers, known as Dairy Farmers, are in the business of raising cows for the sole purpose of producing milk for drinking or making into such other dairy products as cheese, butter, yogurt, ice cream, and buttermilk. They oversee operations that include pasture land and structures for feeding, sheltering, and milking their herds. Some dairy farms do their own milk processing on site, while others send or sell their milk to dairy plants. Most dairy farms are family operations, which farmers own or lease. These farmers retain one or more hired hands, who may be family members, to assist them with the day-to-day operations. Some large dairy farms are owned by dairy corporations; these farms are run by farm managers and technicians.

Dairy Farmers own and manage small herds that range from 50 or fewer cows to several hundred. Their milking operations are complex and sophisticated, not like the traditional images of farmers milking cows by hand. The cows are milked in large buildings called milking parlors. There, machines are operated to efficiently extract milk from each cow's udder and deliver it through tubes to large holding tanks. Dairy Farmers milk their cows two or more times each day. Otherwise, the cows would stop producing milk until they gave birth again.

Some Dairy Farmers convert their operations into organic farms. These farmers modify their farming methods so that their cows produce organic milk, which has been so certified by the U.S. Department of Agriculture (USDA). This federal agency requires farmers to use organic methods to manage their cows for at least one full year. They must refrain from using growth hormones and antibiotics to raise their livestock. They must also feed their cows strictly organically grown grass and feed. In other words, the pastures in which cows graze and the hay and grains they eat must not have been grown from genetically-modified or treated seeds. The pastures and feed crops must also be free of any use of chemical fertilizers, insecticides, or herbicides.

Dairy Farmers perform physically demanding work to keep their operations running smoothly and safely every day. Along with the daily milking, farmers make sure their cows are watered and fed. They provide them with feed and hay in pens and barns, as well as move the cows out to pasture to graze. To keep their costs down, many Dairy Farmers grow hay and feed grains for their cows. Dairy Farmers also schedule breeding, vaccinating, and dehorning of their cows. Furthermore, they attend to the birthing of calves, and bottle-feed the calves with colostrum (their mothers' first milk) and regular milk until they are weaned.

Dairy Farmers check the health of their cows daily and bring in veterinarians to attend to cows that are ill or injured. Some farmers use antibiotics or other medications to treat cows. Any milk produced from cows that have been administered medications is discarded rather than introduced to the market.

Dairy Farmers are responsible for complying with government laws and regulations regarding the production of dairy cows. They are expected to provide comfortable, safe, and healthy living conditions for their cows and adhere to strict sanitation standards.

Dairy Farmers must keep their cows and facilities spotlessly clean to ensure that the milk they produce is free of contaminants. Before cows are milked, their udders are carefully washed. Milking machines, the pipes that carry the milk to holding vats, and the vats themselves are kept clean and sterilized at all times. Dairy Farmers also make sure that the cow stalls, milking parlors, and barn facilities are all thoroughly cleaned and maintained. Before milk is accepted by customers and milk processing plants, the milk is tested to ensure that it is pure and healthful according to standards set by the farmers' states as well as the USDA, the U.S. Environmental Protection Agency, and the U.S. Food and Drug Administration.

Dairy Farmers also perform other farm management duties. They hire, train, and supervise employees. They make sure that farm vehicles, tractors, and other farm equipment are maintained and repaired as needed. Many Dairy Farmers perform their own basic carpentry, mechanical, electrical, and other types of repair work as needed. In addition, Dairy Farmers maintain logs of all farm activities, such as records of each cow's feeding schedule, health status, breeding history, and milk production statistics. Furthermore, Dairy Farmers handle emergencies such as storms, illnesses among their cows, and equipment malfunctions as they occur.

Dairy farm owners manage various business responsibilities as well. They make sure their employees, bills, insurance premiums, mortgage (or rent), and taxes are paid; licenses and permits are up-to-date; payments are collected from customers and purchasers; business records are maintained; and so on. Dairy Farmers also set aside time to plan and implement marketing strategies to generate more sales for their farms.

Dairy Farmers work outdoors in all kinds of weather. They are exposed to dust, animal dander, chemicals, machinery, and other conditions that put them at risk to illnesses and injuries. Dairy Farmers work long hours every day of the year. Some Dairy Farmers also work full-time, part-time, or seasonal jobs to supplement their income.

Salaries

Annual farm income for Dairy Farmers varies each year. Their earnings depend on the size of their farm and geographic location as well as market prices, trends, and such factors as weather conditions that influence production. Their annual net profit is determined after subtracting the total operating expenses from gross annual sales. It is common for small business owners to be unprofitable during their first years in operation.

The U.S. Bureau of Labor Statistics (BLS) reports in its May 2008 Occupational Employment Statistics survey that the estimated annual wage for most farmers ranged from $19,920 to $96,630.

Employment Prospects

Dairy farms are found throughout the United States. According to the Dairy Farming Today Web site (www.dairyfarmingtoday.org), approximately 60,000 dairy farms exist in the nation. Most are family-owned. Some experts in the field state that the trend is toward fewer dairy farms and larger herds.

According to the BLS, approximately 1 million farmers, including Dairy Farmers, were self-employed in the United States in 2008. It further states that during the 2008 to 2018 period, the employment of farmers should decrease by 8 percent. However, opportunities are available for individuals who are willing to invest their money, patience, and hard work into establishing successful farms. Some agricultural experts report that almost 50 percent of today's farmers will reach retirement age in the coming decade.

Advancement Prospects

Dairy Farmers advance according to their own ambitions and interests. Like many other entrepreneurs, they gauge their progress by achieving their business goals and objectives. For example, some Dairy Farmers expand their herds or buy more land. Most, if not all,

Farmers measure their success by being able to make a comfortable living from the profits of their operations.

Education and Training

Although no formal training is required, some experts recommend that individuals obtain education to handle the complex farming, business, and marketing problems and issues that modern farmers face. Many Dairy Farmers have earned college degrees in dairy science, animal science, or other related fields. Every state has at least one college or university that has an agricultural science department.

Dairy Farmers learn their skills on the job. They also complete formal and informal courses in agriculture and business offered through colleges, Cooperative Extension Service offices, farm bureaus, farmers' cooperatives, and other organizations. They also gain knowledge by networking with colleagues, attending trade shows, and through self-study.

Special Requirements

Dairy Farmers must obtain the proper local and state licenses and permits to operate their businesses. Requirements for businesses vary among states. For specific information, contact your local government office that oversees business licensing.

Dairy facilities must also pass local and state inspections regarding animal waste storage, treatment, and disposal. Organic farmers must also be inspected by and certified by the U.S. Department of Agriculture.

Experience, Special Skills, and Personality Traits

Individuals usually have many years of experience working on dairy farms before becoming Dairy Farmers. Many have a few years of experience performing supervisory and managerial responsibilities on dairy farms.

Dairy Farmers need strong marketing and business skills to manage successful operations. In addition, they need excellent leadership, self-management, planning, organizational, problem-solving, communication, interpersonal, and conflict-resolution skills. Some personality traits that Dairy Farmers share include being enterprising, patient, determined, goal-oriented, detail-oriented, resourceful, and self-motivated.

Unions and Associations

Dairy Farmers can join farming organizations, including farmers' cooperatives and associations, to take advantage of networking opportunities, continuing education, and other services and resources. Dairy farmers' cooperatives, for example, assist members with marketing their milk as well as with providing information regarding new developments in dairy farming techniques and technologies. Organizations are available at the local, state, and national levels. For example, the Dairy Farmers of America is a national cooperative that serves the interests of its members from various states. For contact information, see Appendix II.

Tips for Entry

1. While in high school, take one or more business courses to start developing skills needed to run the business aspects of a farm.
2. Work for a dairy farm, particularly in the region where you would like to live, to determine if raising dairy cows is the right career for you.
3. Learn how to use computers proficiently, as they are useful tools for keeping various types of records for farm operations.
4. Join a local farmers' association or farm bureau and get to know other farmers in the area.
5. Use the Internet to learn more about agriculture and farming. You might start by visiting these Web sites: Dairy Farming Today (www.dairyfarmingtoday.org); and Dairyline Radio, (www.dairyline.com). For more links, see Appendix IV.

POULTRY FARMER

CAREER PROFILE

Duties: Oversee commercial poultry operations; perform farming, marketing, management, and administrative duties as required

Alternate Title(s): Chicken Farmer, Turkey Rancher, Duck Farmer

Salary Range: $20,000 to $97,000

Employment Prospects: Fair

Advancement Prospects: Poor

Prerequisites:

    Education or Training—On-the-job training; formal education in agriculture encouraged

    Experience—Several years of poultry farming experience

    Special Skills and Personality Traits—Business, finance, marketing, leadership, organizational, critical-thinking, problem-solving, interpersonal, communication, conflict-resolution, and computer skills; patient, decisive, detail-oriented, orderly, determined, and flexible personality traits

    Special Requirements—Possess appropriate government licenses, permits, and certificates

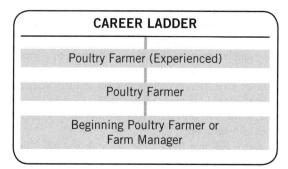

CAREER LADDER

Poultry Farmer (Experienced)

Poultry Farmer

Beginning Poultry Farmer or Farm Manager

Position Description

Poultry Farmers are another type of commercial farmer who produce food for sale. They raise flocks of chickens, turkeys, ducks, and geese for their meat and eggs. Like other agricultural producers, Poultry Farmers make sure their operations run efficiently, economically, and safely every day. Most farmers hire assistants, including family members, to help perform the day-to-day operations of their farm.

Poultry farms manage bird populations that vary in size from several dozen to a few hundred to tens of thousands of birds. Most poultry farms are family-owned businesses.

Many Poultry Farmers focus on tending one type of domesticated fowl. In the United States, the majority of poultry farms raise chickens. Poultry Farmers may specialize further by producing poultry only for their eggs or for their meat. Some farmers breed and nurture birds for showing them at agricultural fairs and exhibitions as well as to market to farmers, retailers, and others.

Poultry Farmers sell their products to food processors, poultry wholesalers and distributors, grocery stores, butcher shops, meat markets, and restaurants. Many small-scale farmers process their animals themselves and sell directly to the public through farmers' markets or from their farms.

Some farmers, particularly chicken farmers, raise birds under contract to poultry integrators. These companies own the hatcheries, feed mills, and processing plants as well as the birds. The companies provide contracted farmers with chicks and poultry feed. The farmers, in turn, manage the poultry and receive payment upon delivery of grown birds or eggs to the companies.

Many farmers raise their flocks indoors for more efficient management as well as to protect their birds from predators. The birds live in climate-controlled facilities to simulate conditions that maximize the production of birds and eggs. Farmers use several buildings to house their birds. Each building has its own purpose and features different interior arrangements to suit its function. For example, in egg-production buildings, hens live without the presence of roosters, as their unfertilized eggs are sold for human consumption.

Some Poultry Farmers prefer to follow sustainable methods to raise their birds. One example is the free-range method, in which birds roam freely in outdoor areas for at least half of their day. They are limited only by fencing, which contains their living area. They eat grasses and other plants as well as worms and insects.

To make sure that the eggs and meat they produce are high quality and suitable for market, Poultry Farmers manage certain tasks every day. They feed and water their flocks. They inspect their birds daily for diseases or injuries and remove sick and injured ones. They keep bird pens and other living areas free of waste, and ensure that proper drainage systems are in good condition. They make sure outdoor areas are clean and free of predators, poisonous plants, and farm equipment. Poultry Farmers also maintain accurate and up-to-date records about their birds, including their birth and death dates, vaccinations, veterinary care, and feeding.

Poultry Farmers work long hours, seven days each week. They work in noisy, smelly, and dusty environments, and are exposed to all weather conditions.

Salaries

Annual farm income for Poultry Farmers varies each year, depending on such factors as the size of their operations, how many products they produce and sell, and the market value for their products. The estimated annual wage for most farmers ranged from $19,920 to $96,630, according to the May 2008 Occupational Employment Statistics survey by the U.S. Bureau of Labor Statistics.

Employment Prospects

Poultry farms are found throughout the United States. According to the U.S. Department of Agriculture Web site, the United States is the largest producer, as well as the second largest exporter, of poultry meat in the world. The U.S. is also a major egg producer.

Opportunities are available for individuals who are willing to invest their money, patience, and hard work in establishing successful farms.

Advancement Prospects

Poultry Farmers define their own criteria for advancement. Like many entrepreneurs, they gauge their progress by achieving their business goals and objectives. For example, some Poultry Farmers buy more land to expand their operations.

Education and Training

Although no formal training is required, many experts in the field encourage individuals to complete educational programs to learn how to handle farming, business, and marketing issues.

Farmers learn their skills on the job. They also complete formal and informal courses in agriculture and business offered through colleges, Cooperative Extension Service offices, farm bureaus, farmers' cooperatives, and other organizations.

Special Requirements

Farmers must obtain the proper local and state licenses and permits to operate their businesses. For specific information, contact your local government office that oversees business licensing. Poultry Farmers may be required to be registered or certified with the proper government agency to sell certain products.

Experience, Special Skills, and Personality Traits

Poultry Farmers normally start a business after many years of experience working in the poultry industry, including managerial experience.

Poultry Farmers need business, finance, and marketing skills to execute their administrative duties well. They must also have leadership, organizational, critical-thinking, problem-solving, interpersonal, communication, and conflict-resolution skills. In addition, they need computer skills to keep track of records and finances. Being patient, decisive, detail-oriented, orderly, determined, and flexible are some personality traits that successful Poultry Farmers have in common.

Unions and Associations

Poultry Farmers can join trade associations, farmers' cooperatives, and other farming organizations to take advantage of networking opportunities, training programs, and other professional services and resources. Some national groups that serve the varied interests of Poultry Farmers are the American Pastured Poultry Producers Association, American Poultry Association, National Chicken Council, National Turkey Federation, and U.S. Poultry & Egg Association. For contact information, see Appendix II.

Tips for Entry

1. While in high school and college, obtain a summer job in the poultry industry.
2. To learn more about starting a poultry farm, contact a Cooperative Extension Service office.
3. Use the Internet to learn more about poultry farming. You might start by visiting the U.S. Poultry and Egg Association Web site at www.poultryegg.org. For more links, see Appendix IV.

MARKET GARDENER

CAREER PROFILE

Duties: Oversee small-scale commercial agricultural operations; perform farming, marketing, management, and administrative duties as required

Alternate Title(s): Market Grower, Truck Farmer

Salary Range: $20,000 to $97,000

Employment Prospects: Fair

Advancement Prospects: Poor

Prerequisites:

Education or Training—On-the-job training; formal education in agriculture encouraged

Experience—Several years of gardening or farming experience

Special Skills and Personality Traits—Management, planning, organizational, problem-solving, interpersonal, communication, conflict-resolution, computer, writing, business, finance, and marketing skills; self-motivated, determined, decisive, patient, flexible, and resourceful personality traits

Special Requirements—Possess appropriate government licenses, permits, and certificates

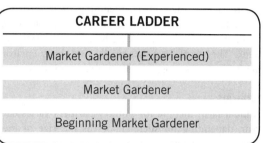

CAREER LADDER

Market Gardener (Experienced)

Market Gardener

Beginning Market Gardener

Position Description

Market Gardeners own and manage commercial mini-farms. Unlike vast farms that produce one or more major crops, Market Gardeners grow several varieties of fruits, vegetables, and flowers on small operations. They might grow their crops on several garden plots that total less than an acre of land or produce crops on as many as 100 acres of land. Some also raise crops in containers or in greenhouses. Market Gardeners are experienced farmers as well as hobby gardeners with little or no farming experience. Their mini-farms may be located in rural areas or suburban backyards, and may even occupy city lots. These agriculturists are also known as market growers, specialty growers, or truck farmers.

Many Market Gardeners raise traditional food crops, such as tomatoes, corn, beans, peppers, lettuces, onions, melons, apples, strawberries, and walnuts. Some grow varieties of flowers that are common to their areas. Other Market Gardeners specialize in producing niche crops such as herbs, Asian vegetables, mushrooms, orchids, or ornamental plants. Some growers also raise poultry, bees, cows, sheep, or other animals in small numbers for their meat, eggs, or by-products, such as wool or honey, to sell.

Market Gardeners promote their products in several different venues to increase their profits. Rather than sell large quantities of produce to grocery conglomerates, the fast-food industry, or other large food distributors, Market Gardeners sell their farm output in a more direct fashion, mostly to local markets. They sell their products to local retailers, such as florists, restaurants, and grocers, as well as to school meal programs, and companies and other institutions that have employee cafeterias.

Market Gardeners also sell their farm products to the public. Many of these growers peddle their products at one or more farmers' markets. Some sell their products from the back of their trucks along roadsides or at busy intersections. Some Market Gardeners set up produce stands or pick-your-own services at their farms, where customers harvest the fruits and vegetables they purchase.

Another source of income for Market Gardeners is through community supported agriculture (CSA) programs, which offer produce subscriptions to local consumers. Every week or month, subscribers receive a certain amount of fresh vegetables, fruits, flowers, and other products from various farms participating in the CSA programs.

Many Market Gardeners find additional ways to earn money from their small operations. For example, some Market Gardeners establish agritourism operations to provide entertainment and educational opportunities on their properties such as horse rides, corn mazes, or pumpkin carving contests, as well as farming workshops, lectures, and garden tours. Some Market Gardeners make finished products from their crops, such as wreaths, flower arrangements, soaps, or jams to sell at farmers' markets or at craft fairs. Others collect seeds to sell to home gardeners.

Market Gardeners often choose to use sustainable farming methods to produce their crops. Consumers increasingly desire sustainably grown foods because of their health benefits and delicious flavors. Moreover, Market Gardeners earn higher incomes from the sale of their sustainable produce than they would from the sale of conventionally grown produce. Sustainable producers do not use chemical-based fertilizers, pesticides, or herbicides to grow their crops or raise their animals. Rather, they amend their soil with manure and compost. They use compatible flowers to draw away insects. They control weeds by hoeing the soil or by using rotor tillers. When they use pesticide or herbicide sprays, they use solutions made from plant products rather than synthetic chemical preparations.

Some sustainable practitioners specifically follow organic methods, and seek certification from the U.S. Department of Agriculture (USDA) to market their products as organic goods. To obtain and maintain USDA organic certification, Market Gardeners must adhere to strict USDA regulations and standards regarding the production, processing, and labeling of organic products. For example, the USDA stipulates that organic farmers must only use organic or untreated seeds as well as keep accurate records of how crops were raised, where they were tended, what products were applied to them, and where the products were stored.

Market Gardeners also incorporate various methods to extend growing seasons or produce crops year-round. They may use such traditional means as cold frames or cloches (glass bell-shaped jars) to protect their plants from cold temperatures and frost. Many Market Gardeners use greenhouses to grow plants year-round or to start seedlings before and throughout the usual growing season. Some farmers are now using plastic sheeting to create row covers, hoop houses, and tunnels to protect entire sections of land from cold weather. They also cover the ground between rows with plastic to prevent the growth of weeds and to provide moisture to crops in a method called drip irrigation.

Market Gardeners, like other farmers, are well versed in business practices and the risks involved in running an agricultural operation. They start their businesses by setting goals, conducting market research, and preparing budgets and business plans. They also research legal aspects of their businesses, purchase or lease land, and determine which crops to grow. They get their businesses established by finding financial assets including loans, obtaining bank accounts, and setting up systems for bookkeeping and other record keeping. Furthermore, they obtain seeds, gardening supplies, tools, and equipment, as well as necessary office equipment and supplies.

In order to make their businesses thrive, Market Gardeners continue to perform careful planning, accounting, record keeping, and other duties. For example, they manage credit and deposit accounts, pay taxes and bills, and comply with various government regulations for farming and business activities. Market Gardeners also keep abreast of developments in market gardening techniques by reading books, attending classes or conferences, and communicating with other growers.

Depending on the size of their operations, Market Gardeners might work alone or with one or more partners. Some of these growers employ family members, apprentices, or hired hands to assist them with their gardening, marketing, and various other tasks. Market Gardeners are responsible for providing their employees with work assignments, training, and supervision.

Market gardens are less mechanized than large farms. Consequently, Market Gardeners perform physically demanding work. They use hand tools or small power tools for cultivating and pruning. They stand, walk, squat, stoop, bend, reach, and lift for long periods. They also endure all kinds of weather conditions including extremes in temperature.

Market Gardeners usually work every day of the week to manage their crops as well as perform their various business and marketing tasks. Their daily schedules vary according to the growing season.

Salaries

Annual farm income for Market Gardeners varies each year, depending on such factors as the size of their operations, how many crops they produce and sell, and the market value for their crops. Their annual net profit is determined after subtracting their total operating expenses from gross annual sales. It is common for small business owners to be unprofitable during their first years in operation.

According to the May 2008 Occupational Employment Statistics survey by the U.S. Bureau of Labor Statistics, the estimated annual wage for most farmers, in general, ranged between $19,920 and $96,630.

Employment Prospects

Any individual willing to invest labor, money, and time may start up a market garden. Market Gardeners operate throughout the United States in rural, suburban, and urban settings. Their success depends on various factors, such as their ambitions and abilities to run a business, the local demand for products, the competition, and the state of the economy.

Some experts in the field express a growing trend of more consumers buying locally-grown harvests. Experts also report that organic farming is one of the fastest growing segments of U.S. agriculture.

Advancement Prospects

Market Gardeners determine their own terms of advancement. Many measure their success by earning higher incomes, by expanding their businesses, and through job satisfaction.

Education and Training

Individuals do not need any formal training to become Market Gardeners. They learn their skills on the job. Many also complete formal and informal courses in agriculture and business offered through colleges, Cooperative Extension Service offices, farm bureaus, farmers' cooperatives, and other organizations. They also gain valuable knowledge by networking with colleagues and through self-study.

Some experts in the field encourage individuals to pursue higher education to handle the complex farming, business, and marketing problems and issues that modern growers face.

Special Requirements

Market Gardeners must obtain the proper local and state licenses and permits to operate their businesses. Requirements for businesses vary among states. For specific information, contact your local government office that oversees business licensing.

They also must acquire proper permits to perform specific activities such as pesticide control. In addition, Market Gardeners may be required to be registered or certified with the proper government agency to sell certain products, such as organic vegetables. Furthermore, they must pass regular government inspections of their products and facilities.

Experience, Special Skills, and Personality Traits

Individuals should have some farming or gardening experience before starting a commercial market gar-

den. They may have gained their experience through employment, volunteer work, or hobbies.

To do well in their business, Market Gardeners must have excellent management, planning, organizational, and problem-solving skills. They also need effective interpersonal, communication, and conflict-resolution skills, as they must be able to get along with many people from diverse backgrounds. In addition, these growers need strong computer, writing, business, finance, and marketing skills. Being self-motivated, determined, decisive, patient, flexible, and resourceful are some personality traits that successful Market Gardeners have in common.

Unions and Associations

Market Gardeners can join local, state, or national marketing gardening associations as well as farming associations and organizations that serve their particular interests. By joining such organizations, they can take advantage of networking opportunities, training programs, and other professional services and resources.

Tips for Entry

1. Work or volunteer for experienced Market Gardeners to learn the business.
2. Enroll in formal or informal educational programs to learn about various aspects of minifarming, horticulture, marketing, and business administration.
3. Developing a strong market plan is as important as creating a business plan for your prospective operations. Contact your local Cooperative Extension Service office or other agricultural group for advice about marketing and preparing a marketing plan.
4. Do your research before starting up a market gardening business. Find out who your competitors are, what establishments (such as restaurants, grocery stores, school cafeterias, and company cafeterias) might be potential markets for you, what farmers' markets are nearby, and so forth.
5. Learn more about market gardening on the Internet. To get a list of relevant Web sites to visit, enter these keywords into a search engine: *market gardening, market growers,* or *micro farming.* For some links, see Appendix IV.

FARMING—
SUPPORT STAFF

FARM MANAGER

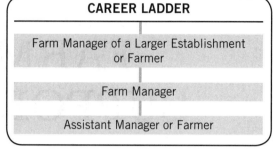

critical-thinking, problem-solving, customer service, negotiation, self-management, writing, and computer skills; outgoing, motivational, patient, ambitious, disciplined, flexible, and resourceful personality traits

Position Description

Farm Managers are employed to oversee all types of commercial operations from market gardens to crop farms to poultry farms to dairy and cattle ranches to tree farms to fish farms. They also manage such other agricultural enterprises as greenhouse operations, nurseries, and harvest-processing centers. In addition, Farm Managers direct the operations of experimental research farms. The primary responsibility of Farm Managers is to ensure the productive capacity of their employers' agricultural operations. Those who are in charge of commercial businesses also make sure that the operations are profitable for their employers.

Farm Managers are experts in both the production and business aspects of running agricultural operations. They attend to tasks that are specific to farm management as well as perform general management tasks similar to the duties that managers carry out in other industries. Farm Managers outline, plan, and coordinate the work of a farm, ranch, or other type of agricultural operation, and direct the farm staff to complete the work. These managers administer budgets, establish goals for farm production, decide what crops or animals to produce, and determine when to purchase materials and sell farm products. They also participate in making marketing decisions.

Many of these men and women are employed by family farmers and agricultural cooperatives as well

as by food manufacturers, seed companies, restaurant chains, supermarkets, and other private companies that own farms for production or research. Other Farm Managers work for firms that offer farm management services on a contractual basis. These Farm Managers may be assigned to oversee two or more operations.

Just as farms differ in size and purpose, the responsibilities of Farm Managers vary in complexity. These experts may attend to many duties or be responsible for only a few aspects of farming while working with owners or a team of Farm Managers. For example, a manager may be hired to supervise farm employees, handle farm accounts and the scheduling of farm tasks, or take charge of marketing responsibilities. In some instances, these professionals have general farming responsibilities, such as operating farm equipment; planting, cultivating, and harvesting crops; or taking care of livestock.

Their working conditions vary according to their job duties and the type of operations they manage. For example, some Farm Managers work mostly in office settings but may also conduct inspections of fields, nurseries, greenhouses, forests, or fishponds. While working outdoors, Farm Managers endure hot and cold temperatures and inclement weather. These managers perform strenuous tasks that may involve walking, standing, climbing, stooping, or bending for long periods or lifting and carrying heavy objects.

Farm Managers are exposed to dust, chemicals (such as pesticide contaminants), loud noises, and the risk of injury from the use of heavy equipment or working with animals.

Farm Managers work all year, although they may be busier during some parts of the year than others. Crop farm managers, for example, work longer hours during growing and harvesting seasons. Farm Managers have flexible work schedules. They may be expected to be available at all hours to handle any work or emergencies that may arise.

Salaries

Salaries for Farm Managers vary, depending on their education, experience, employer, and geographic location, as well as the type and size of their operations. The U.S. Bureau of Labor Statistics reports in its May 2008 Occupational Employment Statistics survey that the estimated annual salary for most Farm Managers ranged from $31,350 to $103,570.

Some employers provide their managers with housing and/or a work vehicle.

Employment Prospects

Job openings for Farm Managers generally become available as individuals retire or transfer to other jobs or careers. Additional positions are created when farmers decide to work part-time or retire and need Farm Managers to oversee their operations.

Advancement Prospects

Farm Managers mark their success by earning higher wages, through job satisfaction, and by being recognized for their work. Some Farm Managers advance by being hired to oversee larger or more complex operations. Entrepreneurial individuals may pursue opportunities to purchase their own farms or to start companies that offer farm management services.

With their experience and knowledge, Farm Managers can also pursue other careers by becoming agricultural sales representatives, teachers, agricultural consultants, Cooperative Extension Service agents, or other agricultural professionals.

Education and Training

Many employers prefer to hire candidates who have an associate's or bachelor's degree in agriculture, farm management, or other related field.

Individuals learn farm production and farm management skills on the job as they work under the direction of farmers, farm supervisors, and Farm Managers.

Experience, Special Skills, and Personality Traits

Employers seek candidates who have extensive experience in farming operations and have knowledge of farm production as well as business management, finance, budgeting, and marketing expertise. Candidates should have previous experience working on the types of farms that they would oversee.

Farm Managers need effective leadership, interpersonal, and communication skills, as they must be able to work well with employers, personnel, and others. Farm Managers also need excellent organizational, critical-thinking, problem-solving, customer service, negotiation, and self-management skills. Having strong writing and computer skills is also important.

Some personality traits that successful Farm Managers share include being outgoing, motivational, patient, ambitious, disciplined, flexible, and resourceful.

Unions and Associations

Some Farm Managers join professional associations to take advantage of networking opportunities, training programs, and other professional services and resources. One national society that serves Farm Managers is the American Society of Farm Managers and Rural Appraisers. For contact information, see Appendix II.

Tips for Entry

1. Being able to speak and understand Spanish may improve your chances of gaining employment.
2. Take basic courses in accounting, bookkeeping, and business management. Be sure to list those courses and skills on your job application.
3. To enhance their employability, some Farm Managers obtain professional certification through the American Society of Farm Managers and Rural Appraisers (ASFMRA). For information, visit ASFMRA (www.asfmra.org) on the Web.
4. Use the Internet to learn more about farm management. To get a list of Web sites, enter the word *farm management* or *farm managers* into a search engine. To learn about some links, see Appendix IV.

BEEF CATTLE MANAGER

CAREER PROFILE

Duties: Oversee the daily production and management of a beef cattle operation; perform other duties as required

Alternate Title(s): Ranch Manager, Livestock Manager, Beef Manager, Herd Manager

Salary Range: $31,000 to $104,000

Employment Prospects: Fair

Advancement Prospects: Poor

Prerequisites:

Education or Training—College degree may be required; on-the-job training

Experience—Several years of experience working on beef cattle ranches; supervisory and management experience needed

CAREER LADDER

Manager of a Larger Establishment or Cattle Rancher

Beef Cattle Manager

Assistant Beef Cattle Manager

Special Skills and Personality Traits—Leadership, organizational, critical-thinking, problem-solving, negotiation, communication, writing, and computer skills; motivational, enterprising, decisive, flexible, and resourceful personality traits

Position Description

Beef cattle ranches are commercial operations that raise as many as thousands of cows for their meat. These ranches typically spread across many acres or several square miles of grassland and rangeland on which cattle graze. Many ranches also have contained areas, called feedlots, where livestock are fed and fattened for market. Beef cattle ranches are owned by individuals and families, as well as by large corporations that may possess several ranches and feedlots. To help them oversee their operations, ranch owners employ Beef Cattle Managers, who are experts in beef cattle production and management.

These livestock managers are responsible for the daily care and well-being of herds. They have expertise in various areas, including husbandry, nutrition, eating habits, bovine behavior, breeding cycles, and the management of injured or sick animals. They are well versed regarding the handling of different types of cows, such as bulls (males), heifers (females), calves, and steers (castrated males). In addition, Beef Cattle Managers are knowledgeable about how to manage rangelands, grasslands, pastures, and feedlots.

Beef Cattle Managers are involved in a wide range of herd production and management duties. Some of their responsibilities include:

- processing cattle as they are received to their ranches or shipped out to feedlots or to purchasers

- monitoring animals for signs of injury, illness, or unusual behavior
- notifying veterinarians when cattle have suffered serious injuries or illnesses
- supervising cattle movements between ranges, pastures, and pens
- branding, castrating, or vaccinating cattle
- administering artificial insemination to breed cattle for desired genetic characteristics

Beef Cattle Managers also perform duties related to ranch administration. Their tasks may include planning budgets, handling financial transactions, preparing financial reports, researching water rights, and scheduling ranch inspections. Some managers keep track of maintenance and repair work and the purchase of ranch equipment and tools. Some managers have knowledge of mechanics and structural design that enables them to perform inspections as well as maintenance and repair tasks on machinery and buildings, or oversee the completion of such activities by ranch staff.

Beef Cattle Managers are responsible for the oversight of ranch hands and other staff. They assign duties to employees, and make sure that employees follow and understand company policies and procedures. Managers evaluate employees on their job performance and discipline employees as needed. These managers are usually responsible for the hiring, firing, and training of employees.

Beef Cattle Managers spend time in offices to perform such tasks as compiling and reviewing records. These experts mostly work in outdoor environments, which includes working in inclement weather. They may be required to drive vehicles to remote areas of their ranch properties. Their work can be physically demanding and involve heavy lifting, walking, stooping, or working in confined spaces. Cattle Managers may risk injury from the use of mechanized equipment, chemicals, and electrical fences.

Beef Cattle Managers work long hours to complete their various tasks. Many are expected to be on call to handle feeding and emergency needs after hours, including weekends and holidays.

Salaries

Salaries for Beef Cattle Managers vary, depending on such factors as their education, experience, and geographic location. The U.S. Bureau of Labor Statistics reports in its May 2008 Occupational Employment Statistics survey that the estimated annual salary for most ranch managers ranged from $31,350 to $103,510.

Employment Prospects

Beef production is a multibillion dollar industry worldwide. According to the U.S. Department of Agriculture, beef cattle operations make up the largest type of farm in the United States. Most of these ranches are family owned.

In addition to private ranches, employers include government agencies, colleges, universities, and nonprofit organizations that operate ranches for research and educational purposes. Some managers are employed by private firms that offer farm management services to livestock ranchers. Job openings generally become available as individuals retire or transfer to other jobs or careers.

Advancement Prospects

Beef Cattle Managers measure their success by earning higher wages, by gaining a professional reputation, and through job satisfaction. Some managers seek opportunities to oversee larger or more complex cattle operations. Entrepreneurial individuals may purchase their own cattle operations or start companies that offer management services to ranchers.

Education and Training

Educational requirements vary with the different employers. More employers prefer to hire candidates who possess an associate's or bachelor's degree in animal science or another related field.

Beef Cattle Managers typically learn their production and management skills on the job while working in lower level positions as ranch hands, supervisors, and assistant managers.

Experience, Special Skills, and Personality Traits

Applicants must have several years of experience working in the different aspects of beef cattle operations, including supervisory and managerial experience.

Beef Cattle Managers must have leadership, organizational, critical-thinking, problem-solving, negotiation, and communication skills. They also need writing and computer skills. Some personality traits that successful managers share include being motivational, enterprising, decisive, flexible, and resourceful.

Unions and Associations

Beef Cattle Managers may join professional, trade, and other organizations to take advantage of networking opportunities, education programs, and other services and resources. Various groups serve the diverse interests of Beef Cattle Managers at the local, state, national, and international levels. For example, some national organizations that these managers might join are the National Cattlemen's Beef Association and the American Farm Bureau. For contact information, see Appendix II.

Tips for Entry

1. While in school, join the FFA or 4-H and raise a steer as part of your livestock project. You can gain valuable experience while taking care of your animal.
2. Contact former coworkers and ranchers for whom you have worked, and ask if they know of any job openings.
3. Use the Internet to learn more about the beef cattle industry. You might start by visiting these Web sites: Explore Beef (www.explorebeef.org) and Cattle Network (www.cattlenetwork.com). For more links, see Appendix IV.

VINEYARD MANAGER

Duties: Oversee the daily activities of a wine-grape vineyard operation; perform other duties as required

Alternate Title(s): Vineyard Manager/Viticulturist

Salary Range: $31,000 to $104,000

Employment Prospects: Fair

Advancement Prospects: Poor

Prerequisites:

Education or Training—Bachelor's degree in viticulture preferred

Experience—Several years of experience working on the type of farm to be managed

Special Skills and Personality Traits—Leadership, teamwork, interpersonal, communication, organizational, critical-thinking, problem-solving, self-management, writing, record-keeping, and computer skills; enthusiastic, congenial, self-motivated, dedicated, and flexible personality traits

CAREER LADDER

Vineyard Manager of a Larger Establishment or Vineyard Owner

Vineyard Manager

Assistant Vineyard Manager

Position Description

Vineyard Managers are responsible for overseeing the smooth, efficient, and economical production of wine grapes for growers. They manage farm operations that are named after the grapevines that stretch along trellises arranged in rows in valleys or on hillsides.

They are knowledgeable about all aspects of vineyard development and care, and they are devoted to helping their employers produce the highest quality product. These farm managers are well versed in the various varieties of wine grapes and how each variety must be cultivated. They are also experts in completing general management tasks such as managing budgets, handling human resource issues, acquiring equipment and supplies, managing work schedules, and keeping records of work activities. Many of these experts are employed directly by vineyards or wineries. Others work for firms that offer vineyard management services to vineyard owners.

Vineyard Managers direct all phases of grape production, from the earliest stages of planning vineyard sites to the planting of vines to the harvesting of grapes. They perform a wide range of duties such as:

- analyzing potential vineyard sites and arranging for the preparation of the land
- planning and scheduling work activities
- preparing plans for the next season's crop
- inspecting vineyards for problems, such as mildew, that affect the health of the vines
- making long-range plans for vineyard operations
- developing and implementing financial plans
- ensuring that quality standards for their vineyard output are achieved and maintained
- keeping current with government regulations regarding environmental and safety standards, pesticide application, and employment conditions

Vineyard Managers oversee a staff of vineyard workers who are both regular and seasonal employees. It is their responsibility to assign staff members to projects and tasks. These managers also carefully monitor workers' performances to make certain that they execute tasks on an exacting schedule to maintain the desired measure of quality.

Depending on their employers, these experts are also hands-on managers. In other words, they perform many of the manual tasks alongside their staff, such as pruning, thinning leaves and grape clusters, applying frost protection measures, harvesting, grafting, spraying, and so on.

Vineyard Managers work closely with viticulturists, who are specialists in the technical aspects of cultivating grapes and monitoring their growth. Together, these managers and viticulturists monitor the progress of each crop's development as well as to control pests, provide adequate water, protect the vines from cold weather, and apply fertilizer.

Vineyard Managers work in offices as well as in the vineyards where they experience all kinds of weather. They sometimes travel to attend trade shows and public relations events. These managers work flexible schedules, which include early mornings, evenings, and weekends. Vineyard Managers generally put in longer hours during planting and harvest seasons.

Salaries

Salaries for Vineyard Managers vary, depending on their experience, employer, and geographic location. Their salaries are similar to the earnings of farm managers. According to the May 2008 Occupational Employment Statistics survey by the U.S. Bureau of Labor Statistics, the estimated annual salary for most farm managers ranged from $31,350 to $103,510.

Employment Prospects

In addition to vineyards and wineries, Vineyard Managers may be employed by government agencies, colleges, and universities that maintain experimental farms for research and educational purposes. Some Vineyard Managers work for private firms that offer vineyard management services to vineyard and winery owners.

Vineyards are found throughout the United States, although not in every state. Wineries, on the other hand, are found in all 50 states. Some wineries own and operate vineyards, while others purchase wine grapes. The wine industry overall is healthy. Some experts in the field report a trend of wineries consolidating.

Job openings for Vineyard Managers generally become available as individuals retire or transfer to other jobs or careers. Opportunities are favorable for experienced managers, particularly those with formal viticulture backgrounds.

Advancement Prospects

Vineyard Managers advance according to their own interests and ambitions. Some pursue positions that involve more complex responsibilities or offer higher salaries. Some seek positions at prestigious vineyards or wineries. Entrepreneurial individuals may purchase their own vineyards or start companies that offer vineyard management services to farmers.

Education and Training

Many employers prefer to hire candidates who have a bachelor's degree in viticulture or a related field. Alternatively, they hire applicants who have many years of experience in vineyard operations.

Experience, Special Skills, and Personality Traits

Employers seek candidates who have extensive experience in vineyard operations, which includes having supervisory and management experience.

Vineyard Managers need excellent leadership, teamwork, interpersonal, and communication skills, as they must able to work well with vineyard workers, professionals, owners, and others from diverse backgrounds. These managers must have strong organizational, critical-thinking, problem-solving, and self-management skills. Having adequate writing, record-keeping, and computer skills is also important. Being enthusiastic, congenial, self-motivated, dedicated, and flexible are some personality traits that successful managers share.

Unions and Associations

Vineyard Managers can join professional associations to take advantage of networking opportunities, training programs, and other professional services and resources. Two national societies that serve their interests are the American Society for Enology and Viticulture and the American Society of Farm Managers and Rural Appraisers. For contact information, see Appendix II.

Tips for Entry

1. Learn about biodynamic and organic farming practices, as some experts report a trend of wineries becoming more interested in moving into environmentally sound growing techniques.
2. Many wineries and vineyards post job announcements on their Web sites.
3. Use the Internet to learn more about vineyard management as well as the wine industry. To get a list of Web sites, enter any of these keywords into a search engine: *vineyard management*, *vineyards*, *wineries*, or *wine industry*. To learn about some links, see Appendix IV.

NURSERY MANAGER

Duties: Oversee daily activities of a nursery operation; perform duties as required

Alternate Title(s): Greenhouse Manager, Farm Manager, Horticulturist

Salary Range: $31,000 to $104,000

Employment Prospects: Fair

Advancement Prospects: Poor

Prerequisites:

Education or Training—College degree usually preferred

Experience—Several years of work experience in the nursery industry

Special Skills and Personality Traits—Leadership, problem-solving, critical-thinking, organizational, negotiation, interpersonal, self-management,

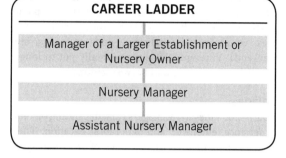

communication, writing, and computer skills; self-directed, detail-oriented, quick-witted, creative, energetic, and flexible personality traits

Position Description

Many of the ornamental and edible plants that we grow in our gardens and use for our landscaping were purchased from commercial farms known as nurseries. At these agricultural operations, plants are propagated from seeds as well as from such plant cuttings as leaves, roots, or branches. The seeds or cuttings may be grown in fields or in containers. Nurseries nurture these young plants until they are a size that they can sell to their customers. Nurseries range in size from an acre or less to hundreds of acres. Many include greenhouses, or hothouses, which are environmentally controlled structures made of glass or plastic.

It is the responsibility of Nursery Managers to make sure their operations run smoothly, efficiently, and safely every day. These men and women are professional horticulturists. They are familiar with the principles and methods of plant cultivation and propagation, and understand plant diseases, weeds, and pests and how to handle and control them. In addition, they are skilled in the maintenance and care of nursery and greenhouse facilities. Some Nursery Managers are also knowledgeable about sustainable nursery practices that focus on building up soil and reducing the use of synthetic chemicals to encourage the growth of healthier plants.

Nursery Managers are accountable to their employers. Many managers are employed by wholesale nurseries, which market their products to other nurseries, retail outlets, and landscape contractors. Many other managers are hired by retail nurseries, including garden centers, that sell their plants to the public. Some Nursery Managers work for landscape services, parks, companies, and other organizations that maintain nurseries to produce plants for their own needs. Still other managers work for academic institutions, government agencies, and nonprofit organizations that maintain nurseries for educational and research purposes.

Nursery Managers are responsible for planning, organizing, and overseeing the propagation, cultivation, and harvest of the different plants that their nurseries grow. They also execute administrative and management duties and may participate in developing and implementing marketing strategies. These managers perform a wide range of tasks each day, such as:

- monitoring the growth of plants
- testing soil and water for quality and cleanliness
- inspecting facilities and equipment for signs of wear, neglect, and safety problems
- planning work schedules
- preparing or administering budgets
- purchasing materials, supplies, and equipment
- maintaining accurate records, such as production reports, inventory lists, employee files, and invoices
- staying abreast of new propagation, gardening, and farming techniques and methods

- making sure that all farm activities and products are in compliance with company and governmental standards and regulations

In addition, Nursery Managers direct, coordinate, and supervise the day-to-day activities of their staff of nursery workers. With the help of crew leaders and supervisors, Nursery Managers make sure that their staffs perform their work in a timely manner and meet quality production standards. These managers also evaluate the job performance of individual staff members regularly, and practice disciplinary actions as needed. Nursery Managers are also responsible for developing and implementing employee training programs. Some managers participate in the recruitment, selection, hiring, and firing of employees.

Their job is physically demanding, as many of their duties may require them to stand, sit, walk, bend, stoop, and reach for long periods as well as to lift and carry heavy objects. They work in all kinds of weather, including rain, wind, and extreme temperatures. Additionally, these managers are exposed to dust, chemicals (such as fertilizers and pesticides), machinery, and other hazards that put them at risk of becoming ill or injured.

Nursery Managers work a 40-hour week but put in additional hours as needed to complete their duties.

Salaries

Salaries for Nursery Managers vary, depending on such factors as their experience, job duties, employer, and geographic location. In general, the estimated annual salary for most agricultural managers ranged between $31,350 and $103,510, according to the May 2008 Occupational Employment Statistics survey by the U.S. Bureau of Labor Statistics.

Employment Prospects

The nursery industry has been steadily growing over the last few decades due to the continual increase in wholesale and retail sales of ornamental plants, trees, and other horticultural plants. However, there may be fewer openings during economic downturns. In general, employers hire managers to replace individuals who have retired or transferred to other jobs or careers.

Advancement Prospects

Becoming a Nursery Manager is the top career goal for many individuals. Entrepreneurial persons might start their own nurseries or plant management consulting services.

Education and Training

There are no educational standards for individuals to follow to become Nursery Managers. Likely candidates have learned their skills on the job, as well as through formal and informal educational programs. Many managers have associate's or bachelor's degrees in horticulture, plant science, nursery management, or other related fields. Many employers prefer to hire Nursery Managers who hold college degrees.

Experience, Special Skills, and Personality Traits

Employers hire candidates who have several years of experience working in the nursery industry. Prospective managers should have extensive plant knowledge and be experienced in all areas of nursery management.

To work effectively at their jobs, Nursery Managers must have excellent leadership, problem-solving, critical-thinking, organizational, negotiation, interpersonal, and self-management skills. They also need strong communication, writing, and computer skills. Being self-directed, detail-oriented, quick-witted, creative, energetic, and flexible are some personality traits that successful Nursery Managers share.

Unions and Associations

Nursery Managers can join professional associations to take advantage of networking opportunities, continuing education, and other services and resources. Various organizations at the local, state, and national levels serve the diverse interests of these professionals. For example, the International Plant Propagator's Society and the American Society for Horticultural Science are two societies that Nursery Managers may join. For contact information, see Appendix II.

Tips for Entry

1. While in school, obtain a part-time job, internship, or work-study position with a nursery to gain valuable work experience.
2. Many professional and trade associations as well as college and university horticulture departments maintain job listings at their Web sites.
3. Use the Internet to learn more about plant nurseries. Your might start by visiting this Web site: American Nursery and Landscape Association (www.anla.org). For more links, see Appendix IV.

FARMWORKER

Duties: Perform various tasks involved in planting, cultivating, harvesting, storing, or marketing crops; perform other tasks as required

Alternate Title(s): Farm Laborer, Agricultural Worker, Farmhand; other title that reflects a specialized job such as Irrigator or Farm Equipment Operator

Salary Range: $16,000 to $25,000

Employment Prospects: Good

Advancement Prospects: Poor

Prerequisites:

    Education or Training—On-the-job training

    Experience—Little or no work experience required

CAREER LADDER

Crew Leader

Skilled Farm Laborer

General Farm Laborer

Special Skills and Personality Traits—Self-management and teamwork skills; hardworking, focused, cooperative, and flexible personality traits

Position Description

Farmworkers play a valuable role in producing sufficient crops to feed people and livestock throughout the world. They are also involved in the cultivation of crops for such purposes as fiber, pharmaceuticals, landscaping, decorations, and energy. These men and women work on farms, in nurseries, and in greenhouses. They are hired by growers to assist with the planting, cultivation, harvesting, storage, and marketing of their commercial crops. Farmworkers might be engaged in the production of corn, wheat, rice, and other grains; vegetable field crops; fruit crops that grow in fields or orchards; walnut, almond, or other nut crops; horticultural crops such as flowers, ornamental plants, trees, and turfgrass; or feed crops for livestock.

Farmwork is characterized as a labor-intensive occupation. In other words, growers need to employ a large number of laborers to perform field tasks, such as transplanting, hoeing, thinning, and harvesting plants, which are physically demanding and which must be done by hand. Field-workers generally work in crews that may range from several to a few hundred workers. Farmworkers may be employed by growers or by farm labor contractors that provide farmers with farmworking services.

Farmworkers perform a wide range of duties that change throughout the year. Their tasks also vary according to their experience and skill levels. For example, Farmworkers might be assigned to:

- prune fruit trees or bushes
- apply pesticides, herbicides, or fertilizers to crops
- irrigate fields
- load or unload harvest crops on or off trucks
- assist in inspecting, grading, and sorting harvested crops for quality
- record information about crops
- transport crops to markets and distribution centers
- maintain farm structures and grounds

Some Farmworkers operate vehicles, tractors, harvesters, and other farm equipment to plow fields, apply fertilizers, harvest crops, collect or deliver heavy materials, and perform other tasks. These employees are usually skilled in maintaining and performing simple repairs on the equipment they use.

On farms that sell their products directly to the public, Farmworkers may be assigned to handle sales at farm stands or to man booths at farmers' markets. They weigh items that customers wish to purchase, calculate amounts, take money from customers, and provide change.

Farmworkers work outdoors in all kinds of weather. They are exposed to dust, pesticides, fertilizers, moving machinery, and other hazards that may cause injuries, illnesses, and diseases.

Farmworkers perform hard physical labor throughout their workday. During the cultivation and harvest seasons, they sometimes work up to 12 hours a day, six or seven days a week. They are continually standing, walking, stooping, crouching, kneeling, bending, and reaching. They may lift or carry objects that weigh 20 pounds or more. Farm equipment operators must sit for long periods.

Some Farmworkers are hired as permanent full-time employees. Most Farmworkers are hired on a seasonal basis. Some farm laborers are known as migrant farmworkers because they do not permanently live in the area where they work. Some travel from their homes, which may be in another country or state, to work at a particular farm. They often go home when the agricultural season is done. Other migrant farmworkers follow the growing and harvesting seasons of different crops throughout the year, working in other parts of a state or in other states.

Salaries

Annual earnings for Farmworkers vary, depending on such factors as their hourly wages, the total number of hours they work in a year, the type of crops with which they work, and their geographic location.

According to the U.S. Bureau of Labor Statistics, in its May 2008 Occupational Employment Statistics survey, the estimated annual salary for most Farmworkers ranged between $15,910 and $24,890. This estimate is for workers involved in crop production, including field crops, vegetables, fruits, nuts, and horticultural specialties.

Employment Prospects

According to the U.S. Department of Agriculture, nearly 1 million Farmworkers were hired in 2006. Approximately half of them were employed in California, Florida, Texas, Washington, Oregon, and North Carolina.

Turnover is high because the pay is low for performing hard, intensive physical work. In recent years, some growers have been reporting a shortage of workers, particularly during the busy parts of the agricultural season. Growers must compete with other local farmers as well as with construction firms, restaurants, and other nonfarming companies that seek qualified employees from the same labor pool.

Advancement Prospects

Farmworkers may advance by earning higher wages and being hired to permanent full-time positions. With additional training and experience, they can become irrigation specialists, farm equipment operators, and other farmwork positions. Farmworkers may also be promoted to supervisory and managerial positions, but

opportunities are limited. Those with entrepreneurial ambitions can establish their own farms.

Education and Training

There are no formal educational requirements needed for individuals to become Farmworkers. However, some employers prefer to hire individuals who hold high school diplomas or general equivalency diplomas.

Farmworkers normally learn their skills on the job. Some employers train interested Farmworkers in operating farm equipment and performing other higher-skilled jobs.

Experience, Special Skills, and Personality Traits

Persons with little or no work experience can usually obtain farmwork positions, as long as they demonstrate an interest in farming and a willingness to perform hard, physical labor.

Farmworkers need to be physically fit and have the stamina and endurance to perform various tough and tiring tasks. In addition, they should have strong self-management and teamwork skills. Being hardworking, focused, cooperative, and flexible are some personality traits that successful Farmworkers have in common.

Unions and Associations

Farmworkers may be members of labor unions that represent them in contract negotiations with employers. One example is the United Farmworkers union. (For contact information, see Appendix II.) Unions seek better terms regarding pay, benefits, and working conditions for their members.

Tips for Entry

1. Migrant Farmworkers who travel from other countries must have the necessary documents to work legally in the United States.
2. Visit or phone state employment offices for help in finding job openings.
3. Being able to operate farm equipment and perform jobs that are more difficult may enhance your ability to obtain full-time positions.
4. Use the Internet to learn more about Farmworkers. To get a list of Web sites, enter the keyword *farmworkers* into a search engine. To learn about some links, see Appendix IV.

FARM EQUIPMENT OPERATOR

CAREER LADDER

Senior Farm Equipment Operator or Farm Supervisor

Farm Equipment Operator

General Farm Laborer

Position Description

Many farmers employ men and women to specifically perform the role of driving and controlling various types of farm equipment. They are generally known as Farm Equipment Operators. Some of these operators own their machines and offer their services to farms on a contractual basis.

Farm Equipment Operators work with a variety of machines, each of which performs specific tasks. They drive tractors to haul equipment and trailers. They may hook tractors to plowing disks that dig the soil into rows for vegetable crops, or to harrows or tillers to rake and loosen soil or remove weeds.

They operate machines called spreaders to scatter seeds evenly in fields or to apply fertilizer, manure, pesticides, or insecticides on rows of plants. They install irrigation equipment to distribute water automatically over fields. They control equipment that harvests all kinds of crops, moves harvested vegetables along conveyors for sorting, threshes grains, or husks corn. They also operate hay-baling machines that collect hay and bundle it into uniform bales.

In addition, some Farm Equipment Operators drive trucks and control earthmoving machinery such as bulldozers or backhoes. Some are trained to operate forklifts and other powered industrial trucks for moving produce, livestock, supplies, and other equipment, as well as for loading and unloading trucks.

These men and women often operate the most modern equipment available. For example, some combines, which are used for harvesting grain crops, feature enclosed operating compartments that are air-conditioned and have radios or CD players. Some operators use global positioning system technologies and self-steering systems to guide harvesting machines.

Because they are involved with the day-to-day processes of growing food, Farm Equipment Operators are well versed in several areas. They understand how to operate their machines to effectively plant, cultivate, and harvest crops. Those operators who apply fertilizers, herbicides, and pesticides have a basic understanding of the chemical properties of these materials, how such chemicals affect the soil and plants they treat, and how to dispose of these substances. All operators are knowledgeable about how their equipment functions and are able to complete rudimentary repair, adjustment, and maintenance tasks as well as install replacement components.

Farm Equipment Operators may also perform general duties similar to other farmworkers, particularly on small farms. For example, they may be assigned to:

- load and drive supply trucks
- assist with the boxing or bagging of crops
- mix pesticide solutions
- handpick fruit or row crops
- use hand tools to prune trees, thin crops, hoe weeds, trim vines, or dig postholes for fences
- help with the construction of farm buildings and perform repair tasks on fences and other structures
- supervise other workers
- keep written records of completed tasks

Farm Equipment Operators work in a hazardous environment. They are exposed to pesticides, herbicides, fertilizers, and other chemicals. They risk injury while working with equipment and tools. They are also vulnerable to continuous loud noises, which may cause discomfort or distraction.

These farmworkers perform a physically demanding job. They labor outdoors in all kinds of weather. They sit for long periods in solitude while operating machinery back and forth over acres of fields. Their job also requires constant standing, walking, bending, and reaching. In addition, they climb onto and off of large equipment, use ladders, and repair roofs on farm structures. Furthermore, they lift objects that may weigh as much as 60 to 100 pounds.

Farm Equipment Operators put in at least 40 hours per week. Their days are longest during planting and harvest seasons. Some of these operators work in shifts that may include weekends.

Salaries

Salaries for Farm Equipment Operators vary, depending on such factors as their experience, job duties, employer, and geographic location. According to the May 2008 Occupational Employment Statistics survey by the U.S. Bureau of Labor Statistics, the estimated annual salary for most of these workers ranged between $15,920 and $35,390.

Employment Prospects

Farm Equipment Operators may be employed directly by farmers or through contractual farm labor services. Some Farm Equipment Operators are independent contractors. In addition to private farms, seed companies, and nurseries, Farm Equipment Operators are hired by colleges, universities, government agencies, and nonprofit institutes to work on experimental farms, which are used for educational and research purposes.

Job openings for Farm Equipment Operators become available as individuals retire or transfer to other jobs. The turnover in farmwork is high due to the physical demands and low wages for this occupation.

Advancement Prospects

Farm Equipment Operators may advance by earning higher wages and by being hired to permanent full-time positions. They may also be promoted to supervisory and managerial positions, but opportunities are limited. Those with entrepreneurial ambitions can lease or purchase land to establish their own farms.

Education and Training

Farm Equipment Operators generally learn their skills on the job while working under the direction of farmers, supervisors, and other experienced farmworkers. Some employers require operators to pass initial training programs for new equipment and procedures.

Experience, Special Skills, and Personality Traits

Employers usually hire applicants who have one or more years of work experience in agriculture or a related field. Some prefer that candidates have experience with farm machinery. All candidates must possess a valid driver's license.

To perform their tasks well, Farm Equipment Operators must have excellent driving skills. They should also have strong communication and teamwork skills, as well as possess good self-management skills, such as the ability to understand and follow instructions, work independently, and organize tasks. Being calm, hardworking, dependable, and self-motivated are some personality traits that successful Farm Equipment Operators have in common.

Unions and Associations

Farm Equipment Operators may be members of labor unions that represent them in contract negotiations for better terms regarding pay, benefits, and working conditions for their members. One union that these operators might join is the United Farmworkers. For contact information, see Appendix II.

Tips for Entry

1. Employers usually prefer to hire Farm Equipment Operators who can perform basic maintenance and simple repairs on farm machinery.
2. Maintain a clean driving record at all times.
3. You can find job openings for Farm Equipment Operators on the Internet. To obtain a list of possible openings, enter any of these words into a search engine: *farm equipment operator*, or *farm machine operator*.

COWBOY

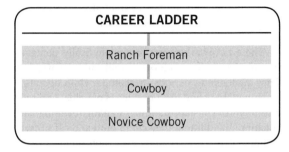

ment skills; enthusiastic, patient, honest, dependable, hardworking, self-motivated, determined, and flexible personality traits

Position Description

Cowboys are highly skilled in riding horses to handle and care for cattle. Both men and women are professional Cowboys.

Cowboys mostly work on cattle ranches that raise cows for selling them for meat or for breeding. Some ranches raise additional types of livestock such as horses, buffaloes, donkeys, or elk. Some ranches grow hay and feed grains, such as barley and sorghum, for their livestock. To bring in additional income, some ranchers have turned their operations into guest ranches (or dude ranches). They offer cattle drives, horseback rides, hunting trips, and other ranch activities to attract tourists, who may stay for one or several days on their ranches.

Taking care of the cattle is the Cowboys' major duty. Cowboys water and feed the cattle daily. They watch over the herd carefully to ensure the cattle are safe. They are responsible for monitoring each cow's health and reporting any injuries and illnesses to their supervisors. Cowboys may be involved with treating sick cattle by helping with the administration of shots and medication. They may also assist in the birthing of calves. In addition, Cowboys participate in the process of branding cattle, which is burning a ranch's identification marks into the animals' skins.

Cowboys work together to move cattle to particular locations. For example, they may need to herd cattle into corrals, to different areas for grazing, or onto trucks for transporting to feedlots or other locales.

In addition to handling animals, Cowboys perform other duties. They make routine patrols of ranch grounds. They check for damaged fences. They make sure water holes have sufficient water. They keep an eye out for cows that have wandered away from the herd, for any evidence of trespassing or cattle rustling, and for any other potential problems. Cowboys might do their rounds on horseback or by vehicle.

Cowboys also perform various tasks needed to maintain ranch facilities and grounds. They clean barns, pens, and stalls. They make basic repairs to fences and other structures as needed. They may also be involved in planting, irrigating, weeding, and harvesting feed crops. They may operate trucks, tractors, backhoes, riding lawn mowers, and other equipment to perform their various tasks.

Some cattle ranches employ Cowboys specifically to perform the role of wranglers. They are responsible for taking care of the horses used for tending livestock or for ranch guests to ride. Wranglers also have the duty of breaking in and training new horses.

On dude ranches, Cowboys, particularly wranglers, interact with guests on a daily basis. Cowboys make sure that children and adults feel comfortable and are enjoying themselves. Cowboys may be assigned any number of tasks. They may teach guests to ride and care for horses. They may lead trail rides or supervise guests with the herding of cattle. Cowboys may also assist with such activities as campfires, cookouts, fishing trips, and daily hikes.

Some Cowboys participate in rodeos during their days off or between jobs. These sport competitions involve events that test their riding, roping, and other cowboy skills. Some rodeos offer monetary prizes to the top winners in the events.

Cowboys may be employed part-time or full-time on a permanent or temporary basis. Many work on a seasonal basis, usually during spring and summer.

Salaries

Salaries for Cowboys vary, depending on such factors as their experience, job duties, employer, and geographic location. According to the May 2008 Occupational Employment Statistics survey by the U.S. Bureau of Labor Statistics, the estimated annual salary ranged between $15,000 and $33,320 for most farmworkers who attend ranch animals.

Employment Prospects

Job opportunities for Cowboys are mostly available in agricultural regions of the United States. Employers generally hire Cowboys to replace individuals who have transferred to other jobs or careers or have left the workforce for various reasons.

In addition to beef cattle ranches, Cowboys can find employment with cattle feedlots, dairy cow farms, and ranches that raise other types of livestock, such as chickens, horses, or buffalo. Colleges and universities, government agencies, nonprofit organizations, and private enterprises that operate experimental ranches for educational and research purposes also hire ranch hands. Dude ranches that cater exclusively to tourists employ Cowboys on both a permanent and seasonal basis. Cowboys are also employed by rodeos, circuses, and other entertainment venues that require livestock handlers.

Advancement Prospects

Supervisory and managerial positions are available, but opportunities are limited. Cowboys generally mark their success by earning higher wages, through job satisfaction, and by gaining a reputation for their skills and work. Some Cowboys pursue opportunities to lease or rent land to establish their own ranches.

Education and Training

Many employers prefer to hire applicants who have high school diplomas or general equivalency diplomas. Some Cowboys have earned college degrees in agriculture and other fields.

Ranch hands learn their skills through on-the-job training while working under the supervision and direction of experienced Cowboys.

Experience, Special Skills, and Personality Traits

Employers prefer to hire applicants who have experience working on ranches, particularly livestock ranches. Candidates should also be experienced in riding, handling, and caring for horses. Some ranchers will hire applicants with little or no experience, if they demonstrate a willingness to work hard.

Cowboys are expected to be physically fit and have the endurance and stamina to work long hours. Cowboys must have strong teamwork, communication, and interpersonal skills to work well with colleagues, ranch owners, and others daily. Additionally, they need excellent self-management skills. Being enthusiastic, patient, honest, dependable, hardworking, self-motivated, determined, and flexible are some personality traits that successful Cowboys have in common.

Unions and Associations

Cowboys may join professional associations to take advantage of networking opportunities, and other professional services and resources. Most local, state, and national cowboy societies serve the interests of men and women who participate in rodeos. One such national organization is the Working Ranch Cowboys Association. For contact information, see Appendix II.

Tips for Entry

1. As children and teenagers, many Cowboys had worked on family ranches, participated in 4-H livestock activities, or enrolled in high school agricultural classes.
2. Complete job applications completely and neatly. Many employers ignore applications that are messy, hard to read, or do not provide the information asked. If a question does not apply to you, write or type *Not Applicable* or *Does Not Apply to Me*.
3. Contact ranches directly about job openings, even if you are seeking summer work. It is never too early to apply or to call about applications in the fall or winter for summer jobs.
4. Use the Internet to learn more about the life of Cowboys. You might start by visiting: Cowboy Showcase (www.cowboyshowcase.com) and the Working Ranch Cowboys Association Web site (www.wrca.org). For more links, see Appendix IV.

NURSERY WORKER

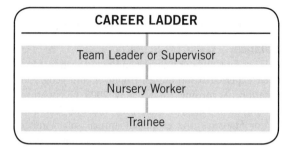

CAREER LADDER

Team Leader or Supervisor

Nursery Worker

Trainee

Position Description

Few of us realize that nurseries are also farms. They grow horticultural specialties, which include edible plants (such as vegetables, herbs, fruits, and nuts) and ornamental plants (such as flowers, foliage, vines, shrubs, trees, and turfgrass). Nurseries nurture plants until they reach a size that can be used by customers who plant them in their own gardens and landscaped areas. Nursery Workers are the men and women who make sure nursery crops grow healthily and meet the quality standards of their employers and the customers.

Nurseries produce crops for commercial, research, educational, transplanting, and other purposes. Many Nursery Workers are employed by retail nurseries and garden centers that sell their plants to the public. Many other Nursery Workers are hired by wholesale nurseries that market their products to retail outlets, landscape contractors, and other nurseries. In addition, Nursery Workers find employment with academic institutions, government agencies, private and public parks, non-profit organizations, landscaping services, and other organizations that maintain nurseries for their particular needs.

In nurseries, plants are grown from seeds as well as propagated from such plant cuttings as leaves, roots, or branches. The seeds or cuttings may be grown in fields or in containers. Some plants are raised in greenhouses, or hothouses, which are environmentally controlled structures made of glass or plastic.

Some nurseries produce a wide variety of edible and ornamental plants, while others focus on raising specific types of crops, such as Asian vegetables, flowers, Christmas trees, turfgrass, or native plants. Some nurseries specialize by using sustainable horticultural practices to produce their crops. Workers are expected to be knowledgeable about the plants with which they work, including the names of the plants, how to care for them, how to identify plant diseases, and how to handle pest problems.

In general, Nursery Workers are responsible for planting, cultivating, and harvesting horticultural crops. Their duties vary, depending on their experience and skills. They are assigned such tasks as:

- preparing land, greenhouse beds, or containers for growing products
- propagating or grafting plants
- applying fertilizers to plants
- irrigating fields or watering containers
- recording information about crops
- digging up field-grown plants and transplanting them into containers
- preparing plants for shipping to customers
- transporting crops to markets and distribution centers
- maintaining farm structures and grounds

Some Nursery Workers perform sales and customer service duties. They help customers by answering questions about plants, suggesting plants that may fit their needs, and loading plants into customers' vehicles.

Nursery Workers use various garden hand tools, such as hoes, pruners, rakes, and shovels, as well as power tools, including chippers, shredders, clippers, and mowers. Some workers operate forklifts and other industrial trucks to carry, load, and unload heavy objects.

These agricultural workers perform physically demanding labor throughout their workday. They are continually standing, walking, stooping, crouching, kneeling, bending, and reaching as they perform their duties. They may lift or carry objects that weigh 20 to 50 pounds or more. Nursery Workers work outdoors in all kinds of weather. They are exposed to dust, pesticides, fertilizers, moving machinery, and other hazards that may cause injuries, illnesses, and diseases.

Year-round Nursery Workers may be employed full-time or part-time. During the growing season, they sometimes work as many as 10 to 12 hours a day, six or seven days a week. Many employers hire additional workers on a temporary basis during this period.

Salaries
Salaries for Nursery Workers vary, depending on such factors as their experience, skills, job duties, employer, and geographic location. According to the May 2008 Occupational Employment Statistics survey by the U.S. Bureau of Labor Statistics, the estimated annual salary for most Nursery Workers ranged between $15,910 and $24,890.

Employment Prospects
In general, openings become available as Nursery Workers advance to higher positions, transfer to other jobs or careers, or leave the workforce for various reasons. Because of the low wages and the physical demand of the work, the turnover rate is high.

Opportunities for Nursery Workers are favorable due to the constant demand for plants to landscape residences, shopping malls, business centers, parks, roads, and other buildings and grounds. In recent years, some employers have expressed concern about finding sufficient applicants, particularly during the busy planting and harvest seasons. Nurseries compete with farms and other agricultural operations as well as nonagricultural employers such as construction companies, for the same labor pool.

Advancement Prospects
Nursery Workers advance by earning higher wages as well as by being hired to permanent, full-time positions. As they gain experience and training, they are assigned duties that are more complex, such as propagating plants and operating farm equipment. They can also be promoted to supervisory and managerial positions, but opportunities are limited. Those with entrepreneurial ambitions can establish their own nurseries, greenhouses, or other agricultural operations.

Education and Training
Employers prefer to hire applicants who have high school diplomas or general equivalency diplomas.

Nursery Workers learn their skills on the job while working under the direction of supervisors and experienced nursery personnel.

Experience, Special Skills, and Personality Traits
Employers generally hire applicants who have some experience working with plants, which they may have gained through employment or volunteer work.

Nursery Workers must also have basic reading, writing, and math skills. In addition, they should have strong teamwork, communication, and self-management skills. Being friendly, dependable, and self-motivated are some personality traits that successful Nursery Workers share.

Unions and Associations
Some Nursery Workers belong to a labor union that represents them in contract negotiations for better pay, benefits, and working conditions. A union may also handle any grievances that members may have against their employers.

Tips for Entry
1. As a high school student, obtain a part-time job in a garden center, nursery, landscaping company, or other site where you work with plants.
2. Contact employers directly for job openings. Some employers will accept job applications even though they have no vacancies.
3. Use the Internet to learn more about the nursery industry. You might start by visiting the American Nursery and Landscape Association Web site at www.anla.org. For more links, see Appendix IV.

AQUACULTURE AND COMMERCIAL FISHING

COMMERCIAL FISHERMAN

Duties: Harvest fish or shellfish from oceans, rivers, or lakes for commercial purposes; perform duties as required of position

Alternate Title(s): Fisher, Fishing Boat Captain, First Mate, Deckhand; a title that reflects a specialty such as Salmon Fisher, Crabber, or Lobsterman

Salary Range: $16,000 to $46,000

Employment Prospects: Poor

Advancement Prospects: Fair

Prerequisites:

    Education or Training—On-the-job training

    Experience—Little or no experience for entry-level positions

    Special Skills and Personality Traits—Teamwork, self-management, communication, and problem-solving skills; management and business skills for

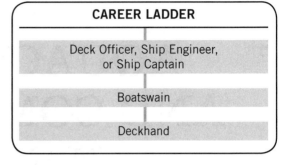

CAREER LADDER

Deck Officer, Ship Engineer, or Ship Captain

Boatswain

Deckhand

fishing boat owners; cooperative, patient, calm, alert, ethical, detail-oriented, and dependable personality traits

Special Requirements—Commercial fishing license needed; mariner license or certificate issued by the U.S. Coast Guard may be required

Position Description

Fish, shellfish, and other types of seafood are vital elements of any healthy diet. Every day, finfish such as cod, herring, and flounder; shellfish such as shrimp, crabs, and scallops; and such foods as calamari and octopus are always available for sale in our supermarkets, fish markets, and other retail outlets. Commercial Fishermen are among the men and women who work hard to bring seafood from the various coastal areas and seas of the United States and the world to our local markets. Some of these men and women also harvest fish species that are used for other purposes, such as pigments, jewelry, and medicines.

Most Commercial Fishermen harvest seafood along ocean coasts or in deeper waters farther out from the coastal areas. Some of them work along rivers or in large inland lakes. The areas where Commercial Fishermen ply their trade are often referred to as fisheries. These fishers may work in particular fisheries, such as salmon or lobster fisheries, during seasons when large populations of the desired species migrate through the areas. Most fisheries are inhabited by wild fish species, but some of them are fish farms. Commercial Fishermen mainly harvest wild species of seafood.

These fishers vary their approach to harvesting fisheries. Some of them operate small fishing vessels alone or with small crews, while others sail in big ships staffed by larger crews. The tools of their trade also vary according to the type of seafood they harvest. Nets, fishing poles, dredges, rakes, and traps of various sizes and descriptions are the types of equipment that Commercial Fishermen use. For example, they may catch tunas in nets, gather crabs or lobsters in traps, or scoop clams from beneath the sand with dredges.

Commercial Fishermen handle their catches in different ways. Many small operators deliver each day's catch to processing companies for cleaning, canning, or preparation for fresh fish markets. Fishers who work on large, company-owned ships perform many processing tasks aboard ship. This type of fishing vessel is called a factory ship because the processing tasks that are otherwise performed in onshore factories are done on board these ships.

Just as their approach to their work varies, Commercial Fishermen also perform different tasks according to their circumstances. In general, however, fishers perform tasks specific to their career. They may:

- prepare for each fishing trip by securing floats or weights to their nets or trap lines
- observe weather and tide conditions
- steer fishing vessels
- use navigational devices to keep track of their location

- put bait in traps or on hooks
- travel to known spots with high fish populations or travel to new locations
- use equipment to lower nets or traps into the water and retrieve them to harvest fish
- use signals to communicate with other fishers about net positions and when to raise or lower them
- sort their catches and return unsatisfactory fish to the water
- clean their catches and place them into storage with ice and salt to keep them cold and fresh
- maintain their boats and equipment
- repair nets, fishing rods, and other gear
- keep records of their daily activities and the location of good fishing sites
- restock their vessels with supplies for the next fishing run
- stay abreast of regulations concerning species protection, fishing seasons, and catch limits

Commercial Fishermen work in crews that vary in size from two crewmembers to several dozen. They hold ranks that denote which duties they perform. Boat captains make plans for each fishing voyage and supervise the work of other crewmembers. They are responsible for acquiring and holding the proper permits and licenses required to run commercial fishing operations. They determine which fish to harvest and where to find them. Captains also decide where to sell their catches.

First mates (also called deck officers) assist captains and are prepared to assume captains' duties when needed. These officers are knowledgeable about navigation and ship operations. They oversee the work of boatswains and deckhands. Boatswains oversee deckhands in the operation of the fishing vessel, casting and retrieving nets, processing catches, and so on. Boatswains also repair nets and equipment, while deckhands clean the ship's decks and maintain engines. Deckhands also unload the catch at the end of the voyage.

Commercial Fishermen have a very strenuous and often dangerous occupation. They may work primarily outdoors in every type of weather condition. They deal with heavy swells in stormy situations. They protect themselves from strong winds and rains by wearing gloves and durable rain suits. Ship decks are frequently wet and slippery. Their working environment may be cramped. Within such tight places, they may work with heavy cranes, winches, and hoists to handle nets and traps. Commercial Fishermen perform repetitive motions for long periods. They risk becoming entangled in nets and fishing lines. Fishers may be exposed to loud noises and hazardous substances, such as diesel fuel and solvents.

Hours vary for Commercial Fishermen. Their voyages may last several days or weeks, or only a few hours out of their day. On long-range voyages, they are separated from their families for extended periods.

Salaries

Salaries for Commercial Fishermen vary, depending on such factors as their position, experience, job duties, employer, type of fishing operation, and geographic location. According to the May 2008 Occupational Employment Statistics survey by the U.S. Bureau of Labor Statistics (BLS), the estimated annual salary for most of these fishers ranged between $16,080 and $45,930. Their annual earnings fluctuate from year to year, depending on the availability of work, the amount and value of the seasonal catch, and other variables. Business owners determine their annual net incomes after subtracting their total operating expenses from their gross incomes.

Fishermen receive a percentage of the their ship's earnings and are normally paid at the end of the season. The ship's owner, who may be the captain, usually receives half of the net proceeds.

During non-fishing seasons, Commercial Fishermen obtain other jobs to supplement their incomes.

Employment Prospects

Many Commercial Fishermen are self-employed; some of them are owners of family-operated fishing concerns. Some are employed by fishing enterprises and seafood and fish processing companies. Commercial Fishermen are mostly employed on the Pacific and Atlantic coasts, particularly on the coastlines of Alaska, California, Virginia, New England, and the Gulf Coast.

Due to the physical and risky nature of the job, as well as financial insecurity, the turnover rate for Commercial Fishermen is high. Many leave the industry for more secure jobs.

Some experts say that opportunities for Commercial Fishermen will continue to be available because eating fish for its health benefits is popular. However, the BLS predicts that employment of Commercial Fishermen should decrease by 8 percent during the 2008 to 2018 decade. Some experts state that these jobs should decrease partly due to technological advancements that allow fishermen to harvest fish more efficiently. In addition, Commercial Fishermen face strong competition from farmed fish producers and seafood importers. Some Commercial Fishermen leave their field because strict regulations limit their catches. Such regulations prevent fish from being over-harvested and allow their populations to replenish.

Advancement Prospects

Commercial Fishermen advance according to their own ambitions and interests. Most begin as deckhands on fishing vessels. As they accrue experience and training, they can obtain higher rankings. The can also become licensed deck officers or ship engineers. For these positions, they are required to have several years of experience in the deck or engineering department or complete formal training programs. With further experience and training, deck officers can qualify to become licensed captains, or masters, of fishing vessels.

Entrepreneurial individuals purchase or lease vessels to start their own commercial fishing operations. Some business owners run fishing charter companies, in which they offer fishing trips to the public.

Many Commercial Fishermen measure their success through job satisfaction and by earning higher incomes.

Education and Training

There are no formal training requirements for individuals to become Commercial Fishermen. However, many employers prefer to hire candidates who hold a high school diploma or a general equivalency diploma.

Commercial Fishermen typically learn their skills on the job while working under the direction and supervision of experienced fishermen.

Special Requirements

All Commercial Fishermen must hold a state commercial fishing license with the proper endorsements for the different fishes and shellfish that they harvest. For specific information, contact the state department office that governs the jurisdiction in which you plan to work.

Fishing boat captains must possess a master license that is issued by the U.S. Coast Guard, a military branch that is part of the U.S. Department of Homeland Security. Their license is limited to the type of vessel they command and the body of water on which they work. Deck officers (such as first mates) may also be required to obtain the proper license for their rank from the U.S. Coast Guard. To work on some fishing vessels, deckhands need to acquire a valid Merchant Mariner Document (MMD) from the same federal agency. To learn more about the master and mate licenses, as well as the MMD, visit the U.S. Coast Guard National Maritime Center Web site at www.uscg.mil/nmc.

Experience, Special Skills, and Personality Traits

Individuals with little or no work experience may obtain entry-level positions as Commercial Fishermen. However, employers prefer to hire applicants who have some work experience in the commercial fishing industry.

Fishermen must be physically fit and have the strength and stamina to perform hard work under difficult and dangerous conditions. Having good coordination and a mechanical aptitude is important for fishermen to have, too. They should have strong teamwork, self-management, communication, and problem-solving skills. Fishing boat owners and captains also need management and business skills. Being cooperative, patient, calm, alert, ethical, detail-oriented, and dependable are some personality traits that successful Commercial Fishermen share.

Unions and Associations

Commercial Fishermen can join professional or trade associations to take advantage of networking opportunities, training programs, and other services and resources. These organizations are available at the local, state, regional, and national levels. Two national organizations that serve the different interests of Commercial Fishermen are the Commercial Fishermen of America and the Small Boat Commercial Salmon Fishermens' Association. For contact information, see Appendix II.

Tips for Entry

1. One way to gain entry into the commercial fishing industry is to first obtain a fish processing job at an onshore plant or on a vessel. Another way is to begin as a deckhand on a fishing vessel.
2. Are you willing to work hard and long hours in the worst conditions? Be sure you understand what is involved to be a professional fisherman. Talk with Commercial Fishermen to learn more about their work.
3. Many jobs are found through word of mouth.
4. For information about working in the Alaskan fishing industry, visit the following Web page of the Division of Employment Security (part of the Alaska Department of Labor and Workforce Development): Seafood and Fishing Jobs in Alaska (labor.state.ak.us/esd_alaska_jobs/seafood.htm).
5. Use the Internet to learn more about Commercial Fishermen. You might start by visiting the Commercial Fishermen of America Web site at www.cfafish.org. For more links, see Appendix IV.

FISH FARMER

Duties: Oversee commercial aquacultural operations; perform farming, marketing, management, and administrative duties as required

Alternate Title(s): Aquaculturist; Catfish Farmer, Oyster Farmer, or other title that reflects a type of farming

Salary Range: $20,000 to $97,000

Employment Prospects: Fair

Advancement Prospects: Poor

Prerequisites:

Education or Training—On-the-job training; formal education in aquaculture encouraged

Experience—Several years of farming experience

Special Skills and Personality Traits—Management, critical-thinking, decision-making, organizational, interpersonal, communication, business, finance, and marketing skills; enterprising, determined, confident, detail-oriented, flexible, and resourceful personality traits

Special Requirements—Possess appropriate government licenses, permits, and certificates

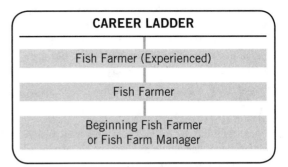

CAREER LADDER

Fish Farmer (Experienced)

Fish Farmer

Beginning Fish Farmer
or Fish Farm Manager

Position Description

Wild fish are caught in their natural habitat, while farmed fish are raised in controlled environments owned and operated by Fish Farmers. Although people have raised fish in controlled conditions for many centuries, several recent social and environmental factors have inspired an increase in the fish farming, or aquaculture, industry. Decreasing supplies of wild fish coupled with an increasing consumer demand for seafood are the two predominant factors that contribute to recent expansion of fish farming.

Many fish farms have been established along seacoasts, but some of them are located inland far from oceans. Fish farms are ponds, partitioned areas of ponds, tanks, or similar facilities in calm ocean waters or on farm properties. Some Fish Farmers are in the business of hatching fingerling fish for stocking large lakes. Some Fish Farmers nurture seaweed, or cultivate oysters for their pearls. Some produce fish for bait, while others raise them for sale to people who have aquariums at home. Most Fish Farmers raise fish or shellfish for food, which they sell to food wholesalers, retailers, and food distributors, as well as to food manufacturers, restaurants, and other food-service establishments. Some Fish Farmers also market their products directly to the public.

Fish Farmers raise any of several dozen different species of fish, shellfish, and aquatic plants, including trout, catfish, sea bass, salmon, tilapia, cod, oysters, clams, shrimp, and seaweed, among others. They produce their crops in both salt water and fresh water, as well as in brackish water—a mixture of salt water and fresh. These farmers also provide a variety of environments for their fish. For example, some fish thrive in tanks, while others are raised in natural or artificial ponds.

In some ways, Fish Farmers are similar to other agricultural producers in how they approach their work and manage their businesses. Their ability to be productive is dependent on weather and climate conditions. Some fish species require cold temperatures and calm waters, for instance. Fish Farmers pay close attention to market and financial conditions, too. They may need to establish credit at banks to set up their fish farms. They must be able to sell mature fish to succeed as well as to make way for another season of productivity. Hence, these experts develop marketing plans for selling their products.

Fish Farmers also work hard to maintain clean environments in which the aquatic species they raise may thrive. In addition, these experts are responsible for maintaining financial and activity records as well as managing staff members. Fish Farmers keep abreast of new developments in aquaculture and in the general field of agriculture. They remain aware of environmental issues and ensure that their operations comply with government regulations.

Fish Farmers experience varying working conditions. Fish Farmers spend much of their time in office settings to maintain business records, complete reports, or manage payroll and handle personnel issues. Many also work in outdoor settings along with employees to feed fish, clean tanks, or harvest fish for market.

Fish Farmers vary their hours, as well. They need to be available around the clock every day of the week to handle emergencies.

Salaries

Annual farm income for Fish Farmers varies each year. Their earnings depend on the size of their farm, market trends, operating expenses, and other factors. According to the May 2008 Occupational Employment Statistics survey by the U.S. Bureau of Labor Statistics, the estimated annual wage for most farmers, including Fish Farmers, ranged between $19,920 and $96,630.

Employment Prospects

Experts state that aquaculture is one of the fastest growing areas of the agriculture industry. Aquaculture operations are established throughout the United States, both in inland and coastal waters. Opportunities to start new fish farms are favorable because of the growing global demand for seafood, as well as increasing concern about over-fishing and the depletion of wildfish species.

Advancement Prospects

Fish Farmers advance according to their own ambitions and interests. Like many other entrepreneurs, they gauge their progress by achieving their business goals and objectives.

Education and Training

Although no formal training is required, some experts recommend that individuals obtain education to handle the technical, business, and marketing problems and issues that Fish Farmers handle. Some high schools, colleges, and universities have aquaculture programs that offer coursework in fish culture, nutrition and feeding practices, reproductive biology, production techniques, marketing, and other areas. Individuals may earn associate's or bachelor's degrees in aquaculture, fisheries technology, or other related fields.

Aquaculturists learn their skills on the job. They also gain further knowledge through self-study, by networking with colleagues, and by attending trade shows.

Special Requirements

Fish Farmers must obtain the proper licenses and permits to operate their businesses. For specific information, contact the appropriate agency that oversees the licensing of fish farms in your area.

Experience, Special Skills, and Personality Traits

Individuals generally need several years of working in aquaculture to obtain sufficient experience to become successful Fish Farmers.

Fish Farmers need effective management, critical-thinking, decision-making, organizational, interpersonal, and communication skills. They should also have fundamental business, finance, and marketing skills. Being enterprising, determined, confident, detail-oriented, flexible, and resourceful are some personality traits that successful Fish Farmers share.

Unions and Associations

Fish Farmers can join trade associations, professional societies, and other organizations to take advantage of networking opportunities, continuing education, and other services and resources. Some groups that serve the diverse interests of Fish Farmers include the American Tilapia Association, Global Aquaculture Alliance, National Aquaculture Association, Striped Bass Growers Association, United States Trout Farmers Association, and World Aquaculture Society.

For contact information for these organizations, see Appendix II.

Tips for Entry

1. Raise fish as a hobby to gain experience.
2. Some Fish Farmers keep their full-time jobs while starting their fish operations on a part-time basis.
3. Use the Internet to learn more about aquaculture. You might start by visiting the Web sites of these organizations: National Aquaculture Association (www.thenaa.net) and Aquaculture Network Information Center, or AquaNIC (aquanic. org). For more links, see Appendix IV.

HATCHERY MANAGER

Duties: Oversee the daily activities of fish hatchery operations; perform other duties as required

Alternate Title(s): Aquacultural Manager

Salary Range: $31,000 to $104,000

Employment Prospects: Fair

Advancement Prospects: Poor

Prerequisites:

    Education or Training—College degree may be required; on-the-job training

    Experience—Several years of work experience

    Special Skills and Personality Traits—Leadership, decision-making, critical-thinking, problem-solving, communication, interpersonal, technical-writing, computer, research, and business skills; motivated, inspirational, detail-oriented, curious, dedicated, and resourceful personality traits

CAREER LADDER

```
┌─────────────────────────────────┐
│  Hatchery Manager of            │
│  a Larger Establishment         │
├─────────────────────────────────┤
│  Hatchery Manager               │
├─────────────────────────────────┤
│  Assistant Manager or Aquaculturist │
└─────────────────────────────────┘
```

Position Description

Some species of fish are born in hatcheries and spend their young days there, where they are fed plenty of food and are safe from predators and environmental hazards. These facilities feature large tanks in which the fish live and grow until they reach a certain size. In addition to raising fish to restock lakes and streams, some fish hatcheries are designed to raise fish for food, while others provide ornamental fish to owners of garden ponds. Fish hatcheries are run by federal, state, and tribal governments as well as by private businesses and nonprofit organizations. Directing these facilities are men and women called Hatchery Managers.

They are experts regarding the management of fish populations and governmental regulations pertinent to wildlife management. They are knowledgeable about biology in general and, in particular, the biology of native fish species, how fish tissues and cells function, and how to identify diseases and parasites that may infect the fish they raise. Hatchery Managers understand how fish interact with each other and their environment. They have knowledge about the foods that fish require to develop properly. They also understand the principles involved with research, data gathering, and statistical analysis as they pertain to managing the life cycles of fish. Furthermore, they stay up to date with techniques for performing the tasks of spawning, fertilizing, incubating, feeding, and releasing fish.

Hatchery Managers oversee the daily operation of fish hatcheries and coordinate the work of hatchery employees. For example, hatchery workers follow the directions of Hatchery Managers to capture fish in the wild, collect their eggs and sperm, and fertilize the eggs. These managers also provide training to their staff members as well as feedback regarding their work performance.

Hatchery Managers consult with scientists and other experts to assist them to determine the proper nutritional and habitat needs of the fish under their care. They also seek advice from hatchery administrators regarding long-range goals and plans. Hatchery Managers observe the life cycle of the fish in their care and keep meticulous records that track their growth, their health, their feeding schedule, and other statistics. They complete and file government-required reports, which include these statistics along with information about hatchery budgets and how money is received and spent by the hatchery. Hatchery Managers also prepare production schedules and feeding charts. Managers of hatcheries that produce fish for ornamental or food markets may also assist with sales tasks.

Hatchery Managers usually perform hands-on tasks at their hatchery facilities, including feeding fish, cleaning tanks, and maintaining equipment such as water filtration systems and release equipment. Hatchery Managers continually monitor water quality and the health of their fish. They identify disease symptoms and administer medications as needed. They may directly handle releasing operations, including transporting fish in specially equipped vehicles to their destination waters. These managers may also assist with the design and construction of new facilities or the repair and maintenance of established hatchery facilities. Some Hatchery Managers interact with the public; for example, they conduct facility tours.

Hatchery Managers work in both outdoor and indoor environments. Most hatchery ponds and tanks are situated outdoors, although some hatcheries also maintain indoor ponds. The work may be physically demanding and these experts may contend with contaminants or disagreeable aromas.

Hatchery Managers often work irregular or long hours. They may be required to work weekends or nights. They may also be required to travel to attend meetings, seminars, conferences, or other events.

Salaries

Salaries for Hatchery Managers vary, depending on such factors as their education, experience, job duties, employer, and geographic location. Their earnings are similar to those of other agricultural managers. According to the May 2008 Occupational Employment Statistics survey by the U.S. Bureau of Labor Statistics, the estimated annual salary for most agricultural managers ranged between $31,350 and $103,510.

Employment Prospects

Fish Hatchery Managers find employment with commercial fish farms and hatcheries, nonprofit fish hatcheries, and local, tribal, and state government agencies that oversee public fisheries. At the federal level, Hatchery Managers are employed at national hatcheries run by the U.S. Fish and Wildlife Service.

Job openings for Hatchery Managers generally become available as individuals retire or transfer to other jobs or careers.

Because of the increasing consumer demand for seafood and the growing concern about the depletion of wildfish species, the number of fish hatcheries and fish farms should increase, according to some experts in the field. As new fish hatcheries and farms are established, new opportunities will open for Hatchery Managers.

Advancement Prospects

Fish Hatchery Managers may measure success by earning higher wages, through job satisfaction, and by being recognized for the quality of their work. Some managers mark their success by being hired to oversee larger or more complex operations.

Entrepreneurial individuals may pursue opportunities to purchase their own fish farms or hatcheries.

Some entrepreneurs establish consulting firms that offer aquaculture or hatchery management services.

Education and Training

Employers prefer to hire candidates for managerial positions who hold either a bachelor's or master's degree in biology, aquaculture, or another related discipline. Some employers are willing to hire applicants who do not have the minimum educational requirement if the applicants possess qualifying work experience.

Fish Hatchery Managers acquired many of their technical and hatchery management skills over the years as they worked in various staff positions.

Experience, Special Skills, and Personality Traits

Employers seek candidates who have extensive experience in fish hatchery operations. They should have at least one year of experience working with the particular type of fish hatchery that they would manage. Additionally, employers hire applicants who have several years of supervisory and general management experience.

Fish Hatchery Managers need excellent leadership, decision-making, critical-thinking, problem-solving, communication, and interpersonal skills. Having strong technical-writing, computer, research, and business skills is essential, too. Being motivated, inspirational, detail-oriented, curious, dedicated, and resourceful are some personality traits that successful managers share.

Unions and Associations

Fish Hatchery Managers can join professional associations to take advantage of networking opportunities, continuing education, and other professional services and resources. One national society that serves their interests is the American Fisheries Society. For contact information, see Appendix II.

Tips for Entry

1. As you begin your career, be willing to work in a public, private, or nonprofit setting to gain experience.
2. Follow the instructions that employers provide for job applications. Some employers, for example, will accept only online applications.
3. Use the Internet to learn more about fish hatcheries. To get a list of Web sites, enter the keywords *fish hatchery* or *fish hatcheries* into a search engine. To learn about some links, see Appendix IV.

FISHERY BIOLOGIST

CAREER PROFILE

Duties: Conduct studies and experiments; assist in fishery management, preservation, and conservation; perform other duties as required

Alternate Title(s): Fisheries Biologist, Fish Biologist, Biologist

Salary Range: $34,000 to $91,000

Employment Prospects: Fair

Advancement Prospects: Good

Prerequisites:

Education or Training—Bachelor's or advanced degree, depending on position

Experience—Previous work experience preferred

Special Skills and Personality Traits—Leadership, teamwork, self-management, research, writing, communication, critical-thinking, and problem-solving skills; tactful, detail-oriented, creative, persistent, and flexible personality traits

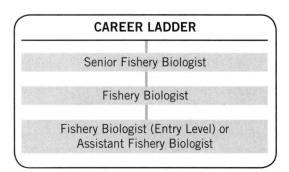

CAREER LADDER

Senior Fishery Biologist

Fishery Biologist

Fishery Biologist (Entry Level) or Assistant Fishery Biologist

Position Description

Catching fish is always a thrill, whether you cast for food or you catch and release for fun. Places where fish are hatched, grow, and live, and where people may catch them, are called fisheries. These lakes, reservoirs, rivers, ocean coastlines, and other habitats need to be managed in order to thrive.

Fishery Biologists are among the experts who assist in protecting and improving the conditions of these public and private fisheries. These scientists specialize in the study of fish and other aquatic organisms that are used for commercial and recreational purposes within a particular fishery. They examine the life cycle and feeding habits of fish species and observe how human fishing habits impact fishery ecosystems. They are also concerned with the social, economic, and management aspects of the fisheries. Their various projects and responsibilities help ensure the vitality of fish populations and the provision of recreational fishing opportunities for the public as well as the vitality of commercial fishing areas.

Fishery Biologists work for government, tribal, and private fisheries, research institutes, and academic institutions. They are employed as staff members or hired as technical consultants.

Many Fishery Biologists are involved in the management of coastal and inland fisheries. Fishery Biologists track the aquatic life in their fisheries and collect data regarding its growth rate, population increases, and health. These scientists catch sample fish and measure them, weigh them, examine tissues and stomach contents microscopically, count sample catches, and observe the incidence of disease or the presence of contaminants in the fishery waters. Fishery Biologists take note of environmental alterations at fisheries and how they impact the life of fish. In addition, these scientists monitor water quality in various locations within their fisheries. They record this information for comparison to earlier reports.

Fishery Biologists also engage in the development and implementation of management programs to protect, improve, or restore the conditions of fisheries. They participate in planning procedures regarding endangered species protection and habitat conservation, for example. They perform such duties as reviewing management proposals and preparing budgets. In addition, they design fishery survey projects and studies to collect data for proposals and programs. For example, Fishery Biologists at a particular fishery might investigate how fish species become infected with disease, how humans alter the life cycle of fish in that fishery, or how human presence affects the way fish reproduce and interact with their surroundings.

Many Fishery Biologists are employed as research scientists whose primary duty is conducting basic and applied research. These scientists mostly work in government and academic settings. Fishery Biologists conduct basic research to seek additional knowledge about fish, shellfish, and aquatic plants, as well as the ecosystems in which they live. Some Fishery Biologists engage in basic studies on socioeconomic issues to understand how fishery management measures affect communities that depend on fisheries. In applied research, Fishery Biologists take the results of basic research to create practices and technologies that may solve fishery management issues and problems. For example, applied researchers may seek ways to prevent fish disease or stop the spread of undesired aquatic species in a fishery.

Fishery Biologists are responsible for designing and conducting their research projects. They perform a wide range of research tasks such as formulating and performing experiments; gathering, analyzing, and interpreting data; writing and presenting reports about their findings; and supervising the work of research assistants. Research scientists may work alone or collaborate with other scientists and engineers. Senior researchers and principal investigators are in charge of the management and coordination of projects, as well as supervision of team members. Some researchers are responsible for obtaining research grants from available sources to fund their projects.

Many academic researchers hold faculty positions at colleges and universities. Along with their research responsibilities, they provide instruction to undergraduate or graduate students. Their duties include preparing and teaching lessons, supervising student research projects, and advising students on technical and career questions. Full-time professors are also responsible for completing scholarly works, performing community service, and completing administrative tasks.

Some senior Fishery Biologists work in the role of technical advisers. They may be consulted by agencies, private enterprises, fisheries commissions, nonprofit organizations involved in sustainable fisheries, Congress, state legislatures, and others. These experts offer assistance in managing fishery resources and other areas. For example, they may be asked to review funding proposals for future fishery projects or examine environmental impact reports regarding commercial or private development near fisheries. Some Fishery Biologists also provide expert testimony to help settle court cases regarding disputed uses of publicly owned fisheries.

Regardless of their work setting and role, Fishery Biologists complete various miscellaneous tasks, such as:

- compiling and analyzing data
- completing reports, paperwork, and correspondence
- drawing fishery maps

- taking inventory of facility supplies and equipment and ordering new stock
- reviewing laboratory procedures and implementing new procedures
- performing maintenance tasks on laboratory or research equipment, boats, and facilities
- providing informational and educational services to the public
- training and overseeing the work of technicians, field crews, and other staff members and evaluating their performance

Fishery Biologists work in offices and laboratories as well as in outdoor settings in all weather conditions. In the field, Fishery Biologists work on or near the water and may camp overnight while conducting water quality or fish population surveys. Their fieldwork may involve lifting, walking, reaching, wading, swimming, hiking, bending, and other strenuous movements. They risk exposure to poisonous plants, biting insects, and rough trail conditions. Those who perform maintenance tasks may be exposed to hazardous solvents and other cleaning chemicals.

Fishery Biologists may put in long hours, working on evenings, weekends, or holidays.

Salaries

Salaries for Fishery Biologists vary, depending on such factors as their education, experience, job duties, employer, and geographic location. Salary information specifically for this profession is unavailable. Their earnings are similar to those received by wildlife biologists. According to the May 2008 Occupational Employment Statistics survey by the U.S. Bureau of Labor Statistics, the estimated annual salary for most wildlife biologists ranged between $33,550 and $90,850.

Employment Prospects

Many Fishery Biologists work for tribal and state fishery agencies, as well as for various federal agencies, such as the National Marine Fisheries Service, the National Oceanic and Atmospheric Administration, the Fish and Wildlife Service, the Forest Service, and the Army Corps of Engineers. Fishery Biologists are also hired by nonprofit organizations, private hatcheries, fish farms, aquaculture companies, power companies, and environmental consulting firms. Some Fishery Biologists are employed as professors at colleges and universities and as Cooperative Extension Service specialists at state land-grant universities. Some Fishery Biologists are independent consultants.

Job competition for Fishery Biologists is strong. Openings generally become available as individuals advance to higher positions, transfer to others jobs, or retire. Employers may create additional positions to fill growing needs, as long as funding is available. Some experts say that a number of biologists employed in government agencies are becoming eligible for retirement in the coming years, which may, in turn, lead to more job openings. However, during economic downturns, employers typically hire fewer workers.

Advancement Prospects

Fishery Biologists advance in their careers according to their interests and ambitions, which typically evolve over the years. Those with administrative, managerial, or consulting career goals pursue such positions. Some professionals seek opportunities to teach at the university level or to conduct independent research.

Education and Training

Educational requirements for Fishery Biologists vary according to the position for which they apply as well as the demands of the employers. To apply for entry-level positions, individuals need at least a bachelor's degree in fishery biology, biology, ecology, environmental science, or another related field. Some employers prefer to hire candidates who have completed minimum units of course work in zoology as well as limnology, ichthyology, fisheries biology, fish culture, or other aquatic subjects.

For research scientist positions, candidates need a master's or doctoral degree. To apply for faculty positions at colleges and universities, individuals must possess doctorates.

Experience, Special Skills, and Personality Traits

Employers usually prefer to hire candidates for entry-level positions who have some work experience related to the job for which they apply. They may have gained their experience through employment, internships, student research projects, and volunteer work.

To perform well at their jobs, Fishery Biologists need strong leadership and teamwork skills, as well as self-management skills, such as the ability to prioritize multiple tasks, work independently, meet deadlines, and handle stressful situations. In addition, they must have effective research, writing, communication, critical-thinking, and problem-solving skills. Being tactful, detail-oriented, creative, persistent, and flexible are some personality traits that successful Fishery Biologists share.

Unions and Associations

Fishery Biologists can join professional associations to take advantage of networking opportunities as well as training programs, publications, and other professional services and resources. Some national societies that serve these professionals are the American Fisheries Society, the National Shellfisheries Association, the American Society of Ichthyologists and Herpetologists, and the American Institute of Fishery Research Biologists. For contact information about these organizations, see Appendix II.

Tips for Entry

1. An employer might hire you even if you do not meet the minimum educational requirement for a job if you have the appropriate work experience.
2. To apply for a job with the federal government, you must usually be a U.S. citizen. You must also successfully pass a thorough background check.
3. If you are interested in working for a federal agency, check the USAJOBS Web site at www.usajobs.gov for current job vacancies.
4. Use the Internet to learn more about the work of Fishery Biologists. You might start by visiting the Web sites of these organizations: the American Fisheries Society (www.fisheries.org) and the U.S. National Marine Fisheries Service (www.nmfs.noaa.gov).

AQUACULTURE TECHNICIAN

Duties: Provide technical and/or research support; perform related duties as required

Alternate Title(s): A title that reflects a particular job such as Fishery Technician, Fish Hatchery Technician, or Wildlife Technician

Salary Range: $23,000 to $67,000

Employment Prospects: Good

Advancement Prospects: Good

Prerequisites:

Education or Training—Educational requirements vary; on-the-job training

Experience—Previous experience preferred

Special Skills and Personality Traits—Communication, analytical, time-management, computer,

teamwork, interpersonal, and self-management skills; motivated, reliable, dedicated, enthusiastic, detail-oriented, innovative, and resourceful personality traits

Position Description

Aquaculture Technicians work in the segment of agriculture that generally pertains to the cultivation of fish, shellfish, crustaceans, aquatic plants, and other aquatic species under controlled conditions. Aquaculture methods are used to produce aquatic organisms in marine and freshwater environments for commercial, recreation, and sporting purposes.

Aquaculture Technicians are employed in different settings in the public and private sectors. Many work for various types of commercial fish farms that produce fish, shellfish, and aquatic plants for food markets. Some technicians work for public and private fish hatcheries that propagate fish and shellfish to stock ponds, streams, and lakes or to release into the wild. Some technicians work for government agencies and nonprofit organizations that manage marine and inland fisheries. Other technicians are employed by research facilities run by nonprofit organizations, government agencies, and academic institutions where they provide research and technical support to fishery biologists and other aquaculture scientists.

Aquaculture Technicians execute a wide range of duties that vary according to their expertise and work setting. They may be involved in the breeding, hatching, rearing, releasing, or harvesting of aquatic life in hatcheries, tanks, ponds, marshes, rivers, lakes, or oceans. They work closely with fish farmers, hatchery managers, fisheries biologists, and other aquaculturists.

These technicians perform duties that are particular to their position and work setting. In fisheries management programs, Aquaculture Technicians may be involved in the collection, organization, and evaluation of biological data for specific management or research projects. Examples of their tasks include performing chemical and biological analyses of water samples, collecting and processing fish samples from lakes and streams, interviewing fishermen, and using various techniques to analyze the age and growth of fish. Some technicians also perform public relations duties, such as conducting tours of facilities and answering questions from the public about their operations.

Aquaculture Technicians complete general routine tasks that are similar in every work setting. Depending on their experience, they may be assigned to:

- stock ponds, lakes, streams, or other waters with fish, shellfish, or aquatic plants
- feed fish, following feeding schedule
- observe fish for disease and illness
- harvest aquatic animals or plants
- load and transport fish to planting sites or other locations
- conduct fish population surveys and inventories
- monitor the flow and quality of water
- use computers and appropriate software applications to collect, analyze, and summarize data

- keep accurate and detailed records and databases of breeding, production, treatment, and other programs
- write reports about fieldwork
- maintain and make basic repairs to equipment, vehicles, buildings, and grounds
- clean, maintain, and repair nets and other fishing gear used to collect or hold fish in enclosures
- assist in the design and construction of habitat improvement projects
- stay abreast of aquaculture technology advances and the latest changes in local, state, and federal laws and regulations

Entry-level technicians perform routine tasks under the supervision and direction of supervisors, scientists, managers, and senior technicians. As they gain experience, they are given higher-level responsibilities and duties. For example, senior technicians may be assigned to plan project or program schedules, maintain inventories of feed and supplies, purchase equipment, and supervise lower-level employees. Some senior technicians assist with the business, economic, or marketing aspects of their operations.

Aquaculture Technicians may work indoors in offices, laboratories, or hatchery buildings. Most technicians perform their duties outdoors in contained or natural environments, including ponds, bays, rivers, sounds, and seas. They may be exposed to water, mud, glare, and unpleasant weather conditions.

These men and women are expected to have the stamina and endurance to perform physically demanding tasks, such as lifting and carrying heavy objects. They may be required to swim, operate boats, or scuba dive to observe fish and perform other duties. Some technicians conduct field studies in remote locations, which may involve overnight stays.

Employers hire Aquaculture Technicians to full-time or part-time positions. From late spring to early fall, employers may employ additional technicians on a temporary basis. Fish hatchery technicians are usually assigned to work shifts, which may include working weekends and holidays.

Salaries

Salaries for Aquaculture Technicians vary, depending on such factors as their education, experience, position, job duties, employer, and geographic location. Usually, individuals with college degrees, as well as those who perform complex duties, earn higher incomes. Specific salary information for Aquaculture Technicians is unavailable. The U.S. Bureau of Labor Statistics (BLS) reports that most life science technicians earned an estimated annual salary that ranged between $22,720 and $67,310. The estimated hourly wage for these technicians ranged between $10.92 and $32.36. These figures come from the BLS's May 2008 Occupational Employment Statistics survey. They are for those life science technicians who were not listed separately in this survey.

Employment Prospects

Aquaculture Technicians may find employment in various settings in the private and public sectors. Private fish hatcheries, fish farms, environmental consulting firms, and aquaculture services are among the businesses that hire these men and women. In the public sector, Aquaculture Technicians are employed by local, state, federal, and tribal government agencies, as well as nonprofit organizations, that manage and preserve fisheries and fish hatcheries. In addition, research technicians are hired by colleges and universities to support research projects in aquaculture.

Aquaculture is a multibillion dollar global industry. According to experts in the field, aquaculture is a growing industry, both in the United States and worldwide. This is partly due to the increased consumer demand in seafood and the concern about over-fishing and depletion of wildfish populations. Hence, opportunities for experienced and qualified Aquaculture Technicians should remain steady through the coming years. However, during economic downturns, employers may hire fewer workers.

Advancement Prospects

Aquaculture Technicians advance according to their interests and ambitions. Some technicians measure their success through job satisfaction, by being assigned duties that are more complex, and by earning higher incomes. Technicians may become specialists in particular areas of aquaculture. Some pursue supervisory and managerial positions. To obtain those positions, technicians may need to complete further education. After gaining sufficient experience, entrepreneurial individuals may establish their own fish farms or other aquaculture businesses.

Education and Training

There are no standard educational requirements for entry-level positions. Employers prefer to hire applicants who have completed course work in aquaculture, ichthyology, biology, fisheries management, environmental science, or other fields relevant to aquaculture.

Depending on the complexity of a job and the employer, applicants may need only a high school diploma or may be required to have an associate's, bachelor's, or master's degree. A bachelor's degree is usually needed for research technician, laboratory technician, or resource management positions. Many fish farms, fisheries, and fish hatcheries require that applicants possess at least an associate's degree in aquaculture or a related field.

Entry-level technicians receive on-the-job training while working under the supervision and direction of experienced Aquaculture Technicians and other aquaculturists.

Experience, Special Skills, and Personality Traits

Employers prefer to hire entry-level candidates who have one or more years of practical experience that is relevant to the position for which they apply. These candidates may have gained their experience through employment, volunteer work, internships, student projects, or self-study.

To perform effectively at their jobs, Aquaculture Technicians need strong communication, analytical, time-management, and computer skills. These technicians also need excellent teamwork and interpersonal skills as well as self-management skills, including the ability to work independently, follow and understand instructions, meet deadlines, and prioritize multiple tasks. Being motivated, reliable, dedicated, enthusiastic, detail-oriented, innovative, and resourceful are some personality traits that successful Aquaculture Technicians share.

Unions and Associations

Some Aquaculture Technicians belong to a labor union that represents them in contract negotiations with their employers for better employee benefits and working conditions. The union also handles any grievances that its members have against their employers.

Some technicians also join professional associations at the local, state, or national level to take advantage of networking opportunities, training programs, and other professional services and resources. The World Aquaculture Society is an example of an organization that serves the interests of aquaculturists, including Aquaculture Technicians. For contact information, see Appendix II.

Tips for Entry

1. Having mechanical skills may enhance your employability. Learn how to use hand and power tools, such as hammers, saws, screwdrivers, and drills, to repair and maintain machinery and engines. Having the ability to perform basic carpentry, electrical, and plumbing tasks may also be an asset.
2. Employers may require that applicants possess a valid driver's license with a clean driving record.
3. Carefully think about what makes you qualified for the position for which you apply. Be sure you highlight your skills, experiences, and training that demonstrate how you can perform the job duties and responsibilities listed on the job announcement.
4. Contact employers directly for information about current vacancies.
5. Use the Internet to learn more about the aquaculture field. You might start by visiting the Aquaculture Network Information Center (AquaNIC) Web site at aquanic.org. For more links, see Appendix IV.

FOREST PRODUCTION AND MANAGEMENT

FORESTER

CAREER PROFILE

Duties: Manage, protect, and conserve forestlands; perform duties as required

Alternate Title(s): Natural Resource Specialist, Forest Scientist, Urban Forester, or other title that reflects a particular job

Salary Range: $35,000 to $78,000

Employment Prospects: Fair

Advancement Prospects: Good

Prerequisites:

Education or Training—Bachelor's or advanced degree in forestry or another related field

Experience—Forest management experience required

Special Skills and Personality Traits—Critical-thinking, problem-solving, decision-making, time-

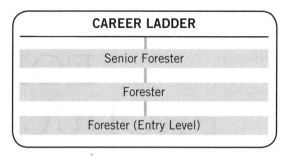

management, conflict-management, interpersonal, communication, and presentation skills; attentive, diplomatic, levelheaded, ethical, curious, innovative, and flexible personality traits

Special Requirements—Professional license or registration may be required

Position Description

Forests are a type of ecosystem, which is a community of plants and animals that live in harmony with one another in one habitat. Forests are mainly recognized for their trees, which appear to be their most abundant life-form. When we visit them, we look closer and notice that birds, insects, reptiles, amphibians, mammals, fish, grasses, flowers, shrubs, and microorganisms also live there. All of the plant and animal species contribute to the vitality and sustenance of forest ecosystems. Forests convert carbon dioxide to oxygen, provide nutrients for plants and animals, and help keep streams and lakes clean and filled with freshwater. Forests also provide our society with useful resources extracted from the living organisms that inhabit them. We mainly use the trees and plants as agricultural crops that can be planted, cultivated, and harvested.

In the United States, our forests are owned by private individuals and corporations as well as by federal, state, and municipal governments. The management, protection, and conservation of forests take a lot of human effort. Men and women called Foresters are responsible for the care and control of forestlands. These experts are knowledgeable about botany, zoology, geology, meteorology, and economics as they pertain to forest development and growth processes. Foresters use their know-how to perform the roles of expert managers, advisers, consultants, researchers, and educators.

Forests take many years to fully develop. After a fire or extensive clearing by humans, forests go through various stages of development culminating in mature trees and rich populations of other wildlife. Consequently, Foresters develop long-term management plans and strategies for achieving the land-use objectives of private owners and public agencies. For example, some Foresters may focus on the management of particular tree species for harvesting to fulfill specific purposes such as selling logs to lumberyards or paper mills. Others may concentrate on protecting watersheds or wildlife habitats. Whichever way their forests are to be used, Foresters are committed to ensuring that forests perpetually thrive to provide benefits now and for future generations to enjoy.

Foresters manage both private and public forests by conducting inventories of trees and other wildlife, making appraisals of harvestable timber, designing and planning for harvesting and reforestation projects, directing logging endeavors, designing forest access roads, and working to prevent fires, disease, or insect infestations. Foresters make decisions about important concerns such as the allotment of sections of forest properties for specific use and the scheduling of logging and other activities. They also determine which methods of care and development of their forests are to be followed.

In public forests, Foresters have additional, more specific responsibilities. They plan and oversee special forest programs, develop regulations, enforce natural resource ordinances, and design recreational sites. They also provide technical support to the public regarding forest usage. Some government Foresters avail themselves to private landowners that live in their region. These experts provide information about the care and development of forestlands as well as about the laws and regulations governing forestry management. They may introduce landowners to private Foresters or forestry consultants to assist them with problems that are more specific.

Some Foresters focus on such areas of concern as land management, industry, procurement, and research. In each of these professional areas, Foresters strive to find a balance between forest conservation and such uses as economic development or recreational opportunities. Land-management Foresters perform such tasks as selecting and overseeing the planning of forest sites. They recommend species of trees to plant and their spacing. They keep an eye on new growth and decide when trees will be ready to harvest as they approach the appropriate size. They examine trees for disease or insect infestation, and contact other professionals who can treat them. These Foresters may also manage controlled burns to prevent the risk of forest fires, as well as direct the clearing of underbrush, weeds, and waste from logging operations.

Industry, or industrial, Foresters manage timberlands that are owned by sawmills, pulp mills, tree nurseries, and other private companies that utilize forest products in their industries. These Foresters make certain that their employers follow all state and federal government laws and regulations pertaining to their stewardship of their forested property.

Other industrial Foresters work as procurement Foresters. They are responsible for purchasing timber from private landowners and overseeing the process of removing timber from these lands. These experts take inventory of harvestable timber on the property, appraise the value of the timber, negotiate purchasing contracts with landowners, and work with subcontractors to perform the timber removal procedures.

Foresters who conduct research are also known as forest scientists. These men and women work in government or academic settings. They conduct either basic or applied research. Basic forestry research is the quest to gain knowledge and understanding about forests, forest ecosystems, and forest management. Foresters involved in applied research seek solutions to particular problems. For example, they research ways to prevent forest fires or maintain urban forests. Forest scientists also develop new forest management technologies and procedures. They work in laboratories as well as in experimental forests. Many forest scientists teach at colleges or universities that offer forestry programs. Those who are full-time professors divide their time among research, teaching, and community service responsibilities.

Other Foresters work as private consultants who offer a variety of forestry services to their clients. Foresters may also work for Cooperative Extension System programs at state land-grant universities. These experts provide technical advice and education outreach programs from their university forestry departments to local landowners.

Foresters learn about their forests and keep track of their development by utilizing a variety of tools and technologies. These professionals use devices called clinometers to measure the height of trees and special measuring tapes called diameter tapes to determine their diameters. They calculate the growth rates of trees by taking samples from trees with such specialized tools as increment borers and bark gauges. Foresters also examine satellite imagery and aerial photographic images of their forests. In addition, these experts use such high-tech tools as geographic information systems, global positioning systems, computers, and Internet resources to compile data, create maps of their forests, and analyze growth trends, among other purposes.

These forest managers may work alone or as part of teams, which may include other Foresters, forestry technicians, ecologists, soil scientists, landscape architects, and engineers. These experts also meet regularly with landowners, loggers, government officials, conservation groups, and the public. Depending on their experience, Foresters may supervise their teams, monitor their performance, and ensure that their work complies with safety, contractual, and regulatory standards.

Most Foresters spend time working outdoors throughout the year and in all types of weather. They also work in such indoor settings as offices, classrooms, or laboratories. Their work may be physically demanding and dangerous. Assisting with forest fires is one example of strenuous and hazardous work they perform. Foresters sometimes work in isolated areas, in which they walk long distances.

Foresters sometimes work during evenings and on weekends to complete tasks, attend meetings and conferences, and participate in other work-related activities.

Salaries

Salaries for Foresters vary, depending on such factors as their position, education, experience, employer, and geographic location. According to the May 2008 Occupational Employment Statistics (OES) survey, by the U.S. Bureau of Labor Statistics (BLS), the estimated annual salary for most Foresters ranged between $34,710 and $78,350.

Foresters in federal agencies earn a salary based on the general schedule (GS), a pay schedule that has several levels and steps. Depending on their position, experience, and education, Forester may be hired at the GS-5 to GS-11 levels. In 2010, the basic pay for these levels ranged from $27,431 to $65,371.

Employment Prospects

According the May 2008 OES survey an estimated 10,160 Foresters were employed in the United States. A large number of Foresters work for federal, state, and municipal agencies. Foresters are also hired by logging companies, forest products manufacturers, utility companies, forestry consulting firms, nonprofit conservation organizations, and academic institutions. Some Foresters are independent consultants.

Opportunities are available nationwide; however, many jobs are concentrated in the west and southeast where most forests exist.

The BLS reports that employment of Foresters is expected to increase by 12 percent between the 2008–18 period. In addition to job growth, Foresters will be needed to replace those who retire, advance to higher positions, or transfer to other jobs.

Advancement Prospects

Foresters advance according to their interests and ambitions. They can become technical specialists or consultants. They can also pursue supervisory, management, and administrative positions. In addition, they can pursue research or teaching careers in four-year colleges and universities. Entrepreneurial Foresters can become independent consultants or business owners of consulting or technical services.

Education and Training

Minimally, Foresters must possess at least a bachelor's degree in forest ecology, forest management, forestry, natural resource management, or another related field. Foresters need a master's or doctoral degree to become forest scientists. They must hold a doctorate to conduct independent research or to teach in four-year colleges and universities.

Forestry degrees are offered in most state land-grant universities. These degree programs generally focus on forest ecology and biology, measurement of forest resources, forest resources management, and public policy.

Special Requirements

In some states, Foresters must be licensed or registered by the professional licensing board. Licensing or registration requirements vary from state to state. In general, applicants must hold a bachelor's degree in forestry and have several years of work experience in forestry. Candidates may need to pass a written exam.

Experience, Special Skills, and Personality Traits

Employers seek candidates, for either entry-level or advanced positions, who have experience related to the positions for which they apply. Entry-level applicants may have gained their experience through internships, volunteer work, student research, or employment.

To be effective at their work, Foresters need strong critical-thinking, problem-solving, decision-making, time-management, and conflict-management skills. They also must have excellent interpersonal, communication, and presentation skills, as they must be able to work well with colleagues, customers, contractors, the public, and others. Being attentive, diplomatic, levelheaded, ethical, curious, innovative, and flexible are some personality traits that successful Foresters have in common.

Unions and Associations

Some Foresters belong to professional associations to take advantage of various professional resources and services such as networking opportunities, continuing education, and professional certification. Some national societies that serve their different interests are the Society of American Foresters, the Forest Guild, and the Association of Consulting Foresters of America. For contact information, see Appendix II.

Tips for Entry

1. Some employers prefer to hire job candidates who have completed a forestry program accredited by the Society of American Foresters. For a list of accredited programs, visit the organization's Web site at safnet.org.
2. Be willing to relocate to another part of the state or country for a job.
3. To learn about job vacancies in the federal government, visit its official employment information system Web site, USAJOBS, at www.usajobs.gov.
4. Use the Internet to learn more about Foresters. You might start by visiting the Society of American Foresters Web site at (safnet.org). For more links, see Appendix IV.

SILVICULTURIST

Duties: Study the care and cultivation of trees on forestlands; assist in the management of public and private forests; perform other duties as required

Alternate Title(s): Forest Silviculturist, Research Silviculturist, Forester (Silviculture), Silvicultural Forester

Salary Range: $35,000 to $78,000

Employment Prospects: Poor

Advancement Prospects: Fair

Prerequisites:

Education or Training—Bachelor's degree in forest management or another related field

Experience—One or more years of forest management experience

Special Skills and Personality Traits—Problem-solving, decision-making, self-management, teamwork, interpersonal, public relations, communication, writing, and computer skills; self-motivated, enthusiastic, ethical, creative, cooperative, and flexible personality traits

Position Description

Forests are a valuable, renewable resource. Their continuation is vital for us so that we may use them for fuel, food, recreation, and commerce. To sustain forests on a long-term basis, they are cultivated within the parameters of their natural ecosystems. Silviculture is the science of taking care of trees in forest ecosystems. The men and women who practice this science are called Silviculturists. They assist foresters and others in the management, protection, and conservation of both public and private forests. They use their knowledge and expertise to provide the technical know-how that foresters need to put their development and management plans into practice.

Silviculturists become experts by studying how trees grow, the conditions in which certain tree species thrive, and how fire or insects impact their life cycle. They know how to control such circumstances to achieve optimum conditions for the use of forests. They are also knowledgeable about the lumber industry.

Silviculturists focus on three major areas of concern: forest regrowth, forest cultivation, and forest harvesting. These men and women plan for new tree generations to grow after harvesting operations or forest fires. They consult with forest managers about how to proceed to prepare sites where seedlings can be planted. Once the young trees are established, Silviculturists help foresters tend to them. Silviculturists make note of which trees have grown to the precise stage of maturity for harvesting.

Silviculturists use different approaches to regrowth and cultivation depending on the needs of forest owners, the species of trees involved, and other factors. They may advise forest managers to plant seedlings of one species or several species of trees. They may allow older trees to regenerate naturally without planting seedlings. They may advise foresters to plant trees at staggered intervals or under older trees if the new trees need shade in their early stages of growth.

As trees mature, Silviculturists have foresters apply various cutting practices, called treatments, at various times to optimize desired growth. Some treatment methods include cutting back underbrush, pruning larger trees, or felling larger trees that are impeding the growth of the younger ones. Silviculturists also recommend the removal of diseased or malformed trees to encourage the growth of more desirable trees. Silviculturists show foresters how to space trees and perform pruning and thinning tasks in such a way that the trees may grow.

Silviculturists take other factors, such as forest diversity, wildlife habitat, and the health of entire ecosystems into consideration when planning for forestry management. These technical experts also consider how their planning impacts terrain, affects watersheds, and concerns neighboring tracts of land.

Silviculturists perform duties that are specific to their occupation, as well as general tasks, such as: developing methods for analyzing and reducing fire hazards;

providing consultations to private companies or government agencies regarding their forestry programs; visiting forests to monitor growth, mark trees for harvest, and observe insect and disease infestations; and writing technical and training materials.

Silviculturists work in both indoor office environments and outdoors. Their work can sometimes be strenuous. For example, they may need to climb tall trees and haul heavy limbs from pruning sites. Silviculturists generally work 40 hours per week but may put in long hours to complete tasks.

Salaries

Salaries for Silviculturists vary, depending on their education, experience, employer, and geographic location. Their earnings are similar to those made by foresters. The estimated annual salary for most foresters ranged between $34,710 and $78,350, according to the May 2008 Occupational Employment Statistics survey by the U.S. Bureau of Labor Statistics.

Silviculturists in the U.S. Forest Service earn a salary based on the general schedule (GS), a pay schedule that has several levels and steps. Entry-level Silviculturists are usually hired at the GS-5, GS-7, or GS-9 level. In 2010, the basic pay for these levels ranged from $27,431 to $54,028.

Employment Prospects

Many Silviculturists are employed by the U.S. Forest Service, state forest services, and other public agencies. Some work for logging companies, consulting firms, and other private firms. They may also find employment with nonprofit and nongovernmental agencies involved in forestry or natural resources management. Some four-year colleges and universities hire Silviculturists for research and teaching positions.

Job openings for Silviculturists generally become available when individuals retire or transfer to other jobs or career fields. Employers may create additional positions if funding is available.

Because of strict budgets, opportunities for Silviculturists at public agencies are limited, according to the Tree Foundation of Kern Web site (www.urbanforest.org).

Advancement Prospects

Silviculturists can advance to management and administrative positions. Entrepreneurial individuals can become independent consultants or business owners of consulting or technical services. Silviculturists can also pursue other career paths by becoming research scientists, college professors, or public policy analysts.

Education and Training

Silviculturists possess at least a bachelor's degree in forest management, forestry, forest biology, or another related field. Many Silviculturists also hold a master's or doctoral degree in silviculture.

Entry-level Silviculturists receive on-the-job training. Some employers also provide Silviculturists with formal instruction.

Experience, Special Skills, and Personality Traits

Employers generally hire entry-level candidates who have one or more years of forest management experience. They may have gained their experience through employment, internships, or work-study programs.

Silviculturists need effective problem-solving, decision-making, self-management, teamwork, interpersonal, and public relations skills for their work. They also need strong communication, writing, and computer skills to perform their various tasks. Being self-motivated, enthusiastic, ethical, creative, cooperative, and flexible are some personality traits that successful Silviculturists share.

Unions and Associations

Silviculturists may join professional associations to take advantage of networking opportunities, continuing education, and other professional resources and services. The Society of American Foresters is one national society that serves their interests. For contact information, see Appendix II.

Tips for Entry

1. Contact district offices of forest services for which you would like to work.
2. Be open to applying for other forestry positions in which you would be able to apply your silviculture knowledge and skills.
3. Use the Internet to learn more about silviculture. To get a list of Web sites, enter the keywords *silviculture* or *silviculturists* into a search engine. To learn about some links, see Appendix IV.

FORESTRY TECHNICIAN

Duties: Provide technical support to managers, scientists, and specialists in the management, conservation, and protection of forests; perform other duties as required

Alternate Title(s): Forest Technician, Natural Resource Specialist

Salary Range: $23,000 to $52,000

Employment Prospects: Fair

Advancement Prospects: Good

Prerequisites:

    Education or Training—Associate's or bachelor's degree preferred

    Experience—Work experience required

    Special Skills and Personality Traits—Communication, interpersonal, teamwork, organizational, critical-thinking, computing, writing, and self-

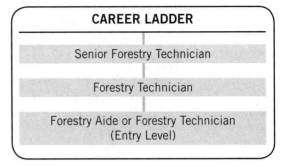

CAREER LADDER

Senior Forestry Technician

Forestry Technician

Forestry Aide or Forestry Technician (Entry Level)

management skills; cooperative, detail-oriented, analytical, dependable, and self-motivated personality traits

    Special Requirements—Incident Qualification Card (or Red Card) required if assigned to firefighting duties

Position Description

Forestry Technicians are forestry professionals who work with and under the oversight of foresters. Their role is to provide foresters, as well as scientists and other forestry specialists, with technical support in the management, protection, and conservation of public and private forest systems.

Forestry Technicians often have academic backgrounds in natural resources and are experts at identifying trees and other vegetation in forestry environments. They collect and record information about forests. They inventory the different species of trees that live in specific forest tracts. Forestry Technicians take tree height and diameter measurements and counts of harvestable tree populations, locate property boundaries, make note of damage caused by insects and disease, monitor the growth of seedling trees, and watch for indications of the likelihood of fire. They estimate how much lumber or pulpwood can be extracted from the trees in a forest. These experts also instruct and supervise seasonal workers in performing such tasks as fighting fires, planting new trees, logging, surveying, and building roads.

These experts use several tools to perform their different tasks. In measuring trees, for example, Forestry Technicians use gadgets called scale sticks to precisely determine how much lumber or plywood the trees can

yield. They also use surveying instruments called transits, which are telescopic sighting devices on tripods, and surveyor's measuring tapes. Forestry Technicians use global positioning system technologies and aerial photos to locate specific points in forests. They record the information they collect into data recorders for future tabulation and analysis. These men and women also operate power tools, such as chain saws, and large equipment, such as road graders.

Besides measuring and collecting information about trees, these experts may fulfill different functions depending upon their employer. For example, some Forestry Technicians have maintenance responsibilities such as installing fences or cleaning kitchens or other campground facilities. Others help maintain forested areas by clearing brush, harvesting diseased trees, and spraying insecticides. Some of these experts monitor the activities of lumbering operations and inspect timber sales facilities. These experts may be educators who train new Forestry Technicians, teach classes about forestry and conservation, or perform research at universities.

These technicians may perform any of a variety of general tasks, including:

- drawing maps, writing reports, and compiling work activity logs
- selecting and marking trees for harvest

- inspecting harvested areas to verify compliance with such regulations as water quality laws
- surveying new areas for reforestation projects
- laying out new boundaries
- overseeing the operations of forest nurseries, including the distribution of seedlings
- conducting experiments with soils, plants, and insects in either field or laboratory settings
- installing devices in forests such as soil moisture measuring instruments and collecting data from them
- standing watch for fires in lookout towers
- assisting engine, helitack, or hotshot crews with fire-fighting activities
- maintaining and marking forest trails
- collecting fees from forest visitors
- distributing information about environmental regulations, fire safety, and other topics
- attending training seminars

Forestry Technicians primarily work in outdoor settings, often in remote wilderness areas far from their homes. However, increasing numbers of these experts work in the area of urban forestry. Some of their tasks, such as data compiling or report writing, are performed indoors.

Forestry Technicians often work alone, but may also work in crews with foresters and conservation workers. They perform their tasks in all weather conditions. These experts hike long distances over rough terrain and steep inclines while carrying equipment and other belongings in backpacks. Some Forestry Technicians ride horses or drive all-terrain vehicles to access remote forested areas. They sometimes must camp overnight or stay in trailers or hotels.

These technicians face exposure to extreme temperatures and occasionally suffer bites, stings, and cuts. They usually wear such safety attire as hard hats and gloves for protection from falling limbs and handling rough surfaces.

Forestry Technicians generally work a standard 40-hour week. They put in varying hours and may work as many as nine hours per day. Technicians may be assigned to work during weekends.

Salaries

Salaries for Forestry Technicians vary, depending on such factors as their position, education, experience, employer, and geographic location. According to the May 2008 Occupational Employment Statistics (OES) survey by the U.S. Bureau of Labor Statistics (BLS), the estimated annual salary for most of these technicians ranged between $22,540 and $51,810. Their estimated hourly wage ranged from $10.84 to $24.91. (In the OES survey, this occupation is classified under forest and conservation technicians.)

Employment Prospects

The BLS reports in its May 2008 OES survey that about 30,850 forest and conservation technicians were employed in the United States. Approximately 75 percent of them worked for the federal government.

Some federal agencies that hire Forestry Technicians are the Forest Service, the Bureau of Land Management, the Fish and Wildlife Service, and the National Park Service. Forestry Technicians are also employed by local and state agencies, as well as by nonprofit and nongovernmental organizations. They may also work in the private sector for such businesses as logging companies, paper companies, wood pulp companies, tree farms, and timber consulting firms. Some Forestry Technicians work for utility, railroad, mining, oil, and other companies that own and manage forested tracts of land.

Job competition for Forestry Technicians is keen. The BLS predicts a 9 percent increase in employment growth for forest and conservation technicians during the 2008–18 period. Opportunities will also become available as Forestry Technicians retire or transfer to other jobs or career fields.

Advancement Prospects

Forestry Technicians advance by earning higher pay and being assigned higher-level responsibilities, as well as through job satisfaction. Some technicians are promoted to supervisory positions.

By obtaining additional education, they can pursue other forestry careers that interest them. They may become professional foresters, forest scientists, or educators, for example.

Education and Training

For entry-level positions, employers prefer to hire applicants who possess an associate's degree in forest technology or a bachelor's degree in forestry or a related field. College programs generally provide instruction in logging, forest protection, land surveying, wildlife management, and other subjects that prepare students for entry-level positions. Alternatively, individuals can work as forestry aides for several years to gain sufficient skills and knowledge to apply for Forestry Technician positions.

Newly hired Forestry Technicians receive on-the-job training while working under the supervision and direction of experienced technicians, foresters, and other forestry professionals.

Forestry Technicians who perform firefighting duties undergo intense training programs, which include both classroom instruction and hands-on experiences. They learn about wildland fire behavior, human factors, firefighting tools, orienteering, fire line construction, and other topics.

Special Requirements

Forestry Technicians who perform firefighting duties must possess the Incident Qualification Card, informally known as the Red Card, which certifies that they are qualified to fight fires on federal land or land that is managed by a federal agency. These cards are issued by a forest service agency or other organizations that have wildland firefighting divisions. Individuals must complete a training program and pass a physical agility test to obtain a Red Card.

Experience, Special Skills, and Personality Traits

Employers generally prefer to hire entry-level candidates who have one or more years of practical experience relevant to the positions for which they apply. They may have gained their experience through employment, internships, work-study programs, student research projects, or volunteer work.

Forestry Technicians must be able to work well with foresters, scientists, and others from diverse backgrounds. Hence, they need excellent communication, interpersonal, and teamwork skills. In addition, these technicians must have strong organizational, critical-thinking, computing, writing, and self-management skills. Being cooperative, detail-oriented, analytical,

dependable, and self-motivated are some personality traits that successful Forestry Technicians share.

Unions and Associations

Forestry Technicians can join professional associations, such as the Society of American Foresters, to take advantage of networking opportunities, training programs, and other professional services and resources. Forestry Technicians may also belong to a labor union that represents them in contract negotiations with their employers. For example, many federal employees are members of the National Federation of Federal Employees.

For contact information to the above organizations, see Appendix II.

Tips for Entry

1. To gain work experience, obtain a part-time or seasonal job with a forest service.
2. Employers may hire applicants with a high school diploma or general equivalency diploma if the applicants have qualifying work experience.
3. According to some experts, the competition is keen for technician positions with the U.S. Forest Service. They suggest that individuals first obtain relevant work experience in other settings before applying with the agency.
4. Check Web sites of prospective employers. Some accept only online applications.
5. Use the Internet to learn more about the forestry field. You might start by visiting the U.S. Forest Service Web site at www.fs.fed.us. For more links, see Appendix IV.

FOREST RANGER

Duties: Protect government-run forestlands; provide technical support in the management and development of forest resources; educate the public about forests; perform other duties as required

Alternate Title(s): Forest Ranger Technician; in federal agencies, known as Forestry Technician

Salary Range: $23,000 to $52,000

Employment Prospects: Fair

Advancement Prospects: Poor

Prerequisites:

    Education or Training—Educational requirements vary; complete employer's training program

    Experience—Previous work experience in forestry operations required

    Special Skills and Personality Traits—Interpersonal, communication, teamwork, self-management, problem-solving, critical-thinking, computer, and writing skills; tactful, calm, sharp-witted, outgoing, inquisitive, detail-oriented, and dependable personality traits

    Special Requirements—Law enforcement officer certification may be required

CAREER LADDER

Senior Forest Ranger or Supervisor

Forest Ranger

Forest Ranger (Entry Level)

Position Description

Millions of acres of public forests in the United States are managed and preserved by the federal and state governments to protect and conserve the natural resources contained within them and to provide for recreational use by all people. Perhaps you have visited some of these beautiful places. Maybe you stopped at a park office to pick up maps and informational brochures that helped you find places to hike, camp, fish, or simply take in the lovely surroundings. In that office, and on the trail, you most likely encountered a friendly, helpful person in a uniform who provided information and some useful tips. That man or woman is one of many experts called Forest Rangers who work for national and state forest services.

Forest Rangers fulfill many functions on the job. These men and women are conservation and wildlife managers; emergency responders; road, trail, and building maintenance experts; tour guides; and educators. Some of them also perform the role of law enforcement officers. Forest Rangers work and live in the national or state forest districts in which they serve. They may occasionally attend to certain duties involving emergencies or other events outside their assigned districts. For the most part, however, they patrol within the boundaries of their districts on foot, on horses, on skis or snowshoes, or by operating such vehicles as bicycles, autos, all-terrain vehicles, boats, or airplanes.

These outdoors professionals spend a considerable amount of time managing their forests and serving the public. Forest Rangers oversee the construction and maintenance of buildings, facilities, roads, trails, campsites, and historical markers. While following environmental guidelines and regulations, these men and women coordinate timber harvesting and reforestation projects; monitor wildlife populations, plant species, and water quality; and observe such factors as bird and animal populations, plant diseases, insect infestations, and soil erosion that impact the healthy growth of their forests. Some Forest Rangers manage the sale of some of their forest's timber.

Forest Rangers promote conservation efforts by educating visitors about how their forests and parks preserve forest ecosystems and habitats. They perform many of their educational services within park boundaries through walking, canoeing, and hiking tours, as well as campfire lecture programs. They may create trail signs and self-guide leaflets that help visitors find their way through parks and forests. Forest Rangers also travel to schools to give presentations. They may take live animals with them to show to the students. These men and women may be involved in research projects concerning the flora and fauna that live in their forest districts.

As law enforcement officers, Forest Rangers are authorized to deal with violations of all laws and regulations that pertain to forests. Like other law enforcement personnel, Forest Rangers handle such crimes as arson, assaults, thefts, and any other type of crimes that violators perpetrate within their jurisdictions. These men and women respond to emergencies such as automobile or boating accidents, missing persons incidents, or injuries that befall their forest's visitors. Forest Rangers conduct investigations, make arrests, interview suspects and witnesses, and present courtroom testimony. In some districts, they may be required to carry firearms.

They also enforce policies that are unique to their forest environment. For example, Forest Rangers enforce rules that pertain to the use of fire by campers, hikers, and other recreational visitors to the forest. Additionally, Forest Rangers work to ensure that loggers who harvest trees in their district comply with regulations governing logging activities within certain distances from waterways, roads, utility lines, and residences. Following logging activities, Forest Rangers inspect sites for compliance with requirements that guarantee forest regeneration.

Forest Rangers are involved with preventing forest fires and managing fire suppression efforts. They also investigate the cause of fires, supervise and train fire lookout staff and firefighting crews, and exercise their authority over such procedures as lighting backfires and the use of other firefighting techniques. In some states, Forest Rangers provide hands-on assistance as firefighters. They may travel to other areas of the country to assist with fighting fires in other forests. Forest Rangers also extend their know-how to neighboring landowners about how to deal with fires or manage controlled burns on their properties.

Forest Rangers perform other tasks, such as creating and maintaining trails; conducting search-and-rescue missions; checking with visitors to make certain they have proper fire, fishing, and hunting permits; maintaining records; writing and submitting reports; reviewing reports submitted by assistants; and manning the forestry office to assist visitors.

Forest Rangers work outdoors for the most part, and are exposed to all types of hot and cold weather conditions. Their work requires them to exert themselves physically. Forest Rangers are exposed to the risks associated with contact with wild animals and law enforcement activities. Forest Rangers also work in office environments to complete some of their tasks, such as writing reports, maintaining park Web sites, or preparing informational brochures. Forest Rangers work alone for extended periods in remote locations far from towns or cities.

Some of these experts work on a seasonal basis, while others are employed in this occupation all year. These men and women may be required to work evenings, weekends, and holidays.

Salaries

Salaries for Forest Rangers vary, depending on their position, education, experience, employer, and other factors. Specific salary information about this occupation is unavailable. Their wages are similar to those earned by forest technicians. According to the May 2008 Occupational Employment Statistics survey by the U.S. Bureau of Labor Statistics, the estimated annual salary for most forest technicians ranged between $22,540 and $51,810.

Employment Prospects

Forest Rangers are employed throughout the United States by state and federal government agencies, particularly in the western and southeastern states. At the federal level, Forest Rangers are hired as forestry technicians with designated responsibilities such as performing wildland firefighting, developing or maintaining wilderness trails, or providing support work to a recreation program. The Forest Service, the Bureau of Land Management, the Fish and Wildlife Service, and the National Park Service are some of the federal agencies that employ forestry technicians.

Jobs are highly competitive for both seasonal and permanent positions. Permanent positions become available when Forest Rangers retire, advance to higher positions, or transfer to other jobs or career fields. Forest service agencies may create additional positions as long as funding is available.

Advancement Prospects

Forest Rangers advance from temporary to permanent positions and progress to higher pay levels. They can also be promoted to supervisory and managerial positions. Usually managers, such as district rangers, spend fewer hours in the field.

Many Forest Rangers measure their success through job satisfaction and by being assigned to field or district offices of their choice.

Education and Training

Minimum educational requirements vary among agencies. Some agencies require only a high school diploma or a general equivalency diploma. Other agencies require applicants to have completed a minimum amount of course work or to possess an associate's or bachelor's degree in forestry, forest management, ecology, botany, biology, environmental science, or another related field.

Forest Ranger recruits complete training programs provided by their employers.

To be appointed to a law enforcement position, Forest Rangers must successfully complete a law enforcement training program. For example, a state forest service may require that its Forest Rangers complete basic peace officer training at a police academy.

Special Requirements

Some employers require that applicants be U.S. citizens and meet age and residency requirements. Candidates may also be required to possess a valid driver's license at the time they obtain an appointment.

To receive a job offer, applicants are usually required to successfully pass any or all of the following reviews: a written test, a medical examination, a physical agility test, a psychological examination, a drug screening, and a background investigation that includes being fingerprinted.

Forest Rangers with law enforcement duties must be certified law enforcement officers.

Experience, Special Skills, and Personality Traits

Requirements vary with the different employers. Generally, applicants for either seasonal or permanent positions need previous experience working in forestry operations, forest fire prevention and control, or related areas. They may have gained their work experience through volunteer work, employment, or work-study programs.

Forest Rangers must be able to work well with colleagues, superiors, the public, and various others from diverse backgrounds. Hence, they need excellent inter-personal, communication, and teamwork skills. They also must have effective self-management, problem-solving, and critical-thinking skills. Having strong computer and writing skills is also important. Being tactful, calm, sharp-witted, outgoing, inquisitive, detail-oriented, and dependable are some personality traits that successful Forest Rangers share.

Unions and Associations

Forest Rangers may be members of labor unions that represent them in contract negotiations for pay, benefits, working conditions, and other terms. For example, some federal Forest Rangers may belong to the National Federation of Federal Employees. For contact information to this organization, see Appendix II.

Tips for Entry

1. While you are a student, whether in high school or college, gain experience by working as a volunteer or a temporary employee for a state or federal forest service agency.
2. The U.S. Forest Service offers various student employment and internship programs. To learn more, contact the agency or visit its Web site at www.fs.fed.us.
3. Employers usually begin hiring in the spring for seasonal positions. Contact agencies for which you would like to work during the fall or winter months for recruitment information about seasonal positions.
4. Contact agencies directly to find out what their job selection process is for permanent positions.
5. Use the Internet to learn more about public forest services and the work of Forest Rangers. To get a list of Web sites, enter any of these keywords into a search engine: *forest service*, *state forest service*, or *forest rangers*. To learn about some links, see Appendix IV.

WILDLAND FIREFIGHTER

CAREER PROFILE

Duties: Control and suppress forest and other wildland fires; save lives and property; perform other duties as required

Alternate Title(s): Forest Firefighter, Firefighter, in federal agencies, known as Forestry Technician

Salary Range: $22,000 to $72,000

Employment Prospects: Fair

Advancement Prospects: Good

Prerequisites:

Education or Training—Educational qualifications vary with agency; complete agency wildland firefighting training program

Experience—Previous firefighting experience required

Special Skills and Personality Traits—Interpersonal, communication, teamwork, self-management, leadership, critical-thinking, problem-solving, and decision-making skills; alert, calm, courageous, caring, quick-witted, determined, persistent, and dependable personality traits

Special Requirements—Possess Incident Qualification Card (or Red Card) and driver's license; fulfill age, residency, and other special requirements

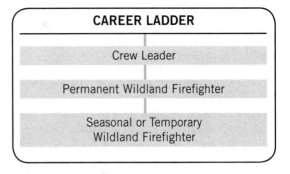

CAREER LADDER

Crew Leader

Permanent Wildland Firefighter

Seasonal or Temporary Wildland Firefighter

Position Description

Each year, thousands of wildland fires burn millions of acres of brush, grasses, and trees in the United States. Whether these fires are caused by lightning or are set by humans, they incur the loss of valuable wilderness habitats for plants and animals. Wildland fires also cause the tragic loss of life and property, because while most of these fires occur in unpopulated areas, many of them encroach on areas where people live, work, or play. Many professional firefighters work to prevent such wildland fires from occurring and fight to contain them. Among these experts are Wildland Firefighters, who specialize in extinguishing fires and saving lives and property in remote outdoor locations.

Many Wildland Firefighters are seasonal and temporary public employees who work during the dry seasons in their regions. Dry seasons vary in different areas of the United States, but Wildland Firefighters generally work during the months between spring and fall. These experts fight fires close to their home areas, although they may be called upon to help firefighters in other regions and states. Wildland Firefighters may also be dispatched to another country to assist with suppressing large out-of-control fires.

Wildland Firefighters work in crews to fulfill several types of firefighting roles. They may be designated by job titles that reflect the kind of firefighting they perform.

Many Wildland Firefighters are assigned to engine crews, who are first responders to fires that occur near their home base of operations. They transport themselves to fire scenes by driving fire engines, which carry as much as 800 gallons of water as well as large quantities of foam or other fire-retardant substances. Engine crews are well versed in using proper hose lines and suitable fittings, as well as operating water pumps. The engines are also equipped for Wildland Firefighters to administer emergency medical care.

Some firefighting crews are specially trained to fight fires in areas that are unreachable by ground vehicles or by foot. They access such remote areas by aircraft. Those who use helicopters are called helitack crews. At 30 to 250 feet in the air, these firefighters rappel down ropes from hovering helicopters to reach fire locations to battle blazes or to clear areas for the helicopters to land. From their vantage point aloft, helitack crews may create maps of the fire area, which are useful to other firefighting crews.

Other Wildland Firefighters are members of airborne firefighting crews called smoke jumpers. These experts parachute from airplanes that fly at higher altitudes than helicopters. Helitack crews and smoke jumpers are able to arrive at remote areas more quickly than firefighters who hike into the areas from the nearest trailheads. Therefore, they are at an advantage by being fully fresh and energized for the difficult task of fighting fires. Helitack and smoke jumper crews usually have to hike out of the fire zones and carry their equipment with them to roadways or clearings.

Wildland Firefighters are also assigned to hand crews or hotshot crews, depending on their experience. Those who work in hand crews are often new at firefighting or are employed in other outdoor occupations as forest rangers or logging professionals but are trained to fight wildland fires.

Hand crews perform such tasks as constructing fire lines. Fire lines are bare sections of ground ranging in width from a few feet to dozens of yards. Their purpose is to keep fires from spreading. These areas are also useful as safety zones to which firefighters can find relief from the fire and rest. Hand-crew members remove vegetation and soil to the mineral depth. That is to say, where the soil contains no flammable organic matter. They also make fire lines by lighting backfires, which keeps the main fire from spreading further. Hand-crew members also spread water, cut open burning trees, and remove burning embers from burned areas. Hotshot crews are composed of men and women who are more experienced and skilled. They perform all aspects of firefighting in the hottest burn areas, hence the name *hotshot*. Hotshot crews also perform search and rescue tasks.

Wildland Firefighters use a variety of tools, including some that are unique to their particular occupation. For example, these firefighting professionals use Pulaskis and McLeods, tools named after the firefighters who invented them. A Pulaski is a combination of an axe and a mattock, which Wildland Firefighters use to chop tree limbs and dig soil. A McLeod is a combination of a rake and a hoe. Firefighters may also carry special backpack pumps containing water to douse embers and cool burned areas.

When they are not involved with firefighting, Wildland Firefighters perform a variety of other duties. They manage controlled fires, which they deliberately set to prevent large wildfires. They also use hand tools to create firebreaks and maintain trails, as well as to thin and dispose of underbrush in high-danger fire areas. In addition, they may:

- write reports about their firefighting activities
- help to build fences, manage wildlife habitats, and construct buildings in campgrounds or other outdoor areas
- plant trees and take inventories of harvestable timber
- maintain equipment and repair tools

- work out to stay in shape
- perform practice firefighting drills
- study fire science and firefighting methods
- attend firefighting workshops, seminars, and conferences

Wildland Firefighters have a physically demanding and rigorous occupation. They risk serious injury from flames, falling trees, and smoke inhalation. These firefighting professionals work in rough, unforgiving terrain and must scramble over fallen trees or rocks and through thick underbrush. They also hike long distances, often up and down steep inclines while carrying heavy loads. They are required to work in all weather conditions.

Wildland Firefighters occasionally spend several days in fire zones and sleep on the ground. They may put in as many as 16 to 20 hour days, and frequently work long hours without breaks.

Salaries

Salaries for Wildland Firefighters vary, depending on such factors as their position, experience, employer, and geographic location. Salary information specifically for this occupation is unavailable. According to the May 2008 Occupational Employment Statistics survey by the U.S. Bureau of Labor Statistics, the estimated annual salary for most firefighters, in general, ranged between $22,440 and $72,210.

Entry-level Wildland Firefighters in the federal agencies usually start at levels 4 or 5 on the general schedule (GS), the pay schedule for many federal employees. In 2010, the basic pay for GS-4 and GS-5 levels ranged from $24,518 to $35,657 per year.

Employment Prospects

The U.S. Forest Service, the U.S. Bureau of Land Management, the U.S. Fish and Wildlife Service, and the U.S. National Park Service are the largest employers of Wildland Firefighters, who usually hold the job title of forestry technician. Wildland Firefighters are also hired by state parks and state forest services. In addition, these firefighters can find employment with private firms that offer wildland firefighting services.

Competition is strong for seasonal, temporary, and permanent positions. Opportunities are continually available due to the low retention rate of these physically demanding jobs. Employers hire professional firefighters for seasonal and temporary positions every year; however, the number of job vacancies fluctuates each year, depending on the availability of funding.

Advancement Prospects

Wildland Firefighters usually work in seasonal or temporary positions for several years before being promoted to full-time, permanent positions. They advance in seniority as well as earn higher pay. Entry-level firefighters are normally assigned to hand or engine crews.

With additional training and experience, Wildland Firefighters can seek specialized firefighting positions as smoke jumpers and engine operators. Those with supervisory and managerial ambitions can be promoted to lead, supervisory, and management positions. Wildland Firefighters may also pursue other career paths by becoming wildland firefighting pilots, dispatchers, specialists, or trainers.

Education and Training

Minimum educational requirements vary with different employers. Some employers require only a high school diploma or general equivalency diploma. Other employers prefer that candidates have completed a minimum amount of college work or hold an associate's or bachelor's degree in wildland fire science, forestry, range management, or another related field.

Recruits complete intense training programs, which include both classroom instruction and hands-on experience. They learn about wildland fire behavior, firefighting tools, orienteering, and other topics.

Special Requirements

Wildland Firefighters must possess the Incident Qualification Card, informally known as the Red Card, which certifies that they are qualified to fight fires on federal land or lands that are managed by a federal agency. These cards are issued by a forest service agency or other organizations that have wildland firefighting divisions. Individuals must complete a training program and pass a physical agility test to obtain a Red Card.

Wildland Firefighters are also required to have a valid driver's license.

Every agency has specific age, residency, and other requirements that applicants must fulfill. Applicants must also successfully pass a physical examination that tests their physical fitness and agility.

Experience, Special Skills, and Personality Traits

Employers hire applicants for entry-level positions who have several years of firefighting experience. Applicants may have gained their experience through volunteer or paid work in seasonal, temporary, or permanent positions. Employers generally favor entry-level applicants who have basic wildland firefighting skills. Some employers also prefer candidates to have logging, forestry, trail-building, and similar work experiences.

Wildland Firefighters need excellent interpersonal, communication, and teamwork skills as they must be able to work well with others from diverse backgrounds. They must also have effective self-management skills. Additionally, these firefighters need strong leadership, critical-thinking, problem-solving, and decision-making skills. Some personality traits that successful firefighters share include being alert, calm, courageous, caring, quick-witted, determined, persistent, and dependable.

Unions and Associations

Wildland Firefighters can join professional associations to take advantage of networking opportunities, continuing education, and other professional services and resources. Some national societies that serve the interests of these professionals include the International Association of Wildland Fire, the International Association of Women in Fire and Emergency Services, and the National Smokejumper Association.

These firefighters may also join labor unions to represent them in contract negotiations with their employers. Federal Wildland Firefighters might join the Federal Wildland Fire Service Association.

For contact information about all of the above organizations, see Appendix II.

Tips for Entry

1. Start gaining firefighting experience by volunteering at your local fire department.
2. Learn such skills as basic first aid, CPR, driving vehicles with manual transmissions, and outdoor skills (such as setting up a campsite, starting a campfire, tying knots, and reading a compass).
3. The U.S. Forest Service provides information about job opportunities on the Internet at www.fs.fed.us/fsjobs. To apply for temporary fire positions with agencies in the U.S. Department of Interior, visit the Wildland Fire Jobs Web site at www.firejobs.doi.gov.
4. Use the Internet to learn more about wildland firefighting. You might start by visiting Wildlandfire.com. For more links, see Appendix IV.

FOREST ENGINEER

Duties: Assist in the management, conservation, and protection of forestlands; develop and execute forest management plans; perform other duties as required

Alternate Title(s): Logging Engineer

Salary Range: $45,000 to $143,000

Employment Prospects: Fair

Advancement Prospects: Good

Prerequisites:

Education or Training—Bachelor's degree in forest engineering or a related natural resources field

Experience—Previous work experience generally required

Special Skills and Personality Traits—Leadership, teamwork, interpersonal, organizational, time-management, problem-solving, decision-making, communication, and writing skills; creative, cooperative, alert, dependable, and adaptable personality traits

Special Requirements—Professional engineer (P.E.) license may be required

CAREER LADDER

Senior Forest Engineer

Forest Engineer

Junior Forest Engineer

Position Description

Forest Engineers work to solve the problems that arise in the process of harvesting trees from forests and taking them to be processed and sold. They help forest managers and other forestry professionals to maintain the sustainability of private and public forests to ensure that they continue to thrive, as well as produce the harvests that society requires, while reducing harmful impacts on the environment. Forest Engineers utilize skills from several disciplines besides engineering. They are also knowledgeable in the fields of mathematics, biology, forestry, plant and animal ecology, watersheds, soil erosion, and business practices, among others.

Forest Engineers conduct research into such areas as forest ecosystems and the impact of human management on these sensitive ecosystems. They study new technologies and techniques of harvesting timber, the cost of operating various types of harvesting equipment, and new planning methods. They may use their know-how to perform such tasks as designing harvesting equipment, laying out plans for new forests, and designing roads and roadway structures such as culverts, bridges, and drains.

Forest Engineers are involved in designing new and efficient machines that cut trees down and do much of the processing on-site that was once performed in off-site mill facilities. Because timber harvesting techniques vary from one region to another in the United States, Forest Engineers face different challenges in creating effective harvesting systems for their particular locations. For example, in northeastern and southeastern forests, harvesting trees is done with different equipment than harvesting in the western and northwestern forests, where the terrain and tree sizes are different. Eastern loggers may use equipment called ground skidders to remove logs from forests, whereas western loggers rely more on cable systems that lift logs from steep terrains.

In all forest regions, Forest Engineers keep environmental concerns in mind. They build roads that drain properly to minimize soil erosion, thereby reducing the contamination of streams. They plan culverts that allow for fish migrations. They design equipment or choose preexisting machinery that efficiently handles harvesting and replanting activities while keeping a balance between their use and the continued health of the forest ecosystem.

Forest Engineers also design and manage the construction of various structures and work areas used by logging concerns. They decide where to place such facilities and plan for the efficient use of roads to access them. They design water supply, drainage, and sewage systems for logging company facilities. Forest Engineers also determine where harvesting should occur and change such locations regularly to ensure proper forest regrowth and to prevent resource depletion. Part of their planning process includes surveying forest areas and drawing maps to the location of new replanting areas, harvesting areas, and staging areas. Forest Engineers also draw up plans for making improvements to older roads and facilities.

Forest Engineers may perform other general tasks, such as contributing engineering consultation for timber sales projects. They may assist with handling emergencies or fill in for other personnel while they handle emergencies, suppress fires, or tend to other tasks. Forest Engineers may provide input to contract preparation by writing clauses that pertain to engineering projects. These experts may also conduct inspections of roadways and facilities to determine compliance with regulations and suggest remediation of problems to meet required standards.

These engineers work indoors and outdoors, depending on the tasks they need to complete. In their offices, they pursue such activities as planning, report and proposal writing, or budget management. They visit outdoor road construction, harvesting, and facility sites to oversee the installation of equipment and maintenance of bridges, culverts, pipelines, and so forth.

Forest Engineers work in rough and remote forest environments. They may be exposed to rain, heat, and cold. They walk on steep inclines and through thick undergrowth. These experts drive to and from job sites along forest access roads that may be muddy and rutted.

Forest Engineers generally work a 40-hour week. They may put in longer hours that include evenings, weekends, or holidays.

Salaries

Salaries for Forest Engineers vary, depending on such factors as their education, experience, employer, and geographic location. Specific salary information for this occupation is unavailable. According to the May 2008 Occupational Employment Statistics survey by the U.S. Bureau of Labor Statistics, most engineers who were not listed in the survey earned an estimated salary that ranged between $49,270 and $132,070. The estimated annual salary for most postsecondary engineering instructors ranged between $45,150 and $142,670.

Employment Prospects

Forest Engineers work for forestry companies, contractors, and consulting firms, as well as timber processing companies and forestry equipment manufacturers. They also find employment with local, state, and federal agencies. Some engineers are independent consultants or business owners of forest engineering services.

In general, openings become available as Forest Engineers advance to higher positions, transfer to other jobs or career fields, retire, or leave the workforce for various reasons. Employers will create new positions as their needs grow and expand, as long as funding is available.

With their training and skills, Forest Engineers can pursue careers in other fields such as logging, surveying, road construction, transportation planning, or natural resource engineering.

Advancement Prospects

Forest Engineers can advance in numerous ways, depending on their interests and ambitions. They can be promoted to supervisory, management, and administrative positions. They can become technical specialists. They can pursue career paths in other areas such as land use planning, marketing, sales, research, or teaching. Engineers with entrepreneurial ambitions can become independent consultants or owners of technical or consulting firms.

Education and Training

Minimally, Forest Engineers need a bachelor's degree in forest engineering, civil engineering, forestry, wildlife management, or another related field. For some positions, employers prefer to hire engineers who hold a master's or doctoral degree in their discipline. For example, consultants, top managers, academic professors, and researchers usually need an advanced degree.

Forest engineering programs generally include instruction in forest management, silviculture, soil science, forest harvesting, forest products processing, harvesting equipment design, road and bridge construction, timber structure design, and production analysis.

Entry-level Forest Engineers normally receive on-the-job training while working under the direction and supervision of experienced engineers.

Throughout their careers, Forest Engineers enroll in continuing education and training programs to update their skills and keep up with advancements in their fields.

Special Requirements

In the United States, Forest Engineers must be licensed professional engineers (P.E.) if they offer their services directly to the public or perform work that affects public safety and welfare. They must be licensed in the jurisdiction where they practice, which may be any of the 50 states, the U.S. territories, or the District of Columbia. For specific information about licensing requirements, visit the board of engineering examiners that oversees the area where you wish to practice.

Experience, Special Skills, and Personality Traits

Employers seek candidates who have work experience related to the positions for which they apply. These may be entry-level or advanced positions. Applicants may have gained their experience through internships, work-study programs, volunteer work, student research projects, postdoctoral training, or employment.

To be effective at their job, Forest Engineers must have strong leadership, teamwork, interpersonal, organizational, time-management, problem-solving, decision-making, communication, and writing skills. Being creative, cooperative, alert, dependable, and adaptable are some personality traits that successful Forest Engineers share.

Unions and Associations

Some Forest Engineers belong to professional associations to take advantage of networking opportunities, continuing education, professional certification, and other professional services and resources. Some national societies that serve the interests of these engineers are the Council on Forest Engineering, the Society of American Foresters, the American Society of Agricultural and Biological Engineers, and the Society of Women Engineers. Many professional engineers join the National Society of Professional Engineers. For contact information, see Appendix II.

Tips for Entry

1. While in college, obtain an internship or summer employment with a forestry service or corporation to gain experience.
2. Many, if not most, employers prefer to hire candidates who have completed engineering programs that are accredited by ABET, Inc. To learn about accredited forest engineering programs, visit the ABET Web site at www.abet.org.
3. Being skilled in computing, mapmaking, and geographic information systems (GIS) may enhance your employability.
4. Read a job announcement carefully and then craft your résumé so that it shows how you are qualified for the vacancy. Many employers contact only applicants whose résumés match the qualifications listed on the job announcement.
5. Use the Internet to learn more about forest engineering. You might start by visiting the Council on Forest Engineering Web site at www.cofe.org. For more links, see Appendix IV.

LOGGER

Duties: Cut and haul trees on forest lands; perform other duties as required of specific position

Alternate Title(s): A title that reflects a particular function such as Faller, or Log Grader

Salary Range: $19,000 to $55,000

Employment Prospects: Fair

Advancement Prospects: Poor

Prerequisites:

Education or Training—High school diploma; on-the-job training

Experience—Logging experience preferred

Special Skills and Personality Traits—Teamwork, problem-solving, decision-making, communication,

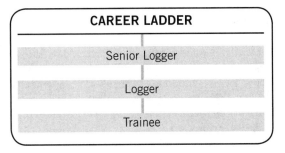

and self-management skills; business and accounting skills for self-employed Loggers; alert, calm, cooperative, levelheaded, dependable, detail-oriented, and self-motivated personality traits

Position Description

Many stories have been written and movies produced that are about lumberjacks who conquer the wilderness through mighty feats of strength. The most famous story, of course, is the legend of Paul Bunyan, the giant lumberjack. Real lumberjacks are not romantic notions or larger-than-life characters, however. They are ordinary men and women who pursue an extraordinary career. Today these hardworking individuals are generally known as Loggers.

These professionals extract logs from forests. They cut down trees, strip them of their branches, and saw them into specific lengths before loading them onto trucks that deliver the logs to sawmills. Some Loggers drive the trucks to the sawmills. At sawmills, logs are further processed to make wood products such as boards, plywood sheets, paper, or large pieces suitable for making common everyday wooden items.

Loggers work in crews. Each of these experts performs specific tasks. They are designated by names that fit the duties they perform. Fallers cut down trees with axes, saws, chain saws, and tree-harvesting machines. Buckers cut the branches off the fallen logs, while scalers measure the portions of the logs that are acceptable for delivery to sawmills. Buckers then trim the logs to the size that the scalers indicate.

Chokers, or choke setters, wrap the logs with chains so they can be hauled away from by tractor to truck loading sites. Chokers are supervised by rigging slingers who also drive the tractors. At some log-

ging sites, Loggers use winches instead of tractors to pull logs from felling sites. Yarders run the winching mechanisms.

At the loading site, loader engineers use large machines to grab the logs and place them on truck beds or flat rail cars.

Other members of logging crews are known as log sorters, markers, movers, and chippers. These Loggers separate logs by certain criteria, such as species, diameter, length, and owner. They mark them and move them to loading areas or to chipping machines.

Logging crews that rely on mechanized methods of performing tree harvesting are designated by such titles as logging equipment operators or logging machine operators. These experts operate various machines mounted on treaded or wheeled chassis that travel over rough terrain and can reach remote locations inaccessible to ordinary vehicles. Some loggers operate machines that combine tasks. For example, they use machines that do the work of buckers, chokers, yarders, and loader engineers.

Whether they use hand tools or sophisticated machinery, Loggers have certain tasks they perform to complete a harvesting operation. They prepare for each operation by inspecting trees for suitability and tag those that are not appropriate for harvest. These experts clear underbrush before cutting down trees. They determine which direction each tree must fall to avoid harming other trees. They always follow the same steps to fell trees, trim them, cut logs to required length, and move them to loading areas. After the trees are harvested, these experts may pull stumps and repair access roads.

Loggers perform dangerous and physically demanding work. They work outdoors in all weather conditions. They do a lot of heavy lifting and clambering over rough terrain to reach their harvest destinations. They may climb trees to cut branches or treetops. Loggers must be continuously aware of safety hazards that threaten them and their crewmembers. They wear eye and ear protections, hard hats, safety boots, back braces, and leather gloves.

Many Loggers work on a seasonal basis. In areas where milder weather permits them to work year-round, these experts may experience long periods without work due to rain or wildfires. Loggers work from 30 to 40 hours per week. They travel to remote wilderness areas to perform their tasks.

Salaries

Salaries for Loggers vary, depending on such factors as their position, experience, skills, employer, and geographic location. The U.S. Bureau of Labor Statistics (BLS) reported in its May 2008 Occupational Employment Statistics (OES) survey the following estimated salary ranges for these different logging professionals:

- fallers: $19,950 to $55,430
- logging equipment operators: $21,660 to $46,780
- log graders and scalers: $21,040 to $50,950
- all other logging workers: $18,860 to $45,650

Employment Prospects

Loggers work throughout the United States, but most opportunities are found in the western and southeastern states where many forests exist. Loggers work for logging companies, logging contractors, lumber companies, sawmills, and other wood product manufacturers. Some loggers are self-employed.

Most job openings will become available as Loggers retire, advance to higher positions, or transfer to other jobs or career fields. According to the BLS, opportunities are favorable for qualified Loggers, particularly those who can operate heavy equipment. A large number of Loggers are expected to reach retirement age in the next several years. In addition, fewer people are interested in committing themselves to a career in logging.

Advancement Prospects

Loggers advance by earning higher incomes and being assigned higher-level responsibilities. Loggers with supervisory and managerial ambitions and skills can be promoted to become crew leaders, supervisors, managers, and trainers. Entrepreneurial individuals might establish companies that offer logging services on a contractual basis.

Education and Training

Many employers prefer to hire applicants who hold at least a high school diploma or a general equivalency diploma.

Novices learn their skills on the job while working under the direction of experienced Loggers.

Experience, Special Skills, and Personality Traits

Employers prefer to hire applicants who have previous experience working in logging companies or sawmills.

Loggers need strong teamwork, problem-solving, decision-making, and communication skills. They also must have excellent self-management skills, including the ability to work independently, handle stressful situations, and follow and understand instructions. Self-employed Loggers need capable business and accounting skills. Being alert, calm, cooperative, levelheaded, dependable, detail-oriented, and self-motivated are some personality traits that successful Loggers share.

Unions and Associations

Some Loggers belong to a labor union that represents them in contract negotiations with their employers. One union that Loggers might join is the Woodworkers Department of the International Association of Machinists and Aerospace Workers. For contact information, see Appendix II.

Tips for Entry

1. Obtain part-time or summer jobs with a logging company or sawmill while in school.
2. Some two-year colleges offer a degree or certificate program in forestry or forest harvesting that prepares students for logging careers.
3. Use the Internet to learn more about loggers. To get a list of Web sites, enter the keywords *loggers*, *professional loggers*, or *logging workers* into a search engine. To learn about some links, see Appendix IV.

AGRISCIENCE

AGRONOMIST

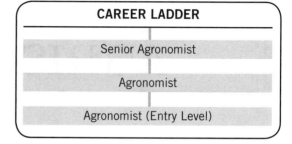

CAREER LADDER

Senior Agronomist

Agronomist

Agronomist (Entry Level)

Position Description

When we travel beyond our cities, we may cross vast fields with rich dark soil on which vegetables, fruits, and grains of all descriptions grow. Much of this abundance ends up on the shelves and bins in our grocery stores. We may ask ourselves how the soil and crops are maintained to keep producing such bounty year after year. Part of the answer is that scientists called Agronomists help to sustain and improve our soils and the output of our crops.

Agronomists engage in conducting scientific studies to help farmers to produce high-quality crops more safely, efficiently, economically, and in greater quantities. The varied backgrounds of these scientists equip them with the expertise they need to develop new methods of crop and soil management as well as techniques for controlling unwanted weeds and pests that can hinder crop production. Agronomists also help agricultural interests around the world to develop and implement the use of new strains of food crops that resist disease, produce higher yields, and thrive in harsh environmental conditions.

Agronomists study the growth and management of all kinds of crops that grow on farms. Food crops include such grains as corn, wheat, barley, rice, and millet. Other types of food crops include potatoes, carrots, beets, turnips, beans, broccoli, cauliflower, lettuce, cabbage, peas, asparagus, basil, tomatoes, and strawberries, among others.

Field crops are grown for other purposes besides food. Farmers may grow feed crops, such as corn, oats, and alfalfa, that are raised specifically for livestock to eat. Some farmers grow cotton, hemp, and other crops that are extracted for fiber. Some crops are grown for various industrial purposes. For example, corn and sugarcane can be converted to fuels that run automobiles and other motor vehicles. Other field crops are useful for making paints, solvents, adhesives, pharmaceuticals, and many other useful products.

Agronomists also study soil and how agricultural processes affect its health and vitality. They examine the organisms, decayed organic matter, and minerals of which soils are composed as well as how soil, water, temperature, and sunlight work together to promote the successful growth of crops. They also investigate how added nutrients such as fertilizers and minerals affect plant growth and food production. Some Agronomists focus on natural or organic fertilizers such as compost and manures as well as organic pest control methods. Others direct their work to the study of chemical fertilizers and pesticides.

These experts approach their work from the standpoint of several scientific and technological disciplines. Agronomy is a combination of the sciences of genetics, chemistry, physics, biology, ecology, plant physiology, cytology, soil science, and meteorology. Agronomists are also knowledgeable about biotechnology, biofuels, sustainable agriculture technologies, plant breeding, and soil building techniques. In addition, many Agronomists work in the new field of nanotechnology.

Agronomists may specialize in different aspects of agronomy, such as crop science and management, soil science, environmental science, weed science, or grassland management. Within these specialty areas, scientists may focus their interest more narrowly in such areas as genetics or biotechnology.

These agricultural scientists collaborate with experts in other scientific fields to conduct basic and applied research. Some Agronomists engage in basic research to enrich their understanding and enhance their use of that knowledge. Others apply the results of basic research to the practical purpose of helping farmers make decisions that not only serve to increase their crop yields but also to conserve natural resources and protect the environment. These scientists develop and introduce to farmers new plant varieties that will thrive in their particular locations as well as their unique climatic and soil conditions. They also assist farmers with integrating increased production with their management of soil erosion, water pollution, ecosystem sustenance, and natural resource conservation on and around their farm properties.

Agronomists work in a variety of career environments from education and research institutions to government agencies to businesses. Many Agronomists teach and conduct research at colleges and universities. Some of these scientists are self-employed consultants who offer their services to individual farmers or ranchers. Agronomists also work as researchers and technicians for nonprofit and nongovernmental organizations.

Some Agronomists pursue careers as educators and researchers with the Cooperative Extension Service at state land-grant universities. These Agronomists research and provide information that help farmers and the public solve their various problems with raising commercial crops or growing personal vegetable gardens.

Agronomists also work in such roles as researchers, technicians, managers, inspectors, and policy analysts in government at the local, state, and federal levels. For example, many Agronomists work for state agricultural departments, as well as for the Agricultural Research Service within the U.S. Department of Agriculture (USDA). Their business affiliations include such varied companies as seed companies, financial institutions, agrochemical companies, agricultural consulting firms, and outfits that supply turf to golf courses.

Agronomists perform duties that are specific to their position. They also do general tasks that are similar regardless of their work setting. For example, they may:

- research new ways to increase crop yields and develop new fertilizers and pesticides
- visit farms and other agriculture businesses to evaluate their processes and to offer advice
- provide information to farmers and the general public through seminars and workshops
- show new products to interested clients
- write informational documents, work logs, and reports about their research findings

Agronomists work in both outdoor and indoor environments. They work on farms, in greenhouses, and at other agricultural operations as well as in offices and laboratories. In outdoor settings, Agronomists contend with all kinds of weather conditions and may walk long distances over uneven or muddy terrain. Some scientists travel to other cities, states, and countries to perform their duties.

Many Agronomists work regular hours on a standard 40-hour schedule. They may put in additional hours, including evenings and weekends, as needed to complete their tasks and meet deadlines.

Salaries

Salaries for Agronomists vary, depending on such factors as their education, experience, employer, and geographic location. The U.S. Bureau of Labor Statistics reports in its May 2008 Occupational Employment Statistics (OES) survey that the estimated annual salary for most plant and soil scientists ranged between $34,260 and $105,340.

According to a 2007 salary survey report by the American Society of Agronomy, the Crop Science Society of America, and the Soil Science Society of America, the average 12-month salary ranged from $72,597 for assistant professors to $103,508 for full professors. The data for this survey were collected from college and university faculty in departments of agronomy, crop, soil, and environmental sciences throughout the United States and Canada.

Employment Prospects

According to the May 2008 OES survey, approximately 10,790 plant and soil scientists were employed in the United States. Nearly 50 percent of those scientists were employed in the federal government, colleges and universities, and scientific research and development services industries.

Opportunities for Agronomists are available worldwide. Job openings generally become available to replace Agronomists who retire, transfer to other jobs, or advance to higher positions. Employers create additional positions to meet their growing needs.

The demand for qualified Agronomists should remain constant through the years, as farmers and other agriculturists are continually seeking ways to improve the quality of crops and to increase crop yields more efficiently and economically. However, during economic downturns, employers may hire fewer employees.

Advancement Prospects

Agronomists advance in their careers according to their interests and ambitions, which typically evolve over the years. Experienced Agronomists normally specialize in particular subject matters and technical areas. Those with administrative, managerial, or consulting career goals pursue such positions. Some Agronomists seek opportunities to teach at the university level or to conduct independent research. A master's or doctoral degree is usually required for Agronomists to advance to careers in management, consulting, research, or teaching.

Some Agronomists become farmers, and some of them move into other career fields by becoming doctors or veterinarians, for example.

Education and Training

For research scientist positions, Agronomists are usually required to possess a master's or doctoral degree in agronomy, crop science, soil science, or another related field. For research assistant or technician positions, candidates must possess at least a bachelor's degree in an appropriate field.

Undergraduate students should obtain a foundation in agricultural and biological sciences. Plant physiology, plant pathology, soil science, entomology, biochemistry, genetics, and statistics are a few courses that experts recommend that students take to prepare for agronomy careers.

Experience, Special Skills, and Personality Traits

Employers usually prefer to hire candidates for entry-level positions who have some work experience related to the job for which they apply. They may have gained their experience through employment, internships, student research projects, and volunteer work.

Agronomists must have excellent leadership, critical-thinking, problem-solving, writing, computer and communication skills. They also need strong interpersonal and teamwork skills, as they must be able to work well with colleagues, technicians, and others from diverse backgrounds. Being organized, detail-oriented, curious, persistent, patient, and self-motivated are some personality traits that successful Agronomists share.

Unions and Associations

Many Agronomists belong to professional associations to take advantage of continuing education, networking opportunities, and other professional services and resources. Some national societies that serve the interests of these scientists are the American Society of Agronomy, the Council for Agricultural Science and Technology, the Crop Science Society of America, and the Soil Science Society of America. For contact information, see Appendix II.

Tips for Entry

1. While in college, become a research assistant to a professor whose work interests you. Be sure to list your experience, whether it was paid or unpaid, on your résumé and job applications.

2. To enhance their employability, some Agronomists obtain professional certification through a recognized organization such as the American Society of Agronomy.

3. Are you interested in working for the federal government? To learn about employment information, visit the USAJOBS Web site, which is run by the U.S. Office of Personnel Management. The URL is www.usajobs.gov.

4. Use the Internet to learn more about the field of agronomy. You might start by visiting the American Society of Agronomy Web site (www.agronomy.org) and Agronomic Links Around the Globe (hosted by Purdue University, www.agry.purdue.edu/links). For more links, see Appendix IV.

PLANT SCIENTIST

CAREER PROFILE

Duties: Study plants and how they relate to each other and their environments; perform other duties as required

Alternate Title(s): Research Scientist, Botanist, Crop Scientist, Plant Pathologist, or another title that reflects a specific occupation

Salary Range: $34,000 to $125,000

Employment Prospects: Good

Advancement Prospects: Good

Prerequisites:

    Education or Training—Master's or doctoral degree required for research scientist positions

    Experience—Previous work experience preferred

CAREER LADDER

Senior Plant Scientist

Plant Scientist

Plant Scientist (Entry Level)

Special Skills and Personality Traits—Leadership, teamwork, organizational, decision-making, self-management, computer, writing, and communication skills; curious, patient, detail-oriented, dedicated, persistent, creative, and flexible personality traits

Position Description

Plants are wondrous organisms. They provide us with so many things. The beauty of flowers and the majesty of big trees inspire and awe us. More importantly, without plants, we simply could not live. Through the process of photosynthesis, plants convert carbon dioxide into oxygen, which we need to breathe. Plants also nourish the soil and keep soil from eroding. We use plants for food as well. Fruits and vegetables all come from plants. The animals we use for food eat plants. Therefore, we consume plants indirectly every time we eat meat or drink milk. Additionally, plants provide us with clothing and shelter, as we derive much of our cloth from cotton or linen and build many of our homes with wood. Many of our medicines are made with ingredients found in plants. Our knowledge and practical applications of plants have been discovered and invented through the dedicated work of many scientists, engineers, technicians, and others. Among them are the men and women known as Plant Scientists, who are also known as botanists.

Plant Scientists study, identify, and classify all the types of plants—fungi, lichens, mosses, ferns, flowers, shrubs, grasses, vines, and trees—that exist among the thousands of known plant species in the world. Plant Scientists learn about the structure and life processes of plants, how plants relate to one another and other organisms, and how they have changed and adapted to their environment throughout Earth's history. These scientists also investigate the practical uses of plants as well as study diseases that infect plants. Plant Scientists research the processes plants use to produce our food or fiber and resist disease. They further study how those processes can be manipulated to increase crop yields. Additionally, they examine how farmers can manage weeds, pests, and soil conditions to improve crop production. Furthermore, Plant Scientists study how environmental changes created by humans affect the growth and vitality of plants of all kinds.

Many Plant Scientists focus their attention on studying certain plant species. They may also specialize by working in one or more fields within plant science such as anatomy, genetics, plant ecology, or molecular botany. They may apply their scientific studies to such fields as:

- horticulture—the development and creation of ornamental plants and their use in landscaping projects, as well as the cultivation of fruit and vegetable crops
- biotechnology—the use of genetic techniques with plants and other organisms to create new products
- agronomy—the study of soils and how they may be managed and used more efficiently to cultivate land and improve crops
- crop science—the study of the breeding, physiology, and management of food and fiber crops
- medical botany—the study of plants that may be used to create medicines

- plant genetics—the study of traits such as size, color, and fertility that plants pass to one another through generations
- plant cytology—the study of the cellular structure of plants
- plant pathology—the study of plant diseases, their causes, and how to control them
- natural resources management—the responsible use of plants and other natural resources to ensure their health and availability for both commercial and non-commercial uses
- food science—the study of how to improve food products made from plants

Many Plant Scientists integrate more than one field of interest within plant science. For example, horticulturists might grow medicinal plants in greenhouse environments and study their properties and growth patterns by using the principles of medical botany, plant genetics, agronomy, or plant pathology.

Like other scientists, Plant Scientists are involved in various types of research projects. They engage in basic research to gain additional knowledge and understanding about their subjects. They perform applied research that involves using the findings of basic research to develop practical solutions to problems in crop production, pest management, natural resource management, and other areas. Plant Scientists also participate in the development of new and improved commercial products.

Plant Scientists work in a variety of occupations where they can pursue their specialized interests in research. They may be research scientists, assistant researchers, technicians, agricultural inspectors, quality professionals, teachers, Cooperative Extension Service agents, or policy analysts, for example.

Plant Scientists are employed in different work settings. In the private sector, some of these professionals work in the pharmaceutical industry. Others find employment with agribusinesses, which are industries associated with large-scale farming and the attendant services used by farms. Some agribusinesses are seed companies, nurseries, paper companies, food products companies, and livestock feed producers. Some Plant Scientists work for biotechnology firms where they help develop new genetically modified plant products.

Many Plant Scientists are in government service. Some Plant Scientists work for government agencies that are concerned with agricultural and environmental policies. These agencies exist at the local, state, and federal levels. They include water districts, regional park districts, agriculture departments, forestry depart-

ments, land management agencies, and environmental agencies, among many others. In addition, Plant Scientists work for colleges, universities, research institutes, museums, parks, and rangeland preserves.

Plant Scientists perform their duties in laboratories, offices, and libraries. They also work in farm fields, orchards, nurseries, and greenhouses. These professionals may occasionally be exposed to hazardous chemicals and solvents. In farm or ranch settings, they may be required to walk long distances over uneven terrain in varying weather conditions. Their hours vary according to the type of projects they need to complete. Most Plant Scientists work regular hours on a 40-hour-per-week schedule.

Salaries

Salaries for Plant Scientists vary, depending on such factors as their education, experience, employer, and geographic location. According to the May 2008 Occupational Employment Statistics survey by the U.S. Bureau of Labor Statistics (BLS), the estimated annual salary for most Plant Scientists ranged between $34,260 and $105,340. The estimated salary range for most college and university agricultural instructors ranged between $38,460 and $124,650

Employment Prospects

According to the BLS, employment of agricultural scientists (including Plant Scientists) should increase by 15 percent during the 2008–18 period. In addition, opportunities become available as scientists transfer to other jobs, advance to higher positions, or retire.

Opportunities are favorable for qualified agricultural scientists, regardless of the state of the economy. However, fewer jobs may be available when the economy is in a downturn. Agricultural producers as well as agribusinesses and food companies are continually seeking efficient and economical ways to grow and process high-quality food for the growing global population.

Advancement Prospects

Plant Scientists advance in their careers according to their ambitions, which typically evolve over the years. As these scientists gain experience, they specialize in subject matter and technical areas that interest them. Those with administrative, managerial, or consulting ambitions can advance to such positions. Examples of management positions include project leaders, program managers, and department or institutional directors.

Some scientists seek permanent academic positions or opportunities to conduct independent research in academic or other settings.

Education and Training

Depending on the employer, Plant Scientists need either a master's or doctoral degree in botany, plant science, or another related field to qualify for research scientist positions. Plant Scientists normally need a doctorate to conduct independent research, hold faculty appointments, or advance to management positions. Individuals with an appropriate bachelor's degree are qualified for laboratory technician or research assistant positions. Some employers prefer to hire applicants who possess master's degrees for these positions.

In general, individuals seeking careers in plant science take courses in botany, crop science, soil science, weed science, plant pathology, and entomology, among others.

Experience, Special Skills, and Personality Traits

Employers usually prefer to hire candidates for entry-level positions who have some work experience related to the job for which they apply. They may have gained their experience through internships, work-study programs, student research projects, employment, or volunteer work.

Plant Scientists need excellent leadership, teamwork, organizational, decision-making, and self-management skills to perform well at their research work. They also must have strong computer, writing, and communication skills. Being curious, patient, detail-oriented, dedicated, persistent, creative, and flexible are some personality traits that successful Plant Scientists share.

Unions and Associations

Many Plant Scientists belong to professional associations to take advantage of professional services and resources, such as networking opportunities, continuing education, job listings, and scientific publications.

Some national societies that serve the diverse interests of these researchers are:

- American Phytopathological Society
- American Society of Agronomy
- American Society of Plant Biologists
- Botanical Society of America
- Council for Agricultural Science and Technology
- Crop Science Society of America
- Weed Science Society of America

For contact information, see Appendix II.

Tips for Entry

1. Are you a high school student? You can start gaining observational and research skills by growing a small flower or vegetable garden, or raising a few houseplants. Watch them carefully as they grow. Take notes about your observations, how often you water them, how you care for them, and so on. Also, read books and articles about your plants, which you can find at your public library or on the Internet.

2. Do research on prospective employers before going to your job interviews. Have a general idea of what they do, what their objectives are, and the kinds of research in which you may be involved. Talk with former or current employees, if possible. You can also find information about potential employers at their Web sites.

3. Check professional and trade association Web sites for job listings.

4. Use the Internet to learn more about plant science. You might start by visiting the World-Wide Web Virtual Library: Botany/Plant Biology at www.ou.edu/cas/botany-micro/www-vl. For more links, see Appendix IV.

ANIMAL SCIENTIST

Position Description

Agriculturists are continually seeking ways to improve the quality and care of the animals that they raise for food, fiber, sport, human companionship, and other purposes. These animals include cattle, swine, poultry, horses, sheep, and other common livestock; exotic species of livestock such as buffalo, llamas, and emus; fishes and shellfishes raised in controlled environments; and species of cats, dogs, mice, and other animals that are sold as pets or research subjects. Animal Scientists are the agricultural specialists who concern themselves with the science of animal agriculture. As research scientists, they engage in studies to find more humane, efficient, and cost-effective ways for producers to raise and manage livestock, aquacultural, and domestic animals. These researchers work in private, academic, governmental, and nongovernmental settings.

Animal Scientists apply the principles of the biological, physical, and social sciences, as well as mathematics, to their studies. Throughout their careers, they are involved in several types of research. They conduct basic research to further scientific knowledge about different animal species and breeds as regards their anatomy, physiology, biochemistry, genetics, reproduction, behavior, nutrition, and other areas. For instance, scientists might examine the genetic composition of certain animals. Animal Scientists also engage in basic research to understand the relationship between animals and their environments, such as the impact the environment has on their reproduction systems.

Applied research is another type of study that Animal Scientists conduct. They utilize the findings of basic research to find practical methods to improve and enhance the production and management of agriculture animals. For example, different scientists might be involved in:

- investigating ways to develop animals that would produce more offspring
- improving the quality of livestock so their meat tastes better
- preventing diseases and keep them from spreading among animals
- improving housing conditions for farmed fish
- refining grazing practices to allow livestock to roam pastures so that riparian areas are less damaged

Animal Scientists are also involved with the research and development or manufacturing of commercial products in the meat processing, food, pharmaceutical, biotechnology, and other private industries. For example, researchers may engage in studies to develop better and more economical foods for household pets or livestock.

Animal Scientists typically specialize in researching specific subject areas, such as animal behavior, reproduction, molecular biology, breeding, diseases, fiber production, animal management, and the marketing concerns of producers. They also focus their interests on specific types, species, and breeds of animals. For example, one Animal Scientist might engage in nutritional studies about dairy cows, while another conducts genetics research on small dog breeds.

Animal Scientists work in laboratories and offices, where they perform various tasks every day. For example, they plan and design research projects, conduct experiments and tests, read research literature, analyze and interpret data, write reports, and perform administrative tasks. Many Animal Scientists also work in the field to perform experiments and collect data. Their fieldwork may involve living and working for extended periods in remote locations.

Animal Scientists often collaborate with producers and other scientists on their projects. They communicate their research findings to their peers and the public by writing books and articles for scientific journals and by making presentations at professional and trade conferences and meetings. Some scientists also build Web sites to disseminate their data, analyses, and conclusions.

Many Animal Scientists hold faculty appointments at colleges and universities where they teach courses in animal science to undergraduate and graduate students. As instructors, Animal Scientists prepare lesson plans, tests, lectures, and class activities. They also supervise student research projects, as well as advise students on academic and career matters. Full-time professors are required to write scholarly works, perform administrative duties, and participate in community service.

Some Animal Scientists are employed as Cooperative Extension Service (Extension) specialists at state land-grant universities. These researchers conduct studies in which the results are used by Extension agents to help farmers, small business owners, consumers, youth, and others in their local communities. Some Extension specialists also hold part-time or full-time faculty positions.

Not all Animal Scientists are researchers. Some work in support positions as research assistants and technicians. Many individuals obtain formal training in animal science, but apply their knowledge and experience to other jobs in agribusiness, education, livestock production, food processing, biotechnology, animal production, animal training, animal health, and livestock marketing, among many other areas. For example, Animal Scientists may be consultants, Extension advisers, high school agriculture teachers, animal nutritionists, animal breeders, ranch managers, fish hatchery managers, meat inspectors, quality control specialists, animal

trainers, kennel operations managers, zookeepers, or veterinary technicians.

Animal Scientists generally work a 40-hour week. They put in additional hours as needed to complete their various tasks or to meet upcoming project deadlines.

Salaries

Salaries for Animal Scientists vary, depending on such factors as their education, experience, occupation, employer, and geographic location. According to the May 2008 Occupational Employment Statistics survey by the U.S. Bureau of Labor Statistics (BLS), the estimated annual salary for most Animal Scientists ranged between $33,060 and $98,980. The estimated mean annual wage was $61,640.

Employment Prospects

Positions usually become available as Animal Scientists retire, advance to higher positions, or transfer to other jobs. Employers create additional positions as their organizations grow, as long as funding is available. The BLS reports that job growth for Animal Scientists is expected to increase by 13 percent during the 2008–18 period. However, during economic downturns, employers may hire fewer employees.

Advancement Prospects

Animal Scientists advance in their careers according to their interests and ambitions, which typically evolve over the years. As they gain experience, these scientists specialize in particular subject areas within their fields. Some scientists pursue administrative, managerial, or consulting positions. Some Animal Scientists seek permanent academic positions or opportunities to conduct independent research in academic or other settings.

Education and Training

Animal Scientists generally earn college degrees in animal science, agricultural science, biological science, or another related discipline. In their undergraduate years, animal science majors take fundamental courses, such as physiology, genetics, reproduction, animal breeding, molecular biology, animal nutrition, animal behavior, and animal management.

Specific educational requirements vary for different positions, as well as for different employers. Employers require that applicants for research assistant and laboratory technician positions possess at least a bachelor's degree. Applicants for research scientist positions must hold either a master's or doctoral degree. To teach in colleges and universities, Animal Scientists must have earned a doctorate.

Applicants for entry-level positions in non-research areas (such as inspection, quality control, education, or food production) may need at least a bachelor's or master's degree, depending on an employer's requirements.

Experience, Special Skills, and Personality Traits

Employers usually prefer to hire candidates for entry-level positions who have some work experience related to the job for which they apply. They may have gained their experience through internships, work-study programs, student research projects, employment, and volunteer work.

To perform well at their jobs, Animal Scientists must have strong computer, writing, communication, interpersonal, teamwork, leadership, and self-management skills. Being detail-oriented, curious, persistent, orderly, creative, and flexible are some personality traits that successful Animal Scientists have in common.

Unions and Associations

Various professional societies serve the different interests of Animal Scientists at the local, state, and national levels. Animal Scientists join these associations to take advantage of networking opportunities, continuing education, professional publications, and other professional services and resources. Some national societies include:

- American Dairy Science Association
- American Meat Science Association
- American Society of Animal Science
- Council for Agricultural Science and Technology
- Equine Science Society
- National Institute for Animal Agriculture
- Poultry Science Association

For contact information, see Appendix II.

Tips for Entry

1. As a teenager, raise a pet or livestock animal to start gaining experience in handling animals.
2. Take advantage of your college career center when you conduct a job hunt. Career counselors can help you to find relevant job openings, write your résumé, and prepare for job interviews. Most college career centers offer their services to alumni.
3. To enhance their employability, some Animal Scientists obtain professional certification through the American Registry of Professional Animal Scientists (ARPAS). For more information, visit the ARPAS Web site at www.arpas.org.
4. Use the Internet to learn more about the field of animal science. You might start by visiting the Web sites of these organizations: the American Society of Animal Science (www.asas.org) and the Federation of Animal Science Societies, www.fass.org). For more links, see Appendix IV.

HORTICULTURAL SCIENTIST

Position Description

Many people confuse horticulture with agriculture. Agriculture is the broader field, of which horticulture is a branch. Agriculture is about the science, art, and practice of farming, while horticulture is the study of the cultivation of fruits, vegetables, herbs, ornamental plants, and other plants used for medicinal and other purposes. Horticulture is often thought of in terms of raising vegetable gardens and flower gardens and landscaping homes, buildings, and parks with lawns, shrubs, trees, and ornamental plants. However, horticulture also involves the cultivation of vegetables, fruits, and grains for crop production for the food supply for both humans and animals.

Many different career opportunities are available in horticulture. Those men and women who are specifically concerned with understanding the science of horticulture are researchers known as Horticultural Scientists. They are also involved with seeking solutions to problems with cultivation and other areas that farmers and gardeners have with their crops and plants.

Horticultural Scientists conduct research in such areas as plant physiology, biochemistry, propagation, breeding, and genetic engineering. They study methods to improve the yield, quality, nutritional value, and beauty of plants that are used for food, medicine, or aesthetic purposes. These research scientists develop new plant varieties by pollination, tissue cultures, grafting, and other methods. They seek ways to make plants grow in different soils and climates, as well as handle diseases and environmental stresses. They also engage in studies to improve techniques for controlling weeds and insect and animal pests. In addition, they address a wide range of issues regarding landscape design, irrigation systems, gardening systems and equipment, the processing, transporting, and storing of horticultural crops, and other matters related to the production and marketing of these crops.

Horticultural Scientists specialize in various ways. They may focus their studies in one of the major subdivisions of horticulture. For example, pomologists study nut and fruit crops, viticulturists examine the science of grape vines, floriculturists investigate the production and use of flowers and foliage plants, and turfgrass scientists research various types of grasses for functional, ornamental, and recreational purposes. Additionally, Horticultural Scientists become experts in certain plants or crop commodities as well as in particular subject areas, such as plant taxonomy, plant physiology, plant pathology, genetics, pest management, or the marketing of horticultural products.

Throughout their careers, Horticultural Scientists become involved in different types of research. They conduct basic research to gain further understanding and knowledge about plants, production, and marketing. They also engage in applied research, in which they use the findings of basic research to find specific solutions to horticultural problems. For example, Horticultural Scientists might be concerned with how to control insect infestation in greenhouses without the use of petrochemicals. Horticultural Scientists may be part of research and development teams in private companies. There, they are involved in creating new or improved commercial products for their employers. Horticultural Scientists may also be part of manufacturing teams in which they seek methods to produce products more safely, efficiently, and economically.

Horticultural Scientists perform a wide range of tasks. They plan and design research projects, conduct literature research, and develop, perform, and monitor experiments and tests. They analyze and interpret their research data to arrive at findings and conclusions. They also maintain accurate records, control equipment, and perform various routine administrative tasks. Many scientists have assistants whom they train and supervise. Horticultural Scientists prepare reports, publications, and presentations about their research to share with scientific colleagues, industry, and the public.

Horticultural Scientists work closely with other research scientists, engineers, technicians, and specialists, who may work in the same organizations or with other companies, government agencies, research centers, or universities.

Many Horticultural Scientists hold faculty appointments at colleges and universities where they teach horticultural or other courses to undergraduate and graduate students. As instructors, these scientists prepare lesson plans, tests, lectures, and class activities. They also supervise student research projects, as well as advise students on academic and career matters. Full-time professors are required to write scholarly works, perform administrative duties, and participate in community service.

At state land-grant universities, some Horticultural Scientists are hired as Cooperative Extension Service (Extension) specialists. The results of their research studies are used by Extension agents to help growers, amateur gardeners, and others in their communities with particular problems raising flowers, vegetables, and other horticultural crops. Extension specialists may also be appointed to faculty positions at their universities.

Horticultural Scientists work in offices, laboratories, and greenhouses. Many of them perform some research tasks outdoors in greenhouses, experimental gardens, or test plots on farms. To ensure safety when exposed to dust, toxic substances, and other dangerous elements, these scientists follow strict safety precautions and wear protective equipment.

Horticultural Scientists sometimes work more than 40-hour weeks to juggle their research and other duties. They might work evenings and weekends to monitor experiments or tests, attend meetings, or complete tasks to meet deadlines.

Salaries

Salaries for Horticultural Scientists vary, depending on such factors as their education, experience, employer, and geographic location. Specific wage information for this occupation is unavailable. In general, they earn wages similar to all plant scientists. The estimated annual salary for most plant scientists ranged between $34,260 and $105,340, according to the May 2008 Occupational Employment Statistics survey by the U.S. Bureau of Labor Statistics (BLS).

Employment Prospects

Many Horticultural Scientists hold faculty positions at colleges and universities. Some are employed as researchers for the Cooperative Extension Service at state land-grant universities. Horticultural Scientists also find research positions with government agencies (such as the USDA Agricultural Research Service) as well as with nongovernmental and nonprofit organizations, such as botanical gardens, arboretums, and research institutes. In addition, Horticultural Scientists are hired by seed, fertilizer, pesticide, biotechnology, and other private companies. They also find research positions with wholesale nursery growers. Some Horticultural Scientists are self-employed consultants.

Opportunities are continually favorable for qualified researchers, as research is always needed to improve and enhance agricultural and horticultural crop production. However, during economic downturns, employers may hire fewer employees.

The BLS predicts that employment for agricultural scientists, in general, should increase by 16 percent during the 2008–18 period. In addition to job growth, opportunities will become available as Horticultural Scientists retire, advance to higher positions, or transfer to other jobs.

Many non-research opportunities are available to horticulturists who are interested in working in production, pest management, inspection, teaching, and other areas. For example, they may seek jobs as gardeners, greenhouse managers, growers, botanical garden curators, Extension agents, landscape designers, plant buyers, crop consultants, gardening writers, and agricultural inspectors.

Advancement Prospects

Horticultural Scientists advance in their careers according to their interests and ambitions, which typically evolve over the years. As they gain experience, these scientists specialize in particular subjects within their fields. Researchers can pursue administrative, managerial, or consulting positions. Some scientists seek permanent academic positions or opportunities to conduct independent research in academic or other settings. A master's or doctoral degree is usually required for Horticultural Scientists to advance to careers in management, consulting, research, or university teaching.

Education and Training

Depending on the employer, Horticultural Scientists may be required to possess a master's or doctoral degree to apply for a research scientist position. The degree may be in horticultural science or another related discipline. For research assistant and technician positions, individuals may need to hold only a bachelor's or master's degree.

Through formal horticulture programs, students learn about plant science, plant nutrition, plant pathology, genetics, plant breeding, entomology, and plant propagation, among other topics.

Experience, Special Skills, and Personality Traits

Employers usually prefer to hire candidates for entry-level positions who have some work experience related to the job for which they apply. They may have gained their experience through internships, student research projects, employment, and postdoctoral work.

Horticultural Scientists must have excellent leadership, teamwork, interpersonal, and communication skills to be able to work well with colleagues and others from diverse backgrounds. They also need strong organizational and self-management skills. Some personality traits that successful Horticultural Scientists share include being creative, patient, persistent, detail-oriented, and flexible.

Unions and Associations

Many scientific societies, plant societies, and trade associations are devoted to the diverse interests of Horticultural Scientists. By joining such organizations, these researchers can take advantage of networking opportunities, continuing education, current research findings, and other professional services and resources. The following are a few examples of different organizations:

- American Horticultural Society
- American Orchid Society
- American Pomological Society
- American Society for Horticultural Science
- International Plant Propagator's Society
- International Society for Horticultural Science
- International Society of Arboriculture
- Potato Association of America

For contact information, see Appendix II.

Tips for Entry

1. As a high school or undergraduate student, gain practical experience working with plants. For example, you might raise a garden or some houseplants; work at a local nursery, landscaping service, or seed company; join a gardening club; or do volunteer gardening work at a botanical garden or nonprofit organization.
2. Job titles for positions vary from employer to employer. Therefore, read the job descriptions and qualifications carefully.
3. Many horticultural organizations post job openings at their Web sites, which nonmembers are welcome to browse.
4. Often, people have found jobs through referrals and tips they receive from past supervisors and fellow workers with whom they formed positive relationships.
5. Use the Internet to learn more about the field of horticultural science. You might start by visiting the Web sites of these organizations: the American Society for Horticultural Science (www.ashs.org) and the Center for Applied Nursery Research (www.canr.org). For more links, see Appendix IV.

ENTOMOLOGIST

CAREER PROFILE

Duties: Study insects and related arthropods; perform related duties as required

Alternate Title(s): A title that reflects an occupation such as Research Scientist, Professor, Extension Specialist, or Pest Control Specialist

Salary Range: 36,000 to $148,000

Employment Prospects: Fair

Advancement Prospects: Good

Prerequisites:

Education or Training—Master's or doctoral degree required for research scientist positions

Experience—Previous work experience preferred

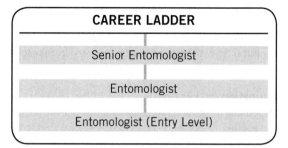

CAREER LADDER

Senior Entomologist

Entomologist

Entomologist (Entry Level)

Special Skills and Personality Traits—Communication, interpersonal, and teamwork skills; curious, creative, patient, persistent, detail-oriented, and flexible personality traits

Position Description

Entomologists are among the various researchers who are involved in finding ways to improve and enhance food production. Entomology is one of the biological sciences that involve the study of living organisms. Entomologists engage in the examination of insects, which are tiny six-legged animals, and related arthropods such as spiders and centipedes. Bees, ladybugs, aphids, and mosquitoes are just a very few of the millions of species of insects that Entomologists have identified thus far. In agriculture, insects are both beneficial and harmful to the production of crops and livestock. For example: bees pollinate plants and make honey; ladybugs eat aphids that can destroy crops; and mosquitoes can spread disease among people and animals.

Entomologists are interested in the relationship that insects have with each other, with humans and other animals, and with the environment. Entomologists also study insects' physical composition, genetics, life cycle, and behavior. Additionally, they are concerned with the classification, distribution, and evolution of the various insects that they study. Entomologists conduct their studies in private, academic, government, and nongovernmental settings. They work in any number of fields, including agriculture, conservation, forestry, public health, the military, and forensic science, among others.

These scientists are involved in different types of research. They engage in basic research to further knowledge and understanding about insects. They perform applied research, which is the utilization of basic

research findings to solve particular problems in crop protection, livestock production, horticulture, public health, the military, and other areas. Entomologists are also involved in creating new or improved consumer products for private companies. For example, Entomologists work on product development teams in such diverse industries as the seed, food processing, pharmaceutical, and agrochemical industries.

In agriculture, many Entomologists are concerned with crop protection. They pursue the understanding of beneficial insects (such as bees and ladybugs) and develop methods to increase their growth rate and distribution. They study insect pests (such as aphids and mosquitoes) that harm crops and seek ways to reduce the numbers of insect pests. Entomologists are also involved with finding ways to control insects, including methods to manage insect pests with minimal or no petrochemicals. Some Entomologists examine how pesticides and other toxic agents affect the environment in which they are applied. Other Entomologists engage in biotechnology studies to design safe methods of pest management.

Entomologists sometimes collaborate on research projects with other scientists. They also work closely with various others such as farmers, pest control advisers, pest specialists, Cooperative Extension Service (Extension) agents, and agricultural engineers. Research scientists perform various tasks every day. For example, they plan and design research projects, conduct experiments and tests, read research literature, analyze and interpret data, write reports, and perform administrative tasks. Some researchers are responsible for seeking grants to fund their projects.

Many academic researchers also hold full-time or part-time faculty positions at colleges and universities where they teach entomology courses, supervise student research projects, and advise students on academic and career matters. Full-time professors are also expected to write scholarly works, perform administrative duties, and participate in community service.

Some researchers at state land-grant universities are employed as Extension specialists. Their role is to conduct research that is used by county Extension agents to help farmers, small business owners, consumers, youth, and others in their local communities. Some of these specialists also teach one or more courses in agriculture, biology, entomology, or another biological science.

Not all agricultural entomologists are research scientists. Some are research assistants and technicians who provide technical and administrative support to scientists. Others apply their entomological backgrounds to jobs in inspection, pest control, consulting, marketing, sales, farming, education, and other areas. These entomologists also conduct research, but it is just one of various tasks that they perform on their jobs. They typically hold job titles that describe their positions, such as beekeeper, farm manager, Extension agent, pest control specialist, agricultural consultant, and curator.

Entomologists work indoors in offices and laboratories, as well as outdoors to perform field research. Due to the nature of their research, they may be required to work and live in remote locations for several days or weeks at a time. Their field studies can involve strenuous work. While performing lab experiments or fieldwork, Entomologists may handle toxic chemicals and poisonous insects.

Entomologists generally work 40 hours a week. They put in additional hours as needed to complete their various tasks or to meet project deadlines.

Salaries

Salaries for Entomologists vary, depending on their education, experience, position, employer, and geographic location. Specific salary information for this profession is unavailable. According to the May 2008 Occupational Employment Statistics survey by the U.S. Bureau of Labor Statistics, the estimated annual salary for most biological scientists, who were not listed separately in its survey, ranged between $35,620 and $101,030. The estimated annual salary for postsecondary biological science teachers ranged between $38,830 and $147,980.

Employment Prospects

Entomologists can find employment as researchers, inspectors, and specialists with local, state, and federal agencies. For example, at the federal level, the U.S. Department of Agriculture, U.S. Food and Drug Administration, the Environmental Protection Agency, and the U.S. military have hired these scientists. Entomologists are also hired to research jobs and other positions in the seed, agrochemical, food, pest control, and other agricultural industries in the private sector. In addition, Entomologists are employed as educators and researchers at academic institutions. Entomologists may also be hired by zoos, natural museums, botanical gardens, and other nongovernmental organizations.

Most positions usually become available as Entomologists retire, transfer to other jobs, or advance to higher positions. The need for qualified Entomologists in agriculture should remain constant through the years, as farmers and other agriculturists are continually seeking ways to improve pest management practices as well as produce plants that are resistant to insects and disease. However, during economic downturns, employers may hire fewer workers.

Advancement Prospects

Entomologists advance in their careers according to their interests and ambitions. As these scientists gain experience, they specialize in particular subject areas within their fields. Those with administrative, managerial, or consulting career goals pursue such positions. Some Entomologists seek opportunities to teach at the university level or to conduct independent research in academic or other settings. A master's or doctoral degree is usually required for Entomologists to advance to careers in management, consulting, research, or teaching.

Education and Training

Educational requirements for Entomologists vary with the different positions as well as among different employers. Employers usually require applicants for research scientist positions to possess either a master's degree or doctorate in entomology or another related field. To teach in colleges and universities, Entomologists must possess a doctoral degree.

For research assistant and laboratory technician positions, applicants must possess a bachelor's degree in entomology, biology, zoology, or another related field. Bachelor's degrees are usually the minimum requirement for entry-level positions in agricultural or food inspection, pest management, industrial sales, and other areas.

Experience, Special Skills, and Personality Traits

Employers usually prefer to hire candidates for entry-level positions who have some work experience related to the job for which they apply. They may have gained their experience through employment, internships, student research projects, and volunteer work.

Entomologists must work well with others; hence, they need excellent communication, interpersonal, and teamwork skills. Being curious, creative, patient, persistent, detail-oriented, and flexible are some personality traits that successful Entomologists share.

Unions and Associations

Many Entomologists belong to professional associations to take advantage of networking opportunities, training programs, and other professional services and resources. Various societies are available at the local, state, and national levels that serve the different interests of Entomologists. Some national societies include:

- American Association of Professional Apiculturists
- Association of Applied IPM Ecologists
- Association of Natural Biocontrol Producers
- Council for Agricultural Science and Technology
- Entomological Society of America
- Lepidopterists' Society
- Society for Integrative and Comparative Biology

For contact information, see Appendix II.

Tips for Entry

1. Involvement in amateur entomology organizations is one way to gain knowledge and experience. For example, young people might find opportunities at a nearby natural museum, a 4-H Club, a scouting unit (such as the Girl Scouts), or a school club.

2. Not all four-year colleges and universities have entomology departments. Therefore, do careful research about an institution before applying for it. If it does not have a department, ask the school such questions as these: Can you obtain a minor in entomology? What entomology courses does the school offer? How often are these courses offered? Does it offer a graduate program in entomology?

3. As a student, obtain a summer job or internship in which you would have the opportunity to work with insects. For example, you might work for a beekeeper, pest control operator, or a forest or agricultural research station, or a Cooperative Extension Service office.

4. When you are conducting a job search, be sure to let current and former professors, work supervisors, and coworkers know of your intentions. You may be able to learn about current and future openings from your contacts.

5. Use the Internet to learn more about Entomologists. You might start by visiting the Entomological Society of America Web site (www.entsoc.org) and Iowa State Entomology Index of Internet Resources (www.ent.iastate.edu/List). For more links, see Appendix IV.

GENETICIST

CAREER PROFILE

Duties: Study the heredity of plants or animals; address problems concerning the production of plants or animals; perform additional duties as required

Alternate Title(s): Research Geneticist, Agricultural Geneticist, Plant Geneticist, Animal Geneticist; a title that reflects a specialty such as Tree Geneticist or Poultry Geneticist

Salary Range: $33,000 to $125,000

Employment Prospects: Good

Advancement Prospects: Good

Prerequisites:

    Education or Training—Bachelor's or advanced degree, depending on position

    Experience—Previous work experience preferred

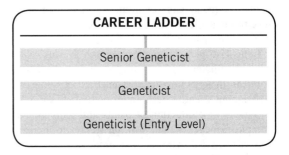

CAREER LADDER

Senior Geneticist

Geneticist

Geneticist (Entry Level)

Special Skills and Personality Traits—Leadership, teamwork, organizational, critical-thinking, writing, communication, and computer skills; inquisitive, patient, goal-driven, persistent, detail-oriented, and flexible personality traits

Position Description

Over the centuries, farmers would save seeds from their best plants to sow for next year's crops. Animal producers would mate their best chickens, cattle, horses, dogs, pigs, and sheep to ensure the continued superior lineage of their animals. Today, scientists engage in research to help agricultural producers raise quality plants and animals for food, fiber, fuel, recreation, and other purposes more efficiently and economically.

Agricultural Geneticists are the research scientists who specialize in the study of heredity. All living organisms—bacteria, plants, animals, and humans—have traits that determine what characteristics or qualities make them what they are. An organism's traits are passed from one generation to the next through the organism's genes, which are found in the nucleus of all its cells. The genes are composed of deoxyribonucleic acid or DNA, and that DNA code, in turn, defines the particular features that a plant, animal, or human has. For example, a horse's genes specify its sex, height, color, speed, and temperament, among other characteristics.

In general, Geneticists examine the traits of living organisms and the different ways that traits are expressed among organisms. They study how traits are inherited as well as how traits evolve through the generations. They also are concerned with studying the molecular structure and function of genes, how DNA is transmitted within the genes, and what causes genes to mutate. In addition, Geneticists are continually devel-

oping new and improved tools and techniques to perform their studies.

Agricultural Geneticists usually focus on either animal or plant genetics. As they become experienced, they concentrate on certain species or varieties. For instance, some animal geneticists might specialize by studying the genetics of dairy cattle, sheep, or turkeys; some plant geneticists might devote their studies to such species as corn, fruit trees, or bamboo. Agricultural Geneticists may further choose to specialize by working in certain areas of genetics, such as

- cytogenetics, which is the study of chromosomes and cell division
- molecular genetics, which is the study of the gene's structure, function, and nature
- population genetics, which is the statistical study of how genes vary and evolve among organisms over time
- quantitative genetics, which is the examination of continuous traits (such an animal's weight or fat content) that are influenced by the environment

Agricultural Geneticists work in academic, private, government, and nongovernmental settings where they are involved in different types of research. They conduct basic research to gain additional knowledge about the genetics of the various species and varieties of plants and animals. For example, plant geneticists might study how genes influence each other, or animal geneticists might compare genetic codes of different breeds of livestock. Basic researchers also seek further understanding about attributes in plants or animals, such as their resistance to disease, their nutritive value, or their cooking or processing quality.

Geneticists perform applied research in which they utilize the findings of basic research to solve practical problems. In agriculture, many Geneticists are engaged in designing scientific techniques or tools to improve the quality or production of plants and animals. For example, Geneticists may work on studies to increase crop yields; raise livestock that produce more meat, fiber, or milk; or produce dogs that have less risk of certain diseases.

Many Geneticists are also employed in agricultural companies where they are involved in the research and development of new or improved commercial products. For instance, animal geneticists might seek ways to make chickens produce more eggs, while plant geneticists might conduct studies to enhance the flavor of vegetables. Geneticists in private companies also engage in the selection and development of new or improved breeds of plants or animals.

Agricultural Geneticists often collaborate on research projects with fellow scientists, including those specializing in other biological or agricultural science fields. Principal investigators are responsible for overseeing the direction and progress of research projects, as well as supervising the work of team members.

Geneticists work in offices and laboratories, as well as in greenhouses and outdoors in fields. Some Geneticists perform breeding duties, which involve planning and executing breeding studies to improve specific characteristics of the varieties of plants or animals on which they are working. They might utilize various technologies that allow them to manipulate the genetic and biochemical characteristics of living organisms at the molecular level. For example, a Geneticist might remove a particular gene from a plant to make it more resistant to drought.

Agricultural Geneticists perform a wide range of tasks in their research work. For example, they plan and design projects, conduct experiments and tests, read research literature, analyze and interpret data, and perform administrative tasks. Some of these experts supervise and direct the work of research assistants and technicians. Geneticists distribute the results of their research to their peers and the public. For example, they might write books, prepare articles for scientific journals, make presentations at scientific or trade conferences, or build Web sites to display their research findings.

Many academic researchers hold faculty appointments in the agricultural sciences or biological sciences department, where they teach genetics, breeding, and other courses to undergraduate and graduate students. Faculty members also supervise student research projects and advise students on academic and career matters. Full-time professors are also responsible for writing scholarly works about their research results, performing administrative duties, and participating in community service.

At state land-grant universities, some Geneticists work as research specialists for the Cooperative Extension System. They conduct studies and seek practical solutions that address concerns of farmers, seed companies, and others within the region that their particular university serves. Their expertise and research findings are distributed by extension agents and educators to the local communities. Some specialists also teach one or more courses at their university.

Geneticists sometimes put in more than 40 hours a week to complete their research tasks and to meet project deadlines. They may work irregular hours, including evenings and weekends.

Salaries

Salaries for Geneticists vary, depending on such factors as their education, experience, employer, and geographic location. The U.S. Bureau of Labor Statistics (BLS) reported in its May 2008 Occupational Employment Statistics survey, the following estimated salary ranges for most professionals working in these positions:

- animal scientists, $33,060 to $98,980
- plant scientists, $34,260 to $105,340
- agricultural instructors in colleges and universities, $38,460 to $124,650

Employment Prospects

Some Agricultural Geneticists are employed by the U.S. Department of Agriculture and other federal, state, and local government agencies, as well as by nonprofit and nongovernmental research institutes. Agricultural Geneticists also find employment in the private sector with plant and animal breeding companies, biotechnology firms, pharmaceutical companies, and others. Many plant and animal geneticists are hired as faculty members in colleges and universities. Some Geneticists are self-employed consultants.

According to the BLS, employment of agricultural scientists should increase by 16 percent during the 2008–18 period. In addition, opportunities will become available for Agricultural Geneticists as scientists transfer to other jobs, advance to higher positions, or retire.

Opportunities are favorable for qualified agricultural scientists, regardless of the state of the economy. However, fewer jobs may be available during economic downturns. Agricultural producers as well as agribusinesses and food companies are continually seeking efficient and economical ways to grow and process high-quality food for the growing global population.

Advancement Prospects

Agricultural Geneticists advance in their careers according to their interests and ambitions, which typically evolve over the years. As Geneticists gain experience, they specialize in subject matter and technical areas that interest them. Those with administrative, managerial, or consulting ambitions can advance to such positions. Examples of management positions include project leaders, program managers, and department or institutional directors.

Some scientists seek permanent academic positions or opportunities to conduct independent research in academic or other settings. Some agricultural Geneticists may choose to apply their backgrounds to other careers by becoming bioinformatics scientists, veterinarians, physicians, attorneys, journalists, policy analysts, or other professionals.

Education and Training

To obtain research scientist positions, Geneticists may be required to possess a master's or doctoral degree in genetics, molecular biology, plant biology, animal science, or another related field. Usually, Geneticists need a doctorate to conduct independent research, hold faculty appointments, or advance to management positions. Individuals with an appropriate bachelor's degree are qualified for laboratory technician or research assistant positions. Some employers may prefer to hire applicants who possess a master's degree for laboratory technician positions.

Agricultural Geneticists generally have a fundamental background in agriculture, biology, molecular biology, biochemistry, genetics, statistics, and bioinformatics. Animal geneticists have also completed courses in animal husbandry, while plant geneticists have completed courses in plant sciences.

Experience, Special Skills, and Personality Traits

Employers usually prefer to hire candidates for entry-level positions who have some work experience related to the job for which they apply. They may have gained their experience through internships, work-study programs, student research projects, employment, and volunteer work.

To do their research work effectively, Geneticists need excellent leadership, teamwork, organizational, critical-thinking, writing, and communication skills. They should also have strong computer skills, particularly in bioinformatics. Being inquisitive, patient, goal-driven, persistent, detail-oriented, and flexible are some personality traits that successful Geneticists share.

Unions and Associations

Geneticists can join professional associations to take advantage of networking opportunities, continuing education, and other professional services and resources. Some national societies that serve the diverse interests of agricultural researchers are:

- American Society of Animal Science
- American Society of Plant Biologists
- Crop Science Society of America
- Genetics Society of America

For contact information, see Appendix II.

Tips for Entry

1. Talk with various agricultural Geneticists to learn about their work and how they obtained their training. To find Geneticists in your area, you might talk with a local Cooperative Extension Service agent or your high school or college agricultural instructors.
2. While in high school or college, gain practical experience breeding animals or plants. For example, if your interest is in plant genetics, obtain part-time or summer employment working as a pollinator or pollination technician.
3. Review a job announcement carefully before filling out a job application. Then think about which of your skills and experience demonstrate how you best qualify for the job. Be sure to highlight that information on your application.
4. Use the Internet to learn more about agricultural genetics. To get a list of relevant Web sites, enter any of these keywords into a search engine: *agricultural genetics*, *crop genetics*, *plant genetics*, *livestock genetics*, or *animal genetics*.

AGRICULTURAL ENGINEER

Duties: Engage in the research, development, design, testing, manufacture, and implementation of solutions to problems involving agricultural, food, and other biological systems; perform related duties as required

Alternate Title(s): Biological Systems Engineer; other title that reflects a specialty (such as Aquacultural Engineer) or an engineering function (such as Project Engineer)

Salary Range: $43,000 to $108,000

Employment Prospects: Good

Advancement Prospects: Good

Prerequisites:

  Education or Training—Bachelor's or advanced degree, depending on position

  Experience—Previous work experience normally required

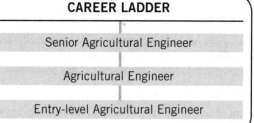

CAREER LADDER

Senior Agricultural Engineer

Agricultural Engineer

Entry-level Agricultural Engineer

Special Skills and Personality Traits—Interpersonal, communication, math, writing, leadership, teamwork, critical-thinking, and problem-solving skills; enthusiastic, curious, creative, and detail-oriented personality traits

Special Requirements—Professional engineer (P.E.) license may be required

Position Description

Agricultural Engineers apply the principles and techniques of engineering, mathematics, and science to create solutions to problems in agriculture, food processing, and related biological systems. They invent products, systems, and processes that are useful and affordable to agricultural producers, amateur gardeners, agribusinesses, food processors, manufacturers, forest and rangeland managers, and many others. In addition, Agricultural Engineers devise technologies that are responsible and safe as well as conserve our natural resources (such as air, water, and soil) and protect the environment.

Besides agriculture, these engineers work in a wide range of industries, including the aquaculture, forest products, food processing, pharmaceuticals, energy, public works, and biotechnology industries, to name just a few. Some conduct basic or applied research in government, private, and academic settings, while others participate in research and development or the production of commercial products. Still other Agricultural Engineers are involved in the construction and operation of agricultural structures, factories and processing plants, and sewage treatment facilities.

Agricultural Engineers engage in diverse types of work; for example, they might:

- develop machinery and equipment for such purposes as crop processing, horticulture production, livestock handling, lawn care, and recreation
- design systems for farming and food processing operations that incorporate electronic and information technologies, such as automation systems, geographic information systems, and global positioning system technology
- devise mechanical systems to improve the storage and distribution of crops, food, or other products
- create pond systems for raising fish (for food, bait, and ornamental purposes) so that less water is used and pollution is reduced
- improve control systems for temperature, humidity, and ventilation in facilities, such as nursery and greenhouse operations
- develop new processes for making plant-based pharmaceuticals
- investigate ways of converting biological products into alternative sources of energy
- develop biodegradable packaging materials for food or pharmaceutical products
- address health and safety issues by finding ways to improve practices, equipment, and materials to lessen the risk of injuries, illnesses, and death

- develop universal standards for equipment, processes, or systems
- evaluate forest operations to solve natural resource and environment problems
- design industrial waste or wastewater treatment systems that are less harmful to the environment
- formulate strategies to clean up mining, construction, or other sites

Many Agricultural Engineers focus on a particular type of engineering, and may hold job titles that reflect their specialties. For example, food engineers engage in the production, packaging, storage, and distribution of food products; aquaculture engineers devise solutions for commercial fish farms as well as for natural fish habitats; and forest engineers participate in developing and executing responsible forest management plants.

Agricultural Engineers work in both the public and private sectors. Employers usually hire engineers to perform specific functions, such as research, design, analysis, testing, or project management. Many engineers engage in a number of these functions during their engineering careers. Some of these experts include:

- research engineers, who conduct studies to find solutions to engineering problems, to develop new or improved products and systems, or to gain new knowledge and understanding about topics of interest
- development engineers, who apply research findings toward creating new or improved products, processes, or systems
- design engineers, who take concepts or working models of products or systems and create designs that meet customers' requirements as well as can be produced economically
- test engineers, who develop and conduct tests to ensure that products are free of defects and meet customers' requirements
- systems engineers, who check system components of a design to ensure they are interfacing correctly
- manufacturing production engineers, who oversee the daily operation of manufacturing processes to ensure that products are being made according to specifications
- process design engineers, who work on developing new or improved manufacturing processes
- facilities engineers, who make sure that the equipment, systems, and structures of a facility, such as a waste treatment plant, factory, or food processing plant are running efficiently and safely at all times

- project engineers, who oversee the daily management and coordination of engineering projects
- sales engineers, who demonstrate to customers how products or services can fulfill their particular needs
- field service engineers, who install, maintain, and repair products and systems at customers' sites

Agricultural Engineers work independently on their tasks, but also work with other engineers, scientists, technologists, technicians, and other personnel to complete projects, manage operations, or market products and services.

Agricultural Engineers work in offices and laboratories. They may spend some time performing tasks at farms, fish hatcheries, rangelands, forests, construction sites, manufacturing plants, or other settings.

Agricultural Engineers work 40 hours a week, but often put in additional hours to complete tasks and meet deadlines. They may be required to travel to other cities to meet with clients or customers, government officials, or suppliers, as well as to participate in professional and trade conferences.

Salaries

Salaries for Agricultural Engineers vary, depending on such factors as their education, experience, position, employer, and geographic location. According to the May 2008 Occupational Employment Statistics (OES) survey by the U.S. Bureau of Labor Statistics (BLS), the estimated annual salary for most Agricultural Engineers ranged between $43,150 and $108,470.

Employment Prospects

The agricultural engineering field is small compared to the other engineering disciplines. The BLS reports in its 2008 OES survey that approximately 2,640 Agricultural Engineers were employed in the United States.

Job opportunities are favorable for qualified Agricultural Engineers. These engineers will continually be needed worldwide to develop and design new and improved technologies for producing crops and conserving natural resources more efficiently. The BLS predicts that employment of these engineers should increase by 12 percent during the 2008–18 period. In addition to job growth, Agricultural Engineers will be needed to replace those who retire, advance to higher positions, and transfer to other jobs or career fields.

Agricultural Engineers are hired by agricultural companies, farm equipment manufacturers, food processing companies, engineering firms, management consulting firms, and research and testing services. They are also employed by government agencies, academic institutions, and nonprofit organizations. Some experts say that two anticipated growth areas are bioengineering and technologies for precision farming.

Advancement Prospects

As Agricultural Engineers gain experience, they receive assignments that are more complex and in which they earn higher pay. Experienced engineers generally specialize in areas that interest them. Those with management and administrative ambitions can pursue positions as supervisory, project, program, and chief engineers. Entrepreneurial engineers often seek opportunities as owners of consulting firms.

Some engineers choose to apply their expertise to other career fields by becoming educators, sales professionals, and marketing experts.

Education and Training

Minimally, Agricultural Engineers must possess a bachelor's degree in agricultural engineering, biological engineering, mechanical engineering, or another related field. A master's or doctoral degree is usually required for engineers to advance to careers in management, consulting, research, or teaching. Engineers must possess a doctorate to teach at the university level.

Agricultural engineering programs are known by various names at different institutions. For example, they may be called biological systems engineering, biosystems and agricultural engineering, or environmental engineering programs. Students in these programs generally gain knowledge in a wide range of topics in biology, agriculture, and engineering to address the diverse problems in the development, production, packaging, and distribution of agricultural products and systems.

Novice engineers typically receive on-the-job training while working under the guidance and direction of experienced staff members.

Special Requirements

Engineers must be state licensed as professional engineers (P.E.) if they perform work that affects the safety and welfare of the public or offer their services directly to the public. The requirements for P.E. licenses vary with each state. For specific requirements, contact the board of engineering examiners in the state where you wish to practice.

Experience, Special Skills, and Personality Traits

Employers typically seek candidates for entry-level positions that have one or more years of work experience related to the position for which they apply. Applicants may have gained their experience through work-study programs, internships, student research projects, or employment.

Agricultural Engineers must have excellent interpersonal and communication skills as they must be able to work well with colleagues, clients, the public, and many others. These engineers also need strong math and writing skills to perform their duties effectively. In addition, they need strong leadership, teamwork, critical-thinking, and problem-solving skills. Being enthusiastic, curious, creative, and detail-oriented are a few personality traits that successful Agricultural Engineers have in common.

Unions and Associations

Many Agricultural Engineers belong to professional associations to take advantage of networking opportunities, continuing education, and other professional services and resources. Some national societies that Agricultural Engineers might join are the American Society of Agricultural and Biological Engineers, the Council for Agricultural Science and Technology, and the National Society of Professional Engineers. For contact information to these organizations, see Appendix II.

Tips for Entry

1. Experts in the field suggest that high school students obtain a solid background in mathematics and science to prepare for college. Additionally, they need to do well in such high school courses as English, humanities, social studies, and computing.
2. Obtain part-time jobs or internships in different areas of agriculture to determine which ones interest you the most.
3. Join student and professional associations that are related to your areas of interest. Go to conferences to network with professionals, as well as to keep up with new developments.
4. Visit Web sites of potential employers to find out about job openings as well as to learn more about what they do.
5. Use the Internet to learn more about agricultural engineering. You might start by visiting the American Society of Agricultural and Biological Engineers Web site at www.asabe.org. For more links, see Appendix IV.

RESEARCH ASSOCIATE

Duties: Provide technical support and research assistance to scientists; perform other duties as required

Alternate Title(s): Research Assistant

Salary Range: $22,000 to $54,000

Employment Prospects: Good

Advancement Prospects: Good

Prerequisites:

Education or Training—Bachelor's or master's degree in a scientific discipline required

Experience—One or more years of work experience preferred

Special Skills and Personality Traits—Writing, computer, communication, critical-thinking,

problem-solving, interpersonal, teamwork, and self-management skills; organized, detail-oriented, creative, innovative, persistent, flexible, and self-motivated personality traits

CAREER LADDER

Senior Research Associate

Research Associate

Research Assistant or Research Associate (Entry Level)

Position Description

Agricultural scientists rely on and work with men and women who assist them in research activities, experiments, and other projects. These individuals are known as Research Associates. They are trained in a particular field of agricultural science, such as plant physiology, agronomics, genetics, entomology, or horticulture.

Research Associates assist scientists with either basic or applied research. They apply scientific principles and techniques to solve a wide array of complex problems in both laboratory and field settings. The combined effort these professionals put into basic and applied research is called research and development.

In basic research, scientists and Research Associates gain knowledge about phenomena that can be utilized in other research projects. They also conduct basic research to develop new scientific theories or concepts.

In applied research, Research Associates assist in finding practical uses for the knowledge revealed by basic research. For example, scientists may use their newfound expertise about genetics to develop new strains of vegetables that will withstand certain climatic conditions.

Research Associates are also engaged in research projects that lead to new or improved products for commercial purposes. For example, agricultural Research Associates may be involved in developing plants that are drought resistant or technologies that run farm equipment more efficiently.

While under the direction of scientists, Research Associates are responsible for conducting specific experiments or tests. They assist in the development, design, and execution of their assigned experiments and tests, as well as with the analysis and reporting of the data collected from them. Research Associates perform such tasks as:

- developing standard operating procedures for experiments or tests
- making careful and detailed observations about an experiment's procedures and results
- troubleshooting problems as they occur
- operating, testing, calibrating, and maintaining laboratory and scientific equipment
- making sure that experiments and tests comply with protocols, policies, and regulations
- keeping detailed and accurate logs and records of observations, data, and findings
- conducting literature searches
- writing technical reports
- attending scientific meetings and conferences

Research Associates may be asked to contribute to scientific papers as well as participate in presentations at scientific conferences. Some senior associates supervise laboratory technicians and research assistants.

Research Associates may be assigned various non-research responsibilities. For example, they might manage nurseries, sow fields, or prune orchards. Some associates oversee the work of field laborers to ensure that experimental crops are grown and harvested according to research specifications.

Research Associates mostly work in laboratories and offices. Those involved in field studies might work in remote locations in varying weather conditions. Research Associates generally work a 40-hour week.

Salaries

Salaries for Research Associates vary, depending on such factors as their education, experience, employer, and geographic location. According to the May 2008 Occupational Employment Statistics survey by the U.S. Bureau of Labor Statistics, the estimated annual salary for most agricultural technicians ranged between $22,190 and $53,880.

Employment Prospects

Agricultural Research Associates work in government agencies, such as the U.S. Department of Agriculture, nongovernmental research institutes, colleges and universities, and nonprofit organizations. They also find research positions in agricultural, food processing, biotechnology, seed, animal breeding, and other companies.

In general, job openings become available when individuals advance to higher positions, transfer to other occupations, or leave the workforce for various reasons. Employers will create additional positions to meet growing needs, as long as funding is available. According to some experts in the field, job prospects are stronger in the biotechnology, food processing, and scientific research and development services industries.

Advancement Prospects

Research Associates can advance according to their interests and ambitions. As they gain experience, they can become technical specialists or pursue supervisory and managerial positions. They may choose to move into production, quality control, marketing, sales, or another area within their company; or they may seek research jobs in government, academic, or other research settings.

Some Research Associates return to school to obtain the appropriate advanced degrees to become research scientists, college professors, or high-level administrators.

Education and Training

Depending on the employer, candidates must have either a bachelor's or master's degree in an appro-priate science discipline. For example, biotechnology companies hire Research Associates who have college degrees in biology, biochemistry, or other related fields.

Employers may hire candidates for entry-level Research Associate positions with associate's degrees, as long as they have extensive experience as laboratory technicians or research assistants.

Experience, Special Skills, and Personality Traits

Employers prefer to hire entry-level candidates who have one or more years of work experience relevant to the position for which they apply. Recent college graduates may have gained experience through internships, work-study programs, research assistantships, or employment.

To perform their various tasks efficiently, Research Associates must have strong writing, computer, and communication skills. They also need effective critical-thinking, problem-solving, interpersonal, teamwork, and self-management skills. Being organized, detail-oriented, creative, innovative, persistent, flexible, and self-motivated are some personality traits that successful Research Associates share.

Unions and Associations

Research Associates can join professional associations that serve their particular interests to take advantage of networking opportunities, continuing education, job listings, and other services and resources. These societies are available at the local, state, national, and international levels. To see a list of scientific societies, go to Appendix II at the back of this book.

Tips for Entry

1. Job titles can mean different occupations to different employers. At some companies, research associates are postdoctoral researchers who hold fellowship positions. Therefore, read job announcements carefully and thoroughly to ensure you meet the qualifications.
2. Contact your current and former employers, as well as instructors and peers, for job referrals.
3. Use the Internet to learn more about the types of agricultural research that are being done. You might start by visiting the U.S. Agricultural Research Service at www.ars.usda.gov.

AGRICULTURAL TECHNICIAN

Duties: Provide technical support to agricultural scientists and engineers involved in research and development; perform related duties as required

Alternate Title(s): Laboratory Technician, Research Assistant; Horticulture Technician, Animal Science Technician, Extension Associate, or other title that reflects a specialty or occupation

Salary Range: $22,000 to $54,000

Employment Prospects: Good

Advancement Prospects: Good

Prerequisites:

Education or Training—Associate's degree usually required

Experience—Work experience preferred

CAREER LADDER

Senior Agricultural Technician

Agricultural Technician

Agricultural Technician (Entry Level)

Special Skills and Personality Traits—Computer, writing, communication, interpersonal, teamwork, self-management, analytical, and problem-solving skills; self-motivated, honest, accurate, detail-oriented, organized, dedicated, and dependable personality traits

Position Description

When we think about farms or ranches, it is generally along the lines of the operations that raise crops and livestock for consumption, whether it is for food, fiber, animal feed, pharmaceuticals, or other commercial purposes. There is another type of farm—the research or experimental farm—that grows crops and livestock to suit a different purpose: to learn more about efficient means to produce food on commercial operations. Scientists and engineers manage these farms along with other members of their staffs. Among those staff members are men and women called Agricultural Technicians.

Agricultural Technicians assist the scientists and engineers at experimental farms to conduct research in crop science, soil science, dairy science, food science, aquaculture, horticulture, and other areas. These technicians play an active role in both basic and applied research projects and contribute to the study of many topics and issues regarding many agricultural fields of interest. For example, they might:

- contribute to the completion of such projects as crop yield and quality improvement studies
- study soil to learn more about its properties and behavior
- experiment with ways to control weeds and insect pests without the use of harmful chemicals
- breed animals or plants to possess desired characteristics

- observe how new foods will impact the growth or health of livestock
- design new methods for producing crops
- develop new seeds, improved food for animals, or new types of farm equipment
- investigate better ways to ensure soil conservation and manage rangelands

Under the direction of scientists, engineers, supervisors, and managers, Agricultural Technicians apply scientific and mathematical principles and techniques to the process of solving problems. These professionals are knowledgeable about research and experimental methods and how they may be applicable to the type of agricultural field in which they work. They also are knowledgeable about local climates and natural resources, as well as which crops are grown and which farming methods are common to their locations. Agricultural Technicians are familiar with the use of various types of equipment including farm tools and vehicles; laboratory equipment such as incubators, weight meters, temperature gauges, and spectrometers; and technologies such as computers, geographic information systems, and global positioning systems.

Depending on their level of expertise and experience, Agricultural Technicians have varying responsibilities. Entry-level technicians perform routine tasks, which may include tending to crops and farm areas.

As they become more knowledgeable and adept at the more technical aspects of their work, they are assigned more responsibilities and work under less supervision. Advanced technicians may assume limited supervisory responsibilities and follow research guidelines and experiment schedules.

Senior Agricultural Technicians may design some of the methods and environmental controls for managing experimental crops. These technicians operate some of the more sophisticated farm equipment and work with new plant species. They maintain databases for research purposes. Senior Agricultural Technicians oversee an entire crew of technicians and laborers. They may design some of the experiments and tests conducted by the staff of technicians.

Agricultural Technicians at all levels perform general tasks to keep experimental farms running smoothly. Some of them are involved with raising plants while others raise animals. Agricultural Technicians may be responsible for:

- pollinating and propagating plants
- harvesting and storing crops
- caring for laboratory animals, livestock, exotic species, fish or shellfish species, or companion animals
- maintaining environmental controls in animal living quarters
- collecting samples from either plants or animals and preparing them for experiments and tests
- estimating local insect populations and collecting sample insects for study and identification
- operating lab equipment including centrifuges, spectrometers, air samplers, and others
- analyzing experimental and test data and preparing summaries and reports regarding the results and findings
- fielding questions from the general public about gardening, small farm management, plant identification, and other areas of concern
- maintaining an inventory of supplies for laboratory and field operations
- performing minor construction, maintenance, and repair of facilities and equipment

Agricultural Technicians conduct their work in several types of indoor or outdoor environments. They work in offices, in laboratories, on farms, or at such locations as rivers, lakes, and ocean shores. They perform physical work that requires them to be able to lift and carry objects weighing 50 pounds or more. Agricultural Technicians must be physically adept to stand, walk, climb, bend, and stoop for long periods.

Their work environment may be dusty and they may endure all kinds of weather conditions while working outdoors. Some Agricultural Technicians may be required to work with toxic chemicals, heavy equipment, or machinery with exposed moving parts. They may work near high-voltage equipment. These technicians must therefore follow strict safety procedures and wear protective clothing such as steel-toed shoes, goggles, and hard hats.

Agricultural Technicians work for 40 hours per week, but they may put in additional hours to complete tasks. Farm activities often take place at irregular hours. Consequently, technicians may work during early mornings, late evenings, or weekends.

Salaries

Salaries for Agricultural Technicians vary, depending on such factors as their education, experience, job duties, employer, and geographic location. According to the May 2008 Occupational Employment Statistics survey by the U.S. Bureau of Labor Statistics (BLS), the estimated annual salary for most Agricultural Technicians ranged between $22,190 and $53,880. The estimated mean hourly wage for this occupation was $17.53.

Employment Prospects

Agricultural Technicians are employed by local, state, and federal agencies, such as the U.S. Department of Agriculture and state fish and wildlife departments. They also work for colleges and universities, nongovernmental organizations, and nonprofit groups. In the private sector, Agricultural Technicians are employed by agricultural, food processing, biotechnology, seed, animal breeding, and other companies.

The BLS reports that employment of Agricultural Technicians is expected to increase by 9 percent between 2008 and 2018. Opportunities are reported to be strongest in the biotechnology, food processing, and scientific research and development services industries. In addition to job growth, openings will become available as technicians advance to higher positions, transfer to other jobs, or leave the workforce for various reasons.

With their training and background, Agricultural Technicians can also seek employment in non-research positions. For example, they may work as technical farm workers for farms and ranches where they oversee the growing and harvesting of crops, or assist in animal breeding, nutrition, and disease control. They may also work as sales representatives for seed, fertilizer, and other companies; farm machinery mechanics; field agents for food processing and packaging companies; field representatives for farmers, growers, or cooperatives; and agricultural inspectors for government agencies.

Advancement Prospects

Agricultural Technicians may advance in various ways, depending on their interests and ambitions. With additional training, laboratory technicians may advance to research assistant and research associate positions. Individuals with supervisory or managerial ambitions can pursue such positions. Some technicians choose to continue their education to become research scientists, engineers, or educators, or to work in other professions that interest them.

Education and Training

Educational requirements vary from position to position. Many employers prefer to hire candidates who possess an associate's degree in agricultural technology or another applied science field. Some employees, such as Cooperative Extension Service associates, are required to possess a bachelor's degree in an appropriate field.

Employers may hire entry-level applicants with a high school diploma or general equivalency diploma if they have prior relevant work experience or demonstrate the ability to learn on the job.

Novice technicians typically receive on-the-job training. Some employers provide their employees with formal classroom training. Throughout their careers, technicians enroll in continuing education programs to update their skills and keep up with advancements in their fields.

Experience, Special Skills, and Personality Traits

Employers prefer to hire entry-level candidates who have one or more years of practical experience relevant to the position for which they apply. Recent college graduates may have gained experience through internships, work-study programs, research assistantships, employment, or volunteer work.

To perform well at their tasks, Agricultural Technicians need strong computer, writing, and communication skills. They also must have excellent interpersonal and teamwork skills, because they work with scientists, managers, and others from diverse backgrounds. Additionally, these technicians need effective self-management, analytical, and problem-solving skills. Some personality traits that successful Agricultural Technicians share include being self-motivated, honest, accurate, detail-oriented, organized, dedicated, and dependable.

Unions and Associations

Agricultural Technicians are usually eligible to join scientific societies that serve their particular areas of interest. Professional associations are available at the local, state, and national levels. By joining a society, technicians may take advantage of networking opportunities, continuing education, and other professional services and resources. For a list of professional associations, see Appendix II.

Tips for Entry

1. While in high school, take courses in English, writing, computing, and science. Enroll in agriculture classes as well, if they are offered.

2. Research formal training programs thoroughly. Ask questions such as these: What courses are offered? How much and what type of practical hands-on training do students receive along with learning theory? Does the school help graduates and alumni find jobs? What kind of jobs have graduates obtained?

3. Learn and maintain your technical skills. Employers prefer to hire applicants who are well-trained on instrumentation and methodologies used in their workplaces.

4. Part-time, seasonal, or temporary jobs can sometimes lead to offers for permanent positions.

5. Use the Internet to learn more about the field of agricultural research. To get a list of relevant Web sites to view, enter the keywords *agricultural research* into a search engine.

AGRICULTURE RESEARCH SERVICE (ARS) RESEARCH SCIENTIST

CAREER PROFILE

Duties: Study a particular area of interest, such as animal health, plant diseases, or rangeland systems; conduct research and development projects; perform other duties as required

Alternate Title(s): A title that reflects a specialty such as Research Microbiologist or Research Animal Scientist

Salary Range: $50,000 to $130,000

Employment Prospects: Fair

Advancement Prospects: Good

Prerequisites:

    Education or Training—Doctoral degree usually required

    Experience—Work experience not required for entry-level positions

    Special Skills and Personality Traits—Leadership, problem-solving, critical-thinking, self-management, teamwork, communication, and interpersonal skills; curious, persistent, enthusiastic, patient, creative, and flexible personality traits

    Special Requirements—U.S. citizenship; a security clearance may be required

CAREER LADDER

Senior or Supervisory Scientist

Research Scientist (Journey Level)

Research Scientist (Entry Level)

Position Description

The United States Department of Agriculture (USDA) develops and executes policy on food, agriculture, natural resources, and other related issues that affect the American people. USDA policies are based on scientific research, some of which is performed by the agency itself. The main research agency of the USDA is called the Agriculture Research Service (ARS). The ARS fulfills the purpose of researching agricultural problems that most affect Americans. For example, the ARS explores such matters as how to keep our agricultural economy competitive in the world market and how to maintain sufficient quality food supplies for all Americans while protecting the environment.

The ARS employs scientists and engineers to various research positions in government and academic research facilities. Those performing the highest level of research are categorized as ARS Research Scientists. They are hired to permanent positions. Some research scientists, such as postdoctoral research associates and visiting scientists, accept temporary (or term) positions that are held for one to four years. Other ARS researchers are classed as support scientists. These men and women are involved in working on one or more phases of research. Still other researchers are known as service scientists. These professionals work on research projects that involve scientific service to other government agencies or to the public.

ARS Research Scientists are engineers, biochemists, food scientists, nutritionists, hydrologists, botanists, immunologists, soil scientists, agronomists, veterinarians, and geneticists. They hold titles that reflect their specialties, such as Research Entomologist or Research Agricultural Engineer.

ARS Research Scientists conduct research in three major areas—nutrition, food safety, and food quality; animal production and protection; and natural resources and sustainable agricultural systems. They investigate a wide range of topics such as insect control, the development of new feed crops, crop production improvements, plant diseases, child and adult nutrition, food safety, the use of different crops to create biofuel, methods of conserving natural resources, and adapting crops to grow in various climates.

ARS Research Scientists engage in either basic research or applied research. Some of them work in both areas. The purpose of basic research is to further scientific knowledge and understanding of phenomena (observable facts). For example, ARS Research Scientists may research salmonella to learn its life span or to find new strains of that bacterium. On the other hand, applied research fulfills the purpose of finding practical applications for what basic research uncovers. For example, scientists may conduct research to find ways to prevent the development and spread of salmonella.

ARS Research Scientists also participate in the development of new or improved products or technologies that are useful in agriculture, as well as products that are made from agricultural resources. For example, scientists may develop such products as infant formulas that are similar to mother's milk, fat substitutes for a variety of processed foods, and more effective mosquito repellents.

ARS Research Scientists work under the supervision of management personnel who assign particular projects that fit within the parameters of the ARS mission. Scientists who are not affiliated by the ARS review the work that ARS Research Scientists perform.

ARS Research Scientists complete a variety of tasks, many of which depend on their area of expertise. For example, horticultural scientists would have different routines and conduct different experiments than would poultry scientists. Nevertheless, all ARS Research Scientists have similar duties for which they are responsible. For example, they:

- plan and conduct research procedures and write reports of their findings
- design and conduct experiments or tests
- assist with or provide input regarding the modification of experiments
- use a variety of laboratory instruments and techniques
- use computers to design experiments, analyze data, manage databases, and write science journal articles
- direct the work of student assistants or technical staff members
- make sure that their work complies with ARS standards and policies as well as laws and regulations
- offer consultation and information to other scientists within ARS as well as to other federal agencies
- present research findings and conclusions at meetings and conferences
- read scientific journals and other research literature
- stay current with the latest developments and technologies in their particular disciplines

Some ARS Research Scientists also hold adjunct faculty positions at colleges and universities. In addition to their full-time research work, these scientists teach one or more courses in their disciplines, such as dairy science, horticultural science, or biosystems engineering. As instructors, they are responsible for preparing lessons and exams, supervising student research papers, and advising students on academic and career matters.

ARS Research Scientists work in offices and laboratories. Depending on their specialties, they may work outdoors on experimental farms or travel to other locations to gather information, to attend meetings, or for other purposes.

ARS Research Scientists work a 40-hour week but put in additional hours as needed to complete their various tasks. Some of them are on a flexible schedule and work according to their own needs.

Salaries

Annual salaries for ARS Research Scientists vary, depending on such factors as their education, experience, position, and pay grade. ARS Research Scientists earn a salary based on the pay scale known as the general schedule (GS), which has several levels and steps. ARS Research Scientists are hired at the GS-11 to GS-15 levels, depending on their qualifications. Most entry-level scientists start at either the GS-11 or GS-12 level.

In 2010, the annual base pay for the GS-11 to GS-15 levels ranged from $50,287 to $129,517. Employees in metropolitan areas, such as New York, Los Angeles, and Washington, D.C., earn additional pay for working in an area where the cost of living is higher.

Employment Prospects

The ARS employs approximately 2,200 scientists, including postdoctoral associates. Most work in ARS research facilities in about 100 locations throughout the United States. Some ARS Research Scientists are assigned to ARS laboratories in other countries.

Job openings generally become available as scientists advance to higher positions, transfer to other jobs, retire, or leave the workforce for various reasons. Additional positions are created to meet needs, as long as funding is available. The ARS budget varies yearly, as it depends on the funds allocated by Congress.

According to one expert in the field, opportunities are favorable for ARS Research Scientists and postdoctoral associates. The agency tends to receive an adequate number of applicants for most openings.

Another expert reports that the agency sometimes experience difficulty hiring in some occupational areas such as veterinary medicine and agricultural engineering, as well as for positions in remote locations.

Advancement Prospects

ARS Research Scientists advance by earning higher wages and through job satisfaction. They can also seek promotions to supervisory or managerial positions.

Individuals may also choose to move into other areas, such as policy analysis, grant applications review, or scientist recruitment and training, with ARS or other federal agencies.

Education and Training

The ARS prefers to hire candidates for entry-level positions who hold doctorates in the life, physical, or engineering sciences. The agency will employ candidates with master's degrees, if they have qualifying work experience. Applicants should hold a degree in a discipline related to the position for which they are applying. For example, to qualify for a position as a research molecular biologist, applicants must possess a doctoral degree in biological sciences, agricultural natural resource management, chemistry, or another related discipline.

Candidates may also qualify by meeting the required combination of education and experience, which varies with the positions.

Novice employees typically receive on-the-job training while working under the guidance and direction of experienced scientists.

Special Requirements

Applicants must be U.S. citizens to qualify for ARS Research Scientist positions.

Applicants for positions that handle sensitive or classified materials must normally undergo a security clearance. This involves a thorough background check of such areas as an applicant's employment, credit, and criminal history.

Experience, Special Skills, and Personality Traits

Job requirements vary with the positions, which may range from no work experience necessary to having several years of appropriate work experience. In general, having work experience is not required of applicants for entry-level positions, as long as they possess doctoral degrees. They should be knowledgeable about the subject matter that they would research. Having practical experience that is relevant to the positions for which they apply may enhance their chances of obtaining employment.

To work effectively at their jobs, ARS Research Scientists must have excellent leadership, problem-solving, critical-thinking, and self-management skills. They also need excellent teamwork, communication, and interpersonal skills, as they must be able to work well with colleagues, managers, and others from diverse backgrounds. Some personality traits that successful research scientists share include being curious, persistent, enthusiastic, patient, creative, and flexible.

Unions and Associations

ARS Research Scientists can join professional associations to take advantage of networking opportunities, continuing education, professional certification, and other professional resources and services. Some of the scientific societies that serve the interests of different ARS scientists are:

- American Chemical Society
- American Dairy Science Association
- American Society for Microbiology
- American Society of Agronomy
- American Society of Animal Science
- American Society of Horticultural Science
- Botanical Society of America
- Crop Science Society of America
- Society for Integrative and Comparative Biology
- Soil Science Society of America

For contact information, see Appendix II.

Tips for Entry

1. To learn more about careers in the ARS, visit the ARS careers Web page on the Internet: www.ars.usda.gov/careers.
2. The ARS attends career fairs on college campuses to recruit applicants. Contact your college career center to find out if the ARS will be coming to your college. You may also be find information at the ARS Web site.
3. Be sure you have attached all the documents that the job application requests before submitting your application package. You may be disqualified if all required documents are not presented.
4. To learn more about the U.S. Agricultural Research Service, visit its Web site at www.ars.usda.gov.

EXTENSION SPECIALIST

Duties: Provide expertise and nonformal educational programs to the public; plan, develop, and evaluate educational programs; perform other duties as required

Alternate Title(s): A title that reflects a specialty, such as Extension Agronomy Specialist, Extension Specialist in Farm Management, or Geospatial Extension Specialist

Salary Range: $34,000 to $148,000

Employment Prospects: Fair

Advancement Prospects: Good

Prerequisites:

Education or Training—Doctoral degree required for university positions

CAREER LADDER

(Full) Extension Specialist

↑

Associate Extension Specialist

↑

Assistant Extension Specialist

Experience—Varies according to program needs

Special Skills and Personality Traits—Leadership, teamwork, organizational, interpersonal, communication, and writing skills; curious, creative, detail-oriented, patient, self-motivated, flexible, and enthusiastic personality traits

Position Description

Extension Specialists are subject-matter experts who work within the Cooperative Extension System, which is part of the National Institute of Food and Agriculture, an agency within the U.S. Department of Agriculture (USDA). Established in 1914, the Cooperative Extension System works in partnership with state land-grant universities. Its purpose is to make the knowledge and resources of the universities available to the public. Cooperative Extension Service (or Extension) offices are found in every U.S. state, as well as in every U.S. territory and the District of Columbia. Through consultations and informational education programs, Extension professionals assist agricultural producers, individuals, families, and communities in the areas of agriculture, natural resources, youth development, family and consumer sciences, and community and economic development.

Extension Specialists are authorities in crop management, entomology, poultry, animal husbandry, horticulture, turf management, farm management, nutrition, food safety, land and home ownership, youth development, geospatial technology, water resources, waste management, and many other areas. These specialists are responsible for developing, implementing, and evaluating various types of programs that address the concerns of Extension clients. For example, they might oversee programs that help:

- crop farmers to market their products
- aquaculturists to manage fish farming operations
- master gardeners to train home gardeners
- home buyers to understand home owner options
- residents to learn how to conserve water resources
- communities to identify and address issues
- 4-H advisers to offer appropriate science activities to middle-school children

Extension personnel are employed by land-grant universities. Every state Extension has main offices at one or more land-grant universities. County and regional field offices, as well as agricultural research stations, are located throughout each state. Extension professionals at the field offices complete the delivery of Extension programs to the public.

Extension Specialists serve as the links between university campuses and Extension field offices. They translate the latest scientific discoveries and applications into terms that the public can understand. Most specialists work at the universities, while the rest work at Extension research stations or field offices. University-based specialists generally provide assistance throughout their states, whereas field-based specialists cover a specific geographic area.

Extension Specialists execute various duties to ensure the success of building statewide or regional Extension programs in their subject matter. Some of their responsibilities include:

- developing educational programs
- obtaining feedback from Extension professionals in field offices for improving programs
- creating informational and educational materials
- utilizing the latest technologies, such as Web sites and CD-ROM, to disseminate information to the public
- presenting information or providing technical assistance to Extension clients through workshops, demonstrations, and on-site visits
- acquiring grants to help fund their programs
- staying up to date with the latest research and knowledge in the fields that concern Extension clients

Extension Specialists are responsible for training Extension professionals and volunteers to deliver the programs as well as to serve in leadership roles within their communities. These specialists may conduct training through group or one-on-one sessions. Extension Specialists are also available to provide Extension personnel in the field with technical consultations.

Part of their job also involves developing and maintaining strong relationships with other Extension personnel, including those in other states. Extension Specialists also establish links with community leaders, businesspersons, farmers, and the public, as well as with government agencies and trade associations.

Additionally, Extension Specialists work closely with faculty members and department heads (including those that are not directly involved with Extension programs) at their particular universities, as well as with others in the Cooperative Extension System. Extension Specialists, for example, consult with their academic colleagues about applications of research findings to ensure they are timely and accurate. Extension Specialists also suggest areas of future research to academic researchers that would be helpful to Extension clients.

Many Extension Specialists conduct applied research to find solutions to specific issues of Extension clients. For example, a geospatial Extension Specialist might research ways that farmers can use technologies to grow crops more efficiently.

Researchers may collaborate with academic and other Extension researchers on projects. Depending on the nature of their studies, researchers may conduct experiments and tests in laboratories, on farms, in greenhouses, in gardens, in forests, on rangelands, along coastlines, or other settings. Extension Specialists publish the results of their research findings in scientific journals and other publications. They may also develop informational or educational materials for use by Extension agents and the public.

Some Extension Specialists also hold teaching appointments in agriculture, biological science, or other academic departments at their universities. They teach one or more courses to undergraduate and graduate students. As instructors, Extension Specialists are responsible for preparing lectures, exams, and other class activities. They attempt to blend their Extension activities with teaching as much as possible. For example, they might bring community and industry experts to classrooms as guest speakers and use their extension work experiences as examples in their lesson plans. Extension Specialists are also responsible for supervising student research projects and advising students on career and academic matters.

Extension Specialists spend most of their working days indoors but work in outdoor environments part of the time. They often work more than 40 hours a week to complete their various duties. They travel to Extension field offices, experimental research stations, and other locations as needed to provide training and assistance to Extension professionals and clients.

Salaries

Salaries for Extension Specialists vary, depending on such factors as their experience, specialty, employer, and geographic location. Formal salary information specifically for these professionals is unavailable. In general, they earn salaries similar to non-extension faculty at academic institutions. The U.S. Bureau of Labor Statistics (BLS) reports the following estimated salary ranges for most of these postsecondary teachers:

- agricultural sciences teachers: $38,460 to $124,650
- biological science teachers: $38,830 to $147,980
- chemistry teachers: $38,960 to $127,740
- engineering teachers: $45,150 to $142,670
- forestry and conservation science teachers: $36,980 to $107,200
- home economics teachers: $33,930 to $117,450

The salary information comes from the May 2008 Occupational Employment Statistics survey by the BLS.

Employment Prospects

All Cooperative Extension Service personnel are employees of state land-grant universities. Extension Specialists are usually hired through an academic department such as an agriculture or biological sciences department. Extension Specialists may be hired to tenured or non-tenured positions. Specialists in non-tenured positions have appointments of one or more years, which may be renewable.

The number of Extension Specialists varies from one university to the next. Each state Extension determines the number and type of Extension Specialist positions it needs.

Job openings generally become available as Extension Specialists advance or transfer to other jobs, retire, or leave the workforce for various reasons. A university will create additional positions to meet needs as long as funding is available.

One expert in the field states that a large number of Extension Specialists are expected to be eligible for retirement over the next few years.

Advancement Prospects

Many Extension Specialists are hired to tenure-track positions, as either Extension or academic appointments. Some specialists have joint appointments. Once they earn tenure at a university, they have gained job security, as well as prestige, for the rest of their career.

Extension Specialists advance through the ranks, starting at the assistant level. They next move to the associate level, and finally to the full specialist level.

Extension Specialists can also seek promotions to administrative and management positions.

Education and Training

Educational requirements vary with the different positions. Candidates should have college degrees in disciplines that are related to the subject areas in which they would work. For example, applicants for agronomy specialist positions need a degree in agronomy, soil science, or another related field.

Extension Specialists who hold faculty positions at land-grant universities must possess doctorates in their chosen disciplines. Those men and women who are based in field offices must possess at least master's degrees.

Experience, Special Skills, and Personality Traits

Experience requirements vary by employer, depending on the research programs for which they are hiring. In general, employers are willing to hire recent Ph.D. graduates who have little or no work experience for new programs. Employers typically seek applicants with several years of experience for established programs.

Extension Specialists need excellent leadership, teamwork, organizational, interpersonal, communication, and writing skills to perform well at their job.

Being curious, creative, detail-oriented, patient, self-motivated, flexible, and enthusiastic are some personality traits that successful Extension Specialists share.

Unions and Associations

Many Extension Specialists join professional associations to take advantage of networking opportunities, continuing education, and other professional services and resources. Organizations that specifically serve the interests of Extension Specialists are available in many states. These professionals may also join organizations that serve the different Extension areas, such as the:

- Association of Natural Resource Extension Professionals
- National Association of Community Development Extension Professionals
- National Extension Association of Family and Consumer Sciences

Some Extension Specialists also belong to professional scientific societies, such as the American Chemical Society, the American Society of Agronomy, the American Society of Animal Science, the American Society of Horticultural Science, and the Institute of Food Technologists.

For contact information to the above organizations, see Appendix II.

Tips for Entry

1. Some Extensions have summer employment and internship programs for students. Contact a local Extension office to find out what may be available in your area.
2. Extension programs and land-grant universities work together to recruit and hire Extension Specialists. Therefore, contact both universities and Extension offices for information about job vacancies.
3. Job vacancies for Extension positions are listed online at the National Job Bank Web site, which is operated by the *Journal of Extension*. The URL is jobs.joe.org.
4. Use the Internet to learn more about the Cooperative Extension System. You might start by visiting these Web sites: *Journal of Extension* (www.joe.org) and Extension (www.nifa.usda.gov/qlinks/extension.html). For more links, see Appendix IV.

AGRICULTURAL SERVICES

AGRICULTURAL CONSULTANT

CAREER PROFILE

Duties: Provide technical or management consulting services to individuals and organizations; perform other duties as required

Alternate Title(s): A title that reflects a specialty such as Soil Science Consultant, Livestock Consultant, Farm Management Consultant, or Agricultural Marketing Consultant

Salary Range: $33,000 to $166,000

Employment Prospects: Good

Advancement Prospects: Fair

Prerequisites:

Education or Training—College degree usually preferred; on-the-job training

Experience—Extensive experience in area of specialty

Special Skills and Personality Traits—Analytical, problem-solving, time-management, organizational, presentation, writing, communication, leadership, interpersonal, and self-management skills; outgoing, tactful, inquisitive, quick-witted, assertive, and flexible personality traits

Special Requirements—Professional license, certification, or registration may be required; business licenses required for company owners

CAREER LADDER

Senior Agricultural Consultant

Agricultural Consultant

Research Associate or Junior Consultant

Position Description

When farmers and agricultural companies lack technical or business expertise in a particular area, they often seek Agricultural Consultants for assistance and advice. These professional experts are agricultural producers, scientists, engineers, researchers, educators, economists, business managers, marketing specialists, entrepreneurs, and others. Agricultural Consultants offer their extensive knowledge and creative problem-solving skills as resources to help clients improve the production, structure, and efficiency of their companies or farms. Consultants may offer their services in one or more subject areas such as farm management, soil science, agronomy, sustainable agriculture, food technology, forest management, aquaculture, regulatory affairs, workplace safety, agricultural economics, land use, or marketing.

Agricultural Consultants are either self-employed or employees of agricultural consulting firms. Clients may seek their assistance for tools, information, or advice on matters in which they specialize. Clients include all types of agricultural producers, including crop farmers, vineyard growers, livestock ranchers, dairy farmers, fish farmers, nursery owners, and tree farmers, among others. Agricultural Consultants are also hired by agribusinesses that are involved in the processing or distribution of food products, the manufacturing of farm supplies and equipment, and other ventures associated with farmers' needs. In addition, nonprofit groups, nongovernmental organizations, and government agencies that have agricultural concerns seek Agricultural Consultants for assistance and advice.

Agricultural Consultants provide different types of services. Some of these professionals offer technical consulting services. For example, a technical consultant might help a farmer with livestock care, crop-system design, soil erosion, pest management, organic farming methods, workplace safety and health regulations, precision agriculture technology, or another area.

Other Agricultural Consultants are management specialists. These professional consultants have expertise in tackling problems involving business operations, such as human resources, marketing, finance, corporate organization, and information systems. They might assist clients with preparing bank loan applications, restructuring the clients' organization, setting up office operations, developing marketing plans, selecting and hiring new employees, or implementing office technology. Some management consultants also offer guidance to corporate clients about such matters as increasing their profitability, buying or selling companies, or consolidating companies.

Agricultural Consultants work on specific assignments on a contractual basis. Their projects may last several days, weeks, or months. They may work on several projects at a time. Their duties vary according to the type of consulting services they offer. All consultants perform various general tasks such as:

- conducting research to gather information about their clients' organizations, which may include interviewing employees, reviewing documents, and observing work procedures and processes
- meeting with specialists, educators, government officials, and others who may provide them with pertinent information about their assignments
- analyzing and evaluating data to offer recommendations for solving problems or issues
- using computer applications, such as spreadsheets and mathematical models, to analyze data
- preparing reports and correspondence as well as completing required forms
- providing clients with frequent updates of their work progress
- maintaining accurate and up-to-date records of their work activities
- working closely with business owners as well as their managers and employees
- scheduling appointments with clients and others
- developing new clients as well as maintaining relationships with current clients
- staying abreast of new developments in their areas of expertise
- supervising and directing the work of research associates and other assistants

Consultants mostly work in offices. Some consulting firms allow employees to work from their homes. Agricultural Consultants travel frequently to other cities, states, or countries to meet with clients or to visit clients' work sites. Depending on their projects, consultants may need to spend several days or weeks away from home to complete assignments. Consulting work can sometimes be stressful, such as when consultants must meet tight deadlines.

Agricultural Consultants work long and irregular hours. They sometimes work evenings and weekends to meet with clients and to complete tasks.

Salaries

Salaries for Agricultural Consultants vary, depending on such factors as their specialty, position (self-employed or staff), education, experience, and geographic location. In some consulting companies, employees receive additional compensation for their job performance.

Salary information specifically for Agricultural Consultants is unavailable, but they generally earn salaries similar to senior workers in their fields. The U.S. Bureau of Labor Statistics (BLS) reported in its May 2008 Occupational Employment Statistics survey the following estimated annual salary ranges for these professions:

- soil and plant scientists: $34,260 to $105,340
- hydrologists: $44,410 to $105,010
- animal scientists: $33,060 to $98,980
- agricultural engineers: $43,150 to $108,470
- foresters: $34,710 to $78,350
- food scientists and technologists: $33,790 to $104,520
- management analysts: $41,910 to $133,850
- marketing managers: $55,270 to $166,400
- economists: $44,050 to $149,110

Employment Prospects

Agricultural Consultants are employed by small and large management and technical consulting firms. Some are independent contractors.

Consulting opportunities are available throughout the United States and the world. Some experts in the field state that agricultural consulting is a fast-growing field. Increasingly, farmers and growers, agricultural, food, and related companies, and government agencies and nonprofit organizations seek the advice and services of experts to assist them with improving their organizations' structure and performance.

The job competition for consulting positions is keen due to the prominent status and high wages that come with the job. In addition, entrepreneurial individuals are attracted to the idea of working independently. Agricultural consulting opportunities vary per specialty. The demand for different Agricultural Consultants is affected by such factors as the health of the economy, the occurrence of natural disasters, and the availability of government funding for research and development. During economic downturns, there may be fewer consulting opportunities.

Advancement Prospects

Individuals start as research associates or junior consultants in companies, depending on their education and experience. They rise through the ranks as consultants, managers, and partners. Individuals usually need advanced degrees to be promoted to higher positions.

Some Agricultural Consultants choose to become independent contractors or to start their own consulting firms. They measure their success by achieving a highly regarded reputation, by earning higher incomes, and through job satisfaction.

Education and Training

Consulting firms prefer to hire candidates for junior consultant positions who hold a master's or doctoral degree in their discipline. They may hire strong candidates without an advanced degree to these positions, if they have years of qualifying work experience. Individuals with bachelor's degrees may qualify for research associate positions.

Consultants learn their skills on the job while working under the direction and supervision of experienced consultants. Some consulting firms provide formal training programs to newly hired consultants.

Throughout their careers, Agricultural Consultants enroll in continuing education programs to update their skills and keep up with advancements in their fields.

Special Requirements

Agricultural Consultants, such as consulting foresters and agricultural engineers, may be required to maintain professional licenses, certificates, or registrations to practice in the state or municipality where they work. Self-employed consultants must possess the proper business licenses to operate their firms.

Experience, Special Skills, and Personality Traits

Agricultural Consultants typically have many years of work experience in their areas of specialization as agricultural producers, managers, research scientists, government regulatory officers, agricultural economists, management analysts, or in other areas.

To perform well at their jobs, Agricultural Consultants need excellent analytical, problem-solving, time-management, organizational, presentation, writing, and communication skills. They also must have strong leadership, interpersonal, and self-management skills. Some personality traits that successful Agricultural Consultants share include being outgoing, tactful, inquisitive, quick-witted, assertive, and flexible.

Unions and Associations

Many Agricultural Consultants belong to professional associations to take advantage of networking opportunities, training programs, and other professional services and resources. Some national societies that serve the interests of different Agricultural Consultants are:

- American Society of Agricultural Consultants
- American Society of Farm Managers and Rural Appraisers
- Institute of Management Consultants USA
- National Alliance of Independent Crop Consultants
- National Society of Consulting Soil Scientists

For contact information about these organizations, see Appendix II.

Tips for Entry

1. Enroll in business courses, especially agricultural business classes, to prepare yourself to become either a technical or management consultant.
2. Do thorough research on the consulting field you wish to enter. For example, answer such questions as: What is the current demand for the areas in which you would consult? What would that demand be in five years and 10 years? What consulting firms would be your competition? How would your services differ from the competition? Why would clients prefer to hire you rather than your competition?
3. To enhance their employability, Agricultural Consultants obtain professional certification from recognized organizations. For example, agricultural management consultants might seek professional certification from the American Society of Farm Managers and Rural Appraisers.
4. Use the Internet to learn more about the agricultural consulting field. To obtain a list of relevant Web sites, enter the keywords *agricultural consulting* or *agricultural consultants* in a search engine. For some links, see Appendix IV.

AGRICULTURAL INSPECTOR

Duties: Enforce agricultural laws and regulations; examine agricultural commodities or facilities; perform other duties as required

Alternate Title(s): A title that reflects a specific job, such as Grain Inspector or Plant Protection Specialist

Salary Range: $25,000 to $59,000

Employment Prospects: Fair

Advancement Prospects: Poor

Prerequisites:

Education or Training—Bachelor's degree usually required; on-the-job training

Experience—Have experience and knowledge in the area in which one would perform inspections

CAREER LADDER

Senior Agricultural Inspector

Agricultural Inspector

Agricultural Inspector (Entry Level)

Special Skills and Personality Traits—Leadership, critical-thinking, problem-solving, communication, writing, computer, customer service, leadership, teamwork, interpersonal, and self-management skills; detail-oriented, accurate, thorough, honest, tactful, courteous, and dependable personality traits

Position Description

Agricultural Inspectors contribute to the welfare of the public by making sure that the food supply is safe to eat. These government officers enforce laws that regulate the quality, health, and safety of agricultural commodities, as well as laws that regulate agricultural production operations, food processing plants, grain warehouses, food distribution centers, and grocery stores and other food outlets. Agricultural Inspectors may work for federal, state, or local government agencies to fulfill the missions of their various regulatory programs.

These men and women specialize in certain areas covered by regulations. Many of these professionals, for example, are involved in inspecting, grading, and certifying the quality of fruits, vegetables, live cattle, meat, fish, poultry, eggs, milk, tree nuts, tobacco, cotton, and other agricultural commodities. These inspectors check the size, labeling, condition, and contract specifications of commodities. They may also certify that commodities meet specific quality standards.

Many other inspectors work to protect the health of consumers by checking plants and animals for harmful pests and diseases. Some Agricultural Inspectors examine agricultural products that are transported between states, or are imported into or exported out of the United States. They check agricultural commodities as well as nursery stock, seeds, livestock, nondomestic animals (such as wildlife), and insects.

Other inspectors examine seed, fertilizer products, and livestock feed before they can be sold to ensure that they meet state and federal quality standards. Local inspectors may be responsible for enforcing regulations and codes regarding the control of noxious weeds or insect pests on private property, or pertaining to the use of pesticides by farmers and growers. Local Agricultural Inspectors test and certify commercial weights and measuring devices to make certain they are accurate.

Many Agricultural Inspectors visit farms, fish hatcheries, nurseries, warehouses, processing plants, or other facilities to conduct their reviews. They follow standard procedures to ensure that they conduct their reviews properly and accurately. These men and women are expected to be unbiased as they conduct their inspections. Any errors they make can strongly affect the health and welfare of the public as well as cause financial loss to the businesses involved and ruin their reputations.

Agricultural Inspectors prepare reports and paperwork about their findings. They explain any problems they have about the products, labeling, processes, personnel, and other matters, as well as offer recommendations to correct them. Inspectors may take enforcement action by issuing citations or notices of violations, for example. If inspectors find commodities are below standards, they may instruct owners to stop selling those products. Inspectors may close production facilities, if they have established that the products would be harmful to consumers.

Agricultural Inspectors perform other duties, which vary according to their experience and skills. For example, inspectors may conduct investigations of complaints or incidents to determine if violations have occurred; they may make educational presentations to the public or to groups of business owners.

Inspection work is physically demanding. Agricultural Inspectors sometimes lift and carry objects weighing 100 pounds or more. They may perform tasks that expose them to loud noises, dusts, odors, chemicals, and other hazards. Their work can also be stressful when they need to handle emotional individuals or other uncomfortable situations.

Agricultural Inspectors work long and irregular hours. They may be assigned to work evenings, holidays, and weekends, or to be on call 24 hours a day.

Salaries

Salaries for Agricultural Inspectors vary, depending on such factors as their education, experience, employer, and geographic location. According to the May 2008 Occupational Employment Statistics (OES) survey by the U.S. Bureau of Labor Statistics (BLS), the estimated annual salary for most Agricultural Inspectors ranged between $25,380 and $59,270.

Employment Prospects

The BLS reported in its May 2008 OES survey that approximately 14,340 Agricultural Inspectors were employed in the United States. Nearly 70 percent of those inspectors were employed by federal and state government agencies. Other inspectors were employed by local government agencies and by private industry.

Most job opportunities become available as Agricultural Inspectors retire, advance to higher positions, or transfer to other jobs or career fields. Employers occasionally create additional positions when funding is available.

Advancement Prospects

Agricultural Inspectors who have supervisory and management ambitions can pursue positions in those areas. Their advancement is based on individual merit. Many inspectors measure their growth by being assigned higher-level responsibilities and by earning higher wages.

Education and Training

Educational requirements vary from position to position. In general, employers prefer to hire applicants for entry-level positions who hold a bachelor's degree in agricultural science, biology, or a related field. Employers may hire applicants with a high school diploma or general equivalency diploma if they have qualifying work experience.

Agricultural Inspectors learn agricultural laws and regulations and inspection techniques and procedures through on-the-job training and classroom instruction.

Experience, Special Skills, and Personality Traits

In general, employers seek candidates who have experience and knowledge in the area in which they would be performing inspections. For instance, applicants for livestock inspectors must be highly familiar with the care and management of livestock.

Agricultural Inspectors need strong leadership, critical-thinking, problem-solving, communication, writing, computer, and customer service skills to perform their various tasks. They also must have excellent leadership, teamwork, and interpersonal skills, as they must be able to work well with colleagues and others from diverse backgrounds every day. Additionally, these inspectors need effective self-management skills. Being detail-oriented, accurate, thorough, honest, tactful, courteous, and dependable are some personality traits that successful Agricultural Inspectors have in common.

Unions and Associations

Some Agricultural Inspectors belong to a labor union that represents them in contract negotiations with their employers. The union also handles any grievances that its members may have against their employers.

Tips for Entry

1. To learn about announcements for federal jobs online, visit USAJOBS at www.usajobs.gov.
2. Many state and local government agencies have job hotlines, which you can find in the white pages of your telephone book.
3. Learn about federal agricultural commodity programs at the USDA Agricultural Marketing Service Web site at www.ams.usda.gov. To learn about federal animal and plant health inspections, visit the USDA Animal and Plant Health Inspection Service Web site at www.aphis.usda.gov. For more links, see Appendix IV.

AGRICULTURAL PILOT

CAREER PROFILE

Duties: Provide aerial applications services to farmers and growers; perform other duties as required

Alternate Title(s): Aerial Applicator, Crop-Duster Pilot, Crop Duster, Ag Pilot

Salary Range: $32,000 to $130,000

Employment Prospects: Fair

Advancement Prospects: Poor

Prerequisites:

Education or Training—High school diploma; on-the-job training

Experience—Previous experience in agricultural and the aerial application industries preferred

Special Skills and Personality Traits—Problem-solving, decision-making, self-management, inter-personal, and communication skills; levelheaded, focused, calm, cooperative, dependable, and self-motivated

Special Requirements—Commercial-pilot certificate with appropriate aircraft ratings; state aerial application license

---

CAREER LADDER

Senior Agricultural Pilot

Journey Level Agricultural Pilot

Apprentice Agricultural Pilot

Position Description

Agricultural piloting is a new type of career. The first Agricultural Pilots flew in the 1920s in what began as an experiment in Ohio to eradicate a pest called the sphinx moth from catalpa trees. The experiment was so successful that soon Agricultural Pilots were spreading pesticides over all kinds of crops in many different regions of the United States. The flyers became known as crop-duster pilots, or simply crop dusters, because the chemicals they sprayed were dry and dusty.

Today, these aerial applicators distribute mostly liquid pesticides to orchards and crop fields in a quick, efficient, and environmentally sensitive manner. Farmers and growers also employ these pilots to spread seeds, fertilizers, or fungicides. Some Agricultural Pilots perform other aerial jobs, as well. For example, they might be hired to deliver fish food to ponds and lakes, or help clean up oil spills or control mosquito populations.

Agricultural Pilots are highly skilled at flying at great speed very close to the ground. They maneuver their planes quickly to avoid colliding with trees, power lines, buildings, and other hazards near their target spray areas. These pilots are also experts at mixing and applying strong chemicals in just the right amount to minimize their impact on the environment.

When they are ready to take flight to a specific location, Agricultural Pilots follow certain procedures. They conduct preflight inspections of their aircraft and spray apparatus—for instance, they perform preflight system checks and make sure there is enough fuel is in their planes. These pilots obtain rural municipality maps and work orders that specify which fields need spraying and that indicate where vulnerable crops, beehives, and other things to avoid are located. They make certain that their ground crews have prepared and loaded the proper spray solutions for the job.

Agricultural Pilots examine their target field before beginning their spraying. They note the presence of roads, livestock, and houses nearby so that they do not distract motorists, harm animals, and disturb nearby residents. They also check for power lines, trees, and other obstacles near their target fields. In addition, these aerial applicators pay attention to the speed and direction of the wind to ensure that their spray is delivered correctly. They plan their flight paths and turns before proceeding with their spraying. Some pilots consult information from global positioning system tools to guide them on each flight path across fields.

Agricultural Pilots precisely calibrate the width of their spray. Some newer airplanes feature onboard computers that control the rate of spray and the size of droplets released from their tanks. As they glide back and forth across their target fields, these experts fly their planes only a few feet above the ground at speeds up to 140 miles per hour. When their supply of spray is depleted, Agricultural Pilots fly back to their base to pick up more and return to the field until their spraying job is finished. They may take off and land their planes as many as 50 times during a typical day of flying.

Agricultural Pilots perform dangerous work. Hence, they follow strict procedures and safety measures. They also wear fire-resistant flight suits, safety helmets, and respirators. These pilots work long hours, which may include working on weekends and holidays.

Salaries

Salaries for Agricultural Pilots vary, depending on such factors as their experience, job duties, employer, and geographic location. In general, their earnings are similar to other commercial pilots. According to the May 2008 Occupational Employment Statistics survey by the U.S. Bureau of Labor Statistics, the estimated annual salary for most commercial pilots ranged between $32,020 and $129,580.

Employment Prospects

According to the National Agriculture Aviation Association, approximately 3,200 Agricultural Pilots are employed in the United States. About 90 percent of them are business owners.

The demand for aerial applicators should remain favorable due to the continuing global demand for food. Some experts in the field express concern that a large number of pilots are reaching retirement age while fewer younger pilots are entering the industry.

Advancement Prospects

Agricultural Pilots generally measure success by earning higher wages, by gaining a professional reputation, and through job satisfaction.

Entrepreneurial individuals start their own aerial application services. Some pilots also pursue opportunities as flight instructors.

Education and Training

Professional pilots possess at least a high school diploma or general equivalency diploma.

Agricultural Pilots generally learn their skills through on-the-job training, while working under the direction of experienced aerial applicators.

Currently, a few flight schools offer formal aerial application programs. Students learn specific skills and maneuvers needed to properly apply various kinds of substances onto crops.

Special Requirements

Agricultural Pilots must possess a commercial pilot certificate granted by the U.S. Federal Aviation Administration (FAA). They must hold appropriate ratings for the type of aircraft that they operate. For specific information about pilot certification, visit the FAA Web site at www.faa.gov. Pilots must also be licensed as aerial applicators in each of the states where they work. For specific information, contact the state department of agriculture that governs the jurisdiction where you wish to work.

Pilots who own their operations must obtain all proper business and pesticide control licenses.

Experience, Special Skills, and Personality Traits

Employers seek applicants for pilot trainee positions who demonstrate the willingness and dedication to work hard. Strong candidates would have previous experience working in the aerial application industry.

To perform their work well, Agricultural Pilots need excellent problem-solving, decision-making, self-management, interpersonal, and communication skills. Some personality traits that successful Agricultural Pilots share include being levelheaded, focused, calm, cooperative, dependable, and self-motivated.

Unions and Associations

Agricultural Pilots can join professional associations to take advantage of networking opportunities and professional services and resources. Some national societies include the National Agricultural Aviation Association and the Aircraft Owners and Pilots Association. For contact information, see Appendix II.

Tips for Entry

1. Many Agricultural Pilots began their careers working in ground crews as mixers and loaders.
2. Seek out Agricultural Pilots to learn more about what they do. You may eventually find someone who would be willing to mentor you.
3. Use the Internet to learn more about the aerial application industry. You might start by visiting the National Agricultural Aviation Association Web site at www.agaviation.org. For more links, see Appendix IV.

FARMERS' MARKET MANAGER

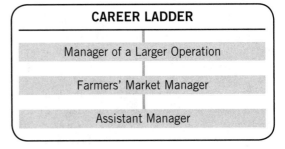

Position Description

In many communities throughout the United States, farmers are able to sell their products directly to customers at farmers' markets that are usually held outdoors in public places. Most farmers' markets are open once or twice a week for several hours. The public may buy fresh produce, meats, chicken, eggs, and flowers, as well as finished food products and handicrafts offered by farmers and other vendors at their makeshift booths. Farmers' markets are nonprofit operations, which may be held year-round or during the local growing season. They are overseen by volunteer or paid Farmers' Market Managers, who are knowledgeable about the foods grown by local farmers.

Farmers' markets are governed by boards of directors, who establish their markets' objectives and policies; develop budgets; determine vendors' fees; and hire and fire farmers' market staff. Farmers' Market Managers are responsible for developing and implementing plans to carry out the directives of their boards. They conduct market research to determine the types of fresh and finished products that customers would be most willing to buy. Managers also have the duty of securing market sites within their communities, which may be such locations as city centers, shopping center parking lots, or city streets that are closed during market hours. In addition, Farmers' Market Managers develop and maintain relationships with local government agencies, businesses, community organizations, and agricultural associations.

Farmers' Market Managers are responsible for recruiting farmers to sell their crops on market days. They work with grower associations, Cooperative Extension Service offices, farm bureaus, and other agricultural organizations to identify farmers to contact. Managers also meet with local bakeries, restaurants, craftspersons, nurseries, and other appropriate businesses that may be interested in selling their products at their markets.

Performing community outreach is another essential duty of Farmers' Market Managers. To promote their markets, they may make presentations at community meetings or events, send press releases, buy advertisements in the local media, and post signs around the community, among other activities. In addition, these managers plan special events and programs on market days to attract customers. For example, they may organize a theme event every month, hold a weekly contest to win a basket of local foods, and schedule local musicians to perform during market hours. Farmers' Market Managers also develop and maintain relationships with local government agencies, businesses, community groups, and agricultural organizations.

On farmers' market days, managers are responsible for ensuring that operations run smoothly and that activities, such as entertainment, take place as scheduled. Managers also supervise the preparation of the market site, such as cleaning up the area, placing market signs and barricades, and assigning vendors to stalls. Throughout the day, managers make sure that the market and vendors comply with all local, state, and federal laws, health codes, and organizational rules. They respond to questions from both vendors and customers, and resolve any disputes or problems that may arise.

These managers also keep count of the number of customers at the market to assess the attendance level throughout the season or year. Some Farmers' Market Managers staff an information booth where educational materials about the farmers' market and local agriculture, as well as recipes and nutritional information, are distributed. At the end of the day, managers collect fees from the vendors and complete required paperwork and reports. In addition, they supervise the cleaning of the market site and make sure that the area is restored to its normal state.

Another major aspect of these managers' job is handling various administrative responsibilities. For example, Farmers' Market Managers perform such tasks as:

- obtaining proper permits and insurance premiums for market sites
- attending public meetings and hearings
- preparing and administering monthly and annual budgets
- staying abreast of food handling, agricultural, organic certification, and other pertinent local, state, and federal laws and regulations
- maintaining records and databases of permits, contracts, leases, and other documents and information
- establishing a market schedule
- developing bookkeeping procedures and systems
- identifying and applying for grants
- planning fund-raising strategies
- preparing performance, accounting, and other required reports

Human resources management is another major duty of Farmers' Market Managers. They are in charge of recruiting and training staff members, who may be volunteer or paid employees. These managers assign staff members to assist with the different aspects of managing and operating markets. Managers also supervise and direct their staff's work activities.

Farmers' Market Managers work in offices, as well as outdoors at market sites. Their job can be stressful when they must handle angry, upset, or otherwise emotional vendors or customers. On occasion, managers must lift and carry heavy items.

These managers may be employed part-time or full-time, year-round or on a seasonal basis. They work at market sites during their hours of operation, which may include working early evening hours or on weekends.

Salaries

Salaries for Farmers' Market Managers vary, depending on such factors as their education, experience, job status, and geographic location. Specific salary information for these professionals is unavailable. An informal search on the Internet revealed that salaries for some full-time Farmers' Market Managers ranged between $28,000 and $45,000 a year. Some managers hold volunteer positions and receive no compensation.

Employment Prospects

Farmers' markets are found throughout the United States. The majority of farmers' markets are open once or twice a week. A few markets, which are usually located in large cities such as in Seattle and Los Angeles, are open daily.

In general, positions for Farmers' Market Managers become available as managers transfer to other jobs or career fields, or leave the workforce for various reasons. As new farmers' markets are established, additional managerial positions are created.

In the United States, the number of farmers' markets has increased in popularity over the last decade. According to the Farmers Market Coalition Web site (www.farmersmarketcoalition.org), about 1,755 farmers' markets existed in 1994 in the nation, while in 2008, the number of these markets had grown to more than 4,685.

In addition, the USDA Agricultural Census reported that direct sales of farm products to consumers nationwide in 2007 were $1.2 billion, which had risen from $812 million in 2002. The number of farms making direct sales through farmers' markets, farm stands, and other methods increased from 116,733 (in 2002) to 136,817 (in 2007). Some experts in the field say that these statistics reflect a growing interest by consumers to buy fresh, local foods from farmers with whom they can interact and trust.

Advancement Prospects

Advancement opportunities are limited for Farmers' Market Managers. In large organizations that oversee several farmers' markets, managers can be promoted to the executive director position. Many managers measure their success by earning higher wages and through job satisfaction. Some individuals seek managerial positions that offer greater challenges or oversee larger or more prestigious farmers' markets.

Some individuals use their experience as Farmers' Markets Managers as stepping-stones to managerial and administrative positions in other areas, such as agricultural associations or nonprofit organizations.

Education and Training

Educational requirements vary with employers. Some prefer to hire candidates who possess bachelor's degrees, while others accept applicants who hold associate's degrees.

Farmers' Market Managers learn their tasks on the job. Many participate in workshops and seminars to update their skills and knowledge. These learning events are offered by organizations that serve the interests of farmers' markets and their staffs.

Experience, Special Skills, and Personality Traits

Employers usually seek candidates who have at least three to four years of experience working in business, nonprofit, and entrepreneurial settings that include supervisory and managerial duties. Candidates should also be experienced or knowledgeable about farmers' markets as well as agriculture, particularly the foods produced in the local areas.

Farmers' Market Managers work with many individuals, such as board members, farmers, community groups, and the public, who come from diverse backgrounds. Hence, these managers must have excellent interpersonal, communication, customer service, and conflict-resolution skills. These managers also need to have effective leadership, teamwork, time-management, organizational, problem-solving, and decision-making skills to perform their various tasks well. In addition, they need strong marketing skills as well as computing competence in word processing, spreadsheets, graphic design, and other software.

Some personality traits that successful Farmers' Market Managers share include being friendly, enthusiastic, tactful, trustworthy, creative, detail-oriented, resourceful, and entrepreneurial.

Unions and Associations

Many Farmers' Market Managers are members of state associations that serve the interests of farmers' markets and their staff. These managers are also eligible to join the Farmers Market Coalition and the North American Farmers' Direct Marketing Association, which advance and promote farmers' markets nationwide. (For contact information about these groups, see Appendix II.) By joining such organizations, Farmers' Market Managers can take advantage of networking opportunities, training programs, and other professional services and resources.

Tips for Entry

1. Managing farmers' markets involves various planning, organizing, and coordinating skills. You can begin gaining such skills by taking part in putting together a fund-raiser, dance, or other special event for your class, club, or other organization.
2. Read job application instructions carefully, and follow them exactly. For example, if the application directs you to submit a résumé and cover letter with your application, then be sure to do so.
3. Many farmers' markets have Web sites on which job announcements are posted.
4. Before you go to a job interview, visit the farmers' market that you are seeking to manage. Observe the operations and think about how you could improve it. Also, talk to some vendors and consumers to find out what they like about the farmers' market, as well as things they would like to have changed.
5. Use the Internet to learn more about farmers' markets. You might start by visiting the Farmers Market Coalition Web site at www.farmersmar ketcoalition.org. For more links, see Appendix IV.

GRAIN ELEVATOR MANAGER

Position Description

Throughout the United States, as well as worldwide, farms produce millions of tons of grains, such as corn, wheat, barley, rice, sorghum, and oats each year. Farmers sell their crops to grain companies and farmers' cooperatives for cash or for contracted prices to be paid upon future delivery. The organizations, in turn, market the grain through futures contracts or directly to exporters, mills, food wholesalers, food processors, and other buyers. Until sales are made, the foodstuffs are kept in complex structures known as grain elevators, which are designed to safely receive and ship grains in bulk as well as to store them so that they will not decompose over time.

Grain elevators are enormous facilities that consist of one or several large buildings and storage silos to contain the different grains. Grain companies and farmers' cooperatives own one or more grain elevators, which are located near farmlands as well as transportation centers. Overseeing the operations of each of these facilities are first-line managers generally known as Grain Elevator Managers. They make sure all details of loading, unloading, cleaning, mixing, and storing grain run smoothly and efficiently from day to day.

Grain elevators are situated at seaports, on the shores of lakes and navigable rivers, next to railroads, and near major roads. Grain deliveries arrive by ships, railcars, and trucks, which also receive loads of grain from the elevators. Managers direct the work of elevator staff to ensure they perform receiving and shipping tasks properly, safely, and in compliance with laws and regulations as well as company policies and procedures.

These managers are responsible for coordinating all grain purchasing, handling, and shipping activities. Modern grain elevators feature computerized systems to automatically control and monitor the flow of grain into and out of the storage silos and register the weights of grains as they are received or shipped. Grain Elevator Managers supervise the use of these systems and have the responsibility to ultimately control them. For example, the automated system may decide to place some grain in a silo, that the Grain Elevator Managers wish to use for another purpose. They override that directive and input new instructions to place the grain in another location.

Elevator managers make sure that grain inventories are properly stored and in good condition at all times. They oversee the classifying and grading of each type of grain as it is received. They also perform regular inspections to monitor the grains for quality, moisture content, and weight, as well as to maintain inventory levels. In addition, these managers ensure that grain elevator property and equipment are maintained and function properly at all times.

Grain Elevator Managers are involved in the marketing and sales activities within their facilities, and they ensure that such activities are profitable. They assist elevator owners with developing marketing plans and establishing sales goals. Elevator Managers also establish prices for grains that are suitable for meeting sales goals and quotas.

Depending on the size of their facilities, Grain Elevator Managers may supervise a few or a large number of full-time and part-time technical, administrative, and professional employees. Managers act as liaisons between elevator employees and owners or higher-level managers. Elevator managers generally handle all personnel issues at their sites. They are responsible for hiring staff members, delegating their work, and evaluating their job performance. They also adjust staff populations for varying seasonal needs.

Grain Elevator Managers work in offices located at grain elevator facilities, as well as in the operating sections of the facilities. They are exposed to noisy and dusty environments. They put in 40-hour workweeks but may work extra hours to complete their tasks.

Salaries

Salaries for Grain Elevator Managers vary, depending on such factors as their education, experience, job duties, employer, and geographic location. Salary information for this occupation is unavailable. The U.S. Bureau of Labor Statistics reported in its May 2008 Occupational Employment Statistics survey that the estimated annual salary for most managers ranged between $46,700 and $153,500. (This salary information concerns managers who were not listed separately in the survey.)

Employment Prospects

Job openings for Grain Elevator Managers become available as individuals advance to higher positions, transfer to other jobs or careers, or retire.

In recent years, there has been a trend throughout the United States of grain companies and farmers' cooperatives merging and consolidating, which has resulted in the closing of some grain elevators.

Advancement Prospects

Grain Elevator Managers are first-line managers. They may advance to district or regional operations manager as well as executive positions.

Many managers measure their success by earning higher salaries and professional recognition.

Education and Training

Minimally, Grain Elevator Managers must possess a high school diploma or a general equivalency diploma. Increasingly, employers prefer to hire candidates who hold an associate's or bachelor's degree in agriculture, agribusiness, or another related field.

Elevator managers normally learn their skills on the job, as they work their way up through the ranks. Some employers have management training programs in which they hire recent or upcoming college graduates to management trainee positions. Employers teach these trainees technical, managerial, and administrative aspects of running grain elevators.

Experience, Special Skills, and Personality Traits

Employers generally hire candidates who have several years of experience working in a grain elevator. Strong candidates also have proven supervisory and facility management experience.

Grain Elevator Managers must have effective leadership, teamwork, interpersonal, and self-management skills. They also need planning, project-management, problem-solving, decision-making, and presentation skills. Being inspirational, organized, collaborative, calm, respectful, and flexible are some personality skills that successful Grain Elevator Managers share.

Unions and Associations

Grain Elevator Managers can join professional associations to take advantage of networking opportunities, continuing education, and other services and resources. One national organization that serves these managers is the Grain Elevator and Processing Society. For contact information, see Appendix II.

Tips for Entry

1. As a grain elevator worker, take the initiative to learn as much as you can about the different aspects of the operations.
2. Having a willingness to relocate may improve your chances of obtaining a management position.
3. Use the Internet to learn more about grain elevators. To get a list of Web sites, enter any of these keywords into a search engine: *grain elevator operations* or *grain elevator management*. To learn about some links, see Appendix IV.

FARM LABOR CONTRACTOR

Duties: Provide work crews to agricultural producers; recruit, hire, train, and supervise agricultural workers; perform other duties as required

Alternate Title(s): None

Salary Range: $19,000 to $55,000

Employment Prospects: Fair

Advancement Prospects: Poor

Prerequisites:

Education or Training—On-the-job training

Experience—Years of experience in the agricultural industry

Special Skills and Personality Traits—Interpersonal, communication, leadership, management, organizational, problem-solving, negotiation, and self-management skills; ability to operate com-

puters and other office equipment; cooperative, enterprising, ethical, resourceful, persistent, composed, detail-oriented, and flexible personality traits

Special Requirements—Possess all required licenses and authorizations

Farm Labor Contractor (Experienced)

Farm Labor Contractor (Novice)

Farm Labor Contractor Foreman, Farmer, or Farm Manager

Position Description

Producing agricultural crops is labor-intensive and seasonal work. Farmers, whether they own small or large operations, seek additional workers on a temporary basis to help cultivate and harvest crops quickly and efficiently. For example, a farmer may need extra workers to hoe weeds and thin plants for a few weeks. Rather than hire temporary workers, many farmers use the services of a Farm Labor Contractor (FLC).

FLCs are small business operators who recruit and hire men and women to perform seasonal work for their clients, who include vegetable farmers, vineyard growers, orchardists, nursery owners, and other agricultural producers. Some FLCs also furnish labor to landscape contractors, landscape maintenance firms, and food processing businesses. Many FLCs serve clients within nearby communities. Some FLCs operate throughout a state or in several states. FLCs form long-term relationships with their clients.

Negotiating contracts is a major responsibility of FLCs. With each client, FLCs agree on such terms as:

- the estimated number of agricultural workers that the FLCs will furnish
- the type of work that agricultural workers will perform, such as planting, cultivating, weeding, irrigating, pruning, or harvesting crops

- the starting and ending dates for which the work will be performed
- the estimated amount to be paid to the FLCs

The agricultural workers are employees of the FLCs and not of the agricultural producers on whose property they work. FLCs usually employ individuals who are considered migrant workers because their permanent place of residence is in another locale, which may be another state or country. After the agricultural season is over, these individuals return home.

FLCs are responsible for the management of agricultural workers at the job sites. Directly, or through their foremen, FLCs train workers in their duties, as well as provide supervision and direction of the workers' daily activities. FLCs also monitor the workers' performance and, if necessary, take any disciplinary action, such as docking their pay or terminating them. FLCs may be responsible for transporting workers to and from their jobs. They may also furnish workers with appropriate tools, such as hoes or pruners, to complete their jobs.

To run a successful farm labor contracting service, owners must complete many administrative responsibilities. For example, FLCs pay employees their wages; maintain accurate personnel records; pay taxes and premiums for workers' compensation, liability, and other required insurance policies; keep business licenses, permits, and registrations up-to-date; and submit required paperwork to appropriate government agencies.

FLCs also endeavor to comply with various laws and regulations pertaining to employment, occupational health and safety, business operations, and other matters. For instance, FLCs must provide workers with access to toilets while working in the fields.

FLCs employ staff to assist them with their operations. They hire foremen who oversee the work activities of the agricultural workers. In addition, FLCs hire office staff to handle business and administrative duties.

FLCs put in long hours, six or seven days a week, to build up their businesses.

Salaries

Annual earnings for FLCs vary from year to year, depending on the size of their operations, the number of clients they have, their competition, and other factors. The U.S. Bureau of Labor Statistics reported in its May 2008 Occupational Employment Statistics survey that the estimated annual wages for most Farm Labor Contractors ranged between $19,040 and $55,400.

Employment Prospects

Agricultural producers seek the services of FLCs for the reduction of personnel paperwork, the convenience, the savings they make from not having to pay employee benefits, and other reasons. In recent years, the pool of farm labor has been decreasing in the United States, according to some experts in the field. This, in turn, has created an increase in growers seeking FLCs to supply them with sufficient workers.

Opportunities for individuals to start farm labor contracting services are favorable. One expert in the field stated that there is a need for FLCs who are customer-oriented, who comply with legal requirements, and who focus on attracting good employees, providing quality work, and exercising workplace safety.

Advancement Prospects

Farm Labor Contractors advance according to their own ambitions and interests. As entrepreneurs, they measure their success by achieving their business goals, as well as by being able to make a comfortable living.

Education and Training

FLCs learn about running a business on the job. Through self-study and enrollment in courses and workshops, they can gain basic business training in bookkeeping, accounting, finance, management, and marketing.

Special Requirements

FLCs must be registered with the U.S. Department of Labor, as required by the Migrant and Seasonal Agricultural Worker Protection Act. Registration is accomplished through a state employment office. In addition, FLCs must be licensed by their state department of labor, and they must possess proper state business licenses.

Experience, Special Skills, and Personality Traits

Individuals usually become FLCs after working many years on farms, in packinghouses, or in other related agricultural businesses, including for Farm Labor Contractors. They also have supervisory and management experience and are familiar with the procedures and principles of recruiting, selecting, and hiring personnel.

FLCs need strong interpersonal and communication skills as they must be able to work well with clients, employees, government officials, and others from diverse backgrounds. They must also have excellent leadership, management, organizational, problem-solving, negotiation, and self-management skills. Additionally, FLCs should be proficient in operating computers and other office equipment. Some personality traits that successful FLCs share include being cooperative, enterprising, ethical, resourceful, persistent, composed, detail-oriented, and flexible.

Unions and Associations

In some states, professional associations that serve the interests of FLCs are available. By joining an association, FLCs can take advantage of networking opportunities, training programs, and other professional services and resources. For example, FLCs in California might join the California Farm Labor Contractors' Alliance (for contact information, see Appendix II).

Tips for Entry

1. Be proficient in speaking and understanding Spanish or another language that the majority of migrant workers speak.
2. Carefully and thoroughly research what is involved in owning a small business. Be sure you understand how much time, energy, and money is involved in starting a business.
3. Learn more about farm labor contracting on the Internet. You might start by visiting the page "Labor Resources" at the Farm Employers Labor Service Web site (www.fels.org/data). For more links, see Appendix IV.

AUCTIONEER

Position Description

Whether we are city dwellers or live in farm country, one of the most pleasant annual pastimes is going to our state or county agricultural fair. There are so many things to see and do. For example, we may pass by an outdoor pavilion where we see people looking at cattle, sheep, goats, or other livestock. We may also see and hear a man or woman behind a podium, holding a microphone, and speaking rapidly and incomprehensibly. If we pay close attention, we begin to understand that what the person is saying has something to do with prices and asking who wants to bid higher prices. Individuals in the audience periodically wave cards or paddles with numbers on them. What we are witnessing is an auction; in this case, it is a livestock auction. The speaker is an Auctioneer.

Auctions are a distinctive way to sell property. They differ from wholesale and retail sales because there are no stores or marketplaces to visit. They differ from direct sales methods, such as swap meets or flea markets, because the buyers at auctions do not haggle over the price of items. Auctions are unique events wherein just about anything can be bought and sold, from antiques to household items to vehicles to equipment and machinery to land. When people sell their property at auctions, they can expect to sell every item they bring, and sell it very quickly to enthusiastic buyers.

There are several kinds of auctions, the most common of which operate like the livestock auctions. Buyers bid competitively and whoever offers the highest bid becomes the new owner of the property. Some auctions sell to the lowest bidder, while others operate on a sealed-bid basis.

Auctioneers are highly knowledgeable about the value of all kinds of property and about how to market properties to the most likely buyers. Auctioneers usually specialize in selling certain types of property. Agricultural auctions are a very important specialty. Besides livestock, such merchandise as farm equipment, farm properties, and even fresh fruits and vegetables are sold at auctions. Agricultural Auctioneers might sell farms, vacant lots, used equipment, antique tractors, farmhouse collectibles, tobacco, wool, wines, or thoroughbred horses, for example. They might also auction commodities, such as grains, soybeans, and pork bellies, or business assets and leases, or even licenses for logging on government-owned land.

Auctioneers are essentially agents who work on behalf of individuals or organizations that wish to sell their property. They may work for either a flat fee or a commission based on a percentage of the sales. Hence, they are motivated to sell all of their clients' items quickly. Auctioneers are governed by ethics standards set by their auction associations. They also comply with appropriate government rules and regulations.

Auctioneers meet with clients to plan and set up the auction. Auctioneers help prepare the items for sale, including cleaning and repairing them if needed. Auctioneers know the fair market value of each piece of property. If they are unsure of the value of an item, they consult with an expert to appraise its value. Auctioneers arrange for the auction venue and pay the appropriate fees for renting space to hold the proceedings.

These auctioneering professionals work to market each auction to groups of buyers who are keenly interested in the types of items to be sold. They advertise upcoming auctions through newspaper notices, flyers, and direct mailings to known auction enthusiasts. They publicize the types of items to be sold as well as the time and location for their auctions, which may take place on courthouse steps or at hotels, auditoriums, warehouses, barns, or large facilities designed specifically for auction activities. As the time approaches for their auctions, Auctioneers determine the sequence of the items to be sold, and arrange them to be sold in groups (or lots) when appropriate.

At the auction, Auctioneers coordinate their staff to keep records of the day's transactions, collect fees, and provide the seller with the proceeds of the sale. They also appoint assistants called ringmen to position themselves in the audience to help keep track of the bids. The ringmen also help auction participants with understanding the bidding process.

From behind the podium, Auctioneers present each item for sale and begin their chant with a bid price. As they chant, they recognize bidders who indicate with their paddles their desire to pay the price the Auctioneers quote. The Auctioneers raise the price repeatedly with their chanting. The highest bidder receives the item and the Auctioneers move on to the next item. These experts repeat this process until they sell every item, which may take as many as four to six hours. Some Auctioneers audiotape or videotape the proceedings at auctions to verify sales and to maintain security. When the auction is over, Auctioneers help with cleaning up the auction facilities. For example, they remove their equipment, such as their podiums, microphones, videotaping machines, and any other items they used during the auction.

Auctioneers' work can be physically demanding, as they must endure standing for long periods and speaking continuously. They must also be able to lift some of the items they sell, which can be quite heavy.

Auctioneers may work full time or part time at this occupation. They may work as many as five days per week and up to eight hours each day. These experts often work during evening hours or on weekends.

Salaries

Auctioneers may earn a flat fee or a commission for their services. Commissions are based on a certain percentage of the total proceeds from an auction. Their fees vary according their experience, the services they provide, and other factors.

Their annual earnings fluctuate from year to year, which depends on how many auctions they perform and how much they earn per auction. According to an online salary survey by PayScale.com, the median salary for Auctioneers in the United States ranged from $30,000 for those with one to four years of experience to $77,419 for those with 20 or more years of experience. (This salary survey was dated May 3, 2009.)

Employment Prospects

The auction industry in the United States is a multibillion-dollar industry. Auctioneers are hired by individuals, farmers, attorneys, banks, corporations, governments, and many others. Some Auctioneers are employed by auction companies, while others are self-employed. According to one expert in the field, the majority of professional Auctioneers own and operate their own auction business.

Staff positions generally become available as Auctioneers transfer to other jobs or career fields, retire, or leave the workforce for various reasons.

Some experts in the field report that opportunities are favorable for qualified Auctioneers. Billions of dollars in goods and services, including produce, livestock, farm equipment and machinery, and farmland, are sold at live auctions every year in the United States.

Advancement Prospects

Auctioneers advance by receiving higher fees and commission rates and by gaining exceptional reputations. Entrepreneurial individuals may start their own businesses.

With their background, Auctioneers can pursue other careers by becoming sales representatives, brokers, buyers, and entrepreneurs.

Education and Training

To become an Auctioneer, individuals must possess at least a high school diploma or a general equivalency diploma.

Auctioneers initially learn their skills in one of two ways. They may serve an apprenticeship under an experienced Auctioneer or complete an auction school or program. Apprentices and students alike receive instruction in such areas as auctioneer jargon, elocution, proper breathing techniques, bid calling, ethics, and appraisals. To become a licensed Auctioneer in some states, individuals must have served their apprenticeships under state-licensed Auctioneers or attended state-approved auction schools.

Throughout their careers, agricultural Auctioneers pursue continuing education to update their auctioneering skills and their knowledge about agricultural auction specialties such as livestock, machinery, or farm estates.

Special Requirements

In some states, as well as in some U.S. cities, Auctioneers are required to hold a professional license. To auction real estate, Auctioneers may need to possess a real estate license. Contact a city or county government office to learn about licensing requirements in the area where you wish to work. Alternatively, contact your state department of agriculture for licensing information for agricultural Auctioneers.

Experience, Special Skills, and Personality Traits

In general, applicants for apprentice positions should have previous experience working in auctions, whether in paid or nonpaid positions. Employers may hire inexperienced applicants if they show a willingness to learn and to work hard.

To perform well at their jobs, Auctioneers must have strong leadership, organizational, self-management, and interpersonal skills. They also need excellent communication, public-speaking, and presentation skills. Being proficient in math and computers is also important. Being entertaining, enthusiastic, quick-witted, tactful, detail-oriented, decisive, and hardworking are some personality traits that successful Auctioneers share.

Unions and Associations

Auctioneers can join professional associations to take advantage of networking opportunities, continuing education, and other professional services and resources. One national society that serves this profession is the National Auctioneers Association. For contact information, see Appendix II.

Tips for Entry

1. Attend agricultural and nonagricultural auctions to get an idea of what takes place as well as to observe styles of different Auctioneers.
2. Volunteer at charity auctions to gain experience.
3. When you go to a job interview, be prepared to demonstrate your auctioneering style.
4. Use the Internet to learn more about auctioneering. You might start by visiting the National Auctioneers Association Web site at www.auctioneers.org. For more links, see Appendix IV.

FARM EQUIPMENT MECHANIC

Duties: Perform maintenance and repairs on farm equipment; perform other duties as required

Alternate Title(s): Agricultural Equipment Technician, Service Mechanic

Salary Range: $21,000 to $59,000

Employment Prospects: Fair

Advancement Prospects: Poor

Prerequisites:

Education or Training—On-the-job training or formal training in agricultural machinery

Experience—Previous experience preferred

Special Skills and Personality Traits—Self-management, interpersonal, communication, problem-solving, critical-thinking, and troubleshooting skills; cooperative, positive, hardworking, flexible, and dependable personality traits

CAREER LADDER

Senior Farm Equipment Mechanic

Farm Equipment Mechanic

Mechanic's Helper or Entry-level Farm Equipment Mechanic

Position Description

Tractors, combines, tree shakers, hay balers, trucks, mowers, milking machines, hydraulic systems, and pumps are among the machines that farmers use regularly to perform their work. These mechanical devices share one characteristic with other machines—they need routine maintenance and occasional repairs. The expert men and women who keep farm machines operating properly are Farm Equipment Mechanics.

Most of these agricultural mechanics work for farm equipment manufacturers or independent repair service companies. Some Farm Equipment Mechanics live on the farms or ranches that hire them. Those mechanics may perform general farm tasks in addition to their machine repair and maintenance duties.

In general, Farm Equipment Mechanics diagnose mechanical problems, replace parts, make adjustments, perform overhauls, and repair broken components on farm vehicles and machines. Mechanics also assemble machines or build new parts and components.

Many farm machines are very sophisticated. For example, some of the newest tractors and combines have global positioning system technologies, computerized monitoring systems, and self-steering mechanisms. Some machines also feature enclosed compartments that are air-conditioned. Farm Equipment Mechanics must, therefore, be well versed in how these machines, their systems, and their components work. They use computerized diagnostic equipment to assist them with their tasks. Such equipment includes devices that measure the flow of current through electrical components. They also utilize computerized equipment to input codes to recalibrate machine components.

Farm Equipment Mechanics are adept at using hand tools, such as hammers, pliers, and screwdrivers, as well as power tools, such as hydraulic jacks and pneumatic wrenches. In addition, these experts work with machine tools to create new engine parts, and welding equipment for attaching components.

Mechanics, particularly those who work for farm equipment manufacturers, may specialize by working on certain types of machines or by performing specific tasks. For example, some specialists may focus on repairing large harvesters, while others may work only on tractors. Similarly, some mechanics may specialize in rebuilding transmissions, while others work on steering mechanisms. Some mechanics work only on machines made by particular manufacturers.

Whether these experts are specialists or general mechanics, they perform tasks that are specific to their farm mechanic careers. For example, they:

- listen to and watch machinery in action to determine malfunctions
- remove parts or components, disassemble them, repair or replace defective parts, reassemble them, and put them back in place
- operate vehicles, machines, and equipment after completing maintenance and repair work to ensure proper function

- read and understand blueprints, schematic diagrams, manuals, and other informational materials
- clean their work areas and keep them orderly
- maintain work tools, equipment, and vehicles

Farm Equipment Mechanics generally work indoors in shop environments. They may be required to travel to remote farm or ranch locations to work on machinery or to bring machinery back to the shop.

Agricultural mechanics need to be in fit condition, as they must work in cramped work areas, lift heavy or greasy objects, kneel, stoop, climb, and reach. They wear safety apparel such as safety boots, hard hats, goggles, and gloves to protect themselves from injury. Farm Equipment Mechanics may be exposed to fumes from fuel and hazardous chemicals contained in various fluids such as motor oil, antifreeze, and hydraulic fluids.

Farm Equipment Mechanics work variable hours, depending on the season. During the winter months, they work fewer days and hours.

Salaries

Salaries for Farm Equipment Mechanics vary, depending on such factors as their training, experience, employer, and geographic location. According to the May 2008 Occupational Employment Statistics survey by the U.S. Bureau of Labor Statistics, the estimated annual salary for most of these mechanics ranged between $21,380 and $46,520. Mechanics who work on diesel engines earn higher wages. The BLS reported that the estimated annual salary for most diesel engine specialists ranged between $26,000 and $59,090.

Employment Prospects

In general, job openings for Farm Equipment Mechanics become available as individuals retire or transfer to other jobs or career fields. Opportunities are more favorable for mechanics who have completed formal training programs, according to some experts in the field.

Advancement Prospects

Farm Equipment Mechanics advance according to their interests and ambitions. Some mechanics rise to supervisory and managerial positions. Some pursue careers in other areas within their companies by becoming sales representatives or service representatives. Entrepreneurial mechanics may establish their own repair shops.

Education and Training

Individuals can enter the field in one of two ways. Some aspiring mechanics learn their skills through on-the-job training while working as mechanics' helpers or trainees. They work under the supervision and direction of experienced mechanics for about three or four years.

Other prospective mechanics complete formal programs in agricultural mechanics or a related field. Community colleges, technical schools, and vocational schools offer associate's degrees, or professional certificate programs that may be six months to two years long.

Experience, Special Skills, and Personality Traits

Employers prefer to hire applicants for entry-level positions who have experience performing repairs and maintenance on farm equipment.

To perform well at their job, Farm Equipment Mechanics need excellent self-management skills. They must also have strong interpersonal, communication, problem-solving, critical-thinking, and troubleshooting skills. Some personality traits that successful mechanics share include being cooperative, positive, hardworking, flexible, and dependable.

Unions and Associations

Some Farm Equipment Mechanics belong to labor unions that represent them in contract negotiations with their employers for better pay, benefits, and working conditions. Unions also handle any grievances that their members may have against their employers.

Tips for Entry

1. Assemble a set of basic tools, as some employers require that you have your own tools.
2. Check your state employment office for job leads.
3. Learn more about agricultural equipment. You might start by visiting the Farm Equipment Manufacturers Association Web site at www.farmequip.org. For other links, see Appendix IV.

AGRIBUSINESS

AGRICULTURAL ECONOMIST

CAREER PROFILE

Duties: Study and apply economic principles and techniques to agricultural issues and problems; perform duties as required of position

Alternate Title(s): A title that reflects a position such as Research Agricultural Economist or Research Analyst

Salary Range: $44,000 to $149,000

Employment Prospects: Fair

Advancement Prospects: Good

Prerequisites:

    Education or Training—Master's or doctoral degree required for research scientist positions

    Experience—Previous work experience preferred

CAREER LADDER

Senior Agricultural Economist

Agricultural Economist

Agricultural Economist (Entry Level)

Special Skills and Personality Traits—Business, leadership, analytical, decision-making, communication, research, writing, computer, and quantitative skills; patient, persistent, curious, creative, and flexible personality traits

Position Description

Economics is a social science concerned with the understanding of commercial activity including the production, distribution, and utilization of goods and services. Agricultural Economists, study how agriculture contributes to the overall economic system. They apply the principles and theories of economics to specific agricultural issues and problems. They strive to accomplish practical goals. For example, they may be engaged in helping government agencies to alleviate rural poverty or agricultural businesses to compete more successfully in the global economy.

Agricultural Economists examine economic factors at every level from local farm and ranch communities to regional, state, national, and international companies and governments. They look for patterns in how consumers purchase and use food and other agricultural products. They analyze how agriculture markets perform within the larger economy. They investigate how agricultural businesses compete or interact with one another. They research the economic implications of farming methods and the process of bringing food to markets and consumers. Agricultural Economists also study commodities markets, ranch management, and environmental policies.

Agricultural Economists approach their studies from several angles. They may use the principles of microeconomics to study how individuals and companies make decisions on how to spend their money, as well as how firms achieve profits and provide goods

or services that their customers require. These economists may also work in the area of macroeconomics to observe how the different components of national or international economies work together to maintain sufficient employment levels. In addition, Agricultural Economists may apply econometrics to their pursuit of understanding. Econometrics is the use of mathematics and statistics to test economic theories and to calculate solutions to problems.

Agricultural Economists may focus their studies on particular agricultural industries, public finance policies, labor conditions, and population demographics to better understand specific areas of agricultural economics. Furthermore, these experts may concentrate on specific economic issues such as farm labor costs, community development in rural areas, the improvement of nutrition standards, government agricultural policies, the utilization of natural resources, or international agricultural trade.

Agricultural Economists are employed in a variety of occupations. For example, some economists teach and conduct research in colleges and universities, while others work as researchers and analysts for government agencies, research institutions, banks, financial institutions, and private companies.

Agricultural Economists perform various duties that are specific to their occupation. They also complete general tasks common to other economists, such as:

- review statistical and economic information

- seek and develop new methods of gathering and analyzing economic data
- keep track of economic changes in agriculture and related industries
- prepare reports of their research findings
- provide economic guidance or counsel to farmers, businesses, government agencies, and others
- testify at public hearings
- speak to community groups about economic issues

These professionals work standard 40-hour weeks, but may put in extra hours to complete projects.

Salaries

Salaries for Agricultural Economists vary, depending on such factors as their education, experience, position, employer, and geographic location. The estimated annual salary for most economists ranged between $44,050 and $149,110, according to the May 2008 Occupational Employment Statistics survey by the U.S. Bureau of Labor Statistics.

Employment Prospects

Agricultural Economics can pursue a wide range of career opportunities. They can work as research scientists, assistants, and analysts in government agencies, academic institutions, nonprofit organizations, and agribusiness companies. They can seek teaching positions in colleges and universities. Individuals can also apply their training and background in agricultural economics to careers as farmers, Cooperative Extension Service agents, bankers, loan officers, market research analysts, sales representatives, and accountants, among other professions.

Advancement Prospects

Agricultural Economists advance in their careers according to their interests and ambitions, which typically evolve over the years. As they gain experience, they usually specialize in particular subject matter. Those with administrative, managerial, or consulting career goals pursue such positions. Some economists seek opportunities to teach at the university level or to conduct independent research.

Education and Training

Employers usually require applicants for research scientist positions to possess either a master's degree or doctorate in economics, agricultural economics, or another related field. For analyst and research assistant positions, applicants may be required to possess either a bachelor's or master's degree. To teach in colleges and universities, Agricultural Economists must possess a doctoral degree.

Experience, Special Skills, and Personality Traits

Employers usually prefer to hire candidates for entry-level positions who have some work experience related to the job for which they apply. They may have gained their experience through employment, internships, student research projects, and volunteer work.

Agricultural Economists need excellent business, leadership, analytical, decision-making, and communication skills. In addition, these professionals need strong research, writing, computer, and quantitative skills. Some personality traits that successful Agricultural Economists share include being patient, persistent, curious, creative, and flexible.

Unions and Associations

Agricultural Economists can join professional associations to take advantage of various services and resources, such as continuing education, professional certification, and networking opportunities. Some national societies that serve the interests of these professionals are the Agricultural and Applied Economics Association, American Economic Association, the Association of Environmental and Resource Economists, the International Association of Agricultural Economists, and the USDA Economists Group. For contact information, see Appendix II.

Tips for Entry

1. Many employers hire economic analysts for specific areas of work, and use job titles (such as market analyst, researcher, and public policy analyst) to reflect those specialties.
2. If economist positions are unavailable at a particular company, be open to applying for an entry-level position.
3. Check Web sites of professional and trade associations. Many of them have job banks or jobs postings that can be accessed by the public.
4. Learn more about the field of agricultural economics. You might start by visiting the Agricultural and Applied Economics Association Web site (www.aaea.org); and AEAweb (www.aeaweb.org). For more links, see Appendix IV.

BUYER (FARM PRODUCTS)

Duties: Purchase farm products for resale to companies and other organizations; perform duties as required

Alternate Title(s): Grain Buyer, Produce Buyer, Cattle Buyer, Seed Buyer, or other title that reflects a particular agricultural product or commodity

Salary Range: $29,000 to $96,000

Employment Prospects: Poor

Advancement Prospects: Fair

Prerequisites:

Education or Training—College degree preferred

Experience—Several years of experience in procurement

Special Skills and Personality Traits—Critical-thinking, time-management, decision-making, teamwork, self-management, interpersonal, communication, customer service, sales, negotiation, computer, mathematical, and writing skills; friendly, patient, ethical, honest, persuasive, resourceful, detail-oriented, adaptable, and self-motivated personality traits

Special Requirements—State license and bonding may be required

CAREER LADDER

Senior Buyer

Buyer

Junior Buyer or Assistant Buyer

Position Description

Agricultural Buyers work for meat processing plants, food processors, produce wholesalers, flower and plant distributors, fiber wholesalers, grocery outlets, and other companies that resell farm products that they purchase. These procurement specialists buy produce, livestock, and other farm products directly from farmers, as well as through farm cooperatives and at agricultural auctions. The Buyers' objective is to purchase products for their employers at the lowest prices possible. Their employers, in turn, sell the products to businesses, shops, manufacturers, government agencies, individual consumers, and others at a higher price to earn a profit.

Agricultural Buyers are highly knowledgeable about the products that they purchase. Typically, they specialize in purchasing one or more types of commodities, such as grains, fruits, produce, livestock, dairy products, poultry, cotton, wool, flowers, or timber. Some Buyers further concentrate by purchasing certain types of goods, such as organically grown products. Buyers may be employees or independent contractors.

Buyers are responsible for locating the producers who can fulfill their employers' requirements in terms of the price, quality, and availability of the farm products. Additionally, Buyers seek reliable producers who can deliver orders on schedule. Some Buyers deal with agricultural producers in other countries.

Buyers carefully research producers who are likely suppliers. They review a producer's history, selection of products, prices, sales records, and so on. Buyers usually examine a potential supplier's products for quality by viewing the products at a trade show or auction, or by visiting the producer's farm or ranch.

Upon selecting suppliers, Buyers negotiate prices, quantities, delivery dates, and other terms of purchase with the different producers. Once suppliers and Buyers agree upon terms, they sign agreements. Buyers are also responsible for overseeing the delivery process of purchased farm products. Some Buyers are involved in arranging the transportation and storage of purchased products. They also monitor contracts to ensure that both suppliers and the Buyers' companies comply with the terms.

Buyers usually work closely with the sales department within their companies. For example, they may teach their company's sales staff about new lines of purchased products or recommend prices for reselling products. Some Buyers are involved in selling the purchased products directly to customers.

Agricultural Buyers are responsible for managing their work schedules and establishing their own daily goals. They perform a wide range of tasks, such as:

- setting up appointments
- preparing contractual agreements

- identifying potential suppliers or purchasers
- tracking the inventory level of products
- resolving problems as they occur with suppliers
- keeping up with the latest price trends, commodity forecasts, and competitors' activities
- maintaining accurate and detailed records

Buyers' work can be stressful at times due to the competitive nature of their job. They often deal with strict deadlines. They are in continual contact with producers and purchasers, as well as with fellow buyers, managers, sales representatives, and others by phone, in person, or through e-mail.

Agricultural Buyers often put in more than 40-hour weeks to complete tasks, attend meetings and conferences, communicate with producers, or meet deadlines.

Salaries

Salaries for agricultural Buyers vary, depending on such factors as their education, experience, employer, and geographic location. According to the May 2008 Occupational Employment Statistics survey by the U.S. Bureau of Labor Statistics, the estimated annual salary for most Buyers of farm products ranged between $28,990 and $96,220.

Employment Prospects

Employment of Buyers of farm products has been decreasing over recent years. This trend is expected to continue because of the consolidation and mergers of agricultural companies and food wholesalers and retailers. Job competition for Buyers is therefore strong.

Advancement Prospects

Buyers generally work their way up the ranks from junior or assistant Buyers to senior Buyers. Agricultural Buyers who have supervisory and managerial aspirations can be promoted to such positions. Continuing education is usually needed for further advancement.

Education and Training

Many employers prefer to hire candidates who hold an associate's or bachelor's degree in business, agricultural business, agriculture, or another related field. Employers may hire candidates who possess a high school diploma or general equivalency diploma if they are highly knowledgeable about the products they would purchase and if they have years of experience in procurement.

Buyers learn their skills on the job, starting as junior or assistant Buyers. These trainees work under the direction and supervision of experienced Buyers.

Special Requirements

Agricultural Buyers may be required to be licensed and bonded in the states in which they wish to make purchases. For more information, contact the state department of agriculture where you wish to work.

Experience, Special Skills, and Personality Traits

Employers generally require that applicants have a few years of work experience in procurement, particularly in their industry (such as the dairy industry). They also seek candidates who are knowledgeable about the farm products that they would purchase.

Buyers must have excellent critical-thinking, time-management, decision-making, teamwork, and self-management skills. They also need effective interpersonal, communication, and customer service skills as they deal with farmers and others of diverse backgrounds every day. In addition, they need strong sales, negotiation, computer, mathematical, and writing skills. Some personality traits that successful Buyers share include being friendly, patient, ethical, honest, persuasive, resourceful, detail-oriented, adaptable, and self-motivated.

Unions and Associations

Agricultural Buyers might join professional or trade organizations to take advantage of networking opportunities, continuing education, and other services and resources. These organizations are found at the local, state, and national levels and serve diverse agricultural interests, including dairy farming, organic farming, flower production, and so on.

Tips for Entry

1. Gain experience working with the products that you may one day purchase as a Buyer. For example, you might work on a farm.
2. Having sales or customer service experience can help prepare you for a purchasing career.
3. Use the Internet to learn more about various agricultural buyers. To get a list of relevant Web sites, enter the name of a particular Buyer, such as *grain buyer* into a search engine.

COMMODITY BROKER

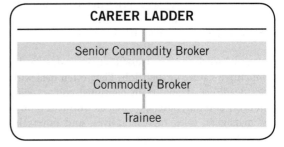

Position Description

We live in an economic system—capitalism—which allows individuals to increase their wealth by investing their money. Depositing our savings into bank accounts is probably the most common way that many of us make investments. Other familiar types of investments are stocks and bonds, which are purchased through brokers who work in institutions known as market exchanges. Many people also invest their money in commodities, such as gold, silver, petroleum, natural gas, soybeans, pork bellies, wheat, and microchips. Commodity Brokers are men and women who trade these items in market exchanges. Some specialize by trading agricultural commodities, and may further focus on one type of goods, such as grains or livestock.

Agricultural Commodity Brokers do business with agricultural producers and buyers, as well as with investors. Some Commodity Brokers are self-employed, but most work for commodity brokerage firms.

The term *Commodity Brokers* refers to either individuals or companies that buy or sell commodity derivatives. One category of these derivatives is called a futures contract. A futures contract is a financial instrument that represents a quantity of a specific commodity. For example, an agricultural Commodity Broker may draw up a contract with a soybean farmer to sell his harvested soybeans. The farmer may have just planted his crop but would like to lock in a certain price for his soybeans when he harvests them several months later. This guarantees that the farmer will receive that set price when he delivers his harvested crop. He consults his broker to arrange for the price on the contract and to arrange for a date when the farmer delivers his crop and receives payment for it. Agricultural buyers, such as a firm that produces soy milk, may purchase the contract from the Commodity Broker and hold it until the farmer delivers his crop.

Many investors are interested in buying into futures contracts. However, they usually do not wish to accept delivery of the commodities for which futures contracts are written. Rather, investors buy commodity options from Commodity Brokers for the purpose of speculation. An option differs from a futures contract in that it represents a commodity to be sold on a specific date, but the option holder is not obligated to purchase the commodity. If, for example, an investor buys an option for a low price but the price of that commodity rises before the contract is due, the investor may sell the option and make a profit. Investors sell their options to other investors or to companies interested in taking delivery of the commodity. Commodity Brokers are the "go-between" professionals who carry out orders to buy or sell futures contracts or options on behalf of their clients, the investors. Commodity Brokers receive a commission for each transaction they make.

Commodity Brokers work in association with marketplaces called commodities exchanges. These professionals fulfill different roles. Some of them work directly on the floor of their exchange where they make actual trades with other brokers. (On the floor, those who trade for their own benefit or that of their employer are referred to as traders, not brokers.) Commodity Brokers who work on exchange floors accept "buy" or "sell" orders by telephone or the Internet and find another trader or broker at the exchange to arrange for each trade. When the trade is completed, the floor broker communicates the result of the transaction by phone or computer back to the brokerage office.

Other Commodity Brokers work in office settings where they field phone calls from their clients to buy or sell derivatives on their behalf. These brokers fulfill various roles under which they are designated by certain titles. Some Commodity Brokers work in the capacity of commodity trading advisers. These brokers teach their clients about how the commodities markets function and they help their clients to make decisions about their investments. They are experts in the commodities markets and use their knowledge to recommend either buy or sell actions for investors who lack that expertise.

Another type of Commodity Broker is known as a commodity pool operator. This individual handles accounts held by groups of investors. Such accounts are similar to stock or bond mutual funds accounts held by investors. Commodity Brokers known as introducing brokers seek and accept orders from customers to buy or sell commodities options but do not accept payment from their clients to make such transactions.

Commodity Brokers use computers to track their accounts, monitor market activities, and relay "buy" or "sell" orders to traders on the floor of the nearest exchange. They also communicate to floor brokers by telephone. The number of their clients varies; for example, a Commodity Brokers might retain a client list of around 100 customers, while another broker has fewer customers. Brokers build their client lists by actively soliciting potential customers via telephone, by networking at business meetings or through civic organizations, or even by teaching investment courses and giving lectures about commodities investment.

Commodity Brokers work at a fast pace under often stressful conditions. Their success depends on how much money they can make on behalf of their clients. Commodity Brokers who work on exchange floors experience the most on-the-job stress. They must make quick decisions in a loud environment among a multitude of other brokers and traders.

Work hours vary for Commodity Brokers depending on whether they work in brokerage office call centers or on exchange floors. These professionals frequently work more than 40 hours per week and often work on weekends or holidays. Call centers operate around the clock and consequently Commodity Brokers may work in shifts.

Salaries

Commodity Brokers earn commissions, which are based on the amount of products that they sell. To provide brokers with a steady income, many employers pay them salaries against the minimum amount of commissions the brokers are expected to earn.

Earnings for Commodity Brokers vary, depending on their experience, ambition, and other factors. Total earnings for Commodity Brokers also vary each year and generally fluctuate with the state of the economy. For example, brokers earn fewer commissions during economic downturns.

Salary information specifically for agricultural Commodity Brokers is unavailable. In general, most commodities sales agents earned an estimated annual wage that ranged between $30,900 and $166,400, according to the May 2008 Occupational Employment Statistics survey by the U.S. Bureau of Labor Statistics (BLS).

Employment Prospects

Opportunities for agricultural Commodity Brokers are available nationwide. Job competition is strong in this field. Because of the fast pace and intensity of the position, there is a high turnover among Commodity Brokers during their first few years on the job.

The BLS groups commodities, securities, and financial services sales agents into one category. Between 2008 and 2018, employment for these professions is expected to increase by 9 percent. In addition to job growth, opportunities will become available as individuals retire or transfer to other jobs. Employment in this field fluctuates with the state of the overall economy. For example, during economic downturns, people invest more conservatively.

Advancement Prospects

Commodity Brokers advance in their careers according to their interests and ambitions. To succeed in this field, Commodity Brokers need to generate and maintain a large client base.

Brokers may pursue supervisory and management positions within their firms. Some Commodity Brokers become partners in their firms. To increase their advancement prospects, some brokers obtain a master's degree in business administration. Entrepreneurial individuals may become independent contractors or establish their own commodity company.

Education and Training

There are no standard minimum educational requirements to become Commodity Brokers. Many agricultural Commodity Brokers, however, possess bachelor's degrees in agribusiness, economics, finance, or another related discipline.

Entry-level brokers typically undergo training programs provided by their employers, which may include classroom instruction. Trainees receive on-the-job training while working under the supervision and direction of experienced Commodity Brokers.

Special Requirements

In the United States, Commodity Brokers must be licensed and registered by the National Futures Association (NFA), which is the self-regulatory organization for the U.S. futures industry. The NFA follows strict guidelines that are established by the Commodity Futures Trading Commission, the federal agency responsible for the overall regulation of the industry.

To become licensed and registered Commodity Brokers, individuals must pass a comprehensive examination that covers futures contracts, regulations, and other topics involved in commodities trading. In addition, individuals must pass a thorough background check. For more information about the licensing and registration process, visit the NFA Web site at www.nfa.futures.org.

Experience, Special Skills, and Personality Traits

Employers prefer to hire candidates for entry-level positions who have experience in sales or finance. Applicants must also be knowledgeable about the commodities that they would be trading.

Agricultural Commodity Brokers work with people from diverse backgrounds; thus, they must possess excellent communication, interpersonal, and customer service skills. To perform their duties effectively, brokers need strong research, writing, organizational, decision-making, time-management, and self-management skills. Being friendly, self-confident, quick-witted, persistent, flexible, honest, and ambitious are some personality traits that successful brokers have in common.

Unions and Associations

Commodity Brokers become mandatory members of the NFA upon becoming registered and licensed by the organization. The NFA, a nonprofit organization, has no affiliation to any futures market. Its purpose is to develop standards, rules, programs, and services that ensure that members comply with federal laws and regulations.

Commodity Brokers may join professional associations to take advantage of networking opportunities, training programs, and other professional services and resources. Two national societies that serve the different interests of Commodity Brokers are the Commodity Floor Brokers and Traders Association and the National Introducing Brokers Association. For contact information, see Appendix II.

Tips for Entry

1. Contact Commodity Brokers to learn more about their jobs. Also, ask them for advice on how to prepare for a career in their field.
2. As a broker, you will be talking with people for several hours a day. Take one or more speech classes to improve your abilities to speak clearly, articulately, and confidently.
3. When you perform a job search, be sure to contact brokerage firms for which you worked during school breaks or completed an internship.
4. Use the Internet to learn more about the field of commodities trading. You might start by visiting About.com: Commodities (commodities.about.com) and the National Futures Association Web site (www.nfa.futures.org). For more links, see Appendix IV.

LOAN OFFICER

Duties: Develop business relationships with current and prospective customers; evaluate loan applications and make recommendations for approval; perform other duties as required

Alternate Title(s): Loan Representative, Financial Services Officer, Agricultural Loan Officer, Farm Loan Specialist

Salary Range: $31,000 to $106,000

Employment Prospects: Good

Advancement Prospects: Fair

Prerequisites:

Education or Training—Bachelor's degree usually required; on-the-job training

Experience—Previous lending or banking experience preferred; have agricultural experience or knowledge

CAREER LADDER

Senior Loan Officer

Loan Officer

Loan Officer Trainee

Special Skills and Personality Traits—Interpersonal, communication, customer service, sales, computer, writing, leadership, organizational, problem-solving, negotiating, and self-management skills; personable, tactful, patient, ethical, dependable, analytical, persistent, and flexible personality traits

Special Requirements—State license may be required for mortgage loan officers

Position Description

When agricultural producers have insufficient funds to run their operations, they often seek loans from banks or other financial institutions. The financial representatives who assist loan applicants through the borrowing process are called Loan Officers. Some Loan Officers, particularly in rural areas, specialize in agricultural loans that are designed for crop farmers, dairy farmers, cattle ranchers, orchardists, flower growers, and other agricultural producers.

Agricultural producers generally apply for loans to make purchases or to finance their operations when financial resources are limited. They may use loans to purchase land, equipment, machinery, supplies, seed, or livestock; repair or replace agricultural tools, equipment, systems, and machinery; or construct or repair buildings, fences, or other structures, among other needs. Agricultural producers may also apply for loans after suffering financial setbacks from drought, freezing temperatures, floods, and other natural disasters.

Agricultural Loan Officers work for commercial banks, savings and loans, credit unions, and other financial institutions. Some agricultural loan specialists are employed by government agencies that offer loan programs directly to agricultural producers. Government loans are usually offered to agricultural producers who cannot obtain loans from commercial lenders.

Loan Officers who process agricultural loans are knowledgeable about the various aspects and risks of agricultural lending, including regulatory requirements. They have a working knowledge of the agricultural industry. They understand the basic elements of farm operations, farm management, the challenges of farming, current prices, trends of commodities, and so forth. Agricultural Loan Officers are also familiar with the different crop, livestock, poultry, greenhouse, and other types of farming operations within their establishments' service area. In addition, Loan Officers are up-to-date with regulatory requirements as well as their employers' policies and procedures.

Agricultural Loan Officers help customers through the loan application process at their institutions. They meet with customers to learn about their loan needs, and then describe the various loan programs for which they may be eligible. Loan Officers answer customers' questions and make sure they understand the requirements and restrictions for each type of loan program. Loan Officers explain how the loan application process works, and may assist customers with filling in the necessary paperwork.

Loan Officers review completed loan applications to determine how much risk is involved in granting customers a loan. In other words, officers verify whether potential borrowers have the ability to repay loans.

Officers analyze such factors as how long agricultural producers have been in business; their successes and failures; what assets they own; and how much they have already invested in their operations. Officers also look at whether applicants have sufficient cash flow to finance their operations as well as pay back the loan. In addition, Loan Officers take into consideration the character, experience, and management skills of the loan applicants. Loan Officers also look at what collateral the applicants have in case they cannot pay the loan.

Loan Officers follow strict guidelines, which are set by their establishments, to make their final assessments. Along with the applications, officers examine supporting documents, such as business plans, financial statements, and income tax returns, that customers provide. Officers also check their applicants' credit histories.

Loan Officers generally do not make the final decisions to grant loans to borrowers. They make recommendations to their establishment on whether to approve or disapprove loan applications. The final decisions are made by managers or loan committees. In some institutions, Loan Officers may have the authority to approve loans for specific amounts.

When loans are approved, Loan Officers go over the terms, rates, and repayment schedules with their clients. After loan documents are signed, officers maintain contact with clients. They remain available to answer questions and address new financial issues that clients may have.

Loan Officers for commercial lenders are responsible for developing new clients for their establishments. They talk with potential customers to learn about their loan needs, and describe how their establishments can best serve customers. Many Loan Officers network with real estate agents, farm equipment dealers, insurance brokers, and others who may refer customers seeking loans for their purchases. Loan Officers also contact agricultural producers, farmers' cooperatives, and other agribusinesses to let them know about their services.

Agricultural Loan Officers perform a variety of tasks every day. For example, they might:

- schedule appointments with current and prospective clients
- attend staff meetings
- return phone calls, respond to e-mails, and write correspondence
- maintain complete and accurate loan records and files
- review loan applications
- examine loan agreements to ensure their accuracy and completeness
- compute payment schedules

- learn about new loan products or programs that their institutions offer
- keep up-to-date with new farming and other agricultural developments, technologies, and issues

Loan Officers work in offices. On occasion, they meet with clients at their offices, farms, or homes. Loan Officers work 40 hours a week and put in additional hours as needed to complete tasks.

Salaries

Salaries for Loan Officers vary depending on such factors as their education, experience, employer, and geographic location. According to the May 2008 Occupational Employment Statistics (OES) survey by the U.S. Bureau of Labor Statistics (BLS), the estimated annual salary for most Loan Officers ranged between $30,850 and $106,360. The estimated mean annual wage for these professionals was $63,540.

Some Loan Officers earn a salary, while others are paid a commission. Some officers receive both a salary and a commission, or bonus, for their loan sales. Commissions are based on the number of loans that officers generate.

Employment Prospects

Opportunities for Loan Officers are found nationwide. The BLS reports in its May 2008 OES survey that an estimated 321,850 Loan Officers were employed in the United States. The majority worked for commercial banks, savings and loans banks, credit unions, and related financial institutions.

Agricultural Loan Officers are employed by commercial lenders and cooperative banking institutions. They also find employment with agencies within the U.S. Department of Agriculture and state agricultural departments that sponsor farm loan programs.

The BLS reports that between 2008 and 2018, employment of Loan Officers is expected to increase by 10 percent. In addition to new positions created by employers, opportunities will become available as individuals retire, advance to higher positions, or transfer to other jobs or careers.

Job opportunities for Loan Officers can fluctuate with the state of the national economy. For example, low interest rates may give rise to a greater number of loan applications, which in turn may create more openings for Loan Officers.

Advancement Prospects

Loan Officers advance according to their interests and ambitions. Many officers measure their success by earning higher incomes, by gaining professional reputation, and through job satisfaction. Some Loan Officers pursue supervisory and managerial positions in their organizations.

Education and Training

Employers generally prefer to hire entry-level candidates who possess a bachelor's degree in finance, economics, agribusiness, or another related field. Employers may hire candidates without a college degree if they have extensive and qualifying work experience in banking or financial institutions.

Novice Loan Officers receive on-the-job training while working under the supervision and direction of supervisors, financial managers, and experienced loan officers. Employers may also provide trainees with formal classroom training.

Many financial institutions train employees at lower-level positions, such as bank tellers, customer service agents, or collection agents, to become Loan Officers. Such training generally takes several years.

Special Requirements

Loan Officers who make mortgage loans may be required to be licensed in the state in which they practice. They must fulfill continuing education requirements to renew their licenses. License requirements vary from state to state. For specific information, contact the appropriate state licensing agency.

Experience, Special Skills, and Personality Traits

Employers seek candidates for entry-level positions who have prior work experience in the lending or banking field. To work in the area of agricultural loans, candidates need one or more years of experience in farming, agribusiness, or in a related field. They also must be knowledgeable about farm operations, farm production, farm business management, land use and value, and agricultural marketing, among other agricultural topics.

Because they meet and handle many people from diverse backgrounds, Loan Officers must possess excellent interpersonal, communication, and customer service skills. They must also have effective sales, computer, writing, leadership, organizational, problem-solving, negotiating, and self-management skills to do well at their jobs. Being personable, tactful, patient, ethical, dependable, analytical, persistent, and flexible are some personality traits that successful Loan Officers have in common.

Unions and Associations

Agricultural Loan Officers can join professional associations to take advantage of networking opportunities, continuing education, and other professional services and resources. Two national societies that Loan Officers can join are the American Bankers Association and the Mortgage Bankers Association. For contact information, see Appendix II.

Tips for Entry

1. Some experts in the field suggest that taking high school or college courses in agriculture, business, computers, accounting, finance, mathematics, and business administration can prepare individuals for a careers as Loan Officers.

2. When you apply for an entry-level position (such as bank teller or customer service agent) at a financial institution, let your interviewer know about your interest in becoming a Loan Officer. Ask about Loan Officer training opportunities that the establishment offers and how you might eventually qualify for them.

3. To apply to work for federal government agencies, you must be a U.S. citizen. You must also be able to pass a rigid background investigation, which includes a fingerprint check.

4. Use the Internet to learn more about agricultural loans. You might start by visiting Agricultural Banking at the American Bankers Association Web site (www.aba.com/Solutions/Agricultural Banking.htm) and USDA Farm Service Agency Web site (www.fsa.usda.gov). For more links, see Appendix IV.

MARKETING SPECIALIST

CAREER PROFILE

Duties: Create, design, and implement effective marketing strategies and activities for clients; perform other duties as required

Alternate Title(s): Marketing Manager, Marketing Coordinator

Salary Range: $55,000 to $166,000

Employment Prospects: Good

Advancement Prospects: Fair

Prerequisites:

Education or Training—Bachelor's degree in marketing or another related field

Experience—Several years of work experience in marketing agricultural products, services, and programs

Special Skills and Personality Traits—Interpersonal, communication, customer service, leadership,

organizational, critical-thinking, problem-solving, self-management, research, writing, and computer skills; tactful, cooperative, persuasive, decisive, detail-oriented, self-motivated, flexible, and creative personality traits

Position Description

To manage successful enterprises, farmers, agribusinesses, and other establishments need effective marketing plans. Marketing refers to all of the activities involved in the promotion, sale, and distribution of products and services. To ensure their success, many farmers and business owners rely on professional men and women known as Marketing Specialists to assist them with their marketing efforts.

Agricultural Marketing Specialists are experts at creating and implementing marketing plans that maximize the profits an organization can make on its products and services while ensuring the satisfaction of its customers. Marketing Specialists also assist in locating or developing new or expanded markets for clients. Many of these specialists also advise clients on ways to improve the quality and marketability of their products and services.

Marketing Specialists who specialize in agriculture may work with farmers, farmers' cooperatives, retail establishments, government agencies, seed companies, manufacturers, academic establishments, and nongovernmental agricultural organizations, among others. Marketing Specialists may be employed as staff members or as consultants.

Agricultural Marketing Specialists are usually concerned with the marketing of one or more agricultural commodities or marketing programs. For example,

different specialists in an agricultural marketing firm might engage in the marketing of poultry, livestock, seafood, or organic products.

Along with understanding the principles of marketing, agricultural Marketing Specialists have a general knowledge of the agricultural commodities or programs on which they work. They are also familiar with the production, processing, and distribution of the commodities. In addition, they have an understanding of agricultural economics and business practices. Furthermore, they are aware of the laws and regulations that apply to agricultural commodities.

Much of these experts' work involve careful research and analysis of such questions as these: What are the client's requirements? Is there a demand for a product or service? Who is the competition? How is the product or service similar and different from the competition's? What groups of customers (or markets) would most likely want or need to purchase the product or service? What must the product or service have in order to interest customers to use it? How much are customers willing to pay for it? What are the most effective ways to attract customers to purchase it? What is the status of the economy?

Marketing Specialists design a marketing plan that is based on their findings and conclusions regarding the data they have gathered. These specialists determine the demand, competition, and potential markets for a product or service. They identify ways that a client can add extra value to it. For example, a vegetable farmer might clean, wash, and cut vegetables and pack them in biodegradable packages. Marketing specialists also formulate pricing strategies for the product or service. Furthermore, they develop marketing programs (such as sales, advertising, and public relations) that would best promote and sell the product or service.

Marketing Specialists establish close working relationships with clients. These marketing professionals also contact subject-matter experts (such as agricultural professors and Cooperative Extension Service agents) and business managers who have specific knowledge of the different aspects of the clients' services and products. In addition, Marketing Specialists seek assistance from other marketing professionals, such as market researchers, analysts, and product development managers, to complete projects. Marketing Specialists also work with advertising executives, promotions managers, sales managers, and public relations personnel to design and implement various marketing activities.

Marketing Specialists perform a wide variety of duties that vary according to their expertise and experience. For example, they might:

- coordinate marketing activities to promote products and services
- conduct market research or other studies for marketing projects
- gather and analyze statistical data
- keep up-to-date on information about marketing, commodities, trends, and other topics
- prepare promotional materials, such as brochures, press releases, and direct-mail materials
- participate in meetings with marketing staff, clients, or others as well as attend conferences with farmers' cooperatives, trade associations, and other organizations
- respond to questions or inquiries from clients, staff, and others through personal contact or correspondence, including letters, memorandums, and e-mail
- conduct training workshops for marketing or technical personnel
- supervise marketing staff

The job of Marketing Specialists is often stressful. They must meet strict deadlines as well as achieve goals set by their clients. Furthermore, Marketing Specialists make decisions and recommendations that may have an impact on the success and failure of agricultural producers and other agribusinesses.

Marketing Specialists mostly work in offices. They often put in more than 40 hours a week to complete their tasks and meet deadlines. It is common for them to work evenings and weekends. Marketing Specialists may be required to travel to other cities and states to meet with clients and others as well as to attend trade and professional conferences.

Salaries

Salaries for Marketing Specialists vary, depending on such factors as their education, experience, job duties, employer, and geographic location. Specific salary information for Marketing Specialists in the agriculture industry is unavailable. Market Specialists are also known as marketing managers. In general, the estimated annual salary for most marketing managers ranges between $55,270 and $166,400, according to the May 2008 Occupational Employment Statistics (OES) survey by the U.S. Bureau of Labor Statistics (BLS).

Employment Prospects

Opportunities for Marketing Specialists are found nationwide and in every industry. The BLS reports in its May 2008 OES survey that an estimated 166,790 marketing managers were employed in the United States. Agricultural Marketing Specialists are employed by government agencies such as the U.S. Department of Agriculture, Cooperative Extension System, and state departments of agriculture. They also find employment with agricultural trade associations, agricultural cooperatives, and other types of nonprofit and nongovernmental organizations that serve agricultural interests. In addition, Marketing Specialists are hired by agricultural businesses, food processing plants, manufacturers, distributors, and other private establishments.

According to the BLS, employment of marketing managers in general is expected to increase by 12 percent between the period of 2008 and 2018. In addition to job growth, openings will become available as Marketing Specialists advance, transfer to other jobs, or retire.

Marketing is a popular career field due to its creative and challenging nature as well as its potential for high earnings. Competition, therefore, is keen for both entry-level and experienced positions.

Advancement Prospects

Marketing professionals typically begin their careers as marketing associates and market researchers. Those with supervisory and managerial talents and ambitions can advance through the management ranks to top executive positions. Entrepreneurial individuals can start their own marketing firms or become independent consultants.

Some Marketing Specialists measure their success by earning higher wages, by receiving assignments of their choice, and through job satisfaction.

Education and Training

Minimally, agricultural Marketing Specialists must possess a bachelor's degree in marketing, business administration, agricultural economics, or another relevant field. Some employers prefer to hire applicants with a master's or doctoral degree. Employers may hire candidates with degrees in agriculture, if they have gained the appropriate training and experience in agricultural marketing.

Throughout their careers, marketing professionals enroll in continuing education programs and company training programs to update their skills and knowledge.

Experience, Special Skills, and Personality Traits

Individuals are hired as Marketing Specialists after several years of working in marketing. Applicants for agricultural specialists usually need one or more years of full-time work experience in the marketing, market research, or economic analysis of agricultural products. Employers also prefer to hire candidates who have previous experience in their particular industry, such as organic farming, farm machinery, or beef cattle ranching.

Marketing Specialists work with customers, colleagues, managers, and many others with diverse backgrounds. Hence, they must have excellent interpersonal, communication, and customer service skills. In addition, they need excellent leadership, organizational, critical-thinking, problem-solving, and self-management skills

to perform their various duties effectively. Having strong research, writing, and computer skills is also essential. Being tactful, cooperative, persuasive, decisive, detail-oriented, self-motivated, flexible, and creative are some personality traits that successful Marketing Specialists share.

Unions and Associations

Agricultural Marketing Specialists can join professional associations to take advantage of networking opportunities, continuing education, and other professional services and resources. Some national societies that serve the interests of these professionals are the National Agri-Marketing Association and the American Marketing Association. For contact information, see Appendix II.

Tips for Entry

1. As you begin your marketing career, seek an entry-level position with a company for which you are interested in working. Be willing to take work assignments that are outside your interests.

2. Speaking another language may enhance your employability, as the agricultural industry is becoming increasingly global.

3. Do you plan to attach your résumé to a job application? Be sure you fill out the application completely. Some employers consider applications with the words *see résumé* on them as being incomplete.

4. Use the Internet to learn more about agricultural marketing. You might start by visiting the Web sites for the Agricultural Marketing Resource Center (www.agmrc.org). For more links, see Appendix IV.

RURAL APPRAISER

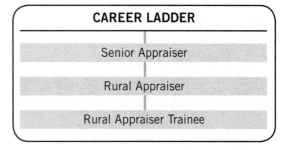

Position Description

When individuals and organizations are interested in knowing the current value of a piece of property, they usually employ the services of appraisers. Their job is to conduct an objective study of the property, and then provide their clients with an estimate of how much the property is currently worth.

Professionals who specialize in assessing the value of agricultural properties are called Rural Appraisers. They assess real property, which refers to parcels of land and all the structures (such as barns and houses), fences, landscaping, natural resources, and rights (such as easement or water rights) that are on them. They also examine such industrial properties as grain storage systems, packing house operations, and food processing plants.

Many Rural Appraisers estimate the value of agricultural chattels, or personal property items, such as livestock, crops, processed products, supplies, equipment, and vehicles. In addition, Rural Appraisers value business operations, which involves reviewing tangible property as well as such intangible assets as patents, trademarks, contracts, and goodwill.

Rural Appraisers conduct appraisals for land owners, agribusinesses, attorneys, accountants, banks, financial institutions, accounting firms, real estate agents, insurance companies, government agencies, nonprofit organizations, and various other individuals and organizations. Appraisals on agricultural property are sought for a wide range of purposes, including property sales or purchases, tax planning, estate settlements, inventory reports, company acquisitions or mergers, litigation support, bank loans, bankruptcies, insurance coverage or claims, and charitable donations, among other personal or business transactions.

Rural Appraisers are highly knowledgeable about the types of agricultural property they assess. They follow standard appraisal procedures established by professional appraisal organizations. They also comply with company policies. These appraisers are responsible for staying up-to-date with relevant markets. Some Rural Appraisers are qualified to provide testimony as expert witnesses in civil and criminal court trials.

Appraisers are expected to perform unbiased and reliable studies and to deliver their results promptly to clients. Their appraisals involve careful physical inspection of properties. Appraisers take thorough notes of their observations, and may take photographs of properties for documentation. Appraisers also collect and review any applicable legal and historical documents about properties, including contracts, maps, receipts, invoices, and financial records. Additionally, they interview owners, employees, and others for information. Appraisers may consult with experts to further understand certain aspects about the properties they are assessing. For example, a Rural Appraiser might contact agricultural scientists, Cooperative Extension Service agents, and economists to ask questions regarding grain crops and markets.

Rural Appraisers also research the current value for similar properties nationwide as well as within local areas. This may entail reading market reports, checking public records, and searching computer and Internet databases. Appraisers analyze and evaluate data to arrive at estimates of the current monetary value of properties. They then prepare comprehensive and concise reports about their research, observations, findings, and conclusions. They also explain in their reports the purpose of the appraisals and the methodologies that they use to conduct their appraisals. Rural Appraisers are expected to present technical concepts in terms that can be clearly understood by clients and others.

Depending on the size and complexity of appraisal projects, Rural Appraisers may work alone, with a partner, or on a team with other appraisers. Rural Appraisers work in offices to complete many of their tasks. They also spend time on sites where they inspect property and review documents.

Rural Appraisers may work full-time or part-time. They often put in long hours to complete tasks and meet deadlines. Their hours are often irregular, which may include working evenings and on weekends. Appraisers make on-site visits when they are convenient to their clients.

Salaries

Salaries for Rural Appraisers vary, depending on such factors as their education, experience, employer, and geographic location. Wage information specifically for this occupation is unavailable. A general idea of their earnings can be gained by looking at what real estate appraisers earn. The estimated annual salary for most real estate appraisers ranged between $25,900 and $88,680, according to the May 2008 Occupational Employment Statistics survey by the U.S. Bureau of Labor Statistics (BLS).

Employment Prospects

Appraisers work for appraisal companies, real estate agencies, financial institutions, accounting firms, insurance companies, government agencies, and other organizations. Some appraisers are self-employed.

Some experts in the field state that opportunities for appraisers, in general, are favorable, regardless of the state of the economy. Appraisals by qualified professionals are continually needed by property owners,

attorneys, insurance companies, financial institutions, government agencies, companies, and various types of organizations. The BLS reports that employment of real estate appraisers is expected to increase by 5 percent during the 2008–18 period.

Advancement Prospects

Rural Appraisers advance according to their interests and ambitions. Many appraisers measure their success by earning higher incomes, by gaining professional reputation, and through job satisfaction. Appraisers also seek higher professional designations, which are offered by professional associations.

As Rural Appraisers gain experience, they may specialize in the types of appraisals they perform. Some appraisers pursue supervisory and managerial positions in their organizations. Entrepreneurial individuals become self-employed appraisers or owners of appraisal companies.

Education and Training

Minimally, trainees must hold a high school diploma or a general equivalency diploma. Some employers require that trainees have some college background. Other employers prefer to hire trainees who possess either an associate's or bachelor's degree in business, economics, finance, real estate, or another related field.

Some appraisers learn their skills on the job or by completing an apprenticeship. Trainees work under the direction and supervision of professional appraisers. Alternatively, individuals can complete appraisal programs or courses offered by professional appraisal associations or academic institutions. Through formal programs, students learn about appraisal theory, procedures, ethics, governmental regulations, report writing, and other subjects. Some programs require enrollees to possess an appropriate bachelor's degree.

Depending on the state, individuals may need to fulfill college-level education requirements, such as a bachelor's degree, to be licensed as real estate appraisers.

Special Requirements

Real estate appraisers are required to be licensed or certified in the states where they practice. Trainees may also be required to be licensed. Those who perform real property appraisals involving federally related transactions are required to hold a state-issued professional appraiser license.

Requirements for appraisal licensing vary from state to state. However, all states conform to the standard requirements established by the Appraisal Qualifications Board, which is part of the Appraisal Foundation.

Appraisers must complete minimum continuing education requirements to maintain their licenses or certifications. For specific information, contact the real property appraiser agency in the state where you wish to practice.

Experience, Special Skills, and Personality Traits

Employers typically hire candidates who have several years of working in the appraisal field. They may have gained their experience through an apprenticeship or on-the-job training. Employers also seek candidates who are highly knowledgeable about the property categories with which they would work. They must also be familiar with local and national markets.

Rural Appraisers must have strong critical-thinking, self-management, research, writing, mathematical, and computer skills. Because they work with many people from diverse backgrounds, appraisers need excellent interpersonal, communication, and customer service skills. Being polite, patient, detail-oriented, honest, unbiased, meticulous, decisive, and dependable are some personality traits that successful Rural Appraisers share.

Unions and Associations

Many Rural Appraisers join professional associations to take advantage of networking opportunities, continuing education, professional certification, and other professional services and resources. Some national societies that serve the diverse interests of Rural Appraisers are:

- American Society of Agricultural Appraisers
- American Society of Appraisers
- American Society of Equine Appraisers
- American Society of Farm Equipment Appraisers
- American Society of Farm Managers and Rural Appraisers
- International Society of Livestock Appraisers
- National Association of Independent Fee Appraisers

For contact information, see Appendix II.

Tips for Entry

1. Contact professional appraisers directly about trainee or apprenticeship opportunities with their firms.
2. Let prospective employers know about any connections you might have to real estate agents, banks, financial institutions, or other businesses that may need future appraisal services.
3. To enhance their employability, some appraisers obtain professional certification on a voluntary basis.
4. Individuals who can appraise different types of property may have a greater number of opportunities for employment.
5. Use the Internet to learn more about the appraisal field. You might start by visiting the Web sites of these organizations: the American Society of Farm Managers and Rural Appraisers (www.asfmra.org) and the Appraisal Foundation (www.appraisalfoundation.org). For more links, see Appendix IV.

SALES REPRESENTATIVE

CAREER PROFILE

Duties: Promote and sell products and services directly to customers in the field; build and maintain a customer base; perform duties as required

Alternate Title(s): Agricultural Sales Representative, Farm Sales Representative

Salary Range: $35,000 to $133,000

Employment Prospects: Good

Advancement Prospects: Good

Prerequisites:

    Education or Training—On-the-job training and instruction from employers

    Experience—Several years of sales experience; agricultural background

    Special Skills and Personality Traits—Interpersonal, communication, customer service, leadership, self-management, organizational, problem-solving, critical-thinking, writing, and computer skills; friendly, trustworthy, persuasive, tactful, goal-oriented, persistent, patient, creative, and flexible personality traits

CAREER LADDER

Senior Sales Representative

Sales Representative

Junior Sales Representative

Position Description

Sales Representatives are essential to the health and vitality of any industry, and agriculture is no exception. They are the professionals who ensure that goods and services provided or used by the agriculture industry are made available for all who benefit from them. These Sales Representatives are experts about the agricultural products and services that they sell. They are familiar with the type of customers they serve and the geographic territories they cover. Many of them became involved with agricultural sales because they were raised on or had worked on farms or had previous sales experience in agricultural communities.

Sales Representatives help support a variety of agricultural areas of concern, including agricultural mechanics, chemicals and pharmaceuticals, animal and feed production, crop production, and general agricultural supplies. In each of these areas, Sales Representatives specialize by selling particular products and providing services to support the use of those products. For example, those who focus on the area of chemicals and pharmaceuticals sell such products as pesticides, fertilizers, animal antibiotic medicines, livestock hormones, and cleaning products directly to farmers. They also sell these products to feed stores and other retail enterprises that are in the business of selling them to farmers and ranchers in their area. Sales Representatives bring with them a thorough knowledge of how these products work and how they may be used safely and effectively to amend soils, improve crop production, fight plant and animal diseases, and more.

For another example, Sales Representatives who specialize in the area of farm mechanics sell farm and ranch machines and equipment to agricultural businesses including ranchers and farmers, equipment dealerships, and any other businesses that utilize such equipment as tractors, harvesters, tillers, milking machines, and other machines or tools. These professionals are also knowledgeable about how these machines work and how they must be maintained. In addition, they carry with them an understanding about basic repair techniques as well as resources for finding repair shops within the boundaries of their sales territories.

Sales Representatives who work in the other agricultural sales areas are likewise knowledgeable about seeds, stone fruit trees, animal nutritional supplements, fencing materials, fuels, and numerous other products that they sell to farmers, food distributors, and other agricultural concerns. They are equipped to make referrals to technical experts who can resolve special problems that their customers may have with the products that Sales Representatives sell.

Agricultural Sales Representatives are assigned to cover specific sales territories within the state or region where their companies market their products and services. Some professionals are assigned to foreign cities.

All Sales Representatives are responsible for developing and maintaining a customer base within their territories. Their customers may include agricultural producers, retailers, distributors, veterinarians, animal clinics, government agencies, private companies, and others.

Sales Representatives complete similar tasks regardless of the products or services they sell. They contact prospective customers in person or by mail, e-mail, or telephone. They also make unannounced visits or calls to prospective customers to present their sales packages. These sales professionals make follow-up calls to set appointments for future visits. Additionally, Sales Representatives:

- maintain a list of customers in their territory
- demonstrate their products and provide samples or catalogs to help their customers select their purchases
- recommend new products that are available from their companies
- provide such information as prices for their products and services along with credit terms
- draw up sales or credit contracts
- provide delivery schedules, installation instructions, warranties, or other documented information pertinent to their customers' needs
- write reports of their sales and other work activities to submit to company administrators
- assist with the development of new or improved products for their companies
- keep up with new developments and technologies in agriculture
- participate in trade shows, professional conferences, and conventions to promote products and make new contacts

Sales Representatives visit customers within their territories on a regular basis.

In general, manufacturing companies and wholesalers employ Sales Representatives. Some Sales Representatives are self-employed and contract themselves to several companies.

Some agriculture Sales Representatives are known as inside sales representatives, who mostly work in office settings. They make contact with potential clients via telephone or letter. Still other Sales Representatives are employed as sales engineers. These men and women are more technically savvy about the products they sell and thus have the additional duties of helping their customers resolve technical problems. For example, they might install products, perform maintenance and repairs on products, or train customers about how to use the products they sell.

Sales Representatives typically work long days and irregular hours. They arrange their own work schedules and often work during evenings or weekends to meet customers. Many Sales Representatives travel great distances within their territories and sometimes stay away from home for several days or weeks at a time.

Salaries

Salaries for Sales Representatives vary, depending on such factors as their education, experience, employer, industry and geographic location. According to the May 2008 Occupational Employment Statistics (OES) survey by the U.S. Bureau of Labor Statistics (BLS), the estimated annual salary for most Sales Representatives who worked for wholesalers and manufacturers ranged between $34,980 and $133,040. (These figures are for sales professionals who sell technical and scientific products.)

In addition to earning a salary, many Sales Representatives receive commissions or a bonus that is based on their job performance. Some employers reimburse Sales Representatives for their expenses, such as lodging, meals, transportation, and home office costs.

Employment Prospects

Agricultural Sales Representatives are employed by a wide range of wholesalers and manufacturers of agricultural products and services, including seeds, farm machinery, dairy equipment, agricultural tools, pesticides, fertilizers, animal feed, and animal pharmaceuticals, among others. They may be hired as employees or independent contractors.

Opportunities for Sales Representatives of scientific and technical products and services are found in virtually every private industry. Agricultural sales professionals may transfer their skills and experience to sales positions in such industries as food processing, grocery products, biotechnology, pharmaceuticals, chemical processing, electronics, construction, and industrial machinery and equipment. According to the May 2008 OES survey by the BLS, approximately 415,120 Sales Representatives of technical and scientific products were employed in the United States.

In general, job openings become available as Sales Representatives transfer to other jobs or career fields or leave the workforce for various reasons. Employers may create additional positions as their enterprises grow. The BLS reports that employment of Sales Representatives that sell technical and scientific products for wholesalers and manufacturers is expected to increase by 10 percent between 2008 and 2018.

Job prospects in sales depend upon such variables as consumer preferences and the health of the economy. During economic downturns, for example, employers may hire fewer employees or lay off employees.

Advancement Prospects

Many Sales Representatives measure their success through job satisfaction, by earning higher incomes, by meeting or exceeding sales goals, and by gaining professional recognition.

Sales professionals with supervisory and management ambitions can rise through the ranks to become executive offices. Entrepreneurial individuals can become independent manufacturer's agents.

Some Sales Representatives use their experience to move into other business areas such as marketing, advertising, purchasing, or finance.

Education and Training

Educational requirements vary among agricultural companies. Minimally, Sales Representatives must hold a high school diploma or a general equivalency diploma. They may also be required to have an associate's or bachelor's degree in agriculture, business, or another field.

Entry-level Sales Representatives receive extensive training from their employers, which in some companies lasts one to two years. Trainees receive instruction about the company, its various departments, and its products and services. In addition, they undergo training in sales techniques, marketing, presentation skills, and other sales topics. Novices also receive on-the-job training. They work under the supervision and direction of experienced Sales Representatives for several months before being allowed to perform sales duties on their own.

Experience, Special Skills, and Personality Traits

Agricultural companies prefer to hire candidates for sales positions who have several years of sales experience. Ideally candidates have a background in agriculture, which they may have gained through employment, studies, or personal experience. Candidates should also have knowledge about the agriculture industry, such as farm equipment or livestock feed, in which they will work.

Because they deal with many people from diverse backgrounds daily, Sales Representatives must have excellent interpersonal, communication, and customer service skills. These professionals also need effective leadership, self-management, organizational, problem-solving, and critical-thinking skills. Having strong writing and computer skills is also essential.

Some personality traits that successful Sales Representatives share include being friendly, trustworthy, persuasive, tactful, goal-oriented, persistent, patient, creative, and flexible.

Unions and Associations

Sales Representatives can join professional and trade associations to take advantage of networking opportunities. These organizations also offer various services and resources such as training programs, professional certification, and publications. A professional association that serves the needs of independent agricultural Sales Representatives is the Agricultural and Industrial Manufacturers Representatives Association. For contact information, see Appendix II.

Tips for Entry

1. Increasingly, employers prefer to hire Sales Representatives who possess a college degree.
2. Before going to a job interview, learn as much as you can about a company's products and services.
3. Employers may require that candidates have a valid driver's license and possess a clean driving record.
4. Many companies post job vacancies on their Web site. Some also take advantage of placing job announcements at online agricultural networks.
5. Use the Internet to learn about the different types of agricultural wholesalers and manufacturers. To get a list of Web sites, enter any of these keywords into a search engine: *agricultural wholesalers*, *agricultural manufacturers*, or *agricultural products*.

FOOD AND
BEVERAGE
INDUSTRIES

BAKER

CAREER PROFILE

Duties: Measure, weigh, mix, and bake breads, cakes, pies, pastries, and other baked goods; perform other duties as required

Alternate Title(s): Production Baker, Pastry Chef; a title that reflects a position (such as Sous-Chef) or specialty (such as Cake Decorator)

Salary Range: $16,000 to $37,000

Employment Prospects: Good

Advancement Prospects: Fair

Prerequisites:

    Education or Training—High school diploma; apprenticeship or completion of a culinary arts program; on-the-job training

    Experience—Previous experience in baking or food preparation and service required

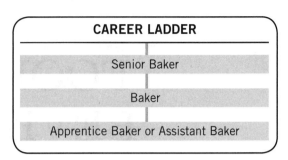

Special Skills and Personality Traits—Organizational, time-management, teamwork, interpersonal, communication skills; reliable, detail-oriented, determined, and self-motivated personality traits

Position Description

People all around the world enjoy eating breads, pastries, and other sweet and savory baked foods made from dough. Many people like to make these foods in their homes, while others rely on experts called Bakers. These baking experts make it possible for people to purchase these delicious products at grocery stores, bakeries, and specialty cake and pastry shops. Bakers are well versed about baking ingredients and the chemistry involved in combining them. They are masters at creating appealing baked goods by using various techniques to produce them efficiently.

Bakers work in bakery facilities of varying sizes, including independently owned neighborhood bakeries, doughnut shops, hotel bakeries, restaurant bake shops, bakery departments in supermarkets, and large factories that produce enormous quantities of baked goods for distribution to retail stores. Those who work in small bakeries make all sorts of baked goods, while production Bakers, who work in factory bakeries, usually perform one or two steps in the baking process of certain products. Production Bakers are also known as batch makers.

Bakers prepare a variety of items according to recipes they create or that were established by their employers. They generally follow the same basic procedures to create their products. They use scales and various sizes of containers to measure flour, water, and other ingre-

dients to create batters, dough, icings, and fillings. They mix their ingredients in mixing bowls; knead, roll, and cut the dough or batter into desired shapes. Bakers may perform their tasks by hand or with the help of electric mixers, blenders, and other appliances. Those who work in factory environments normally use large mixer equipment to help them combine sizeable amounts of ingredients.

They place their creations onto oven sheets, into cake pans, or into muffin tins and bake them in ovens at specific temperatures. Ovens in production bakeries are large enough to bake hundreds of items simultaneously. Bakers put finished baked goods on racks to cool and ready them for sale. For example, Bakers may slice bread, wrap the loaves, and tie or seal the packages; they may decorate baked goods with icings or such toppings as fruit or sprinkles.

Bakers are responsible for adhering to strict hygienic and safety standards. They keep their equipment and work areas maintained and spotlessly clean at all times. These experts monitor mixers and may be required to repair them. Bakers also keep records of their output of baked goods. Some Bakers spend time working bakery counters. They take orders, help customers select items to buy, run the cash register, and make change.

Depending on their experience and level of expertise, Bakers have differing responsibilities. They start their careers as apprentices or assistants. They learn every aspect of the baking trade while working under the direction of established Bakers. Journey-level Bakers keep stocks of ingredients replenished; clean equipment; measure, mix, and form baked goods; attend to ovens; and prepare finished products for sale. Master Bakers oversee production processes and manage the inventory of ingredients and materials. Bakery chefs, also known as pastry chefs, oversee an entire team of Bakers and attend to the administrative tasks of running the business. They organize production schedules and manage their staff of Bakers. These experts continue to produce baked goods but generally focus on decorating custom specialty items in their own signature style.

Bakers may specialize in particular areas of the baking vocation. Some of them are test Bakers who create and try new recipes. They make note of the weight and quantity of each ingredient, compare the various kinds of finished products, and keep records of their endeavors for future reference if their creations are saleworthy. Test Bakers may specialize further by specifically testing cakes. They bake premixed cakes, biscuits, pancakes, or muffins to check how they measure up to preferred criteria before the mixes are produced and packaged for the market. Other Bakers specialize by decorating cakes and creating new designs and techniques for performing this work. Still others focus on baking breads, cookies, pies, cupcakes, or other baked goods.

Production Bakers who work in factories normally are assigned to perform specific tasks. They generally contribute to one process of making baked goods by running the machines that perform certain tasks, such as mixing dough, blending flour, running products through ovens, or placing breads on cooling racks. Many of the machines that production Bakers use are computer-controlled and these experts are well-versed in their operation.

Bakers work in a physically demanding occupation. They perform repetitive work while standing or walking. During the course of their day, they may lift heavy mixing bowls and sacks of ingredients that weigh as much as 100 pounds. Some of the hazards with which they contend include hot temperatures, moving machine components, and flour dust that they might inhale.

Bakers may be required to wear aprons, hairnets, and face masks. Some Bakers wear uniforms and hats.

These professionals generally work five days per week, which may include working on a Saturday or Sunday. Their workdays may begin as early as 2:00 or 3:00 A.M. Some bakeries operate around the clock;

consequently, some Bakers work in shifts. Production Bakers may be required to work on holidays.

Salaries

Salaries for Bakers vary, depending on such factors as their training, experience, position, employer, and geographic location. According to the May 2008 Occupational Employment Statistics (OES) survey by the U.S. Bureau of Labor Statistics (BLS), the estimated annual salary for most Bakers ranged between $16,420 and $37,250. The estimated hourly wage for most of these professionals ranged from $7.89 to $17.91. Pastry chefs and other senior bakers can expect to earn higher wages.

Employment Prospects

The BLS reported in its May 2008 OES survey that an estimated 141,130 Bakers were employed in the United States. The highest levels of employment for Bakers were found in the bakeries and tortilla manufacturing industry, the grocery store industry, and the industry consisting of limited-service eating places such as fast-food restaurants. Some other employers include restaurants, pastry shops, catering companies, hotels and resorts, food-service management companies, government agencies, and academic institutions, among others.

Opportunities are continually favorable for highly skilled bakers. According to the BLS, employment of Bakers is expected to show little or no change in growth between 2008 and 2018. In general, Bakers will be needed to replace those who retire or transfer to other jobs or career fields.

Advancement Prospects

Bakers advance according to their interests and ambitions. Some seek supervisory and managerial positions within their organizations. For example, Bakers in grocery stores can be promoted to team leader, supervisor, and department manager positions. Some Bakers choose to specialize in a particular area, such as cake decorating or baking specialty breads, wedding cakes, or other specific types of products. After gaining experience, entrepreneurial individuals establish their own bakeries or specialty pastry shops.

Education and Training

Most, if not all, employers require that applicants for Baker positions possess at least a high school diploma or general equivalency diploma.

Individuals can pursue several avenues to become Bakers. One path is for persons to complete apprenticeships. Apprentices learn the baking craft while working for several years under highly skilled Bakers.

Culinary apprenticeship programs may be found through schools, colleges, and professional associations, such as the American Culinary Federation.

Another path for individuals is to enroll in a culinary arts program to earn a degree or certificate in professional baking. Vocational schools, private culinary schools, and colleges throughout the United States offer such programs in which students learn about the techniques and theories of baking breads, pastries, and other baked goods.

Individuals can also obtain training while working as assistants in bakeries, restaurants, catering companies, cafeterias, and other food-service establishments and businesses. Assistants learn baking and other culinary skills while working under the direction and supervision of experienced bakers and chefs. Some employers provide employees with formal training opportunities to gain and improve their baking skills.

Experience, Special Skills, and Personality Traits

Employers prefer to hire candidates for entry-level positions who have bakery or food preparation and service experience. Candidates may have gained their experience through training programs, employment, or volunteer work.

To work well in their field, Bakers must have excellent organizational, time-management, teamwork, interpersonal, and communication skills. They must also have the physical stamina and strength to work long hours and perform physically demanding tasks. Being reliable, detail-oriented, determined, and self-motivated are some personality traits that successful Bakers have in common.

Unions and Associations

Some production Bakers belong to a union, such as the Bakery, Confectionery, Tobacco Workers, and Grain Millers International Union, that represents them in contract negotiations for better terms regarding pay, benefits, and working conditions. A union also handles any grievances that its members may have against their employers.

Some Bakers join professional associations to take advantage of networking opportunities, professional certification, continuing education, and other professional services and resources. The Bread Bakers Guild of America and the International Association of Culinary Professionals are two societies that serve the diverse interests of professional Bakers.

Bakery owners might join trade associations such as the Independent Bakers Association and the American Bakers Association.

For contact information to the above organizations, see Appendix II.

Tips for Entry

1. Some experts in the field say that many professional Bakers began as home Bakers who were passionate about making baked goods.
2. While in high school, take home economics or vocational cooking courses. You might also check a local community college or community center for class offerings in baking, cake decorating, or other culinary areas that interest you.
3. If you are interested in one day owning a bakery, take bookkeeping, marketing, and other business courses.
4. Talk to Bakers at the bakeries at which you shop. Ask them about how they got into the field. Also, let them know about your interest in becoming a Baker and what suggestions they might have for you to enter the field.
5. Use the Internet to learn more about Bakers. You might start by visiting Bakery-Net (bakery-net. com). For more links, see Appendix IV.

MEAT CUTTER (RETAIL)

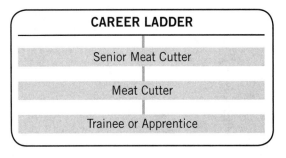

Position Description

Most of us enjoy eating hamburgers, steak, pork ribs, and lamb chops as part of nutritious, balanced diets. What many of us do not realize is how, exactly, the meats we eat end up in neatly wrapped packages at the supermarket. The men and women who work behind the scenes to prepare meats for sale are called Meat Cutters.

Meat cutting or butchery is a trade that has been around for centuries. Traditionally, Meat Cutters are known as butchers. The job titles are often used interchangeably. Some people distinguish the two occupations by the type of work that is performed. Butchers usually engage in primary meat cutting. They select quarters, sides, and carcasses of meat that they will separate into smaller pieces called primal cuts. They trim, prepare, and store primal cuts for secondary butchering that is completed by Meat Cutters. They carve, bone, trim, slice, chop, cube, and mince the pieces of meat for consumers to use in meal preparation. Many Meat Cutters and butchers are able to perform both primary and secondary types of meat cutting.

Meat Cutters, as well as butchers, are highly knowledgeable about the various kinds of standard cuts of beef, pork, lamb, and other types of meat. Steaks, chops, fillets, rib racks, and bacon are among the basic cuts that these experts are skilled at preparing. They also make ground meats and sausages, and shape, lace, and tie roasts. Some prepare meats through corning, smoking, tenderizing, and other preserving methods.

Most Meat Cutters work in the meat departments of grocery and wholesale retailers, as well as at butcher shops. These experts prepare standard cuts of meats for self-service or meat counters. They also cut meats to customer specifications. Some Meat Cutters prepare only one type of meat (such as beef), while others work with all kinds of meats. Many Meat Cutters also cut and debone poultry as well as clean, scale, and cut fish into steaks or fillets.

Many retail Meat Cutters, particularly those who work at meat counters, interact with customers. They fill customers' meat orders, assist them with choosing meats, and even provide advice about cooking meats. Some Meat Cutters are responsible for completing sales transactions, which includes taking money from customers and giving them back the correct change.

Meat Cutters are expected to follow governmental standards concerning weights, measures, and labeling. In addition, they are required to comply with company and governmental safety, health, and sanitation standards.

Meat Cutters perform various general tasks, which vary according to their skill level and experience. For example, they might:

- weigh cuts of meat, wrap them, and label them
- arrange meats, poultry, fish, and shellfish in refrigerated display cases
- receive meat deliveries, inspect all delivered items, and store them properly

- record the amounts of goods received and delivered or sold
- take inventory of meat supplies and order fresh supplies of needed cuts
- inspect and maintain cutting tools and equipment
- clean work areas
- keep up with current pricing schedules
- train novice Meat Cutters

These men and women use a variety of tools, including hand tools such as knives for slicing and removing bones, cleavers for cutting bones, and meat hooks for hanging carcasses. Meat Cutters usually own their knives. Some Meat Cutters handle power tools and machines, such as saws to cut bones, slicers to shave off very thin meat slices, and machines to make sausages. They also use knife sharpeners, cutting blocks, and weight scales, as well as wrapping and vacuum-pack machines to package meats.

Meat Cutters work in cold, damp indoor environments. Meat is stored in refrigerated facilities, which range in temperature from freezing to sub-zero temperatures. Cutting areas are generally kept at temperatures between 40 and 50 degrees Fahrenheit.

Their line of work is hazardous. They are exposed to wastes and cleaning solvents. Blood, fats, and condensation contribute to dampness and slippery floors, which can cause falls. Meat Cutters also contend with the threat of injury from sharp knives, saws, and other cutting devices. Consequently, these experts are required to wear safety gear, such as belly guards, masks, and goggles. Meat Cutters are sometimes exposed to loud sound levels.

Their work is physically demanding, as Meat Cutters must be able to stand for long periods, lift as much as 100 pounds, and perform other physical movements such as reaching and walking. These experts may incur carpal tunnel syndrome or other painful disorders by performing repetitive motions.

These experts generally work for 40 hours per week. Meat plant employees may be assigned to work shifts. Meat Cutters who work in retail and food-service establishments may be required to work on weekends or holidays.

Salaries

Salaries for Meat Cutters vary, depending on their experience, job duties, employer, geographic location, and other factors. The U.S. Bureau of Labor Statistics (BLS) reported in its May 2008 Occupational Employment Statistics (OES) survey that the estimated hourly wage for most Meat Cutters ranged between $8.46 and $21.66. The estimated annual salary for these men and women ranged between $17,600 and $45,060.

In addition to salaries, some Meat Cutters earn bonuses based on their job performance.

Employment Prospects

Meat Cutters are employed throughout the United States. The BLS reported in its May 2008 OES survey that an estimated 128,210 Meat Cutters and butchers were working in the United States. Nearly 70 percent of them were employed by grocery stores. Some other employers of Meat Cutters are independent butcher shops; meatpacking and processing plants; specialty food stores; restaurants and other food-service operations; and the federal government.

The BLS reports that employment of Meat Cutters should remain steady through the 2008–18 period. However, jobs for the Meat Cutters in retail stores is expected to decline as more meat is being cut and processed by Meat Cutters in meat processing and packing plants. Most job openings become available when Meat Cutters advance to higher positions, retire, or transfer to other jobs or career fields.

Advancement Prospects

Meat Cutters advance by earning higher wages and being assigned greater levels of responsibilities. They can also be promoted to become team leaders, supervisors, and department managers. Meat Cutters can also pursue other careers in the meat industry by becoming meat buyers or meat inspectors.

Individuals with entrepreneurial ambitions may choose to open their own meat markets.

Education and Training

Employers prefer to hire applicants who hold at least a high school diploma or general equivalency diploma.

Individuals can learn the craft of meat cutting through on-the-job training. Trainees work under the direction and supervision of experienced butchers and meat cutters. Depending on the meat cutting operations, training may last several days for simple tasks to several months for more complicated tasks. It generally takes one to two years of training to become a highly skilled Meat Cutter.

Alternatively, individuals can complete an apprenticeship, which is sponsored jointly by a union and the apprentice's employer. Apprentices complete classroom instruction in addition to fulfilling supervised on-the-job training. Apprenticeships are usually two years long.

Experience, Special Skills, and Personality Traits

Employers prefer to hire individuals for entry-level positions who have some meat cutting experience. Applicants may have gained their experience through part-time employment, work-study programs, or volunteer work. Many employers hire candidates without experience, as long as the candidates demonstrate a willingness and dedication to learn the meat cutting trade.

Meat Cutters must have strong interpersonal and teamwork skills as well as excellent self-management skills, such as the ability to handle stressful situations, work independently, organize tasks, and follow and understand instructions. Meat Cutters who wait on customers need to have effective communication and customer service skills. All Meat Cutters need to have proficient writing, math, and computer skills. Some personality traits that successful Meat Cutters share include being friendly, courteous, honest, orderly, and dependable.

Unions and Associations

Meat Cutters may join labor unions to represent them in contract negotiations with their employers for better terms regarding pay, benefits, and working conditions. Unions also handle any grievances that officers may have against their employers. The United Food and Commercial Workers International Union (UFCW) is one organization that represents the interests of Meat Cutters. For contact information, see Appendix II.

Tips for Entry

1. Employers usually require that applicants for apprenticeships be at least 18 years old.
2. While in high school, get a part-time job or a work-experience position at a butcher shop or a grocery store to start getting practical experience.
3. Apply directly at butcher shops, grocery stores, and other establishments where you would like to work.
4. When you apply for a job, be sure you are well-groomed to make a strong first impression. Also, bring a pen, and make sure it works, to fill out job applications. In addition, prepare the information you need about your education, work experience, and references beforehand so that you can copy the details onto the application.
5. Use the Internet to learn more about Meat Cutters and their work. To get a list of Web sites, enter the keywords *meat cutting*, *meat cutters*, *butchers*, *meat processing*, or *meat processing plants* into a search engine. For some links, see Appendix IV.

WINEMAKER

Duties: Direct the activities involved in producing wine; perform management and administrative duties; perform other duties as required

Alternate Title(s): Enologist, Vintner

Salary Range: $63,000 to $149,000

Employment Prospects: Fair

Advancement Prospects: Fair

Prerequisites:

Education or Training—Bachelor's degree preferred

Experience—Several years of experience in the wine industry

Special Skills and Personality Traits—Leadership, organizational, planning, time-management,

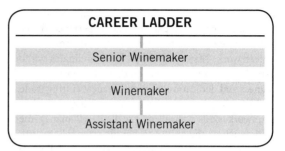

teamwork, interpersonal, communication, public relations, writing, and computer skills; observant, analytical, self-motivated, inspirational, flexible, determined, and detail-oriented personality traits

Position Description

Wine is a favorite beverage of many people worldwide. It is a wonderful complement to food and is an essential component of several cuisines. In addition to its nutritional and flavor values, wine has medicinal properties and health benefits. Although some wine is made from fruits such as apples or blackberries, as well as from honey or rice, most wine is produced from grapes, called varietals, that give wines their different flavors. In the approximately 8,000-year history of wine, men and women called Winemakers have worked to perfect its production.

Professional Winemakers work for commercial wineries that may or may not operate their own grape vineyards. Winemakers follow formulas as well as apply their extensive knowledge and experience to create high-quality types of wine that meet the production and profit goals of their employers. Working closely with winery owners, Winemakers strive to make their wines unique and distinctive.

Making wine is both an art and a science. Winemakers have learned their craft through years of experience working in the different aspects and stages of the wine-making process, from planting and cultivating grape vines to marketing the finished product. Many of these professionals have also completed studies in enology, the science of wine and wine making. In fact, Winemakers are also called enologists.

Professional Winemakers are responsible for overseeing all activities involved in the wine-making pro-

cess, which entails several basic steps. Winemakers work closely with various vineyard and winery personnel throughout the entire process. They maintain contact with viticulturists, or vineyard managers, throughout the cultivation season to make sure grapes are produced and cared for properly. Winemakers conduct laboratory tests on sample grapes to gather various criteria regarding the crop's condition. They also ensure that the grapes are free of pesticide residue and are the correct variety. Winemakers decide when the grapes are ready for harvest. Some Winemakers work alongside vineyard workers to perform harvesting tasks either by hand or by machine.

The grapes are delivered to the winery where Winemakers supervise winery workers through all the stages of wine production, from cleaning the grapes to bottling the wine. Winemakers may direct workers to remove grape stems or crush the stems along with the grapes to provide extra tannin, which is desired in some wine varieties. Workers use machines to crush or press the grapes into juice; they then pour the juice into enormous fermentation vats or barrels. Yeast is added to the juice to start the fermentation process, whereby the sugars in the grape juice convert to alcohol and carbon dioxide. When the fermentation process is complete, the wine is transferred to stainless-steel tanks or wooden barrels to age. Fully aged wine goes through a filtering process before it is bottled and sealed. Winemakers taste finished wines to make sure they are suitable for market.

Winemakers assist the marketing and sales departments to develop strategic advertising, marketing, and sales activities for the different wines their wineries sell. Many Winemakers perform public relations tasks such as conducting tours of winery facilities; arranging for and overseeing wine-tasting events; speaking at industry events; and writing articles for trade journals, food and wine magazines, and other publications. Some Winemakers attend wine trade shows and other wine events as representatives of their wineries.

Along with performing tests to monitor the readiness of grapes and wine, Winemakers conduct research in their laboratories. They study new varieties of wine grapes, for example. Some look for ways to improve techniques and procedures for the fermentation, filtration, aging, or bottling of wine. Many are involved in developing new formulas for creating wine, or combining different varietals to blend into new wines.

Winemakers also perform various tasks relevant to their management and administrative responsibilities. For example, they:

- create and implement work schedules
- develop and manage budgets
- maintain accurate and detailed financial, inventory, and other records
- train, supervise, and develop wine-making staff
- ensure staff compliance with environmental and safety regulations, as well as company policies
- identify problem areas and take corrective actions to resolve them
- develop, review, and monitor winery laboratory procedures such as analytical testing
- manage inventories of finished wines, as well as wine barrels, ingredients, supplies, and equipment
- perform routine maintenance of winery and vineyard equipment
- stay up-to-date with new developments in the wine-making industry by reading technical journals, scientific papers, and financial news reports

Some Winemakers fulfill the additional role of either the winery manager or vineyard manager where they work. As vineyard managers, they oversee the cultivation and harvesting of grapes. As winery managers, they direct and coordinate all winery activities, including winemaking, marketing, sales, finances, business services, and so forth.

Winemakers work in laboratories and offices, as well as in wine cellars that are maintained at cool temperatures ranging between 55 and 65 degrees Fahrenheit. They also perform tasks outdoors in all weather conditions. These professionals experience moderate physical exertion on the job. They walk, stand, climb, reach, and stoop on occasion. They may be required to lift objects that weigh as much as 50 pounds. Winemakers risk hazardous exposure to chemical fumes and moving machinery parts; therefore, they follow strict safety rules and procedures.

Winemakers work long hours, particularly during the harvest season and throughout the wine production process.

Salaries

Salaries for Winemakers vary, depending on their education, experience, employer, and other factors. Formal salary information for Winemakers is unavailable. *Wine Business Monthly* conducted a 2008 salary survey of wineries in California, Washington, and Oregon. The survey reported the following range of average salaries:

- assistant Winemakers: $63,272 (at extra-large wineries) to $69,340 (at small wineries)
- Winemakers: $103,890 (at small wineries) to $111,161 (at midsized wineries)
- wine-making directors: $120,802 (at small wineries) to $148,508 (at large wineries)

Employment Prospects

The U.S. wine industry is a multibillion dollar industry. Nearly 5,000 wineries exist in the United States. Large and small wineries can be found throughout the country. California has nearly 2,500 wineries, which produce about 90 percent of the nation's wine.

Opportunities for Winemakers are available worldwide. In general, job openings become available as Winemakers transfer to other jobs, advance to higher positions, or retire. Additional positions are created when new wineries open and seek Winemakers.

With their training and skills, Winemakers can enter other careers by becoming grape growers, viticulturists, sommeliers, environmental scientists, biotechnologists, agriculture professors, consultants, wine writers, or marketing specialists.

Advancement Prospects

Many Winemakers have worked their way up through the ranks, starting from positions as cellar associates or lab technicians. Winemakers usually have held positions as assistant Winemakers. Winemakers can advance to higher-level management positions to become wine-making directors or vice-presidents. Some Winemakers become wine-making consultants or winery owners.

Many Winemakers measure their success through job satisfaction, by gaining a professional reputation, and by earning higher salaries.

Education and Training

Many employers prefer to hire Winemakers who possess at least a bachelor's degree in enology, viticulture, food technology, or another related discipline.

Students in enology programs take courses in such subjects as math, chemistry, microbiology, botany, and soil science in addition to wine-specific courses in viticulture (the science of growing grapes) and fermentation, as well as courses in the areas of economics and marketing. Along with classroom training, they acquire skills in laboratory settings and in the field through hands-on training by working in vineyards and wineries.

Winemakers learned their wine-making skills over the years as they progressively advanced from lab technician or cellar assistant positions to become assistant Winemakers.

Throughout their careers, Winemakers enroll in workshops and courses as well as study independently to update their knowledge and skills.

Experience, Special Skills, and Personality Traits

Employers seek Winemakers who have extensive experience in the wine industry and are knowledgeable about the various aspects of the winery and the vineyard. Job candidates must be able to demonstrate their ability to produce high-quality wines economically. In addition, candidates must have proven management experience.

To perform their jobs effectively, Winemakers need excellent leadership, organizational, planning, time-management, teamwork, interpersonal, and communication skills. Their other essential skills include strong public relations, writing, and computer skills. Being observant, analytical, self-motivated, inspirational, flexible, determined, and detail-oriented are some personality traits that successful Winemakers share.

Unions and Associations

Winemakers can join professional associations to take advantage of networking opportunities, continuing education, and other professional services and resources. One national society that serves their interests is the American Society for Enology and Viticulture. For contact information, see Appendix II.

Tips for Entry

1. Successful Winemakers have a strong passion for wine, and have refined senses of smell and taste.
2. While in college, obtain an internship or a summer job with a winery to gain experience.
3. Job opportunities vary from location to location. A willingness to relocate may improve your chances of finding the job you want.
4. Check both national and local wine publications for job advertisements.
5. Use the Internet to learn more about enology as well as the wine industry. You might start by visiting the American Society for Enology and Viticulture Web site, (asev.org) and Wine and Vines (www.winesandvines.com). For more links, see Appendix IV.

FOOD TECHNOLOGIST

CAREER PROFILE

Duties: Engage in research and development or production activities in the food industry; perform other duties as required

Alternate Title(s): Food Scientist; a title that reflects a specific job such as Quality Assurance Specialist

Salary Range: $34,000 to $105,000

Employment Prospects: Good

Advancement Prospects: Good

Prerequisites:

　Education or Training—Bachelor's degree in food science or another related field

　Experience—Work experience in the food industry preferred

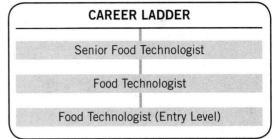

CAREER LADDER

Senior Food Technologist

Food Technologist

Food Technologist (Entry Level)

Special Skills and Personality Traits—Communication, interpersonal, teamwork, leadership, organizational, problem-solving, analytical, and computer skills; outgoing, observant, detail-oriented, curious, creative, flexible, and self-motivated personality traits

Position Description

Most of us have eaten canned vegetables, fruits, or meats at one time or another. Canning food was unheard of until 1810 when Nicolas Appert developed this process of preserving food for extended periods. Not long afterward, in 1864, Louis Pasteur found a way to heat milk to prevent spoilage by disease-bearing microorganisms. Since those early advancements, a discipline known as food science has expanded to encompass research and development in the areas of food preservation and packaging, as well as the introduction of new food products to the market. Many of the packaged, canned, and frozen food products that we consume today are the results of efforts made by men and women known as Food Technologists.

These professionals are food scientists who work in the food industry. Food science is a discipline of agriculture; it is the study of creating food products from raw agricultural products. Food Technologists apply the findings of food science research to developing, processing, preserving, storing, packaging, and distributing safe, nutritious, and convenient food products.

Food Technologists are involved in the various aspects of research and development and production. They apply the principles and techniques of chemistry, microbiology, biology, engineering, and other sciences to their work. Their mission is to create new and improved food products that can be produced economically by their employers as well as satisfy the requirements of customers.

Some Food Technologists work for food companies that manufacture breads, beverages, frozen dinners, canned foods, packaged salads, cheeses, ice cream, sauces, condiments, and many other diverse food products. Other Food Technologists work for companies that produce spices, flavorings, thickeners, preservatives, or other ingredients that food manufacturers need for making their products.

Some Food Technologists specialize by working only with certain types of foods such as fruits, vegetables, meats, beverages, sugars, preservatives, or baked products. These specialists are known by titles that reflect their specialty, such as seafood technologist or additives technologist.

Many Food Technologists are engaged in the area of product development. They are concerned with formulating new food products as well as making improvements in recipes for established products. These experts may be part of development teams to create new processed foods such as snack foods, for example. Food Technologists are familiar with the flavors, binding properties, and other characteristics of both raw and processed foods. They also understand chemical reactions in foods and how to control these reactions during food processing to create products of consistent quality. In addition to formulating new food products, Food Technologists assist with the transition from prototype creation to full-scale production.

Food Technologists also work on various types of applied research projects. Their emphasis is using scientific and engineering principles and techniques to develop practical applications. For example, technologists might substitute ingredients for less-desirable ones while formulating a product. They may develop more efficient preservation techniques. They may design food packages that are economical to make and safe for the environment. In addition, technologists use their knowledge and expertise to create new methods or systems for processing, packaging, storing, or distributing foods.

Food Technologists are also involved in basic research to further their understanding about the nutritional values and other characteristics of food, how food microbes grow in different environments, and other topics. Some technologists conduct basic research to discover new food sources.

Some Food Technologists are involved in inspecting food processing plants for compliance with safety, sanitation, and waste-management standards. Others are part of quality departments where they help ensure the safety and quality of all ingredients and final products. For example, some Food Technologists may be assigned to test products in small quantities for nutritional content and flavor in compliance with company policies and government regulations.

Food Technologists can transfer their knowledge and skills to work in management, marketing, sales, or other areas within food companies. Depending on their position, they might perform such tasks as acting as liaison between their food processing company and ingredients companies; writing information such as nutritional information for food product labels; seeking patents for new products; or providing demonstrations and samples of new products to clients.

These men and women often work independently but also work collaboratively in teams. For example, Food Technologists may work on research teams consisting of other scientists, engineers, technicians, chefs, project managers, and marketing personnel.

All Food Technologists, regardless of their positions, are expected to keep up-to-date with new developments and technologies. They read scientific journals, attend classes and conferences, and network with colleagues, among other activities.

Food Technologists work in offices, laboratories, and test kitchens. They use ovens, microwaves, blenders, food processors, and other cooking implements. These men and women generally work standard schedules of 40 hours per week but may put in extra hours to complete tasks and meet deadlines.

Salaries

Salaries for Food Technologists vary, depending on such factors as their education, experience, employer, and geographic location. According to the May 2008 Occupational Employment Statistics survey by the U.S. Bureau of Labor Statistics (BLS), the estimated annual salary for most Food Technologists ranged between $33,790 and $104,520.

Employment Prospects

Food manufacturers, food ingredient companies, food equipment manufacturers, food store chains, and food research laboratories are some employers in private industry that hire Food Technologists. Government agencies also employ Food Technologists to conduct research or perform regulatory work. Academic institutions hire food scientists to fill instructor and research positions. In addition, food scientists may find employment as Cooperative Extension Service professionals at state land-grant universities.

Because food companies are continually seeking to offer new and improved food products to consumers, opportunities for Food Technologists remain favorable regardless of the state of the economy. However, employers may hire fewer employees during economic downturns. The BLS reports that employment of Food Technologists and food scientists should grow by 16 percent between 2008 and 2018.

Some experts in the field are concerned that the enrollment in food science programs has been decreasing over the last several years.

Advancement Prospects

Food Technologists can advance by earning higher wages and by acquiring higher-level responsibilities. Some scientists pursue supervisory and management positions, which may require seeking work at different companies. Experienced individuals with entrepreneurial ambitions may become independent consultants or establish businesses that offer food technology services to food companies.

Food Technologists can also pursue other careers involving food technology by becoming flavor chemists, food microbiologists, food engineers, food science professors, or food-policy analysts, for example.

Education and Training

Minimally, Food Technologists must possess a bachelor's degree in food science, food engineering, chemical engineering, or another related field. Some employers may prefer to hire candidates who hold master's degrees. To obtain research scientist positions, individuals usually need a master's or doctoral degree.

Entry-level Food Technologists receive on-the-job training while working under the direction and supervision of experienced personnel.

Throughout their careers, Food Technologists enroll in continuing education programs to update their skills and knowledge about the food industry.

Experience, Special Skills, and Personality Traits

Employers prefer to hire candidates for entry-level positions who have experience working in food processing settings, in addition to having knowledge about the job for which they apply. They may have gained their experience through employment, internships, or student research assistantships.

Food Technologists must be able to work well with colleagues and others from diverse backgrounds; hence, they need excellent communication, interpersonal, and teamwork skills. Other essential skills that they need to perform their various tasks successfully are leadership, organizational, problem-solving, analytical, and computer skills. Being outgoing, observant, detail-oriented, curious, creative, flexible, and self-motivated are some personality traits that successful Food Technologists share.

Unions and Associations

Food Technologists can join professional associations to take advantage of networking opportunities, professional certification, continuing education, and other professional services and resources. Some national societies that serve the diverse interests of Food Technologists include the Institute of Food Technologists, AACC International, and the Society of Flavor Chemists. For contact information to these organizations, see Appendix II.

Tips for Entry

1. Having cooking skills may enhance your employability.
2. Obtain a summer job or internship at a food company to gain experience, as well as to learn whether you like working in private industry.
3. Take advantage of your college career center. Counselors are available to help you develop your job search skills and find job leads for possible employment.
4. Use the Internet to learn more about Food Technologists and their field. You might start by visiting the Institute of Food Technologists Web site at www.ift.org. For more links, see Appendix IV.

FLAVOR CHEMIST

Duties: Create natural and artificial flavorings; perform related duties as required

Alternate Title(s): Flavorist, Food Scientist

Salary Range: $38,000 to $113,000+

Employment Prospects: Poor

Advancement Prospects: Fair

Prerequisites:

Education or Training—Bachelor's degree; complete an apprenticeship

Experience—Several years of work experience in food development

Special Skills and Personality Traits—Communication, interpersonal, teamwork, organizational, problem-solving, writing, and self-management

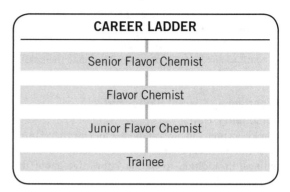

skills; curious, outgoing, self-motivated, persistent, patient, detail-oriented, and creative personality traits

Position Description

In the food industry, Flavor Chemists, or flavorists, play a major role in ensuring that our favorite food products have the flavors we expect to experience and enjoy when we eat them.

The flavors we perceive in our foods are actually a combination of certain chemicals. In the laboratory, Flavor Chemists work with complex chemical formulas, which they combine in slight variations to produce new flavors. These food scientists blend a few or more than a dozen substances together to obtain the taste—and smell—of sweet, sour, savory, and other desired flavors. These manufactured flavors, or flavorings, become ingredients that food companies add to products to enhance the flavors of food.

Flavor Chemists undergo long apprenticeships to be able to identify and memorize the aroma of thousands of chemicals. They are knowledgeable about various flavors and the variety of chemical formulas that create them. They understand how different chemicals work and combine to enhance food flavors. As a result, when Flavor Chemists sample food, they detect many flavors that most people may not be able to distinguish. These experts are more than just scientists—they are also artists who bring a lot of creativity to the process of making flavors.

Flavor Chemists mostly work in the food industry. Some are employed by flavor companies that offer flavor development services to food and beverage compa-

nies, while others work with the flavor divisions within food processing firms. Some flavorists work in the confection, pharmaceutical, and other industries where they develop flavorings for such products as candies, toothpastes, nutritional supplements, and pet foods.

These food scientists produce brand-new flavors as well as develop flavorings that imitate known flavors. They create both natural and artificial flavorings, which are food additives. Their flavoring formulas must only consist of chemicals that have been approved by the U.S. Food and Drug Administration. Natural flavorings are always derived from fruits, vegetables, plant material (such as bark or roots), spices, meats, eggs, dairy products, yeasts, and other natural sources. Artificial flavorings are essentially the same as natural flavors in terms of their chemical composition, but artificial flavors are made from both natural and synthetic chemical sources.

Flavor Chemists work in teams on the development and testing of new flavor compounds. They begin the process by identifying all the chemicals that make up the natural flavor they wish to imitate. They review chemical data that has already been compiled about the particular flavor to pick out the essential chemicals in that flavor. They might also obtain samples of food that have the desired flavor, which they run through tests to determine which molecules contribute to the food's flavor.

With their molecular profiles, flavorists mix various natural and synthetic chemicals into combinations that they think will duplicate the desired flavor. They bear in mind that factors such as consistency and texture are also essential to flavor enjoyment. Flavor Chemists typically mix, test, and critique several formulas until they obtain the precise blend of chemicals that retains the desired flavor characteristics. These experts also work to ensure that the new flavoring is safe for consumption by people who suffer from food allergies. When they are satisfied with the formula, it is used to produce large quantities of the flavor additive.

Flavor Chemists work in laboratory environments. They work in development laboratories, where they create flavors, and in application laboratories, which are set up like test kitchens.

Salaries

Salaries for Flavor Chemists vary, depending on such factors as their education, experience, employer, and geographic location. Formal salary information for these chemists is unavailable. The U.S. Bureau of Labor Statistics reported in its May 2008 Occupational Employment Statistics survey that the estimated annual salary for most chemists ranged between $37,840 and $113,080. According to some sources on the Internet, Flavor Chemists generally earn higher salaries than food scientists, and it is not unusual for master flavorists to earn salaries of $150,000 or more.

Employment Prospects

Flavor Chemists belong to a young and small field. They are employed by food manufacturers as well as by flavor companies and other food ingredient supply companies. Some Flavor Chemists work for such federal government agencies as the Food and Drug Administration. Flavor Chemists also find employment at colleges and universities. In general, job openings become available as flavorists transfer to other jobs or retire.

Advancement Prospects

Flavor Chemists can advance according to their ambitions. Some professionals pursue supervisory and managerial positions within their organizations. Some become independent consultants or establish their own flavor companies.

Education and Training

Individuals usually need at least a bachelor's degree in chemistry, chemical engineering, biology, food science, or another related field to enter the field of flavor chemistry. Some employers prefer candidates who possess a master's or doctoral degree. Individuals must hold a doctorate to teach in four-year colleges or universities.

Flavor Chemists learn their skills on the job while working as assistants to experienced flavorists. It takes several years of on-the-job training for individuals to become flavorists.

Experience, Special Skills, and Personality Traits

Employers prefer to hire applicants for entry-level positions who have experience in product development in foods or beverages, particularly in the area of flavor chemistry.

Flavor Chemists must be able to work well with colleagues and others; hence, they need excellent communication, interpersonal, and teamwork skills. In addition, these chemists need strong organizational, problem-solving, writing, and self-management skills.

Some personality traits that successful Flavor Chemists share include being curious, outgoing, self-motivated, persistent, patient, detail-oriented, and creative.

Unions and Associations

Flavor Chemists can join professional associations to take advantage of networking opportunities and other professional services and resources. Two national associations that serve their interests are the Society of Flavor Chemists and the Institute of Food Technologists. For contact information, see Appendix II.

Tips for Entry

1. While in college, gain experience by obtaining an internship with a food manufacturer.
2. Some employers prefer to hire candidates who are members of the Society of Flavor Chemists.
3. Use the Internet to learn more about the field of flavor chemistry. You might start by visiting the Society of Flavor Chemists Web sites (www.flavorchemist.org). For more links, see Appendix IV.

RESEARCH CHEF

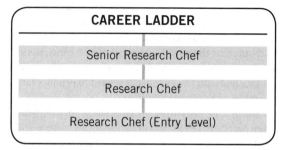

Position Description

In recent years, the number of restaurant chains has increased. Many of the newer franchise operations offer gourmet meals and ethnic cuisines, such as Thai or Italian food, as well as provide a themed dining experience. The appetizers, soups, entrées, desserts, and other dishes served in a franchise of a particular chain are identical, regardless of where the eatery may be located. The fare is also consistent in quality and presentation. Similarly, frozen, canned, and other packaged foods, as well as precooked foods sold in grocery stores, are increasingly prepared to satisfy gourmet palates. These trends are made possible by product development experts known as Research Chefs.

These professional chefs combine knowledge of food technology with culinary expertise in a new field of endeavor called Culinology. Their work is a departure from that of traditional chefs, because Research Chefs create recipes for food dishes and products for large-scale production and distribution. They work for restaurants and other food-service companies, as well as for food and beverage manufacturing companies and retail food companies. The mission of Research Chefs is to develop and test recipes to make high-quality food products more consistently convenient, palatable, and safe for customers. It is also their goal to produce food products more efficiently whether they are gourmet restaurant entrées, fast-food meals, frozen dinners, or barbecue sauces.

Research Chefs have responsibilities that range widely from research to the presentation of new products to customers. These men and women are involved with developing menus, creating and testing recipes, and evaluating final food products. These experts also help their employers plan for expanding and promoting their product lines. Research Chefs typically work with teams of food scientists, food technologists, marketing professionals, and management personnel to develop new products.

Their areas of expertise are as wide-ranging as their responsibilities. Research Chefs are experts in many aspects of food preparation including flavors and flavoring, ingredients and their uses, ethnic cuisines, and recipe creation. They are competent in using both fresh and premixed ingredients to cook and serve a variety of dishes quickly. Research Chefs are also aware of the latest food trends. In addition, these chefs are knowledgeable about the food business, and are well-versed in the operations of their companies. Furthermore, they understand how to use the techniques of food technology to create food products from the research stage to full-scale production.

Research Chefs develop recipes in laboratories that are designed and equipped much like restaurant kitchens, with stoves, ovens, mixing bowls, cutting tools, and so on. These research kitchens are also stocked with precision measuring instruments and scientific scales that allow Research Chefs to follow recipes exactly. In such kitchen environments, Research Chefs experiment with different proportions of ingredients and preparation techniques to develop the type of food products desired by clients. For example, they may dice or julienne vegetables to determine which preparation technique works best in a recipe.

In food sensory laboratories, Research Chefs meet with members of focus groups who assist with testing food products. The taste testers provide feedback about the recipes, which Research Chefs use to decide whether to continue developing new flavors or seasoning mixtures. The chefs also meet with members of their team to work on such issues as marketability, financial concerns, packaging, and food safety to help bring new food products to market.

Research Chefs are responsible for performing a wide range of tasks specific to their occupation. For example, they may:

- manage test kitchens by overseeing the receipt and delivery of product inventories, scheduling projects, ensuring that facilities are maintained and cleaned, and managing subordinate staff members
- lead their teams to complete products within specific deadlines and cost parameters
- ensure that their product development projects comply with food safety regulations
- document information, such as ingredient lists and nutritional data, for use in food product labels
- supervise and train assistants and other staff
- create catalogs of their food products and ingredients for marketing and sales departments
- work with training specialists who help restaurant owners use new recipes, mixes, and other food products in their menus
- read cookbooks and culinary magazines to find suitable recipes to adapt
- stay abreast of food industry trends

As they work in their kitchens, these experts stand for long intervals each day. They perform manual tasks, which include lifting heavy objects such as large pots and ingredient packages. They endure hot temperatures in the proximity of ovens and stoves. They may risk minor injuries such as cuts and burns and risk slipping and falling.

Research Chefs usually work standard 40-hour business weeks. They may put in extra hours to meet deadlines. Many of them travel the world to sample new cuisines at various restaurants.

Salaries

Salaries for Research Chefs vary, depending on such factors as their education, experience, employer, and geographic location. Research Chefs typically earn higher wages than chefs and head cooks in restaurants and other food-service establishments. According to the Web site of the Culinology program at Southwest Minnesota State University (www.smsu.edu/academics/programs/culinology), culinologists earn between $45,000 and $100,000 per year.

Employment Prospects

Culinology is a very young and growing field, which emerged during the 1990s. (The term itself was coined and trademarked by the Research Chefs Association.) Research Chefs are employed by food processing companies, beverage manufacturers, restaurant chains, food-service operations, and food-service management companies. They also work for firms that offer food product development services. Some Research Chefs are independent consultants.

Job opportunities are most favorable for experienced chefs who also have a food science background. Experts in the field report that the demand for Research Chefs should increase as food and beverage companies continue to seek ways to produce safe, wholesome, cost-effective, and quality products that satisfy consumers.

Advancement Prospects

Many Research Chefs mark their success by earning higher wages, by being assigned higher levels of responsibilities, and through job satisfaction. They may also be promoted to supervisory and managerial positions. Entrepreneurial chefs may pursue careers as independent consultants or owners of product development services.

Education and Training

Educational requirements vary among employers. Some employers, for example, prefer to hire chefs with an associate's or bachelor's culinary degree who have completed some course work in food science. Some Research Chefs have earned both culinary arts and food science degrees.

Apprentices learn their skills on the job while working under the direction of experienced Research Chefs, food technologists, and food scientists.

In recent years, academic institutions have begun to offer courses and seminars about food product development to food scientists and culinary students. In addition, some colleges and universities have established bachelor's degree programs in Culinology that combine course work in both the culinary arts and food science.

These programs are accredited by the Research Chefs Association. Students learn about nutrition, food product development, food processing technology, business management, and other topics. Students also receive hands-on experience in culinary arts and research development.

Throughout their careers, Research Chefs enroll in continuing education programs to update their skills and knowledge in food product development.

Experience, Special Skills, and Personality Traits

Employers prefer to hire Research Chefs to entry-level positions who have several years of experience cooking in restaurants and other food-service operations. Many employers also prefer that candidates have food product development experience.

To perform well at their jobs, Research Chefs must have strong problem-solving, organizational, process management, and presentation skills. They also need excellent communication, teamwork, and interpersonal skills, as they must work well with colleagues and others from diverse backgrounds. Having basic computer skills in word processing, spreadsheet, and other applications is also essential. Being enthusiastic, curious, creative, detail-oriented, positive, and dedicated are some personality traits that successful Research Chefs share.

Unions and Associations

Research Chefs can join professional associations to take advantage of networking opportunities as well as various professional services and resources such as continuing education and professional certification. Many belong to the Research Chefs Association, which specifically serves research and development chefs. These chefs are also eligible to join the Institute of Food Technologists, as well as professional culinary societies such as the American Culinary Federation and the International Association of Culinary Professionals. For contact information for these groups, see Appendix II.

Tips for Entry

1. If you are in high school, enroll in vocational cooking courses if your school offers them. They typically teach basic knowledge and skills in cooking, food safety and handling procedures, and other topics to students who are interested in pursuing a career in food service.
2. While you are studying in a culinary program, let your instructors know you are interested in a career in food research and development. Ask them for assistance in finding an appropriate internship with a food company, restaurant chain, or another appropriate business.
3. Learn about the science of food and gain an understanding about how the food development and production systems work through self-study, courses, and workshops.
4. If job vacancies are not available at a company, ask for an informational interview with the food research and development director or head Research Chef. In an informational interview, you can ask questions about the Research Chef position at a company, such as: What are the chef's major duties? What training, experience, skills, and characteristics does the company seek in an applicant? What types of advancement prospects are available?
5. Use the Internet to learn more about Research Chefs and the Culinology field. You might start by visiting the Research Chefs Association Web site (www.culinology.org) and *Culinology* (www. culinologyonline.com). For more links, see Appendix IV.

FOOD PROCESS ENGINEER

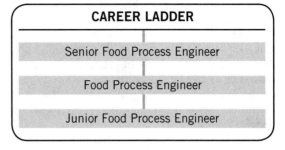

Position Description

People have always processed food in one way or another. When people cook raw meat over a fire, for example, the meat is processed into another form of food. Mixing flour, sugar, salt, flavors, and other ingredients together and baking the batter to make a cake is another example of how food is processed. Over the last few centuries, scientists and engineers have developed more complex food processing methods and techniques that manufacturers have utilized to create a wide range of food products, such as juices, canned soups, frozen dinners, preserved meats, packaged pastas, and candy bars. Every year, in fact, food manufacturers introduce new tasty, quality product lines to satisfy the needs of consumers, who purchase processed foods that they can conveniently prepare and eat in their homes.

Food Process Engineers are among the many professionals that food manufacturers employ to efficiently and economically produce commercial food products. These engineers apply the principles of chemistry, microbiology, and various engineering principles and skills to their work. They are experts in the study, development, design, fabrication, and operation of equipment, processes, and systems used for making, packaging, storing, and distributing safe and wholesome food products in large quantities.

Food Process Engineers (also known as food engineers) seek ways to efficiently produce new food products. These men and women engage in the different aspects of research and development and production within food companies. Those who work in the area of product development study the chemical, physical, and flavor properties of food. They assist in creating food products that can be shipped long distances and retain their nutritional value and flavor without spoiling. They research new methods for using ingredients to produce new foods and for improving qualities in established products by using alternative processing techniques.

Food Process Engineers play a major role in designing the equipment and facilities that are used to produce large quantities of food products. They ensure that the same quality of foods established in prototype samples is consistently maintained on a much larger scale for finished products. Food Process Engineers design or modify food processing plants, equipment, and computerized control systems to efficiently manage the equipment. These experts determine where equipment, machinery, and workstations are to be located, and carefully monitor all the stages of construction.

Food Process Engineers also contribute to designing packaging and storage techniques that serve to preserve food products for extended periods. For example, some Food Process Engineers develop new packaging materials, including new inks for printing product labels on the packages. As with processed foods, these experts make new or improved packaging prototypes, which they test at their lab benches or in pilot plants before approving them for large-scale production.

Some Food Process Engineers focus on ensuring that plant operations function smoothly and efficiently. These engineers continually inspect and adjust food-processing equipment. They also work with other food company personnel to mitigate problems that arise when machines and manufacturing processes fail to perform optimally.

Food Process Engineers also contribute to project management as well as the daily management of programs, units, divisions, facilities, and other technical operations. They direct and coordinate the activities of teams composed of engineers, scientists, technicians, construction crews, and others. Some Food Process Engineers are involved in the business activities of their companies. For example, they may be part of the marketing or sales departments.

Food Process Engineers perform tasks specific to their occupation, as well as general engineering tasks. They may, for example:

- conduct tests during all phases of food production to control such variables as temperature and pressure
- arrange the sequence of production processes for maximum effectiveness
- develop and implement safety rules for the use of processing equipment and materials
- develop or refine laboratory procedures
- design measurement and control systems for production facilities
- estimate production costs
- manage schedules
- prepare reports and required paperwork
- maintain accurate and detailed notes, logs, and records of their work activities
- stay abreast of new food manufacturing processes and technologies

Food Process Engineers work as part of project teams. Throughout their workday, they associate with production workers, equipment manufacturers, technical personnel, managers, accountants, and others that are either directly or indirectly involved with food processing.

These experts work in different environments, depending on the tasks they perform. They work in laboratories where they test production processes. They work in offices where they use computers for creat-

ing machine and facility designs, analyzing laboratory results, and writing reports. Their other tasks may require them to work in test kitchens, pilot plants, or full-production manufacturing facilities.

Food Process Engineers usually work 40 hours each week, but they sometimes put in extra hours to complete tasks and meet deadlines.

Salaries

Salaries for Food Process Engineers vary, depending on such factors as their education, experience, position, employer, and geographic location. Specific salary information for these engineers is unavailable; however, their earnings are similar to those of chemical engineers. The estimated annual salary for most chemical engineers ranged between $53,730 and $130,240, according to the May 2008 Occupational Employment Statistics survey by the U.S. Bureau of Labor Statistics.

Employment Prospects

The food processing industry is a major part of the U.S. economy. In recent years, it has earned over a trillion dollars in annual sales. Jobs are generally more stable in the food processing industry than in other industries during economic downturns because of the constant demand for food, both domestically and worldwide. Furthermore, food companies are constantly enhancing their product lines with new and improved products.

Opportunities for Food Processing Engineers generally become available as individuals advance to higher positions, transfer to other jobs, or retire. Employers will create additional positions to meet the growing needs of their companies. Some experts in the field report that job prospects for food engineers are favorable nationwide.

Food Process Engineers are employed by food manufacturers, as well as by food processing equipment firms, companies that supply food manufacturers with ingredients, and engineering firms that offer design and other consulting services. In addition to the food processing industry, Food Process Engineers work for companies within the biochemical and pharmaceutical industries. They also find work with government agencies and academic institutions. Some Food Process Engineers are independent consultants.

Advancement Prospects

Food Process Engineers advance according to their ambitions and interests. They can become technical specialists in quality assurance, plant engineering, or other areas. They can rise through the ranks of managerial and administrative positions, or become independent consultants or business owners. Engineers may also pursue careers in education.

Education and Training

To become Food Process Engineers, individuals must possess at least a bachelor's degree in chemical engineering, agricultural engineering, biosystems engineering, food science, or physical chemistry with an emphasis in Food Process Engineering. For some positions, employers prefer to hire applicants who hold a master's or doctoral degree in food engineering, chemical engineering, or another related field.

Engineers who plan to conduct research or pursue consulting or management positions normally need an advanced degree. Engineers usually are required to have a doctorate to teach in four-year colleges and universities.

Entry-level engineers receive on-the-job training while working under the supervision and direction of experienced personnel. Some employers also provide trainees with formal classroom instruction.

Throughout their careers, Food Process Engineers enroll in continuing education programs to update their skills and keep up with advancements in their fields.

Special Requirements

All 50 states, as well as the District of Columbia and the U.S. territories, require engineers to be licensed as professional engineers (P.E.), if they offer engineering services directly to the public. Engineers must also be licensed if they perform work that affects the life, health, or property of the public. The requirements for P.E. licensing vary from state to state. For specific information, contact the board of engineers that governs the area where you plan to practice.

Experience, Special Skills, and Personality Traits

Employers generally hire candidates for entry-level positions who have experience related to the position for which they apply. They may have gained their experience through work-study programs, internships, employment, or student research projects.

Food Process Engineers must be able to work well with colleagues and others from diverse backgrounds; hence, they need to have excellent interpersonal, teamwork, and communication skills. To perform their various duties effectively, these engineers also must have strong leadership, planning, project-management, analytical, and problem-solving skills. Being creative, curious, practical, detail-oriented, dedicated, and self-motivated are some personality traits that successful Food Process Engineers share.

Unions and Associations

Food Process Engineers can join professional associations to take advantage of networking opportunities, continuing education, and other professional services and resources. Some national societies that serve their interests are the American Institute of Chemical Engineers, the International Society of Food Engineering, the Institute of Food Technologists, and the American Society of Agricultural and Biological Engineers. Professional engineers may belong to the National Society of Professional Engineers. For contact information to these organizations, see Appendix II.

Tips for Entry

1. Obtain an internship or a part-time job at a food processing facility to get an idea of what it is like to work in such an environment.
2. Do not rely on just one way to find job leads. Many avenues are available. For example, read job ads in newspapers as well as trade and professional publications; attend job fairs; contact professors, colleagues, and former supervisors; check out employment resources offered by professional and trade associations; and call or visit prospective employers.
3. Use the Internet to learn more about the food processing industry. You might start by visiting the Food Engineering Division page of the Institute of Food Technologists Web site (www.ift.org/divisions/food_eng); and FoodProcessing.com (www.foodprocessing.com). For more links, see Appendix IV.

FOOD MICROBIOLOGIST

Duties: Study the characteristics and growth of microorganisms in food; design and conduct research projects; perform duties as required

Alternate Title(s): Microbiologist; a title that reflects a specific position such as Laboratory Technician

Salary Range: $38,000 to $148,000

Employment Prospects: Good

Advancement Prospects: Good

Prerequisites:

    Education or Training—Bachelor's or advanced degree, depending on the position

    Experience—Have work experience related to the position for which one applies

CAREER LADDER

```
          Senior Food Microbiologist

              Food Microbiologist

        Food Microbiologist (Entry Level)
```

Special Skills and Personality Traits—Critical-thinking, problem-solving, organizational, self-management, teamwork, interpersonal, and communication skills; creative, curious, focused, patient, and flexible personality traits

Position Description

Scientists known as Food Microbiologists play a part in ensuring the safety and quality of the foods we consume every day. Microbiology is the study of bacteria, viruses, yeast, molds, and other very tiny single-celled organisms. These microorganisms are both bad and good in the way they affect raw and processed foods. Many of us are aware that microbes can cause food to spoil, which in turn may result in many illnesses and even deaths. Fewer of us, however, know that microorganisms, through fermentation, contribute to the creation of such tasty foods and beverages as cheese, yogurt, sauerkraut, kimchi, pickles, beer, and wine.

Food Microbiologists apply the principles and techniques of microbiology and biochemistry, as well as food science, to understand the dangerous and useful effects that microbes have on foods. They are involved in identifying food microorganisms and investigating how they live and grow in food. These microbiologists are also interested in examining the conditions that cause food microorganisms to multiply and where that may take place during the processing, distribution, storage, or handling of food.

Many Food Microbiologists are research scientists who work in private, government, and academic settings. They engage in various types of research projects. They conduct basic research to further their knowledge about food microorganisms and how they may be controlled. For example, some Food Microbiologists might examine how bacteria spread among plants in fields.

Food Microbiologists also conduct applied research, to solve problems in food spoilage, fermentation, food processing, quality control, and other areas. For example, Food Microbiologists might develop techniques to identify microbial contaminants in perishable foods during food processing.

In food companies, many research scientists are part of product development teams. Their focus is to create new or improved food products. For instance, Food Microbiologists might be involved in designing technologies to improve the quality of meat products.

Some Food Microbiologists are part of the quality assurance programs in their companies. They help create effective plans, techniques, and procedures to identify harmful microorganisms in food products before they can be sold to customers.

Food Microbiologists may work alone or collaborate with other research scientists. These microbiologists perform general tasks that include:

- planning and implementing research studies
- developing laboratory procedures and protocols
- collecting and evaluating experimental data
- preparing required paperwork and reports
- maintaining accurate records and databases
- meeting with research project team members
- preparing and administering budgets

- supervising and training research assistants, technicians, and other staff members

Many academic researchers are employed as instructors at colleges and universities where they teach undergraduate and graduate students. Full-time professors are expected to juggle teaching and research duties with other responsibilities, including advising students, publishing scholarly works, performing administrative duties, and participating in community service.

Some Food Microbiologists are hired as research assistants and technicians. Their role is to provide research scientists with research, technical, and administrative support. Other Food Microbiologists are employed by regulatory agencies, such as the U.S. Food and Drug Administration, to assist in the enforcement of food laws.

Food Microbiologists work in offices and laboratories. They generally work a 40-hour week, but many put in additional hours to complete tasks.

Salaries

Salaries for Food Microbiologists vary, depending on such factors as their position, education, experience, employer, and geographic location. The estimated annual salary for most microbiologists overall ranged from $38,240 to $111,300, according to the May 2008 Occupational Employment Statistics survey by the U.S. Bureau of Labor Statistics (BLS). This survey also reported that most postsecondary biological science instructors, which would include those teaching microbiology, earned a salary that ranged between $38,830 and $147,980.

Employment Prospects

The BLS reports that employment of microbiologists, in general, is expected to grow by 12 percent between 2008 and 2018.

Because of the constant need to maintain a safe and secure food supply, a growing demand for qualified Food Microbiologists is anticipated.

Advancement Prospects

Promotional opportunities vary with the different positions. Laboratory technicians and research assistants may advance to supervisory and managerial positions. Research scientists may advance to become project managers, program managers, and principal research investigators as well as department managers, laboratory directors, and executive officers. College instruc-

tors can rise through the faculty ranks to become full professors and become tenured.

Education and Training

With a bachelor's degree in microbiology, biology, food science, or another related field, individuals can obtain jobs as research assistants and laboratory technicians. Some employers may prefer that applicants hold a master's degree.

To be research scientists, Food Microbiologists must possess either a master's or doctoral degree in microbiology or food microbiology. They must have a doctorate to obtain faculty appointments at four-year colleges and universities.

Experience, Special Skills, and Personality Traits

Employers seek applicants for entry-level positions, whether as laboratory technicians or research scientists, who have relevant experience. They may have gained their experience through employment, internships, work-study programs, or fellowships.

Food Microbiologists need strong critical-thinking, problem-solving, organizational, and self-management skills. They also need teamwork, interpersonal, and communication skills as they must be able to work well with others from diverse backgrounds. Being creative, curious, focused, patient, and flexible are some personality traits that successful microbiologists share.

Unions and Associations

Many Food Microbiologists belong to professional associations to take advantage of networking opportunities and other services and resources. Some national associations they might join are the American Society for Microbiology, the Institute of Food Technologists, and the International Association for Food Protection. For contact information, see Appendix II.

Tips for Entry

1. Check out job forums on the Internet that focus on Food Microbiologists or Microbiologists.
2. Some employers prefer to hire Ph.D. applicants who have completed several years of postdoctoral experience.
3. Use the Internet to learn more about the field of food microbiology. You might start by visiting Microbes.info. For more links, see Appendix IV.

QUALITY ASSURANCE SPECIALIST

CAREER PROFILE

Duties: Implement, evaluate, and improve food quality systems; conduct audits; perform other duties as required

Alternate Title(s): None

Salary Range: $43,000 to $90,000

Employment Prospects: Fair

Advancement Prospects: Fair

Prerequisites:

Education or Training—Bachelor's degree preferred

Experience—Several years of experience working in quality programs

Special Skills and Personality Traits—Leadership, critical-thinking, problem-solving, troubleshooting, self-management, writing, computer, communication, interpersonal, and teamwork skills; analytical, detail-oriented, organized, and flexible personality traits

CAREER LADDER

Senior Quality Assurance Specialist or Quality Manager

Quality Assurance Specialist

Quality Analyst or Quality Engineer

Position Description

Food quality is an all-important issue in the food industry. In food manufacturing, the term *quality* refers to all the characteristics that customers seek in the food products they buy. This includes such features as the flavor and appearance of the product and its cost, packaging, and shelf life. The quality of a product also refers to it being free of contamination or defects.

Quality Assurance (QA) Specialists are among the professionals that food companies hire to ensure that the products they process and manufacture are safe for human or animal consumption. These quality professionals are responsible for enforcing various laws, regulations, policies, and procedures. In addition, they make sure that standards for the manufacturing and packaging of food products are in compliance.

Quality operations in food companies are divided into two distinct units. The quality assurance (QA) department oversees a company's quality system that ensures its products meet all established quality specifications and government regulations. This department may also be in charge of its company's food safety management program. QA Specialists are responsible for planning, developing, and implementing quality programs and activities through which they check all the raw ingredients and final products; the plant, machinery and equipment; the packaging

and labeling of products; the processing procedures; and so forth.

The quality control (QC) unit is responsible for executing the activities and techniques that ensure quality requirements are being met. QC professionals work in plants where they perform daily tests and inspections of raw materials, processes, and final products. QC personnel forward any negative feedback to the QA unit, which in turn analyzes the problems or trends and seek ways to improve quality processes.

QA Specialists perform advisory roles in their companies. Along with being familiar with company-wide quality systems, they are knowledgeable about food safety and other pertinent laws and regulations, food industry standards, recall protocols, best manufacturing practices, company rules and policies, and other areas. Hence, QA Specialists serve as a link between the quality department and the research and development and production departments as well as the finance, marketing, and other business units.

In general, QA Specialists are assigned duties that focus on the implementation, evaluation, and improvement of quality systems within their companies. They perform a wide range of tasks, such as:

- designing product specifications
- reviewing new or revised quality policies, procedures, or work instructions

- recommending measures to improve such areas as quality standards, product safety, plant sanitation, and hygienic practices of employees
- communicating with suppliers, outside laboratories, and customers about quality issues
- conducting training and education programs for quality and food safety
- maintaining accurate and complete records and files
- preparing reports and other paperwork
- staying abreast of laws and regulations, food industry standards, and other matters

QA Specialists also participate in performing inspections of raw materials, manufacturing processes, and finished products. For example, they might review sanitation practices, check scales and weights, or examine facilities for pest infestations. These QA professionals conduct audits of their company plants as well as the facilities of their companies' suppliers and vendors to ensure that they are all in compliance with food safety regulations, good manufacturing practices, company specifications, and other standards and protocols.

These quality professionals work 40-hour weeks. They put in additional hours as needed to complete their various tasks.

Salaries
Salaries for QA Specialists vary, depending on such factors as their education, experience, job duties, employer, and geographic location. Specific salary information for QA Specialists in the food manufacturing industry is unavailable. Salary.com reports the following average salary ranges (as of February 2009) for QA Specialists in general: $42,786 to $54,445 for QA Specialists I, and $73,232 to $90,123 for QA Specialists IV.

Employment Prospects
The demand for qualified QA Specialists in the food industry should remain favorable because of the importance of food safety as well as the delivery of products that achieve customer satisfaction.

In general, opportunities become available as QA Specialists advance to higher positions, transfer to other jobs or career fields, or retire or leave the workforce for various reasons.

Advancement Prospects
Quality Specialists advance by earning higher wages and receiving greater levels of responsibilities. Those with supervisory and managerial ambitions can pursue such positions.

Education and Training
Educational requirements vary with different employers. Employers generally prefer to hire applicants who have a bachelor's degree in food science, chemistry, microbiology, or another related field. For some positions, an associate's degree is the minimum requirement.

Employers provide training to new employees.

Experience, Special Skills, and Personality Traits
Employers seek applicants who have several years of experience working in quality programs in the food industry. Strong candidates would have some experience in the area (such as baking or meat processing) in which they would work.

To perform their duties effectively, QA Specialists must have excellent leadership, critical-thinking, problem-solving, troubleshooting, and self-management skills. They also need proficient writing and computer skills. In addition, these specialists need strong communication, interpersonal, and teamwork skills, as they must work well with many people from diverse backgrounds. Being analytical, detail-oriented, organized, and flexible are some personality traits that successful QA Specialists have in common.

Unions and Associations
QA Specialists can join professional associations to take advantage of networking opportunities, professional certification, and other services and resources. Some national societies that serve quality professionals in the food industry are the Institute of Food Technologists and the American Society for Quality. For contact information, see Appendix II.

Tips for Entry
1. Job titles can differ from company to company. For example, a Quality Specialist could work in either the QC or QA department. Be sure to read job announcements carefully.
2. Contact food companies directly about job vacancies.
3. Learn more about food quality systems. You might start by visiting FoodQualityNews.com. For more links, see Appendix IV.

FOOD INSPECTOR

Duties: Enforce food safety laws, regulations, codes, and standards; conduct inspections of food processing facilities or food service operations; perform related duties as required

Alternate Title(s): Food Inspector; Consumer Safety Inspector, Public Health Inspector, Meat Inspector, or other title that reflects a specific job

Salary Range: $25,000 to $59,000

Employment Prospects: Good

Advancement Prospects: Good

Prerequisites:

Education or Training—Bachelor's degree

Experience—Varies from agency to agency; work experience in food industry preferred

Special Skills and Personality Traits—Organizational, problem-solving, decision-making, interpersonal, writing, communication, computer, and self-management skills; dependable, detail-oriented, quick-witted, inquisitive, tactful, determined, honest, and objective personality traits

Position Description

Food safety is a critical issue worldwide. Every year millions of people become ill due to food contamination. The majority are mild cases, but severe cases have hospitalized people, and, worse, resulted in deaths. In the United States, the local, state, and federal governments work closely together to maintain the safety of the food supply.

Public employees known as Food Inspectors are responsible for monitoring the facilities that produce, process, manufacture, store, and distribute food products, as well as the establishments that sell and serve food to the public. They conduct both routine and surprise visits to farms, ranches, slaughterhouses, food processing plants, beverage plants, food warehouses, wholesale bakeries, supermarkets, restaurants, institutional cafeterias, and other food and food-service companies. They make sure that companies are in compliance with food safety laws, regulations, codes, and standards.

Different government agencies oversee different types of food safety inspections. Federal agencies are responsible for enforcing the federal food safety laws that regulate all food companies involved in interstate and foreign commerce. At the federal level, Food Inspectors mostly work for one of two federal agencies. The Food Safety and Inspection Service (FSIS), an agency within the U.S. Department of Agriculture,

oversees the inspection of all facilities that process, store, distribute, and package meat, poultry, and egg products. The Food and Drug Administration (FDA), part of the U.S. Department of Health and Human Services, has the authority to handle inspections of facilities that manufacture and handle all other foods. FDA inspectors are called consumer safety officers.

All 50 states, as well as the U.S. territories and the District of Columbia, have their own teams of Food Inspectors, who may work under the authority of state agriculture, public health, consumer protection, or other agencies. These inspectors are responsible for enforcing state laws that regulate the production, processing, and sale of foods within state borders. State Food Inspectors may be assigned to review federally regulated companies, if their state has been contracted by the FSIS or the FDA.

At the local level, public health agencies conduct inspections of restaurants and other food-service establishments to ensure that they follow local food safety and public health codes. Local Food Inspectors are usually known as sanitarians, public health inspectors, or environmental health inspectors. Depending on the size of a local public health department, inspectors may be assigned to conduct only food safety inspections or perform environmental health reviews of other types of facilities such as swimming pools, waste disposal sites, or apartment buildings.

Food Inspectors have varying responsibilities, depending on their skills and expertise and the needs of their employers. Inspectors may be responsible for examining a particular type of food, such as milk, fish, or vegetables, or a certain kind of facility, such as vegetable farms, poultry processing plants, or restaurants. Some Food Inspectors are assigned to monitor facilities within a specific geographic area. Food Inspectors may examine food products during their processing, handling, or packaging.

Food Inspectors perform various duties that differ according to the type of inspections they perform. For example, FSIS meat inspectors examine animals before and after they are slaughtered, and determine the grade, quality, and condition of the carcasses.

Food Inspectors also perform general tasks that are similar regardless of the inspections they conduct. They schedule appointments with companies and meet with owners or their representatives. The inspectors conduct physical reviews of facilities to determine that they are in good, clean condition. They check for unsanitary equipment and for any signs of insect or animal (such as rats) infestation. They observe employees to see that they are using proper food handling procedures as well as practicing good personal hygiene.

Food Inspectors also look for evidence of food spoilage. Food Inspectors may collect samples of fresh, processed, or packaged foods and send them to laboratories for chemical, microbiological, and physical analyses. In addition, Food Inspectors review records for accuracy and check that licenses and permits are up-to-date. Some inspectors examine food labels to make sure nutritional and other information about the contents are accurate and truthful.

Food Inspectors take detailed notes about their observations and complete required paperwork and reports about their findings and recommendations. These inspectors may issue warnings or citations to establishments for violations. They make follow-up visits to ensure that noncompliant establishments have resolved their problems. For example, a local Food Inspector might issue a citation to a restaurant for unsanitary kitchen conditions. Some Food Inspectors have the authority to seize food, stop work, close down shops, or prevent the sale of contaminated or mislabeled food items.

Food Inspectors also perform other duties. For example, they may be assigned to:

- assist in the investigation of outbreaks of food-borne illnesses
- investigate consumer complaints about food establishments or products

- respond to questions from the public in person, by phone, or through correspondence
- conduct educational workshops on food safety to food establishments
- issue permits to establishments
- conduct inspections of new or remodeled establishments
- testify as an expert witness at administrative hearings or court trials

These inspectors travel regularly to visit food processing facilities, slaughterhouses, and other establishments. The nature of their inspections requires them to spend long hours of standing and walking, as well as bending, kneeling, reaching, and lifting moderate to heavy objects. These inspectors are exposed to hazardous materials that may place them at risk to infections and disease; hence, they are expected to be alert at all times and to follow strict safety measures. When they are not performing inspections, these professionals work in well-lit, comfortable offices to schedule appointments, prepare reports, and perform other tasks.

Food Inspectors generally work 40 hours a week. Some inspectors have irregular work schedules in order to check restaurants and other facilities at night or on weekends.

Salaries

Salaries for Food Inspectors vary, depending on such factors as their education, experience, job duties, employer, and geographic location. Specific salary information for this occupation is unavailable. Agricultural inspectors perform duties similar to Food Inspectors. According to the May 2008 Occupational Employment Statistics survey by the U.S. Bureau of Labor Statistics, the estimated annual salary for most agricultural inspectors ranged between $25,380 and $59,270.

Depending on their qualifications, entry-level inspectors for federal positions may start on the general schedule (GS) at either the GS-5 or GS-7 level. The general schedule is a pay schedule for most federal employees. In 2010, the base pay for these GS levels ranged from $27,431 to $44,176.

Employment Prospects

In recent years, there has been a growing concern about the increasing number of recalls of fresh and packaged foods. In addition, experts in the field express that there are not enough professionals to effectively conduct food safety inspections. Both factors may lead to the creation of additional positions. However, local, state, and federal agencies are limited by strict budgets in their ability to hire additional inspectors.

Job opportunities generally become available when inspectors retire, advance to higher positions, or transfer to other jobs or career fields.

Advancement Prospects

Supervisory and management opportunities are available, but limited. Many Food Inspectors measure their success by earning higher incomes, by receiving the assignments of their choice, and through job satisfaction.

With their background and knowledge, Food Inspectors may pursue other careers that interest them. For example, they may become Cooperative Extension Service specialists, environmental advocates, policy analysts, researchers, or teachers.

Education and Training

Educational requirements vary from position to position. In general, employers prefer to hire applicants for entry-level positions who hold a bachelor's degree in food science, microbiology, chemistry, epidemiology, environmental health, agricultural science, or another related field. For some positions, applicants may be required to hold a master's or doctoral degree.

Employers may hire applicants with a high school diploma or general equivalency diploma if they have qualifying work experience. They should also be knowledgeable about food safety standards, sanitation practices, and control measures used in the commercial handling and preparation of food products.

Food Inspectors learn laws and regulations and inspection techniques and procedures through on-the-job training and classroom instruction. Novices work under the direction and supervision of experienced Food Inspectors.

Experience, Special Skills, and Personality Traits

Requirements for entry-level positions vary with each employer. For example, applicants for federal inspector positions must have at least three years of work experience if they do not possess a bachelor's degree. In general, employers seek candidates who have experience and knowledge in their inspection area.

Food Inspectors need effective organizational, problem-solving, decision-making, and interpersonal skills. They also must have strong writing, communication, and computer skills. In addition, they must have excellent self-management skills, such as the ability to work independently, handle pressure and stress, and understand and follow instructions. Being dependable, detail-oriented, quick-witted, inquisitive, tactful, determined, honest, and objective are some personality traits that successful Food Inspectors share.

Unions and Associations

Food Inspectors can join professional associations to take advantage of networking opportunities, training programs, and other professional services and resources. Some national organizations that serve the interests of different Food Inspectors are the International Association for Food Protection, the National Environmental Health Association, and the American Public Health Association.

Some Food Inspectors are members of labor unions, which represent them in contract negotiations for better terms regarding pay, benefits, and working conditions. Unions also handle any grievances that their members may have against their employers. Many federal inspectors belong to the American Federation of Government Employees.

For contact information for the above organizations, see Appendix II.

Tips for Entry

1. For information about job vacancies for federal positions, contact a local U.S. Office of Personnel Management. You can also visit the official online job site at www.usajobs.gov.
2. To learn about job openings in local and state governments, visit your state employment office.
3. Be willing to relocate to another city or state to find a job.
4. Use the Internet to learn more about government food safety programs. You might start by visiting the Gateway to Government Food Safety Information Web site, at USA.gov. The URL is www.foodsafety.gov. For more links, see Appendix IV.

FOOD BROKER REPRESENTATIVE

Position Description

Food Broker Representatives are food sales experts. They sell food products to wholesalers, mom-and-pop stores, and grocery chains, as well as to such food-service operations as restaurants, institutional cafeterias, catering services, and food-service management companies. Some of them make sales to food processors. These sales professionals, however, are not employees of food companies. Instead, they work for food brokers, which are businesses that provide sales and marketing services to food producers and manufacturers on a contractual basis.

Essentially, food brokers function as intermediaries between food suppliers and buyers. Food producers and manufacturers seek brokers' services to keep their costs down as well as to access markets that they have difficulty entering. Food brokers may work on behalf of regional, national, or international food companies. Some brokers specialize in representing companies that produce gourmet, organic, ethnic, or other specialty foods. Food brokers may also focus on selling to specific markets such as national or regional retailers, food-service operations, or institutional food operations such as schools, hospitals, and correctional facilities.

Food Broker Representatives are responsible for making personal contact with customers, who may be the establishment owners or their buyers, purchasing agents, or managers. Their primary objective is to make and negotiate sales with the customers. Food Broker Representatives are usually assigned a sales territory that ranges in size from a few cities within a state to several states. Some representatives have global assignments. These sales experts are familiar with the needs of each of their customers. In addition, they are well-versed about every product they promote, which may be meats, fish and shellfish, cheeses, olive oils, pastas, sauces, baked goods, desserts, gourmet foods, condiments, snacks, frozen foods, fruits, beverages, or other products. It is not unusual for Food Broker Representatives to handle several product lines from two or more food companies.

Food brokers hire sales experts to handle either inside or outside sales. Inside sales representatives spend most of their time in the office where they do all their sales pitches over the phone. Outside sales representatives, on the other hand, spend most of their time visiting customers at their businesses, where they use product samples and catalogs to demonstrate their products.

Whether on the phone or in person, Food Broker Representatives strive to generate interest in their different product lines. They describe the products and explain how the products would benefit customers and meet their needs. They answer questions and concerns that customers have about the products, as well as quote prices and estimate the availability and delivery time of products.

These sales experts are responsible for preparing sales contracts. They also follow up on orders to make sure they have been delivered and that customers are satisfied with the products. For retail customers, Food

Broker Representatives may offer suggestions on ways to best display the products as well as provide support in arranging promotional programs for the products.

Food Broker Representatives are expected to establish trusting, long-term working relationships with clients. They contact their customers regularly to ensure that they have sufficient supplies. They also handle any problems that their clients may have with the products, product displays, or promotion of the products.

These sales professionals are also responsible for developing new clients. They seek sales leads from current customers as well as chambers of commerce, trade and professional associations, and other organizations. They also learn about potential clients by reading trade journals and attending trade shows. Food Broker Representatives make cold calls to potential clients by phone or in person. Inside sales representatives, for example, make many unsolicited calls every day to potential customers. Some Food Broker Representatives take prospective clients to lunch or dinner or to entertainment venues to spend time getting to know them and their business needs.

Food Broker Representatives also perform a variety of non-sales duties, which vary according to their experience and position. For example, they may be responsible for:

- checking stock levels of their products at their clients' grocery shelves, warehouses, stockrooms, and walk-in freezers
- analyzing sales statistics
- preparing sales reports and other paperwork
- maintaining accurate records of their sales
- studying literature provided by food companies about the products they sell
- monitoring the sales, prices, and products of their competitors
- participating in company sales meetings and product training sessions
- presenting product lines at food shows and sales meetings
- assisting marketing teams in identifying new markets and products
- performing various administrative tasks such as scheduling appointments, planning work schedules, and making travel plans

Food Broker Representatives work mostly indoors. Outside sales experts are constantly traveling to meet with customers at their offices, warehouses, or stores. Some cover territories that allow them to drive home every night, while others are away from home for several days or weeks. Their jobs can be physically stressful due to the constant travel and standing or walking for long periods. They frequently lift and carry cases of sample products and other objects that weigh up to 50 pounds or more. Whether in person or over the phone, Food Broker Representatives sometimes handle customers who are behaving angrily or are emotionally upset.

Many Food Broker Representatives work flexible schedules. Most sales calls or visits are made on weekdays during regular working hours. Many work evenings and on weekends to prepare reports and paperwork and complete other non-sales tasks.

Salaries

Salaries for Food Broker Representatives vary, depending on such factors as their experience, employer, and geographic location. Specific salary information for these professionals is unavailable; however, their earnings are similar to those of other sales representatives. According to the May 2008 Occupational Employment Statistics survey by the U.S. Bureau of Labor Statistics, the estimated annual salary for most sales representatives who worked for wholesalers and manufacturers ranged between $26,950 and $106,040. These figures are for sales professionals who do not sell technical and scientific products.

Food Broker Representatives may earn a salary, commission, or both.

Employment Prospects

Job opportunities for Food Broker Representatives generally become available as individuals are promoted, transfer to other jobs or career fields, or retire. Employers will create additional positions as their companies grow and expand.

In addition to working for food brokers, food sales representatives are hired directly by food processors, wholesale houses, and food beverage firms.

Some experts in the field report that as food manufacturers and retailers have been consolidating over the last decade, so have food brokerage firms. Until several years ago, hundreds of independent food brokers existed throughout the United States. At the time this book was being written, three national food brokerages fill the demands of large national manufacturers. Some experts expect regional and specialty independent food brokers to emerge to meet the needs of smaller food manufacturers.

Advancement Prospects

Food Broker Representatives advance according to their interests and ambitions. They may be promoted to supervisory and managerial positions. They may also advance to executive sales positions. Entrepreneurial individuals may start their own food brokerages.

Some sales professionals measure their success through job satisfaction, by earning higher incomes, by meeting or exceeding sales goals, or by gaining professional recognition.

Education and Training

There are no formal educational requirements for individuals to become Food Broker Representatives. Many employers prefer to hire applicants who possess a college degree or have some college training. Minimally, applicants should possess at least a high school diploma or a general equivalency diploma.

Newly hired sales professionals work under the supervision and direction of experienced Food Broker Representatives until they become familiar with their responsibilities.

Food Broker Representatives receive training on new product lines that are assigned to them.

Experience, Special Skills, and Personality Traits

Employers prefer to hire candidates who have several years of sales experience in the grocery or food-service industry. Strong candidates would also be knowledgeable about the markets and areas of food sales in which they would work.

To perform well at their sales jobs, Food Broker Representatives need excellent interpersonal, communication, presentation, and customer service skills. They also must have strong organizational, self-management, writing, and computer skills. Being positive, friendly, assertive, persuasive, honest, persistent, energetic, goal-oriented, and flexible are some personality traits that successful Food Broker Representatives share.

Unions and Associations

Trade associations are available for food brokers to join, such as the Independent Food Brokers, a division of the National Association for Retail Marketing Services. (For contact information, see Appendix II.) Through their employers' membership, Food Broker Representatives may be able to take advantage of services and resources such as networking opportunities.

Tips for Entry

1. While in high school or college, get a sales job in a store or other business to see if the sales field may be right for you.
2. Employers usually require applicants to have a valid driver's license along with a good driving record.
3. Check the yellow pages of telephone books for listings of food brokers in your area to contact directly about job openings. If a company does not have any available jobs, ask about their future needs for sales representatives. Also, ask to whom you can send your résumé for potential openings.
4. You can learn more about food brokers on the Internet. To get a list of relevant Web sites, enter the keywords *food brokers* or *food brokerage* into a search engine. For some links, see Appendix IV.

FLORAL, GARDENING, AND LANDSCAPING SERVICES

FLORAL DESIGNER

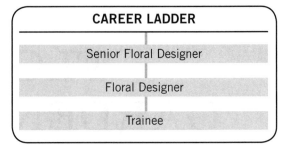

CAREER LADDER

Senior Floral Designer

Floral Designer

Trainee

Position Description

We buy flowers for various reasons. For instance, we give flowers as gifts on special occasions. Sometimes we shop for flowers that we assemble in vases and other containers. Other times we purchase flower arrangements made by professional florists known as Floral Designers.

These floral design artists are trained to create flower arrangements of all sorts and sizes for everyday and special occasions. They fabricate bouquets for weddings, corsages for proms, wreaths for funerals, centerpieces for banquets, swags for home decorations, and so on. Floral Designers use fresh, dried, and artificial flowers. They might also fashion ornamental plants, fruits, or vegetables into arrangements. In addition, Floral Designers add appropriate accessories, such as ribbons, bells, balloons, stuffed animals, candy, or novelty giftware. These professionals assemble standard floral designs as well as customize arrangements to fit the needs of customers.

Floral Designers work in different settings. Many are employed by florists who own storefronts or operate out of their homes or warehouses. Some designers are hired by mass-market florists that have booths in grocery stores and other businesses. Other designers work for wholesale florists who buy flowers from growers and then resell them to retail florists.

Floral Designers work with their customers in person, by phone, by e-mail, or through the Internet. They help their customers decide what flower arrangements to purchase for their particular purposes. Designers advise their customers about types of flowers, colors, designs, prices, and other details that may fulfill their needs and budgets. These designers also provide their customers with information about how to care and maintain arrangements so that they last longer.

Floral Designers generally follow the same routine when completing orders. They comply with instructions that describe the style of the flower arrangements and the types and colors of flowers that their customers want. Some customers provide very specific details, while others give designers the freedom to create arrangements according to their general directions.

Floral Designers perform a number of general tasks, which vary according to their skills, experience, and work setting. They might, for example:

- direct marketing activities
- develop and administer budgets
- supervise, train, and evaluate subordinate staff
- price merchandise
- maintain inventory of fresh flowers, plants, and related merchandise
- purchase flowers, plants, and supplies
- create in-store and window displays or other visual merchandising displays
- perform routine office tasks such as keeping financial records
- sell items, receive payment from their customers, make change, and other retail tasks

Floral Designers work indoors in well-lighted and pleasant workspaces. They may perform some tasks in refrigerated storage rooms or in greenhouses. These professionals work with various tools and materials such as scissors, cutters, shears, knives, glue guns, wires, pins, floral tape, and adhesive spray.

Floral Designers may be employed part time or full time. They may work evenings and on weekends.

Salaries

Salaries for Floral Designers vary, depending on their experience, employer, and other factors. According to the May 2008 Occupational Employment Statistics (OES) survey by the U.S. Bureau of Labor Statistics (BLS), the estimated annual salary for most Floral Designers ranged between $16,210 and $35,010.

Employment Prospects

In addition to working for retail, wholesale, and mass-market florists, Floral Designers find employment with museums, private estates, corporations, and other organizations that require fresh and new arrangements almost daily. Online floral shops are also a source of employment. Some Floral Designers are self-employed.

The BLS reported in its May 2008 OES survey that an estimated 57,500 Floral Designers were employed in the United States. According to the BLS, employment of these professionals is expected to decline between 2008 and 2018; despite this, job opportunities should be favorable due to the turnover rate in retail shops. Many designers leave their jobs because of low wages and lack of advancement opportunities.

Advancement Prospects

Floral Designers can advance to supervisory and managerial positions, but they are limited. After gaining experience, some Floral Designers choose to specialize in creating flower arrangements for special events, such as weddings or corporate parties. Those with entrepreneurial ambitions may start their own flower shops or floral design services.

Education and Training

Minimally, Floral Designers must have a high school diploma or a general equivalency diploma. Some employers may require that applicants hold an asso-

ciate's or bachelor's degree in floriculture or a related field, or have some post–high school training.

There are several ways for individuals to obtain sufficient training to become Floral Designers. One way is to obtain an apprenticeship with an experienced florist. Another path to take is for individuals to enroll in a formal floral design program offered by a college, vocational school, or private floral school. For example, individuals can complete an associate's degree program in floral design, floriculture, horticulture, or ornamental horticulture.

Experience, Special Skills, and Personality Traits

Employers prefer to hire applicants for entry-level positions who have previous experience creating floral arrangements. They may have gained their experience through employment or volunteer work.

Because they deal with customers from diverse backgrounds, Floral Designers need excellent interpersonal, communication, and customer service skills. They must also have effective organizational, problem-solving, time-management, and self-management skills. Some personality traits that successful Floral Designers share include being creative, imaginative, enthusiastic, enterprising, detail-oriented, dependable, and flexible.

Unions and Associations

Floral Designers can join professional associations to take advantage of networking opportunities, training programs, professional certification, and other professional services and resources. Two national societies that serve their interests are the Society of American Florists and the American Institute of Floral Designers. For contact information, see Appendix II.

Tips for Entry

1. While in school, get a part-time job with a florist or garden center to gain work experience.
2. Take photographs of your floral arrangements and present them to prospective employers.
3. Contact retail, wholesale, and mass-market florists directly about job vacancies.
4. Learn more about the flower industry. You might start by visiting the Society of American Florists Web site (www.safnow.org) and The Flower Expert (www.theflowerexpert.com). For more links, see Appendix IV.

INTERIOR PLANT TECHNICIAN

CAREER PROFILE

Duties: Perform plant care maintenance; perform other tasks as required

Alternate Title(s): Horticultural Technician, Interiorscape Technician, Plantscape Technician

Salary Range: $17,000 to $37,000

Employment Prospects: Good

Advancement Prospects: Fair

Prerequisites:

    Education or Training—High school diploma; on-the-job training

    Experience—Work experience preferred

    Special Skills and Personality Traits—Time-management, customer service, communication, interpersonal, teamwork, and self-management skills; energetic, friendly, reliable, trustworthy, ethical, flexible, and self-motivated personality traits

    Special Requirements—Driver's license

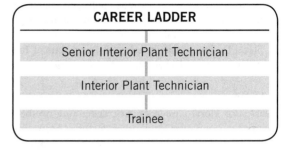

CAREER LADDER

Senior Interior Plant Technician

Interior Plant Technician

Trainee

Position Description

Interior landscaping, also known as interiorscaping and plantscaping, is the art of using green plants to enhance the beauty of indoor environments. This field emerged during the 1970s when growing houseplants became a popular pastime. Today, interior landscaping companies offer customers these basic services: selling or leasing indoor plants, designing and installing plants and containers, and maintaining the plants. These enterprises serve a wide range of customers, including homeowners, apartment complexes, small businesses, medical centers, shopping centers, hotels, restaurants, and nonprofit organizations, among others.

Interior Plant Technicians are responsible for maintaining plants once they have been installed by other interiorscape professionals. These technicians take care of a wide variety of living plants, such as ferns, philodendrons, rubber plants, palms, bamboo, cactus, orchids, African violets, chrysanthemums, and poinsettias. Interior Plant Technicians are knowledgeable about the different indoor plants they maintain; how light, water, and airflow affect each type of plant; and how to specifically care for each plant. They are also experts in methods of watering, fertilizing, pruning, pest control, and identifying plant diseases.

These technicians follow a weekly, biweekly, or other regular schedule to ensure that plants maintain their freshness and beauty. They drive to their clients' residences and buildings in their own vehicles or company vehicles. They work efficiently, quietly, and unobtrusively so as to not disrupt the activities of their clients.

Upon arrival, Interior Plant Technicians assess the overall conditions of the plants and their environments. The technicians look for problems, such as poor lighting, temperatures that are too high for plants, or plant containers being used as garbage cans. They scan the plants for pests and disease and treat the plants as needed. They also check the soil moisture and condition to determine the health of the plants. When needed, they add more topsoil as well as give sufficient fertilizers to plants to build their nutrient levels so that they stay green and healthy.

Interior Plant Technicians water plants accordingly. They remove yellow leaves, trim brown tips off leaves, and prune plants to maintain their shape. These technicians also dust plants and polish leaves to keep them shiny. Furthermore, Interior Plant Technicians rotate plants so that they receive proper lighting and so that the best sides face the room. These technicians remove dying and sickly plants. Depending on their customers' contract, technicians may promptly replace the bad plants with new ones.

Interior Plant Technicians may be assigned other duties. For example, they may maintain plants at greenhouse facilities, assist in the installation of plants, or perform quality inspection checks of the work of other technicians.

The nature of their job is physical. They walk, stand, bend, crouch, and reach for long periods. They climb ladders to reach plants on cabinets and other high places. They also lift, carry, and push heavy objects that may weigh 40 to 50 pounds or more.

Interior Plant Technicians may be employed part-time or full-time. Their work requires constant travel to clients' homes, offices, and buildings.

Salaries

Salaries for Interior Plant Technicians vary, depending on such factors as their education, experience, and geographic location. Formal salary information for these technicians is unavailable. A general idea of their earnings can be gained by looking at similar occupations, such as groundskeeping and landscaping workers. According to the May 2008 Occupational Employment Statistics survey by the U.S. Bureau of Labor Statistics, the estimated annual salary for most groundskeeping and landscaping workers ranged between $16,600 and $36,550.

Employment Prospects

Interiorscape companies are established throughout the United States. In general, job opportunities for Interior Plant Technicians become available as employers need to replace individuals who advance to higher positions, transfer to other jobs or career fields, or leave the workforce for various reasons. As interiorscape companies grow, owners create additional part-time and full-time maintenance positions to fulfill their services.

During economic downturns, there are fewer job opportunities in the interiorscaping industry. In general, though, this green industry has been expanding favorably since its emergence during the 1970s.

Advancement Prospects

Interior Plant Technicians can pursue other career paths by becoming interiorscape sales and design professionals. They can also advance to supervisory and managerial positions. Entrepreneurial individuals can establish their own interiorscape companies.

Education and Training

There are no standard educational requirements for individuals to become Interior Plant Technicians. Most, if not all, employers require that applicants have at least a high school diploma or general equivalency diploma.

These technicians learn their skills on the job, while working under the direction of supervisors and experienced Interior Plant Technicians. Employers also pro-vide technicians with formal training programs that cover such horticultural topics as plant maintenance, methods of pest control, and plant diseases.

Special Requirements

Employers require applicants to hold a valid driver's license as well as have a good driving record. Applicants may be required to supply a vehicle to use for their job.

Experience, Special Skills, and Personality Traits

Employers prefer to hire candidates who have previous experience caring for plants. For example, applicants may have worked for a nursery, greenhouse, garden center, or landscaping or gardening service. Some employers are willing to hire applicants who have no prior work experience, if they demonstrate the ability to learn quickly and the willingness to work hard.

To perform well at their job, Interior Plant Technicians need excellent time-management, customer service, communication, interpersonal, teamwork and self-management skills. Being energetic, friendly, reliable, trustworthy, ethical, flexible, and self-motivated are some personality traits that successful technicians share.

Unions and Associations

The Plantscape Industry Alliance is an organization that serves the interests of interiorscape professionals. Interior Plant Technicians are eligible to join this association to take advantage of networking opportunities, training programs, and other professional services and resources. For contact information, see Appendix II.

Tips for Entry

1. Some technicians seek professional certification through a recognized organization, such as the Professional Landcare Network, to enhance their employability.
2. Do you know any shopping malls, hotels, and other businesses in your area that have interior landscaping? Ask the managers or owners if you could have the name and phone number of the interiorscaping company that they use.
3. Use the Internet to learn more about the interiorscaping industry. You might start by visiting the Plantscape Industry Alliance Web site (www.cipaweb.org) and PlantCare.com. For more links, see Appendix IV.

GARDENER

CAREER PROFILE

Duties: Perform maintenance of private or public gardens, including such tasks as watering, fertilizing, trimming, and treating plant diseases; perform other duties as required

Alternate Title(s): Landscape Gardener, Estate Gardener, Professional Gardener

Salary Range: $17,000 to $48,000

Employment Prospects: Fair

Advancement Prospects: Good

Prerequisites:

Education or Training—On-the-job training, apprenticeship, or formal study in horticulture

Experience—One or more years of work experience

Special Skills and Personality Traits—Self-management, teamwork, interpersonal, communication, and customer service skills; enthusiastic, patient, caring, detail-oriented, and reliable personality traits

Special Requirements—Driver's license; pesticide applicator certificate

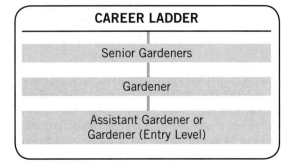

CAREER LADDER

Senior Gardeners

Gardener

Assistant Gardener or Gardener (Entry Level)

Position Description

Many of us like to liven up our living spaces with flower and vegetable gardens wherever we live, from crowded cities to rural farms. Even those of us who are either disinclined or unable to pursue gardening as an avocation appreciate living near plants as much as possible. We enjoy public gardens in parks, arboretums, and city squares. Some of us are fortunate to pass through nice landscaped areas each day where we attend school or work. Gardening, however, is not simply a hobby for some people, it is also a way to make a living. Professional men and women called Gardeners work every day to create and maintain lovely gardens and landscapes in all kinds of public and private places.

These experts bring gardens to life around homes, churches, schools, cemeteries, industrial facilities, and office buildings, as well as in parks and along roadsides. Some of these experts create specialized gardens for display purposes in such venues as fairs and gardening classes, or for stage and screen productions.

Landscaping and groundskeeping service companies may employ Gardeners or they may work directly for homeowners, estates, apartment complex owners, public or private parks, zoos, museums, government agencies, schools and colleges, nurseries, tree farms, golf courses, and various companies in many different industries. Some Gardeners run their own gardening

firms. They contract their gardening services to a variety of clients or to certain categories of clients.

Professional Gardeners are highly skilled and knowledgeable about gardening methods and the more technical aspects of maintaining gardens, particularly on a grander scale than most backyard gardens. For example, these experts are well versed in the use of various chemical or organic soil amendments, pesticides, fungicides, and herbicides. They understand precisely how to mix such preparations and apply them appropriately. They also use high-powered gas or electric tools. In addition, Gardeners work with more extensive irrigation systems and are knowledgeable about proper watering techniques, as well as the proper amounts of watering needed to maximize plant health and growth with a minimum of wastage. Furthermore, Professional Gardeners are skilled in identifying and managing plant diseases and insects that harm plants, and dealing with other problems, such as slow growth.

Most Gardeners cultivate, plant, and maintain gardens that were often designed and installed by other professionals, such as landscape architects and contractors. However, some Gardeners also perform design and installation tasks. In general, Gardeners prepare soil for planting, plant seeds and bulbs at proper soil depths, transplant plants and trees, fertilize, pull weeds, mow lawns, prune shrubs and trees, and remove trash from their work areas. They also perform other related duties such as amending soil, watering plants and lawns, and raking leaves. Gardeners may also be required to install certain garden features such as rock gardens, fences, ponds, raised-bed retaining walls, and so on. Gardeners who work in parks may be assigned to restore and reposition picnic tables or park benches and empty garbage cans.

Gardeners' tasks vary according to the seasons. In cold climates, for example, Gardeners may shovel snow. They may work in greenhouses during winter months to start seedlings and young bulb plants for transplanting in the spring.

Gardeners use a variety of tools to create and maintain their gardens, including both hand and power tools, ranging from small hand clippers and trowels to lawn mowers large enough to ride. Among the hand tools these experts use are shovels, rakes, pitchforks, hoes, edgers, brooms, and pruning shears. Gardeners use such power tools as weed trimmers, leaf blowers, wood chippers, chain saws, hedge trimmers, rotor tillers, and power mowers of all sizes. These men and women are responsible for keeping their tools clean and in operable condition. They may make minor repairs and adjustments to their power tools. Additionally, Gardeners may drive small trucks or vans to their worksites.

Gardeners attend to a variety of tasks during the course of their workdays. Their tasks vary according to their location, their level of experience, client requirements, and season. They may be required to:

- consult with other professionals, such as landscape architects, nursery owners, groundskeepers, and other workers who are involved with gardening projects
- maintain relationships with clients, such as homeowners, business owners, government officials, and others who require gardening services
- assist with maintenance tasks, such as cleaning ponds or creeks or removing debris from rooftops and gutters
- respond to emergencies such as clearing fallen trees following severe storms
- perform some construction tasks on such garden features as pathways, retaining walls, drainage systems, and irrigation systems
- keep records of daily activities to track the progress of gardening projects
- monitor garden areas to determine needed improvements
- prepare grounds for special events, such as garden parties, school assemblies, and athletic games
- assist with garden tours
- comply with company rules and government regulations pertinent to the gardening profession

These experts often work in teams, and may supervise other members of their staff.

Professional Gardeners work primarily in outdoor locations, in which they are exposed to varying temperatures and climatic conditions. Their work may involve some travel to other cities or regions.

Gardeners need to be in good physical condition. They must be able to lift and carry heavy objects including some of their equipment and bags of soil or fertilizer weighing as much as 100 pounds. Gardeners also must possess enough agility to frequently stoop, crouch, reach, bend, and walk.

Because they sometimes work with toxic chemicals, Gardeners must use safety equipment such as goggles, face masks, or respirators. They are also exposed to dust and mud as well as loud noises created by some of their power tools.

Gardeners may be hired to permanent, temporary, or seasonal positions. They may hold part-time or full-time positions. These experts may be scheduled to work flexible or irregular hours that include early mornings, evenings, weekends, or holidays. Their workweeks may be longer during the warmer months, including some weeks that may extend to 48 hours or more.

Salaries

Salaries for Gardeners vary, depending on such factors as their education, experience, job duties, employer, and geographic location. Specific salary information for this profession is unavailable. The U.S. Bureau of Labor Statistics (BLS) reported in its May 2008 Occupational Employment Statistics survey that the estimated annual salary for most grounds maintenance workers ranged between $16,680 and $47,830. (Note: This salary range was cited for all grounds maintenance workers who were not listed separately in the survey.)

Gardeners who work for private estates may receive free housing in addition to their salaries.

Employment Prospects

Opportunities for staff positions usually become available as Gardeners transfer to other jobs or career fields, advance to higher positions, retire, or leave the workforce for various reasons. Employers create additional positions to meet growing needs as long as funding is available.

In general, the BLS reports that employment of grounds maintenance occupations, including Gardeners, is expected to increase by 18 percent through 2018. According to O*NET Online (online.onetcenter. org), landscaping and groundskeeping workers are in demand in the hospitality industry, which includes hotels and other lodging establishments.

Advancement Prospects

Many Gardeners advance by earning higher wages and being assigned greater levels of responsibilities. Some measure success through job satisfaction. Gardeners can also be promoted to supervisor and managerial positions, which may require obtaining additional formal education. Those with entrepreneurial ambitions can start their own gardening services, nurseries, or retail gardening centers.

With additional education, Gardeners can become landscape designers, landscape architects, horticulturists, biologists, agricultural technicians, or environmentalists, or pursue other professions that interest them.

Education and Training

There is no standard educational requirement for individuals to follow to become Gardeners. Most employers, however, prefer to hire applicants who hold at least a high school diploma or a general equivalency diploma.

Individuals can become Gardeners in several ways. One route is for persons to work as assistant Gardeners or grounds maintenance workers and learn skills on the job while working under experienced gardeners and grounds maintenance professionals. Another path is for persons to apply for a gardening apprenticeship program that includes both classroom instruction and on-the-job training. Thirdly, individuals can choose to enroll in a horticulture program, or another related program, at a college or university to earn a degree or a professional certificate.

Special Requirements

Employers may require Gardeners to possess a valid state driver's license and have a good driving record.

Gardeners may also be required to hold a pesticide applicator certificate, which is granted by a state government agency, such as a department of agriculture or environmental protection.

Experience, Special Skills, and Personality Traits

Employers prefer to hire applicants for entry-level positions who have one or more years of experience in plant care and maintenance. Candidates may have gained experience through gardening, nursery, or grounds maintenance work.

Gardeners must have excellent self-management skills, including the ability to work independently, handle stressful situations, follow and understand instructions, and prioritize multiple tasks. They also need effective teamwork, interpersonal, communication, and customer service skills, as they must work well with colleagues, supervisors, customers, and others from diverse backgrounds. Being enthusiastic, patient, caring, detail-oriented, and reliable are some personality traits that successful professional Gardeners have in common.

Unions and Associations

Gardeners who work for academic institutions, government agencies, or large employers may be members of a union, which represents them in contract negotiations with their employers. The union may also handle any grievances that its members may have against their employers.

Gardeners may join associations to take advantage of networking opportunities, professional certification, continuing education, and other professional services and resources. Two national societies that serve the different interests of Gardeners are the Professional Grounds Management Society and the Professional Landcare Network.

Some Gardeners belong to nonprofit gardening organizations such as the American Horticultural Society.

For contact information to the above organizations, see Appendix II.

Tips for Entry

1. As a student, obtain a part-time or summer job with a gardening service, a landscaping service, a nursery, or a garden center to gain work experience.
2. Participate in the Master Gardener program, sponsored through the Cooperative Extension Service, to obtain training as well as experience.
3. Follow application instructions precisely; otherwise, you may be disqualified. For example, submit your application by the deadline date.
4. Contact fellow Gardeners and groundskeepers for leads to job openings. Also, ask employees at local nurseries and garden centers, as well as friends and neighbors who use gardening services, about potential job leads.
5. Use the Internet to find valuable gardening resources. You might start by visiting Garden-Web (www.gardenweb.com) and American Horticultural Society Web site (www.ahs.org). For more links, see Appendix IV.

ARBORIST

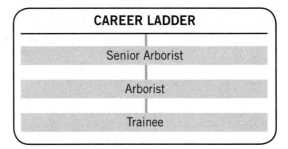

Position Description

For most of our history, people lived in rural areas far from cities and closer to nature. In our present day, most of us live in cities or the metropolitan areas that surround larger cities. As we populated these urban centers, we brought nature with us by planting trees in our yards, along our thoroughfares, and in our parks. Many of us like to live among trees because they add beauty to our surroundings and refresh the air we breathe. Their shade helps us to keep cool in the summer and reduces the glare reflected from windows and other shiny surfaces. Trees provide homes for birds and other wild creatures that would otherwise be displaced by our presence. However, trees have a tendency to live shorter lives in urban environments. Fortunately, professional men and women called Arborists work every day to sustain the health and vitality of trees.

Arborists work with individual trees, shrubs, and any other woody plants that form bark on their trunks and branches. They also work with trees in groups, such as a grove of trees in a park. These professionals understand how certain varieties of trees may be appropriate for specific locations, while other tree species would not thrive there.

Some people call Arborists "tree surgeons" because of the kind of work they do. Trees may need to have their branches trimmed to help them grow properly or stave off certain diseases. Arborists are experts at this process, called pruning. They also have occasion to inject medicines into trees, apply sealing compounds or wrappings to openings in tree bark, provide brace and cabling support to weak limbs, or dig into the soil at the base of trees to work on the roots.

Arborists have varied careers. These professionals help keep trees healthy on constructions sites, plant or transplant trees in yards or parks, remove dead or diseased trees, offer consulting services, and testify in court as expert witnesses, for example. Some Arborists are self-employed, while others work for tree-service firms, city governments, utility companies, arboretums, golf courses, academic institutions, theme parks, resorts, industrial complexes, private estates, landscape architectural firms, and other establishments. In general, they are experts in all aspects of tree growth and the appropriate use of trees in human environments.

Arborists most commonly work in tree crews, consisting of personnel on the ground, climbers, aerialists, and crew leaders. Tree crews work for commercial tree services, utility companies, and municipal governments. Members of the ground crew are often beginning Arborists who learn their profession by cutting and chipping the branches that climbers prune from the trees. Ground crewmembers also provide assistance to other crewmembers and perform cleanup tasks.

Climbers ascend into trees by way of knotted ropes and harnesses. These Arborists secure themselves to high branches in three places and pull themselves up by hand. They prune and install bracing while in the tree canopy. Aerialists, otherwise known as aerial lift operators, also work above the ground to perform pruning and bracing tasks. They use crane mechanisms, sometimes called cherry pickers, in which they are raised into the air while standing in bucket compartments. These Arborists also help to remove trees. Crew leaders supervise the crews and provide instructions for pruning branches, felling operations, and stump removal.

Many Arborists work for commercial tree service companies. These companies contract with clients to provide the services of tree crews. Some commercial Arborists also work in the areas of plant health care, sales, and company management. Plant health care technicians monitor plants and trees for pests, diseases, and other problems, which they treat or offer treatment recommendations for clients to follow. Arborists in sales contact clients and promote business for their companies. Like other salespersons, these experts maintain a sales territory. They may also inspect trees and properties to make estimates of time and costs regarding company services. Arborists in management and executive positions oversee the daily activities of their tree crews, health care technicians, sales force, and other staff members. They manage company budgets and attend to such matters as hiring personnel, acquiring equipment, and managing legal issues.

In addition to tree crews, cities hire technical tree experts. These Arborists work with city governments to specifically manage trees on city properties, such as along streets, in parks, and on the grounds of government buildings. They keep records of all trees and other woody plants on city land and create and enforce municipal regulations regarding their use and care. Municipal Arborists also go over tree-planting projects, manage budgets, develop public education programs about urban forestry, and provide guidelines for managing trees on construction projects, in addition to monitoring tree health and recommending proper treatment for diseases or other problems.

Utility Arborists work for electric utility companies. They maintain trees that grow near power lines to keep their branches from interfering with the delivery of electrical power. They help property owners to keep their trees away from electrical lines and advise them about which tree species are most suitable for planting near electrical wiring. Utility Arborists fulfill different roles. Those who work on tree crews are specially trained to prune and remove trees near power lines. Arborists known as pre-inspectors work alongside utility tree crews to find trees that need work, decide what work needs to be done, and coordinate projects with property owners. Safety coordinators (still other Arborists) write safety rules, train tree crews to work safely,

and conduct site inspections. Supervisory Arborists called utility forest managers assign work, manage budgets, deal with personnel and client issues, and oversee tree crews, pre-inspectors, and safety coordinators.

Some Arborists work as consultants. These men and women use their experience and expertise to offer planning and informational services to their clients regarding the use and placement of trees. Consulting Arborists appraise the value of trees for property owners for settling insurance claims or completing environmental impact reports. They make inspections and advise property owners about preserving their tree resources. They advise lawmakers regarding legislation about trees. Occasionally, consulting Arborists may be called upon to collect data and act as expert witnesses in court cases pertaining to injuries or property damages caused by trees, as well as boundary issues or cases where neighbors feel that trees obstruct their views.

Arborists' work can be very physically demanding and dangerous. They must be able to hoist their own weight and handle sharp pruning shears and saws while negotiating their way around tree canopies at great heights. Aerial lift operators contend with large moving machinery parts. Utility Arborists risk exposure to live power lines. Ground crew members work with powerful machines such as stump grinders. Tree service professionals work amid traffic conditions while being exposed to vehicle fumes, noise, and various lighting conditions. In addition, Arborists are exposed to extremes in temperatures and all kinds of weather.

In general, Arborists work 40 hours per week, but may put in extra hours to complete assignments or to handle emergencies.

Salaries

Salaries for Arborists vary, depending on such factors as their education, experience, job duties, employer, and geographic location. Salary information specifically for Arborists is unavailable. However, the U.S. Bureau of Labor Statistics reported in its May 2008 Occupational Employment Statistics survey that the estimated annual salary for most tree trimmers and pruners ranged between $20,000 and $46,480. In general, experienced Arborists who perform jobs with high-level responsibilities, such as managers and consultants, earn higher wages.

Employment Prospects

According to some experts in the field, job opportunities for Arborists are favorable. The increasing concern about the environment and the conservation of urban forests is expected to contribute to job growth.

In general, job openings become available as Arborists retire, advance to higher positions, or transfer to other jobs or career fields. Employers will also create new positions to meet the growing needs of their organizations.

Advancement Prospects

Arborists can advance in various ways, according to their interests and ambitions. As they gain experience, they earn higher salaries and receive higher-level duties to perform. Some Arborists measure success by seeking opportunities in another tree care field; for example, a municipal Arborist may obtain a desired position in utility arboriculture.

Entry-level Arborists usually start as groundworkers and progress through the ranks as climbers, aerial lift operators, and crew leaders. Arborists can also be promoted to higher positions such as plant health care technicians, safety coordinators, or salespersons, depending on their work setting. Those with management and administrative interests can seek opportunities in those areas as well. Entrepreneurial individuals can start their own tree care services or establish consulting firms.

Arborists can also earn advanced degrees to become research scientists, academic instructors, or Cooperative Extension professionals.

Education and Training

Educational requirements vary for the different Arborist positions. For entry-level ground crew positions, applicants must possess at least a high school diploma or general equivalency diploma. To advance to salesperson, plant health care technician, and other higher positions, employers may prefer that candidates hold an associate's or bachelor's degree in arboriculture, horticulture, forestry, or another related field.

Entry-level Arborists receive on-the-job training. They learn their skills while working under the supervision of crew leaders and other experienced Arborists. Employers also provide Arborists with formal training programs to learn about safety procedures, tree care, and other topics.

Throughout their careers, Arborists enroll in classes and workshops to update their skills and knowledge.

Experience, Special Skills, and Personality Traits

Requirements vary for the different positions available to Arborists. Employers prefer to hire candidates for entry-level positions who have previous work experience in landscaping, groundskeeping, or similar jobs. Many employers are willing to hire applicants without any experience if they demonstrate the ability to learn quickly and to work hard.

To perform well at their job, Arborists need excellent communication, interpersonal teamwork, self-management, and customer service skills. Some personality traits that successful Arborists have in common include being pleasant, responsible, accurate, flexible, and hardworking.

Unions and Associations

Arborists can join professional associations to take advantage of networking opportunities, continuing education, professional certification, and other professional services and resources. Some national societies that serve the diverse interests of these men and women are:

- American Society of Consulting Arborists
- International Society of Arboriculture
- Society of Commercial Arboriculture
- Society of Municipal Arborists
- Utility Arborist Association

For contact information to these organizations, see Appendix II.

Tips for Entry

1. Talk with different Arborists in different settings to find out which type of work would most interest you.
2. Tree crewmembers need to be in good physical condition. So, maintain your physical fitness.
3. For many positions, you will need a valid driver's license and a good driving record. Once you are working, you may eventually need to obtain a commercial driver's license.
4. To enhance their employability, some Arborists obtain professional certification from an organization widely respected in the field, such as the International Society of Arboriculture or the Tree Care Industry Association.
5. Use the Internet to learn more about the field of arboriculture. You might start by visiting the Web sites of these organizations: the International Society of Arboriculture (www.isa-arbor.com/home.aspx) and the Tree Care Industry Association (www.tcia.org). For more links, see Appendix IV.

GOLF COURSE SUPERINTENDENT

Duties: Oversee the daily maintenance and functionality of public or private golf courses; direct the activities of maintenance staff; perform other duties as required

Alternate Title(s): Assistant Golf Course Superintendent

Salary Range: $56,000 to $79,000+

Employment Prospects: Fair

Advancement Prospects: Fair

Prerequisites:

   Education or Training—High school diploma, college degree, or professional certificate, depending on employer

   Experience—Several years of experience in assistant role

CAREER LADDER

Golf Course Superintendent

Assistant Golf Course Superintendent

Golf Course Management Intern

Special Skills and Personality Traits—Leadership, organizational, decision-making, customer service, communication, and interpersonal skills; enthusiastic, outgoing, inspirational, goal-oriented, trustworthy, dedicated, and innovative personality traits

Position Description

Golf courses are expanses of land that are meticulously landscaped to make the game of golf a pleasant pastime for golfing enthusiasts. Several types of lawn areas, trees, shrubs, ponds, and sandy bunkers characterize these recreational grounds. Golf courses often have buildings including clubhouses and shops where golfers may congregate and buy equipment for their games. They also have paved pathways, terraces, and other features that add to golfers' overall experience.

Golf Course Superintendents are in charge of maintaining the appearance and functionality of golf courses. They are experts at keeping these recreational areas in optimum condition. Golf Course Superintendents oversee staffs of groundskeepers, landscape gardeners, arborists, builders, electricians, plumbers, and other trades professionals. They help golf course administrators plan course development. These superintendents implement the construction and ongoing maintenance of entire golf course facilities, including buildings, pathways, and walls, in addition to the fairways, greens, roughs, and other areas where the game of golf is played. These men and women also manage special events held at their golf courses. They handle budgets and equipment inventories.

Golf courses must be mowed and groomed frequently. Some parts of courses, such as putting greens, must be mowed daily and the grass must be maintained at a specific length. Furthermore, various areas of golf courses require varying amounts of water to maintain the right level of moisture. Golf Course Superintendents walk their courses to determine what work needs to be done for each section of the grounds. Some superintendents regularly play golf to become more familiar with conditions on their courses.

These managers schedule such landscaping activities as seeding, cutting, pruning, providing for drainage, leveling, and raking. They plan for the replacement of trees and shrubbery, the application of fertilizers and herbicides, and other landscaping tasks. They arrange for some of these tasks to be performed at specific seasons but also schedule them on a remedial basis. For example, Golf Course Superintendents may decide to move the hole on a green to ensure that the green does not wear unevenly.

Golf Course Superintendents maintain golf courses in consideration of water conservation, wildlife habitat management, pollution control, and other environmental concerns. For example, a superintendent might integrate wildlife sections of their courses with the grassy playing areas to encourage native species of birds, plants, and other wildlife to live in their natural habitats. Golf Course Superintendents also maintain irrigation systems to keep grassy areas green at all times. They continually monitor sprinkler systems, drainage systems, and water pumps to ensure their efficient operation and to ensure water quality.

Golf Course Superintendents are responsible for managing all properties belonging to their golf facilities, including buildings, grounds, tennis courts, swimming pools, and golf carts, as well as the wooded areas, water hazards, access roads, parking lots, and surrounding areas. They oversee new construction and repairs to existing structures. Additionally, they manage equipment maintenance and purchasing, and maintain an inventory of supplies needed for grounds and building repair tasks.

Golf Course Superintendents work closely with golf course owners, general managers, and golf professionals to implement their plans for new courses or the improvement of established courses. Superintendents of public facilities confer with city parks and recreation directors. Golf Course Superintendents also meet with managers and owners to plan for new facilities and coordinate maintenance projects. These superintendents impart their plans to their staffs, which include assistant superintendents, builders, plumbers, landscapists, gardeners, and other trades persons. Golf Course Superintendents ensure that the specifications and standards desired by golf course owners and directors are followed.

Golf Course Superintendents perform various management duties such as:

- interviewing and hiring staff members
- evaluating staff performance and imposing disciplinary measures when needed
- scheduling work activities to minimize conflict with the usage of facilities by patrons
- planning operational budgets and determining how construction and maintenance funds are to be allocated
- keeping records, compiling reports, and writing correspondence
- publishing informational materials regarding golf course activities
- attending professional conferences and training workshops to keep up-to-date with new products and golf course management trends
- organizing and coordinating special events for schools, charitable groups, and other organizations

Golf Course Superintendents mostly work in offices, but also spend time outdoors to monitor the conditions of facilities and grounds, as well as oversee the activities of their staffs. These professionals usually work for 40 hours per week, but may extend their hours to ensure that projects are completed within scheduled time frames. They may work on weekends or holidays.

Salaries

Salaries for Golf Course Superintendents vary, depending on such factors as their education, experience, employer, and geographic location. According to a 2007 compensation survey by the Golf Course Superintendents Association of America, the average salary of Golf Course Superintendents ranged from $56,005 for those who hold high school diplomas to $78,909 for those who earned a two-year professional certificate in golf course management. Some experts in the field report that experienced Golf Course Superintendents may earn six-figure incomes, particularly at private golf courses.

Employment Prospects

Golf Course Superintendents work for public golf courses, private country clubs, hotels, resorts, and golf practice facilities. Some find employment with golf course management companies.

In 2004, there were just over 16,000 golf facilities in the United States. New golf courses are constructed each year, with many of them being planned as part of real estate developments. According to the Golf Channel Solutions Web site (www.golfchannelsolutions. com), there are 26.2 million golfers in the United States. Another 36.7 million Americans are considered to be golf participants in that they either have played one round of golf or visited a golf practice facility.

Job competition is high. Job openings generally become available as Golf Course Superintendents retire or transfer to other jobs. Some experts in the field report that superintendents work an average of seven to 10 years in a position. Job opportunities also open when new golf courses are built.

Advancement Prospects

Golf Course Superintendents typically start their career as assistant superintendents. As they gain experience and establish credentials, they obtain positions at golf course operations that interest them. Many superintendents seek opportunities that offer higher salaries and greater challenges. Some have ambitions to work at prestigious private golf clubs, multicourse facilities, or resorts.

Superintendents can also become general managers of golf courses. Entrepreneurial individuals may pursue opportunities to become consultants or to buy their own golf facility operations.

Education and Training

Educational requirements vary among employers. For example, employers may require that candidates have at least a high school diploma or high school equivalency diploma, while other employers require that candidates possess a college degree in turfgrass management or another related field.

Many two-year colleges, four-year colleges, and universities offer associate degree, bachelor's degree, or professional certificate programs in golf course management. These programs cover agronomy, soil science, horticulture, plant physiology, plant pathology, turfgrass management, irrigation systems management, golf course operations, and other subjects. Many programs also include an internship or practicum in which students get experience working on a golf course.

Throughout their careers, Golf Club Superintendents enroll in continuing education programs to update their skills and keep up with advancements in their fields.

Experience, Special Skills, and Personality Traits

The entry-level position in golf course management is the assistant golf course superintendent. Employers select candidates for assistant positions who have one or more years of responsible work experience in golf course maintenance, which includes supervisory duties. Individuals usually work five to 10 years as assistants before obtaining their first position as a Golf Course Superintendent.

Golf Course Superintendents need excellent leadership, organizational, decision-making, and customer service skills. In addition, they must have strong communication and interpersonal skills as they need to work well with crew, golf club personnel, and others from diverse backgrounds. Being enthusiastic, outgoing, inspirational, goal-oriented, trustworthy, dedicated, and innovative are some personality traits that successful Golf Course Superintendents have in common.

Unions and Associations

Many Golf Course Superintendents belong to state or regional professional associations to take advantage of networking opportunities, professional certification, continuing education, and other professional services and resources. Many also join the Golf Course Superintendents Association of America, which is a national society that serves their interests. For contact information, see Appendix II.

Tips for Entry

1. Are you a high school student? Learn how to play golf. Also, get a part-time or summer job performing groundskeeping work at a local golf course. You will gain work experience as well as determine if golf course management may be the right career for you.
2. Some experts in the field suggest that assistants seek jobs with Golf Course Superintendents who are willing to mentor them.
3. To enhance their professional credibility, some superintendents obtain certification granted by the Golf Course Superintendents Association of America.
4. First impressions count. Dress and act professionally at every job interview. Talk clearly and confidently.
5. Learn more about Golf Course Superintendents on the Internet. You might start by visiting the Golf Course Superintendents Association of America Web site at www.gcsaa.org. For more links, see Appendix IV.

GROUNDSKEEPER

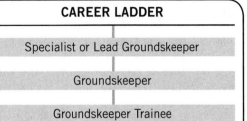

Position Description

Groundskeepers are men and women who take care of cultivated expanses of land such as building landscapes, arboretums, athletic fields, parks, cemetery grounds, golf courses, and school and college campuses, among other areas. The also take care of indoor gardens in such places as office buildings, shopping malls, hotels, and so forth. Their mission is to ensure that such places stay lovely as well as useful to the individuals and communities who use them. These experts perform such tasks as mowing lawns, tending to flower gardens, removing weeds, and pruning trees.

Some Groundskeepers set up new landscaped areas. These men and women are usually known as landscaping workers. They prepare properties for landscaping and plant bushes or trees. They may set up lighting, lay concrete pathways, build terraces for gardens, and install fountains and watering systems. Other Groundskeepers maintain the landscaped areas that the landscaping workers installed. They mow lawns, rake leaves, trim hedges, and repair or maintain such landscape features as sidewalks, walls, and pools. They also maintain groundskeeping equipment and vehicles.

Groundskeepers work in crews that range from small to large according to the size or number of properties on which they work. In large crews, each of these experts performs a specific function, such as mowing lawns or trimming hedges.

Some Groundskeepers specialize by working in certain types of areas, such as at industrial parks or in stadiums. Others specialize by pruning trees and shrubs or by applying fertilizers or other compounds on plants, while others specialize in such tasks as managing lawns, overseeing irrigation systems, or maintaining flower beds. Specialists usually hold a title, such as gardener, pruner, or irrigator, that reflects their particular jobs.

The responsibilities of Groundskeepers also vary according to where they work. For example, in stadiums, Groundskeepers mainly perform lawn care tasks. They may work with either artificial or natural turfs. They maintain padding or soils underneath the turfs to ensure proper drainage of rainwater. They mark lines such as baselines or scrimmage lines. On football fields, they paint the end zones and the midfield area with team names or league logos. On baseball diamonds, they moisten and rake infield areas. They water and mow natural turf or vacuum artificial turfs.

In contrast, Groundskeepers who work at industrial or business parks maintain bushes, trees, pathways, raised beds, and parking lots in addition to their groundskeeping duties. In municipal parks, Groundskeepers may be assigned to paint buildings, clean pools or fountains, pick up litter, and perform similar tasks. At schools, Groundskeepers may be a part of combined maintenance and grounds crews. They may also perform such diverse tasks as installing playground equipment, maintaining asphalt playgrounds, painting play area lines, and attending to other building maintenance tasks.

In general, Groundskeepers perform a variety of tasks specific to their trade. Depending on their work location or specialty, they may:

- add new plants to landscaped grounds by digging holes and transplanting the plants or sowing seeds
- care for plants by watering them regularly, pulling weeds, removing dead leaves and flowers, and applying fertilizer or insecticide
- mow lawns, trim lawn edges, collect clippings, pull weeds, rake leaves, and mulch or fertilize lawn areas
- prune trees, hedges, and bushes
- climb tall trees via ladders or ropes to prune limbs or examine them for disease or insect infestation
- use trucks to remove pruned branches, dried leaves, lawn clippings, and litter from landscape premises and dispose of them properly
- mix batches of fertilizers, herbicides, or insecticides according to specifications
- shovel snow from paved areas in winter and remove mud or dust from paved areas in warmer seasons
- clean fountains and repair cracks
- clean sculptures
- remove debris from roofs, storm sewers, and streets
- fill potholes in streets or parking lots
- repair road signs, fences, planters, park benches, and other man-made items
- attend training classes
- clean and maintain tools, power equipment, and equipment attachments

Groundskeepers use both hand and power tools to complete their various tasks. Among the hand tools they may use are pruning shears, saws, axes or hatchets, hand clippers, rakes, and brooms. They use such power tools as lawn mowers, weed trimmers, lawn edgers, leaf blowers or snowblowers, electric shears, and chain saws. These experts also drive such vehicles as dump trucks and pickup trucks. Some may operate riding lawn mowers, cherry pickers, tractors, wood chippers, and other heavy equipment.

As they gain experience and expertise, these men and women may become supervisors of other Groundskeepers. Supervisory duties include creating work schedules and assigning tasks; providing training to new staff members; evaluating crewmembers' work for quality and compliance with company policies and governmental regulations; keeping records of landscaping and spraying activities; replenishing supplies of seeds, tools, and other items; completing reports; and preparing cost estimates for proposed projects.

Depending on their geographic location, Groundskeepers may work seasonally during spring, summer, and autumn months, or all year. They may work in extreme temperature conditions. These experts work primarily in outdoor locations. Some may work in greenhouse facilities or buildings that have indoor gardens.

Their work is physically demanding. Groundskeepers need to be able to lift, bend, stoop, kneel, and climb. These experts may be exposed to such potentially hazardous situations as operating riding mowers on steep hillsides, using sharp hand and power tools, working on rocky terrain, climbing tall trees, or handling powerful chemical sprays. Groundskeepers may be required to wear gloves, work boots, hearing protection, respiratory equipment, and hard hats during the course of their day.

Groundskeepers work either full-time or part-time. Their schedules may include weekends. During the long hours of summer, they may work in split shifts to fully utilize the available sunlight.

Salaries

Salaries for Groundskeepers vary, depending on such factors as their experience, job duties, employer, and geographic location. The U.S. Bureau of Labor Statistics (BLS) reported the following estimated ranges for most of these groundskeeping workers in its May 2008 Occupational Employment Statistics survey:

- first-line supervisors/managers of lawn service and groundskeeping workers: $26,140 to $65,160
- groundskeeping (and landscaping) workers: $16,600 to $36,550
- pesticide handlers: $19,820 to $44,910
- tree trimmers and pruners: $20,000 to $46,480
- all other grounds maintenance workers: $16,680 to $47,830

Employment Prospects

The BLS reports that approximately 1.5 million ground maintenance workers were employed in the United States in 2008. Nearly 80 percent of them were landscaping and groundskeeping workers.

Employers of Groundskeepers include gardening and landscaping services, educational institutions, private corporations, apartment complexes, real-estate firms, sports stadiums, golf courses, amusement parks, hospitals, shopping malls, parks, government agencies, and homeowners, among others. Some Groundskeepers are self-employed.

Job opportunities should be favorable for experienced Groundskeepers. According to the BLS, employment for the grounds maintenance occupations overall is expected to increase by 18 percent through 2018. In addition to job growth, job openings will become available as Groundskeepers transfer to other jobs or career fields, retire, or leave the workforce for various reasons.

The turnover rate for Groundskeepers is generally high because the work is physically hard and wages for entry-level positions are low.

Advancement Prospects

Groundskeepers advance by earning higher wages and being assigned greater levels of responsibilities. They can also be promoted to supervisory and managerial positions, for which they may be required to obtain additional formal education. Entrepreneurial individuals can establish their own gardening, lawn care, groundskeeping, or landscaping businesses.

With additional education, Groundskeepers can gain entry to other careers that interest them. For example, they may become arborists, landscape architects, horticulturists, biologists, conservation scientists, or agricultural technicians.

Education and Training

Most employees prefer to hire Groundskeepers who possess at least a high school diploma or a general equivalency diploma.

Groundskeepers learn their skills on the job, while working under the supervision and direction of experienced grounds maintenance workers. Trainees are taught the procedures for planting and maintaining lawns, shrubs, trees, and gardens, as well as how to operate mowers, trimmers, and other equipment. They may also learn how to perform basic repair of equipment.

Experience, Special Skills, and Personality Traits

Employers prefer to hire applicants for entry-level positions who have at least one year of experience operating groundskeeping tools as well as performing general groundskeeping tasks. They may have earned their experience through employment, volunteer work, or work-study programs. Some employers hire candidates without any experience if they demonstrate the ability to learn tasks quickly and to work hard.

To perform their job effectively, Groundskeepers must have strong teamwork, interpersonal, and communication skills. They also need excellent self-management skills, such as the ability to work independently, meet deadlines, follow and understand instructions, and prioritize multiple tasks. Having fundamental math, reading, and writing skills is also important. Being cooperative, dependable, detail-oriented, resourceful, and responsible are some personality traits that successful Groundskeepers share.

Unions and Associations

Some Groundskeepers, such as those who work for academic institutions, belong to labor unions. The union represents them in contract negotiations with their employers for better terms regarding pay, benefits, and working conditions. The union also handles any grievances that its members may have against their employers.

Tips for Entry

1. Learn as much as you can about horticulture and gardening. Visit your school or public library and ask the librarian for help finding books and magazines to read.
2. Do you take care of your lawn or do gardening work? Be sure to count that as experience on your application. If that is your only form of experience, you might photograph your handiwork and show the pictures to prospective employers.
3. Many employers seek applicants who possess a valid driver's license and a good driving record.
4. Before they can be hired, applicants may be required to pass a drug screening and a criminal background check.
5. Use the Internet to learn more about grounds maintenance. You might start by visiting the Grounds Maintenance Web site at www.grounds-mag.com. For more links, see Appendix IV.

LANDSCAPE ARCHITECT

Position Description

Landscape Architects are men and women whose profession it is to make our working and living environments pleasant. They design parks, arboretums, and other outdoor places where people can relax and enjoy the outdoors within their towns and cities. They also develop the landscaped areas of amusement parks, stadiums, and other recreational areas. Additionally, Landscape Architects create the small parklike areas surrounding office buildings, town squares, residential complexes, parking lots, government centers, shopping centers, schools, colleges, hospitals, and other public areas. Along streets and highways are strips of land that feature trees, shrubbery, and lawns or other green ground covers that make our driving experience more enjoyable. Landscape Architects design these areas, too. Furthermore, these professionals plan landscaped areas around private residences and estates.

Landscape Architects are not builders or contractors. Their work is primarily in the areas of design and planning. The implementation of construction and maintenance of landscaped areas is the work of other individuals such as landscape contractors, construction workers, and landscape gardeners. However, Landscape Architects monitor the progress of landscape construction. They also offer consultation services to the people who implement their designs.

Landscape Architects apply horticultural principles and methods to their designs, as well as make use of their knowledge of such disciplines as ecology, engineering, mathematics, and geology to plan and design all kinds of land-use projects. Landscape Architects also utilize an artistic sensibility to design lovely spaces that are similar to local natural areas. These men and women create their designs so that the utilization and arrangement of structures and vegetation complement each other. They design pathways and garden areas to follow natural land features or to form geometric patterns. They may incorporate murals, fountains, and sculptures into landscapes to draw visitors' attention to pleasing sights while they stroll through or sit in these public gardens.

When creating landscapes, Landscape Architects think about how their designed areas will be used. They study such site factors as soil quality, natural drainage, weather patterns, and existing plants and trees, and they consider how these may be used in landscape designs. They also read various government documents that may pertain to their sites, such as those regarding laws or regulations enacted to protect historical sites or natural habitats. They observe the presence of power and water lines, adjacent buildings, and nearby thoroughfares to plan how these structures may be incorporated into their designs. Some Landscape Architects use global positioning system devices to note the location of various site features before preparing their preliminary sketches. Landscape Architects also confer with other professionals in such fields as engineering, hydrology, architecture, environmental science, and surveying. With their input, Landscape Architects decide how best to utilize the space required for landscaping projects.

Landscape Architects show their rough designs to their clients before preparing more detailed drawings and models. Landscape Architects also write reports that outline project budgets and summarize environmental and land-use studies, construction schedules, and other project details.

Some Landscape Architects may specialize by working on certain types of projects, such as highway landscaping, shopping center landscaping, or the design of city parks. Others may work on projects that do not involve modifying areas of land that surround structures. For example, some Landscape Architects are employed to preserve historical sites, restore wetlands, and protect other natural areas that have been damaged by people or through natural causes. Some of these professionals contribute their expertise to environmental impact studies, resource management projects, or other endeavors not directly related to landscape design.

Duties for these professionals vary, depending on their experience or particular projects. Landscape Architects may perform such tasks as:

- drawing sketches or maps of project sites
- surveying project sites to ascertain topographical details
- estimating project costs
- writing reports to describe proposed landscaping projects
- choosing and inspecting landscape elements such as plants or structures, or recommending their use
- working out plans for the placement of plants
- implementing quality control processes for installing and maintaining landscaped areas
- ensuring compliance with regulations and codes when reviewing project plans, contracts, and reports
- presenting project proposals and plans with government agencies, landscape contractors, community groups, and other individuals or groups
- providing technical advice to engineers and other professionals on project teams
- keeping up-to-date with new developments in the landscape architecture field including new products, technologies, and design concepts

Experienced Landscape Architects may have supervisory or management responsibilities. They may train staff and oversee their work activities. They manage budgets, develop work plans, schedule work assignments, and perform such other management tasks as reviewing and evaluating employee performance with attention to the level of quality of their work and to their compliance with design specifications and building codes.

Landscape Architects work in both indoor and outdoor environments. They study outdoor locations to understand how landscape projects would work in those locations. Much of their work, however, involves sitting in offices at drawing boards or at computer consoles, which they use to develop completed designs and models of landscapes, as well as to write reports and correspondence.

These professionals usually work 40 hours per week. They may need to put in additional hours to meet project deadlines or complete tasks.

Salaries

Salaries for Landscape Architects vary, depending on such factors as their education, experience, job duties, employer, and geographic location. According to the May 2008 Occupational Employment Statistics (OES) survey by the U.S. Bureau of Labor Statistics (BLS), the estimated annual salary for most of these professionals ranged between $36,520 and $97,370.

Employment Prospects

Landscape Architects are employed in both the public and private sectors throughout the United States. Some Landscape Architects are self-employed. Landscape Architects are needed to assist in the planning and development of new construction of residential homes, commercial buildings, and transportation and transit projects. The BLS reported in its May 2008 OES survey that an estimated 21,130 Landscape Architects were employed in the United States. Approximately 64 percent of them worked in the architectural, engineering, and related services industry. Most were employed by landscape architecture services and firms.

According to some experts, the landscape architecture field is growing fast. *U.S. News & World Report* listed Landscape Architects as members of one of the 30 best careers for 2009, for example. The BLS predicts that employment of Landscape Architects should increase by 20 percent during the 2008–18 period. In addition to the job-growth factor, opportunities will become available as Landscape Architects advance to higher positions, transfer to other jobs or career fields, or retire.

Advancement Prospects

Landscape Architects advance by earning higher wages and being assigned greater levels of responsibility. They may also be promoted to team leader, project manager, and other supervisory and managerial positions. In private firms, individuals may be offered a partnership in the business. Landscape Architects with entrepreneurial ambitions may become independent contractors or start their own firms.

Education and Training

To become Landscape Architects, individuals must complete a formal college program in which they earn either an undergraduate or graduate professional degree. There are two types of bachelor's degree programs in landscape architecture, which take four to five years to complete. One program leads to the professional degree of Bachelor of Landscape Architecture, while the other results in a Bachelor of Science in Landscape Architecture.

Individuals with a bachelor's degree in another discipline can complete the graduate program in landscape architecture in three years. Students who have already earned an undergraduate degree in landscape architecture can finish the program in two years.

The landscape architecture curriculum includes courses in design, landscape construction, the history of landscape architecture, ecology, plant science, soil science, art, urban planning, general management, computer-aided design, geographic information systems, and other subjects. In addition, students complete at least a one-year internship to gain practical experience.

Employers provide entry-level Landscape Architects with on-the-job training.

Throughout their careers, Landscape Architects pursue continuing education to update their skills and knowledge.

Special Requirements

Every state, except for Vermont, requires individuals to be either licensed or registered to practice as professional Landscape Architects. A professional license is not required for them to work in the District of Columbia. Licensing requirements vary from state to state. For specific information, contact the appropriate board of examiners in the state where you wish to practice.

In those states that require professional licenses, Landscape Architects must work one or more years as interns or apprentices before they can qualify for a license. They must be supervised by licensed Landscape Architects until they receive their own professional license.

Landscape Architects are not required to be licensed if they work for the federal government.

Experience, Special Skills, and Personality Traits

Employers prefer to hire candidates for entry-level positions who have work experience, which they may have gained through internships.

Landscape Architects need strong analytical, problem-solving, project-management, teamwork, writing, presentation, and communication skills to perform their various tasks effectively. Being creative, positive, energetic, trustworthy, and detail-oriented are some personality traits that successful Landscape Architects share.

Unions and Associations

Landscape Architects can join professional associations to take advantage of networking opportunities, training programs, and other professional services and resources. One national society that serves their interests is the American Society of Landscape Architects. For contact information, see Appendix II.

Tips for Entry

1. As a high school student, you can start gaining experience by obtaining a summer or part-time job with a Landscape Architect or a landscaping contractor.

2. Employers prefer to hire applicants who have earned a degree from a college program accredited by the Landscape Architectural Accreditation Board.

3. Take advantage of the job search services available at your college career center. Most career centers offer their assistance to college alumni as well.

4. Use the Internet to learn more about landscape architecture. You might start by visiting the American Society of Landscape Architects Web site at www.asla.org. For more links, see Appendix IV.

LANDSCAPE CONTRACTOR

Position Description

Landscape Contractors own and manage businesses that are involved in the planning, installation, and maintenance of such landscape elements as lawns, trees, shrubbery, flower beds, walkways, walls, fences, patios, fountains, outdoor lighting, and other features that enhance a specific area. These experts work in both residential and commercial landscaping. Owners of houses, apartment complexes, shopping malls, office buildings, and industrial parks hire Landscape Contractors and benefit from the services that they provide. They also work in the area of public or environmental landscape design in such locations as public parks and arboretums. Additionally, some contractors offer landscaping services to private and public cemeteries.

Coordinating the design of landscapes as well as performing the work of constructing and maintaining landscapes are team efforts. Such efforts require focus and leadership. Landscape Contractors are men and women who provide such guidance to their crews of gardeners and laborers. They also work with design professionals, as well as with clients who desire appealing landscapes to adorn their properties.

Landscaping projects begin with an idea generated by contractors' clients, and are usually developed into design plans by landscape architects or landscape designers. Some Landscape Contractors are also landscape designers, who may offer clients landscape design ideas. However, only licensed landscape architects can provide clients with construction plans. In their capacity as landscape designers, Landscape Contractors meet with clients to discuss what they want for their landscape projects. They confer about the placement of various landscape elements in the desired locations. They may talk about different configurations or themes, such as the use of drought-resistant or native species, the direction of pathways, whether to use tiles or concrete, raised beds or terraces, lawns or rock gardens, and similar topics.

Landscape Contractors are responsible for making sure that landscaping work is done properly according to client-approved designs. They use blueprints, along with their detailed drawings and computer models of the new landscapes, to determine where to plant which species of vegetation or whether to construct raised beds, lay concrete, create rock gardens, or install restrooms, buildings, fountains, or other man-made elements.

Landscape Contractors are also responsible for assembling tools and materials. They purchase plants, trees, seeds, and topsoil; and acquire bricks, concrete mix, wood, and other building materials. Depending on the size and nature of the project, Landscape Contractors subcontract some of the work to other individuals or firms such as bricklayers, electricians, landscaping companies, construction outfits, irrigation installers, or nurseries.

Landscape Contractors direct the work as it progresses. Many of these contractors perform the same tasks as their crew while providing supervision or instruction. They also confer with their clients to keep them apprised of their progress.

Once landscaping projects are completed, Landscape Contractors may be hired to oversee the upkeep, repairs, and maintenance of the areas. They inspect the grounds to identify problems and assign such tasks as pruning, repairing concrete cracks, pulling weeds, mowing lawns, transplanting shrubbery, and other routine landscape maintenance tasks.

As business owners, Landscape Contractors have additional responsibilities specific to running their own landscaping enterprise. These experts may:

- acquire contracting licenses and business permits and keep them current
- keep office spaces properly maintained and secured
- handle operation budgets
- prepare bids or proposals for jobs
- negotiate contracts with clients, suppliers, and subcontractors
- manage payrolls
- hire, train, and terminate employees
- handle personnel issues such as staff disputes
- review daily work logs
- promote their business through advertising, publicity, and client referrals
- schedule projects to meet client needs
- write and review contracts
- manage and coordinate multiple projects
- maintain inventory of equipment and supplies
- keep all business records current and properly filed
- establish and enforce work policies, operational standards, job procedures, and safety rules
- make sure business is in compliance with all appropriate work safety, employment, and other local, state, and federal laws and regulations

Landscape Contractors work in both indoor and outdoor locations. They attend to their planning, client conferences, and business management responsibilities in offices. Some of their landscaping projects are located indoors, such as in shopping malls or office buildings. Most of their projects are located in outdoor settings, however. Many of their installation and maintenance jobs take place seasonally in areas where winter climates are cold. In warmer climates, such jobs are performed all year.

Landscape Contractors do work that is physically demanding. They spend a lot of time on their feet performing repetitive movements such as lifting, climbing, bending, reaching, raking, and shoveling. They may be exposed to harsh chemicals, including fertilizers and pesticides. They risk injury by using motorized or power equipment. Hearing protection, gloves, work boots, and hard hats are standard for these experts.

Landscape Contractors work 40 hours per week but may put in extra hours to complete jobs.

Salaries

Earnings for Landscape Contractors vary each year, depending on such factors as the size of their companies, their competition, and their geographic location. Their annual income is based on their businesses' annual net profit.

Income information specifically for Landscape Contractors is unavailable. Owners of small business establishments receive earnings similar to salaries made by general managers. According to the May 2008 Occupational Employment Statistics survey by the U.S. Bureau of Labor Statistics, the estimated annual salary for most general managers ranged between $45,410 and $166,400.

Employment Prospects

According to the U.S. Census Bureau, over 76,000 landscaping services existed in the United States in 2002. Experts in the field report that landscaping operations continue to serve a growing market. Homeowners as well as retail and commercial property owners seek reputable Landscape Contractors to plan, construct, upgrade, and maintain landscaping on their grounds.

Some Landscape Contractors work on a part-time basis, on weekends and during evenings, until they have established their businesses. Building any business is hard work. Success depends on various factors, such as a business owner's ambition and ability to run a business, the competition, the local demand for landscaping services, and the state of the economy.

Advancement Prospects

Landscape Contractors typically measure success by earning higher incomes, increasing the size of their companies, and gaining recognition for themselves and their services. They also enjoy job satisfaction.

Education and Training

There are no standard educational requirements for individuals to meet to become Landscape Contractors. However, many of these professionals hold associate's or bachelor's degrees or professional certificates in landscape contracting and management, landscape design, horticulture, or another related field.

Many Landscape Contractors acquire their skills and knowledge through a combination of on-the-job training, self-study, and formal instruction.

In addition to colleges and universities, individuals can obtain formal training through professional and trade associations. Many of these organizations offer workshops and seminars that cover landscape design, landscape management, plant materials, insect control, irrigation installation, and many other topics.

Throughout their careers, Landscape Contractors pursue continuing education to update their skills and knowledge. Contractors may also need to complete continuing education to maintain their professional licenses or certificates.

Special Requirements

Landscape Contractors must possess the appropriate business permits and licenses required by their local and state governments. For specific information about business licenses, contact the local (city or county) governmental administrative office where you plan to operate your business. Landscape Contractors are usually required to carry a surety bond and liability insurance for their business.

Some states require Landscape Contractors to hold a professional license, particularly those contractors who are involved in the installation of walls, walkways, and other hardscape. For specific information about the state where you wish to work, contact the state board of contractors.

Experience, Special Skills, and Personality Traits

Entrepreneurial landscaping experts usually start a landscape service after working several years in the field as landscape technicians or designers. They should be highly knowledgeable and proficient in the types of services they plan to offer to clients. In addition, they should have a foundation in the areas of business, finance, human resources, and marketing.

To be effective business owners, Landscape Contractors need excellent leadership, management, organizational, problem-solving, negotiation, and customer service skills. They must also have excellent interpersonal and communication skills to work well with their staff, customers, subcontractors, govern-ment officials, and various others from diverse backgrounds. In addition, Landscape Contractors need superior self-management skills. Being self-motivated, enthusiastic, dedicated, inspirational, creative, innovative, and flexible are some personality traits that successful Landscape Contractors have in common.

Unions and Associations

Landscape Contractors can join professional associations at the state, regional, or national level to take advantage of professional services and resources, such as professional certification, as well as networking opportunities. Some national societies that serve their different interests are the American Nursery and Landscape Association, the Professional Landcare Network, and the Ecological Landscaping Association. Contractors who are also landscape designers may join the Association of Professional Landscape Designers. For contact information, see Appendix II.

Tips for Entry

1. Learn as much as you can about different types of plants as well as everything about landscaping. You can read books, visit Web sites, and take classes or workshops offered by colleges, community centers, and plant societies.
2. Contact the state landscape contractors' association for advice on how to become a Landscape Contractor in your area.
3. As a landscape technician, be willing to learn how to do the different planning, construction, and maintenance services that your employer offers.
4. The ability to generate new business is an essential skill for business owners. Learn the difference between marketing, public relations, publicity, and advertising techniques and how you can use them cost-effectively.
5. Use the Internet to learn more about landscaping services and Landscape Contractors. You might start by visiting these Web sites: LandscapeOnline.com and the California Landscape Contractors Association Web site (www.clca.org). For more links, see Appendix IV.

PEST CONTROL TECHNICIAN

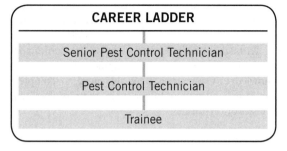

Position Description

Pests are plants and animals that we generally consider unwelcome. Plant pests are unwanted or invasive weeds or poisonous plants, such as berry vines, poison ivy, dandelions, and thistles. Such plants hinder the growth and vitality of food crops or gardens, create traffic hazards, or mar the landscapes along roadways. They can also injure or damage the health of people and animals. Animal pests include such insects as houseflies, cockroaches, aphids, ants, and termites; such mammals as moles, mice, snakes, gophers, raccoons, and deer; and certain birds, such as seagulls. Animal pests eat crops, carry diseases, or destroy property. Such organisms as algae, fungi, or molds are also considered pests. These pests can pollute ponds and cause illnesses in homes or other buildings that people occupy.

People have always battled pests and sought ways to keep them away from homes, wooded areas, croplands, workplaces, food storage facilities, and sailing vessels. Whereas home or business owners may apply some pesticides privately, professionals can apply pesticides that are more powerful. These men and women, called Pest Control Technicians, work every day to keep our living and working environments free of all kinds of pests.

Pest Control Technicians may specialize by concentrating on eradicating certain types of pests, such as termites. Others may specialize by employing beneficial insects to eliminate harmful insects from infesting gardens, landscapes, or croplands.

Pest Control Technicians are experts at identifying pests. They are also authorities on deciding which methods are appropriate and most effective at removing pests from affected areas. Some of their methods include sanitizing affected areas; installing barriers to block pest invasions; spraying; setting traps; injecting pesticides into trees, buildings, or the ground; and using certain species of insects to prey upon or drive away other insects.

They may apply spray from portable tanks they carry by hand or on their backs, or by using trucks or airplanes equipped with spray mechanisms. Some Pest Control Technicians use gases called fumigants to eradicate pests from entire buildings. They seal the buildings and evacuate the inhabitants for the duration of the process.

Pest Control Technicians not only rid buildings and land areas of pests immediately, but also devise strategies for controlling pest populations on a long-term basis. Some of these experts regularly return to these sites to replace insect or rodent traps or spray key spots to keep pest populations at bay.

Pest Control Technicians mix specific chemicals or natural compounds in exact proportions to kill each type of pest. These technicians use both chemical and natural pesticides.

Pest Control Technicians use various basic categories of pesticides, each of which fulfills a particular purpose. Two common pesticides are herbicides and rodenticides. These technicians use herbicides to control or kill undesirable weeds or other plants. Some of these compounds kill all of the plants in an area, while others kill specific species. Pest Control Technicians use rodenticides mainly to hold back populations of rats and mice, but they also use them to control other mammals, as well as birds and fish. Other types of pesticides that these experts use include insecticides for insects, arachnids, and worms; fungicides for mildews, molds, and other fungi; molluscicides for snails and slugs; and nematicides for a type of worm called nematodes that destroy plants by eating their roots.

Pest Control Technicians are careful to apply pesticides only to certain sections of properties, and use strict safety precautions to avoid the spread of toxic chemicals into the environment, to avoid harming people, plants, and animals as well as to minimize their own exposure to the chemicals. Hence, these technicians closely follow the instructions for mixing and applying pesticide compounds that are printed on containers.

Pest Control Technicians are responsible for completing general tasks in addition to performing fumigation or extermination duties. They:

- establish strong relationships with clients
- plan schedules and local routes to serve clients
- inspect job sites to determine population levels of pests and estimate the extent of the damage caused by them
- read blueprints or diagrams of infested areas to choose the most effective treatment methods
- make measurements of areas that require pest control treatments
- prepare cost estimates for each job
- oversee the work of assistants or noncertified Pest Control Technicians
- clean sites at the end of each job and make repairs to properties
- clean, maintain, and calibrate spray devices, tools, and equipment
- keep records of all work activities
- stay up-to-date with developments in the pest control industry
- provide educational services about pest control to clients

Pest Control Technicians have physically demanding jobs. They stand for long periods, climb ladders, and crawl through tight spaces. They may lift and carry equipment weighing 50 pounds or more. These technicians work in both indoor and outdoor environments.

Because they use hazardous and toxic chemicals, Pest Control Technicians wear protective chemical-resistant clothing including coveralls, head and neck coverings, gloves, thick-soled boots, goggles, face shields, and various types of respirators. Each container of chemicals that Pest Control Technicians use is labeled with instructions mandated by the federal government.

These experts generally work full-time but may work according to seasonal schedules. They put in 40-hour weeks and may work on weekends. Their hours may be longer during warmer times of the year.

Salaries

Salaries for Pest Control Technicians vary, depending on their experience, employer, geographic location, and other factors. The U.S. Bureau of Labor Statistics (BLS) reported the following estimated salary ranges for most of these specialists in its May 2008 Occupational Employment Statistics survey:

- pesticide handlers, sprayers, and applicators: $19,820 to $44,910
- pest control workers (who apply chemical solutions to kill animal pests): $19,650 to $44,390

Employment Prospects

Pest Control Technicians who specialize in animal pests mostly work for companies that provide pest control services. Those who specialize in plant pests are employed by groundskeeping, lawn, and landscaping services. Some Pest Control Technicians are self-employed, and have their own extermination companies. Others work for local, state, or federal government agencies. Corporations, sports stadiums, hospitals, schools, colleges, apartment complexes, shopping malls, and other establishments employ Pest Control Technicians as permanent members of their staff to manage their facilities on a full-time basis.

Opportunities are favorable for qualified technicians. The BLS reports that employment of pest control workers is expected to increase by 15 percent between 2008 and 2018. In addition to job growth, openings will become available as these technicians advance to higher positions, transfer to other jobs or career fields, retire, or leave the workforce for various reasons.

Advancement Prospects

Pest Control Technicians advance by earning higher salaries and receiving higher-level responsibilities. They can also be promoted to supervisory and managerial positions. Some technicians become specialists in a particular area of pest control. Entrepreneurial individuals may establish their own services after gaining several years of experience.

Education and Training

Employers usually require that applicants hold a high school diploma or a general equivalency diploma.

Pest control trainees must successfully complete a training program that complies with federal and state standards for pesticide handlers. Pest Control trainees normally must complete one to two years of on-the-job training while working under the direction and supervision of experienced Pest Control Technicians. They also complete formal instruction provided by their employers. They study such topics as general pest control; the proper use of pesticides; signs and symptoms of pesticides poisoning; emergency first aid for pesticide injuries and poisoning; environmental concerns; safety requirements for the handling, transporting, storing, and disposing of pesticides; and the use, care, cleaning, and storage of personal protective equipment. In states that require Pest Control Technicians to be certified, the employer training programs help trainees meet certification requirements.

Special Requirements

The work of Pest Control Technicians is regulated by both state and federal laws. In most states, Pest Control Technicians must be certified or licensed to apply pesticides where they work. Noncertified Pest Control Technicians may only apply toxic substances under the direct supervision of certified professionals.

Requirements for certification vary from state to state. In general, applicants must meet minimum education and experience requirements as well pass an examination. Technicians must usually complete continuing education to renew their certificates.

In addition, Pest Control Technicians are required to possess a valid driver's license.

Experience, Special Skills, and Personality Traits

Employers usually prefer to employ applicants who have previous work experience in the field (such as landscaping or animal pest control) in which they would work. Sometimes employers hire candidates for trainee positions without any work experience, as long as they show a willingness to work hard and the ability to learn quickly.

Because they must work well with colleagues, supervisors, customers, and others from diverse backgrounds, these technicians must have excellent interpersonal and communication skills. They also need strong organizational, problem-solving, self-management, and customer service skills. Some personality traits that successful Pest Control Technicians share include being friendly, courteous, enthusiastic, composed, dependable, detail-oriented, and flexible.

Unions and Associations

Some Pest Control Technicians, such as those who work in academic institutions or government agencies, may belong to a labor union. The union represents them in contract negotiations with their employers for better terms regarding pay, benefits, and working conditions.

Tips for Entry

1. Apply directly to pest control companies, landscaping firms, government agencies, and other employers for whom you would like to work.
2. Take advantage of your state employment office. Along with looking at their listings, you can get help with your job search skills.
3. Job titles vary among employers. Be sure you understand what a job is all about before you apply for it.
4. Use the Internet to learn more about pesticides. You might start by visiting the U.S. Environmental Protection Agency Web page about pesticides www.epa.gov/pesticides/index.htm. For more links, see Appendix IV.

PET AND ANIMAL SERVICES

PET BUSINESS OWNER

Position Description

Millions of households in the United States possess animals as family pets, including dogs, cats, birds, tropical fish, hamsters, rabbits, chicken, lizards, turtles, and snakes, among others. Most, if not all, pet owners treat their pets as members of the family. They make sure that their pets are happy, healthy, clean, and safe at all times. Every day, pet owners purchase products and services for their animal companions from different pet businesses.

Pet store owners are probably the most familiar type of pet business entrepreneur. These men and women own and run independent shops or franchises. They offer for sale a variety of kittens, puppies, birds, rabbits, snakes, lizards, fish, hamsters, and other companion animals. Pet store owners also sell an assortment of packaged and bulk pet foods, as well as pet vitamins, supplies, toys, luxury accessories, and other products. In addition, some pet store owners offer pet grooming, training, or other services to customers. Some pet store owners specialize by selling only natural or organic products, or by focusing their business on one particular type of animal, such as birds or tropical fish.

Pet Business Owners also start up companies that produce and sell pet products that they have created themselves, such as homemade dog biscuits, cat collars, pet clothing, pet furniture, and pet caskets. These entrepreneurs sell their products to retailers and wholesalers as well as directly to customers.

Many Pet Business Owners offer specific pet services. One common service is a kennel operation that boards and cares for pets while their owners are away, whether it is for one night, several nights, or a few weeks. Pet Business Owners known as pet sitters also take care of pets when their owners are away from home. The pets stay home, and the pet sitters check in on them one or more times a day to feed, water, and play with them. Some Pet Business Owners start up pet day-care services to attend to pets while their owners are at work. Pet owners drop off their animals on their way to work and pick them up after work.

Dog obedience training is another pet business that can be found in almost all communities. Dog trainers offer group and one-on-one classes. Some owners operate training schools from their homes or rented spaces, while others offer classes through pet stores, community centers, animal shelters, or other organizations. Dog trainers work closely with both pet owners and their puppies or dogs so that the animals learn to obey their owners.

When pets demonstrate behavioral problems, pet owners may seek the consulting services of pet behavior specialists. These consultants are mostly veterinarians and applied animal behaviorists who have formal training in animal behavior. They identify and understand the causes of pet behavioral problems and advise pet owners on how to resolve the bad behavior of their pets. Some pet behavior specialists also offer animal training sessions.

Pet grooming services make up another type of enterprise that some Pet Business Owners operate. They offer such services as bathing animals, brushing out their coats, cutting and styling animal hair, trimming nails, brushing teeth, and treating animals for fleas and ticks. These entrepreneurs may work with all types of pets or focus on grooming specific animals. Some owners operate mobile salons that allow them to travel to customers' residences or other locations to groom their pets.

A few other pet businesses that entrepreneurs have established include dog walking, pet waste removal, pet breeding, pet photography, and pet spa services, as well as pet cremation and burial services.

Pet Business Owners complete several tasks prior to opening their businesses. They obtain business licenses and permits, as well as professional credentials. They buy insurance policies to safeguard their businesses and themselves against risk. They create business plans that describe their business goals and objectives, what services and products they will offer, how much they will charge for them, and other business matters. These entrepreneurs also establish standard operational policies and procedures, such as customer service policies, billing procedures, and purchasing protocols.

To ensure their success, Pet Business Owners perform a wide range of daily tasks involving financial planning, bookkeeping, client relations, and more. For example, they:

- plan and schedule work activities
- maintain inventory of materials and supplies
- meet with vendors or suppliers
- monitor operational costs
- prepare correspondence and invoices for clients
- pay taxes and bills
- keep accurate records and logs of finances, work activities, and legal matters
- maintain and repair facilities and equipment
- comply with all appropriate local, state, and federal laws and regulations
- stay abreast of industry trends by reading trade and professional publications, attending trade shows, and networking with colleagues

Pet Business Owners who employ staff are responsible for directing and supervising their activities. They also provide their staff with ongoing training and development.

These entrepreneurs also set aside time to generate new business. For example, they may design brochures or flyers and distribute them to pet stores, animal shelters, veterinarian offices, and other businesses that pet owners may visit. Some owners buy ads in the local newspapers and other publications. Many join local business associations (such as the chamber of commerce) and community groups to network with other merchants, civic leaders, and the public.

Some Pet Business Owners run their operations from home, while others purchase or lease commercial property. Some entrepreneurs work out of veterinary offices, pet stores, animal shelters, or other establishments for which they perform subcontract work. For example, an owner of a dog grooming service might work three days a week at facilities owned by a pet store.

Pet Business Owners determine their own work schedules. They typically work hours that are convenient to their customers, which may include evenings, weekends, and holidays. Some owners work part-time at their businesses while holding other full-time or part-time jobs.

Salaries

Formal income information for Pet Business Owners is unavailable. Their earnings vary from year to year and depend on the success of their businesses. Their profits, or net incomes, are determined by subtracting their total operating costs from their gross annual sales.

Employment Prospects

According to the 2009–10 National Pet Owners Survey by the American Pet Products Association (APPA), approximately 71 million households in the United States own pets. The APPA also reported that pet owners in the United States spent $43.2 billion on their pets in 2008.

Some experts in the field state that the pet industry is growing rapidly. This is mostly due to the fact that pet owners consider their pets to be family members and thus purchase basic needs and services, as well as occasional treats, for their animal companions.

Establishing a pet business is hard work. It is common for business owners to have an unprofitable business or go out of business within the first few years. Their success depends on their ambitions and abilities to run a business, the local demand for their products or services, their competition, and other factors.

Advancement Prospects

Most, if not all, Pet Business Owners realize success by being able to make a living from their profits. Owners also measure their progress by achieving their business goals and objectives, such as earning certain annual incomes or expanding their businesses.

Education and Training

To be successful small business owners, individuals need basic instruction in such areas as finance, bookkeeping, business administration, marketing, and sales. Some businessowners took such courses while in high school, while others enrolled in courses offered by community colleges or university extension programs.

Individuals can learn about starting a pet business through independent study, completing workshops or seminars through professional or trade associations, networking with colleagues, and attending trade shows.

Special Requirements

To start a pet service or other type of business, individuals must obtain appropriate business licenses and permits. For specific information about licenses and permits, contact the city or county government administrative office that governs the area where you wish to operate your business.

Pet Business Owners must also comply with all appropriate local, state, and federal laws that govern their jurisdiction. For example, some states have specific laws that mandate the proper care and feeding of animals in pet stores.

Experience, Special Skills, and Personality Traits

Individuals who start pet businesses are passionate about animals, and have years of experience working with them. Those who wish to offer specific types of pet services, such as dog grooming, usually have many years of experience working in those services.

To be successful Pet Business Owners, individuals need excellent leadership, management, critical-thinking, problem-solving, and organizational skills. Because they must be able to handle customers and clients from diverse backgrounds, Pet Business Owners need effective communication, interpersonal, and customer service skills. In addition, they need strong self-management skills, such as the ability to handle stressful situations, meet deadlines, work independently, and prioritize multiple tasks. Being enterprising, foresighted, persistent, optimistic, detail-oriented, creative, and flexible are some personality traits that successful Pet Business Owners share.

Unions and Associations

Pet Business Owners can join professional and trade associations to take advantage of networking opportunities, as well as earn professional certificates, attend training programs, and make use of other professional services and resources. Some organizations that serve the diverse interest of Pet Business Owners include:

- American Pet Products Association
- Association of Pet Dog Trainers
- Association of Professional Animal Waste Specialists
- International Association of Canine Professionals
- National Association of Professional Pet Sitters
- National Dog Groomers Association of America
- Pet Care Services Association
- Pet Industry Joint Advisory Council

For contact information for these organizations, see Appendix II.

Tips for Entry

1. Consult the public library, the U.S. Small Business Administration, or other resources to help you develop business and marketing plans.
2. Do your research. Find out who your competition is in the area that you plan to serve. Learn about a company's products and services and what their customers like and dislike about the company. Also, determine whether you would have enough prospective customers for your business.
3. Network with local business people. You might, for example, join the local chamber of commerce or an area business association. Also, network with local veterinarians, animal clinics, and other animal businesses.
4. Use the Internet to learn more about running a small business in general as well as a pet business in particular. You might start by visiting the U.S. Small Business Administration Web site (www.sba.gov), the Pet Industry Joint Advisory Council (pijac.org), and WorkingwithPets.com. For more links, see Appendix IV.

ANIMAL TRAINER

Duties: Teach animals to exhibit specific behaviors or perform certain skills or tasks upon command; may teach owners to handle their animals; perform other duties as required

Alternate Title(s): Dog Trainer, Horse Trainer, Dolphin Trainer, Guide Dog Trainer, or another title that reflects a specialty

Salary Range: $17,000 to $51,000

Employment Prospects: Good for dog trainers; poor for other trainers

Advancement Prospects: Fair

Prerequisites:

Education or Training—Apprenticeship or other training program

Experience—Experience working with animals

CAREER LADDER

Senior Animal Trainer

Animal Trainer

Apprentice or Trainee

Special Skills and Personality Traits—Teaching, leadership, self-management, organizational, problem-solving, decision-making, and communication skills; business, marketing, public relations, and customer service skills for business owners; enthusiastic, kind, respectful, patient, calm, persistent, detail-oriented, dependable, ethical, and flexible personality traits

Position Description

People own animals for many reasons. Many people keep dogs and other animals as pets or companions. People with disabilities may have service animals to help them live independent lives. Some people use animals to guard their property or to help them perform work. Others raise animals to compete in sporting events or to be part of entertainment venues. Animals need to be trained to perform the specific behaviors, skills, or tasks that their owners require. Many owners, however, do not have the time or skills to teach their animals, so they hire professional Animal Trainers.

Animal Trainers are experts in teaching animals to obey commands, exhibit specific behaviors or skills, and perform certain tasks. These men and women are highly knowledgeable about the domestic and wild animals that they train. They understand the anatomy and physiology of animals, as well as their general nature, behaviors, and habits. Animal Trainers are also familiar with the work and setting in which the animals are expected to perform.

Animal Trainers specialize in the services they offer, whether as employees or independent contractors. They work with certain types of domestic and exotic animals, or train animals for specific purposes.

Dog obedience trainers are probably among the most familiar types of animal instructors. They work closely with pet owners to train their dogs to be respon-

sive to the owners' commands. These trainers also help owners, modify behavior problems that their pets exhibit, such as biting, excessive barking, or inappropriately relieving themselves.

Guide dog instructors train dogs that will be used by blind and visually impaired persons to help them live independently. These instructors teach dogs to handle themselves properly in common situations and environments, such as on crowded sidewalks, or when crossing streets, getting onto a bus, and entering buildings. Once the guide dogs are trained, they are matched with owners and then instructors teach the owners how to handle their guide dogs.

Dogs are also trained by service-animal trainers to assist individuals who have physical, emotional, mental, or other disabilities. These Animal Trainers may teach such other service animals as miniature horses, monkeys, cats, pigs, and parrots to perform specific tasks to help their owners handle their daily routines.

Some Animal Trainers are police dog trainers. Their job is to teach dogs the proper obedience, motivation, balance, and conditioning to help law enforcement officers prevent and deter crime. Police dogs are used to provide one or more services—assist in patrol duty, tactical support, bomb detection, narcotics detection, or search-and-rescue. Police-dog trainers also teach the canine handlers how to work with their dogs.

Professional horse trainers teach both horses and riders for pleasure riding, competitions, or racing. They may also instruct horse owners or riders how to care for their animals. Some trainers work with horses to carry pack loads. Horse trainers are hired by such horse-related businesses as horse stables, horse farms, equestrian centers, dude ranches, and horse training facilities.

Animal Trainers who are experts at handling wild animals—such as lions, tigers, elephants, bears, apes, dolphins, sea lions, and penguins—are employed by circuses, zoos, aquariums, and animal parks. The trainers teach the animals to perform specific behaviors on cue for educational or entertainment programs. Trainers may be involved with the production of these programs, as well as participate in the live performances. These Animal Trainers also teach the animals to obey commands to make it possible to manage them, feed and groom them, and provide them with veterinary care.

Some Animal Trainers specialize in training domestic and wildlife animals to perform specific behaviors or stunts in films or photography shoots. For example, they may train a bear to tear up a campsite, an alligator to wrestle the hero of a movie, or a house cat to open a door to escape from a room. These trainers often own the animals.

Training animals is a slow, precise, and repetitive process. First, trainers interact with animals so that they become used to hearing the human voice and being in contact with humans. When the animals are accustomed to them, trainers begin conditioning them to exhibit specific behaviors by responding to certain cues. A cue is usually a verbal command, a touch to a part of an animal's body, a sound (such a clicking noise), or a hand signal.

Animal Trainers create training sessions and environments that are stimulating and positive for the animals. They also build trust between themselves and animals. When they plan training programs, these professionals consider the nature and temperament of the animals. Trainers apply techniques and methods that are appropriate to the animals with which they work. They teach one behavior or skill at a time, reinforcing the proper response that they want an animal to perform. For example, a dog trainer may reward a dog with a piece of food each time it is ordered to sit or it finds a hidden object. It may take days, weeks, months, or years of repetition for animals to learn skills. Most trainers work with animals on a daily basis, several hours a day.

Animal Trainers perform other duties, which vary according to the type of work they do. Some trainers, for example, are involved in evaluating and selecting animals that they think have the capacity to be trained. Many Animal Trainers take care of animals. They feed them, exercise them, bathe and groom them, administer any prescribed medication to them, and keep their environments neat and clean. Animal Trainers also perform such general tasks as:

- planning training programs and activities
- scheduling training sessions
- maintaining accurate, detailed records of each animal's behavior and learning process
- observing animals for illnesses or injuries, treating minor ailments, and obtaining veterinary care for major medical problems
- maintaining pens, kennels, stalls, cages, and yards
- supervising and directing the work of animal caretakers and inexperienced trainers

Some Animal Trainers are self-employed or are owners of training facilities. They are responsible for the daily management and the success of their operations. They establish policies and procedures, determine fees, bill customers, collect payments, pay bills and taxes, maintain financial accounts, and purchase supplies and materials, among other duties. They also set aside time to implement marketing plans to promote their businesses and generate new customers.

Working with animals can be a physically exhausting job. Trainers constantly walk, run, stand, kneel, crouch, stoop, bend, and twist while working with animals. Animal Trainers follow appropriate precautions to ensure the health and safety of animals as well as themselves, animal owners, or other people. For example, trainers are at risk of being bitten, kicked, or otherwise injured by the animals they handle.

Animal Trainers set their own work schedules. Most work irregular hours, including evenings, weekends, and holidays. Independent trainers particularly work long hours to build and maintain their businesses.

Salaries

Salaries for Animal Trainers vary, depending on such factors as their experience, specialty, employer, and geographic location. According to the May 2008 Occupational Employment Statistics (OES) survey by the U.S. Bureau of Labor Statistics (BLS), the estimated annual wage for most Animal Trainers ranged between $16,700 and $51,400.

Employment Prospects

In general, the BLS predicts that employment of Animal Trainers should increase by 20 percent during the

2008–18 period. The agency reported in its May 2008 OES survey that approximately 10,030 Animal Trainers were employed in the United States.

Job opportunities vary for different trainers. Job opportunities are strongest for dog obedience trainers. The demand for these trainers is expected to grow as the numbers of pet owners increase and seek dog training services. The job outlook for horse, marine mammal, and other types of Animal Trainers is poor. The number of opportunities is limited and the job competition for openings is high.

Staff positions become available as businesses need to replace Animal Trainers who have transferred to other jobs or career fields or have left the workforce for various reasons.

Advancement Prospects

Animal Trainers advance according to their own interests and ambitions. For many trainers, their goal is to become successful business owners. Staff trainers may pursue supervisory and management positions. Some trainers measure success through job satisfaction, by gaining professional reputations, and by earning higher incomes.

Education and Training

There are no standard educational requirements for individuals to fulfill to become Animal Trainers. Many employers require that applicants for entry-level staff positions possess at least a high school diploma or general equivalency diploma. Zoos, animal parks, and aquariums may prefer trainers to hold a bachelor's degree in zoology, biology, animal science, or another related field.

To become Animal Trainers, individuals complete apprenticeships or learn their skills through on-the-job training. Trainees work under the direction of experienced trainers. Initial training may run from one to two years or more, depending on the specialty. For instance, dog guide instructors complete a two- to five-year apprenticeship at a licensed guide dog school.

Police dog trainers are usually required to complete certified training programs, which may be offered through a law enforcement agency or a civilian canine academy.

Throughout their careers, Animal Trainers pursue continuing education to update their skills and knowledge.

Experience, Special Skills, and Personality Traits

Employers prefer to hire applicants for entry-level or trainee positions who have experience training animals, especially in the area of animal obedience. They may have gained their experience through volunteer work or employment, or through training their own pets.

To perform their job well, Animal Trainers must have excellent teaching, leadership, self-management, organizational, problem-solving, and decision-making skills. They also need strong communication skills, as they must be able to deal positively with both people and animals. Business owners also need effective business, marketing, public relations, and customer service skills to run successful firms. Being enthusiastic, kind, respectful, patient, calm, persistent, detail-oriented, dependable, ethical, and flexible are some personality traits that successful Animal Trainers share.

Unions and Associations

Animal Trainers can join professional associations to take advantage of networking opportunities, training programs, and other professional services and resources. The Association of Pet Dog Trainers and the International Marine Animal Trainers' Association are two examples of professional societies that serve the diverse interests of Animal Trainers. For contact information to these organizations, see Appendix II.

Tips for Entry

1. Train your own pet by using professional training techniques.
2. Learn as much as you can about the animals you wish to one day train professionally.
3. Formal training programs are offered by professional Animal Trainers through private schools as well as community colleges. Do your research before enrolling in a program. Ask such questions as: What subjects are taught and how do they prepare you for an animal training career? What types of practical experience will you receive? What are the instructors' qualifications? Where are past students now working? How will the school help you find a job?
4. Gain as much experience as you can working with the animals you wish to train. Do you want to be a dog trainer, for example? Then, you might volunteer at an animal shelter or local rescue group. If you want to be a zoo trainer, volunteer at a zoo or animal park.
5. Use the Internet to learn more about the particular animal training in which you would like to specialize. To get a list of Web sites, enter the name of the training, such as *guide dog training*, *exotic animal training*, or *marine mammal training* into a search engine.

ANIMAL BEHAVIORIST

Duties: Identify and evaluate animal behavioral problems; advise animal owners about their animals' behavioral problems; perform other duties as required

Alternate Title(s): Animal Behavioral Consultant, Applied Animal Behaviorist, Veterinary Behaviorist, Pet Behaviorist

Salary Range: $36,000 to $144,000

Employment Prospects: Fair

Advancement Prospects: Fair

Prerequisites:

Education or Training—A master's or doctoral degree in animal behavior or another field, or a doctor of veterinary medicine degree

Experience—Several years of work experience

Special Skills and Personality Traits—Interpersonal, customer service, communication, and self-management skills; enthusiastic, friendly, respectful, ethical, observant, detail-oriented, and flexible personality traits

Special Requirements—Board certification required for veterinary behaviorists

Position Description

Animal behavior is the scientific study of how animals act. Scientists in this field generally focus on nonhumans, while social scientists, such as anthropologists and psychologists, study human behavior. Animal Behaviorists have backgrounds in animal anatomy, physiology, comparative psychology, ethology, biology, zoology, animal science, and other disciplines. They are interested in understanding the functions, causes, development, and evolution of animals, whether they are single-celled organisms, insects, reptiles, birds, fish, mammals, or other animals.

Some Animal Behaviorists study the behavior issues of animals, such as pets, livestock, service animals, zoo animals, and laboratory animals, that interact with humans. Many of these specialists offer consulting services to animal owners whose animals are exhibiting bad behaviors. For example, an animal may be destroying property, biting people, inappropriately relieving itself, or showing signs of shyness, phobias, aggression, or obsessive-compulsive disorders. Animal Behaviorists may work with pet owners, veterinarians, farmers, animal shelters, animal day-care facilities, kennels, zoos, animal parks, research laboratories, and animal welfare organizations, among others. Some professionals choose to treat specific types of animals.

Animal Behaviorists are not animal trainers. Their role is to counsel animal owners about the behavioral problems their animals exhibit, how to prevent these bad behaviors, and how to strengthen the relationship bond between the owners and their animals. Animal Behaviorists meet with clients at their homes or at an animal facility. They interview clients to understand the problems that the clients have about their animals and how they want their animals to behave. Animal Behaviorists also learn about the daily routines, habits, and lifestyles of specific animals, as well as their training and health history. Animal Behaviorists interact with animals to get an idea about their temperaments and their ability to be trained. If it is safe, these professionals may stimulate animals to misbehave so that they can observe firsthand how the animals act.

Animal Behaviorists evaluate all of their data and make recommendations, including techniques and training exercises, for addressing the behavioral problems. Behaviorists demonstrate the methods as well as provide instructions to pet owners. They also provide owners with referrals to animal trainers, veterinarians, and other animal specialists who may assist the pet owners to carry out the recommendations.

The practice of animal behavior consulting is an unregulated field. Consultants have diverse training backgrounds. Animal Behaviorists described in this profile are either applied Animal Behaviorists or veterinary behaviorists. The latter are trained and licensed veterinarians. They can also diagnose medical problems that may contribute to animals displaying bad behavior. In addition, veterinary behaviorists can prescribe medications as part of their treatment plans.

Animal Behaviorists also offer other services, which vary according to their interests, skills, and experience. For example, these specialists might:

- provide animal training, in which they teach an animal new behaviors, skills, or tasks
- hold staff training workshops for animal shelters, animal day cares, zoos, research laboratories, or other animal facilities
- teach educational workshops, seminars, and classes for pet owners, animal trainers, veterinarians, or other animal specialists
- make presentations at conventions and meetings for professional societies, trade associations, or animal welfare organizations
- write articles and books about animal behavior
- assess animals in animal-rescue facilities to determine whether they are adoptable
- assist in the design of shelters, animal laboratories, and boarding and day-care facilities
- conduct research and development projects for pet- or animal-related companies
- provide expert witness and litigation consulting services to attorneys

Some Animal Behaviorists hold teaching appointments in biology, zoology, animal science, wildlife biology, or other departments at colleges and universities. Animal Behaviorists also teach courses at medical or veterinary colleges. Along with teaching duties, most full-time professors conduct research in their areas of interest.

Animal Behaviorists work as consultants on a part-time or full-time basis. In addition to their consulting activities, they set aside time to manage administrative tasks for their businesses. For example, they invoice customers, pay bills and taxes, do bookkeeping, maintain work records, and promote their business.

These animal specialists keep flexible work hours. They may work evenings and on weekends to accommodate their clients' schedules.

Salaries

Salaries for Animal Behaviorists vary, depending on such factors as their education, experience, and geographic location. Specific salary information for this occupation is unavailable. However, a general idea of their salaries can be gained by looking at the earnings of veterinarians and other biological scientists. The U.S. Bureau of Labor Statistics reported the following estimated annual salaries for these professions in its 2008 Occupational Employment Statistics:

- biological scientists (who were not listed separately in the survey): $35,620 to $101,030
- veterinarians: $46,610 to $143,660

Employment Prospects

The applied animal behavior discipline is small but growing, according to experts in the field. Many Animal Behaviorists are self-employed as independent consultants or they own consulting firms. Animal Behaviorists may find staff positions at zoos, animal parks, animal shelters, veterinary clinics, and other animal-related establishments. Some applied Animal Behaviorists hold part-time or full-time teaching positions at colleges and universities.

Advancement Prospects

Animal Behaviorists advance according to their own interests and ambitions. Many measure their success by earning higher incomes or greater job satisfaction, and by gaining favorable professional reputations.

Education and Training

To become applied Animal Behaviorists, individuals must possess a master's or doctoral degree in animal behavior, biology, zoology, or another related field. They complete an apprenticeship under an experienced Animal Behaviorist for hands-on training. Recent doctoral graduates may seek a postdoctoral fellowship to gain additional training.

To teach in colleges and universities, individuals are usually required to hold doctorates.

Individuals who want to become veterinary behaviorists must first complete a four-year program to earn a veterinary medicine degree (D.V.M. or V.M.D.). They then complete two or more years of training in clinical veterinary behavior, after which they must obtain board certification by the American College of Veterinary Behaviorists.

Throughout their careers, Animal Behaviorists pursue continuing education to update their skills and knowledge.

Special Requirements

Veterinary behaviorists must be board certified by the American College of Veterinary Behaviorists. To become certified, they must successfully pass an examination and fulfill other requirements.

Experience, Special Skills, and Personality Traits

Animal behavioral consultants typically have several years of experience working in the animal behavior field. They may have gained their experience through employment, apprenticeships, postdoctoral training, volunteer work, or a combination of these activities.

Animal Behaviorists must have excellent interpersonal, customer service, and communication skills as they must be able to work well with clients, veterinarians, professionals, and others from diverse backgrounds. In addition, they need self-management skills, such as the ability to work independently, handle stressful situations, meet deadlines, and prioritize multiple tasks. Being enthusiastic, friendly, respectful, ethical, observant, detail-oriented, and flexible are some personality traits that successful Animal Behaviorists share.

Unions and Associations

Animal Behaviorists can join professional associations to take advantage of networking opportunities, continuing education, professional certification, and other professional services and resources. Some national societies that serve their interests are:

- American Veterinary Society of Animal Behavior
- Applied Animal Behavior Section (part of the Animal Behavior Society)
- Association of Companion Animal Behavior Counselors
- International Association of Animal Behavior Consultants
- National Association of Animal Behaviorists

Veterinary Behaviorists who are board-certified by the American College of Veterinary Behaviorists become diplomates of this organization.

Animal Behaviorists may also belong to associations that serve their particular specialty. For example, dog behaviorists might join the International Association of Canine Professionals or the Association of Pet Dog Trainers.

For contact information about all of the above organizations, see Appendix II.

Tips for Entry

1. You can start learning about animal behavior while in high school. Read articles and books about animal behavior, for example. You might raise a pet and keep a log on how it behaves, or you might volunteer at an animal shelter or work in an animal clinic where you may meet animals with behavioral problems.

2. Find an Animal Behaviorist who would be willing to mentor you or let you complete an apprenticeship under him or her.

3. To enhance their employability, Animal Behaviorists obtain professional certificates offered by recognized organizations such as the American Behavior Society or the International Association of Animal Behavior Consultants.

4. One way to market your business is to make personal contact with animal trainers, veterinarians, pet store owners, and other pet professionals in your community. Introduce yourself to each one, and leave some business cards and brochures or flyers about your business.

5. Use the Internet to learn more about Animal Behaviorists and their field. You might start by visiting the Web sites of these groups: American Veterinary Society of Animal Behavior (www.avsabonline.org) and Applied Animal Behavior Section (Animal Behavior Society) (www.animalbehavior.org/ABSAppliedBehavior). For more links, see Appendix IV.

ANIMAL CARETAKER

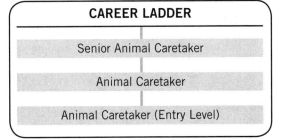

Position Description

Animal Caretakers are responsible for looking after animals in boarding facilities, animal shelters, research laboratories, zoos, veterinary hospitals, and other places that keep them on a temporary or permanent basis. In general terms, Animal Caretakers tend to animals' needs by keeping them and their living areas clean, providing them with food and water, exercising them, and observing their overall health and disposition. They note when animals show behavioral changes or exhibit physical signs of injury or illness, and inform animal owners, handlers, or veterinarians about their observations.

Animal Caretakers work with a wide variety of domestic or exotic animals that live in various environments. These experts are known by many titles, some of which signify more precisely what they do. For example, they may be called zookeepers, pet sitters, dog groomers, veterinary assistants, or laboratory animal care workers. Whatever their job titles, Animal Caretakers all have similar animal care responsibilities, as well as some that vary from one occupation to another.

Many animal care workers tend dogs, cats, and other pets for their owners when they are unable to do so. Animal Caretakers at boarding kennels watch after pets when owners are on vacation or business trips. Pet sitters, on the other hand, attend to pets in their owners' homes during their owners' absence. Both kennel attendants and pet sitters confer with pet owners about

veterinary appointments, medical needs, and dietary restrictions. Some kennels offer obedience training or breeding services to customers. At those facilities, Animal Caretakers may assist trainers and breeders.

Some Animal Caretakers, called grooms, work at stables and exclusively care for horses. They may work at horse farms, racing stables, police stables, or other equine facilities. In addition to the daily care of horses, these animal attendants prepare horses for riding as well as walk horses afterward to help them cool off. Grooms also clean and organize harnesses, saddles, bridles, and other tack items. These Animal Caretakers may manage feed inventories and, with sufficient experience, assist with training horses.

At zoos and animal parks, Animal Caretakers are called zookeepers. They work with exotic animals such as large cats, elephants, monkeys, zebras, giraffes, and the other creatures that reside there. Zookeepers may specialize by working with certain species. They clean their living areas, and observe the animals closely for signs of injury or changes in their behavior. These experts remain in contact with people during their workdays, to answer questions and to educate them about the proper way to watch the animals with respect and kindness.

Animal Caretakers at animal shelters and rescue facilities also have duties that put them in direct contact with the public, in person and by telephone. These attendants work with dogs, cats, and other animals that have been abused or abandoned. Along with their caretaking duties, they interview people who wish to adopt shelter or rescue animals. Animal Caretakers may also teach pet owners about routine care procedures, as well as about spaying and neutering services provided by their facilities.

In veterinary clinics and hospitals, Animal Caretakers assist veterinarians and veterinary technicians with caring for sick and injured animals. They may help with veterinary examinations, dental cleaning, surgeries, and other medical procedures. Under the direction of medical professionals, Animal Caretakers put bandages on wounded animals and administer vaccinations to animals. They also give oral medications to animals and apply medicines directly to their skin. These veterinary assistants may be responsible for preparing lab samples, getting equipment and tools ready for surgery, and keeping operating rooms clean and sterile.

Animal Caretakers also are employed to care for animals that are used in research projects in academic, government, or industry settings. Some of them work in research laboratories, where they care for such animals as mice, rats, rabbits, cats, monkeys, frogs, or fish. Other Animal Caretakers work on experimental farms to tend cows, pigs, sheep, and other livestock. On experimental farms, Animal Caretakers may help with such tasks as birthing, milking, and artificial insemination. In both laboratories and research farms, these experts keep meticulous records of each animal's diet, weight, and the medications administered for research purposes.

Regardless of their work setting, Animal Caretakers have routine tasks to complete. For example, they may:

- use computers to record observations and data regarding the animals in their charge
- clean, disinfect, and repair animal cages, stalls, coops, or other housing
- assist with the euthanization of unwanted or terminally ill animals
- move animal carcasses to disposal or loading areas
- respond to inquiries from the public and requests for appointments
- maintain files of medical tests and treatments, as well as forms, reports, clerical records, and other facility documents
- help to open and close facilities
- order, receive, and store supplies
- keep up-to-date with state and local regulations regarding the care of animals and maintenance of facilities
- participate in staff meetings and training sessions

Animal Caretakers work in both indoor and outdoor locations. Indoors, they work in offices to complete paperwork or confer with veterinarians or members of the public. Some caretakers work in research laboratories. Animal Caretakers who work outdoors are exposed to all kinds of climatic conditions including high and low temperatures and inclement weather. Some of these experts travel with animals, such as dogs and horses, to shows and competitions.

Animal Caretakers need to be in good physical condition. They must be able to lift and carry animals, bales of hay, sacks of feed, and other items that weight 50 pounds or more for distances up to 100 feet. Animal Caretakers may walk, crawl, kneel, reach, squat, bend, or turn while working with animals.

These experts risk exposure to animal wastes and diseases, as well as bites, scratches, and other injuries from animals that may, on occasion, be frightened or angry. They may be required to wear protective equipment including respirators.

Animal Caretakers generally work for 40 hours per week, but may be required to work evenings, weekends, or holidays. In some workplaces, such as animal hospitals, care is needed around the clock. In such locations, Animal Caretakers work in shifts.

Salaries

Salaries for Animal Caretakers vary, depending on such factors as their education, experience, job duties, employer, and geographic location. The U.S. Bureau of Labor Statistics (BLS) reported the following estimated salary ranges for most of these animal care workers in its May 2008 Occupational Employment Statistics (OES) survey:

- nonfarm animal caretakers: $15,140 to $31,590
- veterinary assistants and laboratory animal caretakers: $15,670 to $31,940

Employment Prospects

According to the May 2008 OES survey, approximately 126,740 nonfarm Animal Caretakers and 71,950 veterinary assistants and laboratory animal caretakers were employed in the United States.

Besides dog kennels, dog groomers, horse stables, and other pet care services, Animal Caretakers are hired by pet stores, animal shelters, humane societies, veterinary practices, animal hospitals, zoos, and animal parks. Laboratory animal caretakers find employment in government, academic, and private research settings.

The BLS reports that employment of nonfarm animal caretakers is expected to increase by 21 percent through 2018, while the employment rate of veterinary assistants and laboratory animal caretakers should grow 20 percent or more. Job growth will be mostly due to the expected rise in pet owners with disposable income who demand veterinary, grooming, boarding, and other care services for their pets.

In addition to job growth, Animal Caretakers will be needed to replace individuals who advance to higher positions, transfer to other jobs or careers, or leave the workforce for various reasons.

Advancement Prospects

Animal Caretakers can advance by earning higher wages and being assigned greater levels of responsibilities. They can also be promoted to supervisory and managerial positions, but opportunities are usually limited.

With additional training and experience, Animal Caretakers can pursue other careers by becoming animal control officers or animal trainers, for example. Some individuals continue their education to become veterinary technicians, veterinarians, zookeepers, zoo curators, research scientists, or other professionals. Entrepreneurial persons may open their own boarding kennels, horse stables, or other pet services.

Education and Training

Minimum educational requirements vary with the different positions as well as with employers. In general, individuals who seek positions at zoos and animal parks must possess at least a bachelor's degree in biology, animal science, or another related field. For entry-level positions in animal shelters, veterinary practices, research laboratories, and other work settings, applicants usually need only a high school diploma or general equivalency diploma. Some of these employers may require applicants to have some college background.

Animal Caretakers learn their skills and duties on the job. Entry-level caretakers work under the direction and supervision of experienced staff.

Experience, Special Skills, and Personality Traits

Many employers prefer to hire individuals for entry-level positions who have at least one or more years of experience in animal care, which they may have gained through employment or volunteer work. Employers typically seek applicants who demonstrate that they are able to handle animals with great care, respect, and compassion.

Animal Caretakers need strong self-management skills, such as the ability to handle stressful situations, work independently, prioritize multiple tasks, and understand and follow instructions. Having excellent critical-thinking, problem-solving, communication, interpersonal, and teamwork skills is also important. Being calm, tactful, courteous, patient, observant, detail-oriented, and flexible are some personality traits that successful Animal Caretakers share.

Unions and Associations

Some Animal Caretakers belong to labor unions that represent them in contract negotiations for better terms regarding pay, benefits, and working conditions. Unions also handle any grievances that officers may have against their employers.

Tips for Entry

1. Volunteering at a public or nonprofit group, such as an animal shelter, may sometimes lead to a paid position, if your work is appreciated and if funding is available.
2. Some employers require that applicants hold a valid driver's license.
3. Having basic computer and recordkeeping skills may enhance your employability.
4. Do you need help finding a job or improving your job search skills? Ask for help from a counselor at a local One-Stop Career Center, which is sponsored by the U.S. Department of Labor. To find the nearest center, look in your phone book or visit the CareerOneStop Web site at www.careeronestop.org.
5. Use the Internet to learn more about different work environments for Animal Caretakers. To get a list of Web sites to visit, enter the name of the work setting, such as *animal shelters* or *horse stables,* into a search engine.

ANIMAL CONTROL OFFICER

Duties: Enforce local and state animal control laws and regulations; protect public health and safety; handle abandoned and dangerous animals as needed; perform other duties as required

Alternate Title(s): Animal Services Officer, Community Service Officer

Salary Range: $19,000 to $49,000

Employment Prospects: Fair

Advancement Prospects: Fair

Prerequisites:

Education or Training—High school diploma; on-the-job training

Experience—Experience handling and caring for animals preferred

Special Skills and Personality Traits—Critical-thinking, problem-solving, decision-making, team-work, writing, communication, interpersonal, customer service, and self-management skills; calm, tactful, courteous, quick-witted, and dedicated personality traits

Special Requirements—Driver's license; peace officer certification may be required

CAREER LADDER

Senior or Supervisory
Animal Control Officer

Animal Control Officer

Animal Control Officer (Entry Level)

Position Description

Animal Control Officers were once called dogcatchers because they primarily handled stray dogs. Their work, however, involves all kinds of animals, both domestic and wild. These men and women are responsible for safeguarding the health and welfare of both animals and people within their communities. They also enforce local and state laws and codes pertaining to the treatment, care, and keeping of domestic animals. In addition, they assist with providing care and attention to homeless, lost, abandoned, and neglected animals that are kept at local animal shelters.

Animal Control Officers may work under city or county jurisdictions. Many are municipal, county, or state employees who work for their local animal control program, which may be part of the police or sheriff's department, a public health agency, a parks department, or another government division. In some communities, the animal control services are contracted out to not-for-profit humane societies. Most Animal Control Officers are appointed as full-time employees who work singly or in teams.

Animal Control Officers patrol their communities by driving trucks equipped with holding compartments. As they patrol, Animal Control Officers look for signs of animals exhibiting abnormal behavior or the presence of diseased or injured animals. They also search for violations of laws pertaining to domestic animals. For example, they look for pets that are missing license tags or that are showing clear signs of neglect. Animal Control Officers also retrieve wild or domestic animal carcasses from roadways and dispose of them properly.

These officers respond to calls from citizens concerning animal problems in their neighborhoods. They may settle conflicts between neighbors regarding a dog's continual barking, or a complaint about a neighbor's cat loitering near a bird feeder. They may investigate reports of missing or abandoned pets, allegations of animal cruelty, animal bite incidents, concerns about animal illness, or unsupervised animals wandering through yards. They also help pet owners find ways to keep their animals from wandering away from home. For example, if someone left a gate open and the family dog ran out and dug up a neighbor's flower bed, an Animal Control Officer would advise the dog's owner to make it a habit to make sure that the gate was always secure. Animal Control Officers may also track and capture wild creatures that wander into neighborhoods and release them back into the wild.

When pet owners or others violate regulations, Animal Control Officers explain the law and provide options to the violators. They may urge them to comply with the regulations within a set time frame. Animal Control Officers have the authority to issue warnings and citations. They may file criminal charges when violations are not corrected promptly. Some Animal Control Officers also have arresting powers.

These officers cooperate in criminal cases involving animals, such as animal abuse. For example, they may prepare evidence of crimes or violations of the law. When required, they testify as expert witnesses at court trials.

Animal Control Officers retrieve pets and other domestic animals that cannot be cared for properly or have been abandoned, and bring them to the local animal shelter. If animals need medical care, these experts transport them to veterinary clinics or hospitals. At animal shelters, officers help take care of animals until they are claimed by their rightful owners, adopted by new owners, or transferred to an animal-rescue group. Animal Control Officers may have to administer euthanasia—that is, they kill animals that cannot be adopted or are too ill to recover.

Animal Control Officers also perform responsibilities that address public health and safety. They quarantine animals that suffer from contagious diseases or have bitten other animals or people, for example. In some communities, these officers are assigned to inspect businesses such as pet stores or kennels for compliance with health and safety regulations.

Animal Control Officers provide educational services to members of their communities as well. They inform the public about spaying and neutering their pets, teach people to control their pets' behavior, and conduct clinics to have pets inoculated for rabies. These men and women also promote the adoption of animals held at animal control shelters.

These experts perform a wide range of general tasks every day. At animal shelters, they help visitors identify their missing pets. They contact pet owners regarding missing animals that have been found, animals that have bitten people, or about other concerns. Animal Control Officers provide sheltered animals with food and water, as well as give them daily exercise. In addition, these experts maintain and clean vehicles, equipment, shelter facilities, and grounds.

Animal Control Officers also execute routine administrative tasks. They document all their activities, particularly those that pertain to violations. They may use computers in their vehicles to log reports and document their investigations. Some of them use notebooks or pads of paper to write notes, which they later use as a reference to type more detailed reports. Some officers are responsible for issuing pet licenses for dogs, cats,

ferrets, or other domestic animals. These officers also complete such office routines as answering telephones, filing documents, and typing letters, reports, and other documents.

Depending on their level of seniority, Animal Control Officers may train novice officers, supervise and evaluate the job performance of other staff members, or participate in officer recruitment activities.

Animal Control Officers normally wear uniforms. They use such tools of the trade as traps, nets, ropes, pepper spray, tranquilizer darts, batons, and cages. Depending on their jurisdiction, they may be authorized to carry and use firearms. These experts are trained to administer CPR and first aid to injured animals. They may also operate some types of medical equipment and be responsible for their maintenance and repair.

Animal Control Officers work outdoors in all weather conditions. They travel within their communities by vehicle and on foot. They exert themselves by walking, stooping, reaching, and kneeling, as well as lifting animals and other items that weigh as much as 100 pounds or more. They may risk injury or infection from bites and scratches inflicted on them by animals; hence, they follow strict safety procedures and wear protective equipment such as rubber gloves and biohazard suits.

These officers face a certain amount of stressful situations. They contend with frightened animals and upset pet owners who may exhibit physical aggression and hostile emotions. Animal Control Officers also deal with their own emotional reaction to handling injured, abused, or sick animals, as well as with the requirement to euthanize animals.

These experts may work shifts, including night shifts, as well as during weekends and holidays. Animal Control Officers may be required to be available at all times on an on-call basis.

Salaries
Salaries for Animal Control Officers vary, depending on such factors as their education, experience, employer, and geographic location. The U.S. Bureau of Labor Statistics (BLS) reported in its May 2008 Occupational Employment Statistics (OES) survey that the estimated annual salary for most animal control workers ranged from $18,950 to $48,730. The estimated hourly wage for these workers ranged between $9.11 and $23.43.

Employment Prospects
Approximately 15,480 animal control workers were employed in the United States, according to the May 2008 OES survey.

Job openings for animal control positions usually become available when individuals transfer to other jobs or career fields, advance to higher positions, or retire or leave the workforce for other reasons. The number of positions in an animal control agency depends on the availability of funding. Opportunities are generally better in midsize and large cities. Small cities usually have funds to employ one or two officers.

Advancement Prospects

Animal Control Officers advance by earning higher wages and being assigned greater levels of responsibilities. They may be promoted to supervisory and managerial positions, but opportunities are limited, particularly in small communities.

By seeking further training, Animal Control Officers can pursue careers in law enforcement, veterinary medicine, animal welfare, or animal care and service.

Education and Training

For individuals to become Animal Control Officers, they must hold at least a high school diploma or general equivalency diploma.

Animal Control Officers learn their skills on the job while working under the supervision and direction of experienced officers. They may also complete formal training programs provided by their employers, depending on the requirements of their city or state.

Special Requirements

Animal Control Officers are required to hold a valid driver's license.

In some jurisdictions, these experts are required to hold a peace officer standards and training (POST) certificate, which is earned upon completion of training at a police academy.

Experience, Special Skills, and Personality Traits

Applicants usually do not need any previous work experience when applying for entry-level positions. However, many employers prefer candidates who have at least one year of experience handling and caring for animals.

To perform their job effectively, Animal Control Officers need excellent critical-thinking, problem-solving, decision-making, teamwork, writing, and communication skills. They must also have excellent interpersonal and customer service skills, as they must deal with colleagues, public officials, the public, and others from diverse backgrounds. In addition, Animal Control Officers need strong self-management skills, such as the ability to work independently, meet deadlines, handle stressful situations, and prioritize multiple tasks. Being calm, tactful, courteous, quick-witted, and dedicated are some personality traits that successful Animal Control Officers share.

Unions and Associations

Animal Control Officers may be members of a labor union that represents them in negotiations with their employers for better pay, benefits, and other contract terms. The union also handles any grievances that its members may have against their employer.

Some Animal Control Officers belong to professional associations to take advantage of networking opportunities, continuing education, and other professional services and resources. One national society that serves their interests is the National Animal Control Association. For contact information, see Appendix II.

Tips for Entry

1. To determine if a career in animal control is right for you, volunteer at an animal shelter.
2. Learn as much as you can about animals, how animal shelters work, and the animal control laws that govern the jurisdiction where you would like to work.
3. Obtain a volunteer, temporary, or part-time position at an animal shelter. It may lead to a job offer for a full-time position.
4. City and county governments often post job openings at their Web sites. Individuals may be able to download job applications as well as submit applications through a public agency's Web site.
5. Use the Internet to learn more about Animal Control Officers and animal shelters. You might start by visiting the National Animal Control Association Web site (http://www.nacanet.org) or AnimalSheltering.org. For more links, see Appendix IV.

VETERINARY MEDICINE

VETERINARIAN

Duties: Diagnose and treat animal health problems; may be involved in research, education, regulatory medicine, public health, or other nonclinical area, perform other duties as required

Alternate Title(s): Research Veterinarian; Veterinary Dermatologist, Veterinary Pathologist, or another title that reflects a specialty

Salary Range: $47,000 to $144,000

Employment Prospects: Good

Advancement Prospects: Fair

Prerequisites:

Education or Training—Complete a doctor of veterinary medicine program

Experience—Previous work experience preferred

Special Skills and Personality Traits—Leadership, self-management, critical-thinking, interpersonal, teamwork, and communication skills; business skills, for private practitioners; friendly, compassionate, patient, and dedicated personality traits

Special Requirements—State veterinary license required to practice; veterinary specialists must be board-certified by proper veterinary specialty college or board

CAREER LADDER

Senior Veterinarian

Veterinarian

Veterinarian (Entry Level)

Position Description

Most of us who have pets are familiar with Veterinarians. They are members of the medical profession who are dedicated to improving the life and health of animals as well as humans.

Clinical Veterinarians treat injured or and sick animals for pet owners, agricultural producers, animal shelters, zoos, and others. These medical professionals diagnose diseases, administer shots, set broken bones, perform surgeries, and prescribe medicines for both domestic and wild animals. They also help owners and handlers to learn more about taking care of their animals and keeping them healthy. Clinical Veterinarians mostly work in private practices, animal clinics, and pet hospitals.

Veterinarians may focus on treating certain kinds of animals. Some Veterinarians work with small animals such as pets. Others take care of large farm and ranch animals as well as racehorses. Still others combine their work to include both small and large animals. Some clinical Veterinarians are employed by zoos, aquariums, and animal parks, where they are responsible for the care and treatment of exotic animals in those facilities.

Veterinarians are also hired by research laboratories to support animal testing and research efforts that lead to the development of medicines and lifesaving treatments that benefit the health and welfare of both animals and humans. These Veterinarians make certain that laboratory animals receive the best of care at all times. They also assist researchers in selecting animal models for research projects.

Veterinarians are similar to the doctors who treat humans. They examine animals by listening to their hearts and lungs with stethoscopes. They use special instruments to examine animals' eyes and ears. They take blood tests and use X rays to take closer looks at broken bones and internal organs. What sets these medical professionals apart is that they have to look for subtle indications of pain or discomfort because animals cannot tell them where and how they hurt. Consequently, Veterinarians look at how animals hold themselves, observe how alert they are, or how they respond to touch, for example. These medical professionals also speak to the animals' owners or handlers about symptoms they have observed. Veterinarians evaluate all the information about their patients and then discuss diagnoses and treatment options with their patients' owners or handlers.

In addition to performing various medical treatment procedures, Veterinarians provide emergency care and deliver animal babies. They advise animal owners and handlers about animal nutrition and animal behavior. They also teach them how to administer medications, and how to provide the best of care as their animals recover from their injuries or illnesses.

Many of these doctors practice general veterinary medicine, but others are specialists who are board-certified by a recognized organization to practice a particular veterinary specialty. Some Veterinarians specialize by working with certain animals and obtain the proper certification to open an avian, canine, beef cattle, equine, or other specialized practice. Others focus on excelling in a specific medical discipline such as cardiology, dermatology, internal medicine, surgery, pathology, toxicology, radiology, or oncology. Veterinary specialists have advanced training to make diagnoses and perform medical procedures for which general practitioners may lack expertise.

Veterinarians also fulfill other roles outside of clinical practice. Some of these professionals work as research scientists in academic, government, and industrial laboratory settings. Research Veterinarians are involved in various types of research. They conduct basic studies in animal health to increase their knowledge about different topics such as diseases that afflict animals or how animal diseases spread. They also design applied research projects to find new tools, methodologies, and therapies to diagnose and treat animals. Research Veterinarians also work in pet food, feed, agricultural chemistry, and other industries to create and produce useful products for animals and humans.

Some Veterinarians contribute to biomedical research in which they seek to prevent and treat human health problems. For example, they might assist in the development of new medicines to treat heart disease or new surgical techniques for replacing human organs. Other research Veterinarians conduct studies of infectious diseases that originate in animals. Their concern is to understand the mechanics and development of such a disease, how it can be transmitted to humans, and how to stop it from spreading among both animals and humans. Some of these research professionals work closely with government agencies.

Many Veterinarians work in the field of education as professors at schools or colleges of veterinary medicine. Some teach at medical universities. Professors instruct and advise future Veterinarians and veterinary specialists, as well as supervise postdoctoral fellows. These men and women may perform research activities as part of their academic responsibilities. They are also expected to participate in faculty and school meetings, fulfill community service requirements, and publish scholarly work. Some professors provide consultation services to veterinarians in nearby communities, as well as statewide or nationally.

Veterinarians contribute to the establishment of laws and regulations that protect the health and well being of humans and animals alike. For example, veterinary experts in the field of regulatory medicine may work with agricultural and public health agencies to protect consumers from exposure to diseased meats and poultry. Some Veterinarians monitor the importation of animals from other countries as well as the transport of animals from one region of the United States to another. Government Veterinarians may enforce laws pertaining to the introduction of new vaccines. They investigate disease outbreaks, oversee the safety of food industries and restaurants, or study the impact of pesticides and other contaminants on human and animal populations. Some of these professionals evaluate new medications, food additives, and other products for safety and approval for market.

Veterinarians may also be involved with animal welfare issues, wildlife medicine, or aquatic animal medicine, among other similar fields. In addition, some occupy positions in management, sales, and service departments with various industries such as pharmaceutical manufacturers, food processing enterprises, and animal feed companies.

Veterinarians perform a variety of general tasks, depending on their clinical or nonclinical responsibilities. They may:

- gather tissue and fluid samples from animals for analysis
- prescribe medications and advise animal handlers about how to administer them
- provide required inoculations to pets
- euthanize animals that are terminally ill or too seriously injured to lead normal lives
- use such equipment as ultrasound, X ray, and other diagnostic machines to examine animals
- train and oversee staffs of animal caretakers, veterinary technicians, office support personnel, and other workers
- provide educational services and materials to the public regarding animal care, disease prevention, and other topics

Veterinarians experience work conditions that vary according to their specialties and work settings. Clinical Veterinarians often work 50-hour weeks, and may work on an on-call basis. They are expected to handle emergencies and unscheduled patient visits at any time. Some clinical Veterinarians, particularly those who work with large ranch animals, must travel varying distances to visit their patients.

Research and other nonclinical Veterinarians have standard work schedules of 40 hours per week. They often put in additional hours to complete their various duties.

Salaries

Salaries for Veterinarians vary, depending on such factors as their position, experience, employer, and geographic location. According to the May 2008 Occupational Employment Statistics (OES) survey by the U.S. Bureau of Labor Statistics (BLS) the estimated annual salary for most Veterinarians ranged between $46,610 and $143,660.

Employment Prospects

The BLS reported in its May 2008 OES survey that an estimated 53,110 Veterinarians were employed in the United States.

A large number of Veterinarians work in private clinical practice. Some are independent practitioners or partners in a group practice. Others are salaried employees of a private practice. Some Veterinarians are hired by retail pet stores that offer veterinary services.

Local, state, and federal agencies hire Veterinarians to work in such areas as research, food safety inspection, and public health. Some federal agencies that employ these medical professionals include the Food Safety and Inspection Service, the Agricultural Research Service, the Food and Drug Administration, the Animal and Plant Health Inspection Service, the Environmental Protection Agency, the Centers for Disease Control and Prevention, the National Institutes of Health, the U.S. Army, the U.S. Public Health Service Commissioned Corps, and the U.S. Department of Homeland Security. In the private sector, Veterinarians are hired by pharmaceutical, biotechnology, and animal food companies, among others. Veterinarians also find employment as instructors and researchers in colleges, universities, and medical schools.

Job opportunities for Veterinarians are currently favorable. Some experts in the field say some federal agencies are understaffed. Some express concern that many federal Veterinarians are becoming eligible for retirement over the next several years. Federal agencies are competing with private companies, state agencies, private clinical practices, and other employers for the same pool of experienced and newly licensed Veterinarians.

According to the BLS, the employment growth for Veterinarians is expected to increase by 33 percent through 2018.

Advancement Prospects

Veterinarians advance according to their own interests and ambitions. Those in clinical practice generally start their careers as staff employees. Some general practitioners become veterinary specialists. Entrepreneurial Veterinarians may pursue opportunities to establish their own practices.

Veterinarians who work in research, public health, and other settings may advance to supervisory and managerial positions.

Regardless of their work setting, Veterinarians measure success by earning higher salaries, by gaining professional reputations, and through job satisfaction.

Education and Training

Veterinarians must obtain a doctor of veterinary medicine degree (D.V.M. or V.M.D.) from a college of veterinary medicine accredited by the American Veterinary Medical Association Council on Education. As this book was being written, 28 accredited colleges existed in the United States.

Admission requirements vary among the veterinary colleges. Depending on the school, applicants may be required to hold a bachelor's degree or have completed a minimum number of college units. Veterinary colleges also require that applicants have successfully completed specific course work in biological sciences, physical sciences, mathematics, English, social sciences, humanities, and other subjects. In addition, schools require applicants to submit test scores from the Veterinary College Admission Test (VCAT), the Medical College Admission Test (MCAT), or the Graduate Record Examination (GRE).

D.V.M. programs are four years long. Students study anatomy, pathology, pharmacology, microbiology, and other sciences. They also learn the principles of medicine and surgery in both classroom and clinical settings. Clinical course work includes infectious diseases, diagnostic pathology, obstetrics, public health, preventative medicine, clinical nutrition, business practices, and professional ethics.

To become veterinary specialists, Veterinarians must complete a residency program at an accredited veterinary school in their area of interest, such as cardiology, pathology, anesthesiology, oncology, or exotic animal medicine. Programs may be two to four years or more, depending on the specialty.

Veterinarians who plan to conduct research or teach in academic institutions must earn a master's or doctoral degree in their discipline.

New Veterinarians receive on-the-job training while working under the supervision and direction of experienced staff. All Veterinarians pursue containing education to update their skills and knowledge.

Special Requirements

Every U.S. state, as well as the District of Columbia, requires Veterinarians to be licensed to practice in its jurisdiction. Licensing requirements vary from state to state. For specific licensing information, contact the state veterinary board that governs the area in which you plan to work.

Veterinary specialists must be certified by the appropriate veterinary specialty college or board in order to practice their specialized area of veterinary medicine. For example, veterinary surgeons must be board certified by the American College of Veterinary Surgeons, while veterinary cardiologists must be board certified by the American College of Veterinary Internal Medicine.

Experience, Special Skills, and Personality Traits

Employers hire entry-level applicants who have experience in the type of work, such as clinical practice, research, food safety inspection, or public health, for which they apply. They may have gained their experience through employment, internships, research projects, or volunteer work. Some employers are willing to hire inexperienced candidates if they demonstrate a willingness to learn and work hard.

To perform well at their job, Veterinarians need excellent leadership, self-management, critical-thinking, interpersonal, teamwork, and communication skills. Private practitioners also need strong business skills. Being friendly, compassionate, patient, and dedicated are some personality traits that successful Veterinarians have in common.

Unions and Associations

Many Veterinarians belong to professional associations to take advantage of networking opportunities, continuing education, and other professional services and resources. Some national societies that serve the diverse interests of Veterinarians include:

- Academy of Rural Veterinarians
- American Association of Housecall and Mobile Veterinarians
- American Association of Swine Veterinarians
- American Association of Veterinary Parasitologists
- American Veterinary Dental Society
- American Veterinary Medical Association
- Association of Avian Veterinarians
- Association of Shelter Veterinarians

Veterinary specialists become diplomates of the organizations from which they obtained board certification. For example, veterinary pathologists are members of the American College of Veterinary Pathologists, while veterinary surgeons belong to the American College of Veterinary Surgeons.

For contact information about all of the above organizations, see Appendix II.

Tips for Entry

1. As a student, get a part-time job, or volunteer, at an animal clinic, a petting zoo, a pet store, a dog kennel, an animal shelter, a farm, or another setting where you can gain experience caring for animals.
2. While you are in high school, do research on the veterinary colleges where you would like to enroll. For example, find out what prerequisite courses you must complete to apply for a college.
3. To enhance their employability, some veterinary college graduates complete an internship to gain more experience before looking for work.
4. Take advantage of online job banks that are maintained by professional associations.
5. Use the Internet to learn more about the field of veterinary medicine. You might start by visiting the Web sites of these organizations: the American Veterinary Medical Association (www.avma.org) and the Association of American Veterinary Medical Colleges (www.aavmc.org). For more links, see Appendix IV.

VETERINARY PATHOLOGIST

Duties: Perform laboratory examinations and diagnoses; conduct studies; perform duties as required of position

Alternate Title(s): Veterinary Anatomic Pathologist, Toxicological Pathologist, Research Scientist/Veterinary Pathologist, or another title that reflects a particular job

Salary Range: $47,000 to $144,000

Employment Prospects: Good

Advancement Prospects: Good

Prerequisites:

Education or Training—Complete veterinary and veterinary pathology programs; doctorate needed to become research scientists

Experience—Previous work experience preferred

Special Skills and Personality Traits—Leadership, organizational, problem-solving, communication, interpersonal, and technical writing skills; detail-oriented, precise, unbiased, collaborative, and dedicated personality traits

Special Requirements—Board certification by the American College of Veterinary Pathologists

Position Description

Pathology is the scientific study of the nature and effects of diseases. It is also the medical practice of diagnosing and treating diseases. The men and women who specialize in animal diseases are called Veterinary Pathologists. They work in pathology laboratories where they examine samples of animal tissues, fluids, and wastes for abnormalities. Their diagnoses contribute to the health and well-being of both animals and humans. They work in such diverse areas as animal medicine, wildlife conservation, food safety, public health, pharmaceutical drug development, biomedical research, bioterrorism, and forensic investigations. They work in clinical, government, industry, academic, and other settings.

Veterinary Pathologists are veterinarians who have completed additional training in one or both of these pathology specialties:

- anatomic pathology—the study and diagnosis of specimens by gross or microscopic examinations
- clinical pathology—the study and diagnosis of specimens by conducting various chemical, biological, molecular, and other types of tests

These specialists apply principles and techniques from various biological sciences to their work, including anatomy, biochemistry, microbiology, molecular genetics, immunology, bacteriology, and virology.

Veterinary Pathologists have many career options. In the area of animal health care, they provide laboratory diagnostic services to veterinary practices, veterinary clinics, and animal hospitals as well as to veterinary staffs at zoos, aquariums, animal parks, and other establishments. These pathologists interpret laboratory findings and surgical biopsies to help veterinarians prescribe appropriate treatments for domestic and wild animals. Veterinary Pathologists also perform necropsies on animals to determine the cause of their deaths. Veterinary Pathologists may specialize in working with certain animals, such as pets, livestock, or specific wild animal populations.

Veterinary Pathologists also assist in the conservation of wildlife and the environment by participating in population studies of animals. They may study how a natural or man-made disaster in a particular location has affected animals, how human activities may place certain animal species at risk of extinction, or why the mortality rate of a species is increasing.

Some Veterinary Pathologists work in the area of forensics, which is the application of scientific methods and techniques to legal issues. These experts assist in criminal investigations, civil litigation, and administrative cases that involve violations of government regulations. For example, a Veterinary Pathologist might examine physical evidence that is part of a criminal case in which the suspects are accused of killing birds that are protected by federal wildlife laws. Veterinary Pathologists examine physical evidence—which may be animal bodies, parts, or products—and provide criminal investigators, attorneys, and judges with unbiased evaluations of their findings. They prepare documentation of their evidence and opinions, and may be called on to testify as expert witnesses in court.

Many Veterinary Pathologists work as research scientists in government, private industries, and universities and medical centers to solve animal and human health problems. They conduct independent studies as well as participate in research teams. They may perform basic research to further their understanding about animal diseases, where new diseases come from, the risks of animal diseases to humans, why a disease affects certain species, and other topics. Veterinary Pathologists who focus on public health issues may conduct research to further their understanding of the mechanics and development of contagious diseases.

Veterinary Pathologists also conduct applied research in which they utilize basic research findings to develop solutions to specific problems. For example, Veterinary Pathologists who are part of biomedical research teams may seek cures to cancer, leukemia, and other human diseases. Other Veterinary Pathologists may be involved in the development of pharmaceutical drugs and new approaches for treating illnesses of animals or humans.

Some Veterinary Pathologists engage in regulatory activities for manufacturers of food, pharmaceuticals, medical devices, agricultural chemicals, and other products to ensure their safety for animal or human consumption. These pathologists use their diagnostic skills to identify the level of chemicals and other toxic agents within products. These pathologists also study ways to improve the use of animal toxicology information for human risk assessment.

Many other Veterinary Pathologists perform critical work in the area of public health. They play a big role in diagnosing and monitoring the spread of new and emerging diseases. For example, Veterinary Pathologists were involved in discovering infectious diseases that originated in animals, such as the Ebola virus, the West Nile virus, the hantavirus, and the swine flu virus.

Some Veterinary Pathologists assist authorities in detecting acts of bioterrorism or agricultural terrorism, which can cause economic havoc as well as put the health of large numbers of citizens at risk. Veterinary Pathologists are also employed by the military to identify biological and endemic agents that may cause diseases in countries where the armed forces are deployed.

Veterinary Pathologists hold faculty positions at universities and medical centers where they train and advise future veterinarians and Veterinary Pathologists. Some also supervise postdoctoral fellows. In addition to conducting independent research, Veterinary Pathologists collaborate with other investigators who use animals in their various research projects. Some academic pathologists provide diagnostic pathology and consultation services to veterinarians in surrounding communities, as well as statewide or nationally. Furthermore, academicians participate in faculty and school meetings, fulfill community service, and publish scholarly work.

Veterinary Pathologists carry out various duties, many of which vary according to the type of work they do. Researchers, for example, are responsible for planning, developing, and implementing basic or applied research projects. Veterinary Pathologists also perform certain routine tasks, regardless of their job or setting. For example, they attend meetings, keep records of their work activities, prepare pathology reports, and provide technical consultation to staff and others. Many of these pathologists train others in the proper steps to collect animal tissues and fluids for later examination in the laboratory. Veterinary Pathologists are expected to keep up with new developments in their fields.

Veterinary Pathologists work in laboratories and offices. Researchers work flexible hours, including evenings and weekends, to carry out experiments and complete tasks in a timely manner.

Salaries

Salaries for Veterinary Pathologists vary, depending on such factors as their experience, position, employer, and geographic location. Specific salary information for these professionals is unavailable. In general, they earn higher salaries than veterinarians. The estimated annual salary for most veterinarians ranged between $46,610 and $143,660, according to the May 2008 Occupational Employment Statistics survey by the U.S. Bureau of Labor Statistics.

Employment Prospects

Veterinary pathology is a small but growing field. It is one of the specialties recognized by the American Veterinary Medical Association. Some employers of Veterinary Pathologists include research universities and medical centers, private diagnostic laboratory services, zoos, and animal parks. Veterinary Pathologists also find employment in various private industries including pet product manufacturers, food, pharmaceuticals, biotechnology, and chemical industries, among others.

Veterinary Pathologists are also hired by local and state government agencies as well as such federal agencies as the U.S. Department of Defense, the U.S. Department of Agriculture, the Food and Drug Administration, the National Institutes of Health, and the Centers for Disease Control and Prevention.

Opportunities are favorable for qualified Veterinary Pathologists. Some experts in the field express concern that many Veterinary Pathologists are becoming eligible for retirement in the next several years while, at the same time fewer students are entering the field.

Advancement Prospects

Veterinary Pathologists who hold faculty appointments rise through the ranks from instructor and assistant professor positions to full professorships. They also advance by earning higher incomes, as well as by gaining tenure.

In academic, private, government, and other settings, Veterinary Pathologists can be promoted to supervisory and managerial positions.

Education and Training

Individuals must commit to several years of studies to become Veterinary Pathologists. First, they must complete three or four years of college course work, depending on the veterinary school in which they plan to enroll. They then successfully complete a four-year doctor of veterinary medicine degree (D.V.M. or V.M.D.) program. Next, veterinary pathology candidates undergo three years of training and obtain board certification by the American College of Veterinary Pathologists.

Individuals who plan to become research scientists must earn either a master's or doctoral degree in their discipline, for which they need two to five or more years of study. Usually, those who earn doctorates complete one or more years of postdoctoral training.

Veterinary Pathologists must possess a doctorate if they plan to become college professors.

Special Requirements

Veterinary Pathologists must be board certified by the American College of Veterinary Pathologists in their specialties—veterinary anatomic pathology, veterinary clinical pathology, or both specialties. To become certi-fied, they must successfully pass the appropriate examinations administered by this organization.

Experience, Special Skills, and Personality Traits

Employers hire entry-level applicants who have the appropriate experience and knowledge to qualify them for the positions for which they apply. They may have gained their experience through residencies, postdoctoral training, internships, or employment.

To perform well at their work, Veterinary Pathologists must have effective leadership, organizational, problem-solving, communication, interpersonal, and technical-writing skills. Some personality traits that successful Veterinary Pathologists share include being detail-oriented, precise, unbiased, collaborative, and dedicated.

Unions and Associations

Veterinary Pathologists can join professional associations to take advantage of networking opportunities, professional certification, continuing education, and other professional services and resources. Some national societies that serve the interests of these professionals are the American College of Veterinary Pathologists, the American Veterinary Medical Association, and the Society of Toxicologic Pathology. For contact information to these organizations, see Appendix II.

Tips for Entry

1. While in high school, participate in activities that let you work with animals. For example, you might join a 4-H program or do volunteer work at a humane shelter.
2. As a college student, obtain an internship or part-time job in a medical or veterinary diagnostic laboratory to gain experience. You can also find out if that work setting is right for you.
3. Ask your current, as well as former, professors, supervisors, and classmates about possible job leads.
4. Use the Internet to learn more about veterinary pathology. You might start by visiting the American College of Veterinary Pathologists Web site at www.acvp.org. For more links, see Appendix IV.

VETERINARY TECHNICIAN

Duties: Provide medical and surgical support to veterinarians; perform other duties as required

Alternate Title(s): Veterinary Technologist, Veterinary Laboratory Technician

Salary Range: $20,000 to $41,000

Employment Prospects: Good

Advancement Prospects: Good

Prerequisites:

Education or Training—Associate's or bachelor's degree in veterinary technology required

Experience—One or more years of work experience

Special Skills and Personality Traits—Self-management, interpersonal, communication,

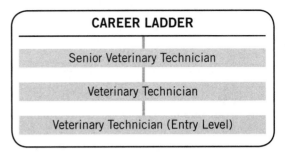

teamwork, organizational, critical-thinking, and problem-solving skills; patient, tactful, sympathetic, gentle, detail-oriented, and flexible personality traits

Special Requirements—State license, certification, or registration required

Position Description

When people take their pets to a veterinarian, they often encounter one or more assistants known as Veterinary Technicians. These men and women work under the direction of veterinarians to vaccinate animals, collect samples of animal body fluids, trim claws, and perform other routine medical procedures. Veterinary Technicians use their knowledge about how to handle and care for animals, as well as about veterinary science, animal physiology, and laboratory or clinical procedures to help veterinarians in all aspects of clinical care. However, Veterinary Technicians are not authorized to perform surgery, diagnose diseases, or prescribe medications.

Most Veterinary Technicians work in private veterinary practices, veterinary clinics, and animal hospitals. Some are part of veterinary staffs employed by animal shelters, zoos, wildlife preserves, and other animal facilities.

Veterinary Technicians help veterinarians by obtaining necessary information about animals before the medical doctors see them. Technicians question pet owners or animal handlers to find out as much as they can about animal patients' history and symptoms. These technicians also perform such preliminary examination tasks as taking the animals' temperatures, listening to their heart and lungs, taking blood pressure readings, making note of pulse rates, and extracting blood samples. When needed, these experts perform CPR and insert breathing tubes to keep animals breathing. Veterinary Technicians look closely at their patients to

make note of the presence of ticks or fleas, missing fur, skin abrasions, or other problems about which doctors would need to know.

As veterinarians perform more in-depth examination procedures, Veterinary Technicians restrain the animals. These technicians further assist the doctors by treating animals under veterinarians' supervision. Veterinary Technicians may dispense medications, clean animals' teeth, help set bones and apply splints or casts, insert intravenous tubes, and treat wounds by dressing or suturing them. Some Veterinary Technicians are responsible for putting extremely sick or injured animals to sleep.

These technicians also assist veterinarians at the operating table. They prepare animal patients for surgery by cleaning and shaving them. They make certain that the necessary equipment and clean instruments are available. They may administer anesthesia, which is needed for many routine surgeries, and perform such procedures as taking and developing X rays. Veterinary Technicians hand instruments to the veterinary surgeon as needed, and monitor the patients throughout the procedures. Following surgery, Veterinary Technicians attend to their patients' needs and observe their recovery. They provide food and water and make certain that their patients are comfortable.

Veterinary Technicians may work with animals of varying sizes in clinical or hospital settings as well as in animal shelters. Their tasks vary depending on the type of animals their employers treat. Different sizes and species of animals require different handling techniques, for example. They use specialized equipment to hold farm animals in place for examinations and to keep them calm, whereas they can hold smaller animals in place by hand. As another example, taking a parakeet's blood pressure would require a different approach than taking a dog's blood pressure.

Veterinary Technicians perform various routine tasks every day. They keep careful records of all examination, surgical, and recovery processes. They write their observations and list the procedures on a chart for each patient. Veterinary Technicians also clean operating rooms, sterilize surgical tools, and complete some maintenance tasks on surgical equipment. Some technicians perform routine office tasks, such as maintaining files, making appointments, and handling phone calls or visitors.

Not all Veterinary Technicians work in clinical settings. Some technicians are involved with veterinary research. They work in academic, government, or private research laboratories, where they provide veterinarians with technical and research support. Veterinarians study animals for a variety of reasons, such as for the purposes of genetic or drug research. Veterinary Technicians assist by making and reporting general observations about the animals being used in research projects. Technicians keep accurate records about the animals' conditions, particularly unusual symptoms or behavior or signs of pain. They make note of animals' weight, eating habits, prescribed medicines, and other pertinent information. They indicate which medications are prescribed for each animal.

Research Veterinary Technicians perform other tasks such as preparing tissue samples for microscopic examination and sterilizing lab equipment. They may assist with designing projects, such as drug trials. In their research capacity, Veterinary Technicians work with certain species or individual animals for extended periods, in contrast to clinical technicians, who work with a variety of animals from day to day.

Veterinary Technicians may specialize in several ways. They may work with certain animals, such as dogs or horses. They may focus their attention to specific work environments, such as animal hospitals or zoos. They may practice in specific technical or medical areas of concern, such as dental care, internal medicine, critical care, or anesthesiology.

These technicians mostly work indoors, but some work in such outdoor environments as ranches, farms, zoos, or wildlife preserves. Their work can be risky or physically demanding. Animals may inflict injury on Veterinary Technicians through bites, kicks, or scratches. Technicians must also be careful when handling animal body fluids and excrement. To ensure their safety, they follow strict procedures and wear protective clothing such as gloves and a mask.

Additionally, dealing with abused, injured, and sick animals, as well as performing euthanasia, can be emotionally stressful for these experts. Sometimes, Veterinary Technicians must contend with hostile or distraught human beings, particularly at pet clinics and animal hospitals.

Veterinary Technicians generally work between 40 and 50 hours per week, depending on their workloads. In some workplaces, these experts work in shifts because their facilities are open around the clock.

Salaries
Salaries for Veterinary Technicians vary, depending on such factors as their education, experience, position, employer, industry, and geographic location. The estimated annual salary for most of these technicians ranged between $19,770 and $41,490, according to the May 2008 Occupational Employment Statistics (OES) survey by the U.S. Bureau of Labor Statistics (BLS). The survey also reported that the estimated hourly wage ranged between $9.50 and $19.95.

Employment Prospects
The May 2008 OES survey estimated that approximately 78,920 Veterinary Technicians were employed in the United States. The majority of them worked in private clinical practices.

Job opportunities are favorable for Veterinary Technicians. There is a demand for qualified technicians in almost all industries. The BLS predicts that between the 2008 and 2018 period, employment of Veterinary Technicians will increase by 36 percent. In addition to job growth, openings will become available as technicians transfer to other jobs or careers, or leave the workforce.

Advancement Prospects
Veterinary Technicians advance by earning higher wages and being assigned greater levels of responsibilities. Technicians may specialize in specific areas such as internal medicine or anesthesia or seek job opportunities in other work settings. Some technicians are promoted to supervisory positions.

Some individuals continue their studies to become veterinarians.

Education and Training
To become Veterinary Technicians, individuals must complete an associate's or bachelor's degree program

in veterinary technology or animal health. Employers prefer to hire applicants who have completed a program accredited by the American Veterinary Medical Association. In general, graduates of associate's programs are hired as Veterinary Technicians, while bachelor's degree holders are hired as veterinary technologists.

Students in veterinary technology programs study animal anatomy, physiology, chemistry, mathematics, medical procedures, and other subjects. They also complete a practicum in which they receive hands-on training in a clinical setting.

Entry-level Veterinary Technicians receive on-the-job training. They perform routine tasks under the direction of veterinarians.

Throughout their careers, Veterinary Technicians pursue continuing education to update their skills and knowledge.

Special Requirements

Veterinary Technicians must be properly credentialed in the state where they work. Depending on the state, they may be required to become licensed veterinary technicians (L.V.T.), certified veterinary technicians (C.V.T.), or registered veterinary technicians (R.V.T.). Credential requirements vary from state to state. For specific information, contact the state board of veterinary examiners that oversees the area in which you wish to work.

Experience, Special Skills, and Personality Traits

Employers prefer to hire applicants for entry-level positions who have one or more years of experience working in the care of animals. They may have gained their experience through employment, internships, or volunteer work.

Veterinary Technicians must have excellent self-management skills, such as the ability to work independently, handle stressful situations, prioritize multiple tasks, and follow and understand instructions. They also need strong interpersonal and communication skills to be able to handle various people from diverse backgrounds on a daily basis. Other essential skills that these technicians need include teamwork,

organizational, critical-thinking, and problem-solving skills. Being patient, tactful, sympathetic, gentle, detail-oriented, and flexible are some personality traits that successful Veterinary Technicians share.

Unions and Associations

Veterinary Technicians can join professional associations to take advantage of networking opportunities, continuing education, and other professional services and resources. Some national societies that serve the different interests of this profession are:

- Academy of Veterinary Emergency and Critical Care Technicians
- Academy of Veterinary Technician Anesthetists
- American Association for Laboratory Animal Science
- Association of Zoo Veterinary Technicians
- National Association of Veterinary Technicians in America
- Society of Veterinary Behavior Technicians

For contact information for the above organizations, see Appendix II.

Tips for Entry

1. As a high school student, find out if working with animals is something you would like to do. You might volunteer or get a part-time job at an animal shelter, zoo pet store, kennel, or animal clinic, for example. You can also read books and periodicals about veterinary technology.
2. To enhance their employability, some Veterinary Technicians obtain professional certification.
3. Ask your college professors, as well as your college career center, for job leads to entry-level positions.
4. Use the Internet to learn more about Veterinary Technicians. To get a list of Web sites, enter the keywords *veterinary technicians* or *veterinary technology* into a search engine. To learn about some links, see Appendix IV.

NATURAL RESOURCES MANAGEMENT AND CONSERVATION

SOIL CONSERVATIONIST

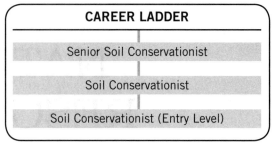

Position Description

Soil is one of our most valuable natural resources. Without it, plant and animal life cannot thrive. Soil is a mixture of mineral and organic substances that are contained in a thin layer across the dry land areas of the Earth. Topsoil, the soil that is most suitable for sustaining all life, varies in thickness from place to place. On average, topsoil is about three feet thick. In some places, topsoil is becoming so thin through erosion or mismanagement that it may disappear. The men and women who are soil scientists study soil to learn as much about it as they can. They approach their studies through research in such areas as soil composition, soil fertility, and the effects that water erosion, chemicals (such as fertilizers or pesticides), crop rotation, water management, and waste management have on the health of soil. Other professionals called Soil Conservationists use the results of soil science research to create practical policies and promote effective actions that landowners can use to protect, increase, and manage their topsoil.

In general, the goal of conservation is to protect and maintain natural resources so that people can use them in productive ways. In the case of soil conservation, the resource is soil that can be used to produce crops for food and industrial purposes. Soil Conservationists work to help landowners, communities, and government land management agencies to prevent soil erosion caused by natural circumstances and human activities. Soil becomes thin when it is washed away by floods, carried away by winds, or depleted by the infusion of harmful pollutants. It may also be diminished by careless growing methods. For example, if a farmer neglects to rotate crops or does not let acreage periodically sit idle, soil loses its vitality and ability to sustain plant growth. Soil Conservationists teach various methods for promoting the increase of soil depth, such as controlling its acid or salt content, introducing helpful minerals and organisms, growing plants that hold soil in place, using natural fertilizers, and practicing alternative plowing methods.

Soil Conservationists visit various locations in need of their services, ranging from rural to urban areas. At each location, they survey the soil quality and observe the impact of gardening, farming, ranching, or forestry activities on the soil within the area concerned. Their focus is on soil depletion and erosion. Soil Conservationists investigate how the land is used at the particular location and look for ways that past and current usage have contributed to problems with the soil. These experts survey properties to establish the boundaries of each affected area. They collect samples to study various characteristics of the soil, such as its pH balance (its degree of acidity or alkalinity), its moisture content, or the amount of mineral or organic matter it contains. Soil Conservationists look for and analyze the causes of the erosion and develop plans for landowners to follow to replace lost soil, as well as to restore proper pH balances and the soil's ability to properly retain moisture.

Using the results of their soil analyses, these experts devise customized plans for landowners to follow so they may revitalize their soil while they simultaneously continue to use it for productive purposes.

Soil Conservationists also provide other services to landowners. They estimate time frames and costs for completing soil-building projects. They suggest how different crops may be planted and rotated to build soils and restore a desired pH balance. They provide information about different plowing methods or how to use terracing to protect soil from depletion. They also advise about the use of natural fertilizers and pesticides.

These experts offer technical assistance for such projects as building ponds or improving drainage systems. Some Soil Conservationists oversee the planting of trees for reforestation or as windbreaks to reduce the incidence of erosion. Additionally, they monitor the progress of soil restoration endeavors and review soil restoration programs with land managers. Furthermore, Soil Conservationists write informative articles about soil conservation for newspapers, give lectures to various organizations, and assist educators with soil conservation lessons for students.

These men and women are sometimes called upon to provide their expertise at the sites of natural disasters, such as wildfires, floods, or mudslides. Rebuilding the soil in such areas is needed to restore land to its natural condition, as well as to prevent further erosion. Soil Conservationists work closely with government agencies to coordinate appropriate responses to such occurrences. They provide agencies with details about their soil restoration projects to help coordinate such endeavors as protection programs for groundwater and other resources.

Soil Conservationists consult with soil scientists, engineers, building contractors, and other specialists in such fields as agronomy, wildlife and livestock management, hydrology, and biology, for assistance with technical information, design concepts, and construction techniques. These conservationists use maps, aerial photographs, soil survey manuals, calculators, and computers to research, study, and analyze information about the areas they survey. Soil Conservationists maintain accurate records of their projects, which they keep in well-organized files.

Soil Conservationists spend a major part of their time working outdoors, often in remote locations to which they may need to travel for extended periods. They may need to access work locations by driving or flying and occasionally by walking through dense woodlands or across uneven terrain. These experts may

be exposed to temperature extremes, as well as to fuels, pesticides, fertilizers, and other harmful contaminants. Soil Conservationists also work in office settings to prepare reports, complete analytical work, and develop soil restoration plans.

These professionals generally keep standard workweeks from Monday through Friday, 40 hours per week. Their hours may vary to fulfill various obligations, such as attending meetings. Some Soil Conservationists work during weekends.

Salaries

Salaries for Soil Conservationists vary, depending on such factors as their education, experience, employer, and geographic location. Formal salary information for this occupation is unavailable. However, their earnings are similar to conservation scientists. The estimated annual salary for most conservation scientists ranged between $35,190 and $86,910, according to the May 2008 Occupational Employment Statistics survey by the U.S. Bureau of Labor Statistics (BLS).

Employment Prospects

Soil Conservationists work for local and state government agencies, such as agriculture, natural resources, water, health, and park and recreation departments. At the federal level, they find employment with the Natural Resources Conservation Service, the Bureau of Land Management, the Fish and Wildlife Service, the U.S. Geological Survey, the Bureau of Indian Affairs, the Army Corps of Engineers, and the National Park Service, among other agencies. Soil Conservationists also work in such private-sector organizations as mining companies, forest products firms, water providers, and environmental concerns. Some conservationists are employed as teachers, researchers, and Cooperative Extension Service professionals at colleges and universities.

In general, job openings become available as Soil Conservationists retire, transfer to other jobs, or advance to higher positions. The BLS predicts that the employment of conservation scientists, including Soil Conservationists, should grow by 12 percent, during the period 2008–18. Opportunities should be favorable for qualified conservation scientists as many of them are expected to retire in the coming years.

Advancement Prospects

Soil Conservationists advance according to their interests and ambition. They can advance to supervisory and managerial positions. They can pursue opportunities in other work settings, by moving from a state position to one in a federal agency, for example. With their backgrounds, they can transfer to related careers by becoming land appraisers or range managers. With advanced degrees, Range Managers can seek positions as research scientists, university professors, and Cooperative Extension specialists. Entrepreneurial individuals can become independent consultants or owners of technical firms.

Education and Training

Applicants for entry-level Soil Consevationist positions are required to hold at least a bachelor's degree in soil conservation, soil science, agronomy, agricultural engineering, or another related field. To teach or conduct research, applicants usually need a master's or doctoral degree.

Entry-level Soil Conservationists receive on-the-job training while working under the direction and supervision of experienced conservationists.

Throughout their careers, Soil Conservationists enroll in continuing education programs to update their skills and knowledge.

Experience, Special Skills, and Personality Traits

Employers seek candidates for entry-level positions who have one or more years of work experience, including fieldwork. They may have gained their experience through internships, work-study programs, research projects, or employment.

To be effective at their job, Soil Conservationists must have excellent teamwork, project-management, communication, writing, and self-management skills. Being enthusiastic, dedicated, detail-oriented, dependable, self-motivated, and flexible are some personality traits that successful Soil Conservationists share.

Unions and Associations

Soil Conservationists can join professional associations to take advantage of networking opportunities, professional certification, continuing education, and other professional services and resources. Some national societies that serve their interests are the Soil Science Society of America, the Soil and Water Conservation Society, and the National Society of Consulting Soil Scientists. For contact information to these organizations, see Appendix II.

Tips for Entry

1. Visit Web sites of prospective employers for job postings. Some employers allow applicants to complete applications online.
2. Carefully and thoroughly read instructions on job applications. For example, if instructions state that you must mail or deliver you application in person, do not fax it. If you improperly submit your application to an employer, you may not be considered for the job.
3. Learn more about soil conservation on the Internet. You might start by visiting the Natural Resources Conservation Service Soils Web site (soils.usda.gov) and the Soil Science Society of America Web site (www.soils.org). For more links, see Appendix IV.

RANGE MANAGER

Position Description

Vast areas of the world are rangelands. These expanses of land are characterized by a variety of vegetation including grasses, broadleaf weeds, and shrubbery. Rangelands are found in most latitudes and climates. They include deserts, alpine meadows, savannahs, arctic tundra, and wetlands, among other types of wild plant and animal communities. Rangelands are used for many purposes, and require a lot of care by the people who use them and work on them. Among the professional men and women who provide that care and oversight are Range Managers.

Although these fragile environments are sparsely populated, rangelands are of great value to the people who live there or visit. Rangelands are mostly unsuitable for the cultivation of crops but they are well suited for raising livestock because many rangeland plant species are nutritious for cattle. Furthermore, the wide spaces, fresh air, and water supplies are beneficial to livestock. Rangelands are also recreation destinations for all kinds of outdoors enthusiasts. These ecosystems benefit everyone whether they live in proximity or far away. Rangelands contain water, minerals, and energy resources of value to many industries. These ecosystems also produce oxygen and reduce carbon dioxide from the air, which circulates to populated areas.

Range Managers are experts in studying rangelands and how to manage and protect them. They work for private landowners, which may be individuals or companies. They also work for government agencies entrusted with the preservation and conservation of publicly-owned rangelands. Range Managers may be known by other job titles, such as range conservationist, range management specialist, range scientist, or ranch manager.

Range Managers are knowledgeable about rangeland ecosystems, including their function and structure, as well as about which natural resources are to be found in each type of rangeland. Range Managers are also familiar with methods and technologies for managing and sustaining the health of rangelands. For example, they utilize appropriate practices to reduce soil erosion, improve the quality of rangeland water supplies, repair damaged ecosystems, and improve habitats for wild plants and animals.

Range Managers use their expertise to create management plans for landowners and government agencies to use for meeting their particular goals for their rangelands with a minimum of damage to fragile species communities. They help land managers:

- establish grazing seasons
- determine boundaries for foraging
- plant new forage vegetation
- use low-impact methods for controlling poisonous plants
- develop fire protection and pest management measures

- restore lands that were damaged by fires, floods, or dry spells, as well as lands hurt by mining and fuel removal

The management and manipulation of rangelands is a process that requires considerable planning. Range Managers design such plans by using facts about the area in question, such as the grazing practices that have been utilized and how those practices may be further used or adapted for use within a new set of goals. Range Managers help landowners make the appropriate changes to their land-use practices to effect a change in how the land is to be used. For example, landowners may wish to convert their rangeland area from cattle grazing purposes to recreational purposes.

The new plans that Range Managers develop take various factors into consideration, such as how such changes will impact the ecosystem. They consider the effect that new trails, salt licks, fencing, and irrigation will have on the plant communities on the rangeland. Range Managers adapt their plans to fit the rate of change desired by landowners and managers. They incorporate such activities or practices as the management of brush, the use of available water supplies, the use of controlled burning, and the application of fertilizers into their plans. They also take into consideration the impact of these activities on surrounding areas, which may be used for other purposes.

Range Managers continually monitor the implementation and progress of their management plans to ensure that landowners' goals are met. They help ranchers or property managers to deal with problems they face with using range management plans. They advise how to resolve such issues as water shortages, the overuse of grazing acreage, and plant or animal species overpopulation. Range Managers are prepared to make alterations to management plans to accommodate needs that are specific to particular land areas.

These experts assist ranchers and land managers to integrate conservation measures with achieving their various aspirations. They help to build up topsoil, determine suitable numbers of cattle to graze per acre, and set up grazing schedules that serve to keep rangelands continually healthy without straining them or depleting them. Range Managers may call into play specific areas of interest to fulfill management planning tasks. They may specialize in certain aspects of land management, such as recreation, wildlife conservation, water management, or livestock production. Their specialties may also be reflective of where Range Managers work. The various types of rangelands require different management techniques, for example. Furthermore, private landowners have needs that differ from government agencies that manage rangelands.

Range Managers are responsible for completing tasks specific to their occupation. Some of these duties include:

- developing technologies that help landowners reseed their rangelands
- creating and utilizing standard methods and technical specifications for range management and teaching other managers to use them
- conducting field trials of rangeland management methods and technologies
- inventorying rangeland resources
- designing plans for structures such as fencing and water storage facilities, and overseeing the installation and care of such structures
- acting as go-betweens to establish agreeable relationships among rangeland users
- ensuring that laws and regulations pertaining to water rights, grazing practices, leasing arrangements, and other range management issues are understood and complied with by rangeland users
- offering advice and technical know-how for rangeland users dealing with environmental impact reports and other processes pertinent to their activities
- providing rangeland management technical help and training services to agency or company staff, as well as to the general public, conservation groups, and legislative bodies

Range Managers may work indoors in office settings or outdoors at rangeland sites, depending on their employer and work assignments. Those managers who work outdoors are exposed to all kinds of weather and may travel to remote or isolated locations. They may need to walk long distances during the course of their assignments.

These experts generally put in standard 40-hour workweeks but may work longer hours to provide assistance with such emergencies as fires or floods. They also may work long hours to help with erosion control efforts.

Salaries

Salaries for Range Managers vary depending on such factors as education, experience, job duties, employer, and geographic location. Formal salary information for this occupation is unavailable. However, their earnings are similar to conservation scientists. According to the May 2008 Occupational Employment Statistics survey by the U.S. Bureau of Labor Statistics (BLS), the estimated annual salary for most conservation scientists ranged between \$35,190 and \$86,910.

Employment Prospects

In the public sector, Range Managers work for various federal agencies such as the Bureau of Land Management, the Forest Service, the Natural Resources Conservation Service, and the Fish and Wildlife Service. They also find employment with state, local, and tribal agencies, including agriculture, fish and wildlife, natural resources, planning, and parks departments, among others. In the private sector, Range Managers work for ranchers, range management consulting firms, land management companies, mining companies, real estate companies, and other private firms. They also find employment with nonprofit land trusts and conservation organizations. In addition, some professionals work at colleges and universities as teachers, researchers, and Cooperative Extension Service professionals.

In general, most job openings become available as Range Managers retire, transfer to other jobs, or advance to higher positions. The BLS reports that employment of conservation scientists, which includes Range Managers, is predicted to increase by 12 percent through 2018.

According to the Society for Range Management Web site (as of September 2009), the demand for range management professionals is high. This professional association also reported that there appears to be an insufficient number of graduates from range programs to meet the demands for new recruits. In addition, about one-third of the rangeland management specialists who work in the Bureau of Land Management, the U.S. Forest Service, and the Natural Resources Conservation Service will be eligible for retirement within the coming years.

Advancement Prospects

As Range Managers gain experience, they earn higher salaries and are assigned duties with greater levels of responsibilities. These men and women can also be promoted to supervisory and managerial positions. Entrepreneurial individuals may pursue careers as independent consultants or owners of range management or consulting firms.

With advanced degrees, Range Managers can seek positions as research scientists, university professors, and Cooperative Extension specialists.

Education and Training

Minimally, Range Managers must possess a bachelor's degree in range management, range science, ecology, or another related discipline. To teach in colleges and universities, conduct independent research, or attain top management positions, Range Managers usually need a doctorate.

Entry-level professionals receive on-the-job training while working under the direction and supervision of experienced personnel.

Throughout their careers, Range Managers enroll in continuing education programs to update their skills and keep up with advancements in their fields.

Experience, Special Skills, and Personality Traits

Employers seek candidates for entry-level positions who are experienced in range management principles and techniques. They may have gained their knowledge and hands-on experience through internships, work-study programs, or employment. Strong applicants would also be familiar with rangeland ecosystems.

To perform well at their work, Range Managers must have effective organizational, decision-making, critical-thinking, communication, interpersonal, teamwork, and self-management skills. Being cooperative, honest, detail-oriented, adaptable, innovative, dependable, and self-motivated are some personality traits that successful Range Managers share.

Unions and Associations

Range Managers belong to professional associations to take advantage of networking opportunities, continuing education, professional certification, and other professional services and resources. One national organization that serves these professionals is the Society for Range Management. For contact information, see Appendix II.

Tips for Entry

1. To enhance their employability, Range Managers obtain professional certification granted by the Society for Range Management when they become eligible.
2. To learn about job openings for range management specialists in the federal government, visit the USAJOBS Web site. This is the official job site of the U.S. federal government. The URL is www.usajobs.gov.
3. Contact prospective employers directly about job vacancies.
4. Use the Internet to learn more about rangeland management. You might start by visiting the Web sites of these groups: the Society for Range Management (www.rangelands.org) and the California Rangelands Research and Information Center (californiarangeland.ucdavis.edu). For more links, see Appendix IV.

WETLAND SCIENTIST

Position Description

Swamps, bogs, marshes, mudflats, vernal pools, and prairie potholes are all examples of valuable natural resources known as wetlands. They protect the quality of watersheds by breaking down and removing sediment, organic waste, and pollutants in water. They either recharge groundwater or serve as sites for groundwater to discharge. Wetlands also absorb and slow down the flow of rain, storm drainage, or melting water to prevent flooding downstream. They protect shorelines and riverbanks from erosion. In addition, wetlands are homes, breeding grounds, and resting areas for many plants, fish, and wildlife, some of which are rare or endangered species. Furthermore, wetlands provide opportunities to the public for recreation, education, and research.

In the United States, wetlands on both public and private lands are protected by state and federal laws. Before landowners can alter wetlands or start construction projects (such as water wells, utility pipelines, roads, or structures), they must get permission from appropriate local, state, tribal, or federal government agencies. Many professionals, known as Wetland Scientists, engage in some technical or regulatory aspects of projects that involve wetlands.

These scientists come from different backgrounds. They include biologists, hydrologists, ecologists, soil scientists, environmental scientists, environmental engineers, and others. Wetland Scientists have an understanding of how the different wetlands are formed, how they work, and how to conserve and manage them. They are also familiar with local, state, and federal laws and regulations regarding wetlands, such as the federal Clean Water Act. They each apply their particular training and expertise to address various wetlands issues.

Wetland Scientists work in private, nonprofit, government, and academic settings. They might work on wetlands projects for homeowners, real estate developers, private companies, architectural firms, waste management companies, law firms, nonprofit groups, and government agencies. Depending on their area of expertise, experience, and work setting, they might assist in such activities as:

- designing construction plans to enhance or restore wetlands
- monitoring wetland restoration projects
- developing plans to integrate wetlands into surrounding watersheds
- conducting studies to determine the function, health, and benefits of wetlands
- identifying, delineating, and mapping the boundaries of wetlands, which may range in size from several acres to thousands of acres
- analyzing the impact that human activities have on wetlands

- conducting field surveys of plant and animal species
- completing necessary application forms for permits, which include maps, reports, and other documents
- designing and implementing mitigation plans to replace wetlands that would be destroyed or lost because of proposed development projects
- enforcing laws and regulations regarding the use of wetlands
- making sure wetlands projects are in compliance with appropriate laws and regulations
- providing litigation support and expert witness services to attorneys
- educating landowners, the public, or others about wetlands, wetland policies, and wetland regulations

Complex projects usually involve several Wetland Scientists working together. These experts bring their expertise in soils, hydrology, wildlife biology, or another area to a project. Wetland Scientists also focus on different areas; for example, one expert may have extensive experience in wetland delineation, while another is more experienced in designing wetlands.

Some Wetland Scientists are employed as research scientists in academic, government, private, and nonprofit settings. Some researchers conduct independent studies, while others engage in research projects on specific wetlands issues for government agencies, construction firms, environmental protection groups, or other organizations.

Research scientists generally engage in two types of research projects. They conduct basic research to gain new knowledge and understanding about wetland environments. For example, a research Wetland Scientist might study the plants and wildlife in freshwater marshes to learn how they interact with each other and the ecosystems in which they live. Research scientists also conduct applied research to seek solutions to specific problems. They use the findings of basic research to design new or improved practices, techniques, and technologies to help protect, conserve, restore, and manage the different types of wetlands. For example, an applied researcher might seek new methods to delineate wetland boundaries under different rainfall conditions.

Many research Wetland Scientists at academic institutions are appointed to faculty positions. In addition to their research work, they teach undergraduate and graduate students in their areas of expertise, such as hydrology, soil science, and wildlife biology. Along with teaching, faculty members advise students on academic and career matters, perform administrative duties, participate in departmental and school committees, and fulfill community service requirements. Full-time professors are expected to publish scholarly works of their research findings, as well as to seek funding for their research projects.

Wetland Scientists work both indoors and outdoors. Most wetland professionals perform fieldwork that may require spending long hours, including early mornings, in undeveloped locations. They are exposed to all types of weather and to dangers such as stinging insects, poisonous snakes and plants, and potentially aggressive wildlife.

Wetland Scientists generally have standard 40-hour workweek schedules. They put in additional evening and weekend hours as needed to complete tasks.

Salaries

Salaries for Wetland Scientists vary, depending on their education, experience, area of expertise, employer, and other factors. Specific salary information for these specialists is unavailable. A general idea can be gained by looking at the salaries of different professionals who work in wetland science. The U.S. Bureau of Labor Statistics (BLS) reported the following estimated salary ranges for most of these scientists in its May 2008 Occupational Employment Statistics survey:

- biological scientists (those not listed separately in the survey): $35,620 to $101,030
- wildlife biologists: $33,550 to $90,850
- environmental engineers: $45,310 to $115,430
- environmental scientists: $36,310 to $102,610
- hydrologists: $44,410 to $105,010
- soil scientists: $34,260 to $105,340
- postsecondary biological science teachers: $38,830 to $147,980
- postsecondary environmental science teachers: $31,550 to $126,010

Employment Prospects

Wetland Scientists work in both the public and private sectors. They are employed by federal agencies such as the Army Corps of Engineers, the Natural Resources Conservation Service, the Environmental Protection Agency, and the U.S. Geological Survey. State departments of natural resources or other regulatory agencies that enforce laws regarding wetlands also employ Wetland Scientists. In addition, these professionals work for local government agencies as well as nonprofit organizations that serve to protect wetlands at a local, state, regional, or national level. In the private sector, many Wetland Scientists are employed by engineering or environmental services consulting firms. Some Wetland Scientists are self-employed consultants. In colleges and universities, Wetland Scientists are employed as teachers, researchers, and Cooperative Extension Service professionals.

Opportunities for Wetland Scientists generally become available as other individuals advance to higher positions, transfer to other jobs or career fields, or retire. Job outlook information for Wetland Scientists is similar to environmental scientists. According to the BLS, employment of this occupation is expected to increase by 28 percent through 2018. Job growth is mostly due to the increasing concern for conserving and protecting the environment. Qualified professionals, for example, are needed to enforce environmental laws and regulations, assess the impact of human activity on ecosystems, and develop plans and strategies for restoring ecosystems.

Advancement Prospects

Wetland Scientists may advance in various ways, depending on their ambitions and interests. They can advance to supervisory and managerial positions by becoming project leaders, program managers, or executive directors. They can become technical specialists. Those with entrepreneurial ambitions can pursue opportunities to become independent contractors or owners of technical consulting firms.

College professors are promoted in rank, from instructor to assistant professor, associate professor, and full professor. They may also earn tenure, which ensures them of job security.

Education and Training

Educational requirements vary with different positions as well as among employers. For non-research scientist positions, employers require that applicants possess at least a bachelor's degree in an appropriate field such as biology, ecology, hydrology, soil science, environmental studies, environmental engineering, or natural resource management. However, many employers prefer to hire candidates who hold a master's or doctoral degree. To teach in colleges and universities, conduct independent research, and advance to managerial positions, Wetland Scientists usually need a doctorate.

Entry-level Wetland Scientists receive on-the-job training while working under the guidance of experienced personnel.

Experience, Special Skills, and Personality Traits

In general, employers prefer to hire candidates to entry-level positions who have one or more years of experience in the areas, such as conducting wetland delineations or research, in which they would work. They may have gained their experience through a combination of employment, work-study programs, internships, or postdoctoral training.

To perform well at their job, Wetland Scientists need strong interpersonal, teamwork, critical-thinking, organizational, self-management, communication, writing, and computer skills. Some personality skills that successful Wetland Scientists share include being positive, flexible, adaptable, trustworthy, honest, and dedicated.

Unions and Associations

Wetland Scientists can join professional associations to take advantage of networking opportunities, training programs, professional certification, and other professional services and resources. Some national societies that serve their interests are the Society of Wetland Scientists and the Association of State Wetland Managers. In addition, they might join associations that serve their particular area of expertise. For contact information, see Appendix II.

Tips for Entry

1. Employers usually seek candidates for non-research positions who have solid field experience and an understanding of such environmental regulations as the federal Clean Water Act.
2. To enhance their employability, Wetland Scientists might obtain professional certification that is granted by the Society of Wetland Scientists. For information, visit its professional certification program Web site at www.wetlandcert.org.
3. Employers use different job titles for the same job. Read all job announcements carefully. If you are still unclear about the job, phone or e-mail the contact person for further information.
4. Use the Internet to learn more about wetlands and the work of Wetland Scientists. You might start by visiting the Association of State Wetland Managers Web site at www.aswm.org. For more links, see Appendix IV.

ENVIRONMENTAL TOXICOLOGIST

Position Description

Any chemical that is consumed in high concentrations may cause serious problems, including the death of living organisms and the destruction of ecosystems. Potentially hazardous chemicals are used in agriculture and industry as well as in homes. Chemicals can enter the environment through accidents (such as oil spills), by improper treatment and disposal of waste, and by other means. Some remain in the environment or break down into harmless substances, while others build up in toxic amounts in the air, water, and soil. Scientists known as Environmental Toxicologists are concerned with the potential consequences that may occur from harmful amounts of chemicals being released into the environment due to human activity. They may be involved in research and development, natural resources management, environmental remediation, regulatory affairs, public health, environmental education, or other areas.

Toxicology is the study of how chemicals affect living things, whether they are humans, animals, plants, or one-celled organisms. There are several areas of concentration within this science. One of these is environmental toxicology. It is a young but rapidly developing field. Environmental toxicology is sometimes confused with ecotoxicology, a related discipline. The former focuses on the effects of environmental chemicals on humans, while the latter concentrates on animals and plants and their ecosystems. Some Environmental Toxicologists are experts in both fields.

Environmental Toxicologists study both natural and synthetic chemicals in the environment. They examine the levels of toxic compounds, such as drugs, pesticides, industrial pollutants, and naturally occurring chemicals, and how these substances move within ecosystems. These scientists also investigate how toxic chemicals are absorbed, circulated, and eliminated by living organisms. Furthermore, Environmental Toxicologists explore the damage that toxic compounds may have on living organisms and the environment.

Environmental toxicology is an interdisciplinary science. Environmental Toxicologists apply principles and techniques from a variety of scientific disciplines to perform their work, including toxicology, environmental chemistry, biology, physiology, computer science, statistics, and social sciences. Depending on their area of expertise, they are also knowledgeable about genetics, nutrition, molecular biology, epidemiology, aquatic toxicology, forensics, or other disciplines.

Many Environmental Toxicologists are employed as research scientists by academic institutions, private companies, government agencies, and nonprofit research institutes. They may conduct basic research to further their understanding and knowledge about the behavior and fate of environmental pollutants. For example, they might examine such questions as: How does a pollutant circulate in soil, water, and the food chain? How does a toxic substance affect different living organisms within an ecosystem? Why are some living organisms resistant to a specific poison, while others are susceptible to it? What are the long-term effects of a pollutant on people's health?

Research Environmental Toxicologists also perform applied research in their areas of expertise. They utilize the findings of basic research to solve specific problems in agriculture, industry, public health, or other areas. In addition, they use the knowledge gained from basic research to develop new techniques to more effectively test and analyze pollutants and their effects on humans and other living organisms, as well as on the environment. In pharmaceutical, food, chemical, and other private companies, research scientists may be part of product development teams. Their mission is to help create new and improved consumer products.

Some researchers at academic institutions hold faculty appointments. Along with maintaining a research program in their area of expertise, they are responsible for instructing undergraduate and graduate students. They teach courses in environmental toxicology and in other areas, such as biology and chemistry, in which they have expertise. As faculty members, they are responsible for advising students on academic and career matters. Their position also involves performing administrative duties, participating in departmental and school committees, and fulfilling community service.

Environmental Toxicologists are also employed as technical experts in the public and private sectors. They may work as staff members or consultants. They help managers and administrators in both private companies and government agencies develop environmental plans, programs, regulations, and policies that safeguard populations, communities, and ecosystems.

Many toxicologists conduct risk assessments to determine whether toxic and hazardous substances in specific locations may be endangering public health or the environment. For example, specialists might examine whether the smoke and other chemicals released into the environment by an oil refinery may be harming residents in nearby neighborhoods. These toxicologists also provide technical consultations to other departments within their organization, or to other companies or government agencies.

Some Environmental Toxicologists evaluate the safety of consumer products, such as drugs, food, cosmetics, household cleaners, paints, fertilizers, and pesticides. They identify, characterize, and interpret any potential health hazards and environmental problems caused by toxic ingredients within products, for example. Other Environmental Toxicologists collect and evaluate environmental data about facilities and sites

to help government agencies determine if the owners should be granted permits to operate.

Regardless of their positions, much of these toxicologists' work involves laboratory and field research. They employ a variety of techniques to study different toxic substances. For example, they might conduct tests using laboratory animals or human subjects.

They perform various duties at work. Some tasks are specific to their occupations. For example, some scientists are responsible for preparing grant proposals to fund their projects. Environmental Toxicologists also perform a variety of general duties such as:

- planning, developing, and implementing studies
- designing and running tests and experiments to measure toxins in water, air, or another medium
- collecting samples or data in the laboratory or field
- conducting literature reviews to obtain relevant information for studies
- developing models to predict the fate and effect of toxic chemicals within an ecosystem
- analyzing and interpreting environmental data
- maintaining accurate records of their work activities
- preparing written reports
- advising others about how to handle toxic and hazardous substances, such as during accidents
- keeping up to date with environmental and public health issues and trends, as well as with developments in their areas of expertise

Environmental Toxicologists primarily work in offices and laboratories. They visit field sites as needed to collect samples. Their lab work and fieldwork expose them to contaminants, fumes, and other toxic and hazardous substances. Hence, they follow strict safety procedures and wear proper safety equipment such as gloves, masks, and full-body suits.

Their hours vary, depending on their occupations. They may put in additional work hours, including evenings and weekends, to complete assignments, meet deadlines, or to respond to emergencies.

Salaries

Salaries for Environmental Toxicologists vary, depending on such factors as their education, experience, employer, and geographic location. Specific salary information for Environmental Toxicologists is unavailable. A general idea of their earnings can be gained by looking at salaries for toxicologists. According to the Society of Toxicology Web site (www.toxicology.org), annual salaries for toxicologists with doctoral degrees ranged from $35,000 to $60,000 for those in entry-level positions to $70,000 to $100,000 for those who have worked for at least 10 years.

Employment Prospects

Job openings for Environmental Toxicologists become available as individuals retire, advance to higher positions, or transfer to other jobs or career fields. In general, opportunities for toxicologists are favorable. Some experts in the field report that many toxicologists are becoming eligible for retirement. Although toxicology is a small field, some employers are unable to find qualified doctorate-level candidates to fill job openings.

Advancement Prospects

Environmental Toxicologists advance in their careers according to their ambitions, which typically evolve over the years. As these scientists gain experience, they specialize in subject matter and technical areas that interest them. They may advance to fill administrative, managerial, or consulting positions. For example, those with management ambitions may become project leaders, program managers, and department directors.

Some Environmental Toxicologists seek permanent academic positions or opportunities to conduct independent research in academic or other settings.

Education and Training

Depending on the employer and the position, Environmental Toxicologists usually need either a master's or doctoral degree in toxicology, environmental toxicology, chemistry, biology, biochemistry, physiology, or another related field. Employers may hire applicants who hold a bachelor's degree as long as they have several years of qualifying work experience. Environmental Toxicologists are typically required to possess a doctorate to conduct independent research, teach in academic institutions, or advance to management positions.

Bachelor's degree holders may qualify for such entry-level toxicology jobs as technicians, research assistants, laboratory assistants, or animal-care specialists.

Experience, Special Skills, and Personality Traits

Employers prefer to hire candidates for entry-level positions who have some work experience related to the job for which they apply. They may have gained their experience through a combination of internships, post-doctoral training, and employment.

To do their work effectively, Environmental Toxicologists need strong leadership, organizational, problem-solving, teamwork, interpersonal, communication, and writing skills. Being collaborative, persistent, detail-oriented, methodical, creative, and self-motivated are some personality traits that successful Environmental Toxicologists have in common.

Unions and Associations

Environmental Toxicologists can join professional associations to take advantage of professional services and resources, such as networking opportunities, continuing education, job listings, and scientific publications. Some national societies that serve the diverse interests of these scientists are the Society of Environmental Toxicology and Chemistry, the Society of Toxicology, and the American College of Toxicology. For contact information regarding these organizations, see Appendix II.

Tips for Entry

1. Postdoctoral scientists can find training opportunities in the private sector. Pharmaceutical, chemical, food, and other companies as well as contract laboratories offer postdoctoral training in toxicology.
2. The National Institute of Environmental Health Sciences offers postdoctoral research opportunities in environmental toxicology, which provide training for postdoctoral scientists. For more information visit its Web site at www.niehs.nih.gov.
3. Some employers require applicants to write a statement that describes how they meet the job requirements stated in the job announcement. First, write a draft, and then edit your statement so that it is brief and yet clearly and comprehensively states how you are qualified.
4. Use the Internet to learn more about environmental toxicology as well as toxicology in general. You might start by visiting the Web sites of these organizations: the Society of Environmental Toxicology and Chemistry (www.setac.org) and the Society of Toxicology (www.toxicology.org). For more links, see Appendix IV.

NATURAL RESOURCES TECHNICIAN

Position Description

Natural Resources Technicians are involved in the study, management, and protection of air, water, soil, plants, wildlife, minerals, timber, and other natural resources on both public and private lands. Their role is to provide technical support to scientists, specialists, and managers who are part of programs and projects relating to water conservation, soil conservation, air quality, forestry management, range management, recycling, and other conservation efforts. These science technicians assist in solving problems and making wise decisions regarding the management of natural resources in agricultural, urban, wilderness, and recreational areas.

Under the general direction of program or project administrators, Natural Resources Technicians help to develop, implement, and coordinate research and management programs. These men and women work in a variety of activities and functions. They may be involved in research and development. They may be engaged in monitoring water supplies; preserving and restoring native habitats; preventing soil erosion; or managing forests, wildlife areas, or fish hatcheries.

Some of these technicians work in the areas of recycling, water conservation, waste management, or the maintenance of parks or other recreational areas. Some

Natural Resources Technicians are hired to enforce environmental or wildlife laws and regulations for government agencies, while others work in private industries to ensure that businesses and companies comply with government regulations. Conducting land surveys, testing the quality of water or air, performing site assessments, handling public relations, maintaining geographic information system (GIS) databases, or providing educational services to the public are a few other diverse activities in which Natural Resources Technicians may also be involved.

Natural Resources Technicians may be hired to perform duties in one or more areas or functions. Some are hired to positions that work in one specific area. These technicians may hold job titles that refer to the specific area in which they work, such as fisheries technician, forestry technician, soil conservation technician, range technician, water technician, and GIS technician.

Natural Resources Technicians find employment in a variety of settings. They work for local, state, and federal government agencies in departments of fish and wildlife, parks and recreation, natural resource conservation, public works, and others. They are hired in the private sector by ranches, logging companies, surveying companies, environmental or engineering consulting firms, environmental laboratories, forest products manufacturers, and various other companies. Natural Resources Technicians also work for nonprofit and nongovernmental organizations as well as academic institutions.

Natural Resources Technicians apply the principles and techniques of science and mathematics to their work. They perform duties that vary according to their experience, skills, and position. Some duties are specific to the position for which they were hired. For example, range technicians engage in such range management tasks as clearing brush and other vegetation from rangelands, building and maintaining fences, and managing prescribed fires.

Many Natural Resources Technicians also execute general duties that are similar regardless of their work setting. For example, they may perform such tasks as:

- recommending administrative policies and procedures
- conducting inventories of vegetation, soil, timber, wildlife, or other natural resources
- running tests on samples
- collecting field or laboratory data
- compiling technical data for reports, duties, or surveys
- monitoring experiments or tests in laboratories or in the field
- identifying and analyzing data
- maintaining accurate and up-to-date records, files, and databases
- preparing reports
- completing general office work
- setting up, operating, and maintaining laboratory instruments
- maintaining and repairing equipment and facilities
- assisting in planning and designing projects and programs
- recommending new or improved job procedures
- supervising and training subordinate staff members

Natural Resources Technicians often perform physically demanding work. They may walk or stand for long periods, or lift or carry objects that weigh 50 pounds or more. Some technicians perform duties in remote locations; for example, forestry technicians maintain trails or gather information about wildlife habitats in wildernesses. Depending on their job, Natural Resources Technicians may be exposed to hazardous chemicals, machinery with moving parts, heavy equipment, or dangerous or poisonous animals. Some technicians perform many of their duties outdoors in all types of weather.

Natural Resources Technicians may be hired to seasonal or permanent positions. Full-time technicians work 40-hour weeks. They may be required to work overtime to complete tasks or to assist in emergencies.

Salaries

Salaries for Natural Resources Technicians vary, depending on their education, experience, position, employer, and geographic location. According to the May 2008 Occupational Employment Statistics survey by the U.S. Bureau of Labor Statistics, the estimated annual salary for most forest and conservation technicians ranged between $22,540 and $51,810. The estimate hourly wage ranged between $10.84 and $24.91.

Employment Prospects

Job openings for Natural Resources Technicians typically become available as individuals transfer to other jobs or career fields, advance to higher positions, or retire. Employers create additional positions to meet their organizations' growing needs, as long as funds are available.

The competition for jobs, in general, is high.

Advancement Prospects

As Natural Resources Technicians gain experience, they earn higher salaries and are assigned to higher levels of responsibility. They can be promoted to supervisory and managerial positions, but opportunities are usually limited.

By obtaining additional education, these technicians can pursue careers as scientists, educators, engineers, and policy makers, or pursue other occupations in which they are interested.

Education and Training

Minimum educational requirements vary with the different positions, as well as among employers. Candidates for some entry-level positions are required to hold an associate's degree or a professional certificate in an applied science field, such as forestry technology. For other entry-level positions, candidates must possess a bachelor's degree in natural resources management, environmental science, botany, ecology, forestry, wildlife management, or another field that is related to the position for which they apply. Employers sometimes hire applicants who have only a high school diploma or a general equivalency diploma, if they have qualifying experience.

Novice technicians typically receive on-the-job training.

Throughout their careers, National Resources Technicians pursue continuing education to update their skills and knowledge.

Experience, Special Skills, and Personality Traits

Employers prefer to hire entry-level applicants who have at least one or more years of practical experience related to the position for which they apply. They may have gained their experience through a combination of internships, student research projects, work-study programs, and employment.

To work well at their job, Natural Resources Technicians need effective interpersonal, teamwork, organizational, critical-thinking, problem-solving, and self-management skills. Having communication, writing, and computer skills is also important. Being enthusiastic, cooperative, tactful, detail-oriented, and dedicated are some personality traits that successful Natural Resources Technicians share.

Unions and Associations

Some Natural Resources Technicians belong to a labor union that represents them in contract negotiations with their employers. The union seeks favorable terms regarding pay, benefits, and working conditions. The union also handles any grievances that its members may have against their employers.

Tips for Entry

1. Have you ever done any volunteer work at a park, hatchery, wildlife area, environmental center, or someplace similar? Do you belong to an environmental group in which you actively participate, such as the Nature Conservancy? Be sure to mention it on your job application.

2. Seasonal or part-time jobs can sometimes lead to permanent and full-time positions, so be willing to consider what is available.

3. Although the deadline for a job vacancy may have passed, you might contact the employer to find out if applications are still being accepted. Sometimes employers continue accepting applications until they find the best candidate.

4. Learn more about natural resources management and conservation on the Internet. You might start by visiting the U.S. Natural Resources Conservation Service Web site at www.nrcs.usda.gov. For more links, see Appendix IV.

CONSERVATION OFFICER

CAREER PROFILE

Duties: Enforce wildlife protection laws and regulations; promote wildlife preservation; perform other duties as required

Alternate Title(s): Wildlife Officer, Game and Fish Warden, Natural Resources Officer, Environmental Police Officer, Special Agent

Salary Range: $30,000 to $82,000

Employment Prospects: Poor

Advancement Prospects: Fair

Prerequisites:

    Education or Training—Bachelor's degree preferred; law enforcement academy training, field training

    Experience—Law enforcement or resource conservation experience preferred

    Special Skills and Personality Traits—Research, writing, public-speaking, teamwork, organizational,

CAREER LADDER

Supervising Conservation Officer

Conservation Officer

Conservation Officer Trainee

decision-making, self-management, interpersonal, and communication skills; enthusiastic, observant, patient, tactful, trustworthy, curious, persistent, adaptable, dependable, and self-motivated personality traits

    Special Requirements—Pass selection process; valid driver's license

Position Description

Conservation Officers are perhaps best known as fish and game wardens. They are the men and women who issue hunting and fishing licenses, and ask outdoors enthusiasts to produce their licenses or make certain that hunters and anglers do not exceed catch limits. However, these are only a few of the many complex duties that these law enforcement officers perform. They also investigate hunting and boating accidents, injurious encounters with wild animals, criminal acts, and incidents of ecological destruction and contamination. In addition, they educate the public to appreciate wildlife preservation and to comply with environmental protection regulations.

In the United States, Conservation Officers are mostly employed by the federal and state governments. They enforce federal and state laws and regulations that serve to protect wildlife and their natural habitats. They safeguard the people who fish, hunt, and boat within state and federal parks, recreation areas, fish and wildlife preserves, and other outdoor areas. These officers make sure that government employees and property within their jurisdictions are safe from harm. Depending on their agency's mission, Conservation Officers may also be responsible for the enforcement of laws and regulations in other areas, such as public safety, environmental protection,

forestry, boating safety, or commercial and marine fisheries.

At the state level, Conservation Officers are employed by departments of fish and wildlife, natural resource conservation, or another state department. These officers have jurisdiction over wildlife species that live within their state. Some state officers have the authority to also enforce certain federal wildlife laws and regulations.

Federal Conservation Officers enforce federal and international laws, as well as international treaties, concerning the protection of migrating wildlife species and endangered species. They also have the authority to deal with regulations pertaining to the importation and exportation of animals and animal parts.

Most federal Conservation Officers work for the U.S. Fish and Wildlife Service (USFWS), an agency within the U.S. Department of the Interior. Some are employed by the USFWS Office of Law Enforcement as special agents. Their role is to conduct criminal investigations. Others in this office are employed as wildlife inspectors. Their job is to monitor the importation and exportation of endangered or protected wildlife species at seaports, border crossings, and other points of entry into the United States. Refuge officers in the U.S. National Wildlife Refuge System are also part of the USFWS. They are responsible for enforcing wildlife protection laws as well as protecting natural and cultural resources on national wildlife refuges and in wetland management areas.

Federal Conservation Officers also work in the U.S. National Oceanic and Atmospheric Administration Fisheries Office for Law Enforcement. Both special agents and uniformed enforcement officers are responsible for enforcing the federal laws and regulations that protect the nation's living marine resources and their habitats. In addition, these officers enforce international treaties on the high seas regarding the conservation and protection of marine resources.

Conservation Officers are assigned to cover specific geographic areas, which may include both urban and remote areas. For example, state officers may be assigned to handle one or more counties within their state. Most Conservation Officers, particularly state officers and federal refuge officers, are responsible for patrolling their territories to ensure that laws and regulations are being followed. They also keep their eyes open to unsafe boating, hunting, or fishing practices; public hazards; and damage to the environment. These field officers also respond to complaints from the public about fishing and hunting violations, illegal dumping of trash, and other matters.

Conservation Officers are similar to other law enforcement officers in that they have the authority to use firearms. They also have the power to give out warnings and citations to lawbreakers as well as to apprehend and arrest criminal suspects. Like other sworn officers, Conservation Officers conduct investigations, prepare cases for trials, and present findings and evidence in court.

Conservation Officers also work in areas besides law enforcement. For example, they may be involved in such diverse duties as:

- gathering biological information on fish and wildlife
- monitoring fish and wildlife for signs of disease
- controlling wildlife damage
- inspecting wildlife rehabilitators, bait dealers, game breeders, and other businesses and organizations for compliance with laws and regulations
- providing educational services to schools, community groups, and the public
- participating in search and rescue operations
- fighting fires

Conservation Officers perform demanding and dangerous work. They work mostly outdoors, where they endure all types of weather and terrain. They usually work alone and in isolated areas, such as wilderness areas, deserts, rivers, wetlands, and beaches. They use various modes of transportation to reach their destinations. For example, they may travel by foot, on horseback, by off-road vehicle, by boat, or by aircraft.

Conservation Officers also work in office settings to attend to such tasks as writing reports, maintaining records, and performing administrative work. Some state officers maintain an office within their homes.

The nature of their job occasionally exposes Conservation Officers to dangerous circumstances, such as dealing with persons who have committed serious crimes or who are on mind-altering drugs. Officers may find that exposure to the pain, suffering, and death of wildlife caused by criminal behavior is a strain on their emotional health. When necessary, they wear protective clothing to safeguard against injury or contact with harmful substances. For example, these officers handle live animals and exotic plants that may be venomous or poisonous.

Conservation Officers have flexible work schedules. Their duties may require them to work weekends and holidays. They are on call 24 hours a day.

Salaries

Salaries for Conservation Officers vary, depending on such factors as their education, experience, employer, and geographic location. According to the May 2008 Occupational Employment Statistics (OES) survey by the U.S. Bureau of Labor Statistics (BLS), the estimated annual salary for most fish and game wardens ranged between $30,400 and $81,710.

Employment Prospects

The BLS reported in its May 2008 OES survey that approximately 7,720 fish and game wardens were employed in the United States. The majority were state employees.

Job openings generally become available when Conservation Officers retire, advance to higher positions, or transfer to other jobs. Job competition for both recruits and experienced candidates is high.

Advancement Prospects

Conservation Officers advance in various ways. They can be promoted in rank, which is based on experience, job performance, and competitive examination scores. They may seek special-duty opportunities by becoming a canine handler, aircraft pilot, field-training officer, firearms instructor, or another specialized position. Some Conservation Officers pursue their career goals by being assigned to the locations of their choice. Others move on to positions in another law enforcement agency; for example, a state conservation officer's career goal may be to become a USFWS special agent.

Education and Training

Law enforcement agencies have different educational requirements. Most agencies prefer to hire applicants who possess a bachelor's degree in wildlife law enforcement, criminal justice, natural resource management, or another related discipline. In some agencies, the minimum education requirement is a high school diploma or general equivalency diploma. Others may require that applicants possess at least an associate's degree.

Recruits must successfully complete several months of formal training at a law enforcement academy. They study topics in both law enforcement and wildlife management, including rules of evidence, investigative procedures, use of firearms, wildlife laws and regulations, wildlife capture techniques, report writing, and court procedures. Upon completion of their academy training, Conservation Officers undergo on-the-job training while working under the close supervision and direction of experienced officers.

Throughout their careers, Conservation Officers enroll in workshops, seminars, and classes to update their skills and knowledge. They also complete in-service training, which is provided by their employers in such areas as defensive tactics, firearms handling and safety, and law enforcement driving.

Special Requirements

Applicants must meet a minimum age requirement, which varies with the different agencies. Some agencies also have a maximum age requirement. Applicants must pass a selection process that may include a written test, an oral interview, a physical agility test, a medical exam, a drug screening, a psychological review, a polygraph examination, and a background investigation. Candidates for federal positions must be U.S. citizens.

Conservation officers are required to hold a valid driver's license.

Experience, Special Skills, and Personality Traits

Requirements vary with different state and federal agencies. For example, federal agencies prefer to hire applicants for entry-level positions who have previous law enforcement experience. In general, employers seek candidates who have some experience with and knowledge about natural resource conservation.

Conservation Officers need strong research, writing, public-speaking, teamwork, organizational, decision-making, and self-management skills. Having excellent interpersonal and communication skills is also essential, as they must be able to work well with the public. Some personality traits that successful Conservation Officers share include being enthusiastic, observant, patient, tactful, trustworthy, curious, persistent, adaptable, dependable, and self-motivated.

Unions and Associations

Many Conservation Officers join a professional association to take advantage of networking opportunities, continuing education, and other services and resources. A national society that serves these officers is the North American Wildlife Enforcement Officers Association. Federal officers are eligible to join the Federal Law Enforcement Officers Association. U.S. Fish and Wildlife Service special agents may join the Federal Wildlife Officers Association. For contact information to these organizations, see Appendix II.

Conservation Officers may be members of labor unions, which represent them in contract negotiations with their employers. Unions also handle any grievances that officers may have against their employers.

Tips for Entry

1. Maintain your physical fitness, as Conservation Officers are expected to be in shape.
2. Some agencies allow applicants to substitute qualifying law enforcement or military experience for part or all of the education requirement.
3. Visit an agency's Web site for information about job vacancies. Some agencies allow job applications to be completed online.
4. Use the Internet to learn more about the wildlife law enforcement field. You might start by visiting the Web sites of these groups: the North American Wildlife Enforcement Officers Association (www.naweoa.org) and the Association of Fish and Wildlife Agencies (www.fishwildlife.org). For more links, see Appendix IV.

WILDLIFE REHABILITATOR

Duties: Provide care for sick, injured, and orphaned wildlife; perform other related duties as required

Alternate Title(s): Avian Rehabilitator, Marine Mammal Rehabilitator, or another title that reflects a specialty

Salary Range: Unavailable

Employment Prospects: Good

Advancement Prospects: Poor

Prerequisites:

    Education or Training—Bachelor's degree in biology, ecology, or another related field preferred; hands-on training

    Experience—One or more years of experience preferred for entry-level staff positions

    Special Skills and Personality Traits—Teamwork, organizational, time-management, problem-solving, crisis-management, self-management, interpersonal, communication, and teamwork skills; caring, tactful, respectful, detail-oriented, self-motivated, dedicated, creative, resourceful, trustworthy, energetic, and flexible personality traits

    Special Requirements—State and federal permits may be required

CAREER LADDER

```
┌─────────────────────────────────────────┐
│          Senior Wildlife Rehabilitator   │
├─────────────────────────────────────────┤
│   Wildlife Rehabilitator (Staff Position)│
├─────────────────────────────────────────┤
│  Wildlife Rehabilitator Volunteer or Intern│
└─────────────────────────────────────────┘
```

Position Description

We rarely experience the sight of wild creatures living in their own territories. Nevertheless, as our populations grow, our cities expand, and new towns are built, we increasingly encroach on wildlife habitats. Consequently, we are more likely than ever to see such wild animals as deer, mountain lions, coyotes, snakes, and eagles near our homes, schools, and workplaces.

Unfortunately, our encounters with these beautiful and magnificent creatures are not always pleasant or inspiring. With increasing frequency, people run over and injure wild animals with automobiles and other vehicles. People shoot them accidentally. New neighborhoods or roads may force animals to move to unfamiliar locations where they become disoriented, sick, or hungry. Sometimes well-meaning humans adopt wild animals as pets and then release them into the wilderness where they can no longer survive. Perhaps most tragically, baby animals are frequently orphaned when their parents are killed. When wild animals in our midst suffer injuries, illness, or displacement, trained experts called Wildlife Rehabilitators help these creatures to recover their health and return to their habitats.

Wildlife Rehabilitators are primarily volunteers, although some of them find paid positions. Many of them work at wildlife centers as well as rehabilitation facilities under the auspices of humane societies, veterinarians, or animal sanctuaries. Wildlife Rehabilitators are dedicated to helping sick and injured animals continue their lives in familiar surroundings as quickly as possible. When the animals have recovered, they are released back into their environments.

Many Wildlife Rehabilitators work with certain species of wild animals. They use their knowledge of particular animals to provide the best appropriate care. When individuals bring other types of animals to them, they often refer them to other rehabilitators who can provide the care needed.

Wildlife Rehabilitators care for animals in both indoor and outdoor environments. Indoor facilities are needed by Wildlife Rehabilitators to closely monitor animals, administer medications, manage food supplies, and provide such comforts as water dispensers and bedding material. Indoor care units include pens or other types of enclosed spaces of varying sizes and configurations to accommodate specific animals. They are well lit by natural or full-spectrum light sources and include storage areas for food, medicines, cleaning supplies, and other needed materials.

Wildlife Rehabilitators also provide outdoor enclosures for animals that are ready to make their transition back into their habitats. These areas are generally larger than those found indoors. They enable animals to move more freely and become accustomed to natural climate conditions. The outdoor facilities are generally protected from severe weather.

Wildlife Rehabilitators begin the rehabilitation process as soon as injured animals are found, seized from illegal hunters, or reported by concerned citizens, who may also bring animals to their facilities. Wildlife Rehabilitators examine each animal carefully to determine the nature of its injury or illness. They decide whether rehabilitation will be a successful course to follow, whether the animal may need permanent care, or whether it must be euthanized.

These experts work closely with veterinarians for injuries and illnesses that require professional medical treatment. Otherwise, Wildlife Rehabilitators provide all other types of high-level care for animals. Some of their duties require daily attendance, while other duties are performed less frequently. In general, these rehabilitators may:

- speak by telephone or in person to members of the public regarding animal behavior, illnesses, or injuries and determine whether their concerns merit animal rehabilitation services
- arrange for the safe transport of injured animals
- accept delivery of injured or sick animals and provide preliminary first aid treatments
- develop diets, as well as feeding and watering schedules, appropriate to each animal
- monitor animal behavior, healing processes, and growth of young animals
- administer medications, change bandages, and provide physical therapy to injured animals
- maintain inventories of food, medicines, and other supplies
- keep accurate records of each animal's progress for the duration of its stay
- clean and sterilize instruments, equipment, and facilities
- repair cages and construct new ones when needed
- determine the suitable place and time for release of an animal and arrange transportation for it to the site
- stay up to date with new developments in their field
- provide outreach to schools, community groups, and other organizations to educate the public about wildlife rehabilitation services

Wildlife Rehabilitators are strongly committed to the rehabilitation process. These men and women are prepared to deal with severe, traumatic injuries, as well as the possibility of having to put some animals to death when they cannot be treated further. They may need to feed other live animals to the animals in their care. These experts may also need to teach animals how to hunt for prey. Wildlife Rehabilitators must be able to manage animals' violent reactions to treatments. Sometimes wild animals may recover from injuries but be unable to return to the wild. In such cases, Wildlife Rehabilitators arrange for permanent care or provide that care themselves.

These men and women are also committed to the amount of time the rehabilitation process takes. Depending on their particular schedules, some experts take care of only one animal at a time, while others are able to handle the responsibilities of caring for more. Some animals may require more time each day for the care they need, or may be members of species with which an individual rehabilitator is unfamiliar. Wildlife Rehabilitators may have to refer some of the animals that people bring to them to other rehabilitators or animal care centers.

Some volunteer rehabilitators offer their services independently of any organization. These experts usually work out of their home. The law forbids Wildlife Rehabilitators to charge fees for their services. They generally do not receive funding from the government; consequently, they often rely on donations and funds raised by wildlife foundations and other organizations. Some rehabilitators, who are able to do so, use their own money to run their facilities. Some of them offer educational services about wildlife rehabilitation to raise money for their operations.

Wildlife rehabilitation can be a physically demanding and emotionally stressful occupation. Wildlife Rehabilitators must be physically fit to lift animals that are heavy or unwilling to be still. Depending on which species of animals are concerned, these experts may risk injury from scratches and bites. They may contract diseases or be infected by bites from parasitic insects that live on the wild animals.

Their hours vary, which may include evenings, nights, weekends, and holidays. Wildlife Rehabilitators may work part-time or full-time in volunteer or paid positions.

Salaries

Many Wildlife Rehabilitators are volunteers and receive no pay. Salaries for staff positions vary, depending on such factors as their education, experience, job duties, employer, and geographic location. Formal salary information for Wildlife Rehabilitators is unavailable. In general, most of these experts work for nonprofit organizations, which usually pay stipends or minimum wage to entry-level and part-time workers.

Employment Prospects

The number of volunteer positions for Wildlife Rehabilitators is endless. Most, if not all, wildlife rehabilitation centers are nonprofit organizations, with much of the work being done by volunteers, according to the Charity Guide Web site (www.charityguide.org).

Volunteer and staff positions are available with wildlife rehabilitation centers, as well as with government-run nature and environmental education facilities. Some licensed Wildlife Rehabilitators are independent and mostly work out of their home.

Advancement Prospects

Advancement opportunities for Wildlife Rehabilitators are few. They may move from volunteer to paid staff positions. In wildlife centers, staff members may advance to supervisory and managerial positions.

Wildlife Rehabilitators typically enter and stay in this field because of their passion and dedication to helping hurt and orphaned wildlife.

Education and Training

There are no minimum educational requirements for individuals to fulfill to become volunteer Wildlife Rehabilitators. However, employers usually hire applicants to staff positions who hold a bachelor's degree in biology, ecology, wildlife management, animal science, veterinary technology, or another related field.

Novice rehabilitators receive hands-on training while working under the direction of experienced rehabilitators. They also participate in formal training programs, offered by rehabilitation facilities, professional associations, state wildlife agencies, and wildlife professionals.

Throughout their careers, Wildlife Rehabilitators pursue continuing education to update their skills and knowledge.

Special Requirements

Wildlife animals are protected by federal and state laws. Wildlife Rehabilitators may be required to hold state permits that allow them to care for wildlife species that are native to their state. In some states, Wildlife Rehabilitators may be covered by the permits issued to facilities where they work.

Wildlife Rehabilitators who work with migratory birds or marine mammals or with species listed under the U.S. Endangered Species Act must obtain appropriate permits from the U.S. Fish and Wildlife Service.

Wildlife Rehabilitators are required to comply with state and federal government regulations pertaining to cage size and requirements for duplicating native habitats, as well as with property zoning permits and health codes.

Experience, Special Skills, and Personality Traits

Individuals do not need prior experience in wildlife rehabilitation to become volunteers or interns. For entry-level staff positions, employers prefer that candidates have one or more years of experience, particularly with the animals, such as marine mammals, with which they will work.

To perform well in this field, Wildlife Rehabilitators need excellent teamwork, organizational, time-management, problem-solving, crisis-management, and self-management skills. Having strong interpersonal, communication, and teamwork skills is also essential as they must be able to work well with colleagues, the public, and others from diverse backgrounds. Being caring, tactful, respectful, detail-oriented, self-motivated, dedicated, creative, resourceful, trustworthy, energetic, and flexible are some personality traits that successful Wildlife Rehabilitators have in common.

Unions and Associations

Many Wildlife Rehabilitators belong to state, regional, and national professional associations to take advantage of networking opportunities, training programs, and other professional services and resources. Some national societies that serve their interests include the National Wildlife Rehabilitators Association and the International Wildlife Rehabilitation Council. For contact information, see Appendix II.

Tips for Entry

1. Read books or visit Web sites about wildlife rehabilitation, as well as visit a wildlife rehabilitation facility in your area, to learn more. You might ask to volunteer for a short period to find out if you can realistically commit yourself to such work.
2. While in college, obtain an internship at a rehabilitation facility to gain experience.
3. Sometimes volunteer positions can lead to paid positions.
4. Use the Internet to learn more about wildlife rehabilitation. You might start by visiting the National Wildlife Rehabilitators Association Web site at www.nwrawildlife.org. For more links, see Appendix IV.

TRAVEL, TOURISM, AND RECREATION

AGRITOURISM OPERATOR

CAREER LADDER

Agritourism Operator (Experienced)

Agritourism Operator

Farmer

Position Description

Farming is a risky business. Many uncontrollable factors, such as weather and market demand, affect farmers' profits every year. Hence, many farmers, ranchers, vineyard growers, and other agricultural producers become Agritourism Operators to increase their profitability. That is, they establish agricultural tourism, or agritourism, enterprises to attract travelers to their farms to buy agricultural products directly and to take part in recreational or educational activities.

Agritourism is sometimes confused with rural tourism. Agritourism is only one segment of the rural tourism industry, which includes resorts, farmers' markets, agricultural fairs, nonprofit agricultural tours, and other activities that attract visitors to rural areas. Agritourism specifically attracts visitors to working farms, and other agricultural operations. Agritourism also generates income for these agricultural businesses, while rural tourism may not.

The agritourism services and attractions that farmers provide visitors depend on their interests, ambitions, consumer demands, local (or regional) competition, and other variables. Agritourism Operators may establish one or several types of agritourism enterprises, such as:

- roadside produce stands or farm stores
- "u-pick" operations in which visitors have the opportunity to harvest the crops that they want to purchase
- farm operation tours, which may include food demonstrations and sampling of foods or beverages

- entertainment venues, such as corn mazes, petting zoos, barn dances, concerts, rodeos, or food festivals
- recreational ventures that promote activities such as fishing, hunting, horseback riding, hiking, picnicking, camping, canoeing, or paintball skirmishing
- farms that rent their land or buildings for weddings, retreats, conferences, or other events
- food venues such as cafés, bakeries, or farm dinners
- dude ranches or other hospitality facilities

The primary business for many Agritourism Operators is farming. They raise crops that they sell to consumers or to businesses for further processing. These agricultural producers establish agritourism activities to supplement their farm income. Other agricultural producers earn their primary incomes with agritourism. For example, a cattle rancher might operate a year-round dude ranch that offers overnight accommodations for vacationers as well as activities for daytime visitors.

Farmers may manage the daily operations of their agritourism enterprises or hire managers and other staff to take charge of the ventures. However, as owners of agritourism operations, farmers perform specific responsibilities to build and maintain successful enterprises. For example, they:

- plan and evaluate business and marketing strategies
- develop and evaluate agritourism activities
- formulate operational policies, procedures, and rules
- pay bills, taxes, fees, and insurance premiums

- maintain up-to-date sales and inventory records
- obtain and keep all necessary legal permits, licenses, and other legal documents current
- comply with appropriate laws and regulations
- promote their businesses
- monitor the quality of products and customer service
- hire, supervise, and train staff about their programs

Agritourism Operators put in long hours, usually every day, to run both their agritourism and farming enterprises.

Salaries

Annual earnings for Agritourism Operators vary from year to year. As self-employed farmers, their earnings are based on the net-profit portion of their farm income. The U.S. Bureau of Labor Statistics reported in its May 2008 Occupational Employment Statistics survey that the estimated annual wage for most farmers ranged between $19,920 and $96,630.

Employment Prospects

Opportunities to start agritourism ventures are available to all farmers who are willing to invest their money, patience, and hard work. Some experts in the field report that agritourism is a growing industry. Millions of students, families, travelers, and others visit working farms and ranches and take part in agritourism activities.

Advancement Prospects

Agritourism Operators generally measure their progress by achieving their business goals and objectives, as well as by increasing their profits each year. Most, if not all, Farmers measure their success by being able to make a comfortable living from their profits.

Education and Training

No formal training is required for farmers to become Agritourism Operators. They generally learn their business on the job.

The Cooperative Extension Service, state departments of agriculture, nonprofit agritourism groups, and other organizations offer workshops to farmers who want to learn about starting agritourism enterprises.

Special Requirements

Agritourism Operators must obtain the proper licenses, permits, or certificates to operate their ventures. They may be required to be registered or certified with the proper government agency to sell certain products, such as organic vegetables. Requirements for businesses vary among states. For specific information, contact your local government office that oversees business licensing.

Experience, Special Skills, and Personality Traits

Becoming an Agritourism Operator requires no prior experience; however, experts in the field recommend that farmers become familiar with the agritourism industry before committing themselves.

To be successful entrepreneurs, Agritourism Operators need strong leadership, management, planning, organizational, and problem-solving skills. They also need excellent interpersonal, communication, and customer service skills. Being creative, innovative, resourceful, bold, foresighted, and determined are some personality traits that successful Agritourism Operators share.

Unions and Associations

Agritourism Operators can join local, state, or national associations to take advantage of networking opportunities, training programs, and other services and resources. At the national level, they might belong to the North American Farmers' Direct Marketing Association. For contact information, see Appendix II.

Tips for Entry

1. Conduct extensive research about the feasibility of starting any agritourism enterprise to determine whether it is right for you.
2. Take advantage of your local Cooperative Extension Service office, state agritourism advisory council, and other resources for advice about starting agritourism ventures.
3. Use the Internet to learn more about agritourism. You might start by visiting Agritourism World (www.agritourismworld.com). For more links, see Appendix IV.

ECOTOUR OPERATOR

Duties: Operate and manage a tour company; plan, design, and offer ecologically friendly tours for sale; may conduct tours; perform other duties as required

Alternate Title(s): Tour Operator

Salary Range: $45,000 to $166,000

Employment Prospects: Fair

Advancement Prospects: Poor

Prerequisites:

Education or Training—Combination of self-study, on-the-job-training, and formal instruction in ecotourism practices

Experience—Extensive background in the ecotourism industry

Special Skills and Personality Traits—Leadership, teamwork, project management, planning, writ-

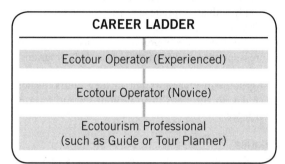

ing, organizational, negotiating, conflict resolution, troubleshooting, interpersonal, communication, customer service, and computer skills; enthusiastic, friendly, patient, resourceful, flexible, enterprising, creative, and dedicated personality traits

Special Requirements—Possess business licenses; obtain permits to visit tour locations

Position Description

Ecotour Operators own travel services that specialize in organizing and selling nature-based trips to wildernesses, rain forests, coastlines, and other remote locations. These tour operators are part of the ecotourism industry, which emerged from the environmental movement during the late 1970s. Ecotourism is also described as sustainable travel and green tourism. Ecotourism proponents—both travelers and travel services—follow these general principles:

- protect and conserve the natural environment
- respect the local culture as well as contribute to the local economy
- have a fun, enjoyable, and educational experience

Ecotour Operators usually have years of experience in the travel industry. They are environmentally conscious and have backgrounds in adventure travel as well as in conservation and wildlife. In addition, they are familiar with the ecosystems to which they organize trips. Ecotour Operators create guided tours that raise awareness about the environment, as well as foster appreciation of the culture of the local people and their social, economic, and political conditions. Their trips may take place within their community or region, in other parts of the United States, and in other countries,

such as Costa Rica, Panama, Peru, Vietnam, China, Nepal, or Kenya. Ecotours usually consist of small groups of travelers so that there is minimum impact to the environment. The trips may last several hours, several days, or weeks.

Ecotours are packaged trips in which groups of people travel together following a preplanned itinerary. They are typically designed for participants to view wildlife and experience the natural surroundings. Tour guests learn about the flora and fauna, as well as the cultural and historical significance of sites from expert naturalists and local guides who accompany them. Some tours also provide guests the opportunity to visit native villages or towns within the area. Birding, wildlife viewing, visiting archeological sites, snorkeling, camping, hiking through a rain forest, and paddling kayaks along a coastline are just a few examples of trips that Ecotour Operators might offer. Sometimes tours are designed to cater to families, senior citizens, or other specific groups of travelers.

Ecotour Operators continually develop new tours to add to their travel packages. Tour operators or their representatives visit destinations to learn about tour opportunities, quality of accommodations and restaurants, reliability of local transportation services, and so forth. Ecotour Operators also conduct research, do market surveys, and obtain feedback from customers and suppliers about travel trends and about popular destinations and attractions. Ecotour Operators analyze and evaluate all their data to create fun, safe, and secure tours and travel programs. They sell their tours directly to consumers and through travel agents.

Ecotour Operators perform various other planning tasks, such as: determining the cost of tours; pricing trips; preparing trip policies; arranging activities and entertainment; organizing transportation, lodging, and meals; and finding local guides. They also negotiate contracts with airlines, hotels, and other suppliers. Ecotour Operators usually seek subcontractors that practice environmental and social sustainability.

Ecotour Operators are also involved in marketing and selling their tour packages.

They perform such tasks as: developing and implementing marketing plans; preparing informational and promotional materials, such as press releases, brochures, and content for Web sites; setting sales targets; and identifying and establishing sales opportunities. Ecotour Operators also make sales and handle inquiries about tours from both customers and travel agents.

Many Ecotour Operators also take part in conducting tours. They may perform the role of tour manager. As such, they are responsible for making sure that trips run smoothly and safely, and that tour members are enjoying themselves. Tour managers coordinate daily schedules and activities. They answer questions, attend to complaints, and accommodate any special needs that members may have. These tour managers supervise the handling of baggage, take charge of checking in and out of lodging, and make sure all members are present during each leg of the trip. Tour managers also troubleshoot problems and handle emergencies as they occur. In addition, they instruct tour members about safety regulations and rules of conduct, as well as provide them with information about the ecological, cultural, and historical aspects of the sites they are visiting.

Ecotour Operators may also work as guides on tours when they are knowledgeable about the locations being visited. As guides, their role is to provide guests with an interpretation of the natural and cultural history of the area. For example, on a rain forest tour, guides may talk about different plants and how people use them for food, medicine, and other purposes. Interpretive guides are expected to explain complex scientific information in simple, interesting terms that are easy for laypeople to understand.

In addition to developing, selling, and conducting tours, Ecotour Operators are responsible for the overall direction and management of their operations. They formulate operational and travel policies and procedures. They plan and coordinate human resources, facilities management, finance, accounting, marketing, sales, and other operational activities. Ecotour Operators make sure that taxes, insurance premiums, and bills are paid; licenses and permits are up-to-date; and all aspects of their businesses comply with regulations and codes. They also promote their businesses by networking with local chambers of commerce, trade associations, and other organizations. To assist with the various business details, they hire, train, and supervise managers, consultants, attorneys, accountants, travel professionals, guides, and others.

Ecotour Operators work in comfortable offices, as well as outdoors in remote locations when they are leading tours or doing research for future trips. These business owners put in long hours, six to seven days a week, to build and maintain successful operations. While working as tour managers, Ecotour Operators are on duty 24 hours a day to assist tour members.

Salaries

Annual earnings for Ecotour Operators vary each year. Their incomes are based on their companies' annual net profits, which are determined by subtracting the total cost of their operating expenses from their gross annual sales. Income information specifically for Ecotour Operators is unavailable. Owners of small business establishments receive earnings similar to salaries made by general managers. According to the May 2008 Occupational Employment Statistics survey by the U.S. Bureau of Labor Statistics, the estimated annual salary for most general managers ranged between $45,410 and $166,400.

Employment Prospects

Opportunities are favorable for Ecotour Operators to start a travel service specializing in ecotourism. The travel industry is one of the largest industries in the world. Some experts in the field report that ecotourism, a multibillion-dollar market, is one of the fastest growing tourism industries worldwide. In the United States, 17 million American travelers consider environmental factors when choosing travel companies, according to a 2003 study by the International Ecotourism Society.

To build a new business, Ecotour Operators must be willing to invest their money and put in long hours. It is common for new companies to be unprofitable or go out of business during their first few years of existence. The success of Ecotour Operators depends on their competition and the demand for their services, their business and market skills, the state of the economy, and other factors.

Advancement Prospects

Ecotour Operators typically measure success by earning higher incomes, increasing the size of their companies, and gaining recognition for themselves and their companies. They also measure success through job satisfaction.

Ecotour Operators may also pursue other career opportunities, in addition to running their travel business. Some individuals become ecotourism consultants, who offer advice on how to develop and implement ecotourism policies and practices to travel companies, hotels, resorts, government agencies, nonprofit groups, and other organizations. Those interested in being educators may seek teaching positions in colleges and universities that offer tourism and travel degrees or professional certification programs.

Education and Training

There are no minimum educational standards for individuals to meet to become Ecotour Operators. In general, these professionals learn about ecotourism practices through a combination of self-study, formal instruction, and on-the-job training. Many have completed formal training in travel and tourism programs.

Some colleges and universities offer programs in which students can earn an associate's degree, bachelor's degree, or professional certificate in ecotourism, or in travel or tourism with a specialization in ecotourism.

Throughout their careers, Ecotour Operators pursue continuing education through various channels to update their skills and knowledge. They may enroll in workshops, seminars, or classes offered by educational institutions, government agencies, community centers, trade associations, or other establishments. They may also attend trade shows, network with colleagues, and read relevant books and publications.

Special Requirements

Ecotour Operators must possess the appropriate business permits and licenses required by their local and state governments. For specific information about business licenses, contact the local—city or county—governmental administrative office where you plan to operate your business.

Operators are usually required to obtain the proper permits to visit the domestic or foreign locations where their tours take place.

Experience, Special Skills, and Personality Traits

Ecotour Operators typically have many years of experience in the travel industry and, in particular, have an extensive background in the ecotourism industry. Many of these professionals have worked for years in such positions as guides, tour managers, tour planners, and travel agents. To be successful Ecotour Operators, they must be familiar with the local culture, economics, politics, ecological systems, and other aspects about the locations in which they offer trips. In addition, they should have basic knowledge in such areas as business administration, finance, accounting, marketing, public relations, sales, and human resources.

Ecotour Operators need excellent leadership, teamwork, project management, planning, writing, organizational, negotiating, conflict resolution, and troubleshooting skills. Because they must work well with many people from diverse backgrounds, they need effective interpersonal, communication, and customer service skills. These professionals must also have strong computer skills, including the ability to use word processing, e-mail, spreadsheet, and other programs. Being enthusiastic, friendly, patient, resourceful, flexible, enterprising, creative, and dedicated are some personality traits that successful Ecotour Operators have in common.

Unions and Associations

Ecotour Operators may join professional associations to take advantage of networking opportunities and other professional services and resources. Two national societies that serve their interests are the United States Tour Operators Association and the International Ecotourism Society. For contact information to these organizations, see Appendix II.

Tips for Entry

1. Are you in college? One way to start gaining experience is to seek an internship position with an ecotour company. Be willing to learn about the different aspects of running a business.
2. If you lack business skills, enroll in workshops and classes offered by a chamber of commerce, community college, or community center.
3. To learn more about establishing a small business, take advantage of online resources offered by the U.S. Small Business Administration. Its URL is www.sba.gov.
4. Use the Internet to learn more about ecotourism. You might start by visiting the EcoTour Web site (www.ecotourdirectory.com) and the International Ecotourism Society Web site (www.ecotourism.org). For more links, see Appendix IV.

PARK NATURALIST

Duties: Plan, conduct, and evaluate interpretive programs, activities, exhibits, and materials; perform other duties as required

Alternate Title(s): Park Ranger, Interpretive Ranger, Park Guide, Interpretive Naturalist

Salary Range: $25,000 to $54,000+

Employment Prospects: Fair

Advancement Prospects: Fair

Prerequisites:

    Education or Training—Bachelor's degree preferred

    Experience—One or more years providing naturalist interpretive work

    Special Skills and Personality Traits—Leadership, teaching, project management, organizational, teamwork, communication, interpersonal, presentation, customer service, writing, and computer skills; enthusiastic, patient, creative, flexible, and self-motivated personality traits

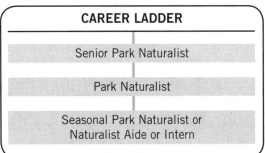

CAREER LADDER

Senior Park Naturalist

Park Naturalist

Seasonal Park Naturalist or Naturalist Aide or Intern

Position Description

When we visit national parks, state parks, and some local public parks, we may encounter uniformed men and women called park rangers. These professionals generally fulfill one of three major roles. Some rangers are law enforcement officers who have the authority to issue citations and parking tickets and arrest law violators. Other park rangers are generalists who perform a wide range of tasks, such as collecting entry and campground fees, maintaining trails, and assisting with fire suppression. Park Naturalists are the third type of rangers. These men and women serve as educators in the parks. They provide visitors with information and opportunities to learn about natural history and science. They teach about the geology, plants, animals, and other natural wonders to be found within their parks.

Park Naturalists present information in different ways. They lead nature hikes and field trips, give talks at campfires, lead crafts programs, and create exhibits for park museums and information centers. They also write pamphlets and brochures that help visitors to find their way on trails and to various park facilities as well as to learn about some of the points of interest they will visit. These park rangers create dioramas, artifact displays, 3-D maps, aquariums, herbariums, and other exhibits for viewing at visitors' centers. They assemble interesting displays that include maps, drawings, photographs, and short articles to post on information kiosks or bulletin boards situated at various points throughout their parks.

Park Naturalists also take photographs, shoot videos, or sketch drawings. They use these to create slide shows or multimedia presentations. They present their slide shows or videos at scheduled group gatherings in their visitors' centers, outdoor amphitheaters, or similar park facilities.

Many of these rangers conduct classes in park nature centers. They cover a variety of topics including nature photography, taxidermy, plant identification, and more. Park Naturalists also visit local schools to give talks about their parks' natural features and services. They bring traveling exhibits with them.

Park Naturalists research their subjects to prepare their materials and programs. They study the plants and animals that inhabit their parks, as well as the geologic formations in their parks. They read books and consult with geologists, botanists, zoologists, historians, and archaeologists to learn more about the minerals, life-forms, and ancient artifacts that may be found within their parks' boundaries. Through their studies, they prepare themselves to be able to explain a wide variety of historical, scientific, and cultural topics about their parks.

These park rangers are also involved in conservation and resource management programs. They strive to achieve a balance between caring for their parks' natural resources and encouraging visitors' enjoyment, which can have an adverse impact on those resources. Park Naturalists develop plans for new trails, campsites, and landscaping projects. Additionally, these experts provide technical advice to government agencies that oversee park development. They review plans for new parks and landscaping projects for both new and existing parks. Park Naturalists provide input for the decision-making process regarding the establishment of new trails, campsites, and buildings. Some of these naturalists advise about timber harvesting and help to eradicate nonnative plant species from their parks. Park Naturalists integrate conservation and resource management information into their guided tour and campfire talks, as well as their park literature and visitor center exhibits. Park Naturalists also teach conservation in more formal educational settings in school-sponsored conservation programs.

Park Naturalists may supervise and train other members of their park's staff, including volunteers and aides. They perform routine administrative tasks such as keeping records and writing reports. Park Naturalists may also be involved with ordering supplies of the materials and equipment used by park staff. Some of these park rangers also help to publicize park programs and activities, including special events.

Some Park Naturalists may be required to fulfill some of the responsibilities of general park rangers. The may collect park entrance fees and distribute general park information to visitors, for example. Some may conduct different types of research, such as monitoring air quality within park boundaries, or gathering statistics about park visitors and programs. Other Park Naturalists may be responsible for patrolling various areas of the park, performing trail maintenance tasks, and assisting in emergencies by fighting fires or searching for lost persons.

Park Naturalists work in parks in a variety of locations. Some parks are very remote, while others are more easily accessible. Some Park Naturalists work in urban locations.

These park rangers work in both indoor and outdoor environments. Their indoor work includes preparing exhibits and educational materials, as well as writing reports and other documents. Much of their research work is conducted outdoors, as are their guided nature walks and campfire presentations. Park Naturalists are routinely exposed to insects and other animals in addition to all kinds of climates and weather conditions. They may handle live creatures and plants during the course of their research and for presentation purposes.

Park Naturalists can work full-time or part-time, seasonally or all year. Their hours are flexible and they may be required to work evening hours or on weekends and holidays. They occasionally travel to locations away from their parks to present educational programs.

Salaries

Salaries for Park Naturalists vary, depending on their education, experience, employer, geographic location, and other factors. According to Salary.com, the median expected salary for Park Naturalists in the United States is $46,546 as of April 2009. The base salary for these professionals ranged between $38,261 and $57,618.

Park rangers in the National Park Service earn salaries based on the general schedule (GS), a federal pay schedule. Seasonal Park Naturalists, also known as park guides, start at the GS-4 level. Depending on their qualifications, newly hired rangers for permanent positions earn a salary that ranges in the GS-5 to GS-9 level. In 2010, the annual base pay for the GS-4 to GS-9 levels ranged between $24,518 and $54,028.

Employment Prospects

Park Naturalists are employed by national, state, county, and municipal parks throughout the United States.

The turnover for park ranger jobs, including naturalists, is low. Because of the popularity of these jobs, the competition for available positions, whether they are permanent, temporary, or seasonal, is high. Opportunities usually become available when Park Naturalists retire, transfer to other jobs or careers, or advance to higher positions. Employers may create additional positions to meet increased workloads, as long as funding is available. When governments face budget crunches, hiring for vacant park positions is often put on temporary hold. Parks may also lay rangers off.

Advancement Prospects

Park Naturalists usually begin their careers in seasonal or temporary positions. It is not unusual for individuals to work for several years in these jobs before being hired to permanent positions.

Qualified Park Naturalists can advance to supervisory, administrative, and management positions, but those opportunities are limited.

Many Park Naturalists measure their success by earning higher incomes, by being assigned to the parks of their choice, and through job satisfaction.

Education and Training

Educational requirements vary with the different employers. Many employers prefer to hire Park Naturalists who possess a bachelor's degree in botany, forestry, zoology, geology, outdoor education, natural resource management, or another related field.

Inexperienced Park Naturalists receive on-the-job training while working under experienced personnel.

Throughout their careers, Park Naturalists enroll in continuing education programs to update their skills and knowledge.

Experience, Special Skills, and Personality Traits

Employers prefer to hire entry-level candidates who have one or more years of experience performing naturalist interpretive work. They are knowledgeable about science education and interpretive principles and techniques, including curriculum planning and exhibit design. Candidates may have gained their experience through a combination of employment, volunteer work, or internships.

Some employers, such as the National Park Service, require that candidates have worked a minimum number of years as seasonal park rangers.

To perform their work effectively, Park Naturalists need leadership, teaching, project management, organizational, and teamwork skills. They must also have excellent communication, interpersonal, presentation, and customer service skills as they deal with many adults and children from diverse backgrounds. Having strong writing and computer skills is also essential for their work. Being enthusiastic, patient, creative, flexible, and self-motivated are some personality traits that successful Park Naturalists have in common.

Unions and Associations

Park Naturalists can join professional associations to take advantage of networking opportunities, continuing education, and other professional services and resources. Two national societies that serve their interests are the National Association for Interpretation and the National Recreation and Park Association. Park Naturalists for the National Park Service are also served by the Association of National Park Rangers. For contact information to these organizations, see Appendix II.

Tips for Entry

1. Many local, state, and national parks accept volunteers to work as interpretive specialists in their summer or year-round programs.
2. Already having a current driver's license as well as CPR and first aid certificates may enhance your employability.
3. Before you go to a job interview, learn as much as you can about the animals, plants, and ecological systems that are found in the park. If you can, check out the interpretive programs that the park offers the public.
4. For information on the Internet about working for the National Park Service, visit its Employment Information Web site at www.nps.gov/personnel.
5. Use the Internet to learn more about the field of park interpretation. You might start by visiting the National Association for Interpretation Web Site at www.interpnet.com. For more links, see Appendix IV.

OUTDOOR GUIDE

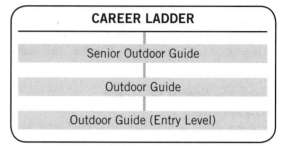

Position Description

Every day, throughout the world, Outdoor Guides lead adventurers, sports enthusiasts, and tourists on trips that involve sports or recreational activities. These professional guides may take interested parties on excursions on the ocean, on rivers, along shorelines, in forests, in parks, in recreational areas, and in wilderness areas. Bird-watching, whale watching, fishing, hunting, hiking, rock climbing, backpacking, horseback riding, bicycling, cross-country skiing, scuba diving, ocean kayaking, and white-water river rafting are just a few of the types of pastimes that different Outdoor Guides organize and conduct.

Outdoor Guides are experts in the sports or recreational activities that they lead. Fishing guides, for example, are knowledgeable about different fish, fishing equipment, fishing techniques, and the best locations for fishing in the area in which they guide. Most Outdoor Guides are employed by travel companies, adventure outfitters, conservation groups, hotels, resorts, dude ranches, sporting goods stores, and other private enterprises and nonprofit organizations.

Outdoor Guides are responsible for directing and assisting the members of their tours throughout the trip. They ensure that customers have memorable, fun, and safe experiences.

Adventure tours may last from a few hours to several weeks. Although guides may lead a trip several times a day, in a week, or in a season, each trip is different because of the varying interests of tour members. Outdoor Guides meet people from all backgrounds with various personalities whom they treat with politeness, respect, and patience. These guides also work with individuals of different skill levels, from beginner to experienced. They sometimes conduct trips that cater to specific types of customers, such as youth, families, singles, women, or senior citizens.

Outdoor Guides work alone or in teams on a trip, depending on the type of excursion, the size of the group, the experience of the guides, and the skill levels of the tour group, and other variables. Outdoor Guides are responsible for organizing and preparing for their trips. They gather all necessary equipment and supplies. They review the itinerary and guest roster, and learn about any special needs or requests that customers might have. They also check weather reports and the status of trails, rivers, oceans, traffic, or other conditions for their trip.

Guides meet and greet their guests at the beginning of each trip. They brief them about what to expect on the trip and go over trip policies and safety rules. Guides also make sure that the members of their group obey all appropriate laws. For example, hunting guides check that all members have proper hunting permits before the tour begins.

Outdoor Guides give instructions on how to perform basic skills for the activity, such as shifting bicycle gears, paddling rafts, or fly casting. They offer tips for improving techniques through the course of the trip.

An important element of these guides' job is making sure that customers are comfortable and enjoying themselves. Outdoor Guides are also responsible for the safety and well-being of all the members of their excursion parties. They talk and listen to their clients as well as observe how they are doing throughout the trip. As guests become tired, for example, Outdoor Guides encourage and motivate them to complete their journey. These guides are prepared to troubleshoot problems and handle emergencies as they occur. For instance, white-water river guides swiftly take charge of events such as when a member has fallen out of the raft.

Many guides provide their parties with information about the local regions. They may talk about the area's history, culture, geography, wildlife, and so on. They may make suggestions to customers about lodging, food, shopping, and current happenings in the area.

Many of these professional guides perform other duties between trips. Those who work at dude ranches, for example, may perform ranch, housekeeping, or wrangler chores, as well as help with entertaining guests at cookouts, dances, and other special events.

At some organizations, Outdoor Guides work in the office to respond to inquiries from the public. Such inquiries may come to them in person, over the phone, by e-mail, or through the Internet. They may also book trips and take payments from customers. Mechanically minded guides may be responsible for maintaining and performing small repairs on equipment and watercraft or vehicles.

Some Outdoor Guides are self-employed. They may run their businesses alone or in partnership with others. Some independent guides offer their services to resorts, adventure outfitters, and other establishments on a contractual basis.

As small-business owners, guides are responsible for attending to various administrative tasks to ensure the success of their operations. For example, they pay bills, taxes, and insurance premiums; establish trip policies, rules, and fees; obtain proper permits and licenses; buy and maintain equipment and supplies; and manage inventory and sales records. Business owners also hire, train, and supervise staff members. In addition, independent guides design and implement marketing plans to generate continued business.

The nature of their job requires Outdoor Guides to be in top physical condition, as they are on the job for the length of the expedition, whether it is a couple of hours or several weeks. They lift and carry heavy loads. Some of them work with horses, mules, llamas, and other animals. Their trips may involve traveling over rough terrain or water currents, as well as experiencing rainy, foggy, or extremely hot weather conditions.

Outdoor Guides are employed part-time or full-time. Some guides work on an on-call basis.

Salaries

Salaries for Outdoor Guides vary, depending on such factors as their experience, skill levels, job duties, and employer. Specific salary information for these guides is unavailable. The estimated annual salary for most travel guides ranged between $17,220 and $56,340, according to the May 2008 Occupational Employment Statistics survey by the U.S. Bureau of Labor Statistics.

Outdoor Guides may be paid an hourly wage or on a per diem basis. Guides may receive tips from customers at the end of a trip. Some employers provide their guides with free room and board during the season.

Because their work tends to be seasonal, many guides supplement their incomes by working at other jobs during the off-season.

Employment Prospects

According to some experts, adventure tourism is a growing industry. Every year, millions of people in the United States and throughout the world participate in adventure vacations and outdoor activities offered by private enterprises and nonprofit organizations.

Outdoor Guides work throughout the United States. Openings for permanent positions generally become available to replace regular guides who have taken other jobs, transferred to other career fields, or left the workforce for various reasons. Opportunities are also created when employers expand their operations to offer more activities to customers.

Most Outdoor Guides work on a seasonal basis. Some of these professionals work throughout the year by obtaining guide jobs with different employers. For example, a guide might work for a ski resort during the winter and a dude ranch the rest of the year. Other seasonal guides hold jobs in teaching, construction, sales, or other fields during the rest of the year.

Advancement Prospects

Outdoor Guides advance according to their own interests and ambitions. Many measure success by gaining professional reputations, by earning higher wages, and through job satisfaction. Guides can also be promoted to lead, supervisory, and management positions.

Entrepreneurial individuals may become independent Outdoor Guides or establish their own outfitting services or other outdoor-related businesses.

Education and Training

There are no standard educational requirements for individuals to fulfill to become Outdoor Guides. Employers generally require that applicants hold at least a high school diploma or general equivalency diploma. Many guides hold college degrees or have completed some college coursework. Some guides have a college degree in outdoor recreation or a related field.

Several options are available for persons who wish to become Outdoor Guides. They may complete an apprenticeship under established guides. They may learn outdoor guiding skills on the job while they work under the direction of experienced guides. They may enroll in guiding programs offered by recognized organizations or adventure guide schools where they learn basic skills to obtain an entry-level position.

Special Requirements

In some states, all Outdoor Guides who offer their services for hire must possess a professional license. In other states, only certain Outdoor Guides, such as fishing or hunting guides, must be licensed.

Most, if not all employers, require that Outdoor Guides have first aid and CPR certificates. Candidates may be hired on the condition that they obtain those certificates within a certain time.

Owners of outfitting services must obtain business licenses to operate within their city or state.

Experience, Special Skills, and Personality Traits

In general, employers prefer to hire applicants for entry-level positions who are already skilled in and knowledgeable about the outdoor activities that they would lead. Additionally, they have previous guiding experience that they may have gained through volunteer work or as part of their duties in such jobs as recreation leaders, park rangers, or outdoor education instructors. Employers also seek candidates who are familiar with the locations in which they would conduct tours. Some employers are willing to hire less experienced candidates if they demonstrate the ability to learn quickly and work hard.

Outdoor Guides meet and deal with many people from diverse backgrounds on their trips; thus, they must have effective communication, interpersonal, and customer service skills. These guides also must have excellent leadership, teaching, organizational, self-management, and teamwork skills. Being lively, positive, calm, patient, supportive, enterprising, levelheaded, dependable, flexible, and resourceful are some personality traits that successful Outdoor Guides share.

Unions and Associations

Outdoor Guides can join professional societies that serve their particular interests, such as mountain climbing or fishing. These organizations may be available at the local, state, or national level. By joining a professional association, Outdoor Guides can take advantage of networking opportunities, professional certification, and other professional services and resources.

Tips for Entry

1. Volunteering is a good way to gain experience, as well as to meet people who may be able to help you find work in the future. Various organizations seek volunteers to help with leading outdoor activities or performing other jobs, such as youth groups, local recreation departments, state or national parks, and conservation groups.

2. Are you a good cook? Do you speak another language? Do you have handyman skills? Have your completed wilderness first responder training? Are you skilled at orienteering? Do you have a background in history or nature? They are all skills and experiences that may enhance your employability.

3. Self-employed guides need strong business, finance, and marketing skills.

4. Use the Internet to learn more about the outdoor recreation field. You might start by visiting the America Outdoors Association Web site (www.americaoutdoors.org), GORP.com, and Outdoor IndustryJobs.com. For more links, see Appendix IV.

EDUCATION AND COMMUNICATIONS

AGRICULTURE TEACHER

Duties: Provide instruction for agriculture education programs in a middle, junior high, or high school; create daily lesson plans; supervise students' agricultural projects; perform other duties as required

Alternate Title(s): Agricultural Science Teacher; a title that reflects a particular position such as Horticulture Teacher or Animal Science Teacher

Salary Range: $34,000 to $78,000

Employment Prospects: Good

Advancement Prospects: Good

Prerequisites:

    Education or Training—Bachelor's degree; for licensed teachers, completion of an accredited teacher-education program

    Experience—Student teaching or other teaching experience

CAREER LADDER

Mentor Teacher or Administrative Position

↑

Agriculture Teacher

↑

Student Teacher or Substitute Teacher

Special Skills and Personality Traits—Leadership, organizational, time-management, critical-thinking, problem-solving, self-management, communication, and interpersonal skills; enthusiastic, patient, outgoing, trustworthy, supportive, inspirational, open-minded, creative, and flexible personality traits

Special Requirements—State teaching credential required in public schools

Position Description

Agricultural education is part of the curriculum in many public and private schools in rural, suburban, and urban communities throughout the United States. It is a vocational program in which Agriculture Teachers prepare students for careers in such areas as agriculture, food, fiber, and natural resources management. Agricultural education programs are designed for grades six through 12. Most programs, however, are found at the high school level where students gain the skills and knowledge they will need to obtain jobs, become entrepreneurs, or pursue college degrees after high school graduation.

No two agricultural education programs are the same. The composition of courses depends on the skill sets needed by local communities and on the interests of the students. Agriculture Teachers may provide instruction in such areas as crop production, ornamental horticulture, livestock management, sustainable agriculture, food science, forestry, soil and water conservation, precision technology, biofuels, pest management, veterinary science, agricultural engineering and mechanics, and agriculture business management, among other fields.

In their courses, agricultural students learn how to apply science, technology, business, management, and

leadership to agriculture. Agriculture Teachers provide formal classroom instruction and manage students under laboratory conditions where they can learn firsthand how to work with plants, animals, and agricultural products. Some examples of laboratory settings are shops, farms, greenhouses, nurseries, nature trails, biotechnology labs, and computer labs. Teachers also enhance their students' learning with field trips and guest speakers.

In addition to providing instruction, Agriculture Teachers act as mentors to their students. They advise students about their career options and help them plan, develop, and complete projects that meet their goals. These teachers also meet with parents, school counselors, school administrators, and other teachers to discuss students' academic performance and, when necessary, behavioral problems.

Vocational agricultural education programs also include two other components that may be required or optional for students to complete. One component is called the supervised agricultural experiences (SAE) program, in which students intern for a farmer or agricultural business, conduct a scientific research project, produce and market crops for sale, or pursue another activity outside of class time. SAE programs allow students to further develop their skills and gain practical experience. Agriculture Teachers help students design SAE programs that are appropriate to their individual career goals. Teachers also supervise and monitor the progress of their activities by visiting students at their work sites.

The FFA (formerly known as the Future Farmers of America) is another component of agricultural education programs. The FFA, a national organization that operates under a federal charter, provides opportunities for students to develop personal growth, leadership skills, and career goals. FFA members participate in competitions, community service projects, state and national leadership conventions, and other activities. Most, if not all, Agriculture Teachers are involved with local FFA chapters. They advise and assist the student officers, committees, and members with the planning and implementation of FFA activities that interest them.

Agriculture Teachers have a busy and intense job. Before their school year begins, they plan each course they will teach. Following instructional standards and curriculum guidelines, teachers identify the goals and student objectives of each course, the sequence of topics to be taught, the textbooks and other student materials that will be used, class rules, grading information, and so on.

These teachers are also responsible for creating daily lesson plans for each of their classes. A lesson plan generally describes what topic will be taught on a particular day and how that lesson will be taught. Teachers prepare for each class by studying the subject matter, gathering teaching materials, creating appropriate student exercises, and setting up lab activities. They present their lessons through lectures, modeling, and demonstrations. Many teachers use films, slide shows, computer databases, and the Internet to supplement their instruction.

To reinforce concepts and skills, teachers assign students classwork, homework, and projects, which the teachers review, correct, add comments to, and grade. They monitor the progress of their students' learning by administering quizzes and tests on a regular basis. Teachers keep a daily record of their students' scores on assignments and examinations. They are also responsible for grading students on their overall performance in class, on examinations, and with their assignments and projects.

Agriculture Teachers in public schools may have special education students, who are children with learning, physical, or other special needs, in their classrooms. Teachers are required to follow an Individualized Education Program (IEP) for each special education student. An IEP describes the instructional goals and objectives for a student, as well as any classroom accommodations or supplementary services or aids that are needed for the student to learn successfully. Agriculture Teachers may seek the help of special education teachers for help with implementing IEPs.

Agriculture Teachers have various nonteaching responsibilities to perform as well. They keep records of students' attendance in their classes. They monitor campus grounds during lunch and other breaks, as well as when students arrive on campus in the morning and leave at the end of the day. Teachers also assist in the supervision of school dances, games, concerts, and other school events. Some Agriculture Teachers oversee and direct the work of teacher aides, student helpers, or student teachers.

Agriculture Teachers are involved in curriculum development for the agricultural education program as well as for the total education program of their school. They also participate in professional development workshops sponsored by their employers. Many Agriculture Teachers take part in community activities such as livestock shows and county fairs. Some teachers serve as resources in their communities about topics in agriculture and natural resources.

Agriculture Teachers work long hours, including evenings and weekends, to perform supervisory duties at afterschool events, grade tests and assignments, prepare lessons, and complete other tasks. Most Agriculture Teachers work a 10-month school year with a two-month summer break. During the summer, many instructors teach in summer school and participate in professional activities to gain new skills and knowledge.

Salaries

Salaries for Agriculture Teachers vary, depending on such factors as their education, experience, employer, and geographic location. Specific salary information for these schoolteachers is unavailable. An idea of their earnings can be gained by looking at the compensation for vocational education teachers in general. The U.S. Bureau of Labor Statistics reported in its May 2008 Occupational Employment Statistics survey the following estimated annual salary ranges for most of these teachers:

- middle school vocational education teachers: $34,020 to $72,270
- secondary school vocational education teachers: $34,980 to $77,950

In addition to their teaching salaries, Agriculture Teachers may earn extra compensation by being FFA advisers, coaching sports, sponsoring extracurricular activities, or teaching summer school classes.

Employment Prospects

Job opportunities for Agriculture Teachers are favorable throughout the United States. According to the National Association of Agricultural Educators Web site (in August 2009), there is a demand for high school Agriculture Teachers. Some experts report that agricultural education programs have closed because of an inability to hire qualified teachers. The shortage of Agriculture Teachers is partly due to fewer students entering the agricultural education field.

In general, positions for Agriculture Teachers become available as individuals retire, or transfer to other teaching jobs, or leave the teaching field. Schools create additional positions to meet growing student interest, as long as funding is available.

Because agriculture is a vital industry, there will always be a need for agricultural education programs to teach and encourage future agricultural producers, scientists, mechanics, economists, educators, and other professions. Currently, the National Council for Agricultural Education is leading an initiative to establish new agricultural education programs throughout the United States. Its goal is expand the total number of programs to 10,000 by 2015.

Advancement Prospects

Agriculture Teachers can advance in various ways. They can earn seniority, tenure, and higher salaries. They can become mentor teachers and chairs of their agriculture or vocational department. Those with higher administrative and managerial ambitions can seek such positions. Public schoolteachers can earn advanced degrees to become principals and district administrators. Private school teachers can become headmasters, deans of students, or other administrators. With further training, schoolteachers can become school counselors, curriculum specialists, educational technologists, or pursue other school-related professions.

Agriculture Teachers may choose other careers in agricultural education. For example, they may become college professors, Cooperative Extension Service professionals, educational consultants, or corporate trainers.

Education and Training

Public and private schools require Agriculture Teachers to possess at least a bachelor's degree in agricultural education, agricultural science, agronomy, agricultural engineering, agricultural economics, or another agricultural discipline. Some schools may waive the require-

ment for highly qualified candidates who have years of experience in their field.

To teach in public schools, prospective teachers must first complete an accredited teacher education program. They receive instruction in such areas as pedagogy, classroom management, technology, and agricultural education. They are also required to complete a supervised field practicum, also known as student teaching.

Beginning Agriculture Teachers are usually assigned to mentor teachers who advise them on such matters as classroom management and creating lesson plans. All schoolteachers undergo in-service workshops throughout the school year.

Special Requirements

Public schools in all 50 states, as well as the District of Columbia and the U.S. territories, require Agriculture Teachers to possess a valid state teaching credential. Licensing requirements vary with each state. In general, applicants must have completed a teacher-education program and pass a test that assesses their basic reading, writing, and mathematics skills. Individuals are first issued a provisional teaching certificate that is valid for three to five years. To qualify for permanent certification, teachers must fulfill further requirements such as completing a minimum number of hours of continuing education or earning a master's degree in education.

Private schools have their own requirements for certification. Some schools, for example, require applicants to be certified by the school itself, a specific school accreditation organization, or the state department of education.

Experience, Special Skills, and Personality Traits

Both public and private schools hire Agriculture Teachers who have one or more years of teaching experience. Novice teachers may have gained their experience through student teaching, substitute teaching, or working in nonformal educational programs such as the Cooperative Extension Service.

To perform well at their jobs, Agriculture Teachers need excellent leadership, organizational, time-management, critical-thinking, problem-solving, and self-management skills. They also need strong communication and interpersonal skills to work well with students, colleagues, administrators, support staff, parents, and others.

Being enthusiastic, patient, outgoing, trustworthy, supportive, inspirational, open-minded, creative, and flexible are some personality traits that successful Agriculture Teachers have in common. Above all, these instructors are passionate about teaching young students about agriculture.

Unions and Associations

Agriculture Teachers can join state or national professional societies that offer networking opportunities, training programs, and other professional services and resources. Two organizations at the national level that serve the particular interests of these teachers are the National Association of Agricultural Educators and the Association of Career and Technical Education.

Many public schoolteachers belong to a union, such as the National Education Association or the American Federation of Teachers, which represents them in contract negotiations with their employers. The union seeks better terms regarding pay, benefits, and working conditions for its membership. The union also handles any grievances that its members may have against their employers.

For contact information to the above organizations, see Appendix II.

Tips for Entry

1. If you are a high school student, let your Agriculture Teacher know about your interest in becoming an agricultural educator. Ask him or her about how you can prepare for a teaching career. You might also ask about an opportunity to work as a teacher's helper in an agricultural class.

2. Gain teaching experience working with middle school and high school students by obtaining a job or volunteering with a school, church, sports, or youth program. For example, you might be a tutor, teacher's aid, sports coach, or 4-H club leader.

3. There are alternative ways to obtain teacher certification, such as by teaching in the classroom under the supervision of experienced instructors. For more information, visit the National Center for Alternative Certification Web site at www.teach-now.org.

4. Before going to a job interview, learn about the agricultural industry in the area where you might work. You might contact Agriculture Teachers, farmers, Cooperative Extension Service agents, your Farm Bureau office, your local Chamber of Commerce, or other local resources for information.

5. Use the Internet to learn more about teaching agriculture in high school. You might start by visiting the Web sites of these groups: the National FFA Organization (www.ffa.org) and the National Association of Agricultural Educators (www.naae.org). For more links, see Appendix IV.

PROFESSOR

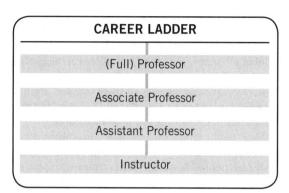

Position Description

Many community colleges, four-year colleges, and universities offer agricultural education programs that prepare individuals for careers in agriculture, food science, and natural resources management and conservation. Professors in these programs teach future agricultural producers, managers, entrepreneurs, scientists, engineers, technicians, food professionals, veterinarians, landscaping experts, Cooperative Extension Service professionals, policy analysts, marketing specialists, economists, foresters, naturalists, inspectors, educators, journalists, and many others.

Agriculture Professors provide instruction in subjects and topics in which they are experts. They teach courses in such diverse fields as animal science, agronomy, biology, horticulture, viticulture, entomology, wildlife and fisheries science, forest science, sustainable agriculture, veterinary science, food science, landscape architecture, conservation science, agricultural and biosystems engineering, agricultural business, agricultural economics, agricultural education, nutrition, family and consumer education, and international agriculture. Many Professors are also involved in conducting research that leads to scientific discoveries and technologies, which benefit the industries of agriculture, food, and others.

Agriculture instructors in community colleges (which are also called two-year colleges, technical colleges, or junior colleges) teach courses that prepare students for jobs and entrepreneurial opportunities in the local communities. Students may earn associate's degrees or occupational certificates. Some students transfer to four-year colleges or universities after fulfilling general education requirements for lower-level undergraduates. In four-year colleges and universities, Professors primarily teach students who are completing programs to earn their bachelor's, master's, or doctoral degrees. Some agriculture instructors teach in continuing education programs at their institutions, in which students can earn professional certificates in a particular area, such as landscape design.

College Professors teach one or more courses per term, preparing for each course before the term begins. This includes creating an outline, or syllabus, for their students, which describes the sequence of topics they will cover in class as well as provides a bibliography of reading materials. Professors also put together individual lessons along with student exercises, activities, and experiments to reinforce concepts and skills. Depending on the nature of their courses, Professors may lecture in large halls, lead small group seminars, or demonstrate experiments in the field or the laboratory. Some Professors teach courses via the Internet or on cable or closed-circuit television.

Most Professors hold regular office hours so that students can confer with them about academic and career concerns. Professors who teach in graduate programs supervise students with their research.

In four-year colleges and universities, many Professors are responsible for developing research programs in their fields of interest. They may conduct basic research to add new knowledge to their fields. For example, entomologists might study certain crop pests to further understand their biology or they might investigate why pesticides do not affect some crop pests. Research Professors may also perform applied research, which is the utilization of basic research findings to solve specific problems in their fields. For example, entomologists might seek ways to develop new techniques to control specific crop pests without chemical pesticides.

As researchers, Professors perform a number of duties. They prepare grant proposals and budgets that they submit to government agencies and other funding sources. They plan and develop research projects; design and conduct experiments and tests; gather, analyze, and interpret data; and review research literature. In addition, they publish the results of their research findings in scholarly journals and books.

At state land-grant universities, some Professors also perform roles as Cooperative Extension (Extension) specialists, or subject-matter experts. The Extension is part of the National Institute of Food and Agriculture, an agency within the U.S. Department of Agriculture. It works in partnership with state land-grant universities to make the knowledge and resources of the universities available to the public.

As Extension specialists, Professors develop, implement, and evaluate research-based programs that address the concerns of Extension clients. For example, they might oversee programs that help aquaculturists to manage fish-farming operations or farmers and residents to conserve water resources. The delivery of Extension programs to the public, however, is the responsibility of Extension professionals who work in field offices. Professors train and maintain close working relationships with field Extension staff. These Professors are also responsible for conducting research to solve specific issues of Extension clients. For instance, an Extension specialist may research new sustainable practices to produce nursery crops.

Performing community service is another essential duty of all Professors. These men and women take part in departmental decisions, such as selecting new faculty members and determining which courses to offer in a term. Some Professors act as advisers to student organizations. Many Professors also participate on administrative and academic committees that deal with matters concerning their institutions as a whole. In addition, Professors are involved in various service activities off campus. They may serve on boards of directors for nonprofit organizations or as members of government commissions, for example.

Professors work in classrooms and offices. Depending on their subject matter, they also spend time in teaching and research laboratories, on experimental farms, and in research stations, processing plants, and other sites. Some Professors conduct field trips for teaching or research purposes to remote locations that may require overnight stays.

Many institutions hire adjunct instructors to teach one to three courses per semester. Adjunct instructors have limited administrative responsibilities.

Full-time Professors are hired to tenured or nontenured positions. Professors with tenure have job security until they resign or retire from their position.

Salaries

Salaries for Professors vary, depending on such factors as their rank, discipline, employer, and geographic location. The U.S. Bureau of Labor Statistics (BLS) reported in its May 2008 Occupational Employment Statistics survey the following estimated annual salary ranges for most of these postsecondary teachers:

- agricultural sciences instructors: $38,460 to $124,650
- biological science instructors: $38,830 to $147,980
- chemistry instructors: $38,960 to $127,740
- economics instructors: $43,720 to $144,140
- engineering instructors: $45,150 to $142,670
- forestry and conservation science instructors: $36,980 to $107,200

Employment Prospects

Academic institutions typically seek Professors to replace individuals who retire or transfer to other jobs. They may create additional positions for new programs, as long as funding is available. Opportunities for college and university instructors, in general, are expected to be favorable in the coming decade because a large number of faculty members will become eligible for retirement. According to the BLS, employment of these educators is expected to increase by 15 percent between 2008 and 2018.

Job competition is keen for Professor positions. In general, opportunities are least favorable for tenure-track positions and better for adjunct positions, as well as for full-time positions that are appointed to limited-term contracts.

Advancement Prospects

College and university faculty hold four academic ranks: instructor, assistant Professor, associate Professor, and full Professor. Academic institutions generally grant appointments, tenure, and promotions to individuals based on their records of teaching, research, scholarly publication, and community service.

Professors who have administrative and managerial ambitions can seek such opportunities. They can rise through the administrative ranks to become department chairs, college deans, administrative directors, provosts, and college presidents.

Education and Training

To teach in two-year colleges, individuals must possess at least a master's degree in their discipline. A doctorate is required to teach at four-year colleges and universities. Institutions may hire individuals without doctoral degrees for part-time or temporary positions.

It takes several years of dedication for students to earn doctoral degrees. They first complete four years of undergraduate work to obtain bachelor's degrees, which is then followed by one or two more years to acquire their master's degrees. After that, they study another four to six years to earn their doctorates.

Experience, Special Skills, and Personality Traits

Employers prefer to hire candidates who have previous teaching experience. Depending on an institution's educational mission, candidates may need to demonstrate that they have a strong teaching, or combined teaching and research, background. Furthermore, candidates must have a strong background in the field in which they would teach. Some Professors spent several years conducting postdoctoral research prior to seeking faculty positions.

Because they must establish rapport with students and others, Professors need excellent communication and interpersonal skills. In addition, they need adequate social skills to handle the various functions they are required to attend. Some personality traits that successful Professors share include being curious, inspirational, self-motivated, flexible, and creative.

Unions and Associations

Professors join various organizations to take advantage of networking opportunities, continuing education, and other services and resources. They may belong to societies for agricultural educators such as the American Association for Agricultural Education, the National Association of Agricultural Educators, and the North American Colleges and Teachers of Agriculture. Some Professors also belong to societies that benefit the interests of academicians in general, such as the National Association of Scholars and the American Association of University Professors.

Many Professors are members of professional associations that serve their particular areas of interest. A few examples of these societies are the American Society of Agricultural and Biological Engineers, American Society of Agronomy, American Society of Animal Science, American Society of Plant Biologists, Entomological Society of America, Institute of Food Technologists, Poultry Science Association, Society of American Foresters, and World Aquaculture Society.

Some Professors belong to the higher education divisions of the National Education Association or the American Federation of Teachers. These two labor unions represent their members in contract negotiations with their employers.

For contact information to all of the above organizations, see Appendix II.

Tips for Entry

1. Teaching positions typically remain open until they are filled. Hence, if you see a job announcement with a past application deadline, contact the institution's human resources office to find out if it is still accepting applications.

2. Employers sometimes hire candidates who have not completed their doctoral thesis on the condition that it is completed by a certain date.

3. What is your teaching philosophy? Can you express it clearly on paper? Employers usually require applicants to submit a written statement that describes their teaching philosophy.

4. To learn more about becoming a college or university instructor, visit the Preparing Future Faculty Web site at www.preparing-faculty.org. For more links, see Appendix IV.

EXTENSION AGENT

Position Description

Cooperative Extension Service (Extension) Agents are educators who provide nonformal educational programs to rural, suburban, and urban communities throughout the United States. These programs are designed to help farmers, individuals, families, businesses, schools, agencies, and others solve problems in their work, lives, and communities. Extension Agents are part of a nationwide system known as the Cooperative Extension System, which was established in 1914 by the U.S. Congress. Its purpose is to give local communities access to the knowledge and resources available at state land-grant universities, with which the system works in partnership.

The Cooperative Extension Service is based at a land-grant university in each state, along with field offices that serve one or more counties. Extension professionals at the land-grant universities and Extension research centers develop practical applications that address agricultural, economic, family, and other issues. They also design nonformal educational programs that are based on unbiased research findings. However, it is the responsibility of Extension Agents to distribute information and implement educational programs in the communities they serve. These professionals are assigned to county or regional field offices.

Extension field offices offer educational programs that meet the particular needs of the communities they serve. Extension Agents lead programs that fall into one of these general areas: agriculture, natural resources, 4-H youth development, family and consumer sciences, or community and economic development. Depending on the size of their offices, Extension Agents may specialize in one or more areas.

Agriculture agents assist farmers, ranchers, home gardeners, nurseries, timber companies, and other agricultural producers with developing and improving their methods of production, processing, and distribution of agricultural products. They cover such topics as farm management, animal husbandry, crop management, entomology, aquaculture, sustainable agriculture, and marketing.

Natural resources agents are experts in the area of natural resources management. They teach landowners and homeowners about methods to protect and conserve water, soil, forests, and other natural resources. They cover such topics as water quality, rangeland ecology, soil conservation, composting, and recycling.

The agents who work in youth development are usually known as 4-H agents. Through 4-H clubs, as well as school enrichment programs and special projects, these agents provide educational activities to children and teenagers to help teach and reinforce academic, life, and social skills. Agents work directly with young participants as well as train volunteer leaders to work with young people.

Extension Agents who specialize in family and consumer sciences conduct educational programs that meet the needs of individuals, families, school staff, childcare providers, and nutrition and health professionals. These Extension Agents cover such subjects as child development, eldercare, nutrition, food safety, health, and money management.

Community and economic development agents help communities identify, create, and plan public programs, activities, and policies that improve their overall economic well-being and the quality of life of their residents. These Extension Agents may offer educational programs that address such community issues as job creation, land use, revitalization of downtown areas, leadership development, and management of community resources. Agents cooperate and collaborate with local, county, state, and tribal agencies as well as with nonprofit organizations.

Extension Agents are responsible for managing and coordinating the different educational programs for their assigned areas. They supervise and train staff, including volunteers, who assist them with implementing, facilitating, and evaluating programs and special projects. Agents also build and maintain relationships with local government agencies, school districts, businesses, community groups, and other organizations.

As educators, these agents' primary role is to inform and teach individuals and groups about various topics in their program area. They use a variety of methods to deliver unbiased and research-based information. They may conduct workshops, classes, or demonstrations in their offices and other locations; lead tours; make presentations at organizational meetings or community events; write articles for local publications; give interviews on local radio or television stations; and build Web sites.

Extension Agents also perform the role of advisers. They assist individuals and groups with specific problems. For example, an agent might advise a resident about how to improve her garden's soil, while another agent might provide guidance to a group of first-time home buyers.

The primary responsibility of developing and planning educational programs belongs to Extension specialists, who are based at land-grant universities or field offices. Extension Agents play a valuable role in ensuring that suitable programs are created for the communities with whom they work. For example, they might suggest that programs be created to help people handle recent critical problems such as droughts, floods, outbreaks of food-borne illnesses, or large numbers of job cuts by local employers. Along with identifying subject matter, they determine the best methods for delivering educational information to the communities. Extension

Agents gather information for future programs through their observations and by conducting surveys. They also confer with local agencies, businesses, civic groups, residents, and others.

Extension Agents perform a wide range of duties, which vary according to their skill level and experience. In general, they may be assigned to:

- promote Extension programs and activities in local media
- provide training and supervision to Extension staff and volunteers
- seek supplemental funding for programs such as conducting fund-raising events and submitting grant proposals to appropriate sources
- prepare educational support materials, such as brochures, fact sheets, newsletters, posters, videos, and content for Web sites
- conduct research about issues or problems requested by clients
- respond to inquiries from clients, the public, Extension staff, and others over the phone, in person, by e-mail, or through Web sites
- prepare required reports and paperwork
- conduct meetings with staff, clients, and others
- comply with civil rights and affirmative action policies
- participate in organizing community events such as 4-H camps and county fairs

Extension Agents may be employed part-time or full-time. They generally work 40 hours a week, but put in additional hours as needed to complete their duties. On occasion, they are required to work evenings and on weekends. They frequently travel to other locations in their county or state for meetings, conferences, training sessions, community functions, and other events. Some travel may involve overnight stays.

Salaries

Salaries for Extension Agents vary, depending on such factors as their education, experience, job duties, and geographic location. According to the May 2008 Occupational Employment Statistics survey by the U.S. Bureau of Labor Statistics, the estimated annual salary for most farm and home management advisers, including Extension Agents, ranged between $21,700 and $70,610.

Employment Prospects

Job competition is strong for agent positions. Opportunities generally become available as Extension Agents retire, advance to higher positions, or transfer to other jobs or career fields.

Although based in field offices, Extension Agents and all other Extension personnel are hired by the land-grant universities. Field offices may have one or more Extension Agents. The number and types of agents depend on the needs of the individual offices, as well as the availability of funds. In August 2009, about 2,900 Extension offices existed in the United States. These include county offices and regional centers.

Advancement Prospects

As Extension Agents gain experience, they earn higher salaries and receive greater levels of responsibility. Agents with supervisory and managerial ambitions may pursue such positions. Many agents measure success through job satisfaction and by being appointed to the offices of their choice. With advanced degrees, agents can seek positions as Extension specialists or as faculty members with land-grant universities.

Education and Training

The educational requirements vary among employers. Minimally, candidates may be required to hold a bachelor's or master's degree in a field related to the position for which they apply. For example, applicants seeking a community and economic development Extension Agent position would need a degree in community development, agricultural economics, business administration, or another related discipline.

Employers sometimes hire applicants with bachelor's degrees on the condition that they earn their master's degree within a certain number of years.

New Extension Agents undergo a comprehensive training and development program during their first year of employment to learn the basic skills and knowledge they need for their job. They complete in-service training programs as well as receive on-the-job training while working under the guidance and supervision of experienced Extension Agents.

Throughout their careers, Extension Agents pursue continuing education to upgrade their skills, gain new knowledge, and keep up with developments in their fields.

Experience, Special Skills, and Personality Traits

Employers usually hire candidates for entry-level positions who have one or more years of experience working with the Cooperative Extension System. They may have gained their experience through a combination of internships, employment, or volunteer work. They also seek candidates who demonstrate knowledge and expertise in the particular subjects, such as agriculture, in which they would work.

To perform well at their job, Extension Agents need strong leadership, organizational, self-management, and teamwork skills. They also must have effective teaching, writing, and computer skills. Additionally, they need excellent communication, interpersonal, and customer service skills, as they must be able to work with colleagues, clients, and the public from diverse backgrounds. Some personality traits that successful Extension Agents share include being tactful, patient, trustworthy, dependable, creative, detail-oriented, inquisitive, and dedicated.

Unions and Associations

Many Extension Agents join professional associations to take advantage of networking opportunities, continuing education, and other professional services and resources. Some national societies that serve their interests are:

- Association of Natural Resource Extension Professionals
- Epsilon Sigma Phi
- National Association of Community Development Extension Professionals
- National Association of County Agricultural Agents
- National Association of Extension 4-H Agents
- National Extension Association of Family and Consumer Sciences

For contact information to the above organizations, see Appendix II.

Tips for Entry

1. Enroll in adult education courses to learn how to teach adult learners. Also, gain experience by being a tutor in an adult literacy program or teaching classes to adults in a community center, senior center, museum, or another institution.
2. Contact or visit Web sites of local Extension offices and state land-grant universities for information about job vacancies.
3. Check the National Job Bank Web site, run by the *Journal of Extension*, for openings nationwide. The URL is jobs.joe.org.
4. Use the Internet to learn more about the Cooperative Extension System. You might start by visiting these Web sites: *Journal of Extension* (www.joe.org) and Extension Collaborative Wiki (collaborate.extension.org). For more links, see Appendix IV.

4-H AGENT

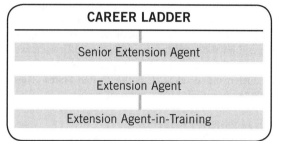

Position Description

In the United States, several million young people, from ages 9 to 19, are participants in a nonformal education program known as 4-H. (The Four H's stand for Head, Heart, Hands, and Health.) The mission of this youth development program is to build leadership and life skills that help girls and boys to become healthy, problem-solving, and successful adults. The 4-H youth development program is administered through the Cooperative Extension System, which is part of the U.S. Department of Agriculture. Each state Cooperative Extension Service (Extension) works in partnership with land-grant universities to develop 4-H educational programs, activities, and projects that are based on research conducted by Extension professionals and university professors.

Extension agents for 4-H, known as 4-H Agents, are responsible for the implementation of the 4-H youth development program in the communities they serve. These professionals are assigned to county and regional Extension field offices. They manage and coordinate different types of nonformal educational programs, including clubs, camps, school enrichment programs, after-school programs, special-interest projects, and child care programs for school-age children. These different types of programs, however, are led and organized by adult and youth volunteer advisers.

The 4-H was established in the early 1900s to serve youth in rural settings. Today, the youth development program meets the needs of young people in urban and suburban communities as well. The 4-H youth development program teaches young people about topics in three basic areas: healthy living; citizenship; and science, engineering, and technology. Through fun, hands-on activities and projects, 4-H participants learn about subject matter that interests them. Raising livestock, training pets, gardening, global positioning system technology, forensic science, rocketry, marine biology, entomology, recycling, photography, crafts, knitting, repairing small engines, computing, fitness, food safety, nutrition, cooking, government systems, and community are among the many subjects that 4-H participants might study.

The 4-H Agents provide leadership and support to Extension paraprofessionals and volunteer advisers, as well as to 4-H youth members and their parents. They work under the supervision of the director of their Extension office. 4-H Agents work collaboratively with Extension colleagues within their field office as well as with Extension professionals at other field offices, research stations, and land-grant universities.

One of the major duties of 4-H Agents is program planning, which involves identifying needs and establishing program priorities. The 4-H Agents conduct assessments as well as monitor trends and issues. These Extension agents also evaluate programs regularly to determine their effectiveness and to seek ways to improve them. The 4-H Agents work closely with Extension colleagues, volunteer 4-H advisers, community advisory boards, and university faculty to develop educational programs that meet the needs of the youth in their particular communities.

The 4-H Agents are also in charge of curriculum development. They plan what will be taught in 4-H programs. For example, they identify learning objectives, outline the concepts and skills to be taught in a session, and decide which teaching method—such as a workshop or demonstration—to use. They also determine what resources are needed for 4-H programs, and develop appropriate educational materials for the projects and activities. It is the agents' job to interpret and integrate research-based information into the educational programs regarding youth development as well as the topics to be taught. Additionally, these educators ensure that their 4-H programs follow Extension guidelines and policies.

Volunteer development is another responsibility of 4-H Agents. They identify and recruit adult and youth volunteers to lead 4-H clubs, camps, and other programs. They train volunteers to conduct 4-H programs and teach them about the content areas through workshops, one-on-one sessions, and online courses. Extension agents provide volunteers with continual support and guidance as they carry out activities, projects, and special events. Additionally, Extension agents monitor the work of volunteers to ensure that they are fulfilling organizational goals and program objectives, as well as complying with policies and appropriate regulations.

Many 4-H Agents also teach youth participants in the different 4-H programs. They might conduct workshops, lead field trips, or instruct youth on an individual basis. These Extension agents also engage in other events involving 4-H participants, such as county fairs, horse shows, livestock judging contests, knowledge bowls, photo exhibitions, poster contests, public speaking competitions, and youth conferences.

The 4-H Agents serve as the liaisons between the Cooperative Extension Service and the community it serves. To ensure the success of the 4-H youth development program in their communities, 4-H Agents build and maintain community support. This includes developing links with schools, civic groups, social agencies, local governments, businesses, other youth groups, and other community organizations.

These Extension professionals perform a wide range of tasks, which vary from day to day. Examples of their duties include:

- planning and carrying out promotional activities to recruit youth participants for 4-H programs
- responding to inquiries about 4-H and Extension activities in person, by phone, by mail, by e-mail, or through Web sites
- preparing information about 4-H activities in such forms as newsletters, press releases, or Web sites
- making presentations about 4-H activities to community groups and other organizations
- planning fund-raising activities
- reading current research information about youth development, teaching techniques, and topics taught in programs
- participating in professional development programs to update skills and knowledge
- preparing required reports and forms
- keeping accurate, complete, and timely records of work activities
- coordinating schedules
- attending meetings

The 4-H youth development is one of several program areas that local Extension offices provide to the public. The other general areas include agriculture, natural resources, family and consumer sciences, and community and economic development. In some field offices, 4-H Agents are also assigned to manage another program area.

The 4-H agents work in comfortable, well-lit offices. Their job requires them to travel throughout their county, district, and state to attend meetings and perform other tasks. The 4-H Agents work a 40-hour week, but may put in additional hours as needed to fulfill their obligations. They often work irregular hours, which may include evenings and weekends.

Salaries

Salaries for Extension agents vary, depending on such factors as their education, experience, job duties, and geographic location. According to the May 2008 Occupational Employment Statistics survey by the U.S. Bureau of Labor Statistics, the estimated annual salary for most farm and home management advisers, including 4-H Agents, ranged between $21,700 and $70,610.

Employment Prospects

The 4-H youth development programs are found in every county of all 50 states, as well as in the District of Columbia, on U.S. military installations worldwide, and in the U.S. territories.

Openings for 4-H Agents usually become available as professionals retire or transfer to others jobs or career fields.

Extension agent positions are sometimes lost when county field offices combine resources due to lack of funds. In some offices, Extension agents are hired to oversee more than one program area.

Advancement Prospects

The 4-H Agents may be promoted to supervisory and managerial positions, but opportunities are limited. Many agents measure success through job satisfaction, by earning higher salaries, and by gaining professional reputations.

With advanced degrees, Extension agents can seek positions as Extension specialists or as faculty members with land-grant universities.

Education and Training

Depending on the employer, candidates for 4-H Agents must possess a bachelor's or master's degree. Employers generally accept a degree in any discipline. Many employers, however, prefer to hire applicants who have a degree or have completed course work in youth development, education, or similar fields.

New Extension Agents undergo a comprehensive training and development program during their first year of employment to learn the basic skills and knowledge required for their job. They complete in-service training programs as well as receive on-the-job training while working under the guidance of experienced Extension agents

Throughout their careers, Extension Agents pursue continuing education to upgrade their skills, gain new knowledge, and keep up with developments in their fields.

Experience, Special Skills, and Personality Traits

Employers hire candidates for entry-level positions who have one or more years of experience working with the Cooperative Extension Service. They may have gained their experience through a combination of internships, employment, or volunteer work. Employ-

ers also prefer to hire 4-H Agent candidates who have experience with working in nonprofit youth development programs and managing volunteers in program delivery and development.

To perform their duties effectively, 4-H Agents need strong leadership, teaching, organizational, management, problem-solving, and teamwork skills. These professionals must also have excellent self-management skills, including the ability to prioritize multiple tasks, meet deadlines, handle stressful situations, and work independently. Furthermore, communication, interpersonal, and customer service skills are essential, as 4-H Agents must work well with youth, parents, volunteers, colleagues, community leaders, and others from diverse backgrounds.

Some personality traits that successful 4-H Agents share include being enthusiastic, patient, tactful, dependable, goal-oriented, determined, creative, resourceful, innovative, and flexible.

Unions and Associations

Many Extension agents join professional associations to take advantage of networking opportunities, continuing education, and other professional services and resources. Some national societies that serve their interests are the National Association of Extension 4-H Agents, the National Association of County Agricultural Agents, the National Extension Association of Family and Consumer Sciences, and Epsilon Sigma Phi. For contact information to these organizations, see Appendix II.

Tips for Entry

1. Are you still in high school? Participate in a 4-H program. Many 4-H Agents were involved in 4-H while still in school.
2. Gain leadership and teaching experience by volunteering to be a 4-H program adviser.
3. Employers who require applicants to have master's degrees sometimes hire persons with bachelor's degrees. Usually, the agents must earn their master's degree within a certain number of years.
4. Learn more about 4-H and 4-H Agents on the Internet. You might start by visiting the 4-H Web site (4-h.org); the National 4-H Headquarters Web site (www.national4-hheadquarters.gov); and the National Association of Extension 4-H Agents Web site (www.nae4ha.org). For more links, see Appendix IV.

AGRICULTURAL JOURNALIST

CAREER PROFILE

Duties: Provide objective and unbiased news reports about agricultural events, issues, and other topics; perform other duties as required

Alternate Title(s): Newspaper Reporter, TV Reporter, Staff Writer, Editor, Photographer, or another title that reflects a specific occupation

Salary Range: $17,000 to $156,000

Employment Prospects: Fair

Advancement Prospects: Fair

Prerequisites:

Education or Training—Bachelor's degree in journalism or another related field; on-the-job training

Experience—Publishing or broadcasting experience usually required

Special Skills and Personality Traits—Writing, research, proofreading, computer, communication,

CAREER LADDER

Senior Agricultural Journalist

Agricultural Journalist

Journalist Trainee

interpersonal, teamwork, problem-solving, and self-management skills; friendly, curious, quick-witted, composed, trustworthy, ethical, resourceful, detail-oriented, persistent, unbiased, and adaptable personality traits

Position Description

Journalists report on breaking news as well as write in-depth features about particular events, persons, places, issues, or trends. Their job is to inform and educate their audiences, who may be newspaper or magazine readers, radio listeners, or television viewers. Some journalists specialize in particular subjects. Those men and women who focus on reporting about topics in the areas of agriculture, food, and natural resources are known as Agricultural Journalists. They provide agricultural producers, agribusiness investors, consumers, and others with stories about market prices, crop conditions, commodities trading trends, farmers and growers, agricultural conferences, food processors, agricultural legislation, technology innovations, agricultural science developments, food recalls, food safety, nutrition, wildlife conservation, environmental sustainability, pet or livestock care, and ecotourism, among many other subjects. Agricultural Journalists may work on stories that take place locally, nationally, or worldwide.

Agricultural Journalists work in different types of media, which may publish or broadcast on a daily, weekly, or monthly basis. Print journalists are employed by newspapers and magazines, while broadcast journalists are hired by radio and television stations. Online journalists work for news services and other companies that publish text, audio, or video content on the World Wide Web. Agricultural Journalists may work specifically for agricultural media or for media that serve general audiences.

Producing news stories for print, online, and broadcast media involves different types of journalists, of which reporters are the most familiar. They are responsible for collecting and assembling accurate facts and details to write news and feature articles that engage their readers or viewers. Agricultural reporters write about scientific and technical news in terms that readers or viewers can easily understand. Reporters may work alone or with other journalists on an assignment.

Much of their job involves gathering information about a story. They observe events firsthand. They interview people who are involved in a story as well as subject-matter experts. Reporters also obtain information from pertinent materials such as public records, company reports, contract specifications, research papers, policy statements, and press releases from reliable sources. Many also seek information from electronic databases and the Internet. Some reporters take their own photographs or videotapes to accompany their stories.

Reporters analyze, interpret, and organize their notes to formulate their stories. They compose stories that explain what happened; who was involved; and when, where, how, and why it happened. Unless they are specifically writing an opinion piece, reporters may not express their personal views about a topic. They are required to present their news or feature stories objectively and without bias.

Most television news reporters are called news correspondents or on-the-scene reporters. They present their stories on news broadcasts live or videotaped. These broadcast journalists integrate both copy and video together to create a visual report of their stories, which are usually two to three minutes long. News analysts are also broadcast journalists. They are more commonly known as newscasters or news anchors. Along with researching and writing news stories, anchors present news stories during broadcast programs. They also introduce videotaped stories and live transmissions from news correspondents. On occasion, anchors write and make commentaries on important issues.

Some Agricultural Journalists are photographers or photojournalists. They use still or video cameras to create images to report news stories. These professionals compose images with their cameras so that they fairly and accurately depict news events. Photographs may run alone or accompany news or feature articles.

Other Agricultural Journalists are editors who work closely with reporters and photographers to help them develop and craft their stories appropriately for publication or broadcast. Some major duties of editors include identifying newsworthy stories; developing story ideas; assigning reporters and photographers to stories; verifying facts and details for accuracy; and revising or rewriting stories for content, tone, language, readability, and length. Editors also make sure stories conform to editorial policies publishing styles and formats. Print and online editors may be involved in designing and laying out pages. Managing editors at print and online publications sometimes write editorials or opinion columns on critical issues that affect their audiences.

Not all Agricultural Journalists are employed as staff members on newspapers, magazines, online news services, or broadcast stations. Some are freelance reporters, photographers, and editors. They work on a contractual basis for different print, online, or broadcast media. In addition to completing their journalist duties, freelancers perform various administrative tasks to ensure the success of their businesses. For example, they pay bills and taxes, invoice clients for their fees, do bookkeeping, plan work schedules, and maintain office supplies and equipment. Freelancers also set aside time to generate future jobs.

Agricultural Journalists' jobs are fast-paced and demanding. They meet strict deadlines. It is not unusual to have only a few hours to research, write, and edit stories for publication or broadcast. Reporters and photographers constantly travel to observe events and interview sources. They also go to libraries, public offices, and other locations to look up information. Editors perform their duties in busy newsrooms.

Agricultural Journalists work varying hours, which may include early mornings, nights, weekends, and holidays. Some professionals work day or evening shifts. Freelance journalists determine their own work schedules.

Salaries

Salaries for Agricultural Journalists vary, depending on such factors as their education, experience, occupation, employer, and geographic location. Specific salary information for these professionals is unavailable. The U.S. Bureau of Labor Statistics reported the following estimated salary ranges for most of these media workers in its May 2008 Occupational Employment Statistics survey:

- reporters and correspondents: $20,180 to $77,480
- broadcast news analysts: $23,470 to $156,200
- photographers: $16,920 to $62,430
- editors: $28,090 to $95,490

Employment Prospects

In addition to print, online, and broadcast media outlets, Agricultural Journalists are employed by news services run by academic institutions and government agencies. They also find employment with professional and trade associations, farm bureaus, farmers' associations, and other agricultural organizations that publish print or online media. With their background and skills, Agricultural Journalists can find work as communications specialists with agribusinesses, nonprofit or nongovernmental agricultural groups, government agencies (such as the U.S. Department of Agriculture), agricultural colleges and universities, nonprofit organizations, and other organizations. Some Agricultural Journalists are self-employed.

Job competition for both entry-level and experienced positions is keen. Staff positions usually become available when journalists advance to higher positions, transfer to other jobs or careers, retire, or leave the workforce for various reasons. Employers create additional positions to meet the growing needs of their organizations, as long as funds are available.

Some experts in the field express that journalists with agricultural knowledge or backgrounds have more opportunities for obtaining staff or freelance jobs with agricultural-based publications and broadcasting companies.

Advancement Prospects

As Agricultural Journalists gain experience, they earn higher pay and receive assignments that are more difficult. They also advance according to their own interests and ambitions. Some seek positions at specific companies. Some move from smaller media companies to larger ones. Others become columnists, news analysts, news anchors, talk show hosts, managing editors, broadcast producers, news bureau directors, book authors, or online publishers, for example. Some journalists switch to teaching careers and become high school journalism teachers or college journalism or communications professors.

Education and Training

Agricultural Journalists possess at least a bachelor's degree in journalism, communications, English, or another related field.

Several academic universities in the United States offer a bachelor's degree program in agricultural journalism or in agricultural communications and journalism. The program offers students the opportunity to develop journalism skills as well as acquire an agricultural background in such areas as animal science, plant science, and agricultural economics.

Novice journalists receive on-the-job training while working under the direction and supervision of editors and senior journalists.

Throughout their careers, Agricultural Journalists enroll in continuing education programs to update their skills and knowledge.

Experience, Special Skills, and Personality Traits

Employers prefer to hire applicants for entry-level positions who have one or more years of publishing or broadcasting experience. They may have gained their practical experience through internships, fellowships, employment, or freelance work. Working in staff positions on college newspapers or radio or TV broadcast stations is also acceptable experience to many employers. Agricultural Journalists must also be familiar about the agricultural subjects and issues about which they would be hired to report.

Along with having excellent writing and research skills, Agricultural Journalists need strong proofreading and computer skills. They also must have effective communication, interpersonal, teamwork, problem-solving, and self-management skills. Being friendly, curious, quick-witted, composed, trustworthy, ethical, resourceful, detail-oriented, persistent, unbiased, and adaptable are some personality traits that successful Agricultural Journalists have in common.

Unions and Associations

Agricultural Journalists may join professional associations to take advantage of networking opportunities, continuing education, and other professional services and resources. Some of the different national societies that serve the diverse interests of these journalists include:

- American Agricultural Editors' Association
- American Society of Journalists and Authors (open to all freelance reporters)
- Association of Food Journalists
- International Federation of Agricultural Journalists
- Investigative Reporters and Editors
- National Association of Broadcasters
- National Press Photographers Association
- North American Agricultural Journalists
- Online News Association
- Radio Television Digital News Association
- Society of Environmental Journalists
- Society of Professional Journalists

For contact information to these organizations, see Appendix II.

Tips for Entry

1. If you plan to be a newspaper reporter, obtain basic photography skills. If you are going to be a television reporter, learn how to operate a TV camera.
2. Be willing to relocate, as well as to work in small communities, to obtain your first job.
3. Contact your professors, colleagues, past supervisors and coworkers, and others for job referrals.
4. Before going to a job interview, learn as much as you can about the media company. For instance: Who is its audience? What agricultural subjects and issues is it currently covering? What major stories has it covered in the past?
5. Use the Internet to learn more about journalism, and agriculture journalism in particular. You might start by visiting CubReporters.org, the International Federation of Agricultural Journalists Web site (www.ifaj.org), and the Agricultural Communicators of Tomorrow Web site (nact-now.org). For more links, see Appendix IV.

COMMUNICATIONS SPECIALIST

Duties: Promote an organization's activities and accomplishments to the public; develop publicity programs and materials; perform other duties as required

Alternate Title(s): Public Relations Specialist, or another title that reflects a specific job

Salary Range: $30,000 to $98,000

Employment Prospects: Good

Advancement Prospects: Fair

Prerequisites:

Education or Training—Bachelor's degree in agricultural communications or a related field

Experience—One or more years of agricultural communications experience preferred

Special Skills and Personality Traits—Writing, editing, interviewing, research, computer, team-

work, self-management, decision-making, problem-solving, organizational, communication, and interpersonal skills; creative, inquisitive, persuasive, tactful, diplomatic, credible, resourceful, detail-oriented, and self-motivated personality traits

CAREER LADDER

Senior Communications Specialist

Communications Specialist

Assistant Communications Specialist

Position Description

The success of businesses, nonprofit groups, government agencies, and all other organizations depend on the support of the people whom they seek to serve with their products and services. Many organizations hire Communications Specialists to build and maintain favorable relationships with their customers as well as with the public and the media.

These professionals develop and implement public relations techniques, strategies, and programs to protect an organization's reputation. Their job is not only to promote public goodwill for the organization, but also reinforce its credibility among the organization's employees and supporters (such as investors or boards of directors). Additionally, these communications professionals strengthen relations within an organization's industry, with local communities, and with the government at all levels. Furthermore, Communications Specialists manage damage control of an organization's public image during critical situations, such as when a company recalls defective products or an agency cuts programs because of lack of funds.

Agricultural Communications Specialists work specifically with organizations that are involved in the areas of agriculture, food, and natural resources, including agricultural production, horticulture, forestry, food processing and distribution, natural resources management, scientific research, marketing,

technologies, legislation, education, and international trade, among other diverse fields. They may work in private, government, academic, or other settings. For example, an agricultural communications professional might work for:

- a nongovernmental organization that encourages agricultural growers, hobby gardeners, and others to use sustainable practices
- a manufacturer that produces agricultural machinery and equipment
- a trade association that promotes and protects the interests of its industry
- an agricultural school that conducts research programs and offers different fields of study to undergraduates and graduates
- a government agency that regulates food safety
- an organization that develops overseas markets for wheat, rice, and other grains

Some agricultural Communications Specialists are hired to staff positions at the different organizations. Others are employed by public relations and marketing firms that offer agricultural communications services on a contractual basis.

Agricultural Communications Specialists usually have experience or training in the fields in which they work. For example, specialists who work in the dairy industry are knowledgeable about the different aspects of dairy farm operations. Communications Specialists maintain a thorough understanding of their employer's (or client's) business—its goals and objectives, its organizational structure, all of its products and services, the markets it serves, and so on. These professionals are also familiar with the different types of agricultural print, broadcast, and online media as well as farm shows, trade conferences, the Internet, organizational publications, and other informational sources that are available.

Communications Specialists are responsible for planning and producing various types of informational materials about the activities and accomplishments of an organization and the issues and trends that may affect the organization's customers or employees. They are also involved in writing, editing, and producing such communications as press releases, magazine articles, radio reports, video scripts, reports, speeches, and promotional materials. They may also prepare copy for Web sites or be in charge of building and maintaining Web sites.

Communications of all kinds are created to educate and inform either external or internal (in-house) audiences. These specialists first research the subject about which they are writing. They observe events, interview sources, and read relevant materials. They then analyze and interpret their notes to prepare clear, accurate, and comprehensive communications. They write technical concepts in language that nontechnical persons can understand. Communications Specialists make sure that all communications are distributed on a timely basis.

Many Communications Specialists serve as media contacts for their organizations. They establish and maintain relationships with both agricultural and general media that serve local, regional, national, and international markets. These specialists put together press kits to provide journalists with information about which to write. They also follow up with the different media to make sure that the coverage about their organizations is favorable.

Communications Specialists perform many other duties, which vary according to their experience, skills, and position. For example, they might be assigned such tasks as:

- advising managers and executives of organizations on effective communications strategies
- administering budgets
- evaluating the effectiveness of public relations programs
- assisting with developing marketing plans
- making presentations about their organizations at trade shows, conferences, and community events

- keeping mailing and e-mail lists up to date, including media contacts, newsletter subscribers, and others
- responding to inquiries that customers, the media, and others may have about an organization

Communications Specialists work in busy office environments. They are under pressure to handle multiple tasks and to meet strict deadlines. They generally work 40 hours a week, but put in additional hours as needed to complete assignments. They sometimes travel to other cities and states to attend meetings, conferences, and events.

Salaries

Salaries for Communications Specialists vary, depending on such factors as their education, experience, job duties, employer, and geographic location. Specific salary information for Communications Specialists in the agricultural industries is unavailable. Their earnings are similar to public relations specialists. The estimated annual salary for most of these specialists ranged between $30,140 and $97,910, according to the May 2008 Occupational Employment Statistics survey by the U.S. Bureau of Labor Statistics (BLS).

Employment Prospects

Agricultural Communications Specialists find employment in both the public and private sectors. These professionals find employment with government agencies as well as with nonprofit and nongovernmental groups that serve the agriculture, fiber, food, natural resources, and related segments of the economy. These include farm bureaus, farmers' associations, professional and trade associations, conservation organizations, food safety programs, agricultural education programs, and public interest groups, among others.

In the private sector, Communications Specialists find employment with agricultural producers, commodity trading firms, farm equipment manufacturers, food processors, timber companies, seed companies, agricultural suppliers, agricultural insurance firms, agricultural media, agricultural biotechnology companies, and many other types of companies. These specialists also work for public relations, marketing, and advertising firms that offer agricultural communications services on a contractual basis. In addition, agricultural schools employ Communications Specialists to promote their academic and research programs.

Job openings for Communications Specialists become available as employees transfer to other jobs or careers, advance to higher positions, or retire. Competition is strong, particularly for entry-level positions.

According to the BLS, employment of public relations specialists, overall, is expected to increase by 24 percent through 2018.

According to some experts in the field, opportunities for qualified Communications Specialists with agricultural backgrounds are favorable. The number of jobs in agricultural communications has been increasing in recent years.

Advancement Prospects

Communications Specialists advance according to their own interests and ambitions. Those interested in supervisory and managerial positions can pursue such opportunities. Entrepreneurial individuals can establish their own consulting firms. With advanced degrees, Communications Specialists can pursue careers as college professors.

Education and Training

Minimally, agricultural Communications Specialists must possess a bachelor's degree in agricultural communications, journalism, marketing, public relations, or another related field. Some employers seek specialists who hold at least a master's degree, preferably in agricultural communications or agricultural journalism. Employers may require that candidates have completed course work in the area (such as animal science) in which they would work.

Novice Communications Specialists undergo on-the-job training while working under experienced staff. Some employers provide formal instruction as well. Throughout their careers, Communications Specialists enroll in continuing education to update their skills and knowledge.

Experience, Special Skills, and Personality Traits

Employers typically hire applicants for entry-level positions who have one or more years of experience in agricultural communications. They may have gained their experience through internships, employment, and volunteer work. Employers also prefer to hire candidates who are knowledgeable about the subject matter in which they would work.

Communications Specialists must have excellent writing, editing, interviewing, research, and computer skills to perform well at their work. They also need strong teamwork, self-management, decision-making, problem-solving, and organizational skills. In addition, they need effective communication and interpersonal skills to work well with colleagues, clients, and others. Some personality traits that successful Communications Specialists share include being creative, inquisitive, persuasive, tactful, diplomatic, credible, resourceful, detail-oriented, and self-motivated.

Unions and Associations

Communications Specialists can join professional associations to take advantage of networking opportunities, professional certification, and other services and resources. Some national societies that serve the interests of these professionals are:

- Agricultural Relations Council
- American Agricultural Editors' Association
- Association for Communication Excellence
- Cooperative Communicators Association
- International Association of Business Communicators
- Livestock Publications Council
- Public Relations Society of America
- Turf and Ornamental Communicators Association

For contact information to these organizations, see Appendix II.

Tips for Entry

1. While in college, participate in student organizations, such as the Agricultural Communicators of Tomorrow, to develop professional skills.
2. Maintain a portfolio of your best work, such as press releases, articles, photographs, brochures, and radio scripts, to show to prospective employers.
3. Contact organizations directly about internships and job opportunities.
4. Use the Internet to learn more about communications. You might start by visiting the Web sites of these organizations: the Public Relations Society of America (www.prsa.org) and the Agricultural Communicators of Tomorrow (nactnow.org). For more links, see Appendix IV.

APPENDIXES

APPENDIX I
EDUCATION AND TRAINING RESOURCES ON THE INTERNET

In this appendix, you will find World Wide Web sources for educational programs pertaining to some of the occupations in this book. To learn about programs for other occupations, talk with school or career counselors as well as with professionals in the fields that interest you. You can also look up schools in college directories, which may be found in your school or public library.

Note: All Web site addresses were current at the time this book was written. If a URL is no longer valid, enter the title of the Web site or the name of the organization or individual into a search engine to find the new URL.

PAYING FOR YOUR EDUCATION
Scholarships, grants, student loans, and other financial aid programs are available to help you pay for your post-secondary education. These programs are sponsored by government agencies, professional and trade associations, unions, private foundations, businesses, and other organizations. (You can find contact information for many professional associations in Appendix II.)

To learn more about financial assistance programs, talk with your high school guidance counselor or college career counselor. Also, consult school catalogs, as they usually include financial aid information. In addition, visit or contact the financial aid office at the college or technical school that you plan to attend or are attending now. Lastly, check out these Web sites for financial aid information:

- FinAid! The Smart Student Guide to Financial Aid (www.finaid.org)
- Student Aid on the Web, U.S. Department of Education Federal Student Aid (studentaid.ed.gov)

GENERAL RESOURCES
The following Web sites provide links to various academic and training programs at postsecondary schools in the United States.

- Peterson's: www.petersons.com
- U.S. College Search: www.uscollegesearch.org

- Web U.S. Higher Education (maintained by the University of Texas at Austin): www.utexas.edu/world/univ

AGRICULTURAL COMMUNICATIONS AND AGRICULTURAL JOURNALISM
The Agricultural, Consumer, and Environmental Sciences College at the University of Illinois in Urbana provides a list of institutions that offer agricultural communications and journalism programs. This is part of the Agriculture Network Information Center (AgNic). The list can be found at www.library.illinois.edu/funkaces/agnic/agcom/info.php?id=31.

The Directory of Science Communication Courses and Programs Web site is a database of universities in the United States that offer undergraduate and graduate communications programs. These programs prepare students to report and write about science topics, such as agriculture, food science, and the environment. This Web site is a project of the School of Journalism and Mass Communication at the University of Wisconsin–Madison. The URL is dsc.journalism.wisc.edu/index.html.

AGRICULTURAL ECONOMICS
The Agricultural and Applied Economics Association (www.aaea.org) has a listing of universities in the U. S. and Canada that have programs or departments in agricultural and applied economics. The Web page is at www.aaea.org/outreach/programs.php.

AGRICULTURAL EDUCATION AND TEACHER EDUCATION
The National Association of Agricultural Educators (www.naae.org) has a listing of colleges and universities in the United States that offer agricultural education programs. This information can be found at www.naae.org/teachag.

The National Council for Accreditation of Teacher Education provides a listing of colleges and universities that offer teacher education programs that meet national standards for preparing teachers and school specialists. This organization's URL is www.ncate.org.

The National Center for Alternative Certification provides information about becoming certified schoolteachers through means other than completing teacher education programs. Its URL is www.teach-now.org.

AGRICULTURAL ENGINEERING, BIOLOGICAL ENGINEERING, AND BIOSYSTEMS ENGINEERING

The American Society of Agricultural and Biological Engineers (www.asabe.org) provides a listing of educational programs in agricultural and biological engineering fields in the United States and other countries. This information can be found at www.asabe.org/membership/students/edprogrm.htm.

AGRICULTURE

Land-grant institutions are designated to receive federal funds to teach agriculture, conduct agricultural research, and provide nonformal educational programs to the public. All 50 states have at least one land-grant college or university. Land-grant institutions are granted their status by either a state legislature or Congress. For a list of institutions, visit the following Web sites:

- Association of Public and Land-Grant Universities: www.aplu.org
- Epsilon Sigma Phi: www.espnational.com
- National Institute of Food and Agriculture (NIFA): www.nifa.usda.gov

ANIMAL BEHAVIOR

The Animal Behavior Society (www.animalbehavior.org) has a listing of institutions that offer undergraduate and graduate programs in animal behavior. This information can be found at www.animalbehavior.org/ABSEducation/programs-in-animal-behavior.

AQUACULTURE

The World Aquaculture Society (www.was.org) has a database of colleges and universities that offer associate's, bachelor's, master's, and doctoral programs in aquaculture or related fields. It lists programs in the United States as well as in other countries. This information can be found at www.was.org/Training/TrainingUniversity.asp?index=a.

ARBORICULTURE AND RELATED FIELDS

The International Society of Arboriculture (www.isa-arbor.com) provides a listing of academic programs in arboriculture and arboriculture-related fields such as forest technology, urban forestry, and landscape horticulture. This information can be found at www.isa-arbor.com/students/degreeSearch.aspx.

CEREAL SCIENCE

AACC International (www.aaccnet.org) provides a list of universities in the United States and Canada that offer graduate degrees in cereal science or in food science with an emphasis in cereal science. This information can be found at www.aaccnet.org/membership/careers brochure.asp#UniversityCerealSciencePrograms.

CRIMINAL JUSTICE, LAW ENFORCEMENT, AND RELATED FIELDS

The American Society of Criminology (www.asc41.com) provides information about some academic programs in criminal justice, criminology, and related fields at the following Web pages:

- Undergraduate programs: www.asc41.com/Crim-CJ_Programs/UNDERGRAD.html
- Graduate programs: www.asc41.com/Crim-CJ_Programs/GRADLINKS.html

The Association of National Park Rangers (www.anpr.org) provides information about the Seasonal Law Enforcement Training Program for seasonal rangers with the U.S. National Park Service. This information can be found at www.anpr.org/academies.htm.

CULINARY ARTS AND CULINOLOGY

The following two Web sites provide information about culinary schools in the United States that offer college degrees and professional certificates:

- Culinary-Careers.org: www.culinary-careers.org
- Culinary Ed: www.culinaryed.com

The Research Chefs Association (www.culinology.com) maintains a listing of accredited schools in the United States that offer Culinology degree programs. This information can be found at www.culinology.com/culinology-degree-programs.

ENGINEERING AND ENGINEERING TECHNOLOGY

The following Web sites provide information about academic programs for different engineering and engineering technology fields:

- ABET, Inc.: www.abet.org

- TryEngineering.org: www.tryengineering.org
- Engineering Education Service Center: www.engineeringedu.com

ENOLOGY AND VITICULTURE

The American Society for Enology and Viticulture (asev.org) has a list of academic institutions in the United States, as well as worldwide, that have programs in enology, viticulture, or related fields. This information can be found at asev.org/links.

ENTOMOLOGY

The Entomological Society of America (www.entsoc.org) provides data about college and universities in North America that offer entomology or entomology-related degrees. This information can be found at www.entsoc.org/resources/education/colleges.htm.

ENVIRONMENTAL SCIENCE, ENVIRONMENTAL STUDIES, AND RELATED FIELDS

The EnviroEducation.com Web site has a database of colleges and universities in the United States that offer degree programs in environmental science, environmental studies, and such related fields as wildlife ecology, conservation biology, and fisheries management. This information can be found at www.enviroeducation.com.

EPIDEMIOLOGY

The World-Wide Virtual Library: Epidemiology Web site provides a list of universities in the United States and worldwide that offer programs in epidemiology or related fields. This information can be found at www.epibiostat.ucsf.edu/epidem/epidem.html#UNI.

FLORAL DESIGN AND FLORICULTURE

The Society of American Florists (www.safnow.org) lists schools that offer degree and certificate programs in floral design, floriculture, and horticulture in its *Careers in Floriculture: Catalog of Schools*. This catalog is available online at www.safnow.org/content/category/6/60/108.

FOOD SCIENCE AND FOOD TECHNOLOGY

The Institute of Food Technologists (www.ift.org) provides a listing of schools that have food science and technology departments or programs. The following information can be found at these Web pages:

- Undergraduate programs: www.ift.org/cms/?pid=1000426
- Graduate programs: www.ift.org/cms/?pid=1000624

FOREST ENGINEERING

The Council on Forest Engineering (www.cofe.org) has a listing of schools in forest engineering and related fields at its Web site. This information can be found at www.cofe.org/index_files/Page395.htm.

FORESTRY, SILVICULTURE, AND FORESTRY TECHNOLOGY

The Society of American Foresters (www.safnet.org) provides listings of accredited professional forestry and forest technology degree programs. This information can be found at www.safnet.org/education/accreditation.cfm.

LANDSCAPE ARCHITECTURE

The American Society of Landscape Architects (www.asla.org) provides a database of academic institutions that have accredited programs in landscape architecture. This information can be found at www.asla.org/schools.aspx.

LANDSCAPE DESIGN

The Association of Professional Landscape Designers (www.apld.com) has a database of academic programs in landscape design. This information can be found at www.apld.com/education/for_students.asp.

NATURAL RESOURCES MANAGEMENT

The EnviroEducation.com Web site provides a listing of academic institutions that offer programs in natural resources management. This information can be found at www.enviroeducation.com.

PARK INTERPRETATION

The National Association for Interpretation (www.interpnet.com) provides a listing of schools that offer interpretive courses and programs that prepare students for careers as park naturalists and other interpretive-related occupations. This information can be found at www.interpnet.com/resources_interp/schools.shtml.

PILOT TRAINING

The Aircraft Owners and Pilots Association (www.aopa.org) offers a database of flight schools in the United

States. This information can be found at www.aopa.org/learntofly/school/index.cfm.

PLANT BIOLOGY
The American Society of Plant Biologists (www.aspb.org) provides a list of colleges and universities that offer master's and doctoral programs in plant biology. This information can be found at www.aspb.org/education/graduate.cfm?CFID=10459715&CFTOKEN=90092664.

PLANT PATHOLOGY
The American Phytopathological Society (www.apsnet.org) provides a list of colleges and universities that offer academic programs in plant pathology or related fields. This information can be found at www.apsnet.org/directories/uprogs.asp.

POULTRY SCIENCE
The Careers in Poultry Web site (www.poultrycareers.org) provide a list of universities that offer poultry science degree programs. This information can be found at www.poultrycareers.org/ucontacts.asp.

RANGE MANAGEMENT
The Society for Range Management (www.rangelands.org) provides a listing of academic institutions that offer programs or courses in range management. This information can be found at www.rangelands.org/education_universities.shtml.

TOXICOLOGY
The Society of Toxicology (www.toxicology.org) has an online version of its *Resource Guide to Careers in Toxicology*, which lists academic and postdoctoral programs in toxicology. This database can be accessed at www.toxicology.org/ai/apt/careerprograms.asp.

VETERINARY MEDICINE
The American Veterinary Medicine Association (www.avma.org) provides a database of veterinary colleges that are accredited by this organization's Council on Education. This database can be found at www.avma.org/education/cvea/colleges_accredited/colleges_accredited.asp.

The Association of American Veterinary Medical Colleges (www.aavmc.org) has a listing of veterinary medical schools and colleges in the United States and Canada, as well as in other countries. This information can be found at www.aavmc.org/students_admissions/vet_schools.htm.

VETERINARY PATHOLOGY
The American College of Veterinary Pathologists (www.acvp.org) provides a list of veterinary pathology programs and residencies at www.acvp.org/career/training_center.php.

VETERINARY TECHNOLOGY
The American Veterinary Medicine Association (www.avma.org) provides a database of veterinary colleges that are accredited by this organization's Committee on Veterinary Technician Education and Activities. This database can be found at www.avma.org/education/cvea/vettech_programs/vettech_programs.asp.

WETLAND SCIENCE
The Society of Wetlands Science (www.sws.org) has a listing of institutions that offer academic programs in wetland science and related fields. This information can be found at www.sws.org/colleges.

WILDERNESS FIREFIGHTING
Wildlandfire.com has a listing of training and educational programs for wildland firefighters. This information can be found at www.wildlandfire.com/links.htm#edu.

APPENDIX II
PROFESSIONAL UNIONS AND ASSOCIATIONS

This appendix provides information about the various professional, trade, and other organizations that were mentioned in this book. You can contact these organizations, or visit their Web sites, to learn more about careers, job opportunities, training programs, conferences, professional certification, and other topics. Many of these organizations have student chapters. Most have branch offices throughout the United States. Contact an organization's headquarters to find out if a branch is in your area.

To learn about other local, state, regional, and national professional organizations, talk with local professionals.

Note: Web site addresses change from time to time. If you come across an address that no longer works, you may be able to find an organization's new URL by entering its name into a search engine.

FARMING

American Pastured Poultry Producers Association
P.O. Box 87
Boyd, WI 54726
Phone: (888) 662-7772
http://www.apppa.org

American Poultry Association
P.O. Box 306
Burgettstown, PA 15021
Phone: (724) 729-3459
http://www.amerpoultryassn.com

Dairy Farmers of America
10220 North Ambassador Drive
Kansas City, MO 64153
Phone: (816) 801-6455 or
    (888) DFA-MILK
http://www.dfamilk.com

National Chicken Council
1015 15th Street NW
Suite 930
Washington, DC 20005
Phone: (202) 296-2622
Fax: (202) 293-4005
http://www.nationalchickencouncil.
    com

National Turkey Federation
1225 New York Avenue NW
Suite 400
Washington, DC 20005
Phone: (202) 898-0100
Fax: (202) 898-0203
http://www.eatturkey.com

Organic Trade Association
60 Wells Street
Greenfield, MA 01301
Phone: (413) 774-7511
Fax: (413) 774-6432
http://www.ota.com

U.S. Poultry and Egg Association
1530 Cooledge Road
Tucker, GA 30084
Phone: (770) 493-9401
Fax: (770) 493-9257
http://www.poultryegg.org

FARMING—SUPPORT STAFF

American Farm Bureau
600 Maryland Avenue SW
Suite 1000W
Washington, DC 20024
Phone: (202) 406-3600
Fax: (202) 406-3602
http://www.fb.org

American Society for Enology and Viticulture
1784 Picasso Avenue
Suite D
Davis, CA 95618
Mailing address:
P.O. Box 1855
Davix, CA 95617
Phone: (530) 753-3142
Fax: (530) 753-3318
http://asev.org

American Society for Horticultural Science
1018 Duke Street
Alexandria, VA 22314
Phone: (703) 836-4606
Fax: (703) 836-2024
http://www.ashs.org

American Society of Farm Managers and Rural Appraisers
950 South Cherry Street
Suite 508
Denver, CO 80246
Phone: (303) 758-3513
Fax: (303) 758-0190
http://portal.asfmra.org

International Plant Propagator's Society
4 Hawthorn Court
Carlisle, PA 17015
Phone: (717) 243-7685
Fax: (717) 243-7691
http://www.ipps.org

National Cattlemen's Beef Association
9110 East Nichols Avenue
Suite 300
Centennial, CO 80112
Phone: (303) 694-0305
http://www.beef.org

United Farmworkers
P.O. Box 62
29700 Woodford-Tehachapi Road
Keene, CA 93531
Phone: (661) 823-6250
http://www.ufw.org

Working Ranch Cowboys Association
P.O. Box 7765
Amarillo, TX 79114
Phone: (806) 374-9722
http://www.wrca.org

FISHERIES AND COMMERCIAL FISHING

American Fisheries Society
5410 Grosvenor Lane
Bethesda, MD 20814
Phone: (301) 897-8616
Fax: (301) 897-8096
http://www.fisheries.org

American Institute of Fishery Research Biologists
http://www.aifrb.org

American Society of Ichthyologists and Herpetologists
http://www.asih.org

American Tilapia Association
P.O. Box 1647
Pine Bluff, AR 71613
Phone: (870) 850-7900
Fax: (870) 850-7902
http://ag.arizona.edu/azaqua/ata. html

Commercial Fishermen of America
991 Marine Drive
San Francisco, CA 94129

Mailing address:
P.O. Box 29196
San Francisco, CA 94129
Phone: (415) 561-FISH, ext. 222
Fax: (415) 561-5464
http://www.cfafish.org

Global Aquaculture Alliance
5661 Telegraph Road
Suite 3A
St. Louis, MO 63129
Phone: (314) 293-5500
Fax: (314) 293-5525
http://www.gaalliance.org

National Aquaculture Association
P.O. Box 1647
Pine Bluff, AR 71613
Phone: (870) 850-7900
Fax: (870) 850-7902
http://www.thenaa.net

National Shellfisheries Association
http://shellfish.org

Small Boat Commercial Salmon Fishermens' Association
http://www.sbcsfa.com

Striped Bass Growers Association
P.O. Box 1647
Pine Bluff, AR 71613
Phone: (870) 850-7900
Fax: (870) 850-7902
http://www.stripedbassgrowers.org

United States Freshwater Prawn and Shrimp Growers Association
655 Napanee Road
Leland, MS 38756
Phone: (662) 686-2894 or (662) 390-3528
http://www.freshwaterprawn.org

United States Trout Farmers Association
P.O. Box 1647
Pine Bluff, AR 71613

Phone: (870) 850-7900
Fax: (870) 850-7902
http://www.ustfa.org

World Aquaculture Society
143 J. M. Parker Coliseum
Louisiana State University
Baton Rouge, LA 70803
Phone: (225) 578-3137
Fax: (225) 578-3493
http://www.was.org

FOREST PRODUCTION AND MANAGEMENT

American Society of Agricultural and Biological Engineers
2950 Niles Road
St. Joseph, MI 49085
Phone: (269) 429-0300
Fax: (269) 429-3852
http://www.asabe.org

Association of Consulting Foresters of America
312 Montgomery Street
Suite 208
Alexandria, VA 22314
Phone: (703) 548-0990
http://www.acf-foresters.org

Council on Forest Engineering
620 SW 4th Street
Corvallis, OR 97333
Phone: (541) 754-7558
Fax: (541) 754-7559
http://www.cofe.org

Federal Wildland Fire Service Association
P.O. Box 517
Inkom, ID 83245
Phone: (208) 775-4577
http://www.fwfsa.org

Forest Guild
P.O. Box 519
Santa Fe, NM 87504
Phone: (505) 983-8992
Fax: (505) 986-0798
http://www.forestguild.org

International Association of
  Wildland Fire
3416 Primm Lane
Birmingham, AL 35216
Phone: (888) 440-4293 or
  (205) 824-7614
http://www.iawfonline.org

International Association
  of Women in Fire and
  Emergency Services
4025 Fair Ridge Drive
Suite 300
Fairfax, VA 22033
Phone: (703) 896-4858
Fax: (703) 273-9363
http://www.i-women.org

National Federation of Federal
  Employees
805 15th Street NW
Suite 500
Washington, DC 20005
Phone: (202) 216-4420
Fax: (202) 898-1861
http://www.nffe.org

National Smokejumper
  Association
http://www.smokejumpers.com

National Society of Professional
  Engineers
1420 King Street
Alexandria, VA 22314
Phone: (888) 285-6773 or
  (703) 684-2800
Fax: (703) 836-4875
http://www.nspe.org

Society of American Foresters
5400 Grosvenor Lane
Bethesda, MD 20814
Phone: (866) 897-8720 or
  (301) 897-8720
http://www.safnet.org

Society of Women Engineers
120 South La Salle Street
Suite 1515
Chicago, IL 60603

Phone: (877) SWE-INFO or
  (312) 596-5223
http://scoietyofwomenengineers.
  swe.org

Woodworkers Department,
  International Association of
  Machinists and Aerospace
  Workers
9000 Machinists Place
Upper Marlboro, MD 20772
http://winpisinger.net/content.
  cfm?cID=405

AGRISCIENCE

American Association of
  Professional Apiculturists
Phone: (225) 767-9293
Fax: (225) 766-9212
http://www.masterbeekeeper.org/
  aapa

American Chemical Society
1155 16th Street NW
Washington, DC 20036
Phone: (800) 227-5558 or
  (202) 872-4600
http://portal.acs.org

American Dairy Science
  Association
2441 Village Green Place
Champaign, IL 61822
Phone: (217) 356-5146
Fax: (217) 398-4119
http://www.adsa.org

American Horticultural
  Society
7931 East Boulevard Drive
Alexandria, VA 22308
Phone: (800) 777-7931 or
  (703) 768-5700
Fax: (703) 768-8700
http://www.ahs.org

American Meat Science
  Association
2441 Village Green Place
Champaign, IL 61874
Phone: (800) 517-AMSA
http://www.meatscience.org

American Orchid Society
16700 AOS Lane
Delray Beach, FL 33446
Phone: (561) 404-2000
Fax: (561) 404-2034 or
  (561) 404-2100
http://www.aos.org

American Phytopathological
  Society
3340 Pilot Knob Road
St. Paul, MN 55121
Phone: (651) 454-7250
Fax: (651) 454-0766
http://www.apsnet.org

American Pomological Society
103 Tyson Building
University Park, PA 16802
Fax: (814) 237-3407
http://americanpomological.org

American Society for
  Horticultural Science
1018 Duke Street
Suite 200
Alexandria, VA 22314
Phone: (703) 836-4606
Fax: (703) 836-2024
http://www.ashs.org

American Society for
  Microbiology
1752 N Street NW
Washington, DC 20036
Phone: (202) 737-3600
http://www.asm.org

American Society of
  Agricultural and Biological
  Engineers
2950 Niles Road
St. Joseph, MI 49085
Phone: (269) 429-0300
Fax: (269) 429-3852
http://www.asabe.org

American Society of Agronomy
5585 Guilford Road
Madison, WI 53711
Phone: (608) 273-8080
Fax: (608) 273-2021
https://www.agronomy.org

American Society of Animal
Science
2441 Village Green Place
Champaign, IL 61822
Phone: (217) 356-9050
Fax: (217) 398-4119
http://www.asas.org

American Society of Plant
Biologists
15501 Monona Drive
Rockville, MD 20855
Phone: (301) 251-0560
Fax: (301) 279-2996
http://www.aspb.org

Association of Applied IPM
Ecologists
P.O. Box 1119
Coarsegold, CA 93614
Phone: (559) 761-1064
http://www.aaie.net

Association of Natural
Biocontrol Producers
P.O. Box 1609
Clovis, CA 93613
Phone: (559) 360-7111
Fax: (800) 553-4817
http://www.anbp.org

Association of Natural Resource
Extension Professionals
http://www.anrep.org

Botanical Society of America
P.O. Box 299
St. Louis, MO 63166
Phone: (314) 577-9566
Fax: (314) 577-9515
http://www.botany.org

Council for Agricultural
Science and Technology
Phone: (515) 292-2125
Fax: (515) 292-4512
http://www.cast-science.org

Crop Science Society of
America
5585 Guilford Road
Madison, WI 53711
Phone: (608) 273-8080

Fax: (608) 273-2021
https://www.crops.org

Entomological Society of
America
10001 Derekwood Lane
Suite 100
Lanham, MD 20706
Phone: (301) 731-4535
Fax: (301) 731-4538
http://www.entsoc.org

Equine Science Society
2441 Village Green Place
Champaign, IL 61822
Phone: (217) 356-3182
Fax: (217) 398-4119
http://www.equinescience.org

Genetics Society of America
9650 Rockville Pike
Bethesda, MD 20814
Phone: (866) 486-GENE or
(301) 634-7300
http://www.genetics-gsa.org

Institute of Food Technologists
525 West Van Buren Street
Suite 1000
Chicago, IL 60607
Phone: (800) 438-3663 or
(312) 782-8424
Fax: (312) 782-8348
http://www.ift.org

International Plant
Propagator's Society
4 Hawthorn Court
Carlisle, PA 17015
Phone: (717) 243-7685
Fax: (717) 243-7691
http://www.ipps.org

International Society for
Horticultural Science
http://www.ishs.org

International Society of
Arboriculture
P.O. Box 3129
Champaign, IL 61826
Phone: (217) 355-9411 or
(888) 472-8733
http://www.isa-arbor.com

Lepidopterists' Society
http://www.lepsoc.org

National Association of
Community Development
Extension Professionals
P.O. Box 4033
Bismarck, ND 58502
Phone: (701) 526-3556
http://nacdep.net

National Extension Association
of Family and Consumer
Sciences
14070 Proton Road
Suite 100
LB 9
Dallas, TX 75244
Phone: (972) 371-2570
Fax: (972) 490-4219
http://www.neafcs.org

National Institute for Animal
Agriculture
13570 Meadowgrass Drive
Suite 201
Colorado Springs, CO 80921
Phone: (719) 538-8843
Fax: (719) 538-8847
http://www.animalagriculture.org

National Society of Professional
Engineers
1420 King Street
Alexandria, VA 22314
Phone: (703) 684-2800
Fax: (703) 836-4875
http://www.nspe.org

Potato Association of America
University of Maine
5719 Crossland Hall
Room 220
Orono, ME 04469
Phone: (207) 581-3042
Fax: (207) 581-3015
http://potatoassociation.org

Poultry Science Association
2441 Village Green Place
Champaign, IL 61822
Phone: (217) 356-5285
Fax: (217) 398-4119
http://www.poultryscience.org

Society for Integrative and Comparative Biology
1313 Dolley Madison Boulevard
Suite 402
McLean, VA 22101
Phone: (800) 955-1236 or
(703) 790-1745
Fax: (703) 790-2672
http://www.sicb.org

Soil Science Society of America
5585 Guilford Road
Madison, WI 53711
Phone: (608) 273-8080
Fax: (608) 273-2021
https://www.soils.org

Weed Science Society of America
Phone: (800) 627-0326 ext. 222
http://www.wssa.net

AGRICULTURAL SERVICES

Aircraft Owners and Pilots Association
421 Aviation Way
Frederick, MD 21701
Phone: (800) 872-2672 or
(301) 695-2000
Fax: (301) 695-2375
http://www.aopa.org

American Society of Agricultural Consultants
N78W14573 Appleton Avenue
Suite 287
Menomonee Falls, WI 53051
Phone: (262) 253-6902
Fax: (262) 253-6903
http://www.agconsultants.org

American Society of Farm Managers and Rural Appraisers
950 South Cherry Street
Suite 508
Denver, CO 80246
Phone: (303) 758-3513
Fax: (303) 758-0190
http://www.asfmra.org

California Farm Labor Contractors' Alliance
http://www.caflca.net

Farmers Market Coalition
P.O. Box 4089
Martinsburg, WV 25402
http://www.farmersmarketcoalition.org

Grain Elevator and Processing Society
4248 Park Glen Road
Minneapolis, MN 55416
Phone: (952) 928-4640
Fax: (952) 929-1318
http://www.geaps.com

Institute of Management Consultants USA
2025 M Street NW
Suite 800
Washington, DC 20036
Phone: (202) 367-1134
http://www.imcusa.org

National Agricultural Aviation Association
1005 E Street SE
Washington, DC 20003
Phone: (202) 546-5722
Fax: (202) 546-5726
http://www.agaviation.org

National Alliance of Independent Crop Consultants
349 East Nolley Drive
Collierville, TN 38017
Phone: (901) 861-0511
Fax: (901) 861-0512
http://www.naicc.org

National Auctioneers Association
8880 Ballentine
Overland Park, KS 66214
Phone: (913) 541-8084
Fax: (913) 894-5281
http://www.auctioneers.org

National Society of Consulting Soil Scientists
P.O. Box 1219
Sandpoint, ID 83864

Phone: (800) 535-7148
Fax: (208) 263-7013
http://www.nscss.org

North American Farmers' Direct Marketing Association
62 White Loaf Road
Southampton, MA 01073
Phone: (888) 884-9270 or
(413) 529-0386
Fax: (413) 529-9101
http://www.nafdma.com

AGRIBUSINESS

Agricultural and Applied Economics Association
555 East Wells Street
Suite 1100
Milwaukee, WI 53202
Phone: (414) 918-3190
Fax: (414) 276-3349
http://www.aaea.org

American Bankers Association
1120 Connecticut Avenue NW
Washington, DC 20036
Phone: (800) 226-5377
http://www.aba.com

American Economic Association
2014 Broadway
Suite 305
Nashville, TN 37203
Phone: (615) 322-2595
Fax: (615) 343-7590
http://www.vanderbilt.edu/AEA

American Marketing Association
311 South Wacker Drive
Suite 5800
Chicago, IL 60606
Phone: (800) AMA-1150 or
(312) 542-9000
Fax: (312) 542-9001
http://www.marketingpower.com

American Society of Agricultural Appraisers
1126 Eastland Drive North
Suite 100
P.O. Box 186

Twin Falls, ID 83303
Phone: (800) 488-7570
Fax: (208) 733-2326
http://www.amagappraisers.com

American Society of Appraisers
555 Herndon Parkway
Suite 125
Herndon, VA 20170
Phone: (800) 272-8258 or
   (703) 478-2228
http://www.appraisers.org

**American Society of Equine
Appraisers**
1126 Eastland Drive North
Suite 100
P.O. Box 186
Twin Falls, ID 83303
Phone: (800) 704-7020
Fax: (208) 733-2326
http://www.equineappraiser.com

**American Society of Farm
Equipment Appraisers**
1126 Eastland Drive North
Suite 100
P.O. Box 186
Twin Falls, ID 83303
Phone: (800) 488-7570 or
   (208) 733-2323
Fax: (208) 733-2326
http://www.amagappraisers.com/
farmeqip.htm

**American Society of Farm
Managers and Rural
Appraisers**
950 South Cherry Street
Suite 508
Denver, CO 80246-2664
Phone: (303) 758-3513
Fax: (303) 758-0190
http://www.asfmra.org

**Association of Environmental
and Resource Economists**
1616 P Street NW
Suite 600
Washington, DC 20036
Phone: (202) 328-5125
Fax: (202) 939-3460
http://www.aere.org

**Commodity Floor Brokers and
Traders Association**
One North End Avenue
Box 204
New York, NY 10282
http://www.cfbta.org

**International Association of
Agricultural Economists**
555 East Wells Street
Suite 1100
Milwaukee, WI 53202
Phone: (414) 918-3199
Fax: (414) 276-3349
http://www.iaae-agecon.org

**International Society of
Livestock Appraisers**
1126 Eastland Drive North
Suite 100
P.O. Box 186
Twin Falls, ID 83303
Phone: (800) 488-7570 or
   (208) 733-2323
Fax: (208) 733-2326
http://www.amagappraisers.com/
livestok.htm

**Mortgage Bankers
Association**
1331 L Street NW
Washington, DC 20005
Phone: (202) 557-2700
http://www.mbaa.org

**National Agri-Marketing
Association**
11020 King Street
Suite 205
Overland Park, KS 66210
Phone: (913) 491-6500
Fax: (913) 491-6502
http://www.nama.org

**National Association
of Independent Fee
Appraisers**
401 North Michigan Avenue
Suite 2200
Chicago, IL 60611
Phone: (312) 321-6830
Fax: (312) 673-6652
http://www.naifa.com

National Futures Association
300 South Riverside Plaza
Suite 1800
Chicago, IL 60606
Phone: (312) 781-1300
Fax: (312) 781-1467
http://www.nfa.futures.org

**National Introducing Brokers
Association**
55 West Monroe Street
Suite 3330
Chicago, IL 60603
Phone: (312) 977-0598
Fax: (312) 977-0121
http://www.theniba.com

USDA Economists Group
http://www.usdaeconomists.org

FOOD AND BEVERAGE
INDUSTRIES

AACC International
3340 Pilot Knob Road
St. Paul, MN 55121
Phone: (651) 454-7250
Fax: (651) 454-0766
http://www.aaccnet.org

American Bakers Association
1300 I Street NW
Suite 700 West
Washington, DC 20005
Phone: (202) 789-0300
Fax: (202) 898-1164
http://www.americanbakers.org

**American Culinary
Federation**
180 Center Place Way
St. Augustine, FL 32095
Phone: (800) 624-9458 or
   (904) 824-4468
Fax: (904) 825-4758
http://www.acfchefs.org

**American Institute of
Chemical Engineers**
3 Park Avenue
New York, NY 10016
Phone: (800) 242-4363 or
   (203) 702-7660

Fax: (203) 775-5177
http://www.aiche.org

American Federation of Government Employees
80 F Street NW
Washington, DC 20001
Phone: (202) 737-8700
http://www.afge.org

American Public Health Association
800 I Street NW
Washington, DC 20001-3710
Phone: (202) 777-2742
Fax: (202) 777-2534
http://www.apha.org

American Society for Enology and Viticulture
1784 Picasso Avenue
Suite D
Davis, CA 95618
Mailing address:
P.O. Box 1855
Davis, CA 95617
Phone: (530) 753-3142
Fax: (530) 753-3318
http://asev.org

American Society for Microbiology
1752 N Street NW
Washington, DC 20036
Phone: (202) 737-3600
http://www.asm.org

American Society for Quality
600 North Plankinton Avenue
Milwaukee, WI 53203
Mailing address:
P.O. Box 3005
Milwaukee, WI 53201
Phone: (800) 248-1946 or
   (414) 272-8575
Fax: (414) 272-1734
http://www.asq.org

American Society of Agricultural and Biological Engineers
2950 Niles Road
St. Joseph, MI 49085

Phone: (269) 429-0300
Fax: (269) 429-3852
http://www.asabe.org

Bakery, Confectionery, Tobacco Workers, and Grain Millers International Union
http://www.bctgm.org

Bread Bakers Guild of America
670 West Napa Street
Suite B
Sonoma, CA 95476
Phone: (707) 935-1468
Fax: (707) 935-1672
http://www.bbga.org

Independent Bakers Association
P.O. Box 3731
Washington, DC 20007
Phone: (202) 333-8190
Fax: (202) 337-3809
http://www.mindspring.com/
   ~independentbaker

Independent Food Brokers Division
National Association for Retail
   Marketing Services
2417 Post Road
Stevens Point, WI 54481
Phone: (715) 342-0948
Fax: (715) 342-1943
http://www.narms.com/about/
   division-ifba

Institute of Food Technologists
525 West Van Buren Street
Suite 1000
Chicago, IL 60607
Phone: (800) 438-3663 or
   (312) 782-8424
Fax: (312) 782-8348
http://www.ift.org

International Association for Food Protection
6200 Aurora Avenue
Suite 200W
Des Moines, IA 50322
Phone: (800) 369-6337 or
   (515) 276-3344

Fax: (515) 276-8655
http://www.foodprotection.org

International Association of Culinary Professionals
1100 Johnson Ferry Road
Suite 300
Atlanta, GA 30342
Phone: (800) 928-4227 or
   (404) 252-3663
http://www.iacp.com

International Society of Food Engineering
Biological Systems Engineering
Washington State University
Pullman, WA 99164
Phone: (509) 335-6188
Fax: (509) 335-2722
http://www.iufost.org/isfe

National Environmental Health Association
720 South Colorado Boulevard
Suite 1000-N
Denver, CO 80246
Phone: (303) 756-9090
Fax: (303) 691-9490
http://www.neha.org

National Society of Professional Engineers
1420 King Street
Alexandria, VA 22314
Phone: (703) 684-2800
Fax: (703) 836-4875
http://www.nspe.org

Research Chefs Association
100 Johnson Ferry Road
Suite 300
Atlanta, GA 30342
Phone: (404) 252-3663
Fax: (404) 252-0774
http://www.culinology.org

Society of Flavor Chemists
3301 Route 66
Suite 205, Building C
Neptune, NJ 07753
Phone: (732) 922-3393
Fax: (732) 922-3590
http://www.flavorchemist.org

United Food and Commercial
Workers International Union
http://www.ufcw.org

FLORAL, GARDENING, AND LANDSCAPING SERVICES

American Horticultural Society
7931 East Boulevard Drive
Alexandria, VA 22308
Phone: (800) 777-7931 or
  (703) 768-5700
Fax: (703) 768-8700
http://www.ahs.org

**American Institute of Floral
  Designers**
720 Light Street
Baltimore, MD 21230
Phone: (410) 752-3318
Fax: (410) 752-8295
http://www.aifd.org

**American Nursery and
  Landscape Association**
1000 Vermont Avenue NW
Suite 300
Washington, DC 20005
Phone: (202) 789-2900
Fax: (202) 789-1893
http://www.anla.org

**American Society of
  Consulting Arborists**
9707 Key West Avenue
Suite 100
Rockville, MD 20850
Phone: (301) 947-0483
Fax: (301) 990-9771
http://www.asca-consultants.org

**American Society of Landscape
  Architects**
636 I Street NW
Washington, DC 20001
Phone: (202) 898-2444
Fax: (202) 898-1185
http://www.asla.org

**Association of Professional
  Landscape Designers**
4305 North Sixth Street
Suite A

Harrisburg, PA 17110
Phone: (717) 238-9780
Fax: (717) 238-9985
http://www.apld.com

**Ecological Landscaping
  Association**
1257 Worcester Road
Suite 262
Framingham, MA 01701
Phone: (617) 436-5838
http://www.ecolanscaping.org

**Golf Course Superintendents
  Association of America**
1421 Research Park Drive
Lawrence, KS 66049
Phone: (800) 472-7878 or
  (785) 841-2240
http://www.gcsaa.org

**International Society of
  Arboriculture**
P.O. Box 3129
Champaign, IL 61826
Phone: (888) 472-8733 or
  (217) 355-9411
http://www.isa-arbor.com

Plantscape Industry Alliance
493 South Highland Avenue
Ukiah, CA 95482
Phone: (707) 462-2276
Fax: (707) 463-6699
http://www.piagrows.org

**Professional Grounds
  Management Society**
720 Light Street
Baltimore, MD 21230
Phone: (410) 223-2861
Fax: (410) 752-8295
http://www.pgms.org

**Professional Landcare
  Network**
950 Herndon Parkway
Suite 450
Herndon, VA 20170
Phone: (800) 395-2522 or
  (703) 736-9666
Fax: (703) 736-9668
http://www.landcarenetwork.org

Society of American Florists
1601 Duke Street
Alexandria, VA 22314
Phone: (703) 836-8700
Fax: (703) 836-8705
http://www.safnow.org

**Society of Commercial
  Arboriculture**
P.O. Box 3129
Champaign, IL 61826
http://sca.isa-arbor.com

Society of Municipal Arborists
http://www.urban-forestry.com

Utility Arborist Association
P.O. Box 3129
Champaign, IL 61826
Phone: (217) 355-9411, ext. 234
Fax: (217) 355-9516
http://www.utilityarborist.org

PET AND ANIMAL SERVICES

**American College of Veterinary
  Behaviorists**
College of Veterinary Medicine
4474 TAMU
Texas A&M University
College Station, TX 77843
http://www.veterinarybehaviorists.
  org

**American Pet Products
  Association**
255 Glenville Road
Greenwich, CT 06831
Phone: (800) 452-1225 or
  (203) 532-0000
Fax: (203) 532-0551
http://americanpetproducts.org

**American Veterinary Society of
  Animal Behavior**
http://www.avsabonline.org

**Applied Animal Behavior
  Section**
Animal Behavior Society
Indiana University
402 North Park Avenue

Bloomington, IN 47408
Phone: (812) 856-5541
Fax: (812) 856-5542
http://www.animalbehavior.org/
ABSAppliedBehavior

Association of Companion Animal Behavior Counselors
P.O. Box 104
Seville, FL 32190
http://animalbehaviorcounselors.org

Association of Pet Dog Trainers
101 North Main Street
Suite 610
Greenville, SC 29615
Phone: (800) PET-DOGS
http://www.apdt.com

Association of Professional Animal Waste Specialists
P.O. Box 2325
Santa Clarita, CA 91386
http://www.apaws.org

International Association of Animal Behavior Consultants
565 Callery Road
Cranberry Township, PA 16066
http://www.iaabc.org

International Association of Canine Professionals
P.O. Box 560156
Montverde, FL 34756
Phone: (877) THE-IACP or
(407) 469-2008
http://www.dogpro.org

International Marine Animal Trainers' Association
1200 South Lake Shore Drive
Chicago, IL 60605
Phone: (312) 692-3193
Fax: (312) 939-2216
http://www.imata.org

National Animal Control Association
101 North Church Street
Suite C
Olathe, KS 66061

Mailing address:
P.O. Box 480851
Kansas City, MO 64148
Phone: (913) 768-1319
Fax: (913) 768-1378
http://www.nacanet.org

National Association of Animal Behaviorists
http://www.animalbehaviorists.org

National Association of Professional Pet Sitters
15000 Commerce Parkway
Suite C
Mount Laurel, NJ 08054
Phone: (856) 439-0324
Fax: (856) 439-0525
http://www.petsitters.org

National Dog Groomers Association of America
P.O. Box 101
Clark, PA 16113
Phone: (724) 962-2711
Fax: (724) 962-1919
http://www.nationaldoggroomers.
com

Pet Care Services Association
2760 North Academy Boulevard
Suite 120
Colorado Springs, CO 80917
Phone: (877) 570-7788 or
(719) 667-1600
Fax: (719) 667-0116
http://www.petcareservices.org

Pet Industry Joint Advisory Council
1220 19th Street NW
Suite 400
Washington, DC 20036
Phone: (800) 553-7387 or
(202) 452-1525
Fax: (202) 293-4377
http://www.pijac.org

VETERINARY MEDICINE

Academy of Rural Veterinarians
1450 Western Avenue
Suite 101

Albany, NY 12203
Phone: (518) 694-0056
Fax: (518) 463-8656
http://www.ruralvets.com

Academy of Veterinary Emergency and Critical Care Technicians
http://avecct.org

Academy of Veterinary Technician Anesthetists
http://www.avta-vts.org

American Association for Laboratory Animal Science
9190 Crestwyn Hills Drive
Memphis, TN 38125
Phone: (901) 754-8620
Fax: (901) 753-0046
http://www.aalas.org

American Association of Housecall and Mobile Veterinarians
http://www.housecallvets.org

American Association of Swine Veterinarians
830 26th Street
Perry, IA 50220
Phone: (515) 465-5255
Fax: (515) 465-3832
http://www.aasv.org

American Association of Veterinary Parasitologists
http://www.aavp.org

American College of Veterinary Pathologists
2810 Crossroads Drive
Suite 3800
Madison, WI 53718
Phone: (608) 443-2466
http://www.acvp.org

American College of Veterinary Surgeons
19785 Crystal Rock Drive
Suite 305
Germantown, MD 20874
Phone: (877) 217-2287 or
(301) 916-0200

Fax: (301) 916-2287
http://www.acvs.org

American Veterinary Dental Society

P.O. Box 803
Fayetteville, TN 37334
Phone: (800) 332-AVDS or
    (931) 438-0238
Fax: (931) 433-6289
http://www.avds-online.org

American Veterinary Medical Association

1931 North Meacham Road
Suite 100
Schaumburg, IL 60173
Phone: (800) 248-2862
Fax: (847) 925-1329
http://www.avma.org

Association of Avian Veterinarians

P.O. Box 811720
Boca Raton, FL 33481
Phone: (561) 393-8901
http://www.aav.org

Association of Shelter Veterinarians

P.O. Box 26007
Lakewood, CO 80226
http://www.sheltervet.org

Association of Zoo Veterinary Technicians

http://www.azvt.org

National Association of Veterinary Technicians in America

50 South Pickett Street
Suite 110
Alexandria, VA 22304
Phone: (703) 740-8737
Fax: (202) 449-8560
http://www.navta.net

Society of Toxicologic Pathology

1821 Michael Faraday Drive
Suite 300
Reston, VA 20190

Phone: (703) 438-7508
Fax: (703) 438-3113
http://www.toxpath.org

Society of Veterinary Behavior Technicians

http://www.svbt.org

NATURAL RESOURCES MANAGEMENT AND CONSERVATION

American College of Toxicology

9650 Rockville Pike
Bethesda, MD 20814
Phone: (301) 634-7840
Fax: (301) 634-7852
http://www.actox.org

Association of State Wetland Managers

2 Basin Road
Windham, ME 04062
Phone: (207) 892-3399
Fax: (207) 892-3089
http://www.aswm.org

Federal Law Enforcement Officers Association

P.O. Box 326
Lewisberry, PA 17339
Phone: (717) 938-2300
Fax: (717) 932-2262
http://www.fleoa.org

Federal Wildlife Officers Association

http://www.fwoa.org

International Wildlife Rehabilitation Council

P.O. Box 8187
San Jose, CA 95155
Phone: (866) 871-1869 or
    (408) 876-6153
http://www.iwrc-online.org

National Society of Consulting Soil Scientists

P.O. Box 1219
Sandpoint, ID 83864
Phone: (800) 535-7148

Fax: (208) 263-7013
http://www.nscss.org

National Wildlife Rehabilitators Association

2625 Clearwater Road
Suite 110
St. Cloud, MN 56301
Phone: (320) 230-9920
Fax: (320) 230-3077
http://www.nwrawildlife.org

North American Wildlife Enforcement Officers Association

http://www.naweoa.org

Society for Range Management

10030 West 27th Avenue
Wheat Ridge, CO 80215
Phone: (303) 986-3309
Fax: (303) 986-3892
http://www.rangelands.org

Society of Environmental Toxicology and Chemistry

1010 North 12th Avenue
Pensacola, FL 32501
Phone: (850) 469-1500
Fax: (850) 469-9778
http://www.setac.org

Society of Toxicology

1821 Michael Faraday Drive
Suite 300
Reston, VA 20190
Phone: (703) 438-3115
Fax: (703) 438-3113
http://www.toxicology.org

Society of Wetland Scientists

1313 Dolley Madison Boulevard
Suite 402
McLean, VA 22101
Phone: (703) 790-1745
Fax: (703) 790-2672
http://www.sws.org

Soil and Water Conservation Society

945 Southwest Ankeny Road
Ankeny, IA 50023
Phone: (515) 289-2331

Fax: (515) 289-1227
http://www.swcs.org

Soil Science Society of America
5585 Guilford Road
Madison, WI 53711
Phone: (608) 273-8080
Fax: (608) 273-2021
https://www.soils.org

TRAVEL, TOURISM, AND RECREATION

Association of National Park Rangers
http://www.anpr.org

International Ecotourism Society
P.O. Box 96503
Number 34145
Washington, DC 20090
Phone: (202) 506-5033
Fax: (202) 789-7279
http://www.ecotourism.org

National Association for Interpretation
P.O. Box 2246
Fort Collins, CO 80522
Phone: (888) 900-8283 or
    (970) 484-8283
Fax: (970) 484-8179
http://www.interpnet.com

National Recreation and Park Association
22377 Belmont Ridge Road
Ashburn, VA 20148
Phone: (800) 626-NRPA
http://www.nrpa.org

North American Farmers' Direct Marketing Association
62 White Loaf Road
Southampton, MA 01073
Phone: (888) 884-9270 or
    (413) 529-0386
Fax: (413) 529-9101
http://www.nafdma.com

United States Tour Operators Association
275 Madison Avenue
Suite 2014
New York, NY 10016
Phone: (212) 599-6599
Fax: (212) 599-6744
http://ustoa.com

EDUCATION AND COMMUNICATIONS

Agricultural Relations Council
http://www.agrelationscouncil.org

American Agricultural Editors' Association
P.O. Box 156
New Prague, MN 56071
Phone: (952) 758-6502
Fax: (952) 758-5813
http://www.ageditors.com

American Association for Agricultural Education
http://aaaeonline.org

American Association of University Professors
1133 19th Street NW
Suite 200
Washington, DC 20036
Phone: (202) 737-5900
Fax: (202) 737-5526
http://www.aaup.org

American Federation of Teachers
555 New Jersey Avenue NW
Washington, DC 20001
Phone: (202) 879-4400
http://www.aft.org

American Society of Agricultural and Biological Engineers
2950 Niles Road
St. Joseph, MI 49085
Phone: (269) 429-0300
Fax: (269) 429-3852
http://www.asabe.org

American Society of Agronomy
5585 Guilford Road

Madison, WI 53711
Phone: (608) 273-8080
Fax: (608) 273-2021
https://www.agronomy.org

American Society of Animal Science
2441 Village Green Place
Champaign, IL 61822
Phone: (217) 356-9050
Fax: (217) 398-4119
http://www.asas.org

American Society of Journalists and Authors
1501 Broadway
Suite 302
New York, NY 10036
Phone: (212) 997-0947
Fax: (212) 937-2315
http://www.asja.org

American Society of Plant Biologists
15501 Monona Drive
Rockville, MD 20855
Phone: (301) 251-0560
Fax: (301) 279-2996
http://www.aspb.org

Association for Career and Technical Education
1410 King Street
Alexandria, VA 22314
Phone: (703) 683-3111 or
    (800) 826-9972
Fax: (703) 683-7424
http://www.acteonline.org

Association for Communication Excellence
P.O. Box 3948
Parker, CO 80134
Phone: (866) 941-3048
http://www.aceweb.org

Association of Food Journalists
http://www.afjonline.com

Association of Natural Resource Extension Professionals
http://anrep.org

Cooperative Communicators Association
174 Crestview Drive
Bellefonte, PA 16823
Phone: (877) 326-5994
Fax: (814) 355-2452
http://www.communicators.coop

Entomological Society of America
10001 Derekwood Lane
Suite 100
Lanham, MD 20706
Phone: (301) 731-4535
Fax: (301) 731-4538
http://www.entsoc.org

Epsilon Sigma Phi
450 Falls Avenue
Suite 106
Twin Falls, ID 83301
Phone: (208) 736-4495
Fax: (208) 736-1916
http://espnational.org

Institute of Food Technologists
525 West Van Buren Street
Suite 1000
Chicago, IL 60607
Phone: (800) 438-3663 or
(312) 782-8424
Fax: (312) 782-8348
http://www.ift.org

International Association of Business Communicators
601 Montgomery Street
Suite 1900
San Francisco, CA 94111
Phone: (800) 776-4222 or
(415) 544-4700
Fax: (415) 544-4747
http://www.iabc.com

International Federation of Agricultural Journalists
http://www.ifaj.org

Investigative Reporters and Editors
141 Neff Annex
University of Missouri
Columbia, MO 65211

Phone: (573) 882-2772
Fax: (573) 882-5431
http://www.ire.org

Livestock Publications Council
910 Currie Street
Fort Worth, TX 76107
Phone: (817) 336-1130
Fax: (817) 232-4820
http://www.livestockpublications.
com

National Association of Agricultural Educators
300 Garrigus Building
University of Kentucky
Lexington, KY 40546
Phone: (800) 509-0204 or
(859) 257-2224
http://www.naae.org

National Association of Broadcasters
1771 N Street NW
Washington, DC 20036
Phone: (202) 429-5300
http://www.nab.org

National Association of Community Development Extension Professionals
http://srdc.msstate.edu/nacdep

National Association of County Agricultural Agents
6584 West Duroc Road
Maroa, IL 61756
Phone: (217) 794-3700
Fax: (217) 794-5901
http://www.nacaa.com

National Association of Extension 4-H Agents
20423 State Road
Suite F6-491
Boca Raton, FL 33498
Phone: (561) 477-8100
http://www.nae4ha.com

National Association of Scholars
1 Airport Place
Suite 7
Princeton, NJ 08540

Phone: (609) 683-7878
http://www.nas.org

National Education Association
1201 16th Street NW
Washington, DC 20036
Phone: (202) 833-4000
http://www.nea.org

National Extension Association of Family and Consumer Sciences
14070 Proton Road
Suite 100, LB 9
Dallas, TX 75244
Phone: (972) 371-2570
Fax: (972) 490-4219
http://www.neafcs.org

National Press Photographers Association
3200 Croasdaile Drive
Suite 306
Durham, NC 27705
Phone: (919) 383-7246
Fax: (919) 383-7261
http://www.nppa.org

North American Agricultural Journalists
http://www.naaj.net

North American Colleges and Teachers of Agriculture
http://www.nactateachers.org

Online News Association
http://journalists.org

Poultry Science Association
2441 Village Green Place
Champaign, IL 61822
Phone: (217) 356-5285
Fax: (217) 398-4119
http://www.poultryscience.org

Public Relations Society of America
33 Maiden Lane
11th Floor
New York, NY 10038
Phone: (212) 460-1400
http://www.prsa.org

Radio Television Digital News Association
529 14th Street NW
Suite 425
Washington, DC 20045
Mailing address:
4121 Plank Road
Suite 512
Fredericksburg, VA 22407
Phone: (202) 659-6510
Fax: (202) 223-4007
http://www.rtnda.org

Society of American Foresters
5400 Grosvenor Lane
Bethesda, MD 20814
Phone: (866) 897-8720 or
    (301) 897-8720
http://www.safnet.org

Society of Environmental Journalists
P.O. Box 2492
Jenkintown, PA 19046
Phone: (215) 884-8174
Fax: (215) 884-8175
http://www.sej.org

Society of Professional Journalists
3909 North Meridian Street
Indianapolis, IN 46208
Phone: (317) 927-8000
Fax: (317) 920-4789
http://www.spj.org

Turf and Ornamental Communicators Association
120 West Main Street

P.O. Box 156
New Prague, MN 56071
Phone: (952) 758-6340
Fax: (952) 758-5813
http://www.toca.org

World Aquaculture Society
143 J. M. Parker Coliseum
Louisiana State University
Baton Rouge, LA 70803
Phone: (225) 578-3137
Fax: (225) 578-3493
http://www.was.org

APPENDIX III
U.S. DEPARTMENTS AND AGENCIES ON THE INTERNET

In this appendix, you will learn about federal agencies that deal with the wide range of issues concerning agricultural production, food safety, and natural resources conservation and management. These agencies are involved in enforcing laws, establishing national safety standards, administering grants, conducting scientific research, developing information resources and tools for the public, and more. You may have come across some of these agencies while reading about the occupations in this book.

Note: All URLs were current when this book was written. If you come across a URL that no longer works, enter the name of the agency into a search engine to get its new address.

DEPARTMENT OF AGRICULTURE (USDA)

The Department of Agriculture was established in 1862 by President Abraham Lincoln to help farmers and growers. Today, the agency has several mission areas, including farm and foreign agricultural services; food safety; food, nutrition, and consumer services; marketing and regulatory programs; rural development; and research, education, and economics. The department's URL is http://www.usda.gov. Some of the agencies within this department include:

- Agricultural Marketing Service (AMS): http://www.ams.usda.gov
- Agricultural Research Service (ARS): http://www.ars.usda.gov
- Animal and Plant Health Inspection Service (APHIS): http://www.aphis.usda.gov
- Economic Research Service (ERS): http://www.ers.usda.gov
- Farm Service Agency (FSA): http://www.fsa.usda.gov
- Food and Nutrition Service (FNS): http://www.fns.usda.gov
- Food Safety and Inspection Service (FSIS): http://www.fsis.usda.go
- Foreign Agricultural Service: http://www.fas.usda.gov

- Forest Service: http://www.fs.fed.us
- Grain Inspection, Packers, and Stockyards Administration: http://www.gipsa.usda.gov
- National Agricultural Library (NAL): http://www.nal.usda.gov
- National Agricultural Statistics Service: http://www.nass.usda.gov
- National Institute of Food and Agriculture (formerly the Cooperative State Research, Education, and Extension Service): http://www.nifa.usda.gov
- Natural Resources Conservation Service (NRCS), http://www.nrcs.usda.gov

DEPARTMENT OF COMMERCE

The Department of Commerce is responsible for advancing and serving businesses within the United States as well as promoting and developing trade with other countries. The department's URL is http://www.commerce.gov. Some agencies within this department that are especially pertinent to agriculture include:

- Census Bureau: http://www.census.gov
- International Trade Administration (ITA): http://www.trade.gov
- National Institute of Standards and Technology (NIST): http://www.nist.gov
- National Oceanic and Atmospheric Administration (NOAA): http://www.noaa.gov
- NOAA National Marine Fisheries Service (NOAA Fisheries Service): http://www.nmfs.noaa.gov
- National Weather Service (NWS): http://www.nws.noaa.gov

DEPARTMENT OF DEFENSE (DoD)

The Department of Defense is responsible for supervising and coordinating all functions and activities related directly to the military and the national security. The department's URL is http://www.defense.gov.

The Army Corps of Engineers is an agency within the U.S. Army that builds and maintains infrastructure for the military in both times of war and peace. This agency also oversees the design, construction, and operation of national public works, infrastructure, and recreational areas. In addition, the agency supports and manages various programs to protect and restore ecosystems on national lands as well as on former military installations. Both civilian and military personnel work for the Army Corps of Engineers. Its URL is http://www.usace.army.mil.

DEPARTMENT OF HEALTH AND HUMAN SERVICES (HHS)

The Department of Health and Human Services is responsible for protecting the health of all Americans as well as providing essential human services to people who need assistance. The department's URL is http://www.hhs.gov. Some agencies within this department that are especially pertinent to agriculture include:

- Agency for Toxic Substances and Disease Registry; http://www.atsdr.cdc.gov
- Centers for Disease Control and Prevention (CDC): http://www.cdc.gov
- Food and Drug Administration (FDA): http://www.fda.gov
- National Institutes of Health (NIH): http://www.nih.gov
- U.S. Public Health Service Commissioned Corps: http://www.usphs.gov

DEPARTMENT OF HOMELAND SECURITY (DHS)

The Department of Homeland Security is responsible for national security within the borders of the United States. The department's URL is http://www.dhs.gov. Some agencies within this department that are especially pertinent to agriculture include:

- Customs and Border Protection (CBP): http://www.cbp.gov
- Federal Law Enforcement Training Center (FLETC): http://www.fletc.gov
- Federal Emergency Management Agency (FEMA): http://www.fema.gov
- Immigration and Customs Enforcement (ICE): http://www.ice.gov
- U.S. Coast Guard (USCG): http://www.uscg.mil

DEPARTMENT OF THE INTERIOR (DOI)

The Department of the Interior is responsible for the protection and management of the United States' natural resources and cultural heritage. The department's URL is http://www.doi.gov. Some agencies within this department that are especially pertinent to agriculture include:

- Bureau of Indian Affairs (BIA): http://www.bia.gov
- Bureau of Land Management (BLM): http://www.blm.gov
- Bureau of Reclamation: http://www.usbr.gov
- National Park Service (NPS): http://www.nps.gov
- U.S. Fish and Wildlife Service (USFWS): http://www.fws.gov
- U.S. Geological Survey (USGS): http://www.usgs.gov

DEPARTMENT OF LABOR (DOL)

The Department of Labor is responsible for promoting the welfare of American workers. It develops and oversees programs that help people find employment, and enforce federal laws and regulations regarding wages, working conditions, occupational safety, employment discrimination, and other labor issues. The department's URL is http://www.dol.gov. Some agencies within this department that are especially pertinent to workers in agriculture include:

- Bureau of Labor Statistics (BLS): http://www.bls.gov
- Employment and Training Administration (ETA): http://www.doleta.gov
- Occupational Safety and Health Administration (OSHA): http://www.osha.gov

INDEPENDENT AGENCIES AND COMMISSIONS

The following federal organizations also address various agricultural and agricultural-related issues. They are some of the independent agencies and commissions that assist with running of the federal government as well as the national economy.

- Commodity Futures Trading Commission (CFTC): http://www.cftc.gov
- Consumer Product Safety Commission (CPSC): http://www.cpsc.gov
- Environmental Protection Agency (EPA): http://www.epa.gov
- Federal Maritime Commission (FMC): http://www.fmc.gov
- Small Business Administration (SBA): http://www.sba.gov

APPENDIX IV
RESOURCES ON THE WORLD WIDE WEB

In this appendix, you will find a list of Web sites that can help you learn more about the occupations that were profiled in this book. In addition, you will find some Web resources that offer career and job search information.

Note: All Web site addresses were current at the time this book was written. If a URL is no longer valid, enter the Web page title or the name of the organization or individual into a search engine to find the new address.

CAREER AND JOB INFORMATION

AgCareers.com
http://www.agcareers.com

Agricultural Career Guide
Vocational Information Center
http://www.khake.com/page39.html

Backdoorjobs.com: Short-term Job Adventures
http://www.backdoorjobs.com

Careers in Food.com
http://www.careersinfood.com

Careers in Forestry and Natural Resources
http://www.forestrycareers.org

Environmental Career Opportunities
http://www.ecojobs.com

Making the Difference
http://www.makingthedifference.org

O*NET OnLine
http://online.onetcenter.org

The Land Lovers
http://www.thelandlovers.org

USA Jobs—The Federal Government's Official Job Site
http://www.usajobs.opm.gov

U.S. Bureau of Labor Statistics: Occupational Employment Statistics
http://www.bls.gov/oes

U.S. Bureau of Labor Statistics: Occupational Outlook Handbook
http://www.bls.gov/oco

USDA Living Science
http://www.agriculture.purdue.edu/USDA/careers/index.html

AGRICULTURE GENERAL INFORMATION

Agriculture Network Information Center
http://www.agnic.org

AgriNet
Agricultural Program, Texas A&M University
http://agrinet.tamu.edu

AgriSeek
http://www.agriseek.com

Agsites.net: The Outdoor World, Agriculture and Weather Information Directory
http://www.agsites.net

American Farm Bureau
http://www.fb.org

American Farmland Trust
http://www.farmland.org

eXtension
Cooperative Extension System
http://www.extension.org

National Association of State Departments of Agriculture
http://www.nasda.org

USA.gov: Environment and Natural Resources
http://www.usa.gov/Citizen/Topics/Environment_Agriculture/Environment.shtml

USDA Rural Development
http://www.rurdev.usda.gov

U.S. Department of Agriculture
http://www.usda.gov

WWW Virtual Library: Agriculture
http://cipm.ncsu.edu/agVL

AGRICULTURAL CONSULTANT

Business.com: Agricultural Consultants Information
http://www.business.com/directory/agriculture/consultants

The Outdoor World Directory:
Agricultural Consultants
http://www.agsites.net/links/
agriculturalconsultants.html

AGRICULTURAL ECONOMIST

Council on Food, Agricultural
and Resource Economics
http://www.cfare.org

RFE: Resources for Economists
on the Internet
http://rfe.org

USDA Economic Research
Service
http://www.ers.usda.gov

AGRICULTURAL EDUCATION

AgGrow Knowledge: The
National Center for
Agriscience and Technology
Education
http://www.agrowknow.org

National FFA Organization
http://www.ffa.org

Team Ag Ed: Agricultural
Education National
Headquarters
http://www.teamaged.org

AGRICULTURAL ENGINEER

Department of Agricultural
and Biosystems
Engineering
Iowa State University
http://www.abe.iastate.edu

Engineering Jobs.net
http://www.engineeringjobs.net

Institute of Biological
Engineering
http://www.ibe.org

International Commission of
Agricultural and Biosystems
Engineering
http://www.cigr.org

AGRICULTURAL INSPECTOR

American Association of Grain
Inspection and Weighing
Agencies
http://www.aagiwa.org

Association of Fruit and
Vegetable Inspection and
Standardization Agencies
http://www.afvisa.org

FoodSafety.gov: Inspections
and Compliance
http://www.foodsafety.gov/
compliance/index.html

International Organic
Inspectors Association
http://www.ioia.net

U.S. EPA: Food Safety
http://www.epa.gov/agriculture/tfsy.
html

AGRICULTURAL JOURNALIST

Agrinet News Network
http://www.agrinetradio.com

BARN: Buckeye Ag Radio
Network
http://www.buckeyeag.com/index.php

Council for the Advancement
of Science Writing
http://www.casw.org

HSJ.org
http://www.highschooljournalism.
org

Journalism.org
http://www.journalism.org

AGRICULTURAL PILOT

Avjobs.com
http://www.avjobs.com/index.asp

Illinois Agricultural Aviation
Association
http://www.agaviation.com

Pacific Northwest Aerial
Applicators Alliance
http://www.pnwaaa.org

AGRICULTURE TEACHER

Agriculture in the Classroom
http://www.agclassroom.org

Curriculum for Agricultural
Science Education
http://www.case4learning.org

Educating About Agriculture
http://www.ageducate.org

Making a Difference: The
Resource for Agriculture
Educators
http://www.ffa.org/ageducators/
mad/index.html

National Association of
Agricultural Educators
http://www.naae.org/links/resources

TeachAg.net
http://www.teachag.net/index.php

AGRITOURISM OPERATOR

Agricultural Marketing
Resource Center:
Agritourism
http://www.agmrc.org/commodities_
_products/agritourism

Agritourism-related Web Sites
UC Davis Small Farm Program
http://www.sfc.ucdavis.edu/
agritourism/links.html

Alternative Enterprises and Agritourism
USDA National Resources Conservation Service
http://www.resourcesfirstfoundation.org/aea/

PickYourOwn.org
http://www.pickyourown.org

Rural Bounty: Fresh Farm Fun
http://ruralbounty.com

AGRONOMIST

Agronomy Research and Information Center
University of California Cooperative Extension
http://groups.ucanr.org/agronomy/index.cfm

Foundation for Agronomic Research
http://www.farmresearch.com

Grain Genes: Links
http://wheat.pw.usda.gov/ggpages/links.shtml

Plant Management Network
http://www.plantmanagementnetwork.org

Weed Science Society of America
http://www.wssa.net

ANIMAL BEHAVIORIST

Animal Behavior Resources Institute
http://abrionline.org

Animal News Network
http://animalnewsnetwork.org

Ark Animal Answers
http://www.arkanimals.com

Center for the Integrative Study of Animal Behavior
Indiana University, Bloomington
http://www.indiana.edu/~animal

ANIMAL CONTROL OFFICER

ACO FunStop.Com: Animal Control and Humane Law Enforcement Portal
http://www.acofunstop.com

American Society for the Prevention of Cruelty to Animals
http://www.aspca.org

Humane Society of the United States
http://www.humanesociety.org

ANIMAL SCIENTIST

Animal Sciences
University of Wisconsin Extension
http://www.uwex.edu/ces/animalscience

CAB International: Animal Science Database
http://www.cabi.org/animalscience

AQUACULTURE TECHNICIAN

Aquaculture Links
Pacific Aquaculture Caucus
http://www.pacaqua.org/links.htm

AquacultureTalk.com
http://www.aquaculturetalk.com

Aquatext: Online Aquaculture Dictionary
http://www.aquatext.com

ARBORIST

Arbor Day Foundation
http://www.arborday.org

Sustainable Urban Forests Coalition
http://www.urbanforestcoalition.com

Trees Are Good
International Society of Arboriculture
http://www.treesaregood.com

Tree World
http://www.treeworld.info

AUCTIONEER

Auction Community
http://www.auctioncommunity.com

Farm Auction Guide
http://www.farmauctionguide.com

Livestock Marketing Association
http://www.lmaweb.com

BAKER

Bakery-Net.com
http://bakery-net.com

Bread Bakers Guild of America
http://www.bbga.org

Retail Bakers of America
http://www.retailbakersofamerica.org

The Fresh Loaf
http://www.thefreshloaf.com

BEEF CATTLE MANAGER

Beef-Cattle.com: Beef Cattle Information and Resources
http://www.beef-cattle.com

Beef Cattle Production
University of Nebraska, Lincoln
http://beef.unl.edu/index.shtml

Livestock Library: Beef Cattle Resources
Department of Animal Science, Oklahoma State University
http://139.78.104.1/library/cattbeef.html

COMMERCIAL FISHERMAN

About Seafood: Industry Links
National Fisheries Institute
http://www.aboutseafood.com/about/about-nfi/industry-links

Commercial Fishery Landings Data
NOAA Fisheries Service
http://www.st.nmfs.noaa.gov/st1/commercial

Commercial Fishing
http://www.commercial-fishing.org

Pacific Coast Federation of Fishermen's Associations
http://www.pcffa.org

COMMODITY BROKER

Agricultural Commodity Market News
http://www.statpub.com

Commodities and Products
USDA Foreign Agricultural Service
http://www.fas.usda.gov/commodities.asp

Commodity Brokers Online
http://www.commoditybrokersonline.com

U.S. Commodity Futures Trading Commission
http://www.cftc.gov

COMMUNICATIONS SPECIALIST

Agricultural Marketing Resource Center
http://www.agmrc.org

Society for Technical Communication
http://www.stc.org

CONSERVATION OFFICER

IOWA DNR: State Conservation Law Enforcement Links
http://www.iowadnr.gov/law/links.html

NOAA Office for Law Enforcement
http://www.nmfs.noaa.gov/ole/index.html

North East Conservation Law Enforcement Chiefs Association
http://www.necleca.org

U.S. Fish and Wildlife Service: Office of Law Enforcement
http://www.fws.gov/le/index.html

COWBOY

DudeRanchJobs.com
http://www.duderanchjobs.com

RanchWork.com
http://www.ranchwork.com

CROP FARMER

Field Crops
National Sustainable Agriculture Information Service
http://attra.ncat.org

GrainFarmer.com
http://www.grainfarmer.com

National Cotton Council of America
http://www.cotton.org

NewCrop: The New Crop Resource Online Program
Center for New Crops and Plant Products, Purdue University
http://www.hort.purdue.edu/newcrop

DAIRY FARMER

Dairy Farmers of Oregon
http://www.dairyfarmersor.com

Dairy Spot
http://dairyspot.com

Gilmer Dairy Farm.com
http://www.gilmerdairyfarm.com

National Milk Producers Federation
http://www.nmpf.org

ECOTOUR OPERATOR

Earthfoot's Ecotour Posterboard
http://www.earthfoot.org

Ecotourism in America
http://www.ecotourisminamerica.com

Ecotravel
http://www.goodmoney.com/ecotravl.htm

WhyGo Ecotourism
http://www.ecotourismlogue.com

Your Travel Choice Blog
International Ecotourism Society
http://www.yourtravelchoice.org

ENTOMOLOGIST

Bug Bios
http://www.insects.org

Extension Entomology
Purdue University
http://extension.entm.purdue.edu

Field and Forage Crop Entomology
University of Wisconsin–Madison Extension and Research
http://www.entomology.wisc.edu/cullenlab/index.html

ENVIRONMENTAL TOXICOLOGIST

Agency for Toxic Substances and Disease Registry
U.S. Department of Health and Human Services
http://www.atsdr.cdc.gov

Environmental Inquiry: Toxicology
Cornell University and Penn State University
http://ei.cornell.edu/toxicology

Environmental Toxicology Department
University of California at Davis
http://www.envtox.ucdavis.edu

EXTOXNET: The Extension Toxicology Network
http://extoxnet.orst.edu

TOXNET: Toxicology Data Network
U.S. National Library of Medicine
http://toxnet.nlm.nih.gov

EXTENSION AGENT

Association for International Agricultural and Extension Education
http://www.aiaee.org

eXtension
http://www.extension.org

Extension
USDA National Institute of Food and Agriculture
http://www.nifa.usda.gov/qlinks/extension.html

EXTENSION SPECIALIST

Cooperative Extension System Offices
http://www.nifa.usda.gov/Extension

Extension Collaborative Wiki
http://collaborate.extension.org/wiki/Main_Page

FARM EQUIPMENT MECHANIC

A History of American Agriculture: Farm Machinery and Technology
http://www.agclassroom.org/gan/timeline/farm_tech.htm

Farm Net Services
http://www.farmnetservices.com

Worldwide Agricultural Machinery and Equipment Directory
http://www.agmachine.com

FARM LABOR CONTRACTOR

Farm Employers Labor Service
http://www.fels.org

Farm Labor Contracting
Agricultural Personnel Management Program, University of California
http://are.berkeley.edu/APMP/pubs/flc/farmlabor.html

Migrant and Seasonal Agricultural Worker Protection Act
http://www.dol.gov/whd/mspa/index.htm

FARM MANAGER

Agricultural Labor Management
University of California
http://www.cnr.berkeley.edu/ucce50/ag-labor

Farm Business Management for the 21st Century
Purdue Extension
http://www.agecon.purdue.edu/extension/programs/fbm21/more.htm

Farm Management: UC Small Farm Program
University of California at Davis
http://www.sfc.ucdavis.edu/management

FARMWORKER

Agricultural Labor Laws
USDA Office of the Chief Economist
http://www.usda.gov/oce/labor/laws.htm

Association of Farmworker Opportunity Programs
http://www.afoprograms.org

Farmworker Justice
http://www.fwjustice.org

National Center for Farmworker Health
http://www.ncfh.org

FARMER

Agriculture Online
http://www.agriculture.com

Farms.com
http://www.farms.com

National Council of Farmer Cooperatives
http://www.ncfc.org

National Farmers Organization
http://www.nfo.org

USA.gov: Agriculture and Farming
http://www.usa.gov/Citizen/Topics/Environment_Agriculture/Agriculture.shtml

FARMER'S MARKET MANAGER

Farmers Market Coalition
http://farmersmarketcoalition.org

Farmers Markets and Local Food Marketing
USDA Agricultural Marketing Service
http://www.ams.usda.gov/AMSv1.0/FarmersMarkets

Local Harvest
http://www.localharvest.org

FISH FARMER

NOAA Aquaculture Program
http://aquaculture.noaa.gov

One Fish Community
Directory
http://www.onefish.org

Pacific Aquaculture Caucus
http://www.pacaqua.org

SeaWeb Aquaculture Resources
http://www.seaweb.org/resources/
aquaculture.php

FLAVORIST

Flavor and Extract
Manufacturers Association
http://www.femaflavor.org

International Organization of
the Flavor Industry
http://www.iofi.org

Monell Chemical Senses Center
http://www.monell.org

National Association of Flavors
and Food-Ingredient
Systems
http://naffs.mytradeassociation.org

Women in Flavor and
Fragrance Commerce
http://www.wffc.org

FLORAL DESIGNER

Aboutflowers
Society of American Florists
http://www.aboutflowers.com

Bella Online: Floral Design Site
http://floraldesign.bellaonline.com/
Site.asp

The Flower Expert
http://www.theflowerexpert.com

FOOD BROKER
REPRESENTATIVE

American Wholesale Marketers
Association
http://www.awmanet.org

Broker Management Council
http://www.bmcsales.com

Specialty Food.com
National Association for the
Specialty Food Trade
http://www.specialtyfood.com

FOOD INSPECTOR

Centers for Disease Control
and Prevention: Food Safety
Office
http://www.cdc.gov/foodsafety

Food HACCP.com: Food Safety
Information Website
http://www.foodhaccp.com/job.html

FoodSafety.gov
http://www.foodsafety.gov

USDA Food Safety and
Inspection Service
http://www.fsis.usda.gov

FOOD MICROBIOLOGIST

FDA: Food Science and
Research
http://www.fda.gov/Food/
ScienceResearch/default.htm

Microbe World
American Society for Microbiology
http://www.microbeworld.org

Microbiology Careers
American Society for Microbiology
http://www.microbiologycareers.
org

Microbiologyprocedure.com
http://microbiologyprocedure.com

FOOD PROCESS ENGINEER

American Society of Baking
http://www.asbe.org

Explore Food Engineering
http://rpaulsingh.com/default.htm

Food Processing Engineering
Links
University of Bristol, United
Kingdom
http://www.frperc.bris.ac.uk/home/
links.html

The Food Processing Center
University of Nebraska–Lincoln
http://fpc.unl.edu

FOOD TECHNOLOGIST

AACC International
http://www.aaccnet.org

Food and Nutrition
Information Center
USDA National Agricultural Library
http://fnic.nal.usda.gov

Food Industry Sites
MSU Agricultural, Food, and
Resource Economics
http://www.aec.msu.edu/
wwwfoodindustry.htm

Food Science Central
http://www.foodsciencecentral.com

Institute of Food Science and
Technology
http://www.ifst.org

Institute of Food Science
and Technology Careers
Homepage
http://www.foodtechcareers.org

FOREST ENGINEER

Links
Forest Engineering, Resources and
Management
College of Forestry, Oregon State
University
http://ferm.forestry.oregonstate.
edu/links

USDA Forest Service
Engineering Home Page
http://www.fs.fed.us/eng/index.htm

FORESTER

American Forest and Paper Association
http://www.afandpa.org

American Forests
http://www.americanforests.org

Forestry Links
Society of American Foresters
http://www.eforester.org/lp/links.cfm

National Association of State Foresters
http://www.stateforesters.org

National Woodland Owners Association
http://www.woodlandowners.org

FOREST RANGER

Park Law Enforcement Association
http://www.myparkranger.org

U.S. Department of Interior: Law Enforcement Jobs
http://olesem.doi.gov/jobs/index.html

U.S. Forest Service: Law Enforcement and Investigations
http://www.fs.fed.us/lei

FORESTRY TECHNICIAN

Forestry AgNic
http://www.lib.umn.edu/forestry/agnic/index.php

Forestry Links
Tennessee Department of Agriculture
http://www.state.tn.us/agriculture/forestry/links.html

Forestry USA.com
http://www.forestryusa.com

4-H AGENT

4-H Project Information and Resources
University of Delaware Cooperative Extension
http://ag.udel.edu/extension/4h/projects/4HProjects.htm

4-H Staff Resources
http://4-h.org/resources/staff.html

National Collegiate 4-H Organization
http://www.collegiate4h.org

GARDENER

American Horticultural Society
http://www.ahs.org

Association of Professional Gardeners
http://www.associationofprofessionalgardeners.org

Gardening Resources
http://www.gardening-resources.com

National Gardening Association
http://www.garden.org

Zone 10
http://www.zone10.com

GOLF COURSE SUPERINTENDENT

National Golf Course Owners Association
http://www.ngcoa.org

Professional Grounds Management Society
http://www.pgms.org

LawnSite.com
http://www.lawnsite.com

TurfNet.com
http://www.turfnet.com

United States Golf Association
http://www.usga.org

GRAIN ELEVATOR MANAGER

Farmers Coop Grain Association
http://www.wellingtoncoop.com

Farm Net Services: Grain Elevators
http://www.farmnetservices.com/farm/index.php?cat=52

GROUNDSKEEPER

Lawn and Garden Network
http://www.lawnandgardennetwork.com

Pro Garden Biz
http://www.progardenbiz.com

HATCHERY MANAGER

Fish Hatcheries
New York State Department of Environmental Conservation
http://www.dec.ny.gov/outdoor/7742.html

U.S. Fish and Wildlife Service National Fish Hatchery System
http://www.fws.gov/fisheries/nfhs

HORTICULTURAL GROWER

Association of Specialty Cut Flower Growers
http://www.ascfg.org

Horticultural Crops
National Sustainable Agriculture Information Service
http://attra.ncat.org/horticultural.html

Horticultural Crops Research Unit
USDA Agricultural Research Service
http://www.ars.usda.gov/Main/site_main.htm?modecode=53-58-10-00

Horticulture Crop Production Information
Department of Horticulture, Oregon State University
http://hort.oregonstate.edu/ research_extension/hort_crop_ info

National Christmas Tree Association
http://www.christmastree.org

HORTICULTURAL SCIENTIST

American Floral Endowment
http://endowment.org

Botanical Society of America
http://www.botany.org

Landscape Plant Development Center
http://www.landscapecenter.org

USDA Plants Database
Natural Resources Conservation Service
http://plants.usda.gov/index.html

INTERIOR PLANT TECHNICIAN

Green Plants for Green Buildings
http://www.greenplantsforgreen buildings.org/index.htm

Interiorplantscaper.com
http://www.interiorplantscaper.com

PLANET: Professional Landcare Network
http://www.landcarenetwork.org

LANDSCAPE ARCHITECT

Council of Landscape Architectural Registration Boards
http://www.clarb.org

International Federation of Landscape Architects
http://www.iflaonline.org

Landscape Architecture
American Society of Landscape Architects
http://www.asla.org

Landscape Architecture Image Resource Project Links
American Society of Landscape Architects
http://www.asla.org/nonmembers/ links.htm

LANDSCAPE CONTRACTOR

California Landscape Contractors Association
http://www.clca.org

Landscape Management
http://www.landscapemanagement. net

LandscapeNetwork.com
http://www.landscapenetwork.com

LIVESTOCK RANCHER

Links
University of Maine Cooperative Extension
http://www.umaine.edu/livestock/ links.htm

Livestock and Pasture
National Sustainable Agriculture Information Service
http://attra.ncat.org/livestock.html

National Livestock Producers Association
http://www.nlpa.org

Ranch and Livestock Links
http://ranchlinks.com

Tejon Ranch
http://www.tejonranch.com

LOAN OFFICER

Business.gov: Farm Loans
http://www.business.gov/industries/ agribusiness/farm-loans.html

National Council of State Agricultural Finance Programs
http://www.stateagfinance.org

LOGGER

American Loggers Council
http://www.americanloggers.org

Discovery Channel: American Loggers
http://dsc.discovery.com/tv/ american-loggers/american- loggers.html

Timber Harvesting (Logging) Machines and Systems
Department of Forest Resources and Environmental Conservation, Virginia Polytechnic Institute and State University
http://www.cnr.vt.edu/ harvestingsystems/index.htm

Van Natta Forestry and Logging
http://www.vannattabros.com

MARKET GARDENER

Garden Web: The Market Gardener Forum
http://forums.gardenweb.com/ forums/market

Market Gardening: A Start Up Guide
http://attra.ncat.org/attra-pub/ marketgardening.html

Tiny Farm Blog
http://tinyfarmblog.com

MARKETING SPECIALIST

Ag Marketing
University of Maryland Extension
http://agmarketing.umd.edu

Foodservice Sales and Marketing Association
http://www.fsmaonline.com

Organic Marketing Resources
National Sustainable Agriculture Information Service
http://attra.ncat.org/attra-pub/markres.html

Student NAMA
National Agri-Marketing Association
http://www.nama.org/student/student-index.html

USDA Agricultural Marketing Service
http://www.ams.usda.gov

MEAT CUTTER

American Association of Meat Processors
http://www.aamp.com

American Meat Institute
http://www.meatami.com

Ask the Meatman
http://www.askthemeatman.com

NATURAL RESOURCES TECHNICIAN

International Union for Conservation of Nature
http://www.iucn.org

National Resources Management Gateway
U.S. Army Corps of Engineers
http://corpslakes.usace.army.mil

U.S. Bureau of Reclamation
http://www.usbr.gov

Wildlife Forever
http://www.wildlifeforever.org

NURSERY MANAGER

Green Industry Links
Spring Meadow Nursery
http://www.springmeadownursery.com/links.htm

Growit.com
http://www.growit.com

Nursery Crop Science
College of Agriculture and Life Sciences, North Carolina State University
http://www.ces.ncsu.edu/depts/hort/nursery

NURSERY WORKER

Garden Centers of America
http://www.gardencentersofamerica.org

Nursery Directory—Local Garden and Plant Nurseries
http://www.gardenguides.com/local-nurseries

Nursery Jobs
http://www.nurseryjobs.com

ORGANIC FARMER

Community Alliance with Family Farmers
http://www.caff.org

CROPP Cooperative
http://www.farmers.coop

How to Go Organic.com
Organic Trade Association
http://www.howtogoorganic.com

National Sustainable Agriculture Information Service
http://attra.ncat.org

Sustainable Agriculture Research and Education
http://www.sare.org

OUTDOOR GUIDE

Adventure Travel Trade Association
http://www.adventuretravel.biz

GuideMeister.com
http://www.guidemeister.com

Top Adventure Tours
http://www.top-adventure-tours.com/index.html

Wilderness Education Association
http://www.weainfo.org

PARK NATURALIST

Eastern National
http://www.easternnational.org

National Association for Interpretation's Blog
http://interpnet.com/naiblog

U.S. Bureau of Land Management: Learning Landscapes
http://www.blm.gov/wo/st/en/res/Education_in_BLM/Learning_Landscapes.html

U.S. National Park Service: Interpretative Development Program
http://www.nps.gov/idp/interp/theprogram.htm

PEST CONTROL TECHNICIAN

National Pesticide Information Center
http://npic.orst.edu/index.html

Pesticide Education Center
http://www.pesticides.org

PestWorld.org
National Pest Management
    Association
http://www.pestworld.org

PET BUSINESS OWNER

IdeaCafe
http://www.businessownersideacafe.
    com

Pet Business
http://www.petbusiness.com

Pet Business Tips and Tools
    Blog
http://workingwithpets.com

Pet Industry Distributors
    Association
http://www.pida.org

PLANT SCIENTIST

Donald Danforth Plant Science
    Center
http://www.danforthcenter.org

Plantstress
http://www.plantstress.com

POULTRY FARMER

Chicken Resources on the Web
http://www.ithaca.edu/staff/
    jhenderson/chooks/chlinks.html

Poultry Science Association
http://www.poultryscience.org

Ranch and Livestock Links:
    Poultry
http://ranchlinks.com/Livestock_/
    Poultry/index.html

The Poultry Site
http://www.thepoultrysite.com

PROFESSOR

Adjunct Nation
http://www.adjunctnation.com

Association of Public and
    Land-Grant Universities
http://www.aplu.org

HigherEdJobs.com
http://www.higheredjobs.com

PostdocJobs.com
http://www.post-docs.com

QUALITY ASSURANCE
SPECIALIST

Food Safety and Quality
    Information Website
http://www.foodhaccp.com

Food Safety Information
    Center
http://foodsafety.nal.usda.gov

Knowledge Center
American Society for Quality
http://www.asq.org/knowledge-
    center/index.html

World Food Programme: Food
    Quality Control
http://foodquality.wfp.org

RANGE MANAGER

American Forage and
    Grassland Council
http://www.afgc.org

Rangelands West
http://rangelandswest.arid.arizona.
    edu/rangelandswest

RESEARCH CHEF

Chef 2 Chef Culinary Portal
http://www.chef2chef.net

Culinary Institute of America
http://www.ciaprochef.com

Research Chefs Foundation
http://www.culinology.com/
    foundation

The Cook's Thesaurus
http://www.foodsubs.com

RURAL APPRAISER

Appraisal Institute
http://www.appraisalinstitute.org

Appraisers Association of
    America
http://www.appraisersassoc.org

Appraisers Forum
http://appraisersforum.com

SILVICULTURIST

Forest Inventory and Analysis
    National Program
U.S. Forest Service
http://www.fia.fs.fed.us

Silviculture Laboratory
Global Institute of Sustainable
    Forestry
http://gisf.research.yale.edu/
    school_forests/silviculture/
    index.html

Silviculture Laboratory
University of Washington College of
    Forest Resources
http://silvae.cfr.washington.edu

SOIL CONSERVATIONIST

Biological Soil Crusts
USGS Canyonlands Research
    Station, Moab, Utah
http://www.soilcrust.org

Soil Erosion Site
http://soilerosion.net

United States Consortium of
    Soil Science Associations
http://soilsassociation.org

USDA-Agricultural Research
    Service Wind Erosion
    Research Unit
http://www.weru.ksu.edu/new_
    weru

World Association of Soil and
Water Conservation
http://www.waswc.org

VETERINARIAN

Resources
Association for Assessment and
Accreditation of Laboratory
Animal Care International
http://www.aaalac.org/resources/
links.cfm

The Animal Pet Doctor
http://animalpetdoctor.homestead.
com

Vet.com: Veterinary
Associations and
Organizations
http://www.vet.com/vet_
associations.html

VETERINARY PATHOLOGIST

ACVP/STP Coalition for
Veterinary Pathology
Fellows
http://www.vetpathcoalition.org

American Association of
Veterinary Laboratory
Diagnosticians
http://www.aavld.org

American Society for
Veterinary Clinical
Pathology
http://www.asvcp.org

Careers in Veterinary Pathology
http://www.vetpathcareers.org

VETERINARY TECHNICIAN

Vet.com
http://www.vet.com

Veterinary Technician National
Examination
http://www.aavsb.org/VTNE

VetLearn.com
http://www.vetlearn.com

VINEYARD MANAGER

Appellation America: All the
Wines of North America
http://wine.appellationamerica.com

Winegrape Growers of America
http://www.winegrapegrowers
ofamerica.org

Wine Grape Varieties
http://www.cellarnotes.net/key_
grape_varieties.html

Wine Market Council
http://www.winemarketcouncil.com

WETLAND SCIENTIST

U.S. Environmental Protection
Agency: Wetlands
http://www.epa.gov/wetlands

U.S. Fish and Wildlife Service
National Wetlands Inventory
http://www.fws.gov/wetlands

U.S. Geological Survey National
Wetlands Research Center
http://www.nwrc.usgs.gov

Wetlands International
http://www.wetlands.org

Wisconsin Wetlands Association
Resources and Links
http://www.wisconsinwetlands.org/
links.htm

Women in Wetlands
http://www.womeninwetlands.
blogspot.com

WILDLAND FIREFIGHTER

InciWeb: Incident Information
System
http://www.inciweb.org

Interagency Fire Program
Management
http://www.ifpm.nifc.gov

United States Wildland
Firefighters Association
http://uswildlandfirefightersasso.
ning.com

WILDLIFE REHABILITATOR

American Association of
Wildlife Veterinarians
http://www.aawv.net

U.S. Geological Survey
National Wildlife Health
Center
http://www.nwhc.usgs.gov

WildAgain
Wildlife Rehabilitation, Inc.
http://www.ewildagain.org

Wildlife Information Network
http://www.wildlifeinformation.org

Wildlife Rehabber
http://wildliferehabber.com

WINEMAKER

All American Wineries
http://www.allamericanwineries.
com

Cellarnotes.net
http://www.cellarnotes.net/index.
html

Wine America
The National Association of
American Wineries
http://www.wineamerica.org

Wine Institute
http://www.wineinstitute.org

Winery Jobs
http://www.wineryjobs.org

administrative   Relating to the daily management of an office, program, or organization.

advanced degree   Any college degree earned beyond a bachelor's degree.

agribusiness   A farm, ranch, or another agricultural operation that produces crops or livestock for commercial purposes; also, any company that sells products or services to agricultural producers, or purchases farm products to resell to others.

agricultural producer   A person, such as a farmer, rancher, or horticultural grower, who raises crops or livestock for commercial purposes.

agriculturist   Someone who is an expert in the art and science of agriculture.

agriscience   Agricultural science.

agritourism   Agricultural tourism; a type of tourism that attracts visitors to farms, ranches, and other agricultural operations to buy products and participate in recreational or educational activities.

agronomy   The study of plants and soils in their environments.

analytical skills   The abilities that workers need to critically examine and solve problems.

animal husbandry   The practice of breeding and caring for farm animals.

apprenticeship   The program or period of time during which a person works under a skilled professional to learn a trade or craft.

aquaculture   Commercial farming of fish, shellfish, and aquatic plants for food or other purposes.

arboretum   An area in which a collection of trees and other woody plants are grown for scientific research, exhibition, and preservation.

attraction   A building, site, or other place that tourists like to see or visit.

bioinformatics   The management of all biological information stored in computer databases.

biotechnology   The study and practice of using living cells and materials to create agricultural and other products.

breed   To mate and reproduce plants or animals.

broker   A person or company who is paid to perform business transactions on the behalf of others.

candidate   A job applicant whom an employer is interested in hiring.

career   The occupation a person chooses as his or her line of work.

certificate   An official document awarded to a person who has completed a course of study or training.   It is also awarded when a person or a product has passed a test to meet certain standards.

certify   To officially confirm that a person or product has passed a test to meet certain standards.

client   A customer.

commercial   Having to do with selling and buying goods or services.

commission   A fee paid to a person for providing a service, such as sales.

commodity   An agricultural product or a raw material that can be bought or sold.

communication skills   The speaking and listening abilities that workers need to perform their job.

compliance   Meeting the conditions required by a specific law, regulation, or policy.

conflict-resolution skills   The abilities that workers need to manage and resolve disagreements or disputes in the workplace.

conservation   The protection of a natural resource, such as air, water, or soil.

consultant   A person who offers the services of his or her technical, business, management, or other expertise to individuals and organizations.

consumer   A person who buys goods or services for his or her personal use.

contractor   An individual or company who is hired to perform specific tasks according to the terms of a written or oral agreement.

Cooperative Extension Service (Extension)   A state-based program (part of the   Cooperative Extension   System) that assists agricultural producers, individuals, families, and communities in the areas of agriculture, natural resources, youth development, family and consumer sciences, and community and economic development.

Cooperative Extension System (Extension)   A federal program, within the U.S. Department of Agriculture, that works in partnership with state land-universities to provide nonformal educational programs to communities.

critical-thinking skills   The abilities that workers need to examine and analyze situations and make sensible judgments on how to handle them.

crop   Any group of vegetable, fruit, or grain that is grown in great amounts for food, fiber, or another purpose.

cultivate   To grow plants or crops.

customer service skills   The abilities that workers need to handle questions, requests, and complaints from customers about an organization's products or services.

data   Information, including facts and figures.

deadline   The date or hour by which something must be completed.

design *(noun)*   The drawing or other graphical description that shows how something is to be made.

design *(verb)*   To create the form or structure of an object or system.

detail-oriented   Paying close attention to the various parts of a task, project, or job.

development   The process by which a product or service is planned and created.

discipline   A field of study, such as agricultural engineering, agronomy, economics, or food science.

distribution   The delivery of items to various individuals or groups.

duty   A task or responsibility that a worker has been hired to do.

ecosystem   A community of animals, plants, and other living organisms that reside and interact within the same physical environment.

ecotourism   A type of tourism that involves traveling to a natural area and causing minimal impact on the environment while visiting it.

endangered species   A species of plant or animal that is at risk of becoming extinct.

enology   The scientific study of wine and wine making.

enterprise   A business; also a project or other organized goal-oriented activity.

entrepreneurial   Willing to take the risks of starting a new business.

entry-level position   A job that individuals can get with little or no experience.

estimated wages   An amount that is close to the actual pay a worker earns.

ethical   Relating to just or honest behavior.

euthanize   To put an animal to death in a merciful way.

experience   Paid and volunteer work that an individual has done that is related to the position for which he or she applies.

Extension   The Cooperative Extension Service or Cooperative Extension System.

facility   A building, structure, or establishment that is used for a specific purpose.

farmers' cooperative   A business organization that is owned by its members; the members share resources for marketing, shipping, and other activities to sell their products.

feedlot   A building or area in which livestock are confined so they can be fed and fattened up before being taken to market.

fertilize   To add nutrients to soil.

FFA   An extracurricular organization that provides opportunities for agricultural students in middle and high schools to develop personal growth, leadership skills, and career goals; it was formerly called the Future Farmers of America.

fishery   A place where fish are hatched, grow, and live, and where people may catch them.

fish hatchery   A place where fish are bred and raised in a controlled environment.

flexible   Able to handle changes.

foliage   The leaves on plants or trees.

4-H   A youth development program that teaches children, ages 9 to 19, about topics in healthy living; citizenship; and science, engineering, and technology.

genetics   The study of how traits are passed from one generation to the next.

Geographic information system (GIS)   The collection of geographic information that is stored in computer databases.

Global positioning system (GPS)   A system for navigation that uses satellites and radio receivers to pinpoint locations anywhere on Earth.

goods   Raw materials, finished products, or other items for sale or use.

grower   A farmer.

habitat   The natural home of a plant or animal.

harvest   To gather crops, or to catch or kill animals for food, clothing, or other purposes.

hazardous   Dangerous.

helitack crew   A group of firefighters who reach remote burn areas in wildland fires by helicopter.

horticulture   The study and practice of growing fruits, vegetables, and ornamental plants.

hotshot crew   A group of highly skilled and experienced firefighters who are assigned to work in the hottest burn areas in wildland fires.

human resources   The employees who work in an organization; also the personnel department that is responsible for recruiting and hiring employees.

husbandry   The practice of raising livestock or growing crops.

independent contractor An individual or business that provides services to clients on a contractual basis.

industry Individuals and organizations that are engaged in the same type of business enterprise.

interdisciplinary Involving two or more fields of study.

internship The period of working as a trainee or a low-level assistant in order to gain experience.

interpersonal skills The abilities that workers need to communicate and work well with others on the job.

inventory A list of items that a person or an organization has on hand.

irrigation The system of supplying additional water to dry lands so that crops can grow.

jurisdiction The area in which certain laws and regulations are applicable.

labor intensive A business activity, such as crop harvesting, that requires a large number of workers to complete the job.

land-grant university A state college or university designated by a state legislature or Congress to receive federal funds to teach agriculture, conduct agricultural research, and provide nonformal educational programs to the public.

landowner The individual or group that owns a piece of property.

land use The way an area of land is used for agriculture, industry, residences, or other purposes.

leadership skills The abilities that workers need to provide supervision and direction to other workers on a project or in a unit.

license A document granted by a government that allows a person to perform certain professional duties, or to legally operate a specific vehicle or machinery.

livestock Animals that are raised to produce food, fiber, or other products, or to perform work.

local Being part of a community, city, or another particular location.

local government A city or county government.

log A detailed record of things that happened during an event or trip.

maintenance Work done to keep equipment, machinery, a building, or an area in good condition.

management consulting The practice of providing assistance to organizations that want to improve how they run their operations.

mentor An adviser, tutor, or coach who helps someone learn skills or gain experience.

method A way of doing something.

microorganism A microbe such as a virus, mold, or bacterium.

nanotechnology The science and technology of creating microscopic devices, circuits, or materials.

natural resources Soil, water, wildlife, timber, or other materials that occur naturally in the Earth.

networking Communicating with colleagues and other people who may provide information about job openings or other career opportunities.

nongovernmental organization A type of nonprofit group that focuses on defending or promoting a particular issue such as the environment, sustainable agriculture, or food safety; it has no connection with any government agency.

nonprofit organization An establishment that conducts business for the purpose of helping the public, and does not seek to make any money from its activities.

novice A new or inexperienced worker.

nursery A place where plants and trees are raised and nurtured until they are big enough to sell.

orchardist A farmer who grows fruit or nut trees.

organic Being produced without the use of chemical fertilizers, pesticides, or other artificial means.

organic farming A type of sustainable agriculture; farms that use ecologically-minded strategies to produce crops in order to protect the environment and to minimize the risk of harming human and animal health.

organism A living thing, such as a one-celled life form, a plant, an animal, or a human being.

ornamental plant Flowering plant, houseplant, or tree that is specifically grown for its beautiful appearance.

pastime An activity, such as a hobby, that a person likes to do in his or her free time.

personnel Human resources; the employees who work in an organization; also the department that is responsible for recruiting and hiring employees.

pest A plant, insect, or animal (such as a rat or gopher) that is not wanted or causes damage to crops, livestock and other animals, or people.

pesticide A chemical substance used to kill weeds or insects that are harmful to the production of crops and livestock.

Ph.D. Doctor of philosophy.

pollutant A substance that contaminates the air, soil, or water.

postdoctoral training Scholarly research conducted by individuals who have recently earned their doctorates to gain further experience in their area.

private sector The part of the national economy that is made up of private companies and is not run by the government.

problem-solving skills The abilities that workers need to analyze and evaluate problems and find ways to solve them.

professional association An organization that serves the interests of a profession; its membership is made up of those particular professionals.

propagate To reproduce.

prune To trim a plant.

public sector The part of the national economy that provides goods and services to the people through local, state, and federal government agencies.

quality Degree to which a product has all the required characteristics and is free of all defects.

rangeland Large area of land suitable for livestock to graze for food.

raw material A natural resource or unprocessed product, such as wheat or wood, which is used for the manufacture or construction of goods or finished products.

regional Being part of a particular geographic area.

register To enter or record the name of a person on an official list.

regulation A rule that a government agency establishes in order to fulfill the requirements of a law.

regulatory Being governed by certain laws.

rehabilitate To care for an animal so its health is restored.

research and development The process of developing new products or improving existing products for commercial purposes.

resource A person or object that is used as a source of information, for assistance, or for economic exploitation.

retail Engaged in the business of selling goods to the public.

retailer A private company that sells goods to the public.

rural Relating to the countryside or agricultural areas.

sample Items picked at random to use in a test or experiment.

schedule A plan that lists the time and order of specific events or activities.

seasonal Happening during a particular time of year.

self-management skills The abilities that workers need to perform their duties without constant supervision.

small business A small company that is owned and operated independently by one or more individuals.

species A group of animals or plants that have the same characteristics.

supervisor An experienced worker who oversees and guides the work activities of a group of workers.

sustainable agriculture The principles and practices of producing healthy plants and livestock that conserve and restore natural resources and enhance the quality of life for farmers and communities, as well as provide profitability to the farmers.

task A duty or job that an employee must perform.

teamwork skills The abilities that workers need to perform effectively as part of a group on a project or in a unit.

technical consulting The practice of providing farming, scientific, engineering, or other type of technical assistance to individuals or organizations.

technician A worker who provides technical support to engineers and other professionals.

technology The application of science for practical purposes.

terrain Land.

time-management skills The abilities that workers need to plan and use their time more efficiently to complete their tasks.

toxic Poisonous.

toxicology The study of how chemicals affect living things, whether they are humans, animals, plants, or one-celled organisms.

trade association An organization that serves the interests of a particular industry; its membership is made up of companies within that industry.

tradespeople Men and women who are trained to perform a particular trade or craft such as plumbing or operating heavy equipment.

turfgrass Grasses that are used specifically for lawns.

USDA United States Department of Agriculture; the federal agency that administers programs to help farmers and growers.

venture A start-up business that involves some risk of failure.

viticulture The scientific study of growing grapes and grapevines.

watershed An area of land where all of the groundwater or surface water that drains from the land goes into the same stream, lake, or other body of water.

wholesale Engaged in the business of selling large quantities of goods to shops and other businesses.

wholesaler A private company that sells goods to businesses that sell them to their customers.

wildland Wilderness.

wildlife Animals that live in their natural habitats; may also include wild plants.

work-study program A financial aid program in which students can earn money working part-time while studying full-time.

wrangler A cowboy who takes care of horses; he or she may also break in and train horses.

BIBLIOGRAPHY

A. PERIODICALS

Print and online publications are available that serve the interests of many of the various occupations described in this book. These include magazines, journals, newspapers, newsletters, webzines, and electronic news services. Many of them are published by professional and trade associations. Listed below are just a few publications. To learn about other print and online publications, talk with librarians, educators, and professionals for recommendations.

You may be able to find some of the following print publications at a public, school, or college library. Some of the print magazines allow limited free access to their articles on the Web. Many of the Web-based publications are free, whereas others require a subscription to access certain issues and other resources. Some publications offer free subscriptions to students or professionals.

To find scholarly journals that may be online, visit the Genamics JournalSeek Web site. This site offers a searchable database of journal information. The URL is http://journalseek.net.

Note: Web site addresses were current when this book was written. If a URL no longer works, you may be able to find the new address by entering the name of the publication into a search engine.

FARMING

Agriculture Online
http://www.agriculture.com

AgWeb.com
http://www.agweb.com

American Livestock Magazine
Phone: (888) 439-2748
http://www.americanlive.com

American Vineyard Magazine
P.O. Box 626
Clovis, CA 93613
http://www.americanvineyardmagazine.com

Dairy Today
Phone: (800) 331-9310
http://www.agweb.com/dairytoday

Farm Journal
http://www.agweb.com/farmjournal

Greenhouse Grower
http://www.greenhousegrower.com

Growing for Market
http://www.growingformarket.com

MetroFarm
http://www.metrofarm.com

Nursery Management and Production
http://www.nmpromagazine.com

Small Farm Today
3903 West Ridge Trail Road
Clark, MO 65243
Phone: (800) 633-2535
http://www.smallfarmtoday.com

The Progressive Farmer
http://www.dtnprogressivefarmer.com

Vineyard and Winery Management Magazine
P.O. Box 2358
Windsor, CA 95492
Phone: (800) 535-5670
Fax: (707) 577-7700
http://www.vwm-online.com

AQUACULTURE AND COMMERCIAL FISHING

Fish Farming News
http://www.fish-news.com/ffn.htm

Hatchery International
http://www.hatcheryinternational.com

National Fisherman
P.O. Box 7438
Portland, ME 04112
http://www.nationalfisherman.com

FORESTRY PRODUCTION AND MANAGEMENT

Forest Magazine
Forest Service Employees for Environmental Ethics
http://www.fseee.org

Forestnet.com
http://www.forestnet.com

Loggers World
4206 Jackson Highway
Chehalis, WA 98532
Phone: (800) 462-8283 or (360) 262-3376
http://www.loggersworld.com

Timber Harvesting and Wood Fiber Operations
225 Hanrick Street
Montgomery, AL 36104
Phone: (334) 834-1170
Fax: (334) 834-4525
http://timberharvesting.com

AGRISCIENCE

Agricultural Research Magazine
USDA Agricultural Research Service
http://www.ars.usda.gov/is/AR

Agronomy Journal
http://agron.scijournals.org

American Scientist
http://www.americanscientist.org

Crop Science
http://crop.scijournals.org

Journal of Agricultural Science
Cambridge University Press
http://journals.cambridge.org

Journal of Extension
http://www.joe.org

Journal of the American Society for Horticultural Science
http://journal.ashspublications.org

Popular Science
http://www.popsci.com

Science magazine
http://www.sciencemag.org

Scientific American
Phone: (800) 333-1199
http://www.scientificamerican.com

The Professional Animal Scientist
http://pas.fass.org

FOOD AND BEVERAGE INDUSTRIES

Baking Management
http://baking-management.com

Culinology
Customer Service
P.O. Box 3439
Northbrook, IL 60065
Phone: (800) 581-1811 or (847) 564-9969
Fax: (847) 564-9453
http://www.culinologyonline.com

Food Manufacturing
http://www.foodmanufacturing.com

Food Navigator–USA.com
http://www.foodnavigator-usa.com

Food Production Daily.com
http://www.foodproductiondaily.com

Food Quality
http://www.foodquality.com

Quality Assurance Magazine
http://www.qualityassurancemag.com

Wine Business Monthly
http://www.winebusiness.com/wbm

Wine Industry Report
http://wineindustryreport.finewinepress.com

FLORAL, GARDENING, AND LANDSCAPING SERVICES

Arbor Age
http://www.arborage.com

Interiorscape Magazine
Phone: (727) 724-0020
Fax: (727) 724-0021
http://www.interiorscape.com

Floral Design Magazine
http://www.floraldesignmagazine.com

Grounds Maintenance
http://www.grounds-mag.com

Landscape and Irrigation
http://www.landscapeirrigation.com

Landscape Architecture
American Society of Landscape Architects
http://archives.asla.org/lamag/subscribe.html

Landscape Online.com
http://www.landscapeonline.com

Lawn and Landscape
http://www.lawnandlandscape.com

Pest Control Technology
http://www.pctonline.com

Superintendent: The Magazine for Golf Course Superintendents
http://www.superintendentmagazine.com

Tree Services
http://www.treeservicesmagazine.com

Tropical Plant Technician
http://www.tropicalplanttechnician.com

PET AND ANIMAL SERVICES

Animal Sheltering Magazine
http://www.animalsheltering.org/publications/magazine

Pet Product News International.com
http://www.petproductnews.com

Pet Style News
http://www.petstylenews.com

VETERINARY MEDICINE

Veterinary Pathology
http://www.vetpathology.org

Veterinary Practice Staff
http://www.veterinarypracticestaff.com

NATURAL RESOURCES MANAGEMENT AND CONSERVATION

Audubon Magazine
http://audubonmagazine.org

Environmental Protection
http://www.eponline.com

National Parks Magazine
http://www.npca.org/magazine

Rangeland Ecology and Management
http://www.srmjournals.org

Rangelands
http://www.srmjournals.org

World Watch Magazine
http://www.worldwatch.org/epublish/1

TRAVEL, TOURISM, AND RECREATION

Adventure Travel News
http://www.adventuretravelnews.com

National Geographic Traveler
Phone: (800) NGS-LINE
http://traveler.nationalgeographic.com

EDUCATION AND COMMUNICATIONS

Agricultural Education Magazine
http://www.naae.org/links/agedmagazine

Journal of Extension
http://www.joe.org

Teacher Magazine
http://www.teachermagazine.org

The Chronicle of Higher Education
http://chronicle.com

B. BOOKS AND OTHER MATERIALS

Listed below are titles of some books and other written materials that can help you learn more about the different occupations in agriculture, food science, and natural resources management. To learn about other resources that may be helpful, ask professionals and librarians for suggestions.

GENERAL CAREER INFORMATION

Devantier, Alecia T., and Carol A. Turkington. *Extraordinary Jobs in Agriculture and Nature*. New York: Infobase Publishing, 2006.

Farr, Michael. *America's 101 Fastest Growing Jobs*. 8th ed. Indianapolis: JIST Publishing Inc., 2005.

Fasulo, Michael, and Paul Walker. *Careers in the Environment*. Lincolnwood, Ill.: VGM Career Horizons, 2000.

Ferguson Editors. *Careers in Focus: Agriculture*. 2d ed. New York: Infobase Publishing, 2006.

Goecker, Allan D., et al. *Employment Opportunities for College Graduates in the U.S. Food, Agricultural, and Natural Resources System 2005–2010*. A report of a USDA study. Available on the Internet at http://faeis.ahnrit.vt.edu/supplydemand/2005-2010.

Henkel, Keri, (ed). *Occupational Guidance for Agriculture*. Minneapolis: Finney Company, 2002.

Shenk, Ellen. *Outdoor Careers*. 2d ed. Mechanicsburg, Penn.: Stackpole Books, 2000.

U.S. Bureau of Labor. *Career Guide to Industries, 2010–2011 Edition*. Washington, D.C.: Bureau of Labor Statistics, 2009. Available on the Internet at http://www.bls.gov/oco/cg.

U.S. Bureau of Labor. *May 2008 National Occupational Employment and Wage Estimates*. Washington, D.C.: Bureau of Labor Statistics, 2009. Available on the Internet at http://www.bls.gov/oes/current/oes_nat.htm.

U.S. Department of Labor. *Occupational Outlook Handbook 2010-2011 Edition*. Washington, D.C.: Bureau of Labor Statistics, 2009. Available on the Internet at http://www.bls.gov/oco.

Yehling, Carol. *Discovering Careers for Your Future: Nature*. Chicago, Ill.: Ferguson Publishing, 2002.

FARMING

Avent, Tony. *So You Want to Start a Nursery*. Portland, Ore.: Timber Press, 2003.

Berry, Wendell. *Bringing It to the Table: On Farming and Food*. Berkeley, Calif.: Counterpoint Press, 2009.

Dohm, Arlene. "Farming in the 21st Century: A Modern Business in a Modern World." *Occupational Outlook Quarterly* 49, No. 1 (Spring 2005) 19–25. Available on the Internet at http://www.bls.gov/opub/ooq/2005/spring/art02.htm.

Fossel, Peter V. *Organic Farming: Everything You Need to Know*. Minneapolis: Voyageur Press, 2007.

Graham, Chris. *Choosing and Keeping Chickens*. Neptune City, N.J.: TFH Publications, 2006.

Greenhorns. *The Greenhorns Guide for Beginning Farmers*. Available on the Internet at http://www.thegreenhorns.net/reading.html.

Grubinger, Vernon. *Sustainable Vegetable Production from Start-Up to Market*. Ithaca, N.Y.: Natural Resource, Agriculture, and Engineering Service, Cooperative Extension, 1999.

Hasheider, Philip. *How to Raise Cattle: Everything You Need to Know*. Minneapolis: Voyageur Press, 2007.

Hoppe, Robert A., et al. *Structure and Finances of U.S. Farms: Family Farm Report, 2007 Edition*. (USDA Economic Research Service, Economic Information Bulletin no. 24 (June 2007). Available on the Internet at http://www.ers.usda.gov/Publications/EIB24.

Hurt, R. Douglas. *American Agriculture: A Brief History*. Rev. ed. West Lafayette, Ind.: Purdue University Press, 2002.

Institute for Career Research. *Career as a Livestock Breeder/Rancher*. Chicago: Institute for Career Research, 2006.

Institute for Career Research. *Careers in Farming: Agriculture-Agribusiness*. Chicago: Institute for Career Research, 2001.

Institute for Career Research. *Careers in the Landscape Nursery Business*. Chicago: Institute for Career Research, 2001.

Kandel, William. *Profile of Hired Farmworkers: A 2008 Update*. USDA Economic Research Service, Economic Research Report No. 60 (July 2008). Available on the Internet at http://www.ers.usda.gov/Publications/ERR60.

Lee, Andy W., and Patricia L. Foreman. *Backyard Market Gardening*. Burlington, Vt.: Good Earth Publications, 1992.

Lopez, Ann Aurelia. *The Farmworkers' Journey*. Berkeley: University of California Press, 2007.

Macher, Ron. *Making Your Small Farm Profitable*. North Adams, Mass.: Storey Publishing, 1999.

Masumoto, David Mas. *Wisdom of the Last Farmer*. New York: Free Press, 2009.

Mazoyer, Marcel, and Laurence Roudart. *A History of World Agriculture: From the Neolithic Age to the Current Crisis*. New York: Monthly Review Press, 2006.

Miller, Daniel. "Living a Cowboy's Life." *Span* (January/February 2007), 30–35. Available on the Internet at http://span.state.gov/wwwhspjanfeb0730.pdf.

Salatin, Joel. *You Can Farm: The Entrepreneur's Guide to Start and Succeed in a Farm Enterprise*. Swoope, Va.: Polyface, 1998.

Thomas, Heather Smith. *Getting Started with Beef and Dairy Cattle*. North Adams, Mass.: Storey Publishing, 2005.

U.S. Department of Agriculture. *Agriculture Fact Book 2001–2002*. Washington, D.C.: U. S. Government Printing Office, 2003. Available on the Internet at http://www.usda.gov/factbook/2002factbook.pdf.

Winch, Tony. *Growing Food: A Guide to Food Production*. Dordrecht, The Netherlands: Springer, 2006.

AQUACULTURE AND COMMERCIAL FISHING

Delgado, Christopher L., et al. *Fish to 2020: Supply and Demand in Changing Global Markets*. Washington, D.C.: International Food Police Research Institute, 2003.

Harris, C. S. *Alaska Commercial Fishing Employment Guide*. Scotts Valley, Calif.: CreateSpace, 2009.

FORESTRY PRODUCTION AND MANAGEMENT

Alvarez, Mila. *The State of America's Forests*. Bethesda, Md.: Society of American Foresters, 2007. Available on the Internet at http://www.safnet.org/publications/index.cfm.

Institute for Career Research. *Careers in Forestry*. Chicago: Institute for Career Research, 2006.

Society of American Foresters. "Choose Forestry" brochure. Available on the Internet at http://www.safnet.org/fs/careers.cfm.

Wille, Christopher. *Opportunities in Forestry Careers*. New York: The McGraw-Hill Companies, 2004.

AGRISCIENCE

American Association for the Advancement of Science. "Career Basics Booklet." Available on the Internet at http://sciencecareers.sciencemag.org/careerbasicspdf.

American Society of Agronomy. "Careers in Agronomy." Available on the Internet at https://www.careerplacement.org/content/careertools/#brochures.

Camenson, Blythe. *Great Jobs for Biology Majors*. 2d ed. New York: VGM Career Books/McGraw-Hill, 2004.

Cassedy, Patrice. *Careers for the Twenty-First Century: Biotechnology*. Farmington Hills, Mich.: Lucent Books, 2003.

Echaore-McDavid, Susan. *Career Opportunities in Science*. 2d ed. New York: Facts on File, 2008.

Entomological Society of America. "Discover Entomology Brochure." Available on the Internet at http://www.entsoc.org/resources/education/index.htm.

Institute for Career Research. *Careers in Agricultural Research*. Chicago: Institute for Career Research, 2005.

McDavid, Richard A., and Susan Echaore-McDavid. *Career Opportunities in Engineering*. New York: Facts on File, 2006.

Ramsey, Alice. "Going 'Green': Environmental Jobs for Scientists and Engineers." *Occupational Outlook Quarterly*, 53, no. 2 (Spring 2009): 2–11. Available on the Internet at http://www.bls.gov/opub/ooq/2009/summer/art01.htm.

Taylor, Robert E., and Thomas G. Field. *Scientific Farm Animal Production*. 9th ed. Upper Saddle River, N.J.: Prentice Hall, 2007.

Sloan Career Cornerstone Center. "Agricultural Engineering Overview." Available on the Internet at http://www.careercornerstone.org/agricultural/agricultural.htm.

USDA Agricultural Research Service Information Staff. "The Agricultural Research Service Research for the Growing World," 2000. Available on the Internet at http://ars.usda.gov/is/np/indexpubs.html.

AGRICULTURAL SERVICES

Barber, Lindsay. "Mentoring New Pilots Into the Aerial Application Industry," *Agricultural Aviation*, (September/October 2007): 16–23. Available on the Internet at http://www.agaviation.org/AgAviationCareers/becomepilot.htm.

Byrne, Lindsay. "The Benefits of Being an Ag Pilot," *Agricultural Aviation* (September/October 2008): 25–27. Available on the Internet at http://www.agaviation.org/AgAviationCareers/becomepilot.htm.

Corum, Vance, Marcie Rosenzweig, and Eric Gibson. *The New Farmers' Market*. Auburn, Calif.: New World Publishing, 2005.

Herren, Ray V. *Agricultural Mechanics: Fundamentals and Applications*. 6th ed. Clifton Park, N.Y.: Delmar Cengage Learning, 2009.

Knudsen, Steven. "Farm Labor Contractors Add Stability." *Farmer & Rancher* (August 2006): 8–9. Available on the Internet at http://www.slofarmbureau. org/News/Farmer-and-Rancher-Archive06.html.

Torpey, Elka Maria. "You're a *What?* Auctioneer," *Occupational Outlook Quarterly*, 50, no. 3 (Fall 2006): 58–59. Available on the Internet at http://www.bls. gov/opub/ooq/2006/fall/yawhat.htm.

AGRIBUSINESS

Appraisal Foundation. "How to Enter the Appraisal Profession." Available on the Internet at http://www. appraisalfoundation.org.

Garner, Carley, and Paul Brittain. *Commodity Options: Trading and Hedging Volatility in the World's Most Lucrative Market.* Upper Saddle River, N.J.: Pearson Education, 2009.

Harrison, Frank E., et al. *The Appraisal of Rural Property.* 2d ed. Chicago: Appraisal Institute, 2000.

Institute for Career Research. *A Career as an Agricultural Economist.* Chicago: Institute for Career Research, 2006.

Penson, John B., Oral Capps, Jr., C. Parr Rosson, and Richard Woodward. *Introduction to Agricultural Economics.* 4th ed. Upper Saddle River, N.J.: Prentice Hall, 2005.

FOOD AND BEVERAGE INDUSTRIES

Alli, Inteaz. *Food Quality Assurance: Principles and Practices.* Boca Raton, Fla.: CRC Press, 2003.

Bell, Chris, Paul Neaves, and Anthony P. Williams. *Food Microbiology and Laboratory Practice.* Oxford: Wiley-Blackwell, 2005.

Brooks, Jim. "FAPC-130 Are Food Brokers Right for You?" Robert M. Kerr Food and Agricultural Products Center, Oklahoma State University, Stillwater, Oklahoma. Available on the Internet at http://www. fapc.okstate.edu/news/factsheets.html.

Crosby, Olivia. "You're a *What?* Research Chef," *Occupational Outlook Quarterly* 46, no. 3 (Fall 2002): 46–47. Available on the Internet at http://www.bls. gov/opub/ooq/2002/fall/yawhat.htm.

Figoni, Paula I. *How Baking Works: Exploring the Fundamentals.* Hoboken, N.J., John Wiley and Sons, 2008.

Fuller, Gordon W. *New Food Product Development: From Concept to Marketplace.* Boca Raton, Fla.: CRC Press, 2005.

Goode, Jamie. *The Science of Wine: From Vine to Glass.* Berkeley: University of California Press, 2006.

Green, Aliza. *Field Guide to Meat: How to Identify, Select, and Prepare Virtually Every Meat, Poultry, and Game Cut.* Philadelphia: Quirk Books, 2005.

Green, Kathleen. "You're a *What?* Flavorist." *Occupational Outlook Quarterly*, 48, no. 4 (Winter 2004–2005): 46–47. Available on the Internet at http://www. bls.gov/opub/ooq/2004/winter/yawhat.htm.

Page, Karen, and Andrew Dornenburg. *The Flavor Bible.* New York: Little, Brown and Company, 2008.

Research Report Task Force. *A Century of Food Science.* Chicago: Institute of Food Technologists, 2000. Available on the Internet at http://www.ift.org/cms/ ?pid=1000107.

Singh, R. Paul. *Introduction to Food Engineering.* 4th ed. Boston: Academic Press, 2008.

Standage, Tom. *An Edible History of Humanity.* New York: Walker and Co., 2009.

FLORAL, GARDENING, AND LANDSCAPING SERVICES

Brickell, Christopher. *The American Historical Society Encyclopedia of Plants and Flowers.* Rev. ed. New York: DK Publishing, 2002.

California Contractors State License Board. "Blueprint for Becoming a Licensed Contractor." Available on the Internet at http://www.cslb.ca.gov/GeneralInfor mation/Library/GuidesAndPamphlets.asp#GCLC.

Camenson, Blythe. *Opportunities in Landscape Architecture, Botanical Gardens, and Arboreta.* Lincolnwood, Ill.: VGM Career Horizons, 1999.

Crosby, Olivia. "You're a *What?* Arborist." *Occupational Outlook Quarterly* 45, no. 1 (Spring 2001): 38–39. Available on the Internet at http://www.bls. gov/opub/ooq/2001/spring/yawhat.htm.

de Jong-Stout, Alisa A. *A Master Guide to the Art of Floral Design.* Portland, Ore.: Timber Press, 2006.

Golf Course Superintendents Association of America. "Picture This: A Career as a GCSAA Golf Course Superintendent." Available on the Internet at http:// www.gcsaa.org/students/default.aspx.

Hall, Charles R., Alan W. Hodges, and John J. Haydu. *Economic Impacts of the Green Industry in the United States.* Department of Food and Resource Economics, Florida Cooperative Extension Service, Institute of Food and Agricultural Sciences, University of Florida: Gainesville, 2005. Available on the Internet at http://edis.ifas.ufl.edu/pdffiles/FE/FE56600.pdf.

Jones, Elka. "You're a *What?* Dog Walker." *Occupational Outlook Quarterly* 48, no. 2 (Spring 2004): 38–39. Available on the Internet at http://www.bls. gov/opub/ooq/2004/summer/yawhat.htm.

McCarron, Kevin M. "Careers in the Green Industry," *Occupational Outlook Quarterly* 49, no. 1 (Spring 2005): 26–35. Available on the Internet at http://www.bls.gov/opub/ooq/2005/spring/art03.htm.

O'Brien, Patrick M. "Profiles of Professional Golf Course Superintendents." USGA Green Section Record (January/February 1998) 1–5. Available on the Internet at http://turf.lib.msu.edu/1990s/1998/980101.pdf.

Simonds, John Ormsbee. *Landscape Architecture*. 4th ed. New York: McGraw-Hill Professional, 2006.

State Landscape Contractors Board of Oregon. "You and Your Landscape Contracting Business." Salem, Ore.: State Landscape Contractors Board. Available on the Internet at http://www.lcb.state.or.us.

PET AND ANIMAL SERVICES

Kasper, Henry T. "Careers for Creature Lovers," *Occupational Outlook Quarterly* (Winter 2006–2007): 2–13. Available on the Internet at http://www.bls.gov/opub/ooq/2006/winter/art01.htm.

Lee, Mary Price, and Richard S. Lee. *Opportunities in Animal and Pet Care Careers*. Lincolnwood, Ill.: VGM Career Books, 2001.

Miller, Louise. *Careers for Animal Lovers and Other Zoological Types, 2d ed.* Lincolnwood, Ill.: VGM Career Books, 2001.

Reeves, Diane Lindsey, and Nancy Heubeck. *Career Ideas for Kids Who Like . . . Animals and Nature*. New York: Facts on File, 2000.

VETERINARY MEDICINE

Cheville, Norman F. *Introduction to Veterinary Pathology*. 3d ed. Ames, Ia.: Wiley-Blackwell, 2006.

Kasper, Henry and Olivia Crosby. "Veterinary Technicians: Nursing Animals to Health." *Occupational Outlook Quarterly* 47, no. 3 (Fall 2003): 24–33. Available on the Internet at http://www.bls.gov/opub/ooq/2003/fall/art03.htm.

Swope, Robert E. *Opportunities in Veterinary Medicine*. Lincolnwood, Ill.: VGM Career Horizons, 1993.

NATURAL RESOURCES MANAGEMENT AND CONSERVATION

Doyle, Kevin, ed. *The Complete Guide to Environmental Careers in the 21st Century*. Washington, D.C.: Island Press, 1999.

Duncan, Dayton, and Ken Burns. *The National Parks: America's Best Idea*. New York: Alfred A. Knopf, 2009.

Ginsberg, Beth, ed. *The ECO Guide to Careers that Make a Difference*. Washington, D.C.: Island Press, 2004.

Miller, Erica A., DVM. *Minimum Standards for Wildlife Rehabilitation*. 3d ed. Saint Cloud, Minn.: National Wildlife Rehabilitators Association, 2000. Available on the Internet at http://www.iwrc-online.org/pub/publications.html.

WildAgain Wildlife Rehabilitation. "Wildlife Rehabilitation: Is It for You?" Available on the Internet at http://www.ewildagain.org/recruiting/recruiting.htm.

TRAVEL, TOURISM, AND RECREATION

Adams, Barbara Berst, and Kipp Davis. *The New Agritourism: Hosting Community and Tourists on Your Farm*. Auburn, Calif.: New World Publishing, 2009.

Colbert, Judy. *Career Opportunities in the Travel Industry*. New York: Facts on File, 2004.

Honey, Martha. *Ecotourism and Sustainable Development*. Washington, D.C.: Island Press, 2008.

Institute for Career Research. *Careers as a Naturalist*. Chicago: Institute for Career Research, 2000.

Kuehn, Diane, et al. *Considerations for Agritourism Development*. State University of New York. Oswego: N.Y. Available on the Internet at http://nsgl.gso.uri.edu/nysgi/nysgig98001.pdf.

Pond, Kathleen Lingle. *The Professional Guide: Dynamics of Tour Guiding*. New York: Van Nostrand Reinhold, 1993.

Ryan, Susan D., Ph.D., and Sean A. Hayes. *Your Agritourism Business in Pennsylvania: A Resource Handbook*. Harrisburg: Center for Rural Pennsylvania, 2009. Available on the Internet at http://www.ruralpa.org/reports.html.

EDUCATION AND COMMUNICATIONS

Boone, Kristina, Terry Meisenbach, and Mark Tucker. *Agricultural Communications: Changes and Challenges*. Ames: Iowa State University Press, 2000.

Echaore-McDavid, Susan. *Career Opportunities in Education and Related Services*. 2d ed. New York: Infobase Publishing, 2006.

Graves, Russell A. *Communicating in the Agricultural Industry*. Clifton Park, N.Y.: Thomson Learning, 2005.

Heck, Katherine E., and Aarti Subramaniam. *Youth Development Frameworks*. Davis, Calif.: 4-H Center for Youth Development, 2009. Available on the Internet at http://cyd.ucdavis.edu/publications/monograph.html.

Institute for Career Research. *A Career with the Cooperative Agricultural Extension Service*. Chicago: Institute for Career Research, 2005.

INDEX